THE

EXPERIENCE

OF

LITERATURE

GENE MONTAGUE
Lecturer in Literature
Massachusetts Institute of Technology

MARJORIE HENSHAW
Assistant Professor of English
Arizona State University

PRENTICE-HALL, INC.

ENGLEWOOD CLIFFS, NEW JERSEY

THE

EXPERIENCE

OF

LITERATURE

Anthology and Analysis

THE EXPERIENCE OF LITERATURE

Gene Montague and Marjorie Henshaw

Library of Congress Catalog Card No.: 66-11698

Printed in the United States of America C 29452

Current printing (last digit):
10 9 8 7 6 5 4 3

PRENTICE-HALL INTERNATIONAL, INC., *London*
PRENTICE-HALL OF AUSTRALIA, PTY., LTD., *Sydney*
PRENTICE-HALL OF CANADA, LTD., *Toronto*
PRENTICE-HALL OF INDIA (PRIVATE) LTD., *New Delhi*
PRENTICE-HALL OF JAPAN, INC., *Tokyo*

ACKNOWLEDGMENTS

Tues. next April 2 theme
+ test

Conrad Aiken   "Silent Snow, Secret Snow" from *Collected Short Stories of Conrad Aiken*. Copyright 1932 by Conrad Aiken. Copyright © 1959 by Conrad Aiken. Reprinted by permission of the publisher, The World Publishing Company.

W. H. Auden   "The Unknown Citizen" from *Another Time*, copyright 1940 by W. H. Auden. Reprinted from *The Collected Poetry of W. H. Auden*, by permission of Random House, Inc. Canadian rights to "The Unknown Citizen" from *Collected Shorter Poems* by W. H. Auden granted by Faber and Faber Ltd.

Sally Benson   "The Overcoat" from *The American Mercury,* November 1934. Reprinted by permission of Sally Benson.

Anton Chekhov   "The New Villa" from *The Witch and Other Stories*. Copyright 1918 by The Macmillan Company, renewed 1946 by Constance Garnett. Rights for U.S.A. granted by The Macmillan Company. Permission to reprint in Canada granted by Chattus and Windus Ltd.

John Ciardi   Permission to reprint "A Sonnet for Robert Frost, But Not About Him" by John Ciardi granted by John Ciardi and The Saturday Review.

Walter Van Tilburg Clark   "The Rapids" copyright 1941 by Walter Van Tilburg Clark. Reprinted from *The Watchful Gods and Other Stories,* by Walter Van Tilburg Clark, by permission of Random House, Inc.

Joseph Conrad   "The Lagoon" from *Tales of Unrest*. Reprinted by permission of J. M. Dent & Sons Ltd. and the trustees of the Joseph Conrad estate.

e. e. cummings   "if everything happens," copyright, 1944, by E. E. Cummings. Reprinted from his volume *Poems 1923-1954* by permission of Harcourt, Brace & World, Inc.

e. e. cummings   "if i/or anybody" copyright, 1938, by E. E. Cummings. Reprinted from his volume *Poems 1923-1954* by permission of Harcourt, Brace & World, Inc.

Emily Dickinson   Selections from *The Poems of Emily Dickinson* reprinted by permission of the publishers and the Trustees of Amherst College from Thomas H. Johnson, Editor, *The Poems of Emily Dickinson*. Cambridge, Mass.: The Belknap Press of Harvard University Press, Copyright 1951, '55 by The President and Fellows of Harvard College.

v

T. S. Eliot "The Love Song of J. Alfred Prufrock" by T. S. Eliot, copyright 1936 by Harcourt, Brace & World, Inc. "Preludes" (Part I-13 lines) Copyright 1963, 1964 by T. S. Eliot. Reprinted by permission of the publishers. Permission to reprint in Canada granted by Faber and Faber Ltd. Publishers.

Richard Erno "Indian Fighter," *Point West Magazine,* September, 1961. Reprinted by permission of the publisher.

Kenneth Fearing "Art Review" from *Afternoon of a Pawnbroker and Other Poems,* copyright, 1943, by Kenneth Fearing. Reprinted by permission of Harcourt, Brace & World, Inc.

Kenneth Fearing "Dirge" from *New and Selected Poems* by Kenneth Fearing. Reprinted by permission of the publisher, Indiana University Press.

Robert Frost Selections from *Complete Poems of Robert Frost.* Copyright 1916, 1921, 1923, 1930, 1939 by Holt, Rinehart and Winston, Inc. Copyright renewed 1944, 1951 by Robert Frost. Reprinted by permission of Holt, Rinehart and Winston, Inc.

Roy Fuller "January, 1940" from *The Middle of a War, 1940.* Reprinted by permission of Curtis Brown Ltd.

Shirley Ann Grau "The Black Prince" copyright 1953, 1954 by Shirley Ann Grau. Reprinted from the *Black Prince and Other Stories* by Shirley Ann Grau, by permission of Alfred A. Knopf, Inc.

Ernest Hemingway "A Clean, Well-Lighted Place" (Copyright 1933 by Charles Scribner's Sons; renewal copyright © 1961 Ernest Hemingway). Reprinted with the permission of Charles Scribner's Sons from *Winner Take Nothing* by Ernest Hemingway.

Gerard Manley Hopkins Selections from *Poems of Gerard Manley Hopkins,* Third Edition, edited by W. H. Gardner. Copyright 1948 by Oxford University Press, Inc. Reprinted by permission.

A. E. Housman "Is my team ploughing" from "A Shropshire Lad"— Authorised Edition—from *Complete Poems* by A. E. Housman. Copyright © 1959 by Holt, Rinehart and Winston, Inc. "The night is freezing fast" from *Complete Poems* by A. E. Housman. Copyright 1922 by Holt, Rinehart and Winston, Inc. Copyright renewed 1950 by Barclays Bank, Ltd., reprinted by permission of Holt, Rinehart and Winston, Inc. Permission for Canada granted by The Society of Authors as the literary representative of the Estate of the late A. E. Housman, and Messrs. Jonathan Cape Ltd., publishers of A. E. Housman's *Collected Poems.*

D. H. Lawrence "The Horse Dealer's Daughter" from *The Complete Short Stories of D. H. Lawrence.* Published by William Heinemann Ltd. American Publishers: The Viking Press Inc. Reprinted with permission of Laurence Pollinger Limited and the Estate of the Late Mrs. Freida Lawrence.

C. Day Lewis Selection from "A Time To Dance" © 1936 by C. Day Lewis. Reprinted by permission of the Harold Matson Company, Inc.

Archibald MacLeish "Ars Poetica" from *Collected Poems of Archibald MacLeish.* Reprinted by permission of the publisher, Houghton Mifflin Company.

Archibald MacLeish " 'Dover Beach': A Note to That Poem" from *Public Speech* by Archibald MacLeish. Copyright 1936, copyright renewed © 1964 by Archibald MacLeish. Reprinted by permission of Holt, Rinehart and Winston, Inc.

Bernard Malamud "The Bill." Reprinted from *The Magic Barrel* by Bernard Malamud, by permission of Farrar, Straus & Company, Inc. Copyright © 1951, 1958 by Bernard Malamud.

Katherine Mansfield "The Fly." Copyright 1922 by Alfred A. Knopf, Inc. Renewed 1950 by J. Middleton Murry. Reprinted from *The Short Stories of Katherine*

Mansfield by permission of Alfred A. Knopf, Inc. Permission to reprint in Canada granted by The Society of Authors as the literary representative of the Estate of the late Katherine Mansfield.

W. Somerset Maugham   "The Colonel's Lady" copyright 1946 by W. Somerset Maugham from *Creatures of Circumstance* by W. Somerset Maugham. Reprinted by permission of Doubleday and Company, Inc. Reprinted in Canada by permission of A. P. Watt & Son.

W. Somerset Maugham   Selection from "Sheppey" by W. Somerset Maugham by permission of the authors and Messrs. William Heineman Ltd.

Guy de Maupassant   "In the Moonlight" from *The Best Stories of Guy de Maupassant,* edited by Saxe Commins. Reprinted by permission of the publishers, Random House, Inc.

Marianne Moore   "Poetry" reprinted with permission of the publisher from *Collected Poems* by Marianne Moore. Copyright 1935 by The Macmillan Company.

Flannery O'Connor   "A Good Man is Hard to Find." Copyright, 1953, by Flannery O'Connor. Reprinted from her volume *A Good Man is Hard to Find* by permission of Harcourt, Brace & World, Inc.

John Crowe Ransom   "Bells for John Whiteside's Daughter," "Janet Waking," "Survey of Literature." Copyright 1924, 1927 by Alfred A. Knopf, Inc. Renewed 1952, 1955 by John Crowe Ransom. Reprinted from *Selected Poems* by John Crowe Ransom, by permission of Alfred A. Knopf, Inc.

Jean Paul Sartre   "The Wall," by Jean Paul Sartre, Translated by Maria Jolas from *Bedside Book of Famous French Stories,* edited by Belle Becker and Robert N. Linscott. Copyright 1945 by Random House, Inc. Reprinted by permission.

William Shakespeare   Alan S. Downer's footnotes to Othello from William Shakespeare's *Twelfth Night—Othello,* edited by Alan S. Downer. Copyright © 1958. (Rinehart Editions). Holt, Rinehart and Winston, Inc.

Max Shulman   "Tread Quietly, Al" from *Barefoot Boy With Cheek.* Copyright 1943 by Max Shulman. Reprinted by permission of Doubleday & Company, Inc.

Sophocles   *The Antigone of Sophocles:* An English Version by Dudley Fitts and Robert Fitzgerald, copyright, 1939, by Harcourt, Brace & World, Inc. and reprinted with their permission.

Dylan Thomas   "Fern Hill" and "Do not go gentle" from *The Collected Poems of Dylan Thomas.* Copyright 1957 by New Directions. Reprinted by permission of New Directions, Publishers. Permission to reprint in Canada granted by J. M. Dent & Sons Ltd.: Publishers.

Eudora Welty   "Death of a Travelling Salesman," from *A Curtain of Green and Other Stories,* copyright 1941, by Eudora Welty. Reprinted by permission of Harcourt, Brace & World, Inc.

Tennessee Williams   *The Glass Menagerie* by Tennessee Williams. Copyright 1945 by Tennessee Williams and Edwina D. Williams. Reprinted from *Six Modern American Plays,* by permission of Random House, Inc.

Richard Wright   "Almos A Man" by Richard Wright. Permission to reprint granted by Paul R. Reynolds & Sons.

William Butler Yeats   "Sailing to Byzantium" reprinted with permission of the publisher from *Collected Poems* by William Butler Yeats. Copyright 1928 by The Macmillan Company, 1956 by Bertha Georgie Yeats.

William Butler Yeats   "The Second Coming" and "The Leaders of the Crowd" reprinted with permission of the publisher from *Collected Poems* by William Butler Yeats. Copyright 1924 by The Macmillan Company, 1952 by Bertha Georgie Yeats.

CONTENTS

General Introduction 1

The Short Story 5

Bernard Malamud, *The Bill* 6

PLOT 9

CHARACTER 13

SETTING 15

SYMBOL 16

Sally Benson, *The Overcoat* 16
W. Somerset Maugham, *Death* (from *Sheppey*) 18
Edgar Allan Poe, *The Masque of the Red Death* 19
Anton Chekhov, *The New Villa* 22
Guy de Maupassant, *In the Moonlight* 29
Joseph Conrad, *The Lagoon* 31
Katherine Mansfield, *The Fly* 38
D. H. Lawrence, *The Horse Dealer's Daughter* 41
- Conrad Aiken, *Silent Snow, Secret Snow* 49
W. Somerset Maugham, *The Colonel's Lady* 58 *ironic*
Eudora Welty, *Death of a Travelling Salesman* 67
James Thurber, *The Secret Life of Walter Mitty* 73
Walter Van Tilburg Clark, *The Rapids* 76
Ernest Hemingway, *A Clean, Well-Lighted Place* 80
Richard Erno, *Indian Fighter* 82

Flannery O'Connor, *A Good Man is Hard to Find*   85
Jean Paul Sartre, *The Wall*   (94)
Richard Wright, *Almos' a Man*   103
Shirley Ann Grau, *The Black Prince*   109

Poetry   123

John Keats, *On First Looking Into Chapman's Homer*   123

CONVENTIONS OF DICTION   130

CONVENTIONS OF RHYTHM AND METER   132

THE MODES OF POETRY   135

NARRATIVE POETRY   135

Anonymous, *Lord Randal*   137
Anonymous, *Sir Patrick Spence*   138
Anonymous, *Jesse James*   138
John Keats, *La Belle Dame Sans Merci*   139
Samuel Taylor Coleridge, *The Rime of the Ancient Mariner*   140
John Keats, *The Eve of St. Agnes*   149
William Morris, *The Defence of Guenevere*   154

DRAMATIC POETRY   158

Alfred, Lord Tennyson, *Ulysses*   158
Robert Browning, *My Last Duchess*   159
Robert Browning, *Fra Lippo Lippi*   160
T. S. Eliot, *The Love Song of J. Alfred Prufrock*   164

LYRIC POETRY   168

Edmund Spenser, *Sonnet 75 (One Day I Wrote Her Name)*   170
William Shakespeare, *Sonnet 73 (That Time of Year)*   170
Michael Drayton, *Sonnet 61 (Since There's No Help)*   170
William Shakespeare, *Sonnet 18 (Shall I Compare Thee)*   170
William Shakespeare, *Sonnet 130 (My Mistress' Eyes)*   171
William Shakespeare, *Sonnet 29 (When In Disgrace)*   171
Sir Thomas Wyatt, *The Lover Compareth*   171
John Donne, *Holy Sonnet 14*   172
John Milton, *On His Blindness*   172
Percy Shelley, *Ozymandias*   172
John Keats, *When I Have Fears*   173
William Wordsworth, *Composed upon Westminster Bridge*   173
William Wordsworth, *The World Is Too Much with Us*   173
Gerard Manley Hopkins, *The Windhover*   174
Gerard Manley Hopkins, *As Kingfishers Catch Fire*   175

John Ciardi, *A Sonnet for Robert Frost*   175
Kenneth Fearing, *Art Review*   176
George Meredith, *Sonnet 1 (By This He Knew)*   176
Christopher Marlowe, *The Passionate Shepherd to His Love*   177
Sir Walter Raleigh, *The Nymph's Reply to the Shepherd*   178
John Donne, *The Bait*   178
Cecil Day Lewis, *from A Time to Dance*   178
John Dryden, *Alexander's Feast*   179
John Keats, *Ode on a Grecian Urn*   182
William Wordsworth, *Ode: Intimations of Immortality*   183
Percy Bysshe Shelley, *Ode to the West Wind*   187
John Milton, *Lycidas*   190
Matthew Arnold, *Thyrsis*   192

Robert Southwell, *The Burning Babe*   195
George Herbert, *The Collar*   196
John Donne, *A Hymn to God the Father*   196
Thomas Campion, *Cherry Ripe*   197
Robert Herrick, *To the Virgins*   197
Robert Herrick, *Delight in Disorder*   197
Andrew Marvell, *To His Coy Mistress*   198
John Donne, *Song*   199
John Donne, *A Valediction Forbidding Mourning*   199
William Blake, *The Little Black Boy*   200
Samuel Taylor Coleridge, *Kubla Khan*   200
Lord Byron, *She Walks in Beauty*   201
Alfred, Lord Tennyson, *from The Princess*   201
Matthew Arnold, *Dover Beach*   202
Arthur Hugh Clough, *Say Not the Struggle*   202
Archibald MacLeish, *'Dover Beach'—A Note to that Poem*   203
William Wordsworth, *A Slumber Did My Spirit Seal*   203
A. E. Housman, *The Night Is Freezing Fast*   203
Edgar Allan Poe, *To Helen*   204
Dante Gabriel Rossetti, *The Woodspurge*   204
A. E. Housman, *Is My Team Ploughing*   205
A. E. Housman, *Loveliest of Trees*   205
Robert Frost, *Stopping by Woods on a Snowy Evening*   205
Gerard Manley Hopkins, *Spring and Fall*   206
William Butler Yeats, *The Second Coming*   206
William Butler Yeats, *Sailing to Byzantium*   206
William Butler Yeats, *The Leaders of the Crowd*   207
Emily Dickinson, *My Life Closed Twice*   207
Emily Dickinson, *Tell All the Truth*   208
Emily Dickinson, *A Bird Came Down the Walk*   208
Dylan Thomas, *Fern Hill*   208
Dylan Thomas, *Do Not Go Gentle*   209
Roy Fuller, *January, 1940*   210
John Crowe Ransom, *Survey of Literature*   210
Robert Frost, *The Road Not Taken*   210

Robert Frost, *Dust of Snow*   211
Robert Frost, *Fire and Ice*   211
Archibald MacLeish, *Ars Poetica*   211
Marianne Moore, *Poetry*   212
John Crowe Ransom, *Janet Waking*   213
John Crowe Ransom, *Bells for John Whiteside's Daughter*   213
Eugene Field, *Little Boy Blue*   214
W. H. Auden, *The Unknown Citizen*   214
E. E. Cummings, *if everything happens*   215
E. E. Cummings, *if i/or anybody*   216
Kenneth Fearing, *Dirge*   216
George Herbert, *Easter Wings*   217
Robert Herrick, *The Pillar of Fame*   217
Sir Walter Raleigh, *In the Grace of Wit, of Tongue and Face*   218

Drama   219

CONVENTIONS OF SYMBOL   220

CONVENTIONS OF CHARACTER   221

CONVENTIONS OF PLOT   223

Sophocles, *Antigone*   225
William Shakespeare, *Othello*   241
Richard Brinsley Sheridan, *The School for Scandal*   297
Oscar Wilde, *The Importance of Being Earnest*   340
Tennessee Williams, *The Glass Menagerie*   370

GENERAL INTRODUCTION

People read poems, novels, short stories, plays for many different reasons. Some read for pleasure, some for profit, some—and these are the lucky ones—for both. Some seek an escape, a temporary respite in another character, another place, another time; others want to experience the feelings of a character, to exist vicariously in another place or time. Most people read for a combination of these reasons.

The kind of enjoyment which people find in literature varies considerably. Those who read to escape, to kill time, to relax, all enjoy what they're doing, but theirs is obviously a limited enjoyment. The reader who adds to these motives a desire to understand thoroughly what he is reading must work harder, but he adds another kind of enjoyment: the satisfaction of encountering and assimilating a new intellectual or emotional experience. This reader does not escape, but rather he expands his personality: he gains something from the experience.

Whatever their motives, all readers have one thing in common: they read to *experience*.

Because literature is one of the arts, it is not, like a science, a body of knowledge; it is a method of handling and presenting knowledge. Literature draws on other bodies of knowledge but retains its own nature. It is not philosophy, although philosophy is inherent in its nature; it is not history, sociology, or economics, although it embodies something of all these. Like any art, literature is basically a manipulation of experience. It recreates an experience—emotional, intellectual, physical—but *manipulates* that experience so that it always emerges distinct from reality through the author's selection of particular aspects of that experience or his isolation of that experience.

Part of the value of all art forms is that they afford experiences that we as readers can get in no other way. There are many reasons for the reader's inability to experience in reality that which he experiences in literature. Perhaps the reader is physically incapable of grasping that experience in the real world because of the limitations of time and space. Literature brings it to him. Perhaps he is incapable of distinguishing the important parts of the experience from the trivial. Literature selects the conse-

1

quential parts and condenses the experience. Perhaps he is incapable of seeing the significance of an often-recurring experience because its monotony obscures its significance. Literature organizes experience so that it can be examined closely and carefully. What the reader has seen only once, and then too quickly to absorb, or what he has seen repeatedly, but never bothered to observe carefully, takes on meaning. Because human beings are often disorganized creatures, they tend to respect and admire order. The difference between a real experience and that same experience in literature is that what may have been chaotic becomes ordered, organized by the author's selection.

If art is the manipulation of experience, that experience will be meaningless to anyone who does not try to participate in it as recreated by the writer; a writer cannot reach an unreceptive reader. The first thing, then, that a reader owes a writer is a fair hearing. Only a very thoughtless person could say that he does not like poetry. Maybe he does not like the poems he has read so far; but they do not represent all poetry, and his taste may mature and change. And since each poem is a recreation of an experience, one cannot say he does not like poetry without being logically absurd. If a reader condemns all poems on the basis of a few, it becomes virtually impossible for him to enjoy a poem, since he has destroyed his receptivity at the beginning. A reader should not go to a new experience, in this case, a poem, with unfair prejudices; rather he should give the writer a fair hearing. Then if he does not like the poem for concrete and specific reasons, he can voice his opinion. Opinions formed without reading the material are meaningless.

Further understanding between reader and writer is also necessary. Like all the arts, literature has certain *conventions*, some of them centuries old, by which it organizes experience. A convention can be defined as a customary artificiality, a device used to organize artistic material. Conventions are a kind of shorthand, convenient ways of condensing and emphasizing and underlining, which make the work of reader and writer easier. The reader must be willing to spend the time necessary to understand the various conventions, or techniques, by which the writer manipulates his material. Otherwise, his concentration will be disturbed by conventions that hamper, even destroy the recreation of experience. For example, rhymed verse in a play will annoy the reader who thinks that "real people" do not talk in rhyme. One can argue that people in a highly emotional state speak a language which differs more from common speech than do most rhymed lines in plays. It is unnecessary to be this ingenious to convince the reader of his mistake. Rhyme is a convention—consciously and subconsciously we are pleased to hear the chime of the recurring sound; rhyme is a guide to the reader and actors—cue lines and scene and act endings are often signaled by strong rhyme; rhyme is a means of emphasis—strongly rhymed lines call attention to themselves and tell the reader that they are important. What one reads in a play or sees on a stage is not real life; it is life manipulated and organized. To say that a play or a novel or a short story was not good because it wasn't real is meaningless criticism. Plays, novels, and short stories never achieve more than an illusion of reality, and many of them do not attempt even that. Literature cannot be real because it never was real; its origin is the imagination, often inspired by experiences that were real.

Nor is it true that short stories and novels achieve something closer to reality than do poems or plays; they are simply easier to read in most cases because they either use fewer conventions or are less condensed and compressed than poems or plays. Finally, such a thing as a poetic experience as distinguished from a prose experience does not exist. Poems, short stories, novels, and plays do not so much render different kinds of experience as they use different conventions to recreate and manipulate similar experiences. A work becomes more highly organized as it uses more conventions because, as we have seen, conventions are a means of ordering, condensing, and unifying raw experience. Poetry is more highly organized than prose; it has at its command more conventions than does prose. Dramatic poetry (that is, a play in verse) is the most highly organized form of literature because it adds to the conventions of verse the conventions of drama. Nondramatic verse is generally more highly organized than prose drama, if only because of its condensation and precision. Certainly the least complicated form is the prose narrative, which in its formally organized shape becomes the novel or short story.

THE SHORT STORY

An Introduction

Defining the short story is like trying to define democracy; the definition is usually too narrow ("a form roughly 2500 words in length, which presents a full-fledged plot aiming at a single effect") or too broad ("a short prose narrative").

Logically, a short story can be defined on the basis of its conventions. Thus, the short story can be defined as

> a fictional prose narrative (distinguishing it from verse and narrative nonfiction);
>
> usually containing a theme (distinguishing it from an incident and giving it an idea around which it is built);
>
> usually embodied in a plot (distinguishing it from a series of random incidents or tales and giving it formal organization)
>
> which is arranged to allow the greatest economy of character and setting (distinguishing it from the novel, which has fewer time and space limitations).

We do not say that only the short story has these separate characteristics; but we do say that only the short story has this combination of these characteristics.

Defining the short story pinpoints the areas of convention that the reader must know in this form: conventions of plot, character, setting, and so forth. The following story illustrates some of the means by which the writer manipulates experience.

BERNARD MALAMUD

The Bill

Though the street was somewhere near a river, it was landlocked and narrow, a crooked row of aged brick tenement buildings. A child throwing a ball straight up saw a bit of pale sky. On the corner, opposite the blackened tenement where Willy Schlegel worked as janitor, stood another like it except that this included the only store on the street—going down five stone steps into the basement, a small, dark delicatessen owned by Mr. and Mrs. F. Panessa, really a hole in the wall.

They had just bought it with the last of their money, Mrs. Panessa told the janitor's wife, so as not to have to depend on either of their daughters, both of whom, Mrs. Schlegel understood, were married to selfish men who had badly affected their characters. To be completely independent of them, Panessa, a retired factory worker, withdrew his three thousands of savings and bought this little delicatessen store. When Mrs. Schlegel, looking around—though she knew the delicatessen quite well for the many years she and Willy had been janitors across the way—when she asked, "Why did you buy this one?" Mrs. Panessa cheerfully replied because it was a small place and they would not have to overwork; Panessa was sixty-three. They were not here to coin money but to support themselves without working too hard. After talking it over many nights and days, they had decided that the store would at least give them a living. She gazed into Etta Schlegel's gaunt eyes and Etta said she hoped so.

She told Willy about the new people across the street who had bought out the Jew, and said to buy there if there was a chance; she meant by that that they would continue to shop at the self-service, but when there was some odd or end to pick up, or something they had forgotten to buy, they could go to Panessa's. Willy did as he was told. He was tall and broad-backed, with a heavy face seamed dark from the coal and ashes he shoveled around all winter, and his hair often looked gray from the dust the wind whirled up at him out of the ash cans when he was lining them up for the sanitation truck. Always in overalls—he complained he never stopped working—he would drift across the street and down the steps when something was needed, and lighting his pipe, would stand around talking to Mrs. Panessa as her husband, a small bent man with a fitful smile, stood behind the counter waiting for the janitor after a long interval of talk to ask, upon reflection, for a dime's worth of this or that, the whole business never amounting to more than half a dollar. Then one day Willy got to talking about how the tenants goaded him all the time and what the cruel and stingy landlord could think up for him to do in that smelly five-floor dungeon. He was absorbed by what he was saying and before he knew it had run up a three-dollar order, though all he had on him was fifty cents. Willy looked like a dog that had just had a licking, but Mr. Panessa, after clearing his throat, chirped up it didn't matter, he could pay the rest whenever he wanted. He said that everything was run on credit, business and everything else, because after all what was credit but the fact that people were human beings, and if you were really a human being you gave credit to somebody else and he gave credit to you. That surprised Willy because he had never heard a storekeeper say it before. After a couple of days he paid the two fifty, but when Panessa said he could trust whenever he felt like it, Willy sucked a flame into his pipe, then began to order all sorts of things.

When he brought home two large bagfuls of stuff, Etta shouted he must be crazy. Willy answered he had charged everything and paid no cash.

"But we have to pay sometime, don't we?" Etta shouted. "And we have to pay higher prices than in the self-service." She said then what she always said, "We're poor people, Willy. We can't afford too much."

Though Willy saw the justice of her remarks, despite her scolding he still went across the street and trusted. Once he had a crumpled ten-dollar bill in his pants pocket and the amount came to less than four, but he didn't offer to pay, and let Panessa write it in the book. Etta knew he had the money so she screamed when he admitted he had bought on credit.

"Why are you doing it for? Why don't you pay if you have the money?"

He didn't answer but after a time he said there were other things he had to buy once in a while. He went into the furnace room and came out with a wrapped package which he opened, and it contained a beaded black dress.

Etta cried over the dress and said she would never wear it because the only time he ever brought her anything was when he had done something wrong. Thereafter she let him do all the grocery shopping and she did not speak when he bought on trust.

Willy continued to buy at Panessa's. It seemed they were always waiting for him to come in. They lived in three tiny rooms on the floor above the store, and when Mrs. Panessa saw him out of her window, she ran down to the store. Willy came up from his basement, crossed the street and went down the steps into the delicatessen, looming large as he opened the door. Every time he bought, it was never less than two-dollars' worth and sometimes it would go as high as five. Mrs. Panessa would pack everything into a deep double bag, after Panessa had called off each item and written the price with a smeary black pencil into his loose-leaf notebook. Whenever Willy walked in, Panessa would open the book, wet his finger tip and flip through a number of blank pages till he found Willy's account in the center of the book. After the order was packed and tied up, Panessa added the amount, touching each figure with his pencil, hissing to himself as he added, and Mrs. Panessa's bird eyes would follow the figuring until Panessa wrote down a sum, and the new total sum (after Panessa had glanced up at Willy and saw that Willy was looking) was twice underscored and then Panessa shut the book. Willy, with his loose unlit pipe in his mouth, did not move until the book was put away under the counter; then he roused himself and embracing the bundle—with which they offered to help him across the street though he always refused—plunged out of the store.

One day when the sum total came to eighty-three dollars and some cents, Panessa, lifting his head and smiling, asked Willy when he could pay something on account. The very next day Willy stopped buying at Panessa's and after that Etta, with her cord market bag, began to shop again at the self-service, and neither of them went across the street for as much as a pound of prunes or box of salt they had meant to buy but had forgotten.

Etta, when she returned from shopping at the self-service, scraped the wall on her side of the street to get as far away as possible from Panessa's.

Later she asked Willy if he had paid them anything.

He said no.

"When will you?"

He said he didn't know.

A month went by, then Etta met Mrs. Panessa around the corner, and though Mrs. Panessa, looking unhappy, said nothing about the bill, Etta came home and reminded Willy.

"Leave me alone," he said. "I got enough trouble of my own."

"What kind of trouble have you got, Willy?"

"The goddam tenants and the goddam land-lord," he shouted and slammed the door.

When he returned he said, "What have I got that I can pay? Ain't I been a poor man every day of my life?"

She was sitting at the table and lowered her arms and put her head down on them and wept.

"With what?" he shouted, his face lit up dark and webbed. "With the meat off of my bones?"

"With the ashes in my eyes. With the piss I mop up on the floors. With the cold in my lungs when I sleep."

He felt for Panessa and his wife a grating hatred and vowed never to pay because he hated them so much, especially the humpback behind the counter. If he ever smiled at him again with those goddam eyes he would lift him off the floor and crack his bent bones.

That night he went out and got drunk and lay till morning in the gutter. When he returned, with filthy clothes and bloodied eyes, Etta held up to him the picture of their four-year-old son who had died from diphtheria, and Willy weeping splashy tears, swore he would never touch another drop.

Each morning he went out to line up the ash cans, he never looked the full way across the street.

"Give credit," he mimicked, "give credit."

Hard times set in. The landlord ordered cut down on heat, cut down on hot water. He cut down on Willy's expense money and wages. The tenants were angered. All day they pestered Willy like clusters of flies and he told them what the landlord had ordered. Then they cursed Willy and Willy cursed them. They telephoned the Board of Health but when the inspectors arrived they said the temperature was within the legal minimum though the house was drafty. However the tenants still complained they were cold and goaded Willy about it all day but he said he was cold too. He said he was freezing but no one believed him.

One day he looked up from lining up four ash cans for the truck to remove and saw Mr. and Mrs. Panessa staring at him from the store. They were staring up through the glass front door and when he looked at them at first his eyes blurred and they appeared to be two scrawny, loose-feathered birds.

He went down the block to get a wrench from another janitor, and when he got back they then reminded him of two skinny leafless bushes sprouting up through the wooden floor. He could see through the bushes to the empty shelves.

In the spring, when the grass shoots were sticking up from the cracks in the sidewalk, he told Etta, "I'm only waiting till I can pay it all."

"How, Willy?"

"We can save up."

"How?"

"How much do we save a month?"

"Nothing."

"How much have you got hid away?"

"Nothing any more."

"I'll pay them bit by bit. I will, by Jesus."

The trouble was there was no place they could get the money. Sometimes when he was trying to think of the different ways there were to get money his thoughts ran ahead and he saw what it would be like when he paid. He would wrap the wad of bills with a thick rubber band and then go up the stairs and cross the street and go down the five steps into the store. He would say to Panessa, "Here it is, little old man, and I bet you didn't think I would do it, and I don't suppose nobody else did and sometimes me myself, but here it is in bucks all held together by a fat rubber band." After hefting the wad a little, he placed it, like making a move on a checkerboard, squarely in the center of the counter, and the diminutive man and his wife both unpeeled it, squeaking and squealing over each blackened buck, and marveling that so many ones had been tied together into such a small pack.

Such was the dream Willy dreamed but he could never make it come true.

He worked hard to. He got up early and scrubbed the stairs from cellar to roof with soap and a hard brush then went over that with a wet mop. He cleaned the woodwork too and oiled the bannister till it shone the whole zigzag way down and rubbed the mailboxes in the vestibule with metal polish and a soft rag until you could see your face in them. He saw his own heavy face with a surprising yellow mustache he had recently grown and the tan felt cap he wore that a tenant had left behind in a closetful of junk

when he had moved. Etta helped him and they cleaned the whole cellar and the dark courtyard under the crisscrossed clotheslines, and they were quick to respond to any kind of request, even from tenants they didn't like, for sink or toilet repairs. Both worked themselves to exhaustion every day, but as they knew from the beginning, no extra money came in.

One morning when Willy was shining up the mailboxes, he found in his own a letter for him. Removing his cap, he opened the envelope and held the paper to the light as he read the trembling writing. It was from Mrs. Panessa, who wrote her husband was sick across the street, and she had no money in the house so could he pay her just ten dollars and the rest could wait for later.

He tore the letter into bits and hid all day in the cellar. That night, Etta, who had been searching for him in the streets, found him behind the furnace amid the pipes, and she asked him what he was doing there.

He explained about the letter.

"Hiding won't do you any good at all," she said hopelessly.

"What should I do then?"

"Go to sleep, I guess."

He went to sleep but the next morning burst out of his covers, pulled on his overalls and ran out of the house with an overcoat flung over his shoulders. Around the corner he found a pawnshop, where he got ten dollars for the coat and was gleeful.

But when he ran back, there was a hearse or something across the street, and two men in black were carrying this small and narrow pine box out of the house.

"Who's dead, a child?" he asked one of the tenants.

"No, a man named Mr. Panessa."

Willy couldn't speak. His throat had turned to bone.

After the pine box was squeezed through the vestibule doors, Mrs. Panessa, grieved all over, tottered out alone. Willy turned his head away although he thought she wouldn't recognize him because of his new mustache and tan cap.

"What'd he die of?" he whispered to the tenant.

"I really couldn't say."

But Mrs. Panessa, walking behind the box, had heard.

"Old age," she shrilly called back.

He tried to say some sweet thing but his tongue hung in his mouth like dead fruit on a tree, and his heart was a black-painted window.

Mrs. Panessa moved away to live first with one stonefaced daughter, then with the other. And the bill was never paid.

A theme is a central idea around which a piece of literature is developed. It is not the plot or subject matter but the idea that they embody. It is not necessarily a moral because not all experiences teach moral lessons—they simply have effects or consequences. The theme of "The Bill" is that trust is easy enough for humans to accept, but difficult to fulfill and destructive when betrayed.

Theme is the simultaneous effect of character, plot, and setting. Theme is therefore largely dependent on conventions of plot, character, and setting.

PLOT

Point of view

Point of view refers to the person who tells the story and determines the grammatical structure of the narrative. *Who* tells the story is very important in determining *what* is in the story: Different narrators will see different things. Some contemporary critics distinguish as many as a dozen different points of view. For our purposes, three are sufficient:

(1) Narrator acting: The narrator is himself an actor in the story, often the main character, and he tells the story in the first person. ("I went to the window . . . ." "I saw her . . . .") Writing from this point of view, the narrator can see only what a normal person would see, hear only what a normal person would hear. He therefore can record only what other people say and do within earshot and eyesight; he cannot read other's minds and he cannot leap great distances.

(2) Narrator observing: The narrator is not directly involved in the story; he tells it from the sidelines. This means that he can see and hear and report the same details that the "narrator acting" does, but he speaks in the third person. ("He went to the window . . . ." "He saw her . . . .") He has the same physical and mental limitations as in the first point of view, but the narrator here is not necessarily emotionally involved in the situations he describes. Therefore, he achieves a degree of objectivity not possible in the first person point of view. At its most objective stage of development, this point of view is often called "reportage"; the story is told by an objective, unemotional observer, totally without personality himself.

(3) Narrator omniscient: The narrator is obviously the author, above and beyond the story. He tells it in the third person ("He went to the window . . . ." "He saw her . . . ."), but he is not restricted by normal human limitations. He can report what people anywhere do, say, and think. He knows all, tells all—or all that he wants to tell.

More than any other age the twentieth century has been concerned with the convention of point of view, which is considered crucial to establishing the illusion of reality necessary in the realistic or naturalistic story. The more rigid (that is, consistent) and restricted the point of view, the more highly organized the experience will be and the easier it will be for the reader to recreate it: The harder it is for the writer, the easier it is for the reader. The easiest point of view for the writer is the omniscient, but it can be the least profitable one if the author meddles too obviously with the story. The reader often finds it hard to share an experience which is being so artificially manipulated by an ever-present author who combines the omnipresence of Superman with the omniscience of a god.

Authors adopt and adapt these points of view as they see fit, choosing the point of view that allows the best manipulation of material to develop the theme. Frequently, six, eight, ten, or even twelve points of view are utilized. For example, the most successful point of view in the popular short story today is a blend of narrator acting and narrator observing; a distinguished writing teacher, K. P. Kempton of Harvard University, calls it "stream of experience." The author tells the story through one main character, but he tells it in the third person. The author, then, is omniscient only about that character and can only observe the others.

The special advantage of this point of view is that the reader will identify himself with the main character as in the acting point of view, and yet the author can avail himself of the objectivity possible in the observing point of view. In other words, the author appropriates some of the psychological advantages of the first two points of view. The stream of experience point of view is a compromise; the author's job is made easier without sacrificing plausibility. This partly accomplishes what seems to be the goal of many twentieth-century authors: the elimination of the author as narrator.

Authors generally are consistent in their point of view. One lapse may destroy the pattern because the reader usually notices the break, and the illusion consequently is shattered. However, interrupting the point of view, like disturbing any pattern, can be a means of emphasis. In his novel *Darkness at Noon*, a story involving Communist brainwashing to produce fraudulent confessions, Arthur Koestler breaks his stream of experience point of view only twice. In each instance the short passage that breaks it summarizes how far the prisoner's breakdown has progressed and predicts what new methods will follow. It may be argued that what Koestler sacrifices in consistency by these breaks is more than offset by the emphasis they receive, largely because of their inconsistency.

Authors often do not so much select a point of view as the story itself imposes its own point of view. Thus "The Bill" could not be told from another point of view without serious loss or without becoming an entirely different story. The author must show us truthfully and dispassionately the resolution of an emotionally charged situation. He cannot allow one of the characters to tell the story since each has such a strong emotional stake in the situation that his feelings of guilt or injury would warp the story. Yet those feelings of guilt and injury have to be communicated to the reader, or the theme of the story will be buried. In addition, the story covers a long period of time. There is, then, only one point of view feasible: the omniscient, disciplined to avoid sentimentality. You will notice that whenever he can, Malamud makes the authority for a statement rest with a character, not with the author, thus making the story as self-contained and self-sustaining as possible.

Narrative structure

The basis of any situation, incident, or action in life itself is conflict. When one person or force says yes and another says no, conflict results and action grows out of it. To be actual this yes-no condition need not be violent or even external. Wanting to buy a meal (yes) but lacking money (no); hating to get up in the morning (no) but finding it necessary to do so (yes); needing a job (yes) but despising work (no); wanting to do the "right thing" (yes) but thinking that doing it is a financial, social, or physical risk (no); desiring to advance yourself (yes) but realizing that the means to that end are not ethical (no)—all these are conflicts. Moreover, in real life, as in literature, conflict resolves itself into a series of steps or divisions of action. In literature they are more easily distinguishable than in life because the author has usually eliminated superfluous material that might clog the action. Nevertheless, the steps are the same. Traditionally, the convention of narrative structure involves seven divisions.

(1) Exposition: The background information necessary to make the story understandable to the reader.

(2) Inciting force: The spark that begins the story itself; before this point the story has not been moving because only the yes or no force was represented; no active conflict has been established.

(3) Rising action: The complication or impetus for the plot, a series of incidents that make the plot "thicken."

(4) Crisis: The turning point of the story, the point past which the story can go only in one direction, although that fact may be obvious to the reader only after he has finished the story.

(5) Climax: The high point, emotionally or intellectually, of the story. Sometimes crisis and climax are combined. If, for instance, the major problem in a story is a character's making up his mind, the moment he does that will probably be both the crisis and climax.

(6) Falling action: The unraveling of the plot, sometimes referred to as "counteraction" as opposed to the "action" of rising action. To avoid anticlimax falling action is generally much shorter than rising action.

(7) Conclusion: The outcome. In tragedy, the conclusion is called "catastrophe," in comedy, often "solution."*

Let us see briefly how this works out in our story. "The Bill" contains several conflicts: Willy vs. the Panessas, Willy vs. Etta, Willy vs. himself, and so on. The central conflict is this last. Willy has accepted a trust without really considering what it involves. He is happy to accept the trust that Mr. Panessa places in him; but he disregards the second half of Mr. Panessa's definition: "If you were really a human being you gave credit to somebody else and he gave credit to you." Willy forgets

---

*One type of story—the "slice-of-life"—does not manifest these divisions. The "slice-of-life" attempts to get as close to reality as possible by presenting a situation with little or no exposition to establish the circumstances or to establish motive, little or no setting, and little or no emphasis to direct the reader's attention to a crisis or climax. In real life we have to think about these things to establish them clearly in our minds; the "slice-of-life" presents the material without "thought" in this sense; it presents it as if we had stumbled on the situation by accident and were dispassionate observers.

that trust involves mutual obligation. He takes without giving, because the taking perhaps makes him feel important and dignified and human. But when the time comes for Willy to validate the dignity and humanity, he will not. He must pay (yes) but he will not (no)—and later he cannot.

"The Bill" has a very simple plot structure because the author has eliminated everything that might distract the reader and has kept all details in strict chronological order.

The story begins with exposition. The reader is told immediately where the action happens, to whom it happens, and how these people happen to be related. Furthermore, in the first two-and-a-half paragraphs, the author suggests that we are to sympathize with the Panessas (who are introduced as timid and alone, with overtones of being born victims) and with Etta Schlegel (whose outward no-nonsense manner is made attractive by her quiet, good-hearted concern for the Panessas), although about Willy, the main character, the author is as yet noncommittal.

So far, however, there is no action because there is no conflict. Mr. Panessa's offer of credit and Willy's acceptance introduces the conflict and incites the action. Willy has assumed an obligation which he does not fully understand and which, we suspect, he will not be able to live up to.

The rising action follows. Mr. Panessa fulfills his side of the bargain; he trusts Willy. Minor conflicts emerge. Etta, for example, knows Willy is involved beyond his depth. She remonstrates, explaining in her own way what mutual trust involves. He will not listen.

The crisis arrives when Mr. Panessa must ask Willy to pay. Willy makes his choice: he will not pay, and he abandons the Panessas. At this point, Willy's decision is not a matter of money so much as a matter of principle. We know he could have paid something earlier, but he would not. Later we learn that even at his poorest he had means of raising some money—not $83, but enough to keep trust alive. However, when Willy decides he will not pay, he has destroyed all possibility of trust by betraying another human being. Willy tries irrationally to shift his guilt by blaming his woes on the tenants, on the landlord, even on the Panessas.

The climax comes when Willy rationalizes a "solution"—that is, a myth that he thinks he can live with. He will pay them in full, he says; he is saving to do it. But the reader knows, and Etta confirms it, that Willy has no way of raising the total amount. Any hope the reader had for Willy evaporates here. He has not decided to pay; he has simply made up another way of not paying.

And when Willy dreams of paying, the reader sees that he is still wrongly motivated. He dreams of tossing the total amount in front of the Panessas, not to discharge his obligation, but to vindicate himself. He still clings to the false pride that brought about his ruin. The climax, then, has grown logically from the inciting force and the crisis.

The falling action shows Willy compensating for his guilt. He becomes the model janitor; working endlessly for the tenants, he does for them what he will not do for the Panessas. But he cannot escape his guilt. The letter from Mrs. Panessa finally shatters Willy's illusions. He runs to get money, but he is too late. Mr. Panessa is dead.

The conclusion is consistent. Mrs. Panessa's ironic cry that Mr. Panessa died of "old age" pierces Willy; he cannot make even the smallest human gesture—he cannot say "some sweet thing" to her. As the author's metaphor ("his heart was a black-painted window") suggests, no light can penetrate or shine out of Willy's heart now. The illusions are gone, and Willy supposedly knows what he is. "And the bill," it is said "was never paid." In one sense, the bill could not have been paid after the crisis; Willy had betrayed what the bill represented.

Although the story is not pat or mechanical, the action is quite balanced. In the rising action Mr. Panessa discharges his side of the trust: he gives and Willy takes. In the falling action Willy responds to trust: he refuses to pay, and the consequences of his action ensue. This narrative structure is natural in one sense but highly artificial in another: Real life is simply not that precise. Furthermore, an enormous amount of material has been left out of the story. The progressive concentration on Willy's consciousness has allowed the author to eliminate many details, and his use of the omniscient point of view has allowed him to cover long periods of time economically and, at the end, to jump far into the future without furnishing connecting links.

But he has used omniscience judiciously. The reader depends on the author only for the *facts* of the story. Nowhere does the author overtly draw an inference for the reader or intrude a value judgment: Thus, he does not destroy plausibility or lessen the impact of compressed experience. The conventions of point of view and narrative structure make the experience vivid, compact, and meaningful.

CHARACTER

Readers and writers talk about major and minor (or supporting) characters; round and flat characters; and dynamic and static characters. These three systems of classifying characters represent three additional conventions that authors use to manipulate experience.

Major and minor characters

In real life, it is often hard to distinguish between important and unimportant people in a situation. When a person is involved in a situation, he regards himself as the most important "character," even if he is not the main actor in the incident. A writer cannot permit himself this luxury; he must distinguish clearly between the leading character or characters and the supporting characters, or the experience loses all focus and meaning. The way he does this is quite simple. First, he observes the convention that a supporting character justifies his existence in a story only by having a significant relationship to a major character; that is, a supporting character is mainly there to *do something* rather than to *be somebody*. When a supporting character opposes a major character or reacts to him or tells the reader something about him or parallels his action or helps him in some way, he is functioning significantly in the story. The relationship, then, between a major and a minor character is the same as that between a major and a minor conflict. Remove the minor character (or conflict) and we do not destroy the major character (or conflict) although we may remove one aspect of it; but remove the major character (or conflict) and the minor character (or conflict) ceases to be meaningful or important.

The two main characters in "The Bill" are Willy and Mr. Panessa. They are the partners to the trust. Mrs. Panessa and Etta are minor characters. Mrs. Panessa exists, so to speak, to get us into the story and out of it. Consider what she does: She tells us who she and her husband are, how they got into the neighborhood, what they hope for. She is the convenient means of communicating Mr. Panessa's plight to Willy. She states, ironically, the point of the story in her two-word explanation of her husband's death. And she illustrates the continuing repercussions of the unpaid bill in the fate she suffers at the very end. All of these things illuminate the two main characters and the theme.

Etta exists first, like Mrs. Panessa, as a means of exposition; second, as a kind of commentator; and third, as Willy's conscience. She exists, in other words, for what she can show us about Willy, by statement and contrast.

Round and flat characters

A round character is one who, because the author has given him sufficient time and detail, projects an illusion of reality, of being a real personality rather than just one aspect of a personality. He is believable and whole. Obviously this kind of treatment is necessary when an author creates a major character.

A flat character is one who is not fully drawn. The author portrays him only enough to qualify him for whatever role he plays in the story. Flat characters are not whole although they are sometimes believable. When a flat character is used as a symbol there is no particular reason why he ought to be believable. Most supporting characters are flat for a number of reasons. First, economy dictates flatness. Second, if all characters were round, the focus of the story would be endangered, because the reader, at the worst, might not be able to distinguish major from minor characters and, at best, would divide his attention among the round characters.

Dynamic and static characters

A dynamic character is one who "develops," that is, he grows and changes, takes on added dimensions as the story or play or poem progresses. He is not the same character at the end of the plot as he was at the beginning. Willy in "The Bill" is dynamic. The young schizoid boy in Conrad Aiken's "Silent Snow, Secret Snow" is strikingly dynamic, since the story concentrates on tracing the disintegration of his sense of reality.

A static character does not develop, does not change. Often he springs full-blown upon the stage, although that is not necessary. He maintains his characteristics unchanged throughout the reader's acquaintance with him. Etta in "The Bill" is static. The title character of Thurber's "The Secret Life of Walter Mitty" is static. He has evolved a method of self-dramatization that helps him escape reality, and he practices it continually in the story. At one point, when he flashes out at his domineering wife, he has, it seems, a chance to change, but he slides back into his fantasies of heroism. The theme of the story depends on his being static.

A writer may choose to tell the story of a character who changes, or he may choose to tell the story of one who maintains his character, with good or bad results. There is nothing inherently better in one plot or the other; they are simply different.

Nor is a round character better than a flat one. These terms are all descriptive; they do not imply value judgments.

We remarked before that the success of a story depends on a close interrelationship between plot, character, setting, and theme. These things can, with some difficulty, be separated for discussion, but they function simultaneously in the story. Nowhere is it more difficult to separate conventions than in dealing with setting, since it is a matter of place and time. Both of these are closely bound up with plot. Moreover, setting can function as a character, and it also is sometimes the strongest determinant of theme.

A story at its simplest level is about something (plot) that happened to someone (character), somewhere, sometime (setting). Setting can, therefore, be only another word for the background of the story. Frequently, however, it functions in other ways.

(1) It can take the place of a character. In Wright's "Almos' a Man," the setting functions as a kind of antagonist. The young Negro's internal conflict is caused by the disparity between what he wants to be and what his environment will let him be.

(2) It can be a determinant of theme when it functions as more than background but less than character. The short stories and novels of William Faulkner are perhaps the best example. In them the South is an all-pervading force. The cast of mind of Faulkner's Southerners seems often only an outgrowth of the tone of the geographical area.

(3) It can also be a communicator of theme. In Conrad's "The Lagoon," although the reader knows none of the details of Arsat's story before Arsat tells it, he knows the result of Arsat's action before he knows what the action was, paradoxical as that sounds, because of the details of setting. These details not only set the tone, the atmosphere, and the mood of the story; they tell the reader in the first six paragraphs what kind of life Arsat has had to lead as a result of his action.

The absence of setting is often significant. In "The Bill" Malamud has reduced setting to a bare minimum. By eliminating details that tie the situation to a specific place and time, Malamud is able to give his theme a wider application, to suggest that the point he is making is applicable at many times in many places.

SYMBOL

A symbol is something that has a real existence in a story, poem, or play but has a significance above and beyond itself. It stands for something more than what it is. The bill itself in "The Bill" is symbolic; it represents much more than a sum of money owed one man by another. It is a gesture of faith and trust that one makes toward another with the understanding that the other will reciprocate. One might even call symbolic a recurring image in "The Bill"—the image of caged birds. One recalls that Malamud says, when Mr. Panessa offers credit and defines trust, that the old man "chirped up"; when the bill is being added up, "Mrs. Panessa's bird eyes would follow the figuring"; and after Willy refuses to pay, "They were staring up through the glass front door and when he looked at them at first his eyes blurred and they appeared to be two scrawny, loose-feathered birds." The association of birds with the Panessas suggests their pitiful, dependent, caged existence. But to call the bird image symbolic is perhaps to use the term so loosely as to make it shed its primary meaning. The term is better preserved for things which are clearly and indisputably emblematic.

In "Silent Snow, Secret Snow," for example, the imaginary snow represents something in the boy's mind. He is unconscious of its symbolic significance, but the reader sees that the boy is hallucinating a creeping death in his desire for what is cold, stifling, secret, and silent. In Conrad's "The Lagoon" multiple symbols appear. The sudden flight of the white eagle obviously symbolizes the departing soul of Arsat's woman. Equally obvious is the "light" symbolism. For example, the last sentence of the story says something symbolic about Arsat. The fly in Mansfield's "The Fly" symbolizes something to the central character; he is not just pestering an insect but recreating part of his past experience. In Clark's "The Rapids" the actions of the main character are not just madcap, Tom Sawyer adventure; they symbolize a kind of life denied him. And the gun that the young Negro in Wright's "Almos' a Man" buys is more than just a firearm; it symbolizes manhood for a boy who, because of his circumstances and birth, will never be a man in any acceptable sense of the word.

In the following story, Sally Benson's "The Overcoat," the overcoat itself is clearly a symbol. It is important to determine what the symbol means to the main character and how the author uses it to convey the theme to the reader.

SALLY BENSON

The Overcoat

It had been noisy and crowded at the Milligan's and Mrs. Bishop had eaten too many little sandwiches and too many iced cakes, so that now, out in the street, the air felt good to her, even if it was damp and cold. At the entrance of the apartment house, she took out her change purse and looked through it and found that by counting the pennies, too, she had just eighty-seven cents, which wasn't enough for a taxi from Tenth Street to Seventy-Third. It was horrid never having enough money in your purse, she thought. Playing bridge, when she lost, she often had to give IOU's and it was faintly embarrassing, although she always managed to make them good. She resented Lila Hardy who could say, "Can anyone change a ten?" and who could take ten dollars from her smart bag while the others scurried for change.

She decided it was too late to take a bus and that she might as well walk over to the subway, although the air down there would probably make her head ache. It was drizzling a little and the sidewalks were wet. And as she stood on the corner waiting for the traffic lights to change, she felt horribly sorry for herself. She remembered as a young girl, she had always assumed she would have lots of money when she was older. She had planned what to do with it— what clothes to buy and what upholstery she would have in her car. Of course, everybody nowadays talked poor and that was a comfort. But it was one thing to have lost your money and quite another never to have had any. It was absurd, though, to go around with less than a dollar in your purse. Suppose something happened? She was a little vague as to what might happen, but the idea fed her resentment.

Everything for the house, like food and things, she charged. Years ago, Robert had worked out some sort of budget for her but it had been impossible to keep their expenses under the right headings, so they had long ago abandoned it. And yet Robert always seemed to have money. That is, when she came to him for five or ten dollars, he managed to give it to her. Men were like that, she thought. They managed to keep money in their pockets but they had no idea you ever needed any. Well, one thing was sure, she would insist on having an allowance. Then she would know where she stood. When she decided this, she began to walk more briskly and everything seemed simpler.

The air in the subway was worse than usual and she stood on the local side waiting for a train. People who took the express seemed to push so and she felt tired and wanted to sit down. When the train came, she took a seat near the door and, although inwardly she was seething with rebellion, her face took on the vacuous look of other faces in the subway. At Eighteenth Street, a great many people got on and she found her vision blocked by a man who had come in and was hanging to the strap in front of her. He was tall and thin and his overcoat which hung loosely on him and swayed with the motion of the train smelled unpleasantly of damp wood. The buttons of the overcoat were of imitation leather and the button directly in front of Mrs. Bishop's eyes evidently had come off and been sewed back on again with black thread, which didn't match the coat at all.

It was what is known as a swagger coat but there was nothing very swagger about it now. The sleeve that she could see was almost threadbare around the cuff and a small shred from the lining hung down over the man's hand. She found herself looking intently at his hand. It was long and pallid and not too clean. The nails were very short as though they had been bitten and there was a discolored callus on his second finger where he probably held his pencil. Mrs. Bishop, who prided herself on her powers of observation, put him in the white-collar class. He most likely, she thought, was the father of a large family and had a hard time sending them all through school. He undoubtedly never spent money on himself. That would account for the shabbiness of his overcoat. And he was probably horribly afraid of losing his job. Mrs. Bishop couldn't decide whether to make his wife a fat slattern or to have her an invalid.

She grew warm with sympathy for the man. Every now and then he gave a slight cough, and that increased her interest and her sadness and made her feel resigned to life. She decided that she would smile at him when she got off. It would be the sort of smile that would make him feel better, as it would be very obvious that she understood and was sorry.

But by the time the train reached Seventy-Second Street, the closeness of the air and the confusion of her own worries had made her feelings less poignant, so that her smile, when she gave it, lacked something. The man looked away embarrassed.

Her apartment was too hot and the smell of broiling chops sickened her after the enormous tea she had eaten. She could see Maude, her maid, setting the table in the dining room for dinner. Mrs. Bishop had bought smart little uniforms for her, but there was nothing smart about Maude and the uniforms never looked right.

Robert was lying on the living room couch, the evening newspaper over his face to shield his eyes. He had changed his shoes, and the gray felt slippers he wore were too short for him and showed the imprint of his toes, and looked depressing. Years ago, when they were first married, he used to dress for dinner sometimes. He would shake up a cocktail for her and things were quite gay and almost the way she had imagined they would be. Mrs. Bishop didn't believe in letting yourself go and it seemed to her that Robert let himself go out of sheer perversity. She hated him as he lay there, resignation in every line of his body. She envied Lila Hardy her husband who drank but who, at least, was somebody. And she felt like tearing the newspaper from his face because her anger and disgust were more than she could bear.

For a minute she stood in the doorway trying to control herself and then she walked over to a window and opened it roughly. "Goodness," she said. "Can't we ever have any air in here?"

Robert gave a slight start and sat up. "Hello, Mollie," he said. "You home?"

"Yes, I'm home," she answered. "I came home in the subway."

Her voice was reproachful. She sat down in the chair facing him and spoke more quietly so that Maude couldn't hear what she was saying.

"Really, Robert," she said, "it was dreadful. I came out from the tea in all that drizzle and couldn't even take a taxi home. I had exactly eighty-seven cents!"

"Say," he said. "That's a shame. Here." He reached in his pocket and took out a small roll of crumpled bills. "Here," he repeated. And handed her one. She saw that it was five dollars.

Mrs. Bishop shook her head. "No, Robert," she told him. "That isn't the point. The point is that I've really got to have some sort of allowance. It isn't fair to me. I never have any money! Never! It's got so it's positively embarrassing!"

Mr. Bishop fingered the five dollar bill thoughtfully. "I see," he said. "You want an allowance. Don't I give you money every time you ask for it?"

"Well, yes," Mrs. Bishop admitted. "But it isn't like my own. An allowance would be more like my own."

"Now, Mollie," he reasoned. "If you had an allowance, it would probably be gone by the tenth of the month."

"Don't treat me like a child," she said. "I just won't be humiliated any more."

Mr. Bishop sat turning the five dollar bill over and over in his hand. "How much do you think you should have?"

"Fifty dollars a month," she told him. And her voice was harsh. "That's the least I can get along on. Why, Lila Hardy would laugh at fifty dollars a month."

"Fifty dollars a month," Mr. Bishop repeated. He ran his fingers through his hair. "I've had a lot of things to attend to this month. But, well, maybe if you would be willing to wait until the first of next month, I might manage."

"Oh, next month will be perfectly all right," she said, feeling it wiser not to press her victory. "But don't forget all about it. Because I shan't."

As she walked toward the closet to put away her wraps, she caught sight of Robert's overcoat on the chair near the door. He had tossed it carelessly across the back of the chair as he came in. One sleeve was hanging down and the vibration of her feet on the floor had made it swing gently back and forth. She saw that the cuff was badly worn and a bit of the lining showed. It looked dreadfully like the sleeve of the overcoat she had seen in the subway. And, suddenly, looking at it, she had a horrible sinking feeling, as though she were falling in a dream.

1. How does the significance of the central symbol change from the time of its first appearance to its second? What details in the story support the meaning of the symbol?

2. What kind of woman is Mrs. Bishop? Why does the author choose to tell the story from Mrs. Bishop's point of view? What would it do to (a) the effect of the story and (b) the symbol if the author were to switch points of view to Mr. Bishop or the maid or to an omniscient point of view?

3. What is ironic and yet typical in Mrs. Bishop's being one "who prided herself on her powers of observation"?

W. SOMERSET MAUGHAM

From *Sheppey*

Death: There was a merchant in Bagdad who sent his servant to market to buy provisions and in a little while the servant came back, white and trembling, and said, Master, just now when I was in the marketplace I was jostled by a woman in the crowd and when I turned I saw it was death that jostled me. She looked at me and made a threatening gesture; now, lend me your horse, and I will ride away from this city and avoid my fate. I will go to Samarra and there death will not find me. The merchant lent him his horse, and the servant mounted it, and he dug his spurs in its flanks and as fast as the horse could gallop he went. Then the merchant went down to the marketplace and he saw me standing in the crowd and he came to me and said, Why did you make a threatening gesture to my servant when you saw him this morning? That was not a threatening gesture, I said, it was only a start of surprise. I was astonished to see him in Bagdad, for I had an appointment with him tonight in Samarra.

FOR ANALYSIS

1. This is a parable, a short narrative that clearly illustrates a moral. How does this short piece differ from a short story?

2. What is not here that you would ordinarily expect in a short story?

EDGAR ALLAN POE

The Masque
of the Red Death

THE "Red Death" had long devastated the country. No pestilence had ever been so fatal, or so hideous. Blood was its Avatar and its seal—the redness and the horror of blood. There were sharp pains, and sudden dizziness, and then profuse bleeding at the pores, with dissolution. The scarlet stains upon the body and especially upon the face of the victim, were the pest ban which shut him out from the aid and from the sympathy of his fellow men. And the whole seizure, progress and termination of the disease, were the incidents of half an hour.

But the Prince Prospero was happy and dauntless and sagacious. When his dominions were half depopulated, he summoned to his presence a thousand hale and light-hearted friends from among the knights and dames of his court, and with these retired to the deep seclusion of one of his castellated abbeys. This was an extensive and magnificent structure, the creation of the prince's own eccentric yet august taste. A strong and lofty wall girdled it in. This wall had gates of iron. The courtiers, having entered, brought furnaces and massy hammers and welded the bolts. They resolved to leave means neither of ingress or egress to the sudden impulses of despair or of frenzy from within. The abbey was amply provisioned. With such precautions the courtiers might bid defiance to contagion. The external world could take care of itself. In the meantime it was folly to grieve, or to think. The prince had provided all the appliances of pleasures. There were buffoons, there were improvisatori, there were ballet dancers, there were musicians, there was Beauty, there was wine. All these and security were within. Without was the "Red Death."

It was toward the close of the fifth or sixth month of his seclusion, and while the pestilence raged most furiously abroad, that the Prince Prospero entertained his thousand friends at a masked ball of the most unusual magnificence.

It was a voluptuous scene, that masquerade. But first let me tell of the rooms in which it was held. There were seven—an imperial suite. In many palaces, however, such suites form a long and straight vista, while the folding doors slide back nearly to the walls on either hand, so that the view of the whole extent is scarcely impeded. Here the case was very different; as might have been expected from the duke's love of the *bizarre*. The apartments were so irregularly disposed that the vision embraced but little more than one at a time. There was a sharp turn at every twenty or thirty yards, and at each turn a novel effect. To the right and left, in the middle of each wall, a tall and narrow Gothic window looked out upon a closed corridor which pursued the windings of the suite. These windows were of stained glass whose color varied in accordance with the prevailing hue of the decorations of the chamber into which it opened. That at the eastern extremity was hung, for example, in blue—and vividly blue were its windows. The second chamber was purple in its ornaments and tapestries, and here the panes were purple. The third was green throughout, and so were the casements. The fourth was furnished and lighted with orange—the fifth with white—the sixth with violet. The seventh apartment was closely shrouded in black velvet tapestries that hung all over the ceiling and down the walls, falling in heavy folds upon a carpet of the same material and hue. But in this chamber only, the color of the windows failed to correspond with the decorations. The panes here were scarlet—a deep blood color. Now in no one of the seven apartments was there any lamp or candelabrum, amid the profusion of golden ornaments that lay scattered to and fro or depended from the roof. There was no light of any kind emanating from lamp or candle within the suite of chambers. But in the corridors that followed the suite, there stood, opposite to each window, a heavy tripod, bearing a brazier of fire that projected its rays through the tinted glass and so glaringly illumined the room. And thus were produced a multitude of gaudy and fantastic appearances. But in the western or black chamber the effect of the fire-light that streamed upon the dark hangings through the blood-tinted panes was ghastly in the extreme, and produced so wild a look upon the countenances of those who entered, that there were few of the company bold enough to set foot within its precincts at all.

It was in this apartment, also, that there stood against the western wall, a gigantic clock of ebony. Its pendulum swung to and fro with a dull, heavy, monotonous clang; and when the minute-hand made the circuit of the face, and the hour was to be stricken, there came from the brazen lungs of the clock a sound which was clear and loud and deep and exceedingly musical, but of so peculiar a note and emphasis that, at each lapse of an hour, the musicians of the orchestra were constrained to pause, momentarily, in their performance, to hearken to the sound; and thus the waltzers perforce ceased their evolutions; and there was a brief disconcert of the whole gay company; and, while the chimes of the clock yet rang, it was observed that the giddiest grew pale, and the more aged and sedate passed their hands over their brows as if in confused reverie or meditation. But when the echoes had fully ceased, a light laughter at once pervaded the assembly; the musicians looked at each other and smiled as if at their own nervousness and folly, and made whispering vows, each to the other, that the next chiming of the clock should produce in them no similar emotion; and then, after the lapse of sixty minutes (which embrace three thousand and six hundred seconds of the Time that flies), there came yet another chiming of the clock, and then were the same disconcert and tremulousness and meditation as before.

But, in spite of these things, it was a gay and magnificent revel. The tastes of the duke were peculiar. He had a fine eye for colors and effects. He disregarded the *decora* of mere fashion. His plans were bold and fiery, and his conceptions glowed with barbaric lustre. There are some who would have thought him mad. His followers felt that he was not. It was necessary to hear and see and touch him to be *sure* that he was not.

He had directed, in great part, the movable embellishments of the seven chambers, upon occasion of this great *fête;* and it was his own guiding taste which had given character to the masqueraders. Be sure they were grotesque. There were much glare and glitter and piquancy and phantasm—much of what has been since seen in "Hernani." There were arabesque figures with unsuited limbs and appointments. There were delirious fancies such as the madman fashions. There was much of the beautiful, much of the wanton, much of the *bizarre*, something of the terrible, and not a little of that which might have excited disgust. To and fro in the seven chambers there stalked, in fact, a multitude of dreams. And these—the dreams— writhed in and about, taking hue from the

rooms, and causing the wild music of the orchestra to seem as the echo of their steps. And, anon, there strikes the ebony clock which stands in the hall of the velvet. And then, for a moment, all is still, and all is silent save the voice of the clock. The dreams are stiff-frozen as they stand. But the echoes of the chime die away—they have endured but an instant—and a light, half-subdued laughter floats after them as they depart. And now again the music swells, and the dreams live, and writhe to and fro more merrily than ever, taking hue from the many-tinted windows through which stream the rays from the tripods. But to the chamber which lies most westwardly of the seven, there are now none of the maskers who venture; for the night is waning away; and there flows a ruddier light through the blood-colored panes; and the blackness of the sable drapery appalls; and to him whose foot falls upon the sable carpet, there comes from the near clock of ebony a muffled peal more solemnly emphatic than any which reaches *their* ears who indulge in the more remote gaieties of the other apartments.

But these other apartments were densely crowded, and in them beat feverishly the heart of life. And the revel went whirlingly on, until at length there commenced the sounding of midnight upon the clock. And then the music ceased, as I have told; and the evolutions of the waltzers were quieted; and there was an uneasy cessation of all things as before. But now there were twelve strokes to be sounded by the bell of the clock; and thus it happened, perhaps, that more of thought crept, with more of time, into the meditations of the thoughtful among those who revelled. And thus, too, it happened, perhaps, that before the last echoes of the last chime had utterly sunk into silence, there were many individuals in the crowd who had found leisure to become aware of the presence of a masked figure which had arrested the attention of no single individual before. And the rumor of this new presence having spread itself whisperingly around, there arose at length from the whole company a buzz, or murmur, expressive of disapprobation and surprise—then, finally, of terror, of horror, and of disgust.

In an assembly of phantasms such as I have painted, it may well be supposed that no ordinary appearance could have excited such sensation. In truth the masquerade license of the night was nearly unlimited; but the figure in question had out-Heroded Herod, and gone beyond the bounds of even the prince's indefinite decorum. There are chords in the hearts of the most reckless which cannot be touched without emotion. Even with the utterly lost, to whom life and death are equally jests, there are matters of which no jest can be made. The whole company, indeed, seemed now deeply to feel that in the costume and bearing of the stranger neither wit nor propriety existed. The figure was tall and gaunt, and shrouded from head to foot in the habiliments of the grave. The mask which concealed the visage was made so nearly to resemble the countenance of a stiffened corpse that the closest scrutiny must have had difficulty in detecting the cheat. And yet all this might have been endured, if not approved, by the mad revellers around. But the mummer had gone so far as to assume the type of the Red Death. His vesture was dabbled in *blood*—and his broad brow, with all the features of the face, was besprinkled with the scarlet horror.

When the eyes of Prince Prospero fell upon this spectral image (which with a slow and solemn movement, as if more fully to sustain its *rôle*, stalked to and fro among the waltzers) he was seen to be convulsed, in the first moment with a strong shudder either of terror or distaste; but, in the next, his brow reddened with rage.

"Who dares?" he demanded hoarsely of the courtiers who stood near him—"who dares insult us with this blasphemous mockery? Seize him and unmask him—that we may know whom we have to hang at sunrise, from the battlements!"

It was in the eastern or blue chamber in which stood the Prince Prospero as he uttered these words. They rang throughout the seven rooms loudly and clearly—for the prince was a bold and robust man, and the music had become hushed at the waving of his hand.

It was in the blue room where stood the prince, with a group of pale courtiers by his side. At first, as he spoke, there was a slight rushing movement of this group in the direction of the intruder, who at the moment was also near at hand, and now, with deliberate and stately step, made closer approach to the speaker. But from a certain nameless awe with which the mad assumptions of the mummer had inspired the whole party, there were found none who put forth hand to seize him; so that, unimpeded, he passed within a yard of the prince's person; and, while the vast assembly, as if with one impulse, shrank from the centers of the rooms to the walls, he made his way uninterruptedly, but with the same solemn and measured step which had distinguished him from the first, through the blue chamber to the purple—through the purple to the green—through the green to the orange—through this again to the white—and even thence to the violet, ere a decided movement had been made to arrest him. It was then, however, that the Prince Prospero, maddening with rage and the shame of his own momentary cowardice, rushed hurriedly through the six chambers, while none followed him on account of a deadly terror that had seized upon all. He bore aloft a drawn dagger, and had approached, in rapid impetuosity, to within three or four feet of the retreating figure, when the latter, having attained the extremity of the velvet apartment, turned suddenly and confronted his pursuer. There was a sharp cry—and the dagger dropped gleaming upon the sable carpet, upon which, instantly afterwards, fell prostrate in death the Prince Prospero. Then, summoning the wild courage of despair, a throng of the revellers at once threw themselves into the black apartment, and, seizing the mummer, whose tall figure stood erect and motionless within the shadow of the ebony clock, gasped in unutterable horror at finding the grave-cerements and corpse-like mask which they handled with so violent a rudeness, untenanted by any tangible form.

And now was acknowledged the presence of the Red Death. He had come like a thief in the night. And one by one dropped the revellers in the blood-bedewed halls of their revel, and died each in the despairing posture of his fall. And the life of the ebony clock went out with that of the last of the gay. And the flames of the tripods expired. And Darkness and Decay and the Red Death held illimitable dominion over all.

FOR ANALYSIS

1. Is this story more akin to the familiar short story form (as in "The Bill") or to the parable (as in the excerpt from *Sheppey*)? Why?
2. The story is replete with symbols. What is the symbolic significance of the Prince's elaborate sealing up of the abbey? of the seven rooms? of the ebony clock? of the musicians' and dancers' response to the striking of the clock?

of the march of the masked figure through the six rooms? of the attack of the Prince on the masked figure?

3. What is the theme of the story?

4. Is there perhaps a double meaning in the word *Masque* in the title?

ANTON CHEKHOV

The New Villa

Two miles from the village of Obrutchanovo a huge bridge was being built. From the village, which stood up high on the steep riverbank, its trellislike skeleton could be seen, and in foggy weather and on still winter days, when its delicate iron girders and all the scaffolding around was covered with hoar frost, it presented a picturesque and even fantastic spectacle. Kutcherov, the engineer who was building the bridge, a stout, broad-shouldered, bearded man in a soft crumpled cap drove through the village in his racing droshky or his open carriage. Now and then on holidays navvies working on the bridge would come to the village; they begged for alms, laughed at the women, and sometimes carried off something. But that was rare; as a rule the days passed quietly and peacefully as though no bridge-building were going on, and only in the evening, when camp fires gleamed near the bridge, the wind faintly wafted the songs of the navvies. And by day there was sometimes the mournful clang of metal, don-don-don.

It happened that the engineer's wife came to see him. She was pleased with the riverbanks and the gorgeous view over the green valley with trees, churches, flocks, and she began begging her husband to buy a small piece of ground and to build them a cottage on it. Her husband agreed. They bought sixty acres of land, and on the high bank in a field, where in earlier days the cows of Obrutchanovo used to wander, they built a pretty house of two stories with a terrace and a verandah, with a tower and a flagstaff on which a flag fluttered on Sundays —they built it in about three months, and then all the winter they were planting big trees, and when spring came and everything began to be

green there were already avenues to the new house, a gardener and two laborers in white aprons were digging near it, there was a little fountain, and a globe of looking glass flashed so brilliantly that it was painful to look at. The house had already been named the New Villa.

On a bright, warm morning at the end of May two horses were brought to Obrutchanovo to the village blacksmith, Rodion Petrov. They came from the New Villa. The horses were sleek, graceful beasts, as white as snow, and strikingly alike.

"Perfect swans!" said Rodion, gazing at them with reverent admiration.

His wife Stepanida, his children and grandchildren came out into the street to look at them. By degrees a crowd collected. The Lytchkovs, father and son, both men with swollen faces and entirely beardless, came up bareheaded. Kozov, a tall, thin old man with a long, narrow beard, came up leaning on a stick with a crook handle: he kept winking with his crafty eyes and smiling ironically as though he knew something.

"It's only that they are white; what is there in them?" he said. "Put mine on oats, and they will be just as sleek. They ought to be in a plough and with a whip, too. . . ."

The coachman simply looked at him with disdain, but did not utter a word. And afterwards, while they were blowing up the fire at the forge, the coachman talked while he smoked cigarettes. The peasants learned from him various details: his employers were wealthy people; his mistress, Elena Ivanovna, had till her marriage lived in Moscow in a poor way as a governess; she was kindhearted, compassionate, and fond of helping the poor. On the new estate, he told them, they were not going to plough or to sow, but simply to live for their pleasure, live only to breathe the fresh air. When he had finished and led the horses back a crowd of boys followed him, the dogs barked, and Kozov, looking after him, winked sarcastically.

"Landowners, too-oo!" he said. "They have built a house and set up horses, but I bet they are nobodies—landowners, too-oo."

Kozov for some reason took a dislike from the first to the new house, to the white horses, and to the handsome, well-fed coachman. Kozov was a solitary man, a widower; he had a dreary life (he was prevented from working by a disease

which he sometimes called a rupture and sometimes worms); he was maintained by his son,
who worked at a confectioner's in Harkov and
sent him money; and from early morning till
evening he sauntered at leisure about the river
or about the village; if he saw, for instance, a
peasant carting a log, or fishing, he would say:
"That log's dry wood—it is rotten," or, "They
won't bite in weather like this." In times of
drought he would declare that there would not
be a drop of rain till the frost came; and when
the rains came he would say that everything
would rot in the fields, that everything was
ruined. And as he said these things he would
wink as though he knew something.

At the New Villa they burned Bengal lights
and sent up fireworks in the evenings, and a
sailing-boat with red lanterns floated by Obrutchanovo. One morning the engineer's wife, Elena
Ivanovna, and her little daughter drove to the
village in a carriage with yellow wheels and a
pair of dark bay ponies; both mother and
daughter were wearing broadbrimmed straw
hats, bent down over their ears.

This was exactly at the time when they were
carting manure, and the blacksmith Rodion, a
tall, gaunt old man, bareheaded and barefooted,
was standing near his dirty and repulsive-looking
cart and, flustered, looked at the ponies, and it
was evident by his face that he had never seen
such little horses before.

"The Kutcherov lady has come!" was whispered around. "Look, the Kutcherov lady has
come!"

Elena Ivanovna looked at the huts as though
she were selecting one, and then stopped at the
very poorest, at the windows of which there
were so many children's heads—flaxen, red, and
dark. Stepanida, Rodion's wife, a stout woman,
came running out of the hut; her kerchief
slipped off her grey head; she looked at the
carriage facing the sun, and her face smiled and
wrinkled up as though she were blind.

"This is for your children," said Elena Ivanovna, and she gave her three roubles.

Stepanida suddenly burst into tears and bowed
down to the ground. Rodion, too, flopped to
the ground, displaying his brownish bald head,
and as he did so he almost caught his wife in
the ribs with the fork. Elena Ivanovna was
overcome with confusion and drove back.

II

The Lytchkovs, father and son, caught in
their meadows two carthorses, a pony, and a
broad-faced Aalhaus bull-calf, and with the help
of red-headed Volodka, son of the blacksmith
Rodion, drove them to the village. They called
the village elder, collected witnesses, and went
to look at the damage.

"All right, let 'em!" said Kozov, winking,
"le-et 'em! Let them get out of it if they can,
the engineers! Do you think there is no such
thing as law? All right! Send for the police
inspector, draw up a statement! . . ."

"Draw up a statement," repeated Volodka.

"I don't want to let this pass!" shouted the
younger Lytchkov. He shouted louder and
louder, and his beardless face seemed to be
more and more swollen. "They've set up a nice
fashion! Leave them free, and they will ruin all
the meadows! You've no sort of right to ill-treat
people! We are not serfs now!"

"We are not serfs now!" repeated Volodka.

"We got on all right without a bridge," said
the elder Lytchkov gloomily; "we did not ask
for it. What do we want a bridge for? We don't
want it!"

"Brothers, good Christians, we cannot leave
it like this!"

"All right, let 'em!" said Kozov, winking.
"Let them get out of it if they can! Landowners,
indeed!"

They went back to the village, and as they
walked the younger Lytchkov beat himself on
the breast with his fist and shouted all the way,
and Volodka shouted, too, repeating his words.
And meanwhile quite a crowd had gathered in
the village round the thoroughbred bull-calf
and the horses. The bull-calf was embarrassed
and looked up from under his brows, but suddenly lowered his muzzle to the ground and
took to his heels, kicking up his hind legs; Kozov
was frightened and waved his stick at him, and
they all burst out laughing. Then they locked
up the beasts, and waited.

In the evening the engineer sent five roubles
for the damage, and the two horses, the pony
and the bull-calf, without being fed or given
water, returned home, their heads hanging with
a guilty air as though they were convicted
criminals.

On getting the five roubles the Lytchkovs,

father and son, the village elder and Volodka, punted over the river in a boat and went to a hamlet on the other side where there was a tavern, and there had a long carousal. Their singing and the shouting of the younger Lytchkov could be heard from the village. Their women were uneasy and did not sleep all night. Rodion did not sleep either.

"It's a bad business," he said, sighing and turning from side to side. "The gentleman will be angry, and then there will be trouble. . . . They have insulted the gentleman. . . . Oh, they've insulted him. It's a bad business. . . ."

It happened that the peasants, Rodion amongst them, went into their forest to divide the clearings for mowing, and as they were returning home they were met by the engineer. He was wearing a red cotton shirt and high boots; a setter dog with its long tongue hanging out, followed behind him.

"Good day, brothers," he said.

The peasants stopped and took off their hats.

"I have long wanted to have a talk with you, friends," he went on. "This is what it is. Ever since the early spring your cattle have been in my copse and garden every day. Everything is trampled down; the pigs have rooted up the meadow, are ruining everything in the kitchen garden, and all the undergrowth in the copse is destroyed. There is no getting on with your herdsmen; one asks them civilly, and they are rude. Damage is done on my estate every day and I do nothing—I don't fine you or make a complaint; meanwhile you impounded my horses and my bull-calf and exacted five roubles. Was that right? Is that neighbourly?" he went on, and his face was so soft and persuasive, and his expression was not forbidding. "Is that the way decent people behave? A week ago one of your people cut down two oak saplings in my copse. You have dug up the road to Eresnevo, and now I have to go two miles round. Why do you injure me at every step? What harm have I done you? For God's sake, tell me! My wife and I do our utmost to live with you in peace and harmony; we help the peasants as we can. My wife is a kind, warmhearted woman; she never refuses you help. That is her dream—to be of use to you and your children. You reward us with evil for our good. You are unjust, my friends. Think of that. I ask you earnestly to think it over. We treat you humanely; repay us in the same coin."

He turned and went away. The peasants stood a little longer, put on their caps and walked away. Rodion, who always understood everything that was said to him in some peculiar way of his own, heaved a sigh and said:

"We must pay. 'Repay in coin, my friends' . . . he said."

They walked to the village in silence. On reaching home Rodion said his prayer, took off his boots, and sat down on the bench beside his wife. Stepanida and he always sat side by side when they were at home, and always walked side by side in the street; they ate and they drank and they slept always together, and the older they grew the more they loved one another. It was hot and crowded in their hut, and there were children everywhere—on the floors, in the windows, on the stove. . . . In spite of her advanced years Stepanida was still bearing children, and now, looking at the crowd of children, it was hard to distinguish which were Rodion's and which were Volodka's. Volodka's wife, Lukerya, a plain young woman with prominent eyes and a nose like the beak of a bird, was kneading dough in a tub; Volodka was sitting on the stove with his legs hanging.

"On the road near Nikita's buckwheat . . . the engineer with his dog . . ." Rodion began, after a rest, scratching his ribs and his elbow. " 'You must pay,' says he . . . 'coin,' says he. . . . Coin or no coin, we shall have to collect ten kopecks from every hut. We've offended the gentleman very much. I am sorry for him. . . ."

"We've lived without a bridge," said Volodka, not looking at anyone, "and we don't want one."

"What next; the bridge is a government business."

"We don't want it."

"Your opinion is not asked. What is it to you?"

" 'Your opinion is not asked,' " Volodka mimicked him. "We don't want to drive anywhere; what do we want with a bridge? If we have to, we can cross by the boat."

Someone from the yard outside knocked at the window so violently that it seemed to shake the whole hut.

"Is Volodka at home?" he heard the voice of the younger Lytchkov, "Volodka, come out, come along."

Volodka jumped down off the stove and began looking for his cap.

"Don't go, Volodka," said Rodion diffidently.

"Don't go with them, son. You are foolish, like a little child; they will teach you no good; don't go!"

"Don't go, son," said Stepanida, and she blinked as thought about to shed tears. "I bet they are calling you to the tavern."

" 'To the tavern,' " Volodka mimicked.

"You'll come back drunk again, you currish Herod," said Lukerya, looking at him angrily. "Go along, go along, and may you burn up with vodka, you tailless Satan!"

"You hold your tongue," shouted Volodka.

"They've married me to a fool, they've ruined me, a luckless orphan, you red-headed drunkard . . ." wailed Lukerya, wiping her face with a hand covered with dough. "I wish I had never set eyes on you."

Volodka gave her a blow on the ear and went off.

III

Elena Ivanovna and her little daughter visited the village on foot. They were out for a walk. It was a Sunday, and the peasant women and girls were walking up and down the street in their brightly colored dresses. Rodion and Stepanida, sitting side by side at their door, bowed and smiled to Elena Ivanovna and her little daughter as to acquaintances. From the windows more than a dozen children stared at them; their faces expressed amazement and curiosity, and they could be heard whispering:

"The Kutcherov lady had come! The Kutcherov lady!"

"Good morning," said Elena Ivanovna, and she stopped; she paused, and then asked: "Well, how are you getting on?"

"We get along all right, thank God," answered Rodion, speaking rapidly. "To be sure we get along."

"The life we lead!" smiled Stepanida. "You can see our poverty yourself, dear lady! The family is fourteen souls in all, and only two breadwinners. We are supposed to be blacksmiths, but when they bring us a horse to shoe we have no coal, nothing to buy it with. We are worried to death, lady," she went on, and laughed. "Oh, oh, we are worried to death."

Elena Ivanovna sat down at the entrance and, putting her arm round her little girl, pondered something, and judging from the little girl's expression, melancholy thoughts were straying through her mind, too; as she brooded she played with the sumptuous lace on the parasol she had taken out of her mother's hands.

"Poverty," said Rodion, "a great deal of anxiety—you see no end to it. Here, God sends no rain . . . our life is not easy, there is no denying it."

"You have a hard time in this life," said Elena Ivanovna, "but in the other world you will be happy."

Rodion did not understand her, and simply coughed into his clenched hand by way of reply. Stepanida said:

"Dear lady, the rich men will be all right in the next world, too. The rich put up candles, pay for services; the rich give to beggars, but what can the poor man do? He has no time to make the sign of the cross. He is the beggar of beggars himself; how can he think of his soul? And many sins come from poverty; from trouble we snarl at one another like dogs, we haven't a good word to say to one another, and all sorts of things happen, dear lady—God forbid! It seems we have no luck in this world nor the next. All the luck has fallen to the rich."

She spoke gaily; she was evidently used to talking of her hard life. And Rodion smiled, too; he was pleased that his old woman was so clever, so ready of speech.

"It is only on the surface that the rich seem to be happy," said Elena Ivanovna. "Every man has his sorrow. Here my husband and I do not live poorly, we have means, but are we happy? I am young, but I have had four children; my children are always being ill. I am ill, too, and constantly being doctored."

"And what is your illness?" asked Rodion.

"A woman's complaint. I get no sleep; a continual headache gives me no peace. Here I am sitting and talking, but my head is bad, I am weak all over, and I should prefer the hardest labour to such a condition. My soul, too, is troubled; I am in continual fear for my children, my husband. Every family has its own trouble of some sort; we have ours. I am not of noble birth. My grandfather was a simple peasant, my father was a tradesman in Moscow; he was a plain, uneducated man, too, while my husband's parents were wealthy and distinguished. They did not want him to marry me, but he disobeyed them, quarrelled with them, and they have not forgiven us to this day. That worries my husband; it troubles him and keeps him in constant agitation; he loves his mother, loves her dearly. So I am uneasy, too, my soul is in pain."

Peasants, men and women, were by now standing round Rodion's hut and listening. Kozov came up, too, and stood twitching his long, narrow beard. The Lytchkovs, father and son, drew near.

"And say what you like, one cannot be happy and satisfied if one does not feel in one's proper place." Elena Ivanovna went on. "Each of you has his strip of land, each of you works and knows what he is working for; my husband builds bridges—in short, everyone has his place, while I, I simply walk about. I have not my bit to work. I don't work, and feel as though I were an outsider. I am saying all this that you may not judge from outward appearances; if a man is expensively dressed and has means it does not prove that he is satisfied with his life."

She got up to go away and took her daughter by the hand.

"I like your place here very much," she said, and smiled, and from that faint, diffident smile one could tell how unwell she really was, how young and how pretty; she had a pale, thinnish face with dark eyebrows and fair hair. And the little girl was just such another as her mother: thin, fair, and slender. There was a fragrance of scent about them.

"I like the river and the forest and the village," Elena Ivanovna went on; "I could live here all my life, and I feel as though here I should get strong and find my place. I want to help you—I want to dreadfully—to be of use, to be a real friend to you. I know your need, and what I don't know I feel, my heart guesses. I am sick, feeble, and for me perhaps it is not possible to change my life as I would. But I have children. I will try to bring them up that they may be of use to you, may love you. I shall impress upon them continually that their life does not belong to them, but to you. Only I beg you earnestly, I beseech you, trust us, live in friendship with us. My husband is a kind, good man. Don't worry him, don't irritate him. He is sensitive to every trifle, and yesterday, for instance, your cattle were in our vegetable garden, and one of your people broke down the fence to the bee-hives, and such an attitude to us drives my husband to despair. I beg you," she went on in an imploring voice, and she clasped her hands on her bosom—"I beg you to treat us as good

neighbours; let us live in peace! There is a saying, you know, that even a bad peace is better than a good quarrel, and, 'Don't buy property, but buy neighbours.' I repeat my husband is a kind man and good; if all goes well we promise to do everything in our power for you; we will mend the roads, we will build a school for your children. I promise you."

"Of course we thank you humbly, lady," said Lytchkov the father, looking at the round; "you are educated people; it is for you to know best. Only, you see, Voronov, a rich peasant at Eresnevo, promised to build a school; he, too, said, 'I will do this for you,' 'I will do that for you,' and he only put up the framework and refused to go on. And then they made the peasants put the roof on and finish it; it cost them a thousand roubles. Voronov did not care; he only stroked his beard, but the peasants felt it a bit hard."

"That was a crow, but now there's a rook, too," said Kozov, and he winked.

There was the sound of laughter.

"We don't want a school," said Volodka sullenly. "Our children go to Petrovskoe, and they can go on going there; we don't want it."

Elena Ivanovna seemed suddenly intimidated; her face looked paler and thinner, she shrank into herself as though she had been touched with something coarse, and walked away without uttering another word. And she walked more and more quickly, without looking round.

"Lady," said Rodion, walking after her, "lady, wait a bit; hear what I would say to you."

He followed her without his cap, and spoke softly as though begging.

"Lady, wait and hear what I will say to you."

They had walked out of the village, and Elena Ivanovna stopped beside a cart in the shade of an old mountain ash.

"Don't be offended, lady," said Rodion. "What does it mean? Have patience. Have patience for a couple of years. You will live here, you will have patience, and it will all come round. Our folks are good and peaceable; there's no harm in them; it's God's truth I'm telling you. Don't mind Kozov and the Lytchkovs, and don't mind Volodka. He's a fool; he listens to the first that speaks. The others are quiet folks; they are silent. Some would be glad, you know, to say a word from the heart and to stand up for themselves, but cannot. They have a heart and a conscience, but no tongue. Don't be offended . . . have patience. . . . What does it matter?"

Elena Ivanovna looked at the broad, tranquil river, pondering, and tears flowed down her cheeks. And Rodion was troubled by those tears; he almost cried himself.

"Never mind . . ." he muttered. "Have patience for a couple of years. You can have the school, you can have the roads, only not all at once. If you went, let us say, to sow corn on that mound you would first have to weed it out, to pick out all the stones, and then to plough, and work and work . . . and with the people, you see, it is the same . . . you must work and work until you overcome them."

The crowd had moved away from Rodion's hut, and was coming along the street towards the mountain ash. They began singing songs and playing the concertina, and they kept coming closer and closer. . . .

"Mamma, let us go away from here," said the little girl, huddling up to her mother, pale and shaking all over; "let us go away, mamma!"

"Where?"

"To Moscow. . . . Let us go, mamma."

The child began crying.

Rodion was utterly overcome; his face broke into profuse perspiration; he took out of his pocket a little crooked cucumber, like a half-moon, covered with crumbs of rye bread, and began thrusting it into the little girl's hands.

"Come, come," he muttered, scowling severely; "take the little cucumber, eat it up. . . . You mustn't cry. Mamma will whip you. . . . She'll tell your father of you when you get home. Come, come. . . ."

They walked on, and he still followed behind them, wanting to say something friendly and persuasive to them. And seeing that they were both absorbed in their own thoughts and their own griefs, and not noticing him, he stopped and, shading his eyes from the sun, looked after them for a long time till they disappeared into their copse.

IV

The engineer seemed to grow irritable and petty, and in every trivial incident saw an act of robbery or outrage. His gate was kept bolted even by day, and at night two watchmen walked up and down the garden beating a board; and

they gave up employing anyone from Obrutchanovo as a labourer. As ill luck would have it someone (either a peasant or one of the workmen) took the new wheels off the cart and replaced them by old ones, then soon afterwards two bridles and a pair of pincers were carried off, and murmurs arose even in the village. People began to say that a search should be made at the Lytchkovs' and at Volodka's, and then the bridles and the pincers were found under the hedge in the engineer's garden; someone had thrown them down there.

It happened that the peasants were coming in a crowd out of the forest, and again they met the engineer on the road. He stopped, and without wishing them good day he began, looking angrily first at one, then at another:

"I have begged you not to gather mushrooms in the park and near the yard, but to leave them for my wife and children, but your girls come before daybreak and there is not a mushroom left. . . . Whether one asks you or not it makes no difference. Entreaties, and friendliness, and persuasion I see are all useless."

He fixed his indignant eyes on Rodion and went on:

"My wife and I behaved to you as human beings, as to our equals, and you? But what's the use of talking! It will end by our looking down upon you. There is nothing left!"

And making an effort to restrain his anger, not to say too much, he turned and went on.

On getting home Rodion said his prayer, took off his boots, and sat down beside his wife.

"Yes . . ." he began with a sigh. "We were walking along just now, and Mr. Kutcherov met us. . . . Yes. . . . He saw the girls at daybreak. . . . 'Why don't they bring mushrooms,' he said . . . 'to my wife and children?' he said. . . . And then he looked at me and he said: 'I and my wife will look after you,' he said. I wanted to fall down at his feet, but I hadn't the courage. . . . God give him health. . . . God bless him! . . ."

Stepanida crossed herself and sighed.

"They are kind, simplehearted people," Rodion went on. " 'We shall look after you.' . . . He promised me that before everyone. In our old age . . . it wouldn't be a bad thing. . . . I should always pray for them. . . . Holy Mother, bless them. . . . "

The Feast of the Exaltation of the Cross, the

fourteenth of September, was the festival of the village church. The Lytchkovs, father and son, went across the river early in the morning and returned to dinner drunk; they spent a long time going about the village, alternately singing and swearing; then they had a fight and went to the New Villa to complain. First Lytchkov the father went into the yard with a long ashen stick in his hands. He stopped irresolutely and took off his hat. Just at that moment the engineer and his family were sitting on the verandah, drinking tea.

"What do you want?" shouted the engineer.

"Your honour . . ." Lytchkov began, and burst into tears. "Show the Divine mercy, protect me . . . my son makes my life a misery . . . your honour. . . ."

Lytchkov the son walked up, too; he, too, was bareheaded and had a stick in his hand; he stopped and fixed his drunken senseless eyes on the verandah.

"It is not my business to settle your affairs," said the engineer. "Go to the rural captain or the police officer."

"I have been everywhere. . . . I have lodged a petition . . ." said Lytchkov the father, and he sobbed. "Where can I go now? He can kill me now, it seems. He can do anything. Is that the way to treat a father? A father?"

He raised his stick and hit his son on the head; the son raised his stick and struck his father just on his bald patch such a blow that the stick bounced back. The father did not even flinch, but hit his son again and again on the head. And so they stood and kept hitting one another on the head, and it looked not so much like a fight as some sort of a game. And peasants, men and women, stood in a crowd at the gate and looked into the garden, and the faces of all were grave. They were the peasants who had come to greet them for the holiday, but seeing the Lytchkovs, they were ashamed and did not go in.

The next morning Elena Ivanovna went with the children to Moscow. And there was a rumour that the engineer was selling his house. . . .

V

The peasants had long ago grown used to the sight of the bridge, and it was difficult to imagine the river at that place without a bridge. The heap of rubble left from the building of it

had long been overgrown with grass, the navvies were forgotten, and instead of the strains of the "Dubinushka" that they used to sing, the peasants heard almost every hour the sounds of a passing train.

The New Villa has long ago been sold; now it belongs to a government clerk who comes here from the town for the holidays with his family, drinks tea on the terrace, and then goes back to the town again. He wears a cockade on his cap; he talks and clears his throat as though he were a very important official, though he is only of the rank of a collegiate secretary, and when the peasants bow he makes no response.

In Obrutchanovo everyone has grown older; Kozov is dead. In Rodion's hut there are even more children. Volodka has grown a long red beard. They are still as poor as ever.

In the early spring the Obrutchanovo peasants were sawing wood near the station. And after work they were going home; they walked without haste one after the other. Broad saws curved over their shoulders; the sun was reflected in them. The nightingales were singing in the bushes on the bank, larks were trilling in the heavens. It was quiet at the New Villa; there was not a soul there, and only golden pigeons —golden because the sunlight was streaming upon them—were flying over the house. All of them—Rodion, the two Lytchkovs, and Volodka—thought of the white horses, the little ponies, the fireworks, the boat with the lanterns; they remembered how the engineer's wife, so beautiful and so grandly dressed, had come into the village and talked to them in such a friendly way. And it seemed as though all that had never been; it was like a dream or a fairy tale.

They trudged along, tired out, and mused as they went. . . . In their village, they mused, the people were good, quiet, sensible, fearing God, and Elena Ivanovna, too, was quiet, kind, and gentle; it made one sad to look at her, but why had they not got on together? Why had they parted like enemies? How was it that some mist had shrouded from their eyes what mattered most, and had let them see nothing but damage done by cattle, bridles, pincers, and all those trivial things which now, as they remembered them, seemed so nonsensical? How was it that with the new owner they lived in peace, and yet had been on bad terms with the engineer?

And not knowing what answer to make to

these questions they were all silent except Volodka, who muttered something.

"What is it?" Rodion asked.

"We lived without a bridge . . ." said Volodka gloomily. "We lived without a bridge, and did not ask for one . . . and we don't want it. . . ."

No one answered him and they walked on in silence with drooping heads.

FOR ANALYSIS

1. Like many Chekhov stories, this one presents a welter of misunderstandings. Why is it that the peasants and the engineer cannot get along? Whose fault is it? Consider, for example, what the peasants are asking the engineer to do when they come and ask him to settle an argument before they begin beating each other. How does he misunderstand them? Consider, on the other hand, the peasants' assaults on the engineer's property. How do they misunderstand him?
2. What does the bridge symbolize?
3. The most enlightening character in the story is Rodion. How do his sentiments and his occasional misunderstandings help explain the basic conflict to the reader?
4. What is the theme of this story?

GUY DE MAUPASSANT

In the Moonlight

Well-merited was the name "soldier of God," by the Abbé Marignan. He was a tall, thin priest, fanatical to a degree, but just, and of an exalted soul. All his beliefs were fixed, with never a waver. He thought that he understood God thoroughly, that he penetrated His designs, His wishes, His intentions.

Striding up and down the garden walk of his little country parsonage, sometimes a question rose in his mind: "Why did God make that?" Then in his thoughts, putting himself in God's place, he searched obstinately, and nearly always was satisfied that he found the reason. He was not the man to murmur in transports of pious humility, "O Lord, thy ways are past finding out!" What he said was: "I am the servant of God; I ought to know the reason of what He does, or to divine it if I do not."

Everything in nature seemed to him created with an absolute and admirable logic. The "wherefore" and the "because" were always balanced. The dawns were made to rejoice you on waking, the days to ripen the harvests, the rains to water them, the evenings to prepare for sleeping, and the nights dark for sleep.

The four seasons corresponded perfectly to all the needs of agriculture; and to him the suspicion could never have come that nature has no intention, and that all which lives has accustomed itself, on the contrary, to the hard conditions of different periods, of climates, and of matter.

But he hated women; he hated them unconsciously, and despised them by instinct. He often repeated the words of Christ, "Woman, what have I to do with thee?" and he would add, "One would almost say that God himself was ill pleased with that particular work of his hands." Woman for him was indeed the "child twelve times unclean" of whom the poet speaks. She was the temptress who had ensnared the first man, and who still continued her damnable work; she was the being who is feeble, dangerous, mysteriously troublous. And even more than her poisonous beauty, he hated her loving soul.

He had often felt women's tenderness attack him, and though he knew himself to be unassailable, he grew exasperated at this need of loving which quivers continually in their hearts.

To his mind, God had only created woman to tempt man and to test him. Man should not approach her without those precautions for defense which he would take, and the fears he would cherish, near an ambush. Woman, indeed, was just like a trap, with her arms extended and her lips open toward a man.

He had toleration only for nuns, rendered harmless by their vow; but he treated them harshly notwithstanding, because, ever at the bottom of their chained-up hearts, their chastened hearts, he perceived the eternal tenderness that constantly went out even to him, although he was a priest.

He had a niece who lived with her mother in a little house near by. He was bent on making her a sister of charity. She was pretty and harebrained, and a great tease. When the abbé sermonized, she laughed; when he was angry at her, she kissed him vehemently, pressing him to her heart, while he would seek involuntarily to free himself from her embrace. Notwithstanding, it made him taste a certain sweet joy, awakening deep within him that sensation of fatherhood which slumbers in every man.

Often he talked to her of God, of his God, walking beside her along the footpaths through the fields. She hardly listened, but looked at the sky, the grass, the flowers, with a joy of living which could be seen in her eyes. Sometimes she rushed forward to catch some flying creature, and bringing it back would cry: "Look, my uncle, how pretty it is; I should like to kiss it." And this necessity to "kiss flies" or sweet flowers worried, irritated, and revolted the priest, who saw, even in that, the ineradicable tenderness which ever springs in the hearts of women.

One day the sacristan's wife, who kept house for the Abbé Marignan, told him, very cautiously, that his niece had a lover!

He experienced a dreadful emotion, and he stood choking, with the soap all over his face, in the act of shaving.

When he found himself able to think and speak once more, he cried: "It is not true; you are lying, Melanie!"

But the peasant woman put her hand on her heart; "May our Lord judge me if I am lying, Monsieur le Curé. I tell you she goes to him every evening as soon as your sister is in bed. They meet each other beside the river. You have only to go there between ten o'clock and midnight, and see for yourself."

He ceased scratching his chin and commenced to pace the room quickly, as he always did in his hours of gravest thought. When he tried to begin his shaving again, he cut himself three times from nose to ear.

All day long, he remained silent, swollen with anger and with rage. To his priestly zeal against the mighty power of love was added the moral indignation of a father, of a teacher, of a keeper of souls, who has been deceived, robbed, played with by a child. He felt the egotistical sorrow that parents feel when their daughter announces that she has chosen a husband without them and in spite of their advice.

After his dinner, he tried to read a little, but he could not attune himself to it; and he grew angrier and angrier. When it struck ten, he took his cane, a formidable oaken club which he always carried when he had to go out at night to visit the sick. Smilingly he regarded the enormous cudgel, holding it in his solid, countryman's fist and cutting threatening circles with it in the air. Then, suddenly, he raised it, and grinding his teeth, he brought it down upon a chair, the back of which, split in two, fell heavily to the ground.

He opened his door to go out; but he stopped upon the threshold, surprised by such a splendor of moonlight as you seldom see.

Endowed as he was with an exalted spirit, such a spirit as must have belonged to those dreamer-poets, the Fathers of the Church, he felt himself suddenly softened and moved by the grand and serene beauty of the palefaced night.

In his little garden, bathed in the soft brilliance, his fruit trees, all a-row, were outlining in shadow upon the walk their slender limbs of wood scarce clothed with green; while the giant honeysuckle climbing on the house wall exhaled delicious, sugared breaths, which hovered through the warm, clear night like a perfumed soul.

He began to breathe deep, drinking the air as drunkards drink their wine, and walking slowly, ravished, surprised, and almost oblivious of his niece.

As he stepped into the open country he stopped to contemplate the whole plain, inundated by this caressing radiance, and drowned in the tender and languishing charm of the serene night. In chorus the frogs threw into space their short, metallic notes, and with the seduction of the moonlight, distant nightingales mingled that fitful music of theirs which brings no thoughts but dreams, a light and vibrant melody which seems attuned to kisses.

The abbé continued his walk, his courage failing, he knew not why. He felt, as it were, enfeebled, and suddenly exhausted; he had a great desire to sit down, to pause right there and praise God in all His works.

Below him, following the bends of the little river, wound a great line of poplars. On and about the banks, wrapping all the tortuous watercourse in a kind of light, transparent wadding, hung suspended a fine mist, a white vapor, which the moon-rays crossed, and silvered, and caused to gleam.

The priest paused yet again, penetrated to the

depths of his soul by a strong and growing emotion. And a doubt, a vague uneasiness, seized on him; he felt that one of those questions he sometimes put to himself was now being born.

Why had God done this? Since the night is destined for sleep, for unconsciousness, for repose, for forgetfulness of everything, why, then, make it more charming than the day, sweeter than dawns and sunsets? And this slow, seductive star, more poetical than the sun, and so discreet that it seems designed to light up things too delicate, too mysterious, for the great luminary—why had it come to brighten all the shades? Why did not the sweetest of all song-sters go to rest like the others? Why set himself to singing in the vaguely troubling dark? Why this half-veil over the world? Why these quiver-ings of the heart, this emotion of the soul, this languor of the body? Why this display of seductions which mankind never sees, since night brings sleep? For whom was this sublime spectacle intended, this flo d of poetry poured from heaven to earth? The abbé did not under-stand it at all.

But then, down there along the edge of the pasture appeared two shadows walking side by side under the arched roof of the trees all soaked in glittering mist.

The man was the taller, and had his arm about his mistress's neck; from time to time he kissed her on the forehead. They animated the lifeless landscape which enveloped them, a divine frame made, as it were, expressly for them. They seemed, these two, a single being, the being for whom this calm and silent night was destined; and they approached the priest like a living answer vouchsafed by his Master to his question.

He stood stock-still, overwhelmed, and with a beating heart. He likened it to some Bible story, such as the loves of Ruth and Boaz, the accomplishment of the will of the Lord in one of those great scenes talked of in holy writ. Through his head ran the versicles of the Song of Songs, the ardent cries, the calls of the body, all the passionate poetry of that poem which burns with tenderness and love. And he said to himself, "God perhaps has made such nights as this to clothe with his ideals the loves of men."

He withdrew before the couple, who went on arm in arm. It was really his niece; and now he

asked himself if he had not been about to disobey God. For does not God indeed permit love, since He surrounds it visibly with splendor such as this?

And he fled, in wonder, almost ashamed, as if he had penetrated into a temple where he had no right to enter.

FOR ANALYSIS

1. Which of the following interpretations of the story seems preferable to you?
   (a) As the story of a priest whose own sense of logic leads him finally to abandon a vicious prejudice that he has held
   (b) As the story of a priest whose pride and passion lead him to believe that he can ex-plain God's universe and that this pride in his own logic finally makes him condone something that he ought to condemn.
2. What details in the story support your choice? What, for example, is the major conflict in the story?

JOSEPH CONRAD

The Lagoon

The white man, leaning with both arms over the roof of the little house in the stern of the boat, said to the steersman:

"We will pass the night in Arsat's clearing. It is late."

The Malay only grunted, and went on look-ing fixedly at the river. The white man rested his chin on his crossed arms and gazed at the wake of the boat. At the end of the straight avenue of forests cut by the intense glitter of the river, the sun appeared unclouded and dazzling, poised low over the water that shone smoothly like a band of metal. The forests, somber and dull, stood motionless and silent on each side of the broad stream. At the foot of big, towering trees, trunkless nipa palms rose from the mud of the bank, in bunches of leaves enormous and heavy, that hung unstirring over the brown swirl of eddies. In the stillness of the air every tree, every leaf, every bough, every tendril of creeper and every petal of minute blossoms seemed to have been bewitched into an immobility perfect and final. Nothing moved on the river but the eight paddles that rose flashing regularly, dipped together with a single splash; while the steersman swept right and left with a periodic and sudden flourish of his blade describing a glinting semicircle above his head. The churned-up water frothed alongside with a confused murmur. And the white man's canoe, advancing upstream in the short-lived disturbance of its own making, seemed to enter the portals of a land from which the very memory of motion had forever departed.

The white man, turning his back upon the setting sun, looked along the empty and broad expanse of the sea-reach. For the last three miles of its course the wandering, hesitating river, as if enticed irresistibly by the freedom of an open horizon, flows straight into the sea, flows straight to the east—to the east that harbors both light and darkness. Astern of the boat the repeated call of some bird, a cry discordant and feeble, skipped along over the smooth water and lost itself, before it could reach the other shore, in the breathless silence of the world.

The steersman dug his paddle into the stream, and held hard with stiffened arms, his body thrown forward. The water gurgled aloud; and suddenly the long straight reach seemed to pivot on its center, the forests swung in a semicircle, and the slanting beams of sunset touched the broadside of the canoe with a fiery glow, throwing the slender and distorted shadows of its crew upon the streaked glitter of the river. The white man turned to look ahead. The course of the boat had been altered at right angles to the stream, and the carved dragon head of its prow was pointing now at a gap in the fringing bushes of the bank. It glided through, brushing the overhanging twigs, and disappeared from the river like some slim and amphibious creature leaving the water for its lair in the forests.

The narrow creek was like a ditch: tortuous, fabulously deep; filled with gloom under the thin strip of pure and shining blue of the heaven. Immense trees soared up, invisible behind the festooned draperies of creepers. Here and there, near the glistening blackness of the water, a twisted root of some tall tree showed amongst the tracery of small ferns, black and dull, writh-

ing and motionless, like an arrested snake. The short words of the paddlers reverberated loudly between the thick and somber walls of vegetation. Darkness oozed out from between the trees, through the tangled maze of the creepers, from behind the great fantastic and unstirring leaves; the darkness, mysterious and invincible; the darkness scented and poisonous of impenetrable forests.

The men poled in the shoaling water. The creek broadened, opening out into a wide sweep of a stagnant lagoon. The forests receded from the marshy bank, leaving a level strip of bright green, reedy grass to frame the reflected blueness of the sky. A fleecy pink cloud drifted high above, trailing the delicate coloring of its image under the floating leaves and the silvery blossoms of the lotus. A little house, perched on high piles, appeared black in the distance. Near it, two tall nibong palms, that seemed to have come out of the forests in the background, leaned slightly over the ragged roof, with a suggestion of sad tenderness and care in the droop of their leafy and soaring heads.

The steersman, pointing with his paddle, said, "Arsat is there. I see his canoe fast between the piles."

The polers ran along the sides of the boat glancing over their shoulders at the end of the day's journey. They would have preferred to spend the night somewhere else than on this lagoon of weird aspect and ghostly reputation. Moreover, they disliked Arsat, first as a stranger, and also because he who repairs a ruined house, and dwells in it, proclaims that he is not afraid to live amongst the spirits that haunt the places abandoned by mankind. Such a man can disturb the course of fate by glances or words; while his familiar ghosts are not easy to propitiate by casual wayfarers upon whom they long to wreak the malice of their human master. White men care not for such things, being unbelievers and in league with the Father of Evil, who leads them unharmed through the invisible dangers of this world. To the warnings of the righteous they oppose an offensive pretense of disbelief. What is there to be done?

So they thought, throwing their weight on the end of their long poles. The big canoe glided on swiftly, noiselessly, and smoothly, towards Arsat's clearing, till, in a great rattling of poles thrown down, and the loud murmurs of "Allah be praised!" it came with a gentle knock against the crooked piles below the house.

The boatmen with uplifted faces shouted discordantly, "Arsat! O Arsat!" Nobody came. The white man began to climb the rude ladder giving access to the bamboo platform before the house. The juragan of the boat said sulkily, "We will cook in the sampan, and sleep on the water."

"Pass my blankets and the basket," said the white man, curtly.

He knelt on the edge of the platform to receive the bundle. Then the boat shoved off, and the white man, standing up, confronted Arsat, who had come out through the low door of his hut. He was a man young, powerful, with broad chest and muscular arms. He had nothing on but his sarong. His head was bare. His big, soft eyes stared eagerly at the white man, but his voice and demeanor were composed as he asked, without any words of greeting:

"Have you medicine, Tuan?"

"No," said the visitor in a startled tone. "No. Why? Is there sickness in the house?"

"Enter and see," replied Arsat, in the same calm manner, and turning short round, passed again through the small doorway. The white man, dropping his bundles, followed.

In the dim light of the dwelling he made out on a couch of bamboos a woman stretched on her back under a broad sheet of red cotton cloth. She lay still, as if dead; but her big eyes, wide open, glittered in the gloom, staring upwards at the slender rafters, motionless and unseeing. She was in a high fever, and evidently unconscious. Her cheeks were sunk slightly, her lips were partly open, and on the young face there was the ominous and fixed expression —the absorbed, contemplating expression of the unconscious who are going to die. The two men stood looking down at her in silence.

"Has she been long ill?" asked the traveler.

"I have not slept for five nights," answered the Malay, in a deliberate tone. "At first she heard voices calling her from the water and struggled against me who held her. But since the sun of today rose she hears nothing—she hears not me. She sees nothing. She sees not me—me!"

He remained silent for a minute, then asked softly:

"Tuan, will she die?"

"I fear so," said the white man, sorrowfully. He had known Arsat years ago, in a far country in times of trouble and danger, when no friendship is to be despised. And since his Malay friend had come unexpectedly to dwell in the hut on the lagoon with a strange woman, he had slept many times there, in his journeys up and down the river. He liked the man who knew how to keep faith in council and how to fight without fear by the side of his white friend. He liked him—not so much perhaps as a man likes his favorite dog—but still he liked him well enough to help and ask no questions, to think sometimes vaguely and hazily in the midst of his own pursuits, about the lonely man and the long-haired woman with audacious face and triumphant eyes, who lived together hidden by the forests—alone and feared.

The white man came out of the hut in time to see the enormous conflagration of sunset put out by the swift and stealthy shadows that, rising like a black and impalpable vapor above the treetops, spread over the heaven, extinguishing the crimson glow of floating clouds and the red brilliance of departing daylight. In a few moments all the stars came out above the intense blackness of the earth and the great lagoon gleaming suddenly with reflected lights resembled an oval patch of night sky flung down into the hopeless and abysmal night of the wilderness. The white man had some supper out of the basket, then collecting a few sticks that lay about the platform, made up a small fire, not for warmth, but for the sake of the smoke, which would keep off the mosquitoes. He wrapped himself in the blankets and sat with his back against the reed wall of the house, smoking thoughtfully.

Arsat came through the doorway with noiseless steps and squatted down by the fire. The white man moved his outstretched legs a little.

"She breathes," said Arsat in a low voice, anticipating the expected question. "She breathes and burns as if with a great fire. She speaks not; she hears not—and burns!"

He paused for a moment, then asked in a quiet, incurious tone:

"Tuan . . . will she die?"

The white man moved his shoulders uneasily and muttered in a hesitating manner:

"If such is her fate."

"No, Tuan," said Arsat, calmly. "If such is my fate. I hear, I see, I wait. I remember. . . . Tuan, do you remember the old days? Do you remember my brother?"

"Yes," said the white man. The Malay rose suddenly and went in. The other, sitting still outside, could hear the voice in the hut. Arsat said: "Hear me! Speak!" His words were succeeded by a complete silence. "O Diamelen!" he cried, suddenly. After that cry there was a deep sigh. Arsat came out and sank down again in his old place.

They sat in silence before the fire. There was no sound within the house, there was no sound near them; but far away on to lagoon they could hear the voices of the boatmen ringing fitful and distinct on the calm water. The fire in the bows of the sampan shone faintly in the distance with a hazy red glow. Then it died out. The voices ceased. The land and the water slept invisible, unstirring and mute. It was as though there had been nothing left in the world but the glitter of stars streaming, ceaseless and vain, through the black stillness of the night.

The white man gazed straight before him into the darkness with wide-open eyes. The fear and fascination, the inspiration and the wonder of death—of death near, unavoidable, and unseen, soothed the unrest of his race and stirred the most indistinct, the most intimate of his thoughts. The ever-ready suspicion of evil, the gnawing suspicion that lurks in our hearts, flowed out into the stillness round him—into the stillness profound and dumb, and made it appear untrustworthy and infamous, like the placid and impenetrable mask of an unjustifiable violence. In that fleeting and powerful disturbance of his being the earth enfolded in the starlight peace became a shadowy country of inhuman strife, a battlefield of phantoms terrible and charming, august or ignoble, struggling ardently for the possession of our helpless hearts. An unquiet and mysterious country of inextinguishable desires and fears.

A plaintive murmur rose in the night; a murmur saddening and startling, as if the great solitudes of surrounding woods had tried to whisper into his ear the wisdom of their immense and lofty indifference. Sounds hesitating and vague floated in the air round him, shaped themselves slowly into words; and at last flowed on gently in a murmuring stream of soft and monotonous sentences. He stirred like a man waking up and changed his position slightly. Arsat, motionless and shadowy, sitting with bowed head under the stars, was speaking in a low and dreamy tone:

". . . for where can we lay down the heaviness of our trouble but in a friend's heart? A man must speak of war and of love. You, Tuan, know what war is, and you have seen me in time of danger seek death as other men seek life! A writing may be lost; a lie may be written; but what the eye has seen is truth and remains in the mind!"

"I remember," said the white man, quietly. Arsat went on with mournful composure:

"Therefore I shall speak to you of love. Speak in the night. Speak before both night and love are gone—and the eye of day looks upon my sorrow and my shame; upon my blackened face; upon my burnt-up heart."

A sigh, short and faint, marked an almost imperceptible pause, and then his words flowed on, without a stir, without a gesture.

"After the time of trouble and war was over and you went away from my country in the pursuit of your desires, which we, men of the islands, cannot understand, I and my brother became again, as we had been before, the sword bearers of the Ruler. You know we were men of family, belonging to a ruling race, and more fit than any to carry on our right shoulder the emblem of power. And in the time of prosperity Si Dendring showed us favor, as we, in time of sorrow, had showed to him the faithfulness of our courage. It was a time of peace. A time of deer hunts and cock fights; of idle talks and foolish squabbles between men whose bellies are full and weapons are rusty. But the sower watched the young rice shoots grow up without fear, and the traders came and went, departed lean and returned fat into the river of peace. They brought news, too. Brought lies and truth mixed together, so that no man knew when to rejoice and when to be sorry. We heard from them about you also. They had seen you here and had seen you there. And I was glad to hear, for I remembered the stirring times, and I always remembered you, Tuan, till the time came when my eyes could see nothing in the past, because they had looked upon the one who is dying there—in the house."

He stopped to exclaim in an intense whisper, "O Mara bahia! O Calamity!" then went on speaking a little louder:

"There's no worse enemy and no better friend than a brother, Tuan, for one brother knows another, and in perfect knowledge is strength for good or evil. I loved my brother. I went to him and told him that I could see nothing but one face, hear nothing but one voice. He told me: 'Open your heart so that she can see what is in it—and wait. Patience is wisdom. Inchi Midah may die or our Ruler may throw off his fear of a woman!' . . . I waited! . . . You remember the lady with the veiled face, Tuan, and the fear of our Ruler before her cunning and temper. And if she wanted her servant, what could I do? But I fed the hunger of my heart on short glances and stealthy words. I loitered on the path to the bathhouses in the daytime, and when the sun had fallen behind the forest I crept along the jasmine hedges of the women's courtyard. Unseeing, we spoke to one another through the scent of flowers, through the veil of leaves, through the blades of long grass that stood still before our lips; so great was our prudence, so faint was the murmur of our great longing. The time passed swiftly . . . and there were whispers amongst women—and our enemies watched—my brother was gloomy, and I began to think of killing and of a fierce death. . . . We are of a people who take what they want —like you whites. There is a time when a man should forget loyalty and respect. Might and authority are given to rulers, but to all men is given love and strength and courage. My brother said, 'You shall take her from their midst. We are two who are like one.' And I answered, 'Let it be soon, for I find no warmth in sunlight that does not shine upon her.' Our time came when the Ruler and all the great people went to the mouth of the river to fish by torchlight. There were hundreds of boats, and on the white sand, between the water and the forests, dwellings of leaves were built for the households of the Rajahs. The smoke of cookingfires was like a blue mist of the evening, and many voices rang in it joyfully. While they were making the boats ready to beat up the fish, my brother came to me and said, 'Tonight!' I looked to my weapons, and when the time came our canoe took its place in the circle of boats carrying the torches. The lights blazed on the water, but behind the boats there was darkness. When the shouting began and the excitement made them like mad we dropped out. The water swallowed our fire, and we floated back to the shore that was dark with only here and there the glimmer of embers. We could hear the talk of slave girls amongst the sheds. Then we found a place deserted and silent. We waited there. She came. She came running along the shore, rapid and leaving no trace, like a leaf driven by the wind into the sea. My brother said gloomily, 'Go and take her;

carry her into our boat.' I lifted her in my arms. She panted. Her heart was beating against my breast. I said, 'I take you from those people. You came to the cry of my heart, but my arms take you into my boat against the will of the great!' 'It is right,' said my brother. 'We are men who take what we want and can hold it against many. We should have taken her in daylight.' I said, 'Let us be off'; for since she was in my boat I began to think of our Ruler's many men. 'Yes. Let us be off,' said my brother. 'We are cast out and this boat is our country now—and the sea is our refuge.' He lingered with his foot on the shore, and I entreated him to hasten, for I remembered the strokes of her heart against my breast and thought that two men cannot withstand a hundred. We left, paddling downstream close to the bank; and as we passed by the creek where they were fishing, the great shouting had ceased, but the murmur of voices was loud like the humming of insects flying at noonday. The boats floated, clustered together, in the red light of torches, under a black roof of smoke; and men talked of their sport. Men that boasted, and praised, and jeered—men that would have been our friends in the morning, but on that night were already our enemies. We paddled swiftly past. We had no more friends in the country of our birth. She sat in the middle of the canoe with covered face; silent as she is now; unseeing as she is now—and I had no regret at what I was leaving because I could hear her breathing close to me —as I can hear her now."

He paused, listened with his ear turned to the doorway, then shook his head and went on:

"My brother wanted to shout the cry of challenge—one cry only—to let the people know we were freeborn robbers who trusted our arms and the great sea. And again I begged him in the name of our love to be silent. Could I not hear her breathing close to me? I knew the pursuit would come quick enough. My brother loved me. He dipped his paddle without a splash. He only said, 'There is half a man in you now—the other half is in that woman. I can wait. When you are a whole man again, you will come back with me here to shout defiance. We are sons of the same mother.' I made no answer. All my strength and all my spirit were in my hands that held the paddle —for I longed to be with her in a safe place beyond the reach of men's anger and of women's spite. My love was so great, that I thought it could guide me to a country where death was unknown, if I could only escape from Inchi Midah's fury and from our Ruler's sword. We paddled with haste, breathing through our teeth. The blades bit deep into the smooth water. We passed out of the river; we flew in clear channels amongst the shallows. We skirted the black coast; we skirted the sand beaches where the sea speaks in whispers to the land; and the gleam of white sand flashed back past our boat, so swiftly she ran upon the water. We spoke not. Only once I said, 'Sleep, Diamelen, for soon you may want all your strength.' I heard the sweetness of her voice, but I never turned my head. The sun rose and still we went on. Water fell from my face like rain from a cloud. We flew in the light and heat. I never looked back, but I knew that my brother's eyes, behind me, were looking steadily ahead, for the boat went as straight as a bushman's dart when it leaves the end of the sumpitan. There was no better paddler, no better steersman than my brother. Many times, together, we had won races in that canoe. But we never had put out our strength as we did then—then, when for the last time we paddled together! There was no braver or stronger man in our country than my brother. I could not spare the strength to turn my head and look at him, but every moment I heard the hiss of his breath getting louder behind me. Still he did not speak. The sun was high. The heat clung to my back like a flame of fire. My ribs were ready to burst, but I could no longer get enough air into my chest. And then I felt I must cry out with my last breath, 'Let us rest!' . . . 'Good!' he answered; and his voice was firm. He was strong. He was brave. He knew not fear and no fatigue . . . My brother!"

A murmur powerful and gentle, a murmur vast and faint; the murmur of trembling leaves, of stirring boughs, ran through the tangled depths of the forests, ran over the starry smoothness of the lagoon, and the water between the piles lapped the slimy timber once with a sudden splash. A breath of warm air touched the two men's faces and passed on with a mournful sound—a breath loud and short like an uneasy sigh of the dreaming earth.

Arsat went on in an even, low voice.

"We ran our canoe on the white beach of a little bay close to a long tongue of land that seemed to bar our road; a long wooded cape going far into the sea. My brother knew that place. Beyond the cape a river has its entrance, and through the jungle of that land there is a narrow path. We made a fire and cooked rice. Then we lay down to sleep on the soft sand in the shade of our canoe, while she watched. No sooner had I closed my eyes than I heard her cry of alarm. We leaped up. The sun was half-way down the sky already and coming in sight in the opening of the bay we saw a prau manned by many paddlers. We knew it at once; it was one of our Rajah's praus. They were watching the shore, and saw us. They beat the gong, and turned the head of the prau into the bay. I felt my heart become weak within my breast. Diamelen sat on the sand and covered her face. There was no escape by sea. My brother laughed. He had the gun you had given him, Tuan, before you went away, but there was only a handful of powder. He spoke to me quickly: 'Run with her along the path. I shall keep them back, for they have no fire-arms, and landing in the face of a man with a gun is certain death for some. Run with her. On the other side of that wood there is a fisherman's house—and a canoe. When I have fired all the shots I will follow. I am a great runner, and before they can come up we shall be gone. I will hold out as long as I can, for she is but a woman—that can neither run nor fight, but she has your heart in her weak hands.' He dropped behind the canoe. The prau was coming. She and I ran, and as we rushed along the path I heard shots. My brother fired—once—twice— and the booming of the gong ceased. There was silence behind us. That neck of land is narrow. Before I heard my brother fire the third shot I saw the shelving shore, and I saw the water again; the mouth of a broad river. We crossed a grassy glade. We ran down to the water. I saw a low hut above the black mud, and a small canoe hauled up. I heard another shot behind me. I thought, 'That is his last charge.' We rushed down to the canoe; a man came running from the hut, but I leaped on him, and we rolled together in the mud. Then I got up, and he lay still at my feet. I don't know whether I had killed him or not. I and Diamelen pushed the canoe afloat. I heard yells behind me, and I saw my brother run across the glade. Many men were bounding after him. I took her in my arms and threw her into the boat, then leaped in myself. When I looked back I saw that my brother had fallen. He fell and was up again, but the men were closing round him. He shouted, 'I am coming!' The men were close to him. I looked. Many men. Then I looked at her. Tuan, I pushed the canoe! I pushed it into deep water. She was kneeling forward looking at me, and I said, 'Take your paddle,' while I struck the water with mine. Tuan, I heard him cry. I heard him cry my name twice; and I heard voices shouting, 'Kill! Strike!' I never turned back. I heard him calling my name again with a great shriek, as when life is going out together with the voice—and I never turned my head. My own name! . . . My brother! Three times he called—but I was not afraid of life. Was she not there in that canoe? And could I not with her find a country where death is forgotten—where death is unknown!"

The white man sat up. Arsat rose and stood, an indistinct and silent figure above the dying embers of the fire. Over the lagoon a mist drifting and low had crept, erasing slowly the glittering images of the stars. And now a great expanse of white vapor covered the land: it flowed cold and gray in the darkness, eddied in noiseless whirls round the tree trunks and about the platform of the house, which seemed to float upon a restless and impalpable illusion of a sea. Only far away the tops of the trees stood outlined on the twinkle of heaven, like a somber and forbidding shore—a coast deceptive, pitiless and black.

Arsat's voice vibrated loudly in the profound peace.

"I had her there! I had her! To get her I would have faced all mankind. But I had her —and—"

His words went out ringing into the empty distances. He paused, and seemed to listen to them dying away very far—beyond help and beyond recall. Then he said quietly:

"Tuan, I loved my brother."

A breath of wind made him shiver. High above his head, high above the silent sea of mist the drooping leaves of the palms rattled together with a mournful and expiring sound. The white man stretched his legs. His chin rested on his chest, and he murmured sadly without lifting his head:

"We all love our brothers."

Arsat burst out with an intense whispering violence:

"What did I care who died? I wanted peace in my own heart."

He seemed to hear a stir in the house—listened—then stepped in noiselessly. The white man stood up. A breeze was coming in fitful puffs. The stars shone paler as if they had retreated into the frozen depths of immense space. After a chill gust of wind there were a few seconds of perfect calm and absolute silence. Then from behind the black and wavy line of the forests a column of golden light shot up into the heavens and spread over the semicircle of the eastern horizon. The sun had risen. The mist lifted, broke into drifting patches, vanished into thin flying wreaths; and the unveiled lagoon lay, polished and black, in the heavy shadows at the foot of the wall of trees. A white eagle rose over it with a slanting and ponderous flight, reached the clear sunshine and appeared dazzlingly brilliant for a moment, then soaring higher, became a dark and motionless speck before it vanished into the blue as if it had left the earth forever. The white man, standing gazing upwards before the doorway, heard in the hut a confused and broken murmur of distracted words ending with a loud groan. Suddenly Arsat stumbled out with outstretched hands, shivered, and stood still for some time with fixed eyes. Then he said:

"She burns no more."

Before his face the sun showed its edge above the treetops rising steadily. The breeze freshened; a great brilliance burst upon the lagoon, sparkled on the rippling water. The forests came out of the clear shadows of the morning, became distinct, as if they had rushed nearer—to stop short in a great stir of leaves, of nodding boughs, of swaying branches. In the merciless sunshine the whisper of unconscious life grew louder, speaking in an incomprehensible voice round the dumb darkness of that human sorrow. Arsat's eyes wandered slowly, then stared at the rising sun.

"I can see nothing," he said half aloud to himself.

"There is nothing," said the white man, moving to the edge of the platform and waving his hand to his boat. A shout came faintly over the lagoon and the sampan began to glide towards the abode of the friend of ghosts.

"If you want to come with me, I will wait all the morning," said the white man, looking away upon the water.

"No, Tuan," said Arsat, softly. "I shall not eat or sleep in this house, but I must first see my road. Now I can see nothing—see nothing! There is no light and no peace in the world; but there is death—death for many. We are sons of the same mother—and I left him in the midst of enemies; but I am going back now."

He drew a long breath and went on in a dreamy tone:

"In a little while I shall see clear enough to strike—to strike. But she has died, and . . . now . . . darkness."

He flung his arms wide open, let them fall along his body, then stood still with unmoved face and stony eyes, staring at the sun. The white man got down into his canoe. The polers ran smartly along the sides of the boat, looking over their shoulders at the beginning of a weary journey. High in the stern, his head muffled up in white rags, the juragan sat moody, letting his paddle trail in the water. The white man, leaning with both arms over the grass roof of the little cabin, looked back at the shining ripple of the boat's wake. Before the sampan passed out of the lagoon into the creek he lifted his eyes. Arsat had not moved. He stood lonely in the searching sunshine; and he looked beyond the great light of a cloudless day into the darkness of a world of illusions.

FOR ANALYSIS

1. Why does Conrad insist repeatedly on the contrast between light and dark in the story? Why is so much of the first part of the story concerned with details of darkness in the setting?
2. How does Conrad's reporting the white man's perception of the woman as having an "audacious face" and "triumphant eyes" affect the story? Does it help focus the problem in the story? What does it tell you about the character of the woman? About the character of Arsat?
3. What is it specifically that tortures Arsat? That he lost his woman? That he lost his brother? That he paid too high a price for her? Or has he lost something even larger? What does the last sentence of the story mean?
4. Where does the crisis, the turning point of the story, occur? Is there a clear-cut moment of choice that determines the outcome?
5. What does the white eagle symbolize? Why does sunshine suddenly invade the dark setting immediately afterward?
6. What will Arsat gain by going back to the village? What will he lose?
7. There is very little immediate action in the story. How is the exposition handled here so that the story doesn't falter?

KATHERINE MANSFIELD

The Fly

"Y'are very snug in here," piped old Mr. Woodifield, and he peered out of the great, green leather armchair by his friend the boss's desk as a baby peers out of its pram. His talk was over; it was time for him to be off. But he did not want to go. Since he had retired, since his . . . stroke, the wife and the girls kept him boxed up in the house every day of the week except Tuesday. On Tuesday he was dressed up and brushed and allowed to cut back to the City for the day. Though what he did there the wife and girls couldn't imagine. Made a nuisance of himself to his friends, they supposed. . . . Well, perhaps so. All the same, we cling to our last pleasures as the tree clings to its last leaves. So there sat old Woodifield, smoking a cigar and staring almost greedily at the boss, who rolled in his office chair, stout, rosy, five years older than he, and still going strong, still at the helm. It did one good to see him.

Wistfully, admiringly, the old voice added, "It's snug in here, upon my word!"

"Yes, it's comfortable enough," agreed the boss, and he flipped *The Financial Times* with a paperknife. As a matter of fact he was proud of his room; he liked to have it admired, especially by old Woodifield. It gave him a feeling of deep, solid satisfaction to be planted there in the midst of it in full view of that frail old figure in the muffler.

"I've had it done up lately," he explained, as he had explained for the past—how many?— weeks. "New carpet," and he pointed to the bright red carpet with a pattern of large white rings. "New furniture," and he nodded towards the massive bookcase and the table with legs like twisted treacle. "Electric heating!" He waved almost exultantly towards the five transparent, pearly sausages glowing so softly in the tilted copper pan.

But he did not draw old Woodifield's attention to the photograph over the table of a grave-looking boy in uniform standing in one of those spectral photographers' parks with photographers' storm clouds behind him. It was not new. It had been there for over six years.

"There was something I wanted to tell you,"

said old Woodifield, and his eyes grew dim remembering. "Now what was it? I had it in my mind when I started out this morning." His hands began to tremble, and patches of red showed above his beard.

Poor old chap, he's on his last pins, thought the boss. And, feeling kindly, he winked at the old man, and said jokingly, "I tell you what. I've got a little drop of something here that'll do you good before you go out into the cold again. It's beautiful stuff. It wouldn't hurt a child." He took a key off his watch chain, unlocked a cupboard below his desk, and drew forth a dark, squat bottle. "That's the medicine," said he. "And the man from whom I got it told me on the strict Q.T. it came from the cellars at Windsor Cassel."

Old Woodifield's mouth fell open at the sight. He couldn't have looked more surprised if the boss had produced a rabbit.

"It's whisky, ain't it?" he piped, feebly.

The boss turned the bottle and lovingly showed him the label. Whisky it was.

"D'you know," said he, peering up at the boss wonderingly, "they won't let me touch it at home." And he looked as though he was going to cry.

"Ah, that's where we know a bit more than the ladies," cried the boss, swooping across for two tumblers that stood on the table with the water bottle, and pouring a generous finger into each. "Drink it down. It'll do you good. And don't put any water with it. It's sacrilege to tamper with stuff like this. Ah!" He tossed off his, pulled out his handkerchief, hastily wiped his moustaches, and cocked an eye at old Woodifield, who was rolling his in his chaps.

The old man swallowed, was silent a moment, and then said faintly, "It's nutty!"

But it warmed him; it crept into his chill old brain—he remembered.

"That was it," he said, heaving himself out of his chair. "I thought you'd like to know. The girls were in Belgium last week having a look at poor Reggie's grave, and they happened to come across your boy's. They're quite near each other, it seems."

Old Woodifield paused, but the boss made no reply. Only a quiver in his eyelids showed that he heard.

"The girls were delighted with the way the place is kept," piped the old voice. "Beautifully looked after. Couldn't be better if they were at home. You've not been across, have yer?"

"No, no!" For various reasons the boss had not been across.

"There's miles of it," quavered old Woodifield, "and it's all as neat as a garden. Flowers growing on all the graves. Nice broad paths." It was plain from his voice how much he liked a nice broad path.

The pause came again. Then the old man brightened wonderfully.

"D'you know what the hotel made the girls pay for a pot of jam?" he piped. "Ten francs! Robbery, I call it. It was a little pot, so Gertrude says, no bigger than a half crown. And she hadn't taken more than a spoonful when they charged her ten francs. Gertrude brought the pot away with her to teach 'em a lesson. Quite right, too; it's trading on our feelings. They think because we're over there having a look around we're ready to pay anything. That's what it is." And he turned towards the door.

"Quite right, quite right!" cried the boss, though what was quite right he hadn't the least idea. He came round by his desk, followed the shuffling footsteps to the door, and saw the old fellow out. Woodifield was gone.

For a long moment the boss stayed, staring at nothing, while the gray-haired office messenger, watching him, dodged in and out of his cubbyhole like a dog that expects to be taken for a run. Then: "I'll see nobody for half an hour, Macey," said the boss. "Understand? Nobody at all."

"Very good, sir."

The door shut, the firm heavy steps recrossed the bright carpet, the fat body plumped down in the spring chair, and leaning forward, the boss covered his face with his hands. He wanted, he intended, he had arranged to weep. . . .

It had been a terrible shock to him when old Woodifield sprang that remark upon him about the boy's grave. It was exactly as though the earth had opened and he had seen the boy lying there with Woodifield's girls staring down at him. For it was strange. Although over six years had passed away, the boss never thought of the boy except as lying unchanged, unblemished in his uniform, asleep for ever. "My son!" groaned the boss. But no tears came yet. In the past, in the first months and even years after the boy's death, he had only to say those words to be overcome by such grief that nothing short of a violent fit of weeping could relieve him. Time, he had declared then, he had told everybody, could make no difference. Other men perhaps might recover, might live their loss down, but not he. How was it possible? His boy was an only son. Ever since his birth the boss had worked at building up this business for him; it had no other meaning if it was not for the boy. Life itself had come to have no other meaning. How on earth could he have slaved, denied himself, kept going all those years without the promise for ever before him of the boy's stepping into his shoes and carrying on where he left off?

And that promise had been so near being fulfilled. The boy had been in the office learning the ropes for a year before the war. Every morning they had started off together; they had come back by the same train. And what congratulations he had received as the boy's father! No wonder; he had taken to it marvellously. As to his popularity with the staff, every man jack of them down to old Macey couldn't make enough of the boy. And he wasn't in the least spoilt. No, he was just his bright, natural self, with the right word for everybody, with that boyish look and his habit of saying, "Simply splendid!"

But all that was over and done with as though it never had been. The day had come when Macey had handed him the telegram that brought the whole place crashing about his head. "Deeply regret to inform you. . . ." And he had left the office a broken man, with his life in ruins.

Six years ago, six years. . . . How quickly time passed! It might have happened yesterday. The boss took his hands from his face; he was puzzled. Something seemed to be wrong with him. He wasn't feeling as he wanted to feel. He decided to get up and have a look at the boy's photograph. But it wasn't a favorite photograph of his; the expression was unnatural. It was cold, even stern-looking. The boy had never looked like that.

At that moment the boss noticed that a fly had fallen into his broken inkpot, and was trying feebly but desperately to clamber out again. Help! help! said those struggling legs. But the sides of the inkpot were wet and slippery; it fell back again and began to swim. The boss took up a pen, picked the fly out of the ink, and shook it onto a piece of blotting paper. For a fraction of a second it lay still on the dark patch that oozed round it. Then the front legs waved, took hold, and, pulling its small sodden body up, it began the immense task of cleaning the ink from its wings. Over and under, over and under, went a leg along a wing, as the stone goes over and under the scythe. Then there was a pause, while the fly, seeming to stand on the tips of its toes, tried to expand first one wing and then the other. It succeeded at last, and, sitting down, it began, like a minute cat, to clean its face. Now one could imagine that the little front legs rubbed against each other lightly, joyfully. The horrible danger was over; it had escaped; it was ready for life again.

But just then the boss had an idea. He plunged his pen back into the ink, leaned his thick wrist on the blotting paper, and as the fly tried its wings down came a great heavy blot. What would it make of that? What indeed! The little beggar seemed absolutely cowed, stunned, and afraid to move because of what would happen next. But then, as if painfully, it dragged itself forward. The front legs waved, caught hold, and, more slowly this time, the task began from the beginning.

"He's a plucky little devil," thought the boss, and he felt a real admiration for the fly's courage. That was the way to tackle things; that was the right spirit. Never say die; it was only a question of . . . But the fly had again finished its laborious task, and the boss had just time to refill his pen, to shake fair and square on the new-cleaned body yet another dark drop. What about it this time? A painful moment of suspense followed. But behold, the front legs were again waving; the boss felt a rush of relief. He leaned over the fly and said to it tenderly, "You artful little b . . ." And he actually had the brilliant notion of breathing on it to help the drying process. All the same, there was something timid and weak about its efforts now, and the boss decided that this time should be the last, as he dipped the pen into the inkpot.

It was. The last blot fell on the soaked blotting paper, and the draggled fly lay in it and did not stir. The back legs were stuck to the body; the front legs were not to be seen.

"Come on," said the boss. "Look sharp!" And he stirred it with his pen—in vain. Nothing happened or was likely to happen. The fly was dead.

The boss lifted the corpse on the end of the paper knife and flung it into the waste-paper

basket. But such a grinding feeling of wretched-
ness seized him that he felt positively frightened.
He started forward and pressed the bell for
Macey.

"Bring me some fresh blotting paper," he said,
sternly, "and look sharp about it." And while
the old dog padded away he fell to wondering
what it was he had been thinking about before.
What was it? It was . . . He took out his handkerchief and passed it inside his collar. For the
life of him he could not remember.

FOR ANALYSIS

1. The key to the meaning of this story is obviously
   the fly. What does it symbolize: The grief of the
   father, which after being resurrected repeatedly
   cannot be revived? His son, who was exploited
   by his father while alive? The father himself?
2. Validate your interpretation by reference to earlier
   details in the story.

D. H. LAWRENCE

The Horse Dealer's Daughter

"Well, Mabel, and what are you going to do
with yourself?" asked Joe, with foolish flippancy.
He felt quite safe himself. Without listening for
an answer, he turned aside, worked a grain of
tobacco to the tip of his tongue, and spat it out.
He did not care about anything, since he felt
safe himself.

The three brothers and the sister sat round the
desolate breakfast table, attempting some sort of
desultory consultation. The morning's post had
given the final tap to the family fortunes, and
all was over. The dreary dining room itself, with
its heavy mahogany furniture, looked as if it
were waiting to be done away with.

But the consultation amounted to nothing.
There was a strange air of ineffectuality about
the three men, as they sprawled at table,
smoking and reflecting vaguely on their own
condition. The girl was alone, a rather short,
sullen-looking young woman of twenty-seven.

She did not share the same life as her brothers.
She would have been good-looking, save for the
impassive fixity of her face, "bulldog," as her
brothers called it.

There was a confused tramping of horses' feet
outside. The three men all sprawled round in
their chairs to watch. Beyond the dark holly
bushes that separated the strip of lawn from the
highroad, they could see a cavalcade of shire
horses swinging out of their own yard, being
taken for exercise. This was the last time. These
were the last horses that would go through their
hands. The young men watched with critical,
callous look. They were all frightened at the
collapse of their lives, and the sense of disaster
in which they were involved left them no inner
freedom.

Yet they were three fine, well-set fellows
enough. Joe, the eldest, was a man of thirty-
three, broad and handsome in a hot, flushed way.
His face was red, he twisted his black moustache
over a thick finger, his eyes were shallow and
restless. He had a sensual way of uncovering his
teeth when he laughed, and his bearing was
stupid. Now he watched the horses with a glazed
look of helplessness in his eyes, a certain stupor
of downfall.

The great draught-horses swung past. They
were tied head to tail, four of them, and they
heaved along to where a lane branched off from
the highroad, planting their great hoofs flouting-
ly in the fine black mud, swinging their great
rounded haunches sumptuously, and trotting a
few sudden steps as they were led into the lane,
round the corner. Every movement showed a
massive, slumbrous strength, and a stupidity
which held them in subjection. The groom at the
head looked back, jerking the leading rope. And
the cavalcade moved out of sight up the lane, the
tail of the last horse, bobbed up tight and stiff,
held out taut from the swinging great haunches
as they rocked behind the hedges in a motion
like sleep.

Joe watched with glazed hopeless eyes. The
horses were almost like his own body to him.
He felt he was done for now. Luckily he was
engaged to a woman as old as himself, and therefore her father, who was steward of a neighbouring estate, would provide him with a job. He
would marry and go into harness. His life was
over, he would be a subject animal now.

He turned uneasily aside, the retreating steps

of the horses echoing in his ears. Then, with foolish restlessness, he reached for the scraps of bacon rind from the plates, and making a faint whistling sound, flung them to the terrier that lay against the fender. He watched the dog swallow them, and waited till the creature looked into his eyes. Then a faint grin came on his face, and in a high, foolish voice he said:

"You won't get much more bacon, shall you, you little b——?"

The dog faintly and dismally wagged its tail, then lowered its haunches, circled round, and lay down again.

There was another helpless silence at the table. Joe sprawled uneasily in his seat, not willing to go till the family conclave was dissolved. Fred Henry, the second brother, was erect, clean-limbed, alert. He had watched the passing of the horses with more *sangfroid*. If he was an animal, like Joe, he was an animal which controls, not one which is controlled. He was master of any horse, and he carried himself with a well-tempered air of mastery. But he was not master of the situations of life. He pushed his coarse brown moustache upwards, off his lip, and glanced irritably at his sister, who sat impassive and inscrutable.

"You'll go and stop with Lucy for a bit, shan't you?" he asked. The girl did not answer.

"I don't see what else you can do," persisted Fred Henry.

"Go as a skivvy," Joe interpolated laconically.

The girl did not move a muscle.

"If I was her, I should go in for training for a nurse," said Malcolm, the youngest of them all. He was the baby of the family, a young man of twenty-two, with a fresh, jaunty *museau*.

But Mabel did not take any notice of him. They had talked at her and round her for so many years, that she hardly heard them at all.

The marble clock on the mantelpiece softly chimed the half hour, the dog rose uneasily from the hearthrug and looked at the party at the breakfast table. But still they sat on in ineffectual conclave.

"Oh, all right," said Joe suddenly, *à propos* of nothing. "I'll get a move on."

He pushed back his chair, straddled his knees with a downward jerk, to get them free, in horsey fashion, and went to the fire. Still he did not go out of the room; he was curious to know what the others would do or say. He began to charge his pipe, looking down at the dog and saying,

in a high, affected voice:

"Going wi' me? Going wi' me are ter? Tha'rt goin' further than tha counts on just now, dost hear?"

The dog faintly wagged its tail, the man stuck out his jaw and covered his pipe with his hands, and puffed intently, losing himself in the tobacco, looking down all the while at the dog with an absent brown eye. The dog looked up at him in mournful distrust. Joe stood with his knees stuck out, in real horsey fashion.

"Have you had a letter from Lucy?" Fred Henry asked of his sister.

"Last week," came the neutral reply.

"And what does she say?"

There was no answer.

"Does she *ask* you to go and stop there?" persisted Fred Henry.

"She says I can if I like."

"Well, then, you'd better. Tell her you'll come on Monday."

This was received in silence.

"That's what you'll do then, is it?" said Fred Henry, in some exasperation.

But she made no answer. There was a silence of futility and irritation in the room. Malcolm grinned fatuously.

"You'll have to make up your mind between now and next Wednesday," said Joe loudly, "or else find yourself lodgings on the kerbstone."

The face of the young woman darkened, but she sat on immutable.

"Here's Jack Fergusson!" exclaimed Malcolm, who was looking aimlessly out of the window.

"Where?" exclaimed Joe, loudly.

"Just gone past."

"Coming in?"

Malcolm craned his neck to see the gate.

"Yes," he said.

There was a silence. Mabel sat on like one condemned, at the head of the table. Then a whistle was heard from the kitchen. The dog got up and barked sharply. Joe opened the door and shouted:

"Come on."

After a moment a young man entered. He was muffled up in overcoat and a purple woollen scarf, and his tweed cap, which he did not remove, was pulled down on his head. He was of medium height, his face was rather long and pale, his eyes looked tired.

"Hello, Jack! Well, Jack!" exclaimed Malcolm

and Joe. Fred Henry merely said, "Jack."

"What's doing?" asked the newcomer, evidently addressing Fred Henry.

"Same. We've got to be out by Wednesday. —Got a cold?"

"I have—got it bad, too."

"Why don't you stop in?"

"*Me* stop in? When I can't stand on my legs, perhaps I shall have a chance." The young man spoke huskily. He had a slight Scotch accent.

"It's a knock-out, isn't it," said Joe, boisterously, "if a doctor goes round croaking with a cold. Looks bad for the patients, doesn't it?"

The young doctor looked at him slowly.

"Anything the matter with *you*, then?" he asked sarcastically.

"Not as I know of. Damn your eyes, I hope not. Why?"

"I thought you were very concerned about the patients, wondered if you might be one yourself."

"Damn it, no, I've never been patient to no flaming doctor, and hope I never shall be," returned Joe.

At this point Mabel rose from the table, and they all seemed to become aware of her existence. She began putting the dishes together. The young doctor looked at her, but did not address her. He had not greeted her. She went out of the room with the tray, her face impassive and unchanged.

"When are you off then, all of you?" asked the doctor.

"I'm catching the eleven-forty," replied Malcolm. "Are you goin' down wi' th' trap, Joe?"

"Yes, I've told you I'm going down wi' th' trap, haven't I?"

"We'd better be getting her in then.—So long, Jack, if I don't see you before I go," said Malcolm, shaking hands.

He went out, followed by Joe, who seemed to have his tail between his legs.

"Well, this is the devil's own," exclaimed the doctor, when he was left alone with Fred Henry. "Going before Wednesday, are you?"

"That's the orders," replied the other.

"Where, to Northampton?"

"That's it."

"The devil!" exclaimed Fergusson, with quiet chagrin.

And there was silence between the two.

"All settled up, are you?" asked Fergusson.

"About."

There was another pause.

"Well, I shall miss yer, Freddy, boy," said the young doctor.

"And I shall miss thee, Jack," returned the other.

"Miss you like hell," mused the doctor.

Fred Henry turned aside. There was nothing to say. Mabel came in again, to finish clearing the table.

"What are *you* going to do, then, Miss Pervin?" asked Fergusson. "Going to your sister's, are you?"

Mabel looked at him with her steady, dangerous eyes, that always made him uncomfortable, unsettling his superficial ease.

"No," she said.

"Well, what in the name of fortune *are* you going to do? Say what you mean to do," cried Fred Henry, with futile intensity.

But she only averted her head, and continued her work. She folded the white tablecloth, and put on the chenille cloth.

"The sulkiest bitch that ever trod!" muttered her brother.

But she finished her task with perfectly impassive face, the young doctor watching her interestedly all the while. The she went out.

Fred Henry stared after her, clenching his lips, his blue eyes fixing in sharp antagonism, as he made a grimace of sour exasperation.

"You could bray her into bits, and that's all you'd get out of her," he said, in a small, narrowed tone.

The doctor smiled faintly.

"What's she *going* to do, then?" he asked.

"Strike me if *I* know!" returned the other.

There was a pause. Then the doctor stirred.

"I'll be seeing you tonight, shall I?" he said to his friend.

"Ay—where's it to be? Are we going over to Jessdale?"

"I don't know. I've got such a cold on me. I'll come round to the Moon and Stars, anyway."

"Let Lizzie and May miss their night for once, eh?"

"That's it—if I feel as I do now."

"All's one—"

The two young men went through the passage and down to the back door together. The house was large, but it was servantless now, and desolate. At the back was a small bricked house-yard, and beyond that a big square, gravelled fine and red, and having stables on two sides.

Sloping, dank, winter-dark fields stretched away on the open sides.

But the stables were empty. Joseph Pervin, the father of the family, had been a man of no education, who had become a fairly large horse dealer. The stables had been full of horses, there was a great turmoil and come-and-go of horses and of dealers and grooms. Then the kitchen was full of servants. But of late things had declined. The old man had married a second time, to retrieve his fortunes. Now he was dead and everything was gone to the dogs, there was nothing but debt and threatening.

For months, Mabel had been servantless in the big house, keeping the home together in penury for her ineffectual brothers. She had kept house for ten years. But previously, it was with unstinted means. Then, however brutal and coarse everything was, the sense of money had kept her proud, confident. The men might be foulmouthed, the women in the kitchen might have bad reputations, her brothers might have illegitimate children. But so long as there was money, the girl felt herself established, and brutally proud, reserved.

No company came to the house, save dealers and coarse men. Mabel had no associates of her own sex, after her sister went away. But she did not mind. She went regularly to church, she attended to her father. And she lived in the memory of her mother, who had died when she was fourteen, and whom she had loved. She had loved her father, too, in a different way, depending upon him, and feeling secure in him, until at the age of fifty-four he married again. And then she had set hard against him. Now he had died and left them all hopelessly in debt.

She had suffered badly during the period of poverty. Nothing, however, could shake the curious sullen, animal pride that dominated each member of the family. Now, for Mabel, the end had come. Still she would not cast about her. She would follow her own way just the same. She would always hold the keys of her own situation. Mindless and persistent, she endured from day to day. Why should she think? Why should she answer anybody? It was enough that this was the end, and there was no way out. She need not pass any more darkly along the main street of the small town, avoiding every eye. She need not demean herself any more, going into the shops and buying the cheapest food. This was at an end. She thought of nobody, not even of herself. Mindless and persistent, she seemed in a sort of ecstasy to be coming nearer to her fulfilment, her own glorification, approaching her dead mother, who was glorified.

In the afternoon she took a little bag, with shears and sponge and a small scrubbing brush, and went out. It was a gray, wintry day, with saddened, dark-green fields and an atmosphere blackened by the smoke of foundries not far off. She went quickly, darkly along the causeway, heeding nobody, through the town to the churchyard.

There she always felt secure, as if no one could see her, although as a matter of fact she was exposed to the stare of everyone who passed along under the churchyard wall. Nevertheless, once under the shadow of the great looming church, among the graves, she felt immune from the world, reserved within the thick churchyard wall as in another country.

Carefully she clipped the grass from the grave, and arranged the pinky-white, small chrysanthemums in the tin cross. When this was done, she took an empty jar from a neighbouring grave, brought water, and carefully, most scrupulously sponged the marble headstone and the coping-stone.

It gave her sincere satisfaction to do this. She felt in immediate contact with the world of her mother. She took minute pains, went through the park in a state bordering on pure happiness, as if in performing this task she came into a subtle, intimate connection with her mother. For the life she followed here in the world was far less real than the world of death she inherited from her mother.

The doctor's house was just by the church. Fergusson, being a mere hired assistant, was slave to the countryside. As he hurried now to attend to the outpatients in the surgery, glancing across the graveyard with his quick eye, he saw the girl at her task at the grave. She seemed so intent and remote, it was like looking into another world. Some mystical element was touched in him. He slowed down as he walked, watching her as if spellbound.

She lifted her eyes, feeling him looking. Their eyes met. And each looked again at once, each feeling, in some way, found out by the other. He lifted his cap and passed on down the road. There remained distinct in his consciousness, like a vision, the memory of her face, lifted from the tombstone in the churchyard, and looking at him with slow, large, portentous eyes. It *was* portentous, her face. It seemed to mesmerize him. There was a heavy power in her eyes which laid hold of his whole being, as if he had drunk some powerful drug. He had been feeling weak and done before. Now the life came back into him, he felt delivered from his own fretted, daily self.

He finished his duties at the surgery as quickly as might be, hastily filling up the bottles of the waiting people with cheap drugs. Then, in perpetual haste, he set off again to visit several cases in another part of his round, before tea-time. At all times he preferred to walk, if he could, but particularly when he was not well. He fancied the motion restored him.

The afternoon was falling. It was grey, deadened, and wintry, with a slow, moist, heavy coldness sinking in and deadening all the faculties. But why should he think or notice? He hastily climbed the hill and turned across the dark-green fields, following the black cinder-track. In the distance, across a shallow dip in the country, the small town was clustered like smouldering ash, a tower, a spire, a heap of low, raw, extinct houses. And on the nearest fringe of the town, sloping into the dip, was Old-meadow, the Pervins' house. He could see the stables and the outbuildings distinctly, as they lay towards him on the slope. Well, he would not go there many more times! Another resource would be lost to him, another place gone: the only company he cared for in the alien, ugly little town he was losing. Nothing but work, drudgery, constant hastening from dwelling to dwelling among the colliers and the ironworkers. It wore him out, but at the same time he had a craving for it. It was a stimulant to him to be in the homes of the working people, moving as it were through the innermost body of their life. His nerves were excited and gratified. He could come so near, into the very lives of the rough, inarticulate, powerfully emotional men and women. He grumbled, he said he hated the hellish hole. But as a matter of fact it excited him, the contact with the rough, strongly-feeling people was a stimulant applied direct to his nerves.

Below Oldmeadow, in the green, shallow, soddened hollow of fields, lay a square, deep pond. Roving across the landscape, the doctor's quick eye detected a figure in black passing through the gate of the field, down towards the pond. He looked again. It would be Mabel Pervin. His mind suddenly became alive and attentive.

Why was she going down there? He pulled up on the path on the slope above, and stood staring. He could just make sure of the small black figure moving in the hollow of the failing day. He seemed to see her in the midst of such obscurity, that he was like a clairvoyant, seeing rather with the mind's eye that with ordinary sight. Yet he could see her positively enough, whilst he kept his eye attentive. He felt, if he looked away from her, in the thick, ugly falling dusk, he would lose her altogether.

He followed her minutely as she moved, direct and intent, like something transmitted rather than stirring in voluntary activity, straight down the field towards the pond. There she stood on the bank for a moment. She never raised her head. Then she waded slowly into the water.

He stood motionless as the small black figure walked slowly and deliberately towards the center of the pond, very slowly, gradually moving deeper into the motionless water, and still moving forward as the water got up to her breast. Then he could see her no more in the dusk of the dead afternoon.

"There!" he exclaimed. "Would you believe it?"

And he hastened straight down, running over the wet, soddened fields, pushing through the hedges, down into the depression of callous wintry obscurity. It took him several minutes to come to the pond. He stood on the bank, breathing heavily. He could see nothing. His eyes seemed to penetrate the dead water. Yes, perhaps that was the dark shadow of her black clothing beneath the surface of the water.

He slowly ventured into the pond. The bottom was deep, soft clay, he sank in, and the water clasped dead cold round his legs. As he stirred he could smell the cold, rotten clay that fouled up into the water. It was objectionable in his lungs. Still, repelled and yet not heeding, he moved deeper into the pond. The cold water rose over his thighs, over his loins, upon his abdomen. The lower part of his body was all sunk in the hideous cold element. And the bottom was so deeply soft and uncertain, he was afraid of pitching with his mouth underneath. He could not swim, and was afraid.

He crouched a little, spreading his hands under the water and moving them round, trying to feel for her. The dead cold pond swayed upon his chest. He moved again, a little deeper, and again, with his hands underneath, he felt all around under the water. And he touched her clothing. But it evaded his fingers. He made a desperate effort to grasp it.

And so doing he lost his balance and went under, horribly, suffocating in the foul earthy water, struggling madly for a few moments. At last, after what seemed an eternity, he got his footing, rose again into the air and looked around. He gasped, and knew he was in the world. Then he looked at the water. She had risen near him. He grasped her clothing, and drawing her nearer, turned to take his way to land again.

He went very slowly, carefully, absorbed in the slow progress. He rose higher, climbing out of the pond. The water was now only about his legs; he was thankful, full of relief to be out of the clutches of the pond. He lifted her and staggered on to the bank, out of the horror of wet, grey clay.

He laid her down on the bank. She was quite unconscious and running with water. He made the water come from her mouth, he worked to restore her. He did not have to work very long before he could feel the breathing begin again in her; she was breathing naturally. He worked a little longer. He could feel her live beneath his hands; she was coming back. He wiped her face, wrapped her in his overcoat, looked round into the dim, dark-grey world, then lifted her and staggered down the bank and across the fields.

It seemed an unthinkably long way, and his burden so heavy he felt he would never get to the house. But at last he was in the stable-yard, and then in the house-yard. He opened the door and went into the house. In the kitchen he laid her down on the hearthrug, and called. The house was empty. But the fire was burning in the grate.

Then again he kneeled to attend to her. She was breathing regularly, her eyes were wide open and as if conscious, but there seemed something missing in her look. She was conscious in herself, but unconscious of her surroundings.

He ran upstairs, took blankets from a bed, and put them before the fire to warm. Then he removed her saturated, earthy-smelling clothing, rubbed her dry with a towel, and wrapped her naked in the blankets. Then he went into the dining room, to look for spirits. There was a little whiskey. He drank a gulp himself, and put some into her mouth.

The effect was instantaneous. She looked full into his face, as if she had been seeing him for some time, and yet had only just become conscious of him.

"Dr. Fergusson?" she said.

"What?" he answered.

He was divesting himself of his coat, intending to find some dry clothing upstairs. He could not bear the smell of the dead, clayey water, and he was mortally afraid for his own health.

"What did I do?" she asked.

"Walked into the pond," he replied. He had begun to shudder like one sick, and could hardly attend to her. Her eyes remained full on him, he seemed to be going dark in his mind, looking back at her helplessly. The shuddering became quieter in him, his life came back in him, dark and unknowing, but strong again.

"Was I out of my mind?" she asked, while her eyes were fixed on him all the time.

"Maybe, for the moment," he replied. He felt quiet, because his strength had come back. The strange fretful strain had left him.

"Am I out of my mind now?" she asked.

"Are you?" he reflected a moment. "No," he answered truthfully, "I don't see that you are." He turned his face aside. He was afraid now, because he felt dazed, and felt dimly that her power was stronger than his, in this issue. And she continued to look at him fixedly all the time. "Can you tell me where I shall find some dry things to put on?" he asked.

"Did you dive into the pond for me?" she asked.

"No," he answered. "I walked in. But I went in overhead as well."

There was silence for a moment. He hesitated. He very much wanted to go upstairs to get into dry clothing. But there was another desire in him. And she seemed to hold him. His will seemed to have gone to sleep, and left him, standing there slack before her. But he felt warm inside himself. He did not shudder at all, though his clothes were sodden on him.

"Why did you?" she asked.

"Because I didn't want you to do such a foolish thing," he said.

"It wasn't foolish," she said, still gazing at him as she lay on the floor, with a sofa cushion under her head. "It was the right thing to do. *I* knew best, then."

"I'll go and shift these wet things," he said. But still he had not the power to move out of her presence, until she sent him. It was as if she had the life of his body in her hands, and he could not extricate himself. Or perhaps he did not want to.

Suddenly she sat up. Then she became aware of her own immediate condition. She felt the blankets about her, she knew her own limbs. For a moment it seemed as if her reason were going. She looked round, with wild eye, as if seeking something. He stood still with fear. She saw her clothing lying scattered.

"Who undressed me?" she asked, her eyes resting full and inevitable on his face.

"I did," he replied, "to bring you round."

For some moments she sat and gazed at him awfully, her lips parted.

"Do you love me then?" she asked.

He only stood and stared at her, fascinated. His soul seemed to melt.

She shuffled forward on her knees, and put her arms round him, round his legs, as he stood there, pressing her breasts against his knees and thighs, clutching him with strange, convulsive certainty, pressing his thighs against her, drawing him to her face, her throat, as she looked up at him with flaring, humble eyes of transfiguration, triumphant in first possession.

"You love me," she murmured, in strange transport, yearning and triumphant and confident. "You love me. I know you love me, I know."

And she was passionately kissing his knees, through the wet clothing, passionately and indiscriminately kissing his knees, his legs, as if unaware of everything.

He looked down at the tangled wet hair, the wild, bare, animal shoulders. He was amazed, bewildered, and afraid. He had never thought of loving her. He had never wanted to love her. When he rescued her and restored her, he was a doctor, and she was a patient. He had had no single personal thought of her. Nay, this introduction of the personal element was very distasteful to him, a violation of his professional honour. It was horrible to have her there embracing his knees. It was horrible. He revolted from it, violently. And yet—and yet—he had not the power to break away.

She looked at him again, with the same supplication of powerful love, and that same transcendent, frightening light of triumph. In view of

the delicate flame which seemed to come from her face like a light, he was powerless. And yet he had never intended to love her. He had never intended. And something stubborn in him could not give way.

"You love me," she repeated, in a murmur of deep, rhapsodic assurance. "You love me."

Her hands were drawing him, drawing him down to her. He was afraid, even a little horrified. For he had, really, no intention of loving her. Yet her hands were drawing him towards her. He put out his hand quickly to steady himself, and grasped her bare shoulder. A flame seemed to burn the hand that grasped her soft shoulder. He had no intention of loving her: his whole will was against his yielding. It was horrible. And yet wonderful was the touch of her shoulders, beautiful the shining of her face. Was she perhaps mad? He had a horror of yielding to her. Yet something in him ached also.

He had been staring away at the door, away from her. But his hand remained on her shoulder. She had gone suddenly very still. He looked down at her. Her eyes were now wide with fear, with doubt, the light was dying from her face, a shadow of terrible greyness was returning. He could not bear the touch of her eyes' question upon him, and the look of death behind the question.

With an inward groan he gave way, and let his heart yield towards her. A sudden gentle smile came on his face. And her eyes, which never left his face, slowly, slowly filled with tears. He watched the strange water rise in her eyes, like some slow fountain coming up. And his heart seemed to burn and melt away in his breast.

He could not bear to look at her any more. He dropped on his knees and caught her head with his arms and pressed her face against his throat. She was very still. His heart, which seemed to have broken, was burning with a kind of agony in his breast. And he felt her slow, hot tears wetting his throat. But he could not move.

He felt the hot tears wet his neck and the hollows of his neck, and he remained motionless, suspended through one of man's eternities. Only now it had become indispensable to him to have her face pressed close to him; he could never let her go again. He could never let her head go away from the close clutch of his arm. He wanted to remain like that for ever, with his heart hurting him in a pain that was also life to him. Without knowing, he was looking down on her damp, soft brown hair.

Then, as it were suddenly, he smelt the horrid stagnant smell of that water. And at the same moment she drew away from him and looked at him. Her eyes were wistful and unfathomable. He was afraid of them, and he fell to kissing her, not knowing what he was doing. He wanted her eyes not to have that terrible, wistful, unfathomable look.

When she turned her face to him again, a faint delicate flush was glowing, and there was again dawning that terrible shining of joy in her eyes, which really terrified him, and yet which he now wanted to see, because he feared the look of doubt still more.

"You love me?" she said, rather faltering.

"Yes." The word cost him a painful effort. Not because it wasn't true. But because it was too newly true, the *saying* seemed to tear open again his newly torn heart. And he hardly wanted it to be true, even now.

She lifted her face to him, and he bent forward and kissed her on the mouth, gently, with the one kiss that is an eternal pledge. And as he kissed her his heart strained again in his breast. He never intended to love her. But now it was over. He had crossed over the gulf to her, and all that he had left behind had shriveled and become void.

After the kiss, her eyes again slowly filled with tears. She sat still, away from him, with her face drooped aside, and her hands folded in her lap. The tears fell very slowly. There was complete silence. He too sat there motionless and silent on the hearthrug. The strange pain of his heart that was broken seemed to consume him. That he should love her? That this was love! That he should be ripped open in this way!—Him, a doctor!—How they would all jeer if they knew! —It was agony to him to think they might know.

In the curious naked pain of the thought he looked again to her. She was sitting there drooped into a muse. He saw a tear fall, and his heart flared hot. He saw for the first time that one of her shoulders was quite uncovered, one arm bare, he could see one of her small breasts; dimly, because it had become almost dark in the room.

"Why are you crying?" he asked, in an altered voice.

She looked up at him, and behind her tears the consciousness of her situation for the first time brought a dark look of shame to her eyes.

"I'm not crying, really," she said, watching him half frightened.

He reached his hand, and softly closed it on her bare arm.

"I love you! I love you!" he said in a soft, low vibrating voice, unlike himself.

She shrank, and dropped her head. The soft, penetrating grip of his hand on her arm distressed her. She looked up at him.

"I want to go," she said. "I want to go and get you some dry things."

"Why?" he said. "I'm all right."

"But I want to go," she said. "And I want you to change your things."

He released her arm, and she wrapped herself in the blanket, looking at him rather frightened. And still she did not rise.

"Kiss me," she said wistfully.

He kissed her, but briefly, half in anger.

Then, after a second, she rose nervously, all mixed up in the blanket. He watched her in her confusion, as she tried to extricate herself and wrap herself up so that she could walk. He watched her relentlessly, as she knew. And as she went, the blanket trailing, and as he saw a glimpse of her feet and her white leg, he tried to remember her as she was when he had wrapped her in the blanket. But then he didn't want to remember, because she had been nothing to him then, and his nature revolted from remembering her as she was when she was nothing to him.

A tumbling, muffled noise from within the dark house startled him. Then he heard her voice:—"There are clothes." He rose and went to the foot of the stairs, and gathered up the garments she had thrown down. Then he came back to the fire, to rub himself down and dress. He grinned at his own appearance when he had finished.

The fire was sinking, so he put on coal. The house was now quite dark, save for the light of a street lamp that shone in faintly from beyond the holly trees. He lit the gas with matches he found on the mantelpiece. Then he emptied the pockets of his own clothes, and threw all his wet things in a heap into the scullery. After which he gathered up her sodden clothes, gently, and put them in a separate heap on the copper-top in the scullery.

It was six o'clock on the clock. His own watch had stopped. He ought to go back to the surgery.

He waited, and still she did not come down. So he went to the foot of the stairs and called:

"I shall have to go."

Almost immediately he heard her coming down. She had on her best dress of black voile, and her hair was tidy, but still damp. She looked at him—and in spite of herself, smiled.

"I don't like you in those clothes," she said.

"Do I look a sight?" he answered.

They were shy of one another.

"I'll make you some tea," she said.

"No, I must go."

"Must you?" And she looked at him again with the wide, strained, doubtful eyes. And again, from the pain of his breast, he knew how he loved her. He went and bent to kiss her, gently, passionately, with his heart's painful kiss.

"And my hair smells so horrible," she murmured in distraction. "And I'm so awful, I'm so awful! Oh, no, I'm too awful." And she broke into bitter, heartbroken sobbing. "You can't want to love me, I'm horrible."

"Don't be silly, don't be silly," he said, trying to comfort her, kissing her, holding her in his arms. "I want you, I want to marry you, we're going to be married, quickly, quickly—tomorrow if I can."

But she only sobbed terribly, and cried:

"I feel awful. I feel awful. I feel I'm horrible to you."

"No, I want you, I want you," was all he answered, blindly, with that terrible intonation which frightened her almost more than her horror lest he should *not* want her.

FOR ANALYSIS

1. Lawrence repeats that Mabel is "mindless and persistent." How is this a key to her survival? What is it that Mabel needs to survive? Is she like the other people in the community?
2. What is it that the doctor needs to survive? He knows he is a slave, working too long and too hard for too little reward. But he feels that he has to be where he is. (Don't confuse this with devotion to duty or a doctor's high calling.) Why? What do these people have? What is this "power" Lawrence keeps mentioning that they have, personified in Mabel, that Fergusson lacks and is therefore drawn to?
3. Fergusson does not capitulate and pretend to love Mabel; he capitulates and does love her. Reread the section which describes his internal turmoil. What is Lawrence saying there about the nature of love?

CONRAD AIKEN

Silent Snow, Secret Snow

1. Just why it should have happened, or why it should have happened just when it did, he could not, of course, possibly have said; nor perhaps would it even have occurred to him to ask. The thing was above all a secret, something to be preciously concealed from Mother and Father; and to that very fact it owed an enormous part of its deliciousness. It was like a peculiarly beautiful trinket to be carried unmentioned in one's trouser pocket—a rare stamp, an old coin, a few tiny gold links found trodden out of shape on the path in the park, a pebble of carnelian, a seashell distinguishable from all others by an unusual spot or stripe—and, as if it were any one of these, he carried around with him everywhere a warm and persistent and increasingly beautiful sense of possession. Nor was it only a sense of possession—it was also a sense of protection. It was as if, in some delightful way, his secret gave him a fortress, a wall behind which he could retreat into heavenly seclusion. This was almost the first thing he had noticed about it—apart from the oddness of the thing itself—and it was this that now again, for the fiftieth time, occurred to him, as he sat in the little schoolroom. It was the half hour for geography. Miss Buell was revolving with one finger, slowly, a huge terrestrial globe which had been placed on her desk. The green and yellow continents passed and repassed, questions were asked and answered, and now the little girl in front of him, Deirdre, who had a funny little constellation of freckles on the back of her neck, exactly like the Big Dipper, was standing up and telling Miss Buell that the equator was the line that ran round the middle.

Miss Buell's face, which was old and grayish and kindly, with gray stiff curls beside the cheeks, and eyes that swam very brightly, like little minnows, behind thick glasses, wrinkled itself into a complication of amusements.

"Ah! I see. The earth is wearing a belt, or a sash. Or someone drew a line round it!"

"Oh no—not that—I mean—"

In the general laughter, he did not share, or only a very little. He was thinking about the Arctic and Antarctic regions, which of course, on the globe, were white. Miss Buell was now telling them about the tropics, the jungles, the steamy heat of equatorial swamps, where the birds and butterflies, and even the snakes, were like living jewels. As he listened to these things, he was already, with a pleasant sense of half-effort, putting his secret between himself and the words. Was it really an effort at all? For effort implied something voluntary, and perhaps even something one did not especially want; whereas this was distinctly pleasant, and came almost of its own accord. All he needed to do was to think of that morning, the first one, and then of all the others—

But it was all so absurdly simple! It had amounted to so little. It was nothing, just an idea—and just why it should have become so wonderful, so permanent, was a mystery—a very pleasant one, to be sure, but also, in an amusing way, foolish. However, without ceasing to listen to Miss Buell, who had now moved up to the north temperate zones, he deliberately invited his memory of the first morning. It was only a moment or two after he had waked up— or perhaps the moment itself. But was there, to be exact, an exact moment? Was one awake all at once? or was it gradual? Anyway, it was after he had stretched a lazy hand up toward the headrail, and yawned, and then relaxed again among his warm covers, all the more grateful on a December morning, that the thing had happened. Suddenly, for no reason, he had thought of the postman, he remembered the postman. Perhaps there was nothing so odd in that. After all, he heard the postman almost every morning, in his life—his heavy boots could be heard clumping round the corner at the top of the little cobbled hill-street, and then, progressively nearer, progressively louder, the double knock at each door, the crossings and recrossings of the street, till finally the clumsy steps came stumbling across to the very door, and the tremendous knock came which shook the house itself.

(Miss Buell was saying, "Vast wheat-growing areas in North America and Siberia."

Deirdre had for the moment placed her left hand across the back of her neck.)

But on this particular morning, the first morning, as he lay there with his eyes closed, he had for some reason *waited* for the postman. He wanted to hear him come round the corner. And that was precisely the joke—he never did. He never came. He never had come—*round the corner*—again. For when at last the steps *were*

heard, they had already, he was quite sure, come a little down the hill, to the first house; and even so, the steps were curiously different—they were softer, they had a new secrecy about them, they were muffled and indistinct; and while the rhythm of them was the same, it now said a new thing—it said peace, it said remoteness, it said cold, it said sleep. And he had understood the situation at once—nothing could have seemed simpler—there had been snow in the night, such as all winter he had been longing for; and it was this which had rendered the postman's first footsteps inaudible, and the later ones faint. Of course! How lovely! And even now it must be snowing—it was going to be a snowy day—the long white ragged lines were drifting and sifting across the street, across the faces of the old houses, whispering and hushing, making little triangles of white in the corners between cobblestones, seething a little when the wind blew them over the ground to a drifted corner; and so it would be all day, getting deeper and deeper and silenter and silenter.

(Miss Buell was saying, "Land of perpetual snow.")

All this time, of course (while he lay in bed), he had kept his eyes closed, listening to the nearer progress of the postman, the muffled footsteps thumping and slipping on the snow-sheathed cobbles; and all the other sounds—the double knocks, a frosty far-off voice or two, a bell ringing thinly and softly as if under a sheet of ice—had the same slightly abstracted quality, as if removed by one degree from actuality—as if everything in the world had been insulated by snow. But when at last, pleased, he opened his eyes, and turned them toward the window, to see for himself this long-desired and now so clearly imagined miracle—what he saw instead was brilliant sunlight on a roof; and when, astonished, he jumped out of bed and stared down into the street, expecting to see the cobbles obliterated by the snow, he saw nothing but the bare bright cobbles themselves.

Queer, the effect this extraordinary surprise had had upon him—all the following morning he had kept with him a sense as of snow falling about him, a secret screen of new snow between himself and the world. If he had not dreamed such a thing—and how could he have dreamed it while awake?—how else could one explain it? In any case, the delusion had been so vivid as to affect his entire behavior. He could not now remember whether it was on the first or the second morning—or was it even the third?—that his mother had drawn attention to some oddness in his manner.

"But my darling"—she had said at the breakfast table—"what has come over you? You don't seem to be listening . . . ."

And how often that very thing had happened since!

(Miss Buell was now asking if anyone knew the difference between the North Pole and the Magnetic Pole. Deirdre was holding up her flickering brown hand, and he could see the four white dimples that marked the knuckles.)

Perhaps it hadn't been either the second or third morning—or even the fourth or fifth. How could he be sure? How could he be sure just when the delicious *progress* had become clear? Just when it had really *begun*? The intervals weren't very precise . . . . All he now knew was, that at some point or other—perhaps the second day, perhaps the sixth—he had noticed that the presence of the snow was a little more insistent, the sound of it clearer; and, conversely, the sound of the postman's footsteps more indistinct. Not only could he not hear the steps come round the corner, he could not even hear them at the first house. It was below the first house that he heard them; and then, a few days later, it was below the second house that he heard them; and a few days later again, below the third. Gradually, gradually, the snow was becoming heavier, the sound of its seething louder, the cobblestones more and more muffled. When he found, each morning, on going to the window, after the ritual of listening, that the roofs and cobbles were as bare as ever, it made no difference. This was, after all, only what he had expected. It was even what pleased him, what rewarded him: the thing was his own, belonged to no one else. No one else knew about it, not even his mother and father. There, outside, were the bare cobbles; and here, inside, was the snow. Snow growing heavier each day, muffling the world, hiding the ugly, and deadening increasingly—above all—the steps of the postman. *Snow Hides the Real world*

"But, my darling"—she had said at the luncheon table—"what has come over you? You don't seem to listen when people speak to you. That's the third time I've asked you to pass your plate . . . ."

How was one to explain this to Mother? or to Father? There was, of course, nothing to be done about it: nothing. All one could do was to laugh embarrassedly, pretend to be a little ashamed, apologize, and take a sudden and somewhat disingenuous interest in what was being done or said. The cat had stayed out all night. He had a curious swelling on his left cheek—perhaps somebody had kicked him, or a stone had struck him. Mrs. Kempton was or was not coming to tea. The house was going to be housecleaned, or "turned out," on Wednesday instead of Friday. A new lamp was provided for his evening work—perhaps it was eyestrain which accounted for this new and so peculiar vagueness of his—Mother was looking at him with amusement as she said this, but with something else as well. A new lamp? A new lamp. Yes, Mother, No, Mother, Yes, Mother. School is going very well. The geometry is very easy. The history is very dull. The geography is very interesting—particularly when it takes one to the North Pole. Why the North Pole? Oh, well, it would be fun to be an explorer. Another Peary or Scott or Shackleton. And then abruptly he found his interest in the talk at an end, stared at the pudding on his plate, listened, waited, and began once more—ah, how heavenly, too, the first beginnings—to hear or feel—for could he actually hear it?—the silent snow, the secret snow.

(Miss Buell was telling them about the search for the Northwest Passage, about Hendrik Hudson, the *Half Moon*.)

This had been, indeed, the only distressing feature of the new experience; the fact that it so increasingly had brought him into a kind of mute misunderstanding, or even conflict, with his father and mother. It was as if he were trying to lead a double life. On the one hand, he had to be Paul Hasleman, and keep up the appearance of being that person—dress, wash, and answer intelligently when spoken to—; on the other, he had to explore this new world which had been opened to him. Nor could there be the slightest doubt—not the slightest—that the new world was the profounder and more wonderful of the two. It was irresistible. It was miraculous. Its beauty was simply beyond anything—beyond speech as beyond thought—utterly incommunicable. But how then, between the two worlds, of which he was thus constantly aware, was he to keep a balance? One must get up, one must go to breakfast, one must talk with Mother, go to school, do one's lessons—and, in all this, try not to appear too much of a fool. But if all the while one was also trying to extract the full deliciousness of another and quite separate existence, one which could not easily (if at all) be spoken of—how was one to manage? How was one to explain? Would it be safe to explain? Would it be absurd? Would it merely mean that he would get into some obscure kind of trouble?

These thoughts came and went, came and went, as softly and secretly as the snow; they were not precisely a disturbance, perhaps they were even a pleasure; he liked to have them; their presence was something almost palpable, something he could stroke with his hand, without closing his eyes, and without ceasing to see Miss Buell and the schoolroom and the globe and the freckles on Deirdre's neck; nevertheless he did in a sense cease to see, or to see the obvious external world, and substituted for this vision the vision of snow, the sound of snow, and the slow, almost soundless, approach of the postman. Yesterday, it had been only at the sixth house that the postman had become audible; the snow was much deeper now, it was falling more swiftly and heavily, the sound of its seething was more distinct, more soothing, more persistent. And this morning, it had been—as nearly as he could figure—just above the seventh house—perhaps only a step or two above; at most, he had heard two or three footsteps before the knock had sounded. . . . And with each such narrowing of the sphere, each nearer approach of the limit at which the postman was first audible, it was odd how sharply was increased the amount of illusion which had to be carried into the ordinary business of daily life. Each day, it was harder to get out of bed, to go to the window, to look out at the—as always—perfectly empty and snowless street. Each day it was more difficult to go through the perfunctory motions of greeting Mother and Father at breakfast, to reply to their questions, to put his books together and go to school. And at school, how extraordinarily hard to conduct with success simultaneously the public life and the life that was secret! There were times when he longed—positively ached—to tell everyone about it—to burst out with it—only to be checked almost at once by a far-off feeling as of some faint absurdity which was inherent in it—but *was* it absurd?—and more importantly by a sense of mysterious power in his very secrecy. Yes; it

must be kept secret. That, more and more, became clear. At whatever cost to himself, whatever pain to others—

(Miss Buell looked straight at him, smiling, and said, "Perhaps we'll ask Paul. I'm sure Paul will come out of his daydream long enough to be able to tell us. Won't you, Paul?" He rose slowly from his chair, resting one hand on the brightly varnished desk, and deliberately stared through the snow toward the blackboard. It was an effort, but it was amusing to make it. "Yes," he said slowly, "it was what we now call the Hudson River. This he thought to be the Northwest Passage. He was disappointed." He sat down again, and as he did so Deirdre half turned in her chair and gave him a shy smile, of approval and admiration.)

At whatever pain to others.

This part of it was very puzzling, very puzzling. Mother was very nice, and so was Father. Yes, that was all true enough. He wanted to be nice to them, to tell them everything—and yet, was it really wrong of him to want to have a secret place of his own?

At bedtime, the night before, Mother had said, "If this goes on, my lad, we'll have to see a doctor, we will! We can't have our boy—" But what was it she had said? "Live in another world"? "Live so far away"? The word "far" had been in it, he was sure, and then Mother had taken up a magazine again and laughed a little, but with an expression which wasn't mirthful. He had felt sorry for her. . .

The bell rang for dismissal. The sound came to him through long curved parallels of falling snow. He saw Deirdre rise, and had himself risen almost as soon—but not quite as soon—as she.

II. On the walk homeward, which was timeless, it pleased him to see through the accompaniment, or counterpoint, of snow, the items of mere externality on his way. There were many kinds of brick in the sidewalks, and laid in many kinds of pattern. The garden walls, too, were various, some of wooden palings, some of plaster, some of stone. Twigs of bushes leaned over the walls: the little hard green winter-buds of lilac, on gray stems, sheathed and fat; other branches very thin and fine and black and desiccated. Dirty sparrows huddled in the bushes, as dull in color as dead fruit left in leafless trees. A single starling creaked on a weather vane. In the gutter, beside a drain, was a scrap of torn and dirty newspaper, caught in a little delta of filth; the word ECZEMA appeared in large capitals, and below it was a letter from Mrs. Amelia D. Cravath, 2100 Pine Street, Fort Worth, Texas, to the effect that after being a sufferer for years she had been cured by Caley's Ointment. In the little delta, beside the fan-shaped and deeply runneled continent of brown mud, were lost twigs, descended from their parent trees, dead matches, a rusty horse chestnut burr, a small concentration of eggshell, a streak of yellow sawdust which had been wet and now was dry and congealed, a brown pebble, and a broken feather. Farther on was a cement sidewalk, ruled into geometrical parallelograms, with a brass inlay at one end commemorating the contractors who had laid it, and, halfway across, an irregular and random series of dog tracks, immortalized in synthetic stone. He knew these well, and always stepped on them; to cover the little hollows with his own foot had always been a queer pleasure; today he did it once more, but perfunctorily and detachedly, all the while thinking of something else. That was a dog, a long time ago, who had made a mistake and walked on the cement while it was still wet. He had probably wagged his tail, but that hadn't been recorded. Now, Paul Hasleman, aged twelve, on his way home from school, crossed the same river, which in the meantime had frozen into rock. Homeward through the snow, the snow falling in bright sunshine. Homeward?

Then came the gateway with the two posts surmounted by egg-shaped stones which had been cunningly balanced on their ends, as if by Columbus, and mortared in the very act of balance; a source of perpetual wonder. On the brick wall just beyond, the letter H had been stenciled, presumably for some purpose. H? H.

The green hydrant, with a little green-painted chain attached to the brass screw-cap.

The elm tree, with the great gray wound in the bark, kidneyshaped, into which he always put his hand—to feel the cold but living wood. The injury, he had been sure, was due to the gnawings of a tethered horse. But now it deserved only a passing palm, a merely tolerant eye. There were more important things. Miracles. Beyond the thoughts of trees, mere elms. Beyond the thoughts of sidewalks, mere stone, mere brick, mere cement. Beyond the thoughts even of his own shoes, which trod these sidewalks obediently, bearing a burden—far above—of elaborate mystery. He watched them. They were not very well polished; he had neglected them, for a very good reason: they were one of the many parts of the increasing difficulty of the daily return to daily life, the morning struggle. To get up, having at last opened one's eyes, to go to the window, and discover no snow, to wash, to dress, to descend the curving stairs to breakfast—

At whatever pain to others, nevertheless, one must persevere in severance, since the incommunicability of the experience demanded it. It was desirable, of course, to be kind to Mother and Father, especially as they seemed to be worried, but it was also desirable to be resolute. If they should decide—as appeared likely—to consult the doctor, Doctor Howells, and have Paul inspected, his heart listened to through a kind of dictaphone, his lungs, his stomach—well, that was all right. He would go through with it. He would give them answer for question, too—perhaps such answers as they hadn't expected? No. That would never do. For the secret world must, at all costs, be preserved.

The birdhouse in the apple tree was empty—it was the wrong time of year for wrens. The little round black door had lost its pleasure. The wrens were enjoying other houses, other nests, remoter trees. But this too was a notion which he only vaguely and grazingly entertained—as if, for the moment, he merely touched an edge of it; there was something further on, which was already assuming a sharper importance; something which already teased at the corners of his eyes, teasing also at the corner of his mind. It was funny to think that he so wanted this, so awaited it—and yet found himself enjoying this momentary dalliance with the birdhouse, as if for a quite deliberate postponement and enhancement of the approaching pleasure. He was aware of his delay, of his smiling and detached and now almost uncomprehending gaze at the little birdhouse; he knew what he was going to look at next: it was his own little cobbled hill-street, his own house, the little river at the bottom of the hill, the grocer's shop with the cardboard man in the window—and now, thinking of all this, he turned his head, still smiling, and looking quickly right and left through the snow-laden sunlight.

And the mist of snow, as he had foreseen, was still on it—a ghost of snow falling in the bright sunlight, softly and steadily floating and turning and pausing, soundlessly meeting the snow that covered, as with a transparent mirage, the bare bright cobbles. He loved it—he stood still and loved it. Its beauty was paralyzing—beyond all words, all experience, all dream. No fairy story he had ever read could be compared with it—none had ever given him this extraordinary combination of ethereal loveliness with a something else, unnameable, which was just faintly and deliciously terrifying. What was this thing? As he thought of it, he looked upward toward his own bedroom window, which was open—and it was as if he looked straight into the room and saw himself lying half awake in his bed. There he was—at this very instant he was still perhaps actually there—more truly there than standing here at the edge of the cobbled hill-street, with one hand lifted to shade his eyes against the snow-sun. Had he indeed ever left his room, in all this time? since that very first morning? Was the whole progress still being enacted there, was it still the same morning, and himself not yet wholly awake? And even now, had the postman not yet come round the corner? . . .

This idea amused him, and automatically, as he thought of it, he turned his head and looked toward the top of the hill. There was, of course, nothing there—nothing and no one. The street was empty and quiet. And all the more because of its emptiness it occurred to him to count the houses—a thing which, oddly enough, he hadn't before thought of doing. Of course, he had known there weren't many—many, that is, on his own side of the street, which were the ones that figured in the postman's progress—but nevertheless it came as something of a shock to find that there were precisely *six*, above his own house—his own house was the seventh.

Six!

Astonished, he looked at his own house—looked at the door, on which was the number thirteen—and then realized that the whole thing was exactly and logically and absurdly what he ought to have known. Just the same, the realization gave him abruptly, and even a little frighteningly, a sense of hurry. He was being hurried—he was being rushed. For—he knit his brow—he couldn't be mistaken—it was just above the *seventh* house, his *own* house, that the postman had first been audible this very morn-

ing. But in that case—in that case—did it mean that tomorrow he would hear nothing? The knock he had heard must have been the knock of their own door. Did it mean—and this was an idea which gave him a really extraordinary feeling of surprise—that he would never hear the postman again?—that tomorrow morning the postman would already have passed the house, in a snow so deep as to render his footsteps completely inaudible? That he would have made his approach down the snow-filled street so soundlessly, so secretly, that he, Paul Hasleman, there lying in bed, would not have waked in time, or waking, would have heard nothing?

But how could that be? Unless even the knocker should be muffled in the snow—frozen tight, perhaps? . . . But in that case—

A vague feeling of disappointment came over him; a vague sadness as if he felt himself deprived of something which he had long looked forward to, something much prized. After all this, all this beautiful progress, the slow delicious advance of the postman through the silent and secret snow, the knock creeping closer each day, and the footsteps nearer, the audible compass of the world thus daily narrowed, narrowed, narrowed, as the snow soothingly and beautifully encroached and deepened, after all this, was he to be defrauded of the one thing he had so wanted—to be able to count, as it were, the last two or three solemn footsteps, as they finally approached his own door? Was it all going to happen, at the end, so suddenly? or indeed, had it already happened? with no slow and subtle gradations of menace, in which he could luxuriate?

He gazed upward again, toward his own window which flashed in the sun; and this time almost with a feeling that it would be better if he *were* still in bed, in that room; for in that case this must still be the first morning, and there would be six more mornings to come—or, for that matter, seven or eight or nine—how could he be sure?—or even more.

III. After supper, the inquisition began. He stood before the doctor, under the lamp, and submitted silently to the usual thumpings and tappings.

"Now will you please say 'Ah!'?"

"Ah!"

"Now again, please, if you don't mind."

"Ah."

"Say it slowly, and hold it if you can—"

"Ah-h-h-h-h-h—"

"Good."

How silly all this was. As if it had anything to do with his throat! Or his heart, or lungs!

Relaxing his mouth, of which the corners, after all this absurd stretching, felt uncomfortable, he avoided the doctor's eyes, and stared toward the fireplace, past his mother's feet (in gray slippers) which projected from the green chair, and his father's feet (in brown slippers) which stood neatly side by side on the hearth rug.

"Hm. There is certainly nothing wrong there ...?"

He felt the doctor's eyes fixed upon him, and, as if merely to be polite, returned the look, but with a feeling of justifiable evasiveness.

"Now, young man, tell me—do you feel all right?"

"Yes, sir, quite all right."

"No headaches? no dizziness?"

"No, I don't think so."

"Let me see. Let's get a book, if you don't mind—yes, thank you, that will do splendidly—and now, Paul, if you'll just read it, holding it as you would normally hold it—"

He took the book and read:

"And another praise have I to tell for this the city our mother, the gift of a great god, a glory of the land most high; the might of horses, the might of young horses, the might of the sea. . . . For thou, son of Cronus, our lord Poseidon, hath throned herein this pride, since in these roads first thou didst show forth the curb that cures the rage of steeds. And the shapely oar, apt to men's hands, hath a wondrous speed on the brine, following the hundred-footed Nereids. . . . O land that art praised above all lands, now is it for thee to make those bright praises seen in deeds."

He stopped, tentatively, and lowered the heavy book.

"No—as I thought—there is certainly no superficial sign of eyestrain."

Silence thronged the room, and he was aware of the focused scrutiny of the three people who confronted him. . . .

"We could have his eyes examined—but I believe it is something else."

"What could it be?" That was his father's voice.

"It's only this curious absent mindedness—" This was his mother's voice.

In the presence of the doctor, they both seemed irritatingly apologetic.

"I believe it is something else. Now Paul—I would like very much to ask you a question or two. You will answer them, won't you—you know I'm an old, old friend of yours, eh? That's right! . . ."

His back was thumped twice by the doctor's fat fist—then the doctor was grinning at him with false amiability, while with one fingernail he was scratching the top button of his waistcoat. Beyond the doctor's shoulder was the fire, the fingers of flame making light prestidigitation against the sooty fireback, the soft sound of their random flutter the only sound.

"I would like to know—is there anything that worries you?"

The doctor was again smiling, his eyelids low against the little black pupils, in each of which was a tiny white bead of light. Why answer him? why answer him at all? "At whatever pain to others"—but it was all a nuisance, this necessity for resistance, this necessity for attention; it was as if one had been stood up on a brilliantly lighted stage, under a great round blaze of spotlight; as if one were merely a trained seal, or a performing dog, or a fish, dipped out of an aquarium and held up by the tail. It would serve them right if he were merely to bark or growl. And meanwhile, to miss these last few precious hours, these hours of which each minute was more beautiful than the last, more menacing—! He still looked, as if from a great distance, at the beads of light in the doctor's eyes, at the fixed false smile, and then, beyond, once more at his mother's slippers, his father's slippers, the soft flutter of the fire. Even here, even amongst these hostile presences, and in this arranged light, he could see the snow, he could hear it—it was in the corners of the room, where the shadow was deepest, under the sofa, behind the half-opened door which led to the dining room. It was gentler here, softer, its seethe the quietest of whispers, as if, in deference to a drawing room, it had quite deliberately put on its "manners"; it kept itself out of sight, obliterated itself, but distinctly with an air of saying, "Ah, but just wait! Wait till we are alone together! Then I will begin to tell you something new! Something white! something cold! something sleepy! something of cease, and peace, and the long bright curve of space! Tell them to go away. Banish them. Refuse to speak. Leave them, go upstairs to your room, turn out the light and get into bed—I will go with you, I will be waiting for you, I will tell you a better story than Little Kay of the Skates, or The Snow Ghost—I will surround your bed, I will close the windows, pile a deep drift against the door, so that none will ever again be able to enter. Speak to them! . . ." It seemed as if the little hissing voice came from a slow white spiral of falling flakes in the corner by the front window—but he could not be sure. He felt himself smiling, then, and said to the doctor, but without looking at him, looking beyond him still—

"Oh no, I think not—"

"But are you sure, my boy?"

His father's voice came softly and coldly then —the familiar voice of silken warning.

"You needn't answer at once, Paul—re- member we're trying to help you—think it over and be quite sure, won't you?"

He felt himself smiling again, at the notion of being quite sure. What a joke! As if he weren't so sure that reassurance was no longer necessary, and all this cross-examination a ridiculous farce, a grotesque parody! What could they know about it? these gross intelligences, these humdrum minds so bound to the usual, the ordinary? Impossible to tell them about it! Why, even now, even now, with the proof so abundant, so formidable, so imminent, so appallingly present here in this very room, could they believe it?—could even his mother believe it? No—it was only too plain that if anything were said about it, the merest hint given, they would be incredulous—they would laugh—they would say "Absurd!"—think things about him which weren't true. . . .

"Why no, I'm not worried—why should I be?"

He looked then straight at the doctor's low-lidded eyes, looked from one of them to the other, from one bead of light to the other, and gave a little laugh.

The doctor seemed to be disconcerted by this. He drew back in his chair, resting a fat white hand on either knee. The smile faded slowly from his face.

"Well, Paul!" he said, and paused gravely,

"I'm afraid you don't take this quite seriously enough. I think you perhaps don't quite realize —don't quite realize—" He took a deep quick breath and turned, as if helplessly, at a loss for words, to the others. But Mother and Father were both silent—no help was forthcoming.

"You must surely know, be aware, that you have not been quite yourself, of late? Don't you know that? . . ."

It was amusing to watch the doctor's renewed attempt at a smile, a queer disorganized look, as of confidential embarrassment.

"I feel all right, sir," he said, and again gave the little laugh.

"And we're trying to help you." The doctor's tone sharpened.

"Yes, sir, I know. But why? I'm all right. I'm just *thinking*, that's all."

His mother made a quick movement forward, resting a hand on the back of the doctor's chair.

"Thinking?" she said. "But my dear, about what?"

This was a direct challenge—and would have to be directly met. But before he met it, he looked again into the corner by the door, as if for reassurance. He smiled again at what he saw, at what he heard. The little spiral was still there, still softly whirling, like the ghost of a white kitten chasing the ghost of a white tail, and making as it did so the faintest of whispers. It was all right! If only he could remain firm, everything was going to be all right.

"Oh, about anything, about nothing—*you* know the way you do!"

"You mean—daydreaming?"

"Oh, no—thinking!"

"But thinking about *what*?"

"Anything."

He laughed a third time—but this time, happening to glance upward toward his mother's face, he was appalled at the effect his laughter seemed to have upon her. Her mouth had opened in an expression of horror. . . . This was too bad! Unfortunate! He had known it would cause pain, of course—but he hadn't expected it to be quite so bad as this. Perhaps—perhaps if he just gave them a tiny gleaming hint—?

"About the snow," he said.

"What on earth?" This was his father's voice. The brown slippers came a step nearer on the hearthrug.

"But my dear, what do you mean?" This was his mother's voice.

The doctor merely stared.

"Just *snow*, that's all. I like to think about it."

"Tell us about it, my boy."

"But that's all it is. There's nothing to tell. *You* know what snow is?"

This he said almost angrily, for he felt that they were trying to corner him. He turned sideways so as no longer to face the doctor, and the better to see the inch of blackness between the windowsill and the lowered curtain—the cold inch of beckoning and delicious night. At once he felt better, more assured.

"Mother—can I go to bed, now, please? I've got a headache."

"But I thought you said—"

"It's just come. It's all these questions—! Can I, mother?"

"You can go as soon as the doctor has finished."

"Don't you think this thing ought to be gone into thoroughly, and *now*?" This was Father's voice. The brown slippers again came a step nearer, the voice was the well-known "punishment" voice, resonant and cruel.

"Oh, what's the use, Norman—"

Quite suddenly, everyone was silent. And without precisely facing them, nevertheless he was aware that all three of them were watching him with an extraordinary intensity—staring hard at him—as if he had done something monstrous, or was himself some kind of monster. He could hear the soft irregular flutter of the flames; the cluck-click-cluck-click of the clock; far and faint, two sudden spurts of laughter from the kitchen, as quickly cut off as begun; a murmur of water in the pipes; and then, the silence seemed to deepen, to spread out, to become world-long and world-wide, to become timeless and shapeless, and to center inevitably and rightly, with a slow and sleepy but enormous concentration of all power, on the beginning of a new sound. What this new sound was going to be, he knew perfectly well. It might begin with a hiss, but it would end with a roar—there was no time to lose—he must escape. It mustn't happen here—

Without another word, he turned and ran up the stairs.

IV. Not a moment too soon. The darkness was coming in long white waves. A prolonged sibilance filled the night—a great seamless seethe of wild influence went abruptly across

it—a cold low humming shook the windows. He shut the door and flung off his clothes in the dark. The bare black floor was like a little raft tossed in waves of snow, almost overwhelmed, washed under whitely, up again, smothered in curled billows of feather. The snow was laughing; it spoke from all sides at once; it pressed closer to him as he ran and jumped exulting into his bed.

"Listen to us!" it said. "Listen! We have come to tell you the story we told you about. You remember? Lie down. Shut your eyes, now —you will no longer see much—in this white darkness who could see, or want to see? We will take the place of everything. . . . Listen—"

A beautiful varying dance of snow began at the front of the room, came forward and then retreated, flattened out toward the floor, then rose fountain-like to the ceiling, swayed, recruited itself from a new stream of flakes which poured laughing in through the humming window, advanced again, lifted long white arms. It said peace, it said remoteness, it said cold—it said— *REPRESENTS REALITY*

But then a gash of <u>horrible light</u> fell brutally across the room from the opening door—the snow drew back hissing—something alien had come into the room—something hostile. This thing rushed at him, clutched at him, shook him—and he was not merely horrified, he was filled with such a loathing as he had never known. What was this? this cruel disturbance? this act of anger and hate? It was as if he had to reach up a hand toward another world for any understanding of it—an effort of which he was only barely capable. But of that other world he still remembered just enough to know the exorcising words. They tore themselves from his other life suddenly— *breaks last link with*

"<u>Mother! Mother! Go away! I hate you!</u>" *REALITY*

And with that effort, everything was solved, everything became all right: the seamless hiss advanced once more, the long white wavering lines rose and fell like enormous whispering sea-waves, the whisper becoming louder, the laughter more numerous.

"Listen!" it said. "<u>We'll tell you the last, the most beautiful and secret story—shut your eyes</u>—it is a very small story—a story that gets smaller and smaller—it comes inward instead of opening like a flower—it is a flower becoming a seed—a little cold seed—do you hear? we are leaning closer to you—"

Snow draws him to death.
He doesn't realize his
want to die

The hiss was now becoming a roar—the whole world was a vast moving screen of snow—but even now it said peace, it said remoteness, it said cold, it said sleep.   *death.*

FOR ANALYSIS

1. What is the major conflict in this story?
2. A clinical psychologist would probably call this story a study in schizophrenia; Paul begins to live in two worlds, and finally the illusory world overwhelms the real world. Why should it be snow that he hallucinates? What does snow symbolize to him? What does it symbolize to the reader?
3. Is there any hint in the story of the cause of Paul's sickness?
4. Why the author chose this particular point of view is obvious. But why did he choose to begin the story where he did? Why not earlier? Why not later?   *extent of his Knowledge*

W. SOMERSET MAUGHAM

The Colonel's Lady
ironic

All this happened two or three years before the outbreak of the war.

The Peregrines were having breakfast. Though they were alone and the table was long they sat at opposite ends of it. From the walls George Peregrine's ancestors, painted by the fashionable painters of the day, looked down upon them. The butler brought in the morning post. There were several letters for the Colonel, business letters, the *Times* and a small parcel for his wife Evie. He looked at his letters and then, opening the *Times*, began to read it. They finished breakfast and rose from the table. He noticed that his wife hadn't opened the parcel.

"What's that?" he asked.

"Only some books."

"Shall I open it for you?"

"If you like."

He hated to cut string and so with some difficulty untied the knots.

"But they're all the same," he said when he had unwrapped the parcel. "What on earth d'you want six copies of the same book for?"

He opened one of them. "Poetry." Then he looked at the title page. *When Pyramids Decay*, he read, by E. K. Hamilton. Eva Katherine Hamilton: that was his wife's maiden name. He looked at her with smiling surprise. "Have you written a book, Evie? You are a slyboots."

"I didn't think it would interest you very much. Would you like a copy?"

"Well, you know poetry isn't much in my line, but—yes, I'd like a copy; I'll read it. I'll take it along to my study. I've got a lot to do this morning."

He gathered up the *Times*, his letters and the book and went out. His study was a large and comfortable room, with a big desk, leather armchairs and what he called "trophies of the chase" on the walls. In the bookshelves were works of reference, books on farming, gardening, fishing and shooting, and books on the last war, in which he had won an M.C. and a D.S.O. For before his marriage he had been in the Welsh Guards. At the end of the war he retired and settled down to the life of a country gentleman in the spacious house, some twenty miles from Sheffield, which one of his forebears had built in the reign of George II. George Peregrine had an estate of some fifteen hundred acres which he managed with ability; he was a justice of the peace and performed his duties conscientiously. During the season he rode to hounds two days a week. He was a good shot, a golfer and though now a little over fifty could still play a hard game of tennis. He could describe himself with propriety as an all-round sportsman.

He had been putting on weight lately, but was still a fine figure of a man; tall, with gray curly hair, only just beginning to grow thin on the crown, frank blue eyes, good features and a high colour. He was a public-spirited man, chairman of any number of local organizations and, as became his class and station, a loyal member of the Conservative party. He looked upon it as his duty to see to the welfare of the people on his estate and it was a satisfaction to him to know that Evie could be trusted to tend the sick and succour the poor. He had built a cottage hospital on the outskirts of the village and paid the wages of a nurse out of his own pocket. All he asked of the recipients of his bounty was that at elections, county or general, they should vote for his candidate. He was a friendly man, affable to his inferiors, considerate with his tenants and popular with the neighbouring gentry. He would have been pleased and at the same time slightly embarrassed if someone had told him he was a jolly good fellow. That was what he wanted to be. He desired no higher praise. *(handwritten: ¢ is definition of colonel)*

It was hard luck that he had no children. He would have been an excellent father, kindly but strict, and would have brought up his sons as a gentleman's sons should be brought up, sent them to Eton, you know, taught them to fish, shoot and ride. As it was, his heir was a nephew, son of his brother killed in a motor accident, not a bad boy, but not a chip off the old block, no, sir, far from it; and would you believe it, his fool of a mother was sending him to a co-educational school. Evie had been a sad disappointment to him. Of course she was a lady, and she had a bit of money of her own; she managed the house uncommonly well and she was a good hostess. The village people adored her. She had been a pretty little thing when he married her, with a creamy skin, light brown hair and a trim figure, healthy too and not a bad tennis player; he couldn't understand why she'd had no children; of course she was faded now, she must be getting on for five and forty; her skin was drab, her hair had lost its sheen and she was as thin as a rail. She was always neat and suitably dressed, but she didn't seem to bother how she looked, she wore no makeup and didn't even use lipstick; sometimes at night when she dolled herself up for a party you could tell that once she'd been quite attractive, but ordinarily she was—well, the sort of woman you simply didn't notice. A nice woman, of course, a good wife, and it wasn't her fault if she was barren, but it was tough on a fellow who wanted an heir of his own loins; she hadn't any vitality, that's what was the matter with her. He supposed he'd been in love with her when he asked her to marry him, at least sufficiently in love for a man who wanted to marry and settle down, but with time he discovered that they had nothing much in common. She didn't care about hunting, and fishing bored her. Naturally they'd drifted apart. He had to do her the justice to admit that she'd never bothered him. There'd been no scenes. They had no quarrels. She seemed to take it for granted that he should go his own way. When he went up to London now and then she never wanted to come with him. He had a girl there, well, she wasn't exactly a girl, she was thirty-five if she was a day, but she was blonde and luscious and he only had to wire ahead of time and they'd dine, do a show and spend the night together. Well, a man, a healthy normal man had to have some fun in his life. The thought crossed his mind that if Evie hadn't been such a good woman she'd have been a better wife; but it was not the sort of thought that he welcomed and he put it away from him.

George Peregrine finished his *Times* and being a considerate fellow rang the bell and told the butler to take the paper to Evie. Then he looked at his watch. It was half past ten and at eleven he had an appointment with one of his tenants. He had half an hour to spare.

"I'd better have a look at Evie's book," he said to himself.

He took it up with a smile, Evie had a lot of highbrow books in her sitting room, not the sort of books that interested him, but if they amused her he had no objection to her reading them. He noticed that the volume he now held in his hand contained no more than ninety pages. That was all to the good. He shared Edgar Allan Poe's opinion that poems should be short. But as he turned the pages he noticed that several of Evie's had long lines of irregular length and didn't rhyme. He didn't like that. At his first school, when he was a little boy, he remembered learning a poem that began: *The boy stood on the burning deck* and later, at Eton, one that started: *Ruin seize thee, ruthless king;* and then there was Henry V; they'd had to take that one half. He stared at Evie's pages with consternation.

"That's not what I call poetry," he said.

Fortunately it wasn't all like that. Interspersed with the pieces that looked so odd, lines of three or four words and then a line of ten or fifteen, there were little poems, quite short, that rhymed, thank God, with the lines all the same length. Several of the pages were just headed with the word *Sonnet*, and out of curiosity he counted the lines; there were fourteen of them. He read them. They seemed all right, but he didn't quite know what they were all about. He repeated to himself: *Ruin seize thee, ruthless king.*

"Poor Evie," he sighed.

At that moment the farmer he was expecting was ushered into the study, and putting the book down he made him welcome. They embarked on their business.

"I read your book, Evie," he said as they sat down to lunch.

"Jolly good. Did it cost you a packet to have it printed?"

"No, I was lucky, I sent it to a publisher and he took it."

"Not much money in poetry, my dear," he said in his good-natured, hearty way.

"No, I don't suppose there is. What did Bannock want to see you about this morning?"

Bannock was the tenant who had interrupted his reading of Evie's poems.

"He's asked me to advance the money for a pedigree bull he wants to buy. He's a good man and I've half a mind to do it."

George Peregrine saw that Evie didn't want to talk about her book and he was not sorry to change the subject. He was glad she had used her maiden name on the title page; he didn't suppose anyone would ever hear about the book, but he was proud of his own unusual name and he wouldn't have liked it if some damned penny-a-liner had made fun of Evie's effort in one of the papers.

During the few weeks that followed he thought it tactful not to ask Evie any questions about her venture into verse and she never referred to it. It might have been a discreditable incident that they had silently agreed not to mention. But then a strange thing happened. He had to go to London on business and he took Daphne out to dinner. That was the name of the girl with whom he was in the habit of passing a few agreeable hours whenever he went to town.

"Oh, George," she said, "is that your wife who's written a book they're all talking about?"

"What on earth d'you mean?"

"Well, there's a fellow I know who's a critic. He took me out to dinner the other night and he had a book with him. 'Got anything for me to read?' I said. 'What's that?' 'Oh, I don't think that's your cup of tea,' he said. 'It's poetry. I've just been reviewing it.' 'No poetry for me,' I said. 'It's about the hottest stuff I ever read,' he said. 'Selling like hot cakes. And it's damned good.'"

"Who's the book by?" asked George.

"A woman called Hamilton. My friend told me that wasn't her real name. He said her real name was Peregrine. 'Funny,' I said, 'I know a fellow called Peregrine.' 'Colonel in the army,' he said. 'Lives near Sheffield.'"

"I'd just as soon you didn't talk about me to your friends," said George with a frown of vexation.

"Keep your shirt on, dearie. Who'd you take me for? I just said, 'It's not the same one.'" Daphne giggled. "My friend said: 'They say he's a regular Colonel Blimp.'" *DAPHNE IS SO DIFFERENT FROM EV*

George had a keen sense of humour.

"You could tell them better than that," he laughed. "If my wife had written a book I'd be the first to know about it, wouldn't I?"

"I suppose you would."

Anyhow the matter didn't interest her and when the Colonel began to talk of other things she forgot about it. He put it out of his mind too. There was nothing to it, he decided, and that silly fool of a critic had just been pulling Daphne's leg. He was amused at the thought of her tackling that book because she had been told it was hot stuff and then finding it just a lot of stuff cut up into unequal lines.

He was a member of several clubs and next day he thought he'd lunch at one in St. James's Street. He was catching a train back to Sheffield early in the afternoon. He was sitting in a comfortable armchair having a glass of sherry before going into the dining room when an old friend came up to him.

"Well, old boy, how's life?" he said. "How d'you like being the husband of a celebrity?"

George Peregrine looked at his friend. He thought he saw an amused twinkle in his eyes.

"I don't know what you're talking about," he answered.

"Come off it, George. Everyone knows E. K. Hamilton is your wife. Not often a book of verse has a success like that. Look here, Henry Dashwood is lunching with me. He'd like to meet you."

"Who the devil is Henry Dashwood and why should he want to meet me?"

"Oh, my dear fellow, what do you do with yourself all the time in the country? Henry's about the best critic we've got. He wrote a wonderful review of Evie's book. D'you mean to say she didn't show it you?"

Before George could answer his friend had called a man over. A tall, thin man, with a high forehead, a beard, a long nose and a stoop, just the sort of man whom George was prepared to dislike at first sight. Introductions were effected. Henry Dashwood sat down.

"Is Mrs. Peregrine in London by any chance? I should very much like to meet her," he said.

"No, my wife doesn't like London. She prefers the country," said George stiffly.

"She wrote me a very nice letter about my review. I was pleased. You know, we critics get more kicks than halfpence. I was simply bowled over by her book. It's so fresh and original, very modern without being obscure. She seems to be as much at her ease in free verse as in the classical metres." Then because he was a critic he thought he should criticize. "Some times her ear is a trifle at fault, but you can say the same of Emily Dickinson. There are several of those short lyrics of hers that might have been written by Landor."

All this was gibberish to George Peregrine. The man was nothing but a disgusting highbrow. But the Colonel had good manners and he answered with proper civility: Henry Dashwood went on as though he hadn't spoken.

"But what makes the book so outstanding is the passion that throbs in every line. So many of these young poets are so anemic, cold, bloodless, dully intellectual, but here you have real naked, earthy passion; of course deep, sincere emotion like that is tragic—ah, my dear Colonel, how right Heine was when he said that the poet makes little songs out of his great sorrows. You know, now and then, as I read and reread those heartrending pages I thought of Sappho." GREEK LOVE POET.

This was too much for George Peregrine and he got up.

"Well, it's jolly nice of you to say such nice things about my wife's little book. I'm sure she'll be delighted. But I must bolt, I've got to catch a train and I want to get a bite of lunch."

"Damned fool," he said irritably to himself as he walked upstairs to the dining room.

He got home in time for dinner and after Evie had gone to bed he went into his study and looked for her book. He thought he'd just glance through it again to see for himself what they were making such a fuss about, but he couldn't find it. Evie must have taken it away.

"Silly," he muttered.

He'd told her he thought it jolly good. What more could a fellow be expected to say? Well, it didn't matter. He lit his pipe and read the *Field* till he felt sleepy. But a week or so later it happened that he had to go into Sheffield for the day. He lunched there at his club. He had nearly finished when the Duke of Haverel came in. This was the great local magnate and of course the Colonel knew him, but only to say how d'you do to; and he was surprised when the Duke stopped at his table.

"We're so sorry your wife couldn't come to us for the week end," he said, with a sort of shy cordiality. "We're expecting rather a nice lot of people."

George was taken aback. He guessed that the Haverels had asked him and Evie over for the week end and Evie, without saying a word to him about it, had refused. He had the presence of mind to say he was sorry too.

"Better luck next time," said the Duke pleasantly and moved on.

Colonel Peregrine was very angry and when he got home he said to his wife:

"Look here, what's this about our being asked over to Haverel? Why on earth did you say we couldn't go? We've never been asked before and it's the best shooting in the county."

"I didn't think of that. I thought it would only bore you."

"Damn it all, you might at least have asked me if I wanted to go."

"I'm sorry."

He looked at her closely. There was something in her expression that he didn't quite understand. He frowned.

"I suppose *I* was asked?" he barked.

Evie flushed a little.

"Well, in point of fact you weren't."

"I call it damned rude of them to ask you without asking me."

"I suppose they thought it wasn't your sort of party. The Duchess is rather fond of writers and people like that, you know. She's having Henry Dashwood, the critic, and for some reason he wants to meet me."

"It was damned nice of you to refuse, Evie."

"It's the least I could do," she smiled. She hesitated a moment. "George, my publishers want to give a little dinner party for me one day towards the end of the month and of course they want you to come too."

"Oh, I don't think that's quite my mark. I'll come up to London with you if you like. I'll find someone to dine with."

Daphne.

"I expect it'll be very dull, but they're making rather a point of it. And the day after, the American publisher who's taken my book is giving a cocktail party at Claridge's. I'd like you to come to that if you wouldn't mind."

"Sounds like a crashing bore, but if you really want me to come I'll come."

"It would be sweet of you."

George Peregrine was dazed by the cocktail party. There were a lot of people. Some of them didn't look so bad, a few of the women were decently turned out, but the men seemed to him pretty awful. He was introduced to everybody as Colonel Peregrine, E. K. Hamilton's husband, you know. The men didn't seem to have anything to say to him, but the women gushed.

"You *must* be proud of your wife. Isn't it *wonderful*? You know, I read it right through at a sitting, I simply couldn't put it down, and when I'd finished I started again at the beginning and read it right through a second time. I was simply *thrilled*."

The English publisher said to him:

"We've not had a success like this with a book of verse for twenty years. I've never seen such reviews."

The American publisher said to him:

"It's swell. It'll be a smash hit in America. You wait and see."

The American publisher had sent Evie a great spray of orchids. Damned ridiculous, thought George. As they came in, people were taken up to Evie and it was evident that they said flattering things to her, which she took with a pleasant smile and a word or two of thanks. She was a trifle flushed with the excitement, but seemed quite at her ease. Though he thought the whole thing a lot of stuff and nonsense George noted with approval that his wife was carrying it off in just the right way.

"Well, there's one thing," he said to himself, "you can see she's a lady and that's damned sight more than you can say of anyone else here."

He drank a good many cocktails. But there was one thing that bothered him. He had a notion that some of the people he was introduced to looked at him in rather a funny sort of way, he couldn't quite make out what it meant, and once when he strolled by two women who were sitting together on a sofa he had the impression that they were talking about him and after he passed he was almost certain they tittered. He was very glad when the party came to an end.

In the taxi on their way back to their hotel Evie said to him:

"You were wonderful, dear. You made quite a hit. The girls simply raved about you; they thought you so handsome."

"Girls," he said bitterly. "Old hags."

"Were you bored, dear?"

"Stiff."

She pressed his hand in a gesture of sympathy.

"I hope you won't mind if we wait and go down by the afternoon train. I've got some things to do in the morning."

"No, that's all right. Shopping?"

"I do want to buy one or two things, but I've got to go and be photographed. I hate the idea, but they think I ought to be. For America, you know."

He said nothing. But he thought. He thought it would be a shock to the American public when they saw the portrait of the homely, desiccated little woman who was his wife. He'd always been under the impression that they liked glamour in America.

He went on thinking and next morning when Evie had gone out he went to his club and up to the library. There he looked up recent numbers of the *Times Literary Supplement*, the *New Statesman* and the *Spectator*. Presently he found reviews of Evie's book. He didn't read them very carefully, but enough to see that they were extremely favourable. Then he went to the bookseller's in Piccadilly where he occasionally bought books. He'd made up his mind that he had to read this damned thing of Evie's properly, but he didn't want to ask her what she'd done with the copy she'd given him. He'd buy one for himself. Before going in he looked in the window and the first thing he saw was a display of *When Pyramids Decay*. Damned silly title! He went in. A young man came forward and asked if he could help him.

"No, I'm just having a look round." It embarrassed him to ask for Evie's book and he thought he'd find it for himself and then take it to the salesman. But he could't see it anywhere and at last, finding the young man near him, he said in a carefully casual tone: "By the way, have you got a book called *When Pyramids Decay*?"

"The new edition came in this morning. I'll get a copy."

In a moment the young man returned with it. He was a short, rather stout young man, with a shock of untidy carroty hair and spectacles. George Peregrine, tall, upstanding, very military, towered over him.

"Is this a new edition then?" he asked.

"Yes, sir. The fifth. It might be a novel the way it's selling."

George Peregrine hesitated a moment.

"Why d'you suppose it's such a success? I've always been told no one reads poetry."

"Well, it's good, you know. I've read it meself."

The young man, though obviously cultured, had a slight Cockney accent, and George quite instinctively adopted a patronizing attitude.

"It's the story they like. Sexy, you know, but tragic."

George frowned a little. He was coming to the conclusion that the young man was rather impertinent. No one had told him anything about there being a story in the damned book and he had not gathered that from reading the reviews. The young man went on.

"Of course it's only a flash in the pan, if you know what I mean. The way I look at it, she was sort of inspired like by a personal experience, like Housman was with *The Shropshire Lad*. She'll never write anything else."

"How much is the book?" said George coldly to stop his chatter. "You needn't wrap it up, I'll just slip it in my pocket."

The November morning was raw and he was wearing a greatcoat.

At the station he bought the evening papers and magazines and he and Evie settled themselves comfortably in opposite corners of a first-class carriage and read. At five o'clock they went along to the restaurant car to have tea and chatted a little. They arrived. They drove home in the car which was waiting for them. They bathed, dressed for dinner, and after dinner Evie, saying she was tired out, went to bed. She kissed him, as was her habit, on the forehead. Then he went into the hall, took Evie's book out of his greatcoat pocket and going into the study began to read it. He didn't read verse very easily and though he read with attention, every word of it, the impression he received was far from clear. Then he began at the beginning again and read it a second time. He read with increasing malaise, but he was not a stupid man and when he had finished he had a distinct understanding of what it was all about. Part of the book was in free verse, part in conventional metres, but the story it related was coherent and plain to the meanest intelligence. It was the story of a passionate love affair between an older woman, married, and a young man. George Peregrine made out the steps of it as easily as if he had been doing a sum in simple addition.

Written in the first person, it began with the tremulous surprise of the woman, past her youth, when it dawned upon her that the young man was in love with her. She hesitated to believe it. She thought she must be deceiving herself. And she was terrified when on a sudden she discovered that she was passionately in love with him. She told herself it was absurd; with the disparity of age between them nothing but unhappiness could come to her if she yielded to her emotion. She tried to prevent him from speaking, but the day came when he told her that he loved her and forced her to tell him that she loved him too. He begged her to run away with him. She couldn't leave her husband, her home; and what life could they look forward to, she an aging woman, he so young? How could she expect his love to last? She begged him to have mercy on her. But his love was impetuous. He wanted her, he wanted her with all his heart, and at last trembling, afraid, desirous, she yielded to him. Then there was a period of ecstatic happiness. The world, the dull, humdrum world of every day, blazed with glory. Love songs flowed from her pen. The woman worshipped the young, virile body of her lover. George flushed darkly when she praised his broad chest and slim flanks, the beauty of his legs and the flatness of his belly.

Hot stuff, Daphne's friend had said. It was that all right. Disgusting.

There were sad little pieces in which she lamented the emptiness of her life when as must happen he left her, but they ended with a cry that all she had to suffer would be worth it for the bliss that for a while had been hers. She wrote of the long, tremulous nights they passed together and the languor that lulled them to sleep in one another's arms. She wrote of the rapture of brief stolen moments when, braving all danger, their passion overwhelmed them and they surrendered to its call.

She thought it would be an affair of a few weeks, but miraculously it lasted. One of the poems referred to three years having gone by without lessening the love that filled their hearts. It looked as though he continued to press her to go away with him, far away, to a hill town in Italy, a Greek island, a walled city in Tunisia, so that they could be together always, for in another of the poems she besought him to let things be as they were. Their happiness was precarious. Perhaps it was owing to the difficulties they had to encounter and the rarity of their meetings that their love had retained for so long its first enchanting ardour. Then on a sudden the young man died. How, when or where George could not discover. There followed a long, heartbroken cry of bitter grief, grief she could not indulge in, grief that had to be hidden. She had to be cheerful, give dinner parties and go out to dinner, behave as she had always behaved, though the light had gone out of her life and she was bowed down with anguish. The last poem of all was a set of four short stanzas in which the writer, sadly resigned to her loss, thanked the dark powers that rule man's destiny that she had been privileged at least for a while to enjoy the greatest happiness that we poor human beings can ever hope to know.

It was three o'clock in the morning when George Peregrine finally put the book down. It had seemed to him that he heard Evie's voice in every line, over and over again he came upon turns of phrase he had heard her use, there were details that were as familiar to him as to her: there was no doubt about it; it was her own story she had told, and it was as plain as anything could be that she had had a lover and her lover had died. It was not anger so much that he felt, or horror or dismay, though he was dismayed and he was horrified, but amazement. It was as inconceivable that Evie should have had a love affair, and a wildly passionate one at that, as that the trout in a glass case over the chimney piece in his study, the finest he had ever caught, should suddenly wag its tail. He understood now the meaning of the amused look he had seen in the eyes of that man he had spoken with at the club, he understood why Daphne when she was talking about the book had seemed to be enjoying a private joke and why those two women at the cocktail party had tittered when he strolled past them.

He broke out into a sweat. Then on a sudden he was seized with fury and he jumped up to go and awake Evie and ask her sternly for an explanation. But he stopped at the door. After all what proof had he? A book. He remembered that he'd told Evie he thought it jolly good. True, he hadn't read it, but he'd pretended he had. He would look a perfect fool if he had to admit that.

"I must watch my step," he muttered.

He made up his mind to wait for two or three days and think it all over. Then he'd decide what to do. He went to bed, but he couldn't sleep for a long time.

"Evie," he kept on saying to himself. "Evie, of all people."

They met at breakfast next morning as usual. Evie was as she always was, quiet, demure and self-possessed, a middle-aged woman, who made

no effort to look younger than she was, a woman who had nothing of what he still called It. He looked at her as he hadn't looked at her for years. She had her usual placid serenity. Her pale blue eyes were untroubled. There was no sign of guilt on her candid brow. She made the same little casual remarks she always made.

"It's nice to get back to the country again after those two hectic days in London. What are you going to do this morning?"

It was incomprehensible.

Three days later he went to see his solicitor. Henry Blane was an old friend of George's as well as his lawyer. He had a place not far from Peregrine's and for years they had shot over one anothers' preserves. For two days a week he was a country gentleman and for the other five a busy lawyer in Sheffield. He was a tall, robust fellow, with a boisterous manner and a jovial laugh, which suggested that he liked to be looked upon essentially as a sportsman and a good fellow and only incidentally as a lawyer. But he was shrewd and worldly-wise.

"Well, George, what's brought you here today?" he boomed as the Colonel was shown into his office. "Have a good time in London? I'm taking my missus up for a few days next week. How's Evie?"

"It's about Evie I've come to see you," said Peregrine, giving him a suspicious look. "Have you read her book?"

His sensitivity had been sharpened during those last days of troubled thought and he was conscious of a faint change in the lawyer's expression. It was as though he were suddenly on his guard.

"Yes, I've read it. Great success, isn't it? Fancy Evie breaking out into poetry. Wonders will never cease."

George Peregrine was inclined to lose his temper.

"It's made me look a perfect damned fool."

"Oh, what nonsense, George! There's no harm in Evie's writing a book. You ought to be jolly proud of her."

"Don't talk such rot. It's her own story. You know it and everyone else knows it. I suppose I'm the only one who doesn't know who her lover was."

"There is such a thing as imagination, old boy. There's no reason to suppose the whole thing isn't just made up."

"Look here, Henry, we've known one another all our lives. We've had all sorts of good times together. Be honest with me. Can you look me in the face and tell me you believe it's a made-up story?"

Henry Blane moved uneasily in his chair. He was disturbed by the distress in old George's voice.

"You've got no right to ask me a question like that. Ask Evie."

"I daren't," George answered after an anguished pause. "I'm afraid she'd tell me the truth."

There was an uncomfortable silence.

"Who was the chap?"

Henry Blane looked at him straight in the eye.

"I don't know, and if I did I wouldn't tell you."

"You swine. Don't you see what a position I'm in? Do you think it's very pleasant to be made absolutely ridiculous?"

The lawyer lit a cigarette and for some moments silently puffed it.

"I don't see what I can do for you," he said at last.

"You've got private detectives you employ, I suppose. I want you to put them on the job and let them find everything out."

"It's not very pretty to put detectives on one's wife, old boy; and besides, taking for granted for a moment that Evie had an affair, it was a good many years ago and I don't suppose it would be possible to find out a thing. They seem to have covered their tracks pretty carefully."

"I don't care. You put the detectives on. I want to know the truth."

"I won't, George. If you're determined to do that you'd better consult someone else. And look here, even if you got evidence that Evie had been unfaithful to you what would you do with it? You'd look rather silly divorcing your wife because she'd committed adultery ten years ago."

"At all events I could have it out with her."

"You can do that now, but you know just as well as I do, that if you do she'll leave you. D'you want her to do that?"

George gave him an unhappy look.

"I don't know. I always thought she'd been a damned good wife to me. She runs the house perfectly, we never have any servant trouble; she's done wonders with the garden and she's

splendid with all the village people. But damn it, I have my self-respect to think of. How can I go on living with her when I know that she was grossly unfaithful to me?"

"Have you always been faithful to her?"

"More or less, you know. After all we've been married for nearly twenty-four years and Evie was never much for bed."

The solicitor slightly raised his eyebrows, but George was too intent on what he was saying to notice.

"I don't deny that I've had a bit of fun now and then. A man wants it. Women are different."

"We only have mens' word for that," said Henry Blane, with a faint smile.

"Evie's absolutely the last woman I'd have suspected of kicking over the traces. I mean, she's a very fastidious, reticent woman. What on earth made her write the damned book?"

"I suppose it was a very poignant experience and perhaps it was a relief to her to get it off her chest like that."

"Well, if she had to write it why the devil didn't she write it under an assumed name?"

"She used her maiden name. I suppose she thought that was enough and it would have been if the book hadn't had this amazing boom."

George Peregrine and the lawyer were sitting opposite one another with a desk between them. George, his elbow on the desk, his cheek resting on his hand, frowned at his thought.

"It's so rotten not to know what sort of a chap he was. One can't even tell if he was by way of being a gentleman. I mean, for all I know he may have been a farmhand or a clerk in a lawyer's office."

Henry Blane did not permit himself to smile and when he answered there was in his eyes a kindly, tolerant look.

"Knowing Evie so well I think the probabilities are that he was all right. Anyhow I'm sure he wasn't a clerk in my office."

"It's been such a shock to me," the Colonel sighed. "I though she was fond of me. She couldn't have written that book unless she hated me." *She wrote it because she once loved him.*

"Oh, I don't believe that. I don't think she's capable of hatred."

"You're not going to pretend that she loves me."

"No."

"Well, what does she feel for me?"

Henry Blane leaned back in his swivel chair and looked at George reflectively.

"Indifference, I should say."

The Colonel gave a little shudder and reddened.

"After all, you're not in love with her, are you?"

George Peregrine did not answer directly.

"It's been a great blow to me not to have any children, but I've never let her see that I think she's let me down. I've always been kind to her. Within reasonable limits I've tried to do my duty by her."

The lawyer passed a large hand over his mouth to conceal the smile that trembled on his lips.

"It's been such an awful shock to me," Peregrine went on. "Damn it all, even ten years ago Evie was no chicken and God knows, she wasn't much to look at. It's so ugly." He sighed deeply. "What would you do in my place?"

"Nothing."

George Peregrine drew himself bolt upright in his chair and he looked at Henry with the stern set face that he must have worn when he inspected his regiment.

"I can't overlook a thing like this. I've been made a laughingstock. I can never hold up my head again."

"Nonsense," said the lawyer sharply, and then in a pleasant, kindly manner: "Listen, old boy: the man's dead; it all happened a long while back. Forget it. Talk to people about Evie's book, rave about it, tell 'em how proud you are of her. Behave as though you had so much confidence in her, you *know* she could never have been unfaithful to you. The world moves so quickly and people's memories are so short. They'll forget."

"I shan't forget."

"You're both middle-aged people. She probably does a great deal more for you than you think and you'd be awfully lonely without her. I don't think it matters if you don't forget. It'll be all to the good if you can get it into that thick head of yours that there's a lot more in Evie than you ever had the gumption to see."

"Damn it all, you talk as if *I* was to blame."

"No, I don't think you were to blame, but I'm not so sure that Evie was either. I don't suppose she wanted to fall in love with this boy. D'you remember those verses right at the end? The impression they gave me was that though she

was shattered by his death, in a strange sort of way she welcomed it. All through she'd been aware of the fragility of the tie that bound them. He died in the full flush of his first love and had never known that love so seldom endures; he'd only known its bliss and beauty. In her own bitter grief she found solace in the thought that he'd been spared all sorrow."

"All that's a bit above my head, old boy. I see more or less what you mean."

George Peregrine stared unhappily at the inkstand on the desk. He was silent and the lawyer looked to him with curious, yet sympathetic, eyes.

"Do you realize what courage she must have had never by a sign to show how dreadfully unhappy she was?" he said gently.

Colonel Peregrine sighed.

"I'm broken. I suppose you're right; it's no good crying over spilt milk and it would only make things worse if I made a fuss."

"Well?"

George Peregrine gave a pitiful little smile.

"I'll take your advice. I'll do nothing. Let them think me a damned fool and to hell with them. The truth is, I don't know what I'd do without Evie. But I'll tell you what, there's one thing I shall never understand till my dying day: What in the name of heaven did the fellow ever see in her?"

FOR ANALYSIS

1. The title of this story comes from a ballad by Rudyard Kipling: "The Colonel's lady and Judy O'Grady are sisters under the skin." Exactly what does that mean? Who in the story does not realize that it is true?

2. Is there an implication in the story of who the young man in Evie's book really was? What leads you to this conclusion?

3. Describe the character of George Peregrine. What are his special blindspots? Would you call him tragic or pathetic? What matters most in the world to him? How is his reaction to the story told in Evie's book of poems typical of him? What is Maugham telling you of his character when he has Peregrine say that he doesn't dare ask Evie about the book because "I'm afraid she'd tell me the truth"?

4. Who in the story functions as the author's "mouthpiece"—that is, who speaks for Maugham?

EUDORA WELTY

Death of a Travelling Salesman

Symbolic

R. J. Bowman, who for fourteen years had travelled for a shoe company through Mississippi, drove his Ford along a rutted dirt path. It was a long day! The time did not seem to clear the noon hurdle and settle into soft afternoon. The sun, keeping its strength here even in winter, stayed at the top of the sky, and every time Bowman stuck his head out of the dusty car to stare up the road, it seemed to reach a long arm down and push against the top of his head, right through his hat—like the practical joke of an old drummer, long on the road. It made him feel all the more angry and helpless. He was feverish, and he was not quite sure of the way.

This was his first day back on the road after a long siege of influenza. He had had very high fever, and dreams, and had become weakened and pale, enough to tell the difference in the mirror, and he could not think clearly. . . . All afternoon, in the midst of his anger, and for no reason, he had thought of his dead grandmother. She had been a comfortable soul. Once more Bowman wished he could fall into the big feather bed that had been in her room. . . . Then he forgot her again.

This desolate hill country! And he seemed to be going the wrong way—it was as if he were going back, far back. There was not a house in sight. . . . There was no use wishing he were back in bed, though. By paying the hotel doctor his bill he had proved his recovery. He had not even been sorry when the pretty trained nurse said good-bye. He did not like illness, he distrusted it, as he distrusted the road without signposts. It angered him. He had given the nurse a really expensive bracelet, just because she was packing up her bag and leaving.

But now—what if in fourteen years on the road he had never been ill before and never had an accident? His record was broken, and he had even begun almost to question it. . . . He had gradually put up at better hotels, in the bigger towns, but weren't they all, eternally, stuffy in summer and draughty in winter? Women? He could only remember little rooms within little rooms, like a nest of Chinese paper boxes, and if he thought of one woman he saw the worn loneliness that the furniture of that room seemed built of. And he himself—he was a man who always wore rather wide-brimmed black hats, and in the wavy hotel mirrors had looked something like a bullfighter, as he paused for that inevitable instant on the landing, walking downstairs to supper. . . . He leaned out of the car again, and once more the sun pushed at his head.

Bowman had wanted to reach Beulah by dark, to go to bed and sleep off his fatigue. As he remembered, Beulah was fifty miles away from the last town, on a graveled road. This was only a cow trail. How had he ever come to such a place? One hand wiped the sweat from his face, and he drove on.

He had made the Beulah trip before. But he had never seen this hill or this petering-out path before—or that cloud, he thought shyly, looking up and then down quickly—any more than he had seen this day before. Why did he not admit he was simply lost and had been for miles? . . . He was not in the habit of asking the way of strangers, and these people never knew where the very roads they lived on went to; but then he had not even been close enough to anyone to call out. People standing in the fields now and then, or on top of the haystacks, had been too far away, looking like leaning sticks or weeds, turning a little at the solitary rattle of his car across their countryside, watching the pale sobered winter dust where it chunked out behind like big squashes down the road. The stares of these distant people had followed him solidly like a wall, impenetrable, behind which they turned back after he had passed.

The cloud floated there to one side like the bolster on his grandmother's bed. It went over a cabin on the edge of a hill, where two bare chinaberry trees clutched at the sky. He drove through a heap of dead oak leaves, his wheels stirring their weightless sides to make a silvery melancholy whistle as the car passed through their bed. No car had been along this way ahead of him. Then he saw that he was on the edge of a ravine that fell away, a red erosion, and that this was indeed the road's end.

He pulled the brake. But it did not hold, though he put all his strength into it. The car, tipped toward the edge, rolled a little. Without doubt, it was going over the bank.

He got out quietly, as though some mischief had been done him and he had his dignity to remember. He lifted his bag and sample case out, set them down, and stood back and watched the car roll over the edge. He heard something—not the crash he was listening for, but a slow unuproarious crackle. Rather distastefully he went to look over, and he saw that his car had fallen into a tangle of immense grape vines as thick as his arm, which caught it and held it, rocked it like a grotesque child in a dark cradle, and then, as he watched, concerned somehow that he was not still inside it, released it gently to the ground.

He sighed.

Where am I? he wondered with a shock. Why didn't I do something? All his anger seemed to have drifted away from him. There was the house, back on the hill. He took a bag in each hand and with almost childlike willingness went toward it. But his breathing came with difficulty, and he had to stop to rest.

It was a shotgun house, two rooms and an open passage between, perched on the hill. The whole cabin slanted a little under the heavy heaped-up vine that covered the roof, light and green, as though forgotten from summer. A woman stood in the passage.

He stopped still. Then all of a sudden his heart began to behave strangely. Like a rocket set off, it began to leap and expand into uneven patterns of beats which showered into his brain, and he could not think. But in scattering and falling it made no noise. It shot up with great power, almost elation, and fell gently, like acrobats into nets. It began to pound profoundly, then waited irresponsibly, hitting in some sort of inward mockery first at his ribs, then against his eyes, then under his shoulder blades, and against the roof of his mouth when he tried to say, "Good afternoon, madam." But he could not hear his heart—it was as quiet as ashes falling. This was rather comforting; still, it was shocking to Bowman to feel his heart beating at all.

Stockstill in his confusion, he dropped his bags, which seemed to drift in slow bulks gracefully through the air and to cushion themselves on the grey prostrate grass near the doorstep.

As for the woman standing there, he saw at once that she was old. Since she could not possibly hear his heart, he ignored the pounding and now looked at her carefully, and yet in his distraction dreamily, with his mouth open.

She had been cleaning the lamp, and held it, half blackened, half clear, in front of her. He saw her with the dark passage behind her. She was a big woman with a weather beaten but unwrinkled face; her lips were held tightly together, and her eyes looked with a curious dulled brightness into his. He looked at her shoes, which were like bundles. If it were summer she would be barefoot. . . . Bowman, who automatically judged a woman's age on sight, set her age at fifty. She wore a formless garment of some grey coarse material, rough-dried from a washing, from which her arms appeared pink and unexpectedly round. When she never said a word, and sustained her quiet pose of holding the lamp, he was convinced of the strength in her body.

"Good afternoon, madam," he said.

She stared on, whether at him or at the air around him he could not tell, but after a moment she lowered her eyes to show that she would listen to whatever he had to say.

"I wonder if you would be interested—" He tried once more. "An accident—my car . . ."

Her voice emerged low and remote, like a sound across a lake. "Sonny he ain't here."

"Sonny?"

"Sonny ain't here now."

Her son—a fellow able to bring my car up, he decided in blurred relief. He pointed down the hill. "My car's in the bottom of the ditch. I'll need help."

"Sonny ain't here, but he'll be here."

She was becoming clearer to him and her voice stronger, and Bowman saw that she was stupid.

He was hardly surprised at the deepening postponement and tedium of his journey. He took a breath, and heard his voice speaking over the silent blows of his heart. "I was sick. I am not strong yet. . . . May I come in?"

He stooped and laid his big black hat over the handle on his bag. It was a humble motion, almost a bow, that instantly struck him as absurd and betraying of all his weakness. He looked up at the woman, the wind blowing his hair. He might have continued for a long time in this unfamiliar attitude; he had never been a patient man, but when he was sick he had learned to sink submissively into the pillows, to wait for his medicine. He waited on the woman.

Then she, looking at him with blue eyes, turned and held open the door, and after a moment Bowman, as if convinced in his action, stood erect and followed her in.

Inside, the darkness of the house touched him

like a professional hand, the doctor's. The wo-man set the half-cleaned lamp on a table in the center of the room and pointed, also like a pro-fessional person, a guide, to a chair with a yellow cowhide seat. She herself crouched on the hearth, drawing her knees up under the shapeless dress.

At first he felt hopefully secure. His heart was quieter. The room was enclosed in the gloom of yellow pine boards. He could see the other room, with the foot of an iron bed showing, across the passage. The bed had been made up with a red-and-yellow pieced quilt that looked like a map of a picture, a little like his grandmother's girl-hood painting of Rome burning.

He had ached for coolness, but in this room it was cold. He stared at the hearth with dead coals lying on it and iron pots in the corners. The hearth and smoked chimney were of the stone he had seen ribbing the hills, mostly slate. Why is there no fire? he wondered.

And it was so still. The silence of the fields seemed to enter and move familiarly through the house. The wind used the open hall. He felt that he was in a mysterious, quiet, cool danger. It was necessary to do what? . . . To talk.

"I have a nice line of women's low-priced shoes . . ." he said.

But the woman answered, "Sonny'll be here. He's strong. Sonny'll move your car."

"Where is he now?"

"Farms for Mr. Redmond."

Mr. Redmond. Mr. Redmond. That was some-one he would never have to encounter, and he was glad. Somehow the name did not appeal to him. . . . In a flare of touchiness and anxiety, Bowman wished to avoid even mention of un-known men and their unknown farms.

"Do you two live here alone?" He was sur-prised to hear his old voice, chatty, confidential, inflected for selling shoes, asking a question like that—a thing he did not even want to know.

"Yes. We are alone."

He was surprised at the way she answered. She had taken a long time to say that. She had nodded her head in a deep way too. Had she wished to affect him with some sort of premoni-tion? he wondered unhappily. Or was it only that she would not help him, after all, by talking with him? For he was not strong enough to receive the impact of unfamiliar things without a little talk to break their fall. He had lived a month in which nothing had happened except in his head and his body—an almost inaudible life of heartbeats and dreams that came back,

a life of fever and privacy, a delicate life which had left him weak to the point of—what? Of beg-ging. The pulse in his palm leapt like a trout in a brook.

He wondered over and over why the woman did not go ahead with cleaning the lamp. What prompted her to stay there across the room, silently bestowing her presence upon him? He saw that with her it was not a time for doing little tasks. Her face was grave; she was feeling how right she was. Perhaps it was only polite-ness. In docility he held his eyes stiffly wide; they fixed themselves on the woman's clasped hands as though she held the cord they were strung on.

Then, "Sonny's coming," she said.

He himself had not heard anything, but there came a man passing the window and then plung-ing in at the door, with two hounds beside him. Sonny was a big enough man, with his belt slung low about his hips. He looked at least thirty. He had a hot, red face that was yet full of silence. He wore muddy blue pants and an old military coat stained and patched. World War? Bowman wondered. Great God, it was a Confederate coat. On the back of his light hair he had a wide filthy black hat which seemed to insult Bowman's own. He pushed down the dogs from his chest. He was strong with dignity and heaviness in his way of moving. . . . There was the resemblance to his mother.

They stood side by side. . . . He must account again for his presence here.

"Sonny, this man, he had his car to run off over the prec'pice an' wants to know if you will git it out for him," the woman said after a few minutes.

Bowman could not even state his case.

Sonny's eyes lay upon him.

He knew he should offer explanations and show money—at least appear either penitent or authoritative. But all he could do was to shrug slightly.

Sonny brushed by him going to the window, followed by the eager dogs, and looked out. There was effort even in the way he was looking, as if he could throw his sight out like a rope. Without turning Bowman felt that his own eyes could have seen nothing: it was too far.

"Got me a mule out there an' got me a block an' tackle," said Sonny meaningfully. "I *could* catch me my mule an' git me my ropes, an' before long I'd git your car out the ravine."

He looked completely round the room, as if in meditation, his eyes roving in their own distance. Then he pressed his lips firmly and yet shyly together, and with the dogs ahead of him this time, he lowered his head and strode out. The hard earth sounded, cupping to his powerful way of walking—almost a stagger.

Mischievously, at the suggestion of those sounds, Bowman's heart leapt again. It seemed to walk about inside him.

"Sonny's goin' to do it," the woman said. She said it again, singing it almost, like a song. She was sitting in her place by the hearth.

Without looking out, he heard some shouts and the dogs barking and the pounding of hoofs in short runs on the hill. In a few minutes Sonny passed under the window with a rope, and there was a brown mule with quivering, shining, purple-looking ears. The mule actually looked in the window. Under its eyelashes it turned targetlike eyes into his. Bowman averted his head and saw the woman looking serenely back at the mule, with only satisfaction in her face.

She sang a little more, under her breath. It occurred to him, and it seemed quite marvelous, that she was not really talking to him, but rather following the thing that came about with words that were unconscious and part of her looking.

So he said nothing, and this time when he did not reply he felt a curious and strong emotion, not fear, rise up in him.

This time, when his heart leapt, something—his soul—seemed to leap too, like a little colt invited out of a pen. He stared at the woman while the frantic nimbleness of his feeling made his head sway. He could not move; there was nothing he could do, unless perhaps he might embrace this woman who sat there growing old and shapeless before him.

But he wanted to leap up, to say to her, I have been sick and I found out then, only then, how lonely I am. Is it too late? My heart puts up a struggle inside me, and you may have heard it, protesting against emptiness. . . . It should be full, he would rush on to tell her, thinking of his heart now as a deep lake, it should be holding love like other hearts. It should be flooded with love. There would be a warm spring day. . . . Come and stand in my heart, whoever you are, and a whole river would cover your feet and rise higher and take your knees in whirlpools, and draw you down to itself, your whole body, your heart too.

But he moved a trembling hand across his eyes, and looked at the placid crouching woman

across the room. She was still as a statue. He felt ashamed and exhausted by the thought that he might, in one more moment, have tried by simple words and embraces to communicate some strange thing—something which seemed always to have just escaped him . . . .

Sunlight touched the farthest pot on the hearth. It was late afternoon. This time tomorrow he would be somewhere on a good gravelled road, driving his car past things that happened to people, quicker than their happening. Seeing ahead to the next day, he was glad, and knew that this was no time to embrace an old woman. He could feel in his pounding temples the readying of his blood for motion and for hurrying away.

"Sonny's hitched up your car by now," said the woman. "He'll git it out the ravine right shortly."

"Fine!" he cried with his customary enthusiasm.

Yet it seemed a long time that they waited. It began to get dark. Bowman was cramped in his chair. Any man should know enough to get up and walk around while he waited. There was something like guilt in such stillness and silence.

But instead of getting up, he listened. . . . His breathing restrained, his eyes powerless in the growing dark, he listened uneasily for a warning sound, forgetting in wariness what it would be. Before long he heard something—soft, continuous, insinuating.

"What's the noise?" he asked, his voice jumping into the dark. Then wildly he was afraid it would be his heart beating so plainly in the quiet room, and she would tell him so.

"You might hear the stream," she said grudgingly.

Her voice was closer. She was standing by the table. He wondered why she did not light the lamp. She stood there in the dark and did not light it.

Bowman would never speak to her now, for the time was past. I'll sleep in the dark, he thought, in his bewilderment pitying himself.

Heavily she moved on to the window. Her arm, vaguely white, rose straight from her full side and she pointed out into the darkness.

"That white speck's Sonny," she said, talking to herself.

He turned unwillingly and peered over her

shoulder; he hesitated to rise and stand beside her. His eyes searched the dusky air. The white speck floated smoothly toward her finger, like a leaf on a river, growing whiter in the dark. It was as if she had shown him something secret, part of her life, but had offered no explanation. He looked away. He was moved almost to tears, feeling for no reason that she had made a silent declaration equivalent to his own. His hand waited upon his chest.

Then a step shook the house, and Sonny was in the room. Bowman felt how the woman left him there and went to the other man's side.

"I done got your car out, mister," said Sonny's voice in the dark. "She's settin' a-waitin' in the road, turned to go back where she come from."

"Fine!" said Bowman, projecting his own voice to loudness. "I'm surely much obliged—I could never have done it myself—I was sick . . . ."

"I could do it easy," said Sonny.

Bowman could feel them both waiting in the dark, and he could hear the dogs panting out in the yard, waiting to bark when he should go. He felt strangely helpless and resentful. Now that he could go, he longed to stay. From what was he being deprived? His chest was rudely shaken by the violence of his heart. These people cherished something here that he could not see, they withheld some ancient promise of food and warmth and light. Between them they had a conspiracy. He thought of the way she had moved away from him and gone to Sonny, she had flowed toward him. He was shaking with cold, he was tired, and it was not fair. Humbly and yet angrily he stuck his hand into his pocket.

"Of course I'm going to pay you for everything—"

"We don't take money for such," said Sonny's voice belligerently.

"I want to pay. But do something more . . . Let me stay—to-night. . . ." He took another step toward them. If only they could see him, they would know his sincerity, his real need! His voice went on, "I'm not very strong yet, I'm not able to walk far, even back to my car, maybe, I don't know—I don't know exactly where I am—"

He stopped. He felt as if he might burst into tears. What would they think of him!

Sonny came over and put his hands on him. Bowman felt them pass (they were professional too) across his chest, over his hips. He could feel Sonny's eyes upon him in the dark.

"You ain't no revenuer come sneakin' here, mister, ain't got no gun?"

To this end of nowhere! And yet *he* had come. He made a grave answer. "No."

"You can stay."

"Sonny," said the woman, "you'll have to borry some fire."

"I'll go git it from Redmond's," said Sonny.

"What?" Bowman strained to hear their words to each other.

"Our fire, it's out, and Sonny's got to borry some, because it's dark an' cold," she said.

"But matches—I have matches—"

"We don't have no need for 'em," she said proudly. "Sonny's goin' after his own fire."

"I'm goin' to Redmond's," said Sonny with an air of importance, and he went out.

After they had waited a while, Bowman looked out the window and saw a light moving over the hill. It spread itself out like a little fan. It zigzagged along the field, darting and swift, not like Sonny at all. . . . Soon enough, Sonny staggered in, holding a burning stick behind him in tongs, fire flowing in his wake, blazing light into the corners of the room.

"We'll make a fire now," the woman said, taking the brand.

When that was done she lit the lamp. It showed its dark and light. The whole room turned golden-yellow like some sort of flower, and the walls smelled of it and seemed to tremble with the quiet rushing of the fire and the waving of the burning lampwick in its funnel of light.

The woman moved among the iron pots. With the tongs she dropped hot coals on top of the iron lids. They made a set of soft vibrations, like the sound of a bell far away.

She looked up and over at Bowman, but he could not answer. He was trembling. . . .

"Have a drink, mister?" Sonny asked. He had brought in a chair from the other room and sat astride it with his folded arms across the back. Now we are all visible to one another, Bowman thought, and cried, "Yes, sir, you bet, thanks!"

"Come after me and do just what I do," said Sonny.

It was another excursion into the dark. They went through the hall, out to the back of the house, past a shed and a hooded well. They came to a wilderness of thicket.

"Down on your knees," said Sonny.

"What?" Sweat broke out on his forehead.

He understood when Sonny began to crawl through a sort of tunnel that the bushes made over the ground. He followed, startled in spite of himself when a twig or a thorn touched him gently without making a sound, clinging to him and finally letting him go.

Sonny stopped crawling and, crouched on his knees, began to dig with both his hands into the dirt. Bowman shyly struck matches and made a light. In a few minutes Sonny pulled up a jug. He poured out some of the whisky into a bottle from his coat pocket, and buried the jug again. "You never know who's liable to knock at your door," he said, and laughed. "Start back," he said, almost formally. "Ain't no need for us to drink outdoors, like hogs."

At the table by the fire, sitting opposite each other in their chairs, Sonny and Bowman took drinks out of the bottle, passing it across. The dogs slept; one of them was having a dream.

"This is good," said Bowman. "That is what I needed." It was just as though he were drinking the fire off the hearth. *waemth + security*

"He makes it," said the woman with quiet pride.   *Sonny is the source of it.*

She was pushing the coals off the pots, and the smells of corn bread and coffee circled the room. She set everything on the table before the men, with a bone-handled knife stuck into one of the potatoes, splitting out its golden fibre. Then she stood for a minute looking at them, tall and full above them where they sat. She leaned a little toward them.

"You-all can eat now," she said, and suddenly smiled.

Bowman had just happened to be looking at her. He set his cup back on the table in unbelieving protest. A pain pressed at his eyes. He saw that she was not an old woman. She was young, still young. He could think of no number of years for her. She was the same age as Sonny, and she belonged to him. She stood with the deep dark corner of the room behind her, the shifting yellow light scattering over her head and her grey formless dress, trembling over her tall body when it bent over them in its sudden communication. She was young. Her teeth were shining and her eyes glowed. She turned and walked slowly and heavily out of the room, and he heard her sit

down on the cot and then lie down. The pattern on the quilt moved.

"She goin' to have a baby," said Sonny, popping a bite into his mouth.

Bowman could not speak. He was shocked with knowing what was really in this house. A marriage, a fruitful marriage. That simple thing. Anyone could have had that.

Somehow he felt unable to be indignant or protest, although some sort of joke had certainly been played upon him. There was nothing remote or mysterious here—only something private. The only secret was the ancient communication between two people. But the memory of the woman's waiting silently by the cold hearth, of the man's stubborn journey a mile away to get fire, and how they finally brought out their food and drink and filled the room proudly with all they had to show, was suddenly too clear and too enormous within him for response. . . .

"You ain't as hungry as you look," said Sonny.

The woman came out of the bedroom as soon as the men had finished, and ate her supper while her husband stared peacefully into the fire.

Then they put the dogs out, with the food that was left.

"I think I'd better sleep here by the fire, on the floor," said Bowman. *cheated because he thought of they as his, they don't ooffed.* He felt that he had been cheated, and that he could afford now to be generous. Ill though he was, he was not going to ask them for their bed. He was through with asking favours in this house, now that he understood what was there.

"Sure, mister."

But he had not known yet how slowly he understood. They had not meant to give him their bed. After a little interval they both rose and looking at him gravely went into the other room.

He lay stretched by the fire until it grew low and dying. He watched every tongue of blaze lick out and vanish. "There will be special reduced prices on all footwear during the month of January," he found himself repeating quietly, and then he lay with his lips tight shut.

How many noises the night had! He heard the stream running, the fire dying, and he was sure now that he heard his heart beating, too, the sound it made under his ribs. He heard breathing, round and deep, of the man and his wife in the room across the passage. And that was all. But emotion swelled patiently within him, and he wished that the child were his.

He must get back to where he had been before.

Free + warmth die

He stood weakly before the red coals, and put on his overcoat. It felt too heavy on his shoulders. As he started out he looked and saw that the woman had never got through with cleaning the lamp. On some impulse he put all the money from his billfold under its fluted glass base, almost ostentatiously.

Ashamed, shrugging a little, and then shivering, he took his bags and went out. The cold of the air seemed to lift him bodily. The moon was in the sky.

On the slope he began to run, he could not help it. Just as he reached the road, where his car seemed to sit in the moonlight like a boat, his heart began to give off tremendous explosions like a rifle, bang bang bang.

He sank in fright on to the road, his bags falling about him. He felt as if all this had happened before. He covered his heart with both hands to keep anyone from hearing the noise it made. *No one she's him die*

But nobody heard it. *& No one cares so he is isolated.*

FOR ANALYSIS

1. Ordinarily one would expect the salesman to feel superior to Sonny and his wife. But he doesn't. What kind of life has he led? How is their life superior to his?
2. What significance do Miss Welty's repeated references to the beating of Bowman's heart have?

JAMES THURBER

The Secret Life
of Walter Mitty

"We're going through!" The Commander's voice was like thin ice breaking. He wore his full-dress uniform, with the heavily braided white cap pulled down rakishly over one cold gray eye. "We can't make it, sir. It's spoiling for a hurricane, if you ask me." "I'm not asking you, Lieutenant Berg," said the Commander. "Throw on the power light! Rev her up to 8,500! We're going through!" The pounding of the cylinders increased: ta-pocketa-pocketa-pocketa-*pocketa-*

pocketa. The Commander stared at the ice forming on the pilot window. He walked over and twisted a row of complicated dials. "Switch on No. 8 auxiliary!" he shouted. "Switch on No. 8 auxiliary!" repeated Lieutenant Berg. "Full strength in No. 3 turret!" shouted the Commander. "Full strength in No. 3 turret!" The crew, bending to their various tasks in the huge, hurtling eight-engined Navy hydroplane, looked at each other and grinned. "The Old Man'll get us through," they said to one another. "The Old Man ain't afraid of Hell!" . . .

"Not so fast! You're driving too fast!" said Mrs. Mitty. "What are you driving so fast for?"

"Hmm?" said Walter Mitty. He looked at his wife, in the seat beside him, with shocked astonishment. She seemed grossly unfamiliar, like a strange woman who had yelled at him in a crowd. "You were up to fifty-five," she said. "You know I don't like to go more than forty. You were up to fifty-five." Walter Mitty drove on toward Waterbury in silence, the roaring of the SN202 through the worst storm in twenty years of Navy flying fading in the remote, intimate airways of his mind. "You're tensed up again," said Mrs. Mitty. "It's one of your days. I wish you'd let Dr. Renshaw look you over."

Walter Mitty stopped the car in front of the building where his wife went to have her hair done. "Remember to get those overshoes while I'm having my hair done," she said. "I don't need overshoes," said Mitty. She put her mirror back into her bag. "We've been all through that," she said, getting out of the car. "You're not a young man any longer." He raced the engine a little. "Why don't you wear your gloves? Have you lost your gloves?" Walter Mitty reached in a pocket and brought out the gloves. He put them on, but after she had turned and gone into the building and he had driven on to a red light, he took them off again. "Pick it up, brother!" snapped a cop as the light changed, and Mitty hastily pulled on his gloves and lurched ahead. He drove around the streets aimlessly for a time, and then he drove past the hospital on his way to the parking lot.

. . . "It's the millionaire banker, Wellington McMillan," said the pretty nurse. "Yes?" said Walter Mitty, removing his gloves slowly. "Who has the case?" "Dr. Renshaw and Dr. Benbow, but there are two specialists here, Dr. Remington from New York and Mr. Pritchard-Mitford from London. He flew over." A door opened down a long, cool corridor and Dr. Renshaw came out. He looked distraught and haggard. "Hello, Mitty," he said. "We're having the devil's own time with McMillan, the millionaire banker and close personal friend of Roosevelt. Obstreosis of the ductal tract. Tertiary. Wish you'd take a look at him." "Glad to," said Mitty.

In the operating room there were whispered introductions: "Dr. Remington, Dr. Mitty. Mr. Pritchard-Mitford, Dr. Mitty." "I've read your book on streptothricosis," said Pritchard-Mitford, shaking hands. "A brilliant performance, sir." "Thank you," said Walter Mitty. "Didn't know you were in the States, Mitty," grumbled Remington. "Coals to Newcastle, bringing Mitford and me up here for a tertiary." "You are very kind," said Mitty. A huge, complicated machine, connected to the operating table, with many tubes and wires, began at this moment to go pocketa-pocketa-pocketa. "The new anesthetizer is giving way!" shouted an interne. "There is no one in the East who knows how to fix it!" "Quiet, man!" said Mitty, in a low, cool voice. He sprang to the machine, which was now going pocketa-pocketa-queep-pocketa-queep. He began fingering delicately a row of glistening dials.

"Give me a fountain pen!" he snapped. Someone handed him a fountain pen. He pulled a faulty piston out of the machine and inserted the pen in its place. "That will hold for ten minutes," he said. "Get on with the operation." A nurse hurried over and whispered to Renshaw, and Mitty saw the man turn pale. "Coreopsis has set in," said Renshaw nervously. "If you would take over, Mitty?" Mitty looked at him and at the craven figure of Benbow, who drank, and at the grave, uncertain faces of the two great specialists. "If you wish," he said. They slipped a white gown on him; he adjusted a mask and drew on thin gloves; nurses handed him shining . . .

"Back it up, Mac! Look out for that Buick!" Walter Mitty jammed on the brakes. "Wrong lane, Mac," said the parking lot attendant, looking at Mitty closely. "Gee. Yeh," muttered Mitty. He began cautiously to back out of the lane marked "Exit Only." "Leave her sit there," said the attendant. "I'll put her away." Mitty got out of the car. "Hey, better leave the key." "Oh," said Mitty, handing the man the ignition key. The attendant vaulted into the car, backed it up with insolent skill, and put it where it belonged.

They're so damn cocky, thought Walter Mitty, walking along Main Street; they think they know everything. Once he had tried to take his chains off, outside New Milford, and he had got them wound around the axles. A man had had to come out in a wrecking car and unwind them, a young, grinning garageman. Since then Mrs. Mitty always made him drive to a garage to have the chains taken off. The next time, he thought, I'll wear my right arm in a sling; they won't grin at me then. I'll have my right arm in a sling and they'll see I couldn't possibly take the chains off myself. He kicked at the slush on the sidewalk. "Overshoes," he said to himself, and he began looking for a shoe store.

When he came out into the street again, with the overshoes in a box under his arm, Walter Mitty began to wonder what the other thing was his wife had told him to get. She had told him twice, before they set out from their house for Waterbury. In a way he hated these weekly trips to town—he was always getting something wrong. Kleenex, he thought, Squibb's, razor blades? No. Toothpaste, toothbrush, bicarbonate, carborundum, initiative and referendum? He gave it up. But she would remember it. "Where's the what's-its-name?" she would ask. "Don't tell me you forgot the what's-its-name."

A newsboy went by shouting something about the Waterbury trial.

. . . "Perhaps this will refresh your memory." The District Attorney suddenly thrust a heavy automatic at the quiet figure on the witness stand. "Have you ever seen this before?" Walter Mitty took the gun and examined it expertly. "This is my Webley-Vickers 50.80," he said calmly. An excited buzz ran around the courtroom. The judge rapped for order. "You are a crack shot with any sort of firearms, I believe?" said the District Attorney, insinuatingly. "Objection!" shouted Mitty's attorney. "We have shown that the defendant could not have fired the shot. We have shown that he wore his right arm in a sling on the night of the fourteenth of July." Walter Mitty raised his hand briefly and the bickering attorneys were stilled. "With any known make of gun," he said evenly, "I could have killed Gregory Fitzhurst at three hundred feet *with my left hand.*" Pandemonium broke loose in the courtroom. A woman's scream rose above the bedlam and suddenly a lovely, dark-haired girl was in Walter Mitty's arms. The District Attorney struck at her savagely. Without rising from his chair, Mitty let the man have it on the point of the chin. "You miserable cur!" . . .

"Puppy biscuit," said Walter Mitty. He stopped walking and the buildings of Waterbury rose up out of the misty courtroom and surrounded him again. A woman who was passing laughed. "He said 'Puppy biscuit,'" she said to her companion. "That man said 'Puppy biscuit' to himself." Walter Mitty hurried on. He went into an A. & P., not the first one he came to but a smaller one farther up the street. "I want some biscuit for small, young dogs," he said to the clerk. "Any special brand, sir?" The greatest pistol shot in the world thought a moment. "It says 'Puppies Bark for It' on the box," said Walter Mitty.

His wife would be through at the hairdresser's in fifteen minutes, Mitty saw in looking at his watch, unless they had trouble drying it; sometimes they had trouble drying it. She didn't like to get to the hotel first; she would want him to be there waiting for her as usual. He found a big leather chair in the lobby, facing a window, and he put the overshoes and the puppy biscuit on the floor beside it. He picked up an old copy of *Liberty* and sank down into the chair. "Can Germany Conquer the World Through the Air?" Walter Mitty looked at the pictures of bombing planes and of ruined streets.

. . . "The cannonading has got the wind up in young Raleigh, sir," said the sergeant. Captain Mitty looked up at him through tousled hair. "Get him to bed," he said wearily. "With the others. I'll fly alone." "But you can't, sir," said the sergeant anxiously. "It takes two men to handle that bomber and the Archies are pounding hell out of the air. Von Richtman's circus is between here and Saulier." "Somebody's got to get that ammunition dump," said Mitty. "I'm going over. Spot of brandy?" He poured a drink for the sergeant and one for himself. War thundered and whined around the dugout and battered at the door. There was a rending of wood and splinters flew through the room. "A bit of a near thing," said Captain Mitty carelessly. "The box barrage is closing in," said the sergeant. "We only live once, Sergeant," said Mitty, with his faint, fleeting smile. "Or do we?" He poured another brandy and tossed it off. "I never see a man could hold his brandy like you, sir," said the sergeant. "Begging your pardon, sir." Captain Mitty stood up and strapped

on his huge Webley-Vickers automatic. "It's forty kilometers through hell, sir," said the sergeant. Mitty finished one last brandy. "After all," he said softly, "what isn't?" The pounding of the cannon increased; there was the rat-tat-tatting of machine guns, and from somewhere came the menacing pocketa-pocketa-pocketa of the new flamethrowers. Walter Mitty walked to the door of the dugout humming "Auprès de Ma Blonde." He turned and waved to the sergeant. "Cheerio!" he said. . . .

Something struck his shoulder. "I've been looking all over this hotel for you," said Mrs. Mitty. "Why do you have to hide in this old chair? How did you expect me to find you?" "Things close in," said Walter Mitty vaguely. "What?" Mrs. Mitty said. "Did you get the what's-its-name? The puppy biscuit? What's in that box?" "Overshoes," said Mitty. "Couldn't you have put them on in the store?" "I was thinking," said Walter Mitty. "Does it ever occur to you that I am sometimes thinking?" She looked at him. "I'm going to take your temperature when I get you home," she said.

They went out through the revolving doors that made a faintly derisive whistling sound when you pushed them. It was two blocks to the parking lot. At the drugstore on the corner she said, "Wait here for me. I forgot something. I won't be a minute." She was more than a minute. Walter Mitty lighted a cigarette. It began to rain, rain with sleet in it. He stood up against the wall of the drugstore, smoking. . . . He put his shoulders back and his heels together. "To hell with the handkerchief," said Walter Mitty scornfully. He took one last drag on his cigarette and snapped it away. Then, with that faint, fleeting smile playing about his lips, he faced the firing squad; erect and motionless, proud and disdainful, Walter Mitty the Undefeated, inscrutable to the last.

FOR ANALYSIS

1. What do all of Mitty's daydreams have in common? What do these things tell you of the basic nature of the man? In what way is his resolve to wear his arm in a sling when he goes to the garage to have his tire chains removed an extension of his daydreams into the world of reality?

2. In what way is Mitty's remark, "Things close in," a key to his mental processes?

3. Is there a plot in this narrative, that is, does Mitty

ever come to grips with a real problem? Does he try to assert himself in the real world? If so, where is the crisis? Is the conclusion then ironic?

WALTER VAN TILBURG CLARK

The Rapids

Where the unpaved road curved over the top of the hill and descended to the river, a man appeared, walking by himself. He was thin, and wore spectacles, and his legs, when they showed through the flapping wings of his red and blue dressing gown, were very white. He carried a towel in one hand. Walking carefully, for his slippers were thin, he came down between the fir trees, then between the alders and the willows, and stood at the edge of the river.

Four terraces of red rock lay diagonally across the river at this point, but they were tilted away from him, so that the heavy water gushed all on the farther side, and narrowed until, from the lowest ledge, it jetted forth in a single head, making a big, back-bellying bubble rimmed with foam in the pool below. Closer to him, eddies from the main stream came over the terraces at intervals, making thin, transparent falls a foot or two high. Swarms of midget flies danced against these falls, keeping just free of the almost invisible mist which blew from them.

Climbing cautiously from the bank to the rocks, the man walked out onto the second terrace, which was the broadest, and had a gentle incline. He bent over and felt of the rock. It was warm with sun. He took off his dressing gown and sat down. Then he fished in the pocket of the gown, drew out a piece of soap, and put it beside the towel. Finally he pulled off his slippers and placed them on the edge of the towel, to hold it down if the wind blew. After this preparation, he sat with his arms around his knees and stared at the running water.

The sun felt good on his back. He wondered if he dared to remove his shorts, but the bridge from his road lay across the river close above him, so he decided not to. Also there was a building on the opposite bank at the point where the river jumped out into the pool. There were only two and a half walls of the building stand-

ing, and the windows had been out of those for a long time. Vines grew over the gray-tan stones and into the windows, and nothing was left of the roof. Still, it was a building, four stories high. So he kept on his shorts and sat in the sun and looked at the building, remembering the bit of its history he had heard. It had been a mill, way back toward the days of the Revolution. Since then this part of the country had failed. There were only small, poor farms in it now, and the remnants of villages. It gave him a queer feeling to look through the empty windows and see trees growing inside, and the steep, green bank behind them. The ruin was old for America. He was used to seeing empty mills that weren't ten years old. This one went a long way back.

After a time the draft in the river canyon felt chilly in spite of the sun. The man removed his spectacles with both hands, placed them on his dressing gown, picked up the cake of soap, and approached the nearest of the little falls. Standing beside it, with his feet in the shallow basin of turning water, he shivered before the breath of the river. Timidly he began to wash, laving his forearms and the back of his neck, determinedly splashing a palmful of water over his white chest and belly. Encouraged, he wet himself all over and rubbed on the soap vigorously, ducking his head into the fall and then working up a great lather on it, like a shining white wig. When he was well soaped, he couldn't open his eyes. Feeling for the rim of the fall, he moved gingerly, for the basin was slimy. Having come close enough, he squatted under the fall and let it drive the soap down from him until he could open his eyes and see the irridescent trail of the soap, like an oil mark, draining away from him down the gutter of rock. All of this time he moved his arms as much as he dared, because the water was cold.

Back out in the sun, he realized that he would have to do more. He had been too cramped in the basin, and much of his body was still greasy with soap. He walked carefully down the terrace toward the pool, gripping the stone with his toes, for his wet feet were uncertain. They left a trail of increasingly perfect tracks from the small puddle where he had stood beside his dressing gown to the last print at the edge of the terrace, which showed each toe faintly but distinctly, and the ball, the arch, and the heel—clearly a man's foot.

After hesitating, he let himself down over the

edge until the cool water was about his shins. Then he stood on slimy stone like that in the basin. On all fours, he moved slowly, crabwise, along this submerged ledge, and slid off into deeper water. This was at the center of the pool, and the water was quiet, moved only by a side flow circling the pool from the falls, and occasionally by a light wind-ripple along the surface. Awkwardly, and with some splashing, he rubbed himself under water until the last slickness of soap was gone and his hands adhered to his thighs. Then he paddled aimlessly in the pool for a few minutes, treading water and observing himself below. His arms and legs appeared dwarfed and misshapen, his hands and feet immense and square. All of him that was under water looked yellow, and was hairy with particles of the slime he had stirred getting in. Altogether, he was a much more powerful and formidable man, seen through the glass of the pool. He began to feel adventurous.

He noticed that the green darkness of the pool paled on the side across from the ledges. A subaqueous, changeable gold was visible there under the black surface reflection of the forest on the hill. He paddled toward it, keeping his head above water and feeling before him with his hands. When he came to rest, balanced on his hands, he was on a sunken sandbar—the dam which made the pool. The sand was coarse and white, and felt clean to his touch after the scum in the basin and on the ledge. Letting his feet down, he planted them firmly and walked up the incline of the sandbar, feeling himself emerge into gusty air. At last he was on top, the water ankle-deep. Looking down from this eminence, he saw a boat farther along the ridge of the bar. It lay bottom up, and was so waterlogged that it had ground into the sand until no part of it but the very center of the bottom was above water. Now and then a wind-ripple passed over even that.

The man was excited by the discovery. He waded to the boat and attempted to turn it right side up. The vacuum under it, or simply its weight, held it solidly. He was angered, and put forth all his thin might in repeated efforts, standing upright between tries, to breathe deeply and let the blood subside from his head. To the best of his efforts the boat rocked, and straining, he raised the gunwale as far as his knee. This encouraged him, but when he lifted again, the boat came no higher, and then remained passively immovable. He had to let it fall back into the

water, where it rolled lightly, splashing around its shape like a stubborn live thing, run aground, but insisting upon its element. The man's feet had been driven down into the sand until he could not lift well from his position. Freeing himself, he climbed onto the crest of the bar again and stood with his legs apart, glaring at the boat. He considered leaving it and relinquishing himself to placid floating in the pool, whence he could eye the useless boat disdainfully. But when the blood in his temples ceased pounding, he had a cunning thought. Moving down into the water until he was on the outer side of the boat, he slid it backwards off the bar. Once it floated free, he could get his shoulder under it. This stratagem succeeded. The boat rolled bulkily over, sending out a wave which broke on the sandbar.

"That fixes you," the man said aloud.

However, the water in the boat was level with the water in the pool. Only a portion of the prow and of the square stern protruded. The man found that tilting the boat let in as much water as it let out. He laid hold of a chain at the prow and drew the boat onto the crest of the bar. It followed him with lumbering unwillingness. On the bar, a great deal more of it stood above water, and by teetering it fore and aft, he drove several belches of water out over the stern. Still the boat would not rise. The man climbed into it and began to scoop with both hands. The water flew in silver sheets, spread into silver drops, and splattered on the pool, but more of it fell through his hands than went overboard. He stood up and looked around. On a flat rock at the west edge of the pool, there sat a shining two-quart tin can. He clambered out of the boat, went down into the water, paddled industriously across, hoisted himself up the irregular rock steps, and procured the can.

Shortly he had all but an inch or two of water out of the boat. That persisted because of three little leaks, through which he could see minute streams gliding steadily in. He pushed the boat, with the can in it, off the sandbar, and kicking noisily, propelled it to shore. Here he pulled grass and made small wads of it, with the heads standing up in tufts. These plugged the leaks quite effectively, and the man began to hum to himself while he bailed out the last water.

The boat, clumsy and flat-bottomed, with two bowed planks forming each side, had been battered downstream in the flood of the spring rains.

Much of the orange paint had been beaten from it, and the single thwart had been torn out, leaving four rusty nails projecting from each scar. The man searched out a squarish stone and hammered the nails down, humming more loudly. He was formulating a daring plan. He would work the boat around in front of the falls, where the big bubble bellied, and see how far he could go down the stony rapids below the pool. A man taking a risk like that couldn't have nails sticking out where they'd rake his legs if he had to move quickly.

At last he drifted on the pool, keeping the can with him. "Quite a boat," he maintained in a clear voice, and then, argumentatively, but with satisfaction, "I say it's quite a boat."

The boat, dull with the water it had soaked up, rode low and heavily. It refused to be coerced by hand paddling, and cruised, half sidewards, out into the middle of the pool, where it spun slowly three times in the circular current and then headed—or rather tailed—for the stagnant backwash between the shore boulders and the terrace of red rock. The man ceased humming and paddled frantically with his hands, first on one side and then on the other, for the boat was too wide for him to reach water on both sides at once. The boat turned completely around once more, and continued to back toward the extremely green scum in the crevice. The man abandoned himself, held onto the sides, and rode in backwards, muttering. The boat bumped gently, grated along the stone, stirred sinuously, and succeeded in wedging itself. The man sat and observed the pond scum with aversion.

Then he saw a long bamboo pole caught under a ledge. His spirits rose. The pole was within reach, and by bruising his knees a little, slithering on the wet mossiness of the boat, he grasped it. It was heavy, and rotten from enduring the river and from its long hiding in the pool, but having it, he felt confident again. "You'll do," he told the pole. He stood erect, and brandished it in both hands, like a cudgel. "Swell pole." He pressed it firmly against the holding rock, and leaned on it. The boat gave way and swam sluggishly out through the scum. The man, still standing, was immensely elated. "And now, Mr. Boat," he cried.

Maintaining his heroic erectness, he jabbed at rocks along the side and bottom, and brought the boat circuitously toward the back-rolling bubble. As he poled, he hummed grandly, even venturing some openmouthed tra-las. Approaching the bubble more closely, he became quiet and knelt, preparatory to sitting. In this position, he watched the water fall steadily. Coming very close, he was suddenly alarmed by the rapid streaming-away of the foam towards the rocks where the water jumped at a hundred points and turned white, like a miniature surf in a cross-rip. He made a spasmodic thrust with the pole. The boat swung sedately around, slid its stern directly under the fall, lifted its snout, and sank backwards. The man clung amazed until the water was under his chin, and then, with a shout, let go and struck out wildly to avoid the rise of the boat.

He continued to swim, growing calmer, until he bumped on the sandbar and could stand up in the water. Thence he saw his boat lodged against a rock below the bar, the waters protesting around it. The sight enraged him. He remained angry until he had secured the boat, bailed it out, recovered his pole, and returned round the edge of the pool to the fall. Then he swore at the fall to keep his temper up, and this time managed to enter the current just below the bubble. He sat down quickly, nervous because of the speed he expected, believing all at once that his pole was useless. But the boat was too waterlogged. Slow and stately it turned upon the stream, let the anxious waters divide about it, coasted past the sandbar, knocked gently from one rock to another at the head of the shallow rapids, and came to rest between two of them. The man relaxed and took his hands from the sides. "Well," he said, "Well, well."

Thereafter he became pink over his whole body from the exertion of dragging his boat back to the pool. He scraped his feet among the stones of the river bed and never noticed. He took three more rides, going a little farther each time, as he became acquainted with the most prominent rocks. He was so confident on the fifth ride that during the burdensome start he sat with his pole in his hands and regarded the world before him.

In the canyon below the rapids, where the rocky shores grew into cliffs with dense cedar and spruce forests above them, was a splendid curve which hid the lower river. Over the cliff and the forest, a great rounded thunderhead swelled voluminously out of the west and darkened the trees. It appeared to fill the sky, and its upper bosses were bright with sun. The man felt this cloud to be a recognition of the dimension of his undertaking, and gazed at it with stern exultation.

In the late afternoon a woman came over the hill on the road. When she first appeared, irritation was in her walk. The clouds had spread far east and were no longer gilded. The wind kept blowing her hair.

Part way down, she stopped, and stood with her hands on her hips. "For goodness sake," she exclaimed. "For goodness sake, what does that man think he's doing?" She stared. "And yelling his head off like a lunatic," she exclaimed.

The man was just launching out from the jade-colored, white-streaked, back-bellying bubble. He was standing upright in the orange boat, the bamboo pole held aloft like a spear. As he gravitated toward the rapids, his mouth could be seen to open tremendously and repeatedly. He waved his left arm in accompaniment. Faintly, even over the wind and the rush of the falls, the woman could hear the words. "Sailing, sailing," roared the man in the boat. He shook his spear. "Sailing, sailing," he roared, until the boat stumbled and knocked him to his knees. Even then his mouth opened and closed in the same way. Only when the boat stalled, with a white fan of water behind it, did he close his mouth. Then he scrambled out, grabbed the chain on the prow, and dragged, tugged and jerked the boat up the slope of rock and froth.

When the boat was in the pool again, he commenced at once to climb into it and to work his mouth. "Sailing, sailing," he bellowed.

The woman said, "Gracious heavens, he's absolutely crazy," and recovered herself. She advanced to the edge of the rock and yelled at the man. He was then halfway over the stern and kicking valiantly. The woman yelled, "John!" She leaned forward and stuck her chin out when she yelled. The man lay perfectly still for an instant, halfway over the stern. Then he slid back into the water and held onto the stern with one hand. He looked across at the woman. "Yes?" he asked.

The woman could see his mouth move. She looked angry but relieved, and eased her voice a little. "D. L. called you," she cried. "He wants you back in town."

"Bother D. L.," the man said to himself.

"What's that you said?" cried the woman.

"I said all right," the man yelled suddenly.

The woman put one hand on her hip. "He called hours ago. He'll be wild."

The man let go of the boat reluctantly and paddled across to the terrace. The woman stood where she was, waiting. The man drew himself out of the water slowly, with great care for his battered toes. Crabwise he ascended the slimy, submerged rock and crawled up onto the red rock in the wind. Cautiously he walked across the red rock to the spot where he had left his things. His tracks grew more distinct as he went.

"For goodness sake, get a move on," the woman called up at him.

His thin, unmuscular body was turning blue in the wind. Bending stiffly, he removed his slippers from the towel, straightened up, and began to wipe himself. He sat down to wipe his feet, and was tender of his toes. He put his spectacles on, using both hands. Then he stood up and donned the red and blue dressing gown and the leather slippers. He wobbled on one leg at a time while putting on his slippers, and screwed his face up while each rubbed over his toes. He searched a moment for the cake of soap. When he found it, he put it in his pocket and, carrying his towel in one hand, descended carefully to where the woman was waiting.

"What on earth were you doing out there?" she asked. But having seen what he was doing, she went on. "D. L. called up hours ago. How on earth did I know I'd have to come way down here after you? How could I know you'd be . . ."

They went on up the road.

"Well, I'm sure I don't know what you were doing," said the woman. "You're so cold your teeth are chattering."

The man was avoiding sharp pebbles in the road, and said nothing. His peeled knees worked in and out of the opening of the dressing gown, which occasionally fled out behind him on the wind.

"How would I know you'd take all afternoon?" asked the woman sharply. "D. L. will be wild. And all because—well, what on earth *were* you doing out there?"

"Oh, I don't know," said the man. "I found an old boat."

The woman was unpleasantly silent.

"I was just fooling around with an old boat," the man explained, and again, "That's all I was doing, just fooling around with an old boat I found."

The wind on top of the hill was unexpectedly sustained. The woman, holding down her hair with both hands, made no reply. The man had to clutch at his dressing gown tightly, to keep it from streaming out and leaving him uncovered.

FOR ANALYSIS

1. What can you infer about the main character here after reading only the first paragraph? What additional inference can you draw, three paragraphs later, from his refusal to remove his shorts because of the ruined building across from him?

2. In what way is the early remark, "Altogether, he was a much more powerful and formidable man, seen through the glass of the pool," a key to what happens in the story? What significance does the author's careful and detailed description of the man's footprints as he enters and leaves the water have? Notice his final comment on the tracks both times. What is the significance of the final sentence of the story? Is there a connection between this sentence and the footprint details?

3. What symbolic significance does the man's adventure with the boat have for him and for the reader?

4. Compare this story with "The Secret Life of Walter Mitty." What do the two main characters have in common? How do they differ? How does the author's attitude toward his main character differ in the two stories?

ERNEST HEMINGWAY

A Clean
Well-Lighted Place

It was late and every one had left the café except an old man who sat in the shadow the leaves of the tree made against the electric light. In the day time the street was dusty, but at night the dew settled the dust and the old man liked to sit late because he was deaf and now at night it was quiet and he felt the difference. The two waiters inside the café knew that the old man was a little drunk, and while he was a good client they knew that if he became too drunk he would leave without paying, so they kept watch on him.

"Last week he tried to commit suicide," one waiter said.

"Why?"

"He was in despair."

"What about?"

"Nothing."

"How do you know it was nothing?"

"He has plenty of money."

They sat together at a table that was close against the wall near the door of the café and looked at the terrace where the tables were all empty except where the old man sat in the shadow of the leaves of the tree that moved slightly in the wind. A girl and a soldier went by in the street. The street light shone on the brass number on his collar. The girl wore no head covering and hurried beside him.

"The guard will pick him up," one waiter said.

"What does it matter if he gets what he's after?"

"He had better get off the street now. The guard will get him. They went by five minutes ago."

The old man sitting in the shadow rapped on his saucer with his glass. The younger waiter went over to him.

"What do you want?"

The old man looked at him. "Another brandy," he said.

"You'll be drunk," the waiter said. The old man looked at him. The waiter went away.

"He'll stay all night," he said to his colleague. "I'm sleepy now. I never get into bed before three o'clock. He should have killed himself last week."

The waiter took the brandy bottle and another saucer from the counter inside the café and marched out to the old man's table. He put down the saucer and poured the glass full of brandy.

"You should have killed yourself last week," he said to the deaf man. The old man motioned with his finger. "A little more," he said. The waiter poured on into the glass so that the brandy slopped over and ran down the stem into the top saucer of the pile. "Thank you," the old man said. The waiter took the bottle back inside the café. He sat down at the table with his colleague again.

"He's drunk now," he said.

"He's drunk every night."

"What did he want to kill himself for?"

"How should I know?"

"How did he do it?"

"He hung himself with a rope."

"Who cut him down?"

"His niece."

"Why did they do it?"

"Fear for his soul."

"How much money has he got?"

"He's got plenty."

"He must be eighty years old."

"Anyway I should say he was eighty."

"I wish he would go home. I never get to bed before three o'clock. What kind of hour is that to go to bed?"

"He stays up because he likes it."

"He's lonely. I'm not lonely. I have a wife waiting in bed for me."

"He had a wife once too."

"A wife would be no good to him now."

"You can't tell. He might be better with a wife."

"His niece looks after him."

"I know. You said she cut him down."

"I wouldn't want to be that old. An old man is a nasty thing."

"Not always. This old man is clean. He drinks without spilling. Even now, drunk. Look at him."

"I don't want to look at him. I wish he would go home. He has no regard for those who must work."

The old man looked from his glass across the square, then over at the waiters.

"Another brandy," he said, pointing to his glass. The waiter who was in a hurry came over.

"Finished," he said, speaking with that omission of syntax stupid people employ when talking to drunken people or foreigners. "No more tonight. Close now."

"Another," said the old man.

"No. Finished." The waiter wiped the edge of the table with a towel and shook his head.

The old man stood up, slowly counted the saucers, took a leather coin purse from his pocket and paid for the drinks, leaving half a peseta tip.

The waiter watched him go down the street, a very old man walking unsteadily but with dignity.

"Why didn't you let him stay and drink?" the unhurried waiter asked. They were putting up the shutters. "It is not half past two."

"I want to go home to bed."

"What is an hour?"

"More to me than to him."

"An hour is the same."

"You talk like an old man yourself. He can buy a bottle and drink at home."

"It's not the same."

"No, it is not," agreed the waiter with a wife. He did not wish to be unjust. He was only in a hurry.

"And you? You have no fear of going home before your usual hour?"

"Are you trying to insult me?"

"No, hombre, only to make a joke."

"No," the waiter who was in a hurry said, rising from pulling down the metal shutters. "I have confidence. I am all confidence."

"You have youth, confidence, and a job," the older waiter said. "You have everything."

"And what do you lack?"

"Everything but work."

"You have everything I have."

"No. I have never had confidence and I am not young."

"Come on. Stop talking nonsense and lock up."

"I am of those who like to stay late at the café," the older waiter said. "With all those who do not want to go to bed. With all those who need a light for the night."

"I want to go home and into bed."

"We are of two different kinds," the older waiter said. He was now dressed to go home. "It is not only a question of youth and confidence although those things are very beautiful. Each night I am reluctant to close up because there may be some one who needs the café."

"Hombre, there are bodegas open all night long."

"You do not understand. This is a clean and pleasant café. It is well lighted. The light is very good and also, now, there are shadows of the leaves."

"Good night," said the younger waiter.

"Good night," the other said. Turning off the electric light he continued the conversation with himself. It is the light of course but it is necessary that the place be clean and pleasant. You do not want music. Certainly you do not want music. Nor can you stand before a bar with dignity although that is all that is provided for these hours. What did he fear? It was not fear or dread. It was a nothing that he knew too well. It was all a nothing and a man was nothing too. It was only that and light was all it needed and a certain cleanness and order. Some lived in it and never felt it but he knew it all was nada y pues nada y nada y pues nada. Our nada who art in nada, nada be thy name thy kingdom nada

Nada means Nothing.

thy will be nada in nada as it is in nada. Give us this nada our daily nada and nada us our nada as we nada our nadas and nada us not into nada but deliver us from nada; pues nada. Hail nothing full of nothing, nothing is with thee. He smiled and stood before a bar with a shining steam pressure coffee machine.

"What's yours?" asked the barman.

"Nada."

"Otro loco mas," said the barman and turned away.

"A little cup," said the waiter.

The barman poured it for him.

"The light is very bright and pleasant but the bar is unpolished," the waiter said.

The barman looked at him but did not answer. It was too late at night for conversation.

"You want another copita?" the barman asked.

"No, thank you," said the waiter and went out. He disliked bars and bodegas. A clean, well-lighted café was a very different thing. Now, without thinking further, he would go home to his room. He would lie in the bed and finally, with daylight, he would go to sleep. After all, he said to himself, it is probably only insomnia. Many must have it.

FOR ANALYSIS

1. All three major characters in this story have problems. Their problems are different because they live philosophically in different worlds. How would the younger waiter define the world and the "good life"? How would the older waiter define those things?
2. In what way are the older waiter and the old man similar? In what way different? (Look closely at the concluding paragraph.)
3. What point of view is Hemingway using here? Discuss the suitability of this point of view for this story.

RICHARD ERNO

Indian Fighter

At that time my grandfather and Aunt Eleanor were living on 16th Street. I was ten years old the year I went there, and I remember coming alone up the narrow walk between the hedges after the taxi driver pointed out the house to me, took my last few cents and drove off.

Here in Phoenix it was spring already, and I wondered if it was still winter in Kansas City where my mother and father were staying for the next few months. Here on 16th Street there could be no doubt that it was spring. The hedges had already lost that spindly adolescent angularity of twigs and branches interwoven, and had fattened with new green leaves.

The house itself, squatting before me in stuccoed ugliness like a great toad, was somnolent, old. As I looked at the heavy pillars supporting the roof of the porch and the lacework of vines that would soon plunge the porch into deep shadows even with the sun bright in summer, I felt that I was going to be stifled and choked by the age and quiet and dust—for even then I knew that there is always the feel of dust and dry sweetness around old people, despite the cleanliness of their houses—even Aunt Eleanor's.

My Aunt Eleanor met me at the door with a flour-powdered apron on and she led me into the study with its generous scattering of rose-shaded lamps and tintypes and glass-footed tables. There she stood with me before my grandfather.

"This is Harry, Pa," she said.

He looked up as if he had been dozing, his eyes rheumy with age, and said, "Harry?"

"Harry," she repeated. Then she burst out, "For Heaven's sake, Pa, I told you two days ago that John and Agnes were sending him down." She was a tall spare woman, the kind who, when angry, suddenly grow in stature, shooting up and looming over one with wide-opened eyes like glaring suns.

"Oh, yes," he said. "Pull the curtain there, Eleanor, so I can see him."

When she pulled the curtain I got my first good look at him. He must have been about eighty or eighty-one at the time. He wore a white mustache, full and turned up at the ends. He was bald and his forehead jutted at me huge and forbidding, and he wore a black wool sweater I later learned he wore every day in any temperature. His eyes cleared in the sunlight and became suddenly almost blue, like the sky. He looked at me for a full minute while Aunt Eleanor came back to stand beside me, and put her hand on my shoulder.

"This is your grandson," she said. "He's a nice-looking boy, isn't he?"

"He's skinny," Grandfather said.

All this was a long time ago. Children respected their elders then, so I didn't tell him any of the things my own grandchildren are likely to say to me any day now. I stood as still as I could, as small as I could.

"He's skinny as hell," Grandfather said.

"Stop using profanity," Aunt Eleanor told him.

"Come over here," he said to me.

I went to him, not without some trepidation, and he grabbed my arm and then my shoulder.

"Skinny, all right," he said. "They don't feed kids right nowadays."

"I was thin when I was a child," Aunt Eleanor said.

"You were sick," Grandfather said without looking at her.

"I was *not* sick," she answered.

"I smell something burning," Grandfather said. "You got something in the oven?"

Aunt Eleanor sniffed, throwing her long face up and back. Then she said, "The cake," and ran out of the room.

As soon as she was gone, my grandfather changed. His eyes crinkled and he pointed to the footstool and told me to pull it up close to him. "I'll tell you a story," he said. "Did you know I fought Indians out west?"

"No," I said.

"Well, I did," he said. "Eleanor will tell you it's not true, but it is."

"Pa?" her voice echoed from the kitchen. "Pa?"

"Yes?" His voice was still powerful. It seemed to me that it came from time that was miles and miles and years and years away.

"Harry better take a bath," she shouted. "He came a long ways on the train and he's probably dirty."

"Are you dirty?" he asked me.

"No," I said.

He tilted back his head, the thin neck expanding, and shouted, "He's not dirty. He don't need a bath."

It was quiet for a moment and then we could hear her footsteps in the hall. When she stood tall in the doorway she said, "He's in need of a bath."

"He says he don't need a bath," Grandfather persisted.

"I say he does."

"He ain't dirty."

"Harry," she said, turning to me, "Come with me."

I looked at my grandfather. For a moment he frowned at me over the blue eyes, and then he winked and said, "Maybe you better go, Harry. I'll tell you later."

"Yes," I said.

"Sir."

I didn't know for a moment what he meant. I said, "What?"

"Say sir to me when you speak."

"Yes, sir," I said.

I heard that first story later. And then I heard a lot more. There were so many that even as a child I began to wonder if they were true. One day my Aunt took me into the kitchen and closed the door to the hall and told me I musn't believe the stories Grandfather told me.

"Why?" I asked her.

"Because they aren't true."

But the stories were good stories nevertheless. They were about Indian raids and cavalry troops and hunting, and always Grandfather was in the thick of things. He would get excited and the huge bony hands would summon up whole multitudes of screaming red savages over the top of the green davenport or thundering herds of buffalo on to the lawn outside the window. They were the stories that comic strips tell today, but when he told them, I was there with him, in the room and on the prairies. And though I was sure by now that they weren't true, they were so real that I lived them anyway.

The third week I was there the pigeons arrived. Two of them. They squatted on the peak of the roof or walked with that fat dowager strut of theirs along the tin gutters at the eaves. All through the house, all, we could hear the throaty, purring sounds they made. When I went out with Grandfather to see them for the first time in the afternoon sun, their colors astonished me, for I was used to the flat colors of robins and sparrows and woodpeckers instead of the lambent colors of the pigeons.

"We'll have to get rid of them," Grandfather said.

"Why?"

"Sir."

"Why, sir?"

"Because they'll dirty the house all up."

We went inside then and he told Aunt Eleanor that he'd have to shoot them.

"Why?" she asked.

"They'll dirty the house up." He sounded more convinced of it than he had when we were outside. "And they'll drive us crazy with their noise."

"Pshaw!"

I could tell that she didn't really believe he meant what he said. She swept vigorously up the hallway toward us, and we had to step into the study to get out of her way.

"I'll have to shoot them," Grandfather said again.

She stopped sweeping and looked at him. "No," she said, "They won't bother anyone and anyway you wouldn't know how to shoot a gun if you had to. You leave them alone. And leave the guns alone too."

"I'll have to shoot them," Grandfather said.

Pleading now, she returned, "Don't be stubborn, Pa. You'll just hurt yourself if you start playing with guns." She leaned back against the wall and drew her thin hand across her forehead as if she were suddenly willing to give up the battle with him that had been going on for so long. Then she straightened up and said, "I won't have it, Pa." She turned away and began sweeping again. "I just won't have it."

We went out on the porch. Behind us in the hall we could hear the swish of the broom and the shuffle of her feet and around the corner of the house came the scratchy sounds of the pigeons' feet on the tin gutter and the chuckling noises they made. It was almost noon and the sun was getting hot. The swish of the broom had stopped behind us and we could hear the clatter of pans as Aunt Eleanor began preparing lunch.

"Go across to that white house and see if Mr. Bradford is home," Grandfather told me, pointing.

"Why?" I asked.

"Sir."

"Why, sir?"

"Don't ask questions, just do as I say."

When I came back and told him that Mr. Bradford would get home about three in the afternoon he told me not to say anything to Aunt Eleanor, and we went in to wash up for lunch.

I watched the pigeons all that afternoon while Grandfather tried to sleep in the study on the green couch. I had already inspected all the lamps and glass-footed tables and albums, had even looked at the huge Bible with the velvet cover on the library table. Now the pigeons were something new to watch. The sun was hot and I sat under on of the trees and watched them. About three in the afternoon a boy came along the sidewalk and stopped to look at them too. I went out and said "hello" to him.

"Those your pigeons?" he asked.

"No. We're going to have to get rid of them."

"Why?"

"They'll dirty the house up."

When he was gone I turned to find Grandfather sitting on the porch. He had pulled the chair around so he could see Mr. Bradford's house across the street. You could see how really old he was out in the sun like that. He had been tall once but his shoulders were stooped now, rounded like old things that have been handled a lot and have shaped themselves to the demands put upon them.

"I want to borrow your shotgun," Grandfather said when he caught Mr. Bradford between the house and the garage. "And a couple of shells if you have them. Bird shot."

Mr. Bradford smirked openly. He was a big man, probably forty now and going prematurely bald. A big, white-faced man with a briefcase in his hand, he asked, "What are you planning to do with the shotgun, Grandpa?"

"Kill those pigeons, I'll get you some more shells for the one I'll use."

"One shell for more than one pigeon? You must be a crack shot," Mr. Bradford said. He was laughing at my gradfather and I was ashamed—not for Mr. Bradford—for my grandfather.

"Could I borrow it?" Grandfather repeated.

"Sure," he said, "But what about the police? You have to have a permit to shoot inside the city limits."

"I'll take care of that," my grandfather said.

"Well, that's your worry," Mr. Bradford said.

When he came out of the house he handed Grandfather a double-barreled 16-gauge shotgun and a couple of shells.

"Don't really need two shells," Grandfather said. "One should do."

I was sure he was boasting. Aunt Eleanor had said already that he didn't know how to shoot a gun. And walking back across the street I hoped she was wrong. Although I liked to watch the pigeons, liked to hear them even, I wanted him to prove that he hadn't lied to me. I wanted him to prove that Aunt Eleanor was wrong.

We stood in the yard just outside the shade of the tree and he broke the gun and put the two shells in. His shoulders had straightened suddenly and he held the gun loosely in both hands, his eyes drawn down tight against the sun, some old, easy, assured grace seeping back into the stiff bones and slack muscles.

On the peak of the roof the two pigeons were moving aimlessly back and forth. They were about eight feet apart, and I wondered why he didn't shoot them. Then they began to move together and I knew he was waiting until they were close together so he could get them in one shot.

They were four feet apart now.

"What will Aunt Eleanor say?" I asked.

"Sir," he said, moving only his lips.

"Yes, sir."

"This is a man's job, Harry," he said, still without looking at me. "A man has to keep his job his own."

"Aunt Eleanor won't like it," I said.

He didn't notice how I'd left off the "Sir."

"Aunt Eleanor's a woman."

The pigeons were a foot apart now.

A moment later he fired. It was one of those beautiful things you see sometimes, the way he brought the shotgun up to his shoulder, I mean, and aimed and fired in the same movement. It was all one—all one movement, like the way a seagull dives toward the water and a moment later rises with a fish in her mouth, magic, swift, and graceful. The single blast made me close my eyes in surprise and when I opened them the shotgun was at his side again, lowered with the assured air of a man who knows he never misses a shot. Above the roof of the house the two pigeons whirled wildly on fluttering wings, quite alive and quite unharmed. When I turned to my grandfather I found him standing as before. With his right hand he rubbed brutally at his eyes, as if to vent some anger on them in reproof of their failure. The corners of his mouth were drawn down grimly and I was not sure whether it was anger or sorrow that caused it. For a moment he seemed to totter drunkenly in the hot sunlight. But that may have been my imagination, for he went striding off toward the back of the house, past the shrubs and then up the steps onto the back porch. I followed him.

My Aunt Eleanor was standing just inside the screen. My grandfather must not have seen her until he was almost upon her, for suddenly, as he reached for the door to pull it open, he stopped short, and they stood face to face, through the dark screen.

For a long moment they said nothing to each other, and all three of us stood in attitudes of waiting, caught in the shadows of the porch roof, motionless as eternity is motionless, unfixed from time.

Suddenly, without turning, he thrust the shotgun in my direction. "Take this," he said. "I don't need it any more." His eyes still fixed on my Aunt Eleanor, he stood in that black wool sweater seeming taller to me than he had been before.

"Yes, sir," I said. "I'll take it back."

When I went around the corner of the house I didn't look back. In the street the sun was very hot. I went slowly to Mr. Bradford's house, carrying the gun freely in my hand, knowing for the first time what age could do to a man. Behind me the pigeons cooed softly, and then I heard the flutter of their wings.

FOR ANALYSIS

1. Why did the writer choose the point of view that he did? Consider what kind of economy he gains by telling the story through the boy.
2. Explain how a piece of exposition is made to seem like something else in the second paragraph.
3. How has the ending been foreshadowed by the end of first section of the story?
4. What one word, carefully repeated in the story, explains a shift in sympathy in the boy?

FLANNERY O'CONNOR

A Good Man
Is Hard to Find

The grandmother didn't want to go to Florida. She wanted to visit some of her connections in east Tennessee and she was seizing at every chance to change Bailey's mind. Bailey was the son she lived with, her only boy. He was sitting on the edge of his chair at the table, bent over the orange sports section of the *Journal*. "Now look here, Bailey," she said, "see here, read this," and she stood with one hand on her thin hip and the other rattling the newspaper at his bald head. "Here this fellow that calls himself The Misfit is aloose from the Federal Pen and headed toward Florida and you read here what it says he did to these people. Just you read it. I wouldn't take my children in any direction with a criminal like that aloose in it. I couldn't answer to my conscience if I did."

Bailey didn't look up from his reading so she wheeled around then and faced the children's mother, a young woman in slacks, whose face was broad and innocent as a cabbage and was tied around with a green head-kerchief that had two points on the top like rabbit's ears. She was sitting on the sofa, feeding the baby his apricots out of a jar. "The children have been to Florida before," the old lady said. "You all ought to take them somewhere else for a change so they would see different parts of the world and be broad. They never have been to east Tennessee."

The children's mother didn't seem to hear her but the eight-year-old boy, John Wesley, a stocky child with glasses, said, "If you don't want to go to Florida, why dontcha stay at home?" He and the little girl, June Star, were reading the funny papers on the floor.

"She wouldn't stay at home to be queen for a day," June Star said without raising her yellow head.

"Yes and what would you do if this fellow, The Misfit, caught you?" the grandmother asked.

"I'd smack his face," John Wesley said.

"She wouldn't stay at home for a million bucks," June Star said. "Afraid she'd miss something. She has to go everywhere we go."

"All right, Miss," the grandmother said. "Just remember that the next time you want me to curl your hair."

June Star said her hair was naturally curly.

The next morning the grandmother was the first one in the car, ready to go. She had her big black valise that looked like the head of a hippopotamus in one corner, and underneath it she was hiding a basket with Pitty Sing, the cat, in it. She didn't intend for the cat to be left alone in the house for three days because he would miss her too much and she was afraid he might brush against one of the gas burners and accidentally asphyxiate himself. Her son, Bailey, didn't like to arrive at a motel with a cat.

She sat in the middle of the back seat with John Wesley and June Star on either side of her. Bailey and the children's mother and the baby sat in front and they left Atlanta at eight forty-five with the mileage on the car at 55890. The grandmother wrote this down because she thought it would be interesting to say how many miles they had been when they got back. It took them twenty minutes to reach the outskirts of the city.

The old lady settled herself comfortably, removing her white cotton gloves and putting them up with her purse on the shelf in front of the back window. The children's mother still had on slacks and still had her head tied up in a green kerchief, but the grandmother had on a navy blue straw sailor hat with a bunch of white violets on the brim and a navy blue dress with a small white dot in the print. Her collars and cuffs were white organdy trimmed with lace and at her neckline she had pinned a purple spray of cloth violets containing a sachet. In case of an accident, anyone seeing her dead on the highway would know at once that she was a lady.

She said she thought it was going to be a good day for driving, neither too hot nor too cold, and she cautioned Bailey that the speed limit was fifty-five miles an hour and that the patrolmen hid themselves behind billboards and small clumps of trees and sped out after you before you had a chance to slow down. She pointed out interesting details of the scenery: Stone Mountain; the blue granite that in some places came up to both sides of the highway; the brilliant red clay banks slightly streaked with purple; and the various crops that made rows of green lace-work on the ground. The trees were full of silver-white sunlight and the meanest of them sparkled. The children were reading comic magazines and their mother had gone back to sleep.

"Let's go through Georgia fast so we won't have to look at it much," John Wesley said.

"If I were a little boy," said the grandmother, "I wouldn't talk about my native state that way. Tennessee has the mountains and Georgia has the hills."

"Tennessee is just a hillbilly dumping ground," John Wesley said, "and Georgia is a lousy state too."

"You said it," June Star said.

"In my time," said the grandmother, folding her thin veined fingers, "children were more respectful of their native states and their parents and everything else. People did right then. Oh look at the cute little pickaninny!" she said and pointed to a Negro child standing in the door of a shack. "Wouldn't that make a picture, now?" she asked and they all turned and looked at the little Negro out of the back window. He waved.

"He didn't have any britches on," June Star said.

"He probably didn't have any," the grandmother explained. "Little niggers in the country don't have things like we do. If I could paint, I'd paint that picture," she said.

The children exchanged comic books.

The grandmother offered to hold the baby and the children's mother passed him over the front seat to her. She set him on her knee and bounced him and told him about the things they were passing. She rolled her eyes and screwed up her mouth and stuck her leathery thin face into his smooth bland one. Occasionally he gave her a faraway smile. They passed a large cotton field with five or six graves fenced in the middle of it, like a small island. "Look at the grave-yard!" the grandmother said, pointing it out. "That was the old family burying ground. That belonged to the plantation."

"Where's the plantation?" John Wesley asked.

"Gone With the Wind," said the grandmother. "Ha. Ha."

When the children finished all the comic books they had brought, they opened the lunch and ate it. The grandmother ate a peanut butter sandwich and an olive and would not let the children throw the box and the paper napkins out the window. When there was nothing else to do they played a game by choosing a cloud and making the other two guess what shape it suggested. John Wesley took one the shape of a cow and June Star guessed a cow and John Wesley said, no, an automobile, and June Star said he didn't play fair, and they began to slap each other over the grandmother.

The grandmother said she would tell them a story if they would keep quiet. When she told a story, she rolled her eyes and waved her head and was very dramatic. She said once when she was a maiden lady she had been courted by a Mr. Edgar Atkins Teagarden from Jasper, Georgia. She said he was a very good-looking man and a gentleman and that he brought her a watermelon every Saturday afternoon with his initials cut in it, E. A. T. Well, one Saturday, she said, Mr. Teagarden brought the water-melon and there was nobody at home and he left it on the front porch and returned in his buggy to Jasper, but she never got the water-melon, she said, because a nigger boy ate it when he saw the initials, E. A. T.! This story tickled John Wesley's funny bone and he giggled and giggled but June Star didn't think it was any good. She said she wouldn't marry a man that just brought her a watermelon on Saturday. The grandmother said she would have done well to marry Mr. Teagarden bacause he was a gentleman and had bought Coca-Cola stock when it first came out and that he had died only a few years ago, a very wealthy man.

They stopped at The Tower for barbecued sandwiches. The Tower was a part stucco and part wood filling station and dance hall set in a clearing outside of Timothy. A fat man named Red Sammy Butts ran it and there were signs stuck here and there on the building and for miles up and down the highway saying, TRY RED SAMMY'S FAMOUS BARBECUE. NONE LIKE FAMOUS RED SAMMY'S! RED SAM! THE FAT BOY WITH THE HAPPY LAUGH. A VETERAN! RED SAMMY'S YOUR MAN!

Red Sammy was lying on the bare ground outside The Tower with his head under a truck while a gray monkey about a foot high, chained to a small chinaberry tree, chattered nearby. The monkey sprang back into the tree and got on the highest limb as soon as he saw the children jump out of the car and run toward him.

Inside, The Tower was a long dark room with a counter at one end and tables at the other and dancing space in the middle. They all sat down at a board table next to the nickelodeon and Red Sam's wife, a tall burnt-brown woman with hair and eyes lighter than her skin, came and took their order. The children's mother put a dime in the machine and played "The Tennessee Waltz," and the grandmother said that tune always made her want to dance. She asked Bailey if he would like to dance but he only glared at her. He didn't have a naturally sunny disposition like she did and trips made him nervous. The grandmother's brown eyes were very bright. She swayed her head from side to side and pretended she was dancing in her chair. June Star said play something she could tap to so the children's mother put in another dime and played a fast number and June Star stepped out onto the dance floor and did her tap routine.

"Ain't she cute?" Red Sam's wife said, leaning over the counter. "Would you like to come be my little girl?"

"No I certainly wouldn't," June Star said. "I wouldn't live in a broken-down place like this for a million bucks!" and she ran back to the table.

"Ain't she cute?" the woman repeated, stretching her mouth politely.

"Aren't you ashamed?" hissed the grandmother.

Red Sam came in and told his wife to quit lounging on the counter and hurry up with these people's order. His khaki trousers reached just to his hip bones and his stomach hung over them like a sack of meal swaying under his shirt. He came over and sat down at a table nearby and let out a combination sigh and yodel. "You can't win," he said. "You can't win," and he wiped his sweating red face off with a gray handkerchief. "These days you don't know who to trust," he said. "Ain't that the truth?"

"People are certainly not nice like they used to be," said the grandmother.

"Two fellers come in here last week," Red Sammy said, "driving a Chrysler. It was a old beat-up car but it was a good one and these boys looked all right to me. Said they worked at the mill and you know I let them fellers charge the gas they bought? Now why did I do that?"

"Because you're a good man!" the grandmother said at once.

"Yes'm, I suppose so," Red Sam said as if he were struck with this answer.

His wife brought the orders, carrying the five plates all at once without a tray, two in each hand and one balanced on her arm. "It isn't a soul in this green world of God's that you can trust," she said. "And I don't count nobody out of that, not nobody," she repeated, looking at Red Sammy.

"Did you read about that criminal, The Misfit, that's escaped?" asked the grandmother.

"I wouldn't be a bit surprised if he didn't attact this place right here," said the woman. "If he hears about it being here, I wouldn't be none surprised to see him. If he hears it's two cent in the cash register, I wouldn't be a tall surprised if he . . ."

"That'll do," Red Sam said. "Go bring these people their Co'-Colas," and the woman went off to get the rest of the order.

"A good man is hard to find," Red Sammy said. "Everything is getting terrible. I remember the day you could go off and leave your screen door unlatched. Not no more."

He and the grandmother discussed better times. The old lady said that in her opinion Europe was entirely to blame for the way things were now. She said the way Europe acted you would think we were made of money and Red Sam said it was no use talking about it, she was exactly right. The children ran outside into the white sunlight and looked at the monkey in the lacy chinaberry tree. He was busy catching fleas on himself and biting each one carefully between his teeth as if it were a delicacy.

They drove off again into the hot afternoon. The grandmother took cat naps and woke up every few minutes with her own snoring. Outside of Toombsboro she woke up and recalled an old plantation that she had visited in this neighborhood once when she was a young lady. She said the house had six white columns across the front and that there was an avenue of oaks leading up to it and two little wooden trellis arbors on either side in front where you sat down with your suitor after a stroll in the garden. She recalled exactly which road to turn off to get to it. She knew that Bailey would not be willing to lose any time looking at an old house, but the more she talked about it, the more she wanted to see it once again and find out if the little twin arbors were still standing. "There was a sercret panel in this house," she said craftily, not telling the truth but wishing that she were, "and the story went that all the family silver was hidden in it when Sherman came through but it was never found . . ."

"Hey!" John Wesley said. "Let's go see it! We'll find it! We'll poke all the woodwork and find it! Who lives there? Where do you turn off at? Hey Pop, can't we turn off there?"

"We never have seen a house with a secret panel!" June Star shrieked. "Let's go to the house with the secret panel! Hey Pop, can't we go see the house with the secret panel!"

"It's not far from here, I know," the grandmother said. "It wouldn't take over twenty minutes."

Bailey was looking straight ahead. His jaw was as rigid as a horseshoe. "No," he said.

The children began to yell and scream that they wanted to see the house with the secret panel. John Wesley kicked the back of the front seat and June Star hung over her mother's shoulder and whined desperately into her ear that they never had any fun even on their vacation, that they could never do what THEY wanted to do. The baby began to scream and John Wesley kicked the back of the seat so hard that his father could feel the blows in his kidney.

"All right!" he shouted and drew the car to a stop at the side of the road. "Will you all shut up? Will you all just shut up for one second? If you don't shut up, we won't go anywhere."

"It would be very educational for them," the grandmother murmured.

"All right," Bailey said, "but get this: this is the only time we're going to stop for anything like this. This is the one and only time."

"The dirt road that you have to turn down is about a mile back," the grandmother directed. "I marked it when we passed."

"A dirt road," Bailey groaned.

After they had turned around and were headed toward the dirt road, the grandmother recalled other points about the house, the beautiful glass over the front doorway and the candle-lamp in the hall. John Wesley said that the secret panel was probably in the fireplace.

"You can't go inside this house," Bailey said. "You don't know who lives there."

"While you all talk to the people in front, I'll run around behind and get in a window," John Wesley suggested.

"We'll all stay in the car," his mother said.

They turned onto the dirt road and the car raced roughly along in a swirl of pink dust. The grandmother recalled the times when there were no paved roads and thirty miles was a day's journey. The dirt road was hilly and there were sudden washes in it and sharp curves on danger-ous embankments. All at once they would be on a hill, looking down over the blue tops of trees for miles around, then the next minute, they would be in a red depression with the dust-coated trees looking down on them.

"This place had better turn up in a minute," Bailey said, "or I'm going to turn around."

The road looked as if no one had traveled on it in months.

"It's not much farther," the grandmother said and just as she said it, a horrible thought came to her. The thought was so embarrassing that she turned red in the face and her eyes dilated and her feet jumped up, upsetting her valise in the corner. The instant the valise moved, the newspaper top she had over the basket under it rose with a snarl and Pitty Sing, the cat, sprang onto Bailey's shoulder.

The children were thrown to the floor and their mother, clutching the baby, was thrown out the door onto the ground; the old lady was thrown into the front seat. The car turned over once and landed right-side-up in a gulch off the side of the road. Bailey remained in the driver's seat with the cat—gray-striped with a broad white face and an orange nose—clinging to his neck like a caterpillar.

As soon as the children saw they could move their arms and legs, they scrambled out of the car, shouting, "We've had an ACCIDENT!" The grandmother was curled up under the dashboard, hoping she was injured so that Bailey's wrath would not come down on her all at once. The horrible thought she had had before the accident was that the house she had re-membered so vividly was not in Georgia but in Tennessee.

Bailey removed the cat from his neck with both hands and flung it out the window against the side of a pine tree. Then he got out of the car and started looking for the children's mother. She was sitting against the side of the red gutted ditch, holding the screaming baby, but she only had a cut down her face and a broken shoulder. "We've had an ACCIDENT!" the children screamed in a frenzy of delight.

"But nobody's killed," June Star said with disappointment as the grandmother limped out of the car, her hat still pinned to her head but the broken front brim standing up at a jaunty angle and the violet spray hanging off the side. They all sat down in the ditch, except the children, to recover from the shock. They were all shaking.

"Maybe a car will come along," said the children's mother hoarsely.

"I believe I have injured an organ," said the grandmother, pressing her side, but no one answered her. Bailey's teeth were clattering. He had on a yellow sport shirt with bright blue parrots designed in it and his face was as yellow as the shirt. The grandmother decided that she would not mention that the house was in Tennessee.

The road was about ten feet above and they could see only the tops of the trees on the other side of it. Behind the ditch they were sitting in there were more woods, tall and dark and deep. In a few minutes they saw a car some distance away on top of a hill, coming slowly as if the occupants were watching them. The grandmother stood up and waved both arms dramatically to attract their attention. The car continued to come on slowly, disappeared around a bend and appeared again, moving even slower, on top of the hill they had gone over. It was a big black battered hearse-like automobile. There were three men in it.

It came to a stop just over them and for some minutes, the driver looked down with a steady expressionless gaze to where they were sitting, and didn't speak. Then he turned his head and muttered something to the other two and they got out. One was a fat boy in black trousers and a red sweat shirt with a silver stallion embossed on the front of it. He moved around on the right side of them and stood staring, his mouth partly open in a kind of loose grin. The other had on khaki pants and a blue striped coat and a gray hat pulled down very low, hiding most of his face. He came around slowly on the left side. Neither spoke.

The driver got out of the car and stood by the side of it, looking down at them. He was an older man than the other two. His hair was just beginning to gray and he wore silver-rimmed spectacles that gave him a scholarly look. He had a long creased face and didn't have on any shirt or undershirt. He had on blue jeans that were too tight for him and was holding a black hat and a gun. The two boys also had guns.

"We've had an ACCIDENT!" the children screamed.

The grandmother had the peculiar feeling that the bespectacled man was someone she knew.

His face was as familiar to her as if she had known him all her life but she could not recall who he was. He moved away from the car and began to come down the embankment, placing his feet carefully so that he wouldn't slip. He had on tan and white shoes and no socks, and his ankles were red and thin. "Good afternoon," he said. "I see you all had you a little spill."

"We turned over twice!" said the grandmother.

"Oncet," he corrected. "We seen it happen. Try their car and see will it run, Hiram," he said quietly to the boy with the gray hat.

"What you got that gun for?" John Wesley asked. "Whatcha gonna do with that gun?"

"Lady," the man said to the children's mother, "would you mind calling them children to sit down by you? Children make me nervous. I want all you all to sit down right together there where you're at."

"What are you telling US what to do for?" June Star asked.

Behind them the line of woods gaped like a dark open mouth. "Come here," said their mother.

"Look here now," Bailey began suddenly, "we're in a predicament! We're in . . ."

The grandmother shrieked. She scrambled to her feet and stood staring. "You're The Misfit!" she said. "I recognized you at once!"

"Yes'm," the man said, smiling slightly as if he were pleased in spite of himself to be known, "but it would have been better for all of you, lady, if you hadn't of reckernized me."

Bailey turned his head sharply and said something to his mother that shocked even the children. The old lady began to cry and The Misfit reddened.

"Lady," he said, "don't you get upset. Sometimes a man says things he don't mean. I don't reckon he meant to talk to you thataway."

"You wouldn't shoot a lady, would you?" the grandmother said and removed a clean handkerchief from her cuff and began to slap at her eyes with it.

The Misfit pointed the toe of his shoe into the ground and made a little hole and then covered it up again. "I would hate to have to," he said.

"Listen," the grandmother almost screamed, "I know you're a good man. You don't look a bit like you have common blood. I know you must come from nice people!"

"Yes mam," he said, "finest people in the world." When he smiled he showed a row of strong white teeth. "God never made a finer woman than my mother and my daddy's heart was pure gold," he said. The boy with the red sweat shirt had come around behind them and was standing with his gun at his hip. The Misfit squatted down on the ground. "Watch them children, Bobby Lee," he said. "You know they make me nervous." He looked at the six of them huddled together in front of him and he seemed to be embarrassed as if he couldn't think of anything to say. "Ain't a cloud in the sky," he remarked, looking up at it. "Don't see no sun but don't see no cloud neither."

"Yes, it's a beautiful day," said the grandmother. "Listen," she said, "you shouldn't call yourself The Misfit because I know you're a good man at heart. I can just look at you and tell."

"Hush!" Bailey yelled. "Hush! Everybody shut up and let me handle this!" He was squatting in the position of a runner about to sprint forward but he didn't move.

"I pre-chate that, lady," The Misfit said and drew a little circle in the ground with the butt of his gun.

"It'll take a half a hour to fix this here car," Hiram called, looking over the raised hood of it.

"Well, first you and Bobby Lee get him and that little boy to step over yonder with you," The Misfit said, pointing to Bailey and John Wesley. "The boys want to ast you something," he said to Bailey. "Would you mind stepping back in them woods there with them?"

"Listen," Bailey began, "we're in a terrible predicament! Nobody realizes what this is," and his voice cracked. His eyes were as blue and intense as the parrots in his shirt and he remained perfectly still.

The grandmother reached up to adjust her hat brim as if she were going to the woods with him but it came off in her hand. She stood staring at it and after a second she let it fall on the ground. Hiram pulled Bailey up by the arm as if he were assisting an old man. John Wesley caught hold of his father's hand and Bobby Lee followed. They went off toward the woods and just as they reached the dark edge, Bailey turned and supporting himself against a gray naked pine trunk, he shouted, "I'll be back in a minute, Mamma, wait on me!"

"Come back this instant!" his mother shrilled but they all disappeared into the woods.

"Bailey Boy!" the grandmother called in a tragic voice but she found she was looking at The Misfit squatting on the ground in front of her. "I just know you're a good man," she said desperately. "You're not a bit common!"

"Nome, I ain't a good man," The Misfit said after a second as if he had considered her statement carefully, "but I ain't the worst in the world neither. My daddy said I was a different breed of dog from my brothers and sisters. 'You know,' Daddy said, 'it's some that can live their whole life out without asking about it and it's others has to know why it is, and this boy is one of the latters. He's going to be into everything!'" He put on his black hat and looked up suddenly and then away deep into the woods as if he were embarrassed again. "I'm sorry I don't have on a shirt before you ladies," he said, hunching his shoulders slightly. "We buried our clothes that we had on when we escaped and we're just making do until we can get better. We borrowed these from some folks we met," explained.

"That's perfectly all right," the grandmother said. "Maybe Bailey has an extra shirt in his suitcase."

"I'll look and see terrectly," The Misfit said.

"Where are they taking him?" the children's mother screamed.

"Daddy was a card himself," The Misfit said. "You couldn't put anything over on him. He never got in trouble with the Authorities though. Just had the knack of handling them."

"You could be honest too if you'd only try," said the grandmother. "Think how wonderful it would be to settle down and live a comfortable life and not have to think about somebody chasing you all the time."

The Misfit kept scratching in the ground with the butt of his gun as if he were thinking about it. "Yes'm, somebody is always after you," he murmured.

The grandmother noticed how thin his shoulder blades were just behind his hat because she was standing up looking down on him. "Do you ever pray?" she asked.

He shook his head. All she saw was the black hat wiggle between his shoulder blades. "Nome," he said.

There was a pistol shot from the woods, followed closely by another. Then silence. The old lady's head jerked around. She could hear the wind move through the tree tops like a long satisfied insuck of breath. "Bailey Boy!" she called.

"I was a gospel singer for a while," The Misfit said. "I been most everything. Been in the arm service, both land and sea, at home and abroad, been twict married, been an undertaker, been with the railroads, plowed Mother Earth, been in a tornado, seen a man burnt alive oncet," and he looked up at the children's mother and the little girl who were sitting close together, their faces white and their eyes glassy; "I even seen a woman flogged," he said.

"Pray, pray," the grandmother began, "pray, pray . . ."

"I never was a bad boy that I remember of," The Misfit said in an almost dreamy voice, "but somewheres along the line I done something wrong and got sent to the penitentiary. I was buried alive," and he looked up and held her attention to him by a steady stare.

"That's when you should have started to pray," she said. "What did you do to get sent to the penitentiary that first time?"

"Turn to the right, it was a wall," The Misfit said, looking up again at the cloudless sky. "Turn to the left, it was a wall. Look up it was a ceiling, look down it was floor. I forget what I done, lady. I set there and set there, trying to remember what it was I done and I ain't recalled it to this day. Oncet in a while, I would think it was coming to me, but it never come."

"Maybe they put you in by mistake," the old lady said vaguely.

"Nome," he said. "It wasn't no mistake. They had the papers on me."

"You must have stolen something," she said.

The Misfit sneered slightly. "Nobody had nothing I wanted," he said. "It was a head-doctor at the penitentiary said what I had done was kill my daddy but I known that for a lie. My daddy died in nineteen ought nineteen of the epidemic flu and I never had a thing to do with it. He was buried in the Mount Hopewell Baptist churchyard and you can go there and see for yourself."

"If you would pray," the old lady said, "Jesus would help you."

"That's right," The Misfit said.

"Well then, why don't you pray?" she asked trembling with delight suddenly.

"I don't want no hep," he said. "I'm doing all right by myself."

Bobby Lee and Hiram came ambling back from the woods. Bobby Lee was dragging a yellow shirt with bright blue parrots in it.

"Thow me that shirt, Bobby Lee," The Misfit said. The shirt came flying at him and landed on his shoulder and he put it on. The grandmother couldn't name what the shirt reminded her of. "No, lady," The Misfit said while he was buttoning it up, "I found out the crime don't matter. You can do one thing or you can do another, kill a man or take a tire off his car, because sooner or later you're going to forget what it was you done and just be punished for it."

The children's mother had begun to make heaving noises as if she couldn't get her breath. "Lady," he asked, "would you and that little girl like to step off yonder with Bobby Lee and Hiram and join your husband?"

"Yes, thank you," the mother said faintly. Her left arm dangled helplessly and she was holding the baby, who had gone to sleep, in the other. "Hep that lady up, Hiram," The Misfit said as she struggled to climb out of the ditch, "and Bobby Lee, you hold onto that little girl's hand."

"I don't want to hold hands with him," June Star said. "He reminds me of a pig."

The fat boy blushed and laughed and caught her by the arm and pulled her off into the woods after Hiram and her mother.

Alone with The Misfit, the grandmother found that she had lost her voice. There was not a cloud in the sky nor any sun. There was nothing around her but woods. She wanted to tell him that he must pray. She opened and closed her mouth several times before anything came out. Finally she found herself saying, "Jesus. Jesus," meaning, Jesus will help you, but the way she was saying it, it sounded as if she might be cursing.

"Yes'm," The Misfit said as if he agreed. "Jesus thown everything off balance. It was the same case with Him as with me except He hadn't committed any crime and they could prove I had committed one because they had the papers on me. Of course," he said, "they never shown me my papers. That's why I sign myself now. I said long ago, you get you a signature and sign everything you do and keep a copy of it. Then you'll know what you done and you can hold up the crime to the punishment and see do they match and in the end you'll have something to prove you ain't been treated right. I call myself The Misfit," he said, "because I can't make what all I done wrong fit what all I gone through in punishment."

There was a piercing scream from the woods followed closely by a pistol report. "Does it seem right to you, lady, that one is punished a heap and another ain't punished at all?"

"Jesus!" the old lady cried. "You've got good blood! I know you wouldn't shoot a lady! I know you come from nice people! Pray! Jesus, you ought not to shoot a lady. I'll give you all the money I've got!"

"Lady," The Misfit said, looking beyond her far into the woods, "there never was a body that give the undertaker a tip."

There were two more pistol reports and the grandmother raised her head like a parched old turkey hen crying for water and called, "Bailey Boy, Bailey Boy!" as if her heart would break.

"Jesus was the only One that ever raised the dead," The Misfit continued, "and He shouldn't have done it. He thown everything off balance. If He did what He said, then it's nothing for you to do but thow away everything and follow Him, and if He didn't, then it's nothing for you to do but enjoy the few minutes you got left the best way you can—by killing somebody or burning down his house or doing some other meanness to him. No pleasure but meanness," he said and his voice had become almost a snarl.

"Maybe He didn't raise the dead," the old lady mumbled, not knowing what she was saying and feeling so dizzy that she sank down in the ditch with her legs twisted under her.

"I wasn't there so I can't say He didn't," The Misfit said. "I wisht I had of been there," he said, hitting the ground with his fist. "It ain't right I wasn't there because if I had of been there I would of known. Listen lady," he said in a high voice, "if I had of been there I would of known and I wouldn't be like I am now." His voice seemed about to crack and the grandmother's head cleared for an instant. She saw the man's face twisted close to her own as if he were going to cry and she murmured, "Why

you're one of my babies. You're one of my own children!" She reached out and touched him on the shoulder. The Misfit sprang back as if a snake had bitten him and shot her three times through the chest. Then he put his gun down on the ground and took off his glasses and began to clean them.

Hiram and Bobby Lee returned from the woods and stood over the ditch, looking down at the grandmother who half sat and half lay in a puddle of blood with her legs crossed under her like a child's and her face smiling up at the cloudless sky.

Without his glasses, The Misfit's eyes were red-rimmed and pale and defenseless-looking. "Take her off and thow her where you thown the others," he said, picking up the cat that was rubbing itself against his leg.

"She was a talker, wasn't she?" Bobby Lee said, sliding down the ditch with a yodel.

"She would of been a good woman," The Misfit said, "if it had been somebody there to shoot her every minute of her life."

"Some fun!" Bobby Lee said.

"Shut up, Bobby Lee," The Misfit said. "It's no real pleasure in life."

FOR ANALYSIS

1. As a critic once remarked, "Miss O'Connor's sense of humor takes a little getting used to." Sometimes when she seems to be clowning she is deadly serious—and sometimes the most outwardly serious remark is downright ridiculous. You can find examples of these reversals throughout this story. Consider, for example, the bare contents of the story: a serious car accident and six murders by a homicidal maniac. But most readers feel no deep sense of horror at the killings themselves. What is it that Miss O'Connor has done to make the murders seem incidental?

2. In what sense is the Misfit's impossible remark, "She would of been a good woman . . . if it had been somebody there to shoot her every minute of her life," a true summation of the grandmother's character?

3. Evaluate the Misfit's analysis of Christian theology.

4. How is the title of the story to be taken? Is there a "Good Man" in it? What, then do you take to be the theme of the story?

JEAN-PAUL SARTRE *french philosopher*
atheist, man must rely on himself
"Existentialist"

The Wall

must take advantage of freedom of will + are responsible for it + man can't predict outcome

They pushed us into a large white room and my eyes began to blink because the light hurt them. Then I saw a table and four fellows seated at the table, civilians, looking at some papers. The other prisoners were herded together at one end and we were obliged to cross the entire room to join them. There were several I knew, and others who must have been foreigners. The two in front of me were blond with round heads. They looked alike. I imagine they were French. The smaller one kept pulling at his trousers, out of nervousness.

This lasted about three hours. I was dog-tired and my head was empty. But the room was well-heated, which struck me as rather agreeable; we had not stopped shivering for twenty-four hours. The guards led the prisoners in one after the other in front of the table. Then the four fellows asked them their names and what they did. Most of the time that was all—or perhaps from time to time they would ask such questions as: "Did you help sabotage the munitions?" or, "Where were you on the morning of the ninth and what were you doing?" They didn't even listen to the replies, or at least they didn't seem to. They just remained silent for a moment and looked straight ahead, then they began to write. They asked Tom if it was true he had served in the International Brigade. Tom couldn't say he hadn't because of the papers they had found in his jacket. They didn't ask Juan anything, but after he told them his name, they wrote for a long while.

"It's my brother José who's the anarchist," Juan said. "You know perfectly well he's not here now. I don't belong to any party. I never did take part in politics." They didn't answer.

Then Juan said, "I didn't do anything. And I'm not going to pay for what the others did."

His lips were trembling. A guard told him to stop talking and led him away. It was my turn.

"Your name is Pablo Ibbieta?"

I said yes.

The fellow looked at his papers and said, "Where is Ramon Gris?"

"I don't know."

"You hid him in your house from the sixth to the nineteenth."

"I did not."

They continued to write for a moment and the guards led me away. In the hall, Tom and Juan were waiting between two guards. We started walking. Tom asked one of the guards, "What's the idea?" "How do you mean?" the guard asked. "Was that just the preliminary questioning, or was that the trial?" "That was the trial," the guard said. "So now what? What are they going to do with us?" The guard answered drily, "The verdict will be told you in your cell." *can't control own destiny*

In reality, our cell was one of the cellars of the hospital. It was terribly cold there because it was very drafty. We had been shivering all night long and it had hardly been any better during the day. I had spent the preceding five days in a cellar in the archbishop's palace, a sort of dungeon that must have dated back to the Middle Ages. There were lots of prisoners and not much room, so they housed them just anywhere. But I was not homesick for my dungeon. I hadn't been cold there, but I had been alone, and that gets to be irritating. In the cellar I had company. Juan didn't say a word; he was afraid, and besides, he was too young to have anything to say. But Tom was a good talker and knew Spanish well.

In the cellar there were a bench and four straw mattresses. When they led us back we sat down and waited in silence. After a while Tom said, "Our goose is cooked."

"I think so too," I said. "But I don't believe they'll do anything to the kid."

Tom said, "They haven't got anything on him. He's the brother of a fellow who's fighting, and that's all."

I looked at Juan. He didn't seem to have heard.

Tom continued, "You know what they do in Saragossa? They lay the guys across the road and then they drive over them with trucks. It was a Moroccan deserter who told us that. They say it's just to save ammunition."

I said, "Well, it doesn't save gasoline."

I was irritated with Tom; he shouldn't have said that.

He went on, "There are officers walking up and down the roads with their hands in their pockets, smoking, and they see that it's done right. Do you think they'd put'em out of their misery? Like hell they do. They just let 'em holler. Sometimes as long as an hour. The

Interrogation meaning less

Moroccan said the first time he almost puked."

"I don't believe they do that here," I said, "unless they really are short of ammunition."

The daylight came in through four air vents and a round opening that had been cut in the ceiling, to the left, and which opened directly onto the sky. It was through this hole, which was ordinarily closed by means of a trapdoor, that they unloaded coal into the cellar. Directly under the hole, there was a big pile of coal dust; it had been intended for heating the hospital, but at the beginning of the war they had evacuated the patients and the coal had stayed there unused; it even got rained on from time to time, when they forgot to close the trapdoor.

Tom started to shiver, "God damn it," he said, "I'm shivering. There, it is starting again."

He rose and began to do gymnastic exercises. At each movement, his shirt opened and showed his white, hairy chest. He lay down on his back, lifted his legs in the air and began to do the scissors movement. I watched his big buttocks tremble. Tom was tough, but he had too much fat on him. I kept thinking that soon bullets and bayonet points would sink into that mass of tender flesh as though it were a pat of butter.

I wasn't exactly cold, but I couldn't feel my shoulders or my arms. From time to time, I had the impression that something was missing and I began to look around for my jacket. Then I would suddenly remember they hadn't given me a jacket. It was rather awkward. They had taken our clothes to give them to their own soldiers and had left us only our shirts and these cotton trousers the hospital patients wore in midsummer. After a moment, Tom got up and sat down beside me, breathless.

"Did you get warmed up?"

"Damn it, no. But I'm all out of breath."

Around eight o'clock in the evening, a Major came in with two falangists.

"What are the names of those three over there?" he asked the guard.

"Steinbock, Ibbieta and Mirbal," said the guard.

The Major put on his glasses and examined his list.

"Steinbock—Steinbock . . . Here it is. You are condemned to death. You'll be shot tomorrow morning."

He looked at his list again.

"The other two, also," he said.

"That's not possible," said Juan. "Not me."

The Major looked at him with surprise. "What's your name?"

"Juan Mirbal."

"Well, your name is here," said the Major, "and you're condemned to death."

"I didn't do anything," said Juan.

The Major shrugged his shoulders and turned toward Tom and me.

"You are both Basque?"

"No, nobody's Basque."

He appeared exasperated.

"I was told there were three Basques. I'm not going to waste my time running after them. I suppose you don't want a priest?"

We didn't even answer.

Then he said, "A Belgian doctor will be around in a little while. He has permission to stay with you all night."

He gave a military salute and left.

"What did I tell you?" Tom said. "We're in for something swell."

"Yes," I said. "It's a damned shame for the kid."

I said that to be fair, but I really didn't like the kid. His face was too refined and it was disfigured by fear and suffering, which had twisted all his features. Three days ago, he was just a kid with a kind of affected manner some people like. But now he looked like an aging fairy, and I thought to myself he would never be young again, even if they let him go. It wouldn't have been a bad thing to show him a little pity, but pity makes me sick, and besides, I couldn't stand him. He hadn't said anything more, but he had turned gray. His face and hands were gray. He sat down again and stared, round-eyed, at the ground. Tom was good-hearted and tried to take him by the arm, but the kid drew himself away violently and made an ugly face. "Leave him alone," I said quietly. "Can't you see he's going to start to bawl?" Tom obeyed regretfully. He would have liked to console the kid; that would have kept him occupied and he wouldn't have been tempted to think about himself. But it got on my nerves. I had never thought about death, for the reason that the question had never come up. But now it had come up, and there was nothing else to do but think about it.

Tom started talking. "Say, did you ever bump anybody off?" he asked me. I didn't answer. He started to explain to me that he had bumped off six fellows since August. He hadn't yet realized what we were in for, and I saw clearly he didn't *want* to realize it. I myself hadn't quite taken it in. I wondered if it hurt very much. I thought about the bullets; I imagined their fiery hail going through my body. All that was beside the real question; but I was calm, we had all night in which to realize it. After a while Tom stopped talking and I looked at him out of the corner of my eye. I saw that he, too, had turned gray and that he looked pretty miserable. I said to myself, "It's starting." It was almost dark, a dull light filtered through the air vents across the coal pile and made a big spot under the sky. Through the hole in the ceiling I could already see a star. The night was going to be clear and cold.

The door opened and two guards entered. They were followed by a blond man in a tan uniform. He greeted us.

"I'm the doctor," he said. "I've been authorized to give you any assistance you may require in these painful circumstances."

He had an agreeable, cultivated voice.

I said to him, "What are you going to do here?"

"Whatever you want me to do. I shall do everything in my power to lighten these few hours."

"Why did you come to us? There are lots of others: the hospital's full of them."

"I was sent here," he answered vaguely. "You'd probably like to smoke, wouldn't you?" he added suddenly. "I've got some cigarettes and even some cigars."

wouldn't accept anything from Enemy. He passed around some English cigarettes and some *puros*, but we refused them. I looked him straight in the eye and he appeared uncomfortable.

"You didn't come here out of compassion," I said to him. "In fact, I know who you are. I saw you with some fascists in the barracks yard the day I was arrested."

I was about to continue, when all at once something happened to me which surprised me: the presence of this doctor had suddenly ceased to interest me. Usually, when I've got hold of a man I don't let go. But somehow the desire to speak had left me. I shrugged my shoulders and turned away. A little later, I looked up and saw he was watching me with an air of curiosity. The guards had sat down on one of the mat-

tresses. Pedro, the tall thin one, was twiddling his thumbs, while the other one shook his head occasionally to keep from falling asleep.

"Do you want some light?" Pedro suddenly asked the doctor. The other fellow nodded "Yes." I think he was not over-intelligent, but doubtless he was not malicious. As I looked at his big, cold, blue eyes, it seemed to me the worst thing about him was his lack of imagination. Pedro went out and came back with an oil lamp which he set on the corner of the bench. It gave a poor light, but it was better than nothing; the night before we had been left in the dark. For a long while I stared at the circle of light the lamp threw on the ceiling. I was fascinated. Then, suddenly, I came to, the light circle paled, and I felt as if I were being crushed under an enormous weight. It wasn't the thought of death, and it wasn't fear; it was something anonymous. My cheeks were burning hot and my head ached.

I roused myself and looked at my two companions. Tom had his head in his hands and only the fat, white nape of his neck was visible. Juan was by far the worst off; his mouth was wide open and his nostrils were trembling. The doctor came over to him and touched him on the shoulder, as though to comfort him; but his eyes remained cold. Then I saw the Belgian slide his hand furtively down Juan's arm to his wrist. Indifferent, Juan let himself be handled. Then, as though absentmindedly, the Belgian laid three fingers over his wrist; at the same time, he drew away somewhat and managed to turn his back to me. But I leaned over backward and saw him take out his watch and look at it a moment before relinquishing the boy's wrist. After a moment, he let the inert hand fall and went and leaned against the wall. Then, as if he had suddenly remembered something very important that had to be noted down immediately, he took a notebook from his pocket and wrote a few lines in it. "The son-of-a-bitch," I thought angrily. "He better not come and feel my pulse; I'll give him a punch in his dirty jaw."

He didn't come near me, but I felt he was looking at me. I raised my head and looked back at him. In an impersonal voice, he said, "Don't you think it's frightfully cold here?"

He looked purple with cold.

"I'm not cold," I answered him.

He kept looking at me with a hard expression.

Suddenly I understood, and I lifted my hands to my face. I was covered with sweat. Here, in this cellar, in midwinter, right in a draft, I was sweating. I ran my fingers through my hair, which was stiff with sweat; at the same time, I realized my shirt was damp and sticking to my skin. I had been streaming with perspiration for an hour, at least, and had felt nothing. But this fact hadn't escaped that Belgian swine. He had seen the drops rolling down my face and had said to himself that it showed an almost pathological terror; and he himself had felt normal and proud of it because he was cold. I wanted to get up and go punch his face in, but I had hardly started to make a move before my shame and anger had disappeared. I dropped back onto the bench with indifference.

I was content to rub my neck with my handkerchief because now I felt the sweat dripping from my hair onto the nape of my neck and that was disagreeable. I soon gave up rubbing myself, however, for it didn't do any good; my handkerchief was already wringing wet and I was still sweating. My buttocks, too, were sweating, and my damp trousers stuck to the bench.

Suddenly, Juan said, "You're a doctor, aren't you?"

"Yes," said the Belgian.

"Do people suffer—very long?"

"Oh! When . . .? No, no," said the Belgian, in a paternal voice, "it's quickly over."

His manner was as reassuring as if he had been answering a paying patient.

"But I . . . Somebody told me—they often have to fire two volleys."

"Sometimes," said the Belgian, raising his head, "it just happens that the first volley doesn't hit any of the vital organs."

"So then they have to reload their guns and aim all over again?" Juan thought for a moment, then added hoarsely, "But that takes time!"

He was terribly afraid of suffering. He couldn't think about anything else, but that went with his age. As for me, I hardly thought about it any more and it certainly was not fear of suffering that made me perspire.

I rose and walked toward the pile of coal dust Tom gave a start and looked at me with a look of hate. I irritated him because my shoes squeaked. I wondered if my face was as putty-colored as his. Then I noticed that he, too, was sweating. The sky was magnificent; no light at all came into our dark corner and I had only to lift my head to see the Big Bear. But it didn't look the way it had looked before. Two days ago, from my cell in the archbishop's palace, I could see a big patch of sky and each time of day brought back a different memory. In the morning, when the sky was a deep blue, and light, I thought of beaches along the Atlantic; at noon, I could see the sun, and I remembered a bar in Seville where I used to drink manzanilla and eat anchovies and olives; in the afternoon, I was in the shade, and I thought of the deep shadow which covers half of the arena while the other half gleams in the sunlight: it really gave me a pang to see the whole earth reflected in the sky like that. Now, however, no matter how much I looked up in the air, the sky no longer recalled anything. I liked it better that way. I came back and sat down next to Tom. There was a long silence.

Then Tom began to talk in a low voice. He had to keep talking, otherwise he lost his way in his own thoughts. I believe he was talking to me, but he didn't look at me. No doubt he was afraid to look at me, because I was gray and sweating. We were both alike and worse than mirrors for each other. He looked at the Belgian, the only one who was alive. *only one w[h]o thinks of lif[e]*

"Say, do you understand? I don't."

Then I, too, began to talk in a low voice. I was watching the Belgian.

"Understand what? What's the matter?"

"Something's going to happen to us that I don't understand." *whole philosophy*

There was a strange odor about Tom. It seemed to me that I was more sensitive to odors than ordinarily. With a sneer, I said, "You'll understand, later."

"That's not so sure," he said stubbornly. "I'm willing to be courageous, but at least I ought to know . . . Listen, they're going to take us out into the courtyard. All right. The fellows will be standing in line in front of us. How many of them will there be?"

"Oh, I don't know. Five, or eight. Not more."

"That's enough. Let's say there'll be eight of them. Somebody will shout 'Shoulder arms!' and I'll see all eight rifles aimed at me. I'm sure I'm going to feel like going through the wall.

Tom speaks for everyone.

I'll push against the wall as hard as I can with my back, and the wall won't give in. The way it is in a nightmare. . . . I can imagine all that. Ah, if you only knew how well I can imagine it!"

"Skip it!" I said. "I can imagine it too."

"It must hurt like the devil. You know they aim at your eyes and mouth so as to disfigure you," he added maliciously. "I can feel the wounds already. For the last hour I've been having pains in my head and neck. Not real pains—it's worse still. They're the pains I'll feel tomorrow morning. And after that, then what?"

I understood perfectly well what he meant, but I didn't want to seem to understand. As for the pains, I, too, felt them all through my body, like a lot of little gashes. I couldn't get used to them, but I was like him, I didn't think they were very important.

"After that," I said roughly, "you'll be eating daisies."

He started talking to himself, not taking his eyes off the Belgian, who didn't seem to be listening to him. I knew what he had come for, and that what we were thinking didn't interest him. He had come to look at our bodies, our bodies which were dying alive.

"It's like in a nightmare," said Tom. "You want to think of something, you keep having the impression you've got it, that you're going to understand, and then it slips away from you, it eludes you and it's gone again. I say to myself, afterwards, there won't be anything. But I don't really understand what that means. There are moments when I almost do—and then it's gone again. I start to think of the pains, the bullets, the noise of the shooting. I am a materialist, I swear it; and I'm not going crazy, either. But there's something wrong. I see my own corpse. That's not hard, but it's *I* who see it, with *my* eyes. I'll have to get to the point where I think —where I think I won't see anything more. I won't hear anything more, and the world will go on for the others. We're not made to think that way, Pablo. Believe me, I've already stayed awake all night waiting for something. But this is not the same thing. This will grab us from behind, Pablo, and we won't be ready for it."

"Shut up," I said. "Do you want me to call a father confessor?"

He didn't answer. I had already noticed that he had a tendency to prophesy and call me "Pablo" in a kind of pale voice. I didn't like

that very much, but it seems all the Irish are like that. I had a vague impression that he smelled of urine. Actually, I didn't like Tom very much, and I didn't see why, just because we were going to die together, I should like him any better. There are certain fellows with whom it would be different—with Ramon Gris, for instance. But between Tom and Juan, I felt alone. In fact, I liked it better that way. With Ramon I might have grown soft. But I felt terribly hard at that moment, and I wanted to stay hard.

Tom kept on muttering, in a kind of absent-minded way. He was certainly talking to keep from thinking. Naturally, I agreed with him, and I could have said everything he was saying. It's not *natural* to die. And since I was going to die, nothing seemed natural any more: neither the coal pile, nor the bench, nor Pedro's dirty old face. Only it was disagreeable for me to think the same things Tom thought. And I knew perfectly well that all night long, within five minutes of each other, we would keep on thinking things at the same time, sweating or shivering at the same time. I looked at him sideways and, for the first time, he seemed strange to me. He had death written on his face. My pride was wounded. For twenty-four hours I had lived side by side with Tom, I had listened to him, I had talked to him, and I knew we had nothing in common. And now we were as alike as twin brothers, simply because we were going to die together. Tom took my hand without looking at me.

"Pablo, I wonder . . . I wonder if it's true that we just cease to exist."

I drew my hand away.

"Look between your feet, you dirty dog."

There was a puddle between his feet and water was dripping from his trousers.

"What's the matter?" he said, frightened.

"You're wetting your pants," I said to him.

"It's not true," he said furiously. "I can't be . . . I don't feel anything."

The Belgian had come closer to him. With an air of false concern, he asked, "Aren't you feeling well?"

Tom didn't answer. The Belgian looked at the puddle without comment.

"I don't know what that is," Tom said savagely, "but I'm not afraid. I swear to you, I'm not afraid."

The Belgian made no answer. Tom rose and went to the corner. He came back, buttoning his fly, and sat down, without a word. The Belgian was taking notes.

We were watching the doctor. Juan was watching him too. All three of us were watching him because he was alive. He had the gestures of a living person, the interests of a living person; he was shivering in this cellar the way living people shiver; he had an obedient, well-fed body. We, on the other hand, didn't feel our bodies any more—not the same way, in any case. I felt like touching my trousers, but I didn't dare to. I looked at the Belgian, well-planted on his two legs, master of his muscles—and able to plan for tomorrow. We were like three shadows deprived of blood; we were watching him and sucking his life like vampires.

Finally he came over to Juan. Was he going to lay his hand on the nape of Juan's neck for some professional reason, or had he obeyed a charitable impulse? If he had acted out of charity, it was the one and only time during the whole night. He fondled Juan's head and the nape of his neck. The kid let him do it, without taking his eyes off him. Then, suddenly, he took hold of the doctor's hand and looked at it in a funny way. He held the Belgian's hand between his own two hands and there was nothing pleasing about them, those two gray paws squeezing that fat red hand. I sensed what was going to happen and Tom must have sensed it, too. But all the Belgian saw was emotion, and he smiled paternally. After a moment, the kid lifted the big red paw to his mouth and started to bite it. The Belgian drew back quickly and stumbled toward the wall. For a second, he looked at us with horror. He must have suddenly understood that we were not men like himself. I began to laugh, and one of the guards started up. The other had fallen asleep with his eyes wide open, showing only the whites.

I felt tired and overexcited at the same time. I didn't want to think any more about what was going to happen at dawn—about death. It didn't make sense, and I never got beyond just words, or emptiness. But whenever I tried to think about something else I saw the barrels of rifles aimed at me. I must have lived through my execution twenty times in succession; one time I thought it was the real thing; I must have dozed off for a moment. They were drag-

ging me toward the wall and I was resisting; I was imploring their pardon. I woke with a start and looked at the Belgian. I was afraid I had cried out in my sleep. But he was smoothing his mustache; he hadn't noticed anything. If I had wanted to, I believe I could have slept for a while. I had been awake for the last forty-eight hours, and I was worn out. But I didn't want to lose two hours of life. They would have had to come and wake me at dawn. I would have followed them, drunk with sleep, and I would have gone off without so much as "Gosh!" I didn't want it that way, I didn't want to die like an animal. I wanted to understand. Besides, I was afraid of having nightmares. I got up and began to walk up and down and, so as to think about something else, I began to think about my past life. Memories crowded in on me, helter-skelter. Some were good and some were bad—at least that was how I had thought of them *before*. There were faces and happenings. I saw the face of a little *novilero* who had gotten himself horned during the *Feria*, in Valencia. I saw the face of one of my uncles, of Ramon Gris. I remembered all kinds of things that had happened: how I had been on strike for three months in 1926, and had almost died of hunger. I recalled a night I had spent on a bench in Granada; I hadn't eaten for three days, I was nearly wild, I didn't want to give up the sponge. I had to smile. With what eagerness I had run after happiness, and women, and liberty! And to what end? I had wanted to liberate Spain, I admired Py Margall, I had belonged to the anarchist movement, I had spoken at public meetings. I took everything as seriously as if I had been immortal.

At that time I had the impression that I had my whole life before me, and I thought to myself, "It's all a god-damned lie." Now it wasn't worth anything because it was finished. I wondered how I had ever been able to go out and have a good time with girls. I wouldn't have lifted my little finger if I had ever imagined that I would die like this. I saw my life before me, finished, closed, like a bag, and yet what was inside was not finished. For a moment I tried to appraise it. I would have liked to say to myself, "It's been a good life." But it couldn't be appraised, it was only an outline. I had spent my time writing checks on eternity, and had understood nothing. Now, I didn't miss anything. There were a lot of things I might have missed: the taste of manzanilla, for instance, or the swims I used to take in summer in a little creek near Cadiz. But death had taken the charm out of everything.

Suddenly the Belgian had a wonderful idea.

"My friends," he said to us, "if you want me to—and providing the military authorities give their consent—I could undertake to deliver a word or some token from you to your loved ones. . . ."

Tom growled, "I haven't got anybody."

I didn't answer. Tom waited for a moment, then he looked at me with curiosity. "Aren't you going to send any message to Concha?"

"No." *Isolated from Concha*

I hated that sort of sentimental conspiracy. Of course, it was my fault, since I had mentioned Concha the night before, and I should have kept my mouth shut. I had been with her for a year. Even as late as last night, I would have cut my arm off with a hatchet just to see her again for five minutes. That was why I had mentioned her. I couldn't help it. Now I didn't care any more about seeing her. I hadn't anything more to say to her. I didn't even want to hold her in my arms. I loathed my body because it had turned gray and was sweating—and I wasn't even sure that I didn't loathe hers too. Concha would cry when she heard about my death; for months she would have no more interest in life. But still it was I who was going to die. I thought of her beautiful, loving eyes. When she looked at me something went from her to me. But I thought to myself that it was all over; if she looked at me *now* her gaze would not leave her eyes, it would not reach out to me. I was alone.

Tom too, was alone, but not the same way. He was seated astride his chair and had begun to look at the bench with a sort of smile, with surprise, even. He reached out his hand and touched the wood cautiously, as though he were afraid of breaking something, then he drew his hand back hurriedly, and shivered. I wouldn't have amused myself touching that bench, if I had been Tom, that was just some more Irish playacting. But somehow it seemed to me too that the different objects had something funny about them. They seemed to have grown paler, less massive than before. I had only to look at the bench, the lamp or the pile of coal dust to feel I was going to die. Naturally, I couldn't

think clearly about my death, but I saw it everywhere, even on the different objects, the way they had withdrawn and kept their distance, tactfully, like people talking at the bedside of a dying person. It was *his own death* Tom had just touched on the bench.

In the state I was in, if they had come and told me could go home quietly, that my life would be saved, it would have left me cold. A few hours, or a few years of waiting are all the same, when you've lost the illusion of being eternal. Nothing mattered to me any more. In a way, I was calm. But it was a horrible kind of calm—because of my body. My body—I saw with its eyes and I heard with its ears, but it was no longer I. It sweat and trembled independently, and I didn't recognize it any longer. I was obliged to touch it and look at it to know what was happening to it, just as if it had been someone else's body. At times I still felt it, I felt a slipping, a sort of headlong plunging, as in a falling airplane, or else I heard my heart beating. But this didn't give me confidence. In fact, everything that came from my body had something damned dubious about it. Most of the time it was silent, it stayed put and I didn't feel anything other than a sort of heaviness, a loathsome presence against me. I had the impression of being bound to an enormous vermin.

The Belgian took out his watch and looked at it.

"It's half-past three," he said.

The son-of-a-bitch! He must have done it on purpose. Tom jumped up. We hadn't yet realized the time was passing. The night surrounded us like a formless, dark mass; I didn't even remember it had started.

Juan started to shout. Wringing his hands, he implored, "I don't want to die! I don't want to die!"

He ran the whole length of the cellar with his arms in the air, then he dropped down onto one of the mattresses, sobbing. Tom looked at him with dismal eyes and didn't even try to console him any more. The fact was, it was no use; the kid made more noise than we did, but he was less affected, really. He was like a sick person who defends himself against his malady with a high fever. When there's not even any fever left, it's much more serious.

He was crying. I could tell he felt sorry for himself; he was thinking about death. For one second, one single second, I too felt like crying,

crying out of pity for myself. But just the contrary happened. I took one look at the kid, saw his thin, sobbing shoulders, and I felt I was inhuman. I couldn't feel pity either for these others or for myself. I said to myself, "I want to die decently."

Tom had gotten up and was standing just under the round opening looking out for the first signs of daylight. I was determined, I wanted to die decently, and I only thought about that. But underneath, ever since the doctor had told us the time, I felt time slipping, flowing by, one drop at a time.

It was still dark when I heard Tom's voice.

"Do you hear them?"

"Yes."

People were walking in the courtyard.

"What the hell are they doing? After all, they can't shoot in the dark."

After a moment, we didn't hear anything more. I said to Tom, "There's the daylight."

Pedro got up yawning, and came and blew out the lamp. He turned to the man beside him. "It's hellish cold."

The cellar had grown gray. We could hear shots at a distance.

"It's about to start," I said to Tom. "That must be in the back courtyard."

Tom asked the doctor to give him a cigarette. I didn't want any; I didn't want either cigarettes or alcohol. From that moment on, the shooting didn't stop.

"Can you take it in?" Tom said.

He started to add something, then he stopped and began to watch the door. The door opened and a lieutenant came in with four soldiers. Tom dropped his cigarette.

"Steinbock?"

Tom didn't answer. Pedro pointed him out.

"Juan Mirbal?"

"He's the one on the mattress."

"Stand up," said the Lieutenant.

Juan didn't move. Two soldiers took hold of him by the armpits and stood him up on his feet. But as soon as they let go of him he fell down.

The soldiers hesitated a moment.

"He's not the first one to get sick," said the Lieutenant. "You'll have to carry him, the two of you. We'll arrange things when we get there." He turned to Tom. "All right, come along."

Tom left between two soldiers. Two other soldiers followed, carrying the kid by his arms and legs. He was not unconscious; his eyes were wide open and tears were rolling down his cheeks. When I started to go out, the Lieutenant stopped me.

"Are you Ibbieta?"

"Yes."

"You wait here. They'll come and get you later on."

They left. The Belgian and the two jailers left too, and I was alone. I didn't understand what had happened to me, but I would have liked it better if they had ended it all right away. I heard the volleys at almost regular intervals; at each one, I shuddered. I felt like howling and tearing my hair. But instead, I gritted my teeth and pushed my hands deep into my pockets, because I wanted to stay decent.

An hour later, they came to fetch me and took me up to the first floor in a little room which smelt of cigar smoke and was so hot it seemed to me suffocating. Here there were two officers sitting in comfortable chairs, smoking, with papers spread out on their knees.

"Your name is Ibbieta?"

"Yes."

"Where is Ramon Gris?"

"I don't know."

The man who questioned me was small and stocky. He had hard eyes behind his glasses.

"Come nearer," he said to me.

I went nearer. He rose and took me by the arms, looking at me in a way calculated to make me go through the floor. At the same time he pinched my arms with all his might. He didn't mean to hurt me; it was quite a game; he wanted to dominate me. He also seemed to think it was necessary to blow his fetid breath right into my face. We stood like that for a moment, only I felt more like laughing than anything else. It takes a lot more than that to intimidate a man who's about to die: it didn't work. He pushed me away violently and sat down again.

"It's your life or his," he said. "You'll be allowed to go free if you tell us where he is."

After all, these two bedizened fellows with their riding crops and boots were just men who were going to die one day. A little later than I, perhaps, but not a great deal. And there they were, looking for names among their papers, running after other men in order to put them in prison or do away with them entirely. They had their opinions on the the future of Spain and on other subjects. Their petty activities seemed to me to be offensive and ludicrous. I could no longer put myself in their place. I had the impression they were crazy.

The little fat fellow kept looking at me, tapping his boots with his riding crop. All his gestures were calculated to make him appear like a spirited, ferocious animal.

"Well? Do you understand?"

"I don't know where Gris is," I said. "I thought he was in Madrid."

The other officer lifted his pale hand indolently. This indolence was also calculated. I saw through all their little tricks, and I was dumbfounded that men should still exist who took pleasure in that kind of thing.

"You have fifteen minutes to think it over," he said slowly. "Take him to the linen-room, and bring him back here in fifteen minutes. If he continues to refuse, he'll be executed at once."

They knew what they were doing. I had spent the night waiting. After that, they had made me wait another hour in the cellar, while they shot Tom and Juan, and now they locked me in the linen-room. They must have arranged the whole thing the night before. They figured that sooner or later people's nerves wear out and they hoped to get me that way.

They made a big mistake. In the linen-room I sat down on a ladder because I felt very weak, and I began to think things over. Not their proposition, however. Naturally I knew where Gris was. He was hiding in his cousins' house, about two miles outside of the city. I knew, too, that I would not reveal his hiding place, unless they tortured me (but they didn't seem to be considering that). All that was definitely settled and didn't interest me in the least. Only I would have liked to understand the reasons for my own conduct. I would rather die than betray Gris. Why? I no longer liked Ramon Gris. My friendship for him had died shortly before dawn along with my love for Concha, along with my own desire to live. Of course I still admired him—he was hard. But it was not for that reason that I was willing to die in his place; his life was no more valuable than mine. No life was of any value. A man was going to be stood up against a wall and fired at till he dropped dead. It didn't make any difference whether it was I or Gris or somebody else. I knew perfectly well he was more useful to the Spanish cause than I was, but I didn't give a

God damn about Spain or anarchy, either; nothing had any importance now. And yet, there I was. I could save my skin by betraying Gris and I refused to do it. It seemed more ludicrous to me than anything else; it was stubbornness.

I thought to myself, "Am I hard-headed!" And I was seized with a strange sort of cheerfulness.

They came to fetch me and took me back to the two officers. A rat darted out under our feet and that amused me. I turned to one of the falangists and said to him, "Did you see that rat?"

He made no reply. He was gloomy, and took himself very seriously. As for me, I felt like laughing, but I restrained myself because I was afraid that if I started, I wouldn't be able to stop. The falangist wore mustaches. I kept after him, "You ought to cut off those mustaches, you fool."

I was amused by the fact that he let hair grow all over his face while he was still alive. He gave me a kind of half-hearted kick, and I shut up.

"Well," said the fat officer, "have you thought things over?"

I looked at them with curiosity, like insects of a very rare species,

"I know where he is," I said. "He's hiding in the cemetery. Either in one of the vaults, or in the gravediggers' shack."

I said that just to make fools of them. I wanted to see them get up and fasten their belts and bustle about giving orders.

They jumped to their feet.

"Fine. Moles, go ask Lieutenant Lopez for fifteen men. And as for you," the little fat fellow said to me, "if you've told the truth, I don't go back on my word. But you'll pay for this, if you're pulling our leg."

They left noisily and I waited in peace, still guarded by the falangists. From time to time I smiled at the thought of the face they were going to make. I felt dull and malicious. I could see them lifting up the gravestones, or opening the doors of the vaults one by one. I saw the whole situation as though I were another person: the prisoner determined to play the hero, the solemn falangists with their mustaches and the men in uniform running around among the graves. It was irresistibly funny.

After half an hour, the little fat fellow came back alone. I thought he had come to give the order to execute me. The others must have stayed in the cemetery.

The officer looked at me. He didn't look at all foolish.

"Take him out in the big couryard with the others," he said. "When military operations are over, a regular tribunal will decide his case."

I thought I must have misunderstood.

"So they're not—they're not going to shoot me?" I asked.

"Not now, in any case. Afterwards, that doesn't concern me."

I still didn't understand.

"But why?" I said to him.

He shrugged his shoulders without replying, and the soldiers led me away. In the big courtyard there were a hundred or so prisoners, women, children and a few old men. I started to walk around the grass plot in the middle. I felt absolutely idiotic. At noon we were fed in the dining hall. Two or three fellows spoke to me. I must have known them, but I didn't answer. I didn't even know where I was.

Toward evening, about ten new prisoners were pushed into the courtyard. I recognized Garcia, the baker.

He said to me, "Lucky dog! I didn't expect to find you alive."

"They condemned me to death," I said, "and then they changed their minds. I don't know why."

"I was arrested at two o'clock," Garcia said.

"What for?"

Garcia took no part in politics.

"I don't know," he said. "They arrest everybody who doesn't think the way they do."

He lowered his voice.

"They got Gris."

I began to tremble.

"When?"

"This morning. He acted like a damned fool. He left his cousins' house Tuesday because of a disagreement. There were any number of fellows who would have hidden him, but he didn't want to be indebted to anybody any more. He said, 'I would have hidden at Ibbieta's, but since they've got him, I'll go hide in the cemetery.'"

"In the cemetery?"

"Yes. It was the god-damnedest thing. Natu-rally they passed by there this morning; that had to happen. They found him in the grave-diggers' shack. They opened fire at him and they finished him off."

"In the cemetery!"

Everything went around in circles, and when I came to I was sitting on the ground. I laughed so hard the tears came to my eyes.

FOR ANALYSIS

1. What is the point of view in this story?
2. Notice in the early part of the story Pablo's attitude toward abstract justice (Juan's predicament) and pity (Tom's gesture toward Juan). What does he think of them? Does this harmonize with his attitude toward friendship?
3. How does Tom's attitude toward approaching death differ from Pablo's? What does Tom mean by "I'm willing to be courageous, but at least I ought to know . . ."? What ought he to know?
4. In what way is Pablo's reflection, "I took everything as seriously as if I had been immortal," a key to his mental makeup?
5. In an ordinary, rational world, Gris's running to the cemetery would seem an incredible coincidence. Why is it that in this story, Gris's being there is entirely fitting and proper? How does it bear out Pablo's view of the world?

RICHARD WRIGHT

Almos' a Man

Dave struck out across the fields, looking home-ward through paling light. Whut's the usa talkin wid em niggers in the field? Anyhow, his mother was putting supper on the table. Them niggers can't understan nothing. One of these days he was going to get a gun and practice shooting, then they can't talk to him as though he were a little boy. He slowed, looking at the ground. Shucks, Ah ain scareda them even ef they are biggern me! Aw, Ah know whut Ahma do. . . . Ahm going by ol Joe's sto n git that Sears Roebuck catlog n look at them guns. Mabbe Ma will lemme buy one when she gits mah pay from ol man Hawkins. Ahma beg her t gimme some money. Ahm ol ernough to hava gun. Ahm seventeen. Almost a man. He strode, feeling his long, loose-jointed limbs. Shucks, a man oughta hava little gun aftah he done worked hard all day. . . .

He came in sight of Joe's store. A yellow lantern glowed on the front porch. He mounted steps and went through the screen door, hearing it bang behind him. There was a strong smell of coal oil and mackerel fish. He felt very confident until he saw fat Joe walk in through the rear door, then his courage began to ooze.

"Howdy, Dave! Whutcha want?"

"How yuh, Mistah Joe? Aw, Ah don wanna buy nothing. Ah jus wanted t see ef yuhd lemme look at tha ol catlog erwhile."

"Sure! You wanna see it here?"

"Nawsuh. Ah wans t take it home wid me. Ahll bring it back termorrow when Ah come in from the fiels."

"You plannin on buyin something?"

"Yessuh."

"Your ma letting you have your own money now?"

"Shucks. Mistah Joe, Ahm gittin t be a man like anybody else!"

Joe laughed and wiped his greasy white face with a red bandanna.

"Whut you plannin on buyin?"

Dave looked at the floor, scratched his head, scratched his thigh, and smiled. Then he looked up shyly.

"Ahll tell yuh, Mistah Joe, ef yuh promise yuh won't tell."

"I promise."

"Waal, Ahma buy a gun."

"A gun? Whut you want with a gun?"

"Ah wanna keep it."

"You ain't nothing but a boy. You don't need a gun."

"Aw, lemme have the catlog, Mistah Joe. Ahll bring it back."

Joe walked through the rear door. Dave was elated. He looked around at barrels of sugar and flour. He heard Joe coming back. He craned his neck to see if he were bringing the book. Yeah, he's got it! Gawddog, he's got it!

"Here, but be sure you bring it back. It's the only one I got."

"Sho, Mistah Joe."

"Say, if you wanna buy a gun, why don't you buy one from me? I gotta gun to sell."

"Will it shoot?"

"Sure it'll shoot."

"Whut kind is it?"

"Oh, it's kinda old. . . . A lefthand Wheeler. A pistol. A big one."

"Is it got bullets in it?"

"It's loaded."

"Kin Ah see it?"

"Where's your money?"

"Whut yuh wan fer it?"

"I'll let you have it for two dollars."

"Just two dollahs? Shucks, Ah could buy tha when Ah git mah pay."

"I'll have it here when you want it."

"Awright, suh. Ah be in fer it."

He went through the door, hearing it slam again behind him. Ahma git some money from Ma n buy me a gun! Only two dollahs! He tucked the thick catalogue under his arm and hurried.

"Where yuh been, boy?" His mother held a steaming dish of black-eyed peas.

"Aw, Ma, Ah jus stopped own the road t talk wid th boys."

"Yuh know bettah than t keep suppah waitin."

He sat down, resting the catalogue on the edge of the table.

" Yuh git up from there and git to the well n wash yosef! Ah ain feedin no hogs in mah house!"

She grabbed his shoulder and pushed him. He stumbled out of the room, then came back to get the catalogue.

"Whut this?"

"Aw, Ma, it's jusa catlog."

"Who yuh git it from?"

"From Joe, down at the sto."

"Waal, thas good. We kin use it around the house."

"Naw, Ma." He grabbed for it. "Gimme mah catlog, Ma."

She held onto it and glared at him.

"Quit hollerin at me! Whut's wrong wid yuh? Yuh crazy?"

"But Ma, please. It ain mine! It's Joe's! He tol me t bring it back t im termorrow."

She gave up the book. He stumbled down the back steps, hugging the thick book under his arm. When he had splashed water on his face and hands, he groped back to the kitchen and fumbled in a corner for the towel. He bumped into a chair; it clattered to the floor. The catalogue sprawled at his feet. When he had dried his eyes he snatched up the book and held it again under his arm. His mother stood watching him.

"Now, ef yuh gonna acka fool over that ol book, Ahll take it n burn it up."

"Naw, Ma, please."

"Waal, set down n be still!"

He sat down and drew the oil lamp close. He thumbed page after page, unaware of the food his mother set on the table. His father came in. Then his small brother.

"Whutcha got there, Dave?" his father asked.

"Jusa catlog," he answered, not looking up.

"Ywah, here they is!" His eyes glowed at blue and black revolvers. He glanced up, feeling sudden guilt. His father was watching him. He eased the book under the table and rested it on his knees. After the blessing was asked, he ate. He scooped up peas and swallowed fat meat without chewing. Buttermilk helped to wash it down. He did not want to mention money before his father. He would do much better by cornering his mother when she was alone. He looked at his father uneasily out of the edge of his eye.

"Boy, how come yuh don quit foolin wid tha book n eat yo suppah?"

"Yessuh."

"How you n ol man Hawkins gittin erlong?"

"Suh?"

"Can't yuh hear? Why don yuh lissen? Ah ast yu how wuz yuh n ol man Hawkins gittin erlong?"

"Oh, swell, Pa. Ah plows mo lan than anybody over there."

"Waal, yuh oughta keep you min on whut yuh doin."

"Yessuh."

He poured his plate full of molasses and sopped at it slowly with a chunk of cornbread. When all but his mother had left the kitchen, he still sat and looked again at the guns in the catalogue. Lawd, ef Ah only had tha pretty one! He could almost feel the slickness of the weapon with his fingers. If he had a gun like that he would polish it and keep it shining so it would never rust. N Ahd keep it loaded, by Gawd!

"Ma?"

"Hunh?"

"Ol man Hawkins give yuh mah money yit?"

"Yeah, but ain no usa yuh thinkin bout thowin nona it erway. Ahm keepin tha money sos yuh kin have cloes t go to school this winter."

He rose and went to her side with the open catalogue in his palms. She was washing dishes, her head bent low over a pan. Shyly he raised the open book. When he spoke his voice was husky, faint.

"Ma, Gawd knows Ah wans one of these."

"One of whut?" she asked, not raising her eyes.

"One of these, "he said again, not daring even to point. She glanced up at the page, then at him with wide eyes.

"Nigger, is yuh gone plum crazy?"

"Aw, Ma—"

"Git outta here! Don yuh talk t me bout no gun! Yuh a fool!"

"Ma, Ah kin buy one fer two dollahs."

"Not ef Ah knows it yuh ain!"

"But yuh promised me one—"

"Ah don care whut Ah promised! Yuh ain nothing but a boy yit!"

"Ma, ef yuh lemme buy one Ahll never ast yuh fer nothing no mo."

"Ah tol yuh t git outta here! Yuh ain gonna toucha penny of tha money fer no gun! Thas how come Ah has Mistah Hawkins t pay yo wages t me, cause Ah knows yuh ain got no sense."

"But Ma, we needa gun. Pa ain got no gun. We needa gun in the house. Yuh kin never tell whut might happen."

"Now don yuh try to maka fool outta me, boy! Ef we did hava gun yuh wouldn't have it!"

He laid the catalogue down and slipped his arm around her waist.

"Aw, Ma, Ah done worked hard alla summer n ain ast yuh fer nothin, is Ah, now?"

"Thas whut yuh spose t do!"

"But Ma, Ah wans a gun. Yuh kin lemma have two dollahs outta mah money. Please, Ma. I kin give it to Pa . . . Please, Ma! Ah loves yuh, Ma."

When she spoke her voice came soft and low.

"Whut yu wan wida gun, Dave? Yuh don need no gun. Yuhll git in trouble. N ef yo Pa jus thought Ah let yuh have money t buy a gun he'd hava fit."

"Ahll hide it, Ma. It ain but two dollahs."

"Lawd, chil, whuts wrong wid yuh?"

"Ain nothin wrong, Ma. Ahm almos a man now. Ah wans a gun."

"Who gonna sell yuh a gun?"

"Ol Joe at the sto."

"N it don cos but two dollahs?"

"Thas all, Ma. Just two dollahs. Please, Ma."

She was stacking the plates away; her hands

moved slowly, reflectively. Dave kept an anxious silence. Finally, she turned to him.

"Ahll let yuh git tha gun ef yuh promise me one thing."

"Whuts tha, Ma?"

"Yuh bring it straight back t me, yuh hear? It be fer Pa."

"Yessum! Lemme go now, Ma."

She stooped, turned slightly to one side, raised the hem of her dress, rolled down the top of her stocking, and came up with a slender wad of bills.

"Here," she said. "Lawd knows yuh don need no gun. But yer Pa does. Yuh bring it right back t me, yuh hear? Ahma put it up. Now ef yuh don, Ahma have yuh Pa lick yuh so hard yuh won ferget it."

"Yessum."

He took the money, ran down the steps, and across the yard.

"Dave! Yuuuuuh Daaaaave!"

He heard, but he was not going to stop now. "Naw, Lawd!"

The first movement he made the following morning was to reach under his pillow for the gun. In the gray light of dawn he held it loosely, feeling a sense of power. Could killa man wida gun like this. Kill anybody, black or white. And if he were holding his gun in his hand nobody could run over him; they would have to respect him. It was a big gun, with a long barrel and a heavy handle. He raised and lowered it in his hand, marveling at its weight.

He had not come straight home with it as his mother had asked; instead he had stayed out in the fields, holding the weapon in his hand, aiming it now and then at some imaginary foe. But he had not fired it; he had been afraid that his father might hear. Also he was not sure he knew how to fire it.

To avoid surrendering the pistol he had not come into the house until he knew that all were asleep. When his mother had tiptoed to his bedside late that night and demanded the gun, he had first played 'possum; then he had told her that the gun was hidden outdoors, that he would bring it to her in the morning. Now he lay turning it slowly in his hands. He broke it, took out the cartridges, felt them, and then put them back.

He slid out of bed, got a long strip of old flannel from a trunk, wrapped the gun in it, and tied it to his naked thigh while it was still loaded. He did not go in to breakfast. Even though it was not yet daylight, he started for Jim Hawkins' plantation. Just as the sun was rising he reached the barns where the mules and plows were kept.

"Hey! That you, Dave?"

He turned. Jim Hawkins stood eying him suspiciously.

"What're yuh doing here so early?"

"Ah didn't know Ah wuz gittin up so early, Mistah Hawkins. Ah wuz fixin t hitch up ol Jenny n take her t the fiels."

"Good. Since you're here so early, how about plowing that stretch down by the woods?"

"Suits me, Mistah Hawkins."

"O. K. Go to it!"

He hitched Jenny to a plow and started across the fields. Hot dog! This was just what he wanted. If he could get down by the woods, he could shoot his gun and nobody would hear. He walked behind the plow, hearing the traces creaking, feeling the gun tied tight to his thigh.

When he reached the woods, he plowed two whole rows before he decided to take out the gun. Finally, he stopped, looked in all directions, then untied the gun and held it in his hand. He turned to the mule and smiled.

"Know whut this is, Jenny? Naw, yuh wouldn't know! Yuhs jusa ol mule! Anyhow, this is a gun, n it kin shoot, by Gawd!"

He held the gun at arm's length. Whut t hell, Ahma shoot this thing! He looked at Jenny again.

"Lissen here, Jenny! When Ah pull this ol trigger Ah don wan yuh t run n acka fool now."

Jenny stood with head down, her short ears pricked straight. Dave walked off about twenty feet, held the gun far out from him, at arm's length, and turned his head. Hell, he told himself, Ah ain afraid. The gun felt loose in his fingers; he waved it wildly for a moment. Then he shut his eyes and tightened his forefinger. Bloom! A report half-deafened him and he thought his right hand was torn from his arm. He heard Jenny whinnying and galloping over the field, and he found himself on his knees, squeezing his fingers hard between his legs. His hand was numb; he jammed it into his mouth, trying to warm it, trying to stop the pain. The gun lay at his feet. He did not quite know what happened. He stood up and stared at the gun as though it were a live thing. He gritted his teeth and kicked the gun. Yuh almos broke mah arm! He turned to look for Jenny; she was far over the fields, tossing her head and kicking wildly.

"Hol on there, ol mule!"

When he caught up with her she stood trembling, walling her big white eyes at him. The plow was far away; the traces had broken. Then Dave stopped short, looking, not believing. Jenny was bleeding. Her left side was red and wet with blood. He went closer. Lawd have mercy! Wondah did Ah shoot this mule? He grabbed for Jenny's mane. She flinched, snorted, whirled, tossing her head.

"Hol on now! Hol on."

Then he saw the hole in Jenny's side, right between the ribs. It was round, wet, red. A crimson stream streaked down the front leg, flowing fast. Good Gawd! Ah wuznt shootin at tha mule. . . . He felt panic. He knew he had to stop that blood, or Jenny would bleed to death. He had never seen so much blood in all his life. He ran the mule for half a mile, trying to catch her. Finally she stopped, breathing hard, stumpy tail half arched. He caught her mane and led her back to where the plow and gun lay. Then he stopped and grabbed handfuls of damp black earth and tried to plug the bullet hole. Jenny shuddered, winnied, and broke from him.

"Hol on! Hol on now!"

He tried to plug it again, but blood came anyhow. His fingers were hot and sticky. He rubbed dirt hard into his palms, trying to dry them. Then again he attempted to plug the bullet hole, but Jenny shied away, kicking her heels high. He stood helpless. He had to do something. He ran at Jenny; she dodged him. He watched a red stream of blood flow down Jenny's leg and form a bright pool at her feet.

"Jenny . . . Jenny . . ." he called weakly.

His lips trembled. She's bleeding t death! He looked in the direction of home, wanting to go back, wanting to get help. But he saw the pistol lying in the damp black clay. He had a queer feeling that if he only did something, this would not be; Jenny would not be there bleeding to death.

When he went to her this time, she did not move. She stood with sleepy, dreamy eyes; and when he touched her she gave a low-pitched whinny and knelt to the ground, her front knees slopping in blood.

"Jenny . . . Jenny . . ." he whispered.

For a long time she held her neck erect; then her head sank, slowly. Her ribs swelled with a mighty heave and she went over.

Dave's stomach felt empty, very empty. He picked up the gun and held it gingerly between his thumb and forefinger. He buried it at the foot of a tree. He took a stick and tried to cover the pool of blood with dirt—but what was the use? There was Jenny lying with her mouth open and her eyes walled and glassy. He could not tell Jim Hawkins he had shot his mule. But he had to tell something. Yeah, Ahll tell em Jenny started gittin wil n fell on the joint of the plow. . . . But that would hardly happen to a mule. He walked across the field slowly, head down.

It was sunset. Two of Jim Hawkins' men were over near the edge of the woods digging a hole in which to bury Jenny. Dave was surrounded by a knot of people; all of them were looking down at the dead mule.

"I don't see how in the world it happened," said Jim Hawkins for the tenth time.

The crowd parted and Dave's mother, father, and small brother pushed into the center.

"Where Dave?" his mother called.

"There he is," said Jim Hawkins.

His mother grabbed him.

"Whut happened, Dave? Whut yuh done?"

"Nothing."

"C'mon, boy, talk," his father said.

Dave took a deep breath and told the story he knew nobody believed.

"Waal," he drawled. "Ah brung ol Jenny down here sos Ah could do mah plowin. Ah plowed bout two rows, just like yuh see." He stopped and pointed at the long rows of up-turned earth. "Then something musta been wrong wid ol Jenny. She wouldn't ack right a-tall. She started snortin n kickin her heels. Ah tried to hol her, but she pulled erway, rearin n goin on. Then when the point of the plow was stickin up in the air, she swung erroun n twisted herself back on it. . . . She stuck hersef n started t bleed. N fo Ah could do anything, she wuz dead."

"Did you ever hear of anything like that in all your life?" asked Jim Hawkins.

There were white and black standing in the crowd. They murmured. Dave's mother came close to him and looked hard into his face. "Tell the truth, Dave," she said.

"Looks like a bullet hole ter me," said one man.

"Dave, whut yuh do wid tha gun?" his mother asked.

The crowd surged in, looking at him. He jammed his hands into his pockets, shook his head slowly from left to right, and backed away. His eyes were wide and painful.

"Did he hava gun?" asked Jim Hawkins.

"By Gawd, Oh tol yuh tha wuz a gun wound," said a man, slapping his thigh.

His father caught his shoulders and shook him till his teeth rattled.

"Tell whut happened, yuh rascal! Tell whut. . . ."

Dave looked at Jenny's stiff legs and began to cry.

"Whut yuh do wid tha gun?" his mother asked.

"Whut wuz he doin wida gun?" his father asked.

"Come on and tell the truth," said Hawkins. "Ain't nobody going to hurt you . . . ."

His mother crowded close to him.

"Did yuh shoot tha mule, Dave?"

Dave cried, seeing blurred white and black faces.

"Ahh ddinnt gggo tt sshoooot hher. . . . Ah ssswear ffo Gawd Ahh ddint. . . . Ah wuz a-trying t sssee ef the ol gggun would sshoot—"

"Where yuh git the gun from?" his father asked.

"Ah got it from Joe, at the sto."

"Where yuh git the money?"

"Ma give it t me."

"He kept worryin me, Bob. . . . Ah had t. . . . Ah tol im t bring the gun right back t me. . . . It was fer yuh, the gun."

"But how yuh happen to shoot that mule?" asked Jim Hawkins.

"Ah wuznt shootin at the mule, Mistah Hawkins. The gun jumped when Ah pulled the trigger . . . N fo Ah knowed anything Jenny was there a-bleedin."

Somebody in the crowd laughed. Jim Hawkins walked close to Dave and looked into his face.

"Well, looks like you have bought you a mule, Dave."

"Ah swear fo Gawd, Ah didn't go t kill the mule, Mistah Hawkins!"

"But you killed her!"

All the crowd was laughing now. They stood on tiptoe and poked heads over one another's shoulders.

"Well, boy, looks like yuh done bought a dead mule! Hahaha!"

"Ain tha ershame."

"Hohohohoho."

Dave stood, head down, twisting his feet in the dirt.

"Well, you needn't worry about it, Bob," said Jim Hawkins to Dave's father. "Just let the boy keep on working and pay me two dollars a month."

"Whut yuh wan fer yo mule, Mistah Hawkins?"

Jim Hawkins screwed up his eyes.

"Fifty dollars."

"Whut yuh do wid tha gun?" Dave's father demanded.

Dave said nothing.

"Yuh wan me t take a tree lim n beat yuh till yuh talk!"

"Nawsuh!"

"Whut yuh do wid it?"

"Ah thowed it erway."

"Where?"

"Ah . . . Ah thowed it in the creek."

"Waal, c mon home. N firs thing in the mawnin git to tha creek n fin tha gun."

"Yessuh."

"Whut yuh pay fer it?"

"Two dollahs."

"Take tha gun n git yo money back n carry it t Mistah Hawkins, yuh hear? N don fergit Ahma lam you black bottom good fer this! Now march yosef on home, suh!"

Dave turned and walked slowly. He heard people laughing. Dave glared, his eyes welling with tears. Hot anger bubbled in him. Then he swallowed and stumbled on.

That night Dave did not sleep. He was glad that he had gotten out of killing the mule so easily, but he was hurt. Something hot seemed to turn over inside him each time he remembered how they had laughed. He tossed on his bed, feeling his hard pillow. N Pa says he's gonna beat me. . . . He remembered other beatings, and his back quivered. Naw, naw, Ah sho don wan im t beat me tha way no mo. . . . Dam em all! Nobody ever gave him anything. All he did was work. They treat me like a mule. . . . N then they beat me. . . . He gritted his teeth. Ma had t tell on me.

Well, if he had to, he would take old man Hawkins that two dollars. But that meant selling the gun. And he wanted to keep that gun. Fifty dollahs fer a dead mule.

He turned over, thinking how he had fired the gun. He had an itch to fire it again. Ef other men kin shoota gun, by Gawd, Ah kin! He was still listening. Mebbe they all sleepin now. . . . The house was still. He heard the soft breathing of his brother. Yes, now! He would go down and get that gun and see if he could fire it! He eased out of bed and slipped into overalls.

The moon was bright. He ran almost all the way to the edge of the woods. He stumbled over the ground, looking for the spot where he had buried the gun. Yeah, here it is. Like a hungry dog scratching for a bone he pawed it up. He puffed his black cheeks and blew dirt from the trigger and barrel. He broke it and found four cartridges unshot. He looked around; the fields were filled with silence and moonlight. He clutched the gun stiff and hard in his fingers. But as soon as he wanted to pull the trigger, he shut his eyes and turned his head. Naw, Ah can't shoot wid mah eyes closed n mah head turned. With effort he held his eyes open; then he squeezed. Blooooom! He was stiff, not breathing. The gun was still in his hands. Dammit, he'd done it! He fired again. Blooo- oom! He smiled. Blooooom! Blooooom! Click, click. There! It was empty. If anybody could shoot a gun, he could. He put the gun into his hip pocket and started across the fields.

When he reached the top of a ridge he stood straight and proud in the moonlight, looking at Jim Hawkins' big white house, feeling the gun sagging in his pocket. Lawd, ef Ah had jus one mo bullet Ahd taka shot at tha house. Ahd like t scare ol man Hawkins jussa little. . . . Jussa enough t let im know Dave Sanders is a man.

To his left the road curved, running to the tracks of the Illinois Central. He jerked his head, listening. From far off came a faint hoooof- hoooof; hoooof-hoooof; hoooof-hoooof . . . That's number eight. He took a swift look at Jim Hawkins' white house; he thought of pa, of ma, of his little brother, and the boys. He thought of the dead mule and heard hoooof- hoooof; hoooof-hoooof; hoooof-hoooof . . . He stood rigid. Two dollas a mont. Les see now . . . Tha means itll take bout two years. Shucks! Ahll be dam!

He started down the road, toward the tracks.

Yeah, here she comes! He stood beside the track and held himself stiffly. Here she comes, erroun the ben. . . . C mon, yuh slow poke! C mon! He had his hand on his gun; something quivered in his stomach. Then the train thundered past, the gray and brown box cars rumbling and clinking. He gripped the gun tightly; then he jerked his hand out of his pocket. Ah betcha Bill wouldn't do it! Ah betcha. . . . The cars slid past, steel grinding upon steel. Ahm riding yuh ternight so hep me Gawd! He was hot all over. He hesitated just a moment; then he grabbed, pulled atop of a car, and lay flat. He felt his pocket; the gun was still there. Ahead the long rails were glinting in moonlight, stretching away, away to somewhere, somewhere where he could be a man. . . .

FOR ANALYSIS

1. How would the young hero of this story define a "man"?

2. What does the gun symbolize to the boy? How much of this does he consciously realize?

3. Is the dialect necessary here?

SHIRLEY ANN GRAU

The Black Prince

"How art thou fallen from heaven,
O Lucifer, son of the morning!"

Winters are short and very cold; sometimes there is even a snow like heavy frost on the ground. Summers are powdery hot; the white ball sun goes rolling around and around in a sky behind the smoke from the summer fires. There is always a burning somewhere in sum- mer; the pines are dry and waiting; the sun itself starts the smoldering. A pine fire is quiet; there is only a kind of rustle from the flames inside the trunks until the branches and needles go up with a whistling. A whole hill often burns that way, its smoke rising straight up to the white sun, and quiet.

In the plowed patches, green things grow quickly: the ground is rich and there are under- ground rivers. But there are no big farms: only patches of corn, green beans, and a field or two of cotton (grown for a little cash to spend on Saturdays at Luther's General Store or Willie's Café; these are the only two places for forty miles in any direction). There is good pasture: the green places along the hillsides with pines for shade and sure water in the streams that come down from the Smokies to the north; even in the burnt-out land of five seasons back, shrubs are high. But in the whole county there are only fifty cows, gone wild most of them and dry because they were never milked. They are afraid of men and feed in the farthest ridges and the swamps that are the bottoms of some littlest of the valleys. Their numbers are slowly increasing because no one bothers them. Only once in a while some man with a hankering for cow meat takes his rifle and goes after them. But that is not often; the people prefer pork. Each family keeps enough razorbacks in a run of bark palings.

It is all colored people here, and it is the poorest part of the smallest and worst county in the state. The place at the end of the dirt road leading from the state highway, the place where Luther's Store and Willie's Café stand, does not even have a name in the county records.

The only cool time of the summer day is very early, before the mists have shriveled away. There is a breeze then, a good stiff one out of the Smokies. During the day there is no sound: it is dead hot. But in the early mornings, when the breeze from the north is blowing, it is not so lonesomely quiet: crickets and locusts and the birds that flutter about hunting them, calling frantically as if they had something of importance to settle quick before the heat sets in. (By seven they are quiet again, in the invisible places they have chosen to wait out the day.)

A pine cone rattled down on Alberta's head and bounced from her shoulder. She scooped it from the ground and threw it upward through the branches. "You just keep your cone, mister birds. I got no cause to want it." With a pumping of wings the birds were gone, their cries sliding after them, back down the air. "You just yell your head off. I can hit you any time I want. Any time I want." There was a small round piece of granite at her feet and she tossed it, without particular aim, into the biggest of the bay trees: a gray squirrel with a thin rattail tumbled from the branches and peeped at her from behind the

trunk with a pointed little rat face. She jammed her hands in the pockets of her dress and went on, swaggering slightly, cool and feeling good.

She was a handsome girl, taller than most people in her part of the county, and light brown —there had been a lot of white blood in her family, back somewhere, they'd forgot where exactly. She was not graceful—not as a woman is —but light on her feet and supple as a man. Her dress, which the sun had bleached to a whitish color, leaving only a trace of pink along the seams, had shrunk out of size for her: it pulled tight across her broad, slightly hunched, muscled back, even though she had left all the front buttons open down to the waist.

As she walked along, the birds were making even more of a row, knocking loose cones and dry pine needles and old broad bay leaves, and twice she stopped, threw back her head, and called up to them: "Crazy fool birds. Can't do nothing to me. Fool jackass birds." Up ahead, a couple of minutes' walk, was the field and the cotton, bursting white out of the brown cups and waiting to be picked. And she did not feel like working. She leaned against a tree, stretching so that the bark crumbled in her fingers, listening to the birds.

Something different was in their calling. She listened, her head bent forward, her eyes closed, as she sorted the sounds. One jay was wrong: its long sustained note ended with the cluck of a quail. No bird did that. Alberta opened her eyes and looked slowly around. But the pines were thick and close and full of blue night shadow and wrapped with fog that moved like bits of cloth in the wind. Leaving the other birdcalls, the whistle became distinct, high, soaring, mocking, like some rare bird, proudly, insolently.

Alberta moved a few steps out from the tree and turned slowly on her heels. The whistle was going around her now, in slow circles, and she turned with it, keeping her eye on the sound, seeing nothing. The birds were still calling and fluttering in the branches, sending bits of twig and bark tumbling down.

Alberta said: "A fool thing you doing. A crazy fool jackass thing." She sat down on a tumbled pile of bricks that had been the chimney of a sugarhouse burned during the Civil War. She spoke in her best tone, while the whistling went round and round her faster. "I reckon you got nothing better to do than go around messing up folks. You got me so riled up I don't reckon I know what way I'm heading in." The sound went around her and around her, but she held her head steady, talking to the pine directly in front of her. "I don't reckon there's nothing for me but set here till you tires out and goes away." The whistle circled her twice and then abruptly stopped, the last high clear note running off down the breeze. Alberta stood up, pulling down her faded dress. "I am mighty glad you come to stopping. I reckon now I can tell what direction I got to go in."

He was right there, leaning on the same pine she had been staring at, cleaning his front teeth with a little green twig and studying her, and she told him to his face: "That was a crazy mean thing, and you ain't got nothing better to do."

"Reckon not," he said, moving the little green twig in and out of the hole between his lower front teeth.

She pushed her hands in the pockets of her dress and looked him over. "Where you come from?"

"Me?" The little green twig went in and out of his teeth with each breath. "I just come straight out the morning."

She turned and walked away. "I be glad to see you go."

He stood in front of her: he had a way of moving without a sound, of popping up in places. "I be sorry to see you go, Alberta Lacy."

She studied him before she answered: tall, not too big or heavy, and black (no other blood but his own in him, she thought). He was dressed nice—a leather jacket with fringe on the sleeves, a red plaid shirt, and new blue denim pants. "How you know what I'm called?" she asked him politely.

He grinned, and his teeth were white and perfect. "I done seen it in the fire," he said. "I done seen it in the fire and I read it clear: Alberta Lacy."

She frowned. "I don't see as how I understand."

He blew the little green twig out of his mouth. "I might could be seeing you again real soon, Alberta Lacy." Then he slipped around the tree like the last trail of night shadow and disappeared.

Alberta stood listening: only the birds and the insects and the wind. Then everything got quiet, and the sun was shining white all around, and she climbed down the slope to the field.

A little field—just a strip of cotton tucked in between two ridges. Her father and her two biggest brothers had planted it with half a morning's work, and they hadn't gone back to tend it once. They didn't even seem to remember it: whatever work they did was in the older fields closer to home. So Alberta had taken it over. Sometimes she brought along the twins: Sidney and Silvia; they were seven: young enough for her to order around and big enough to be a help. But usually she couldn't find them; they were strange ones, gone out of the house for a couple of days at a time in summer, sleeping out somewhere, always sticking together. They were strange little ones and not worth trouble looking for. So most times Alberta worked with Maggie Mary Evans, who was Josh Evans's daughter and just about the only girl her age she was friendly with. From the field there'd be maybe three bales of real early stuff; and they'd split the profit. They worked all morning, pulling off the bolls and dropping them in the sacks they slung crosswise across their shoulders. They worked very slowly, so slowly that at times their hands seemed hardly to move, dozing in the heat. When it got to be noon, when they had no shadow any more, they slipped off the sacks, leaving them between the furrows, and turned to the shade to eat their lunch.

He was waiting for them there, stretched out along the ground with his head propped up on the slender trunk of a little bay tree. He winked lazily at Alberta; his eyes were big and shiny black as oil. "How you, Miss Alberta Lacy?"

Alberta looked down at him, crooking her lips. "You got nothing to do but pester me?"

"Sure I got something to do, but ain't nothing nice like this."

Alberta looked at him through half-closed lids, then sat down to the lunch.

"You hungry, mister?" Maggie Mary asked. She had stood watching, both hands jammed into the belt of her dress, and her eyes moving from one to the other with the quickness and the color of a sparrow.

The man rolled over and looked up at her. "Reckon I am."

"You can have some of our lunch," Maggie Mary said.

Crazy fool, Alberta thought, standing so close with him on the ground like that. He must can see all the way up her. And from the way he lay there, grinning, he must be enjoying it.

"That real nice," he said to Maggie Mary, and crawled over on his stomach to where the lunch bucket was.

Alberta watched his smooth, black hand reaching into the bucket and suddenly she remembered. "How you called?"

He put a piece of corn bread in his mouth, chewed it briefly, and swallowed it with a gulp. "I got three names."

"No fooling," Maggie Mary said, and giggled in her hand. "I got three names, too."

"Stanley Albert Thompson."

"That a good-sounding name," Alberta said. She began to eat her lunch quickly, her mouth too full to talk. Stanley Albert was staring at her, but she didn't raise her eyes. Then he began to sing, low, pounding time with the flat of his hand against the ground.

> *"Alberta, let you hair hang low,*
> *Alberta, let you hair hang low,*
> *I'll give you more gold than you apron can hold*
> *If you just let you hair hang low."*

Alberta got up slowly, not looking at him. "We got work to finish."

Stanley Albert turned over so that his face was pressed in the grass and pine needles. "All you get's the muscles in you arm."

"That right." Maggie Mary nodded quickly. "That right."

"Maggie Mary," Alberta said, "iffen you don't come with me I gonna bop you so hard you land in the middle of tomorrow."

"Goodby, Mr. Stanley Albert Thompson," Maggie Mary said, but he had fallen asleep.

By the time they finished work he was gone; there wasn't even a spot in the pine needles and short grass to show where he had been.

"Ain't that the strangest thing?" Maggie Mary said.

Alberta picked up the small bucket they carried their lunch in. "I reckon not."

"Seemed like he was fixing to wait for us."

"He ain't fixing to wait for nobody, that kind." Alberta rubbed one hand across her shoulders, sighing slightly. "I got a pain fit to kill."

Maggie Mary leaned one arm against a tree and looked off across the little field where they had spent the day. "You reckon he was in here most all morning watching us?"

"Maybe." Alberta began to walk home. Maggie Mary followed slowly, her head still turned, watching the field.

"He musta spent all morning just watching."

"Nothing hard about doing that, watching us break our back out in the sun."

Maggie Mary took one long, loping step and came up with Alberta. "You reckon he coming back?"

Alberta stared full at her, head bent, chewing on her lower lip. "Maggie Mary Evans," she said, "you might could get a thought that he might be wanting you and you might could get a thought that you be wanting him—"

Maggie Mary bent down and brushed the dust off her bare feet carefully, not answering.

"You a plain crazy fool." Alberta planted both hands on her hips and bent her body forward slightly. "A plain crazy fool. You wouldn't be forgetting Jay Mastern?" Jay Mastern had gone off to Ramsey to work at the mill and never come back, but left Maggie Mary to have his baby. So one day Maggie Mary took her pa's best mule and put a blanket on it for a saddle and rode over to Blue Goose Lake, where the old woman lived who could tell her what to do. The old woman gave her medicine in a beer can: whisky and calomel and other things that were a secret. Maggie Mary took the medicine in one gulp, because it tasted so bad, waded way out into Blue Goose Lake so that the water came up to her neck, then dripping wet got up on the mule and whipped him up to a good fast pace all the way home. The baby had come off all right: there wasn't one. And Maggie Mary nearly died. It was something on to three months before she was able to do more than walk around, her arms hanging straight down and stiff and black skin overtinged with gray.

"You wouldn't be forgetting Jay Mastern?"

"Sure," Maggie Mary said, brushing the dust off her bare feet lightly. "I clean forgot about him."

"Don't you be having nothing to do with this here Stanley Albert Thompson."

Maggie Mary began to walk again, slowly, smiling just a little bit with one corner of her mouth. "Sounds like you been thinking about him for yourself."

Alberta jammed both hands down in the

pockets of her dress. "I been thinking nothing of the sort."

"Willie'll kill him."

Alberta chewed on one finger. "I reckon he could care for himself."

Maggie Mary smiled to herself softly, remembering. "I reckon he could; he's real fine-appearing man."

"He was dressed good."

"Where you reckon he come from?" Maggie Mary asked.

Alberta shrugged. "He just come walking out of the morning fog."

That was how he came into this country: he appeared one day whistling a birdcall in the woods in high summer. And he stayed on. The very first Saturday night he went down to Willie's and had four fights and won them all.

Willie's was an ordinary house made of pine slabs, older than most of the other houses, but more solid. There were two rooms: a little one where Willie lived (a heavy scrolled ironwork bed, a square oak dresser, a chest, a three-footed table, and on its cracked marble top a blue-painted mandolin without strings). And a big room: the café. Since anybody could remember, the café had been there with Willie's father or his grandfather, as long as there had been people in these parts. And that had been a long while: long before the Civil War even, runaways were settling here, knowing they'd be safe and hidden in the rough, uneven hills and the pines.

Willie had made some changes in the five or six years since his father died. He painted the counter that was the bar with varnish; that had not been a good idea: the whisky took the varnish off in a few weeks. And he painted the walls: bright blue. Then he went over them again, shaking his brush so that the walls were flecked like a mockingbird's eggs. But Willie used red to fleck—red against blue. And the mirror, gilt-edged, and hanging from a thick gold cord: that had been Willie's idea, too. He'd found it one day, lying on the shoulder alongside the state highway; it must have fallen from a truck somehow. So he took it home. It was cracked in maybe two dozen pieces. Anyone who looked into it would see his face split up into a dozen different parts, all separate. But Willie hung it right over the shelves where he kept his whisky and set one of the kerosene lamps in front of it so that the light should reflect yellow-

bright from all the pieces. One of them fell out (so that Willie had to glue it back with flour and water) the night Stanley Albert had his fourth fight, which he won like the other three. Not a man in the country would stand up like that, because fighting at Willie's on Saturday night is a rough affair with razors, or knives, or bottles.

Not a man in the country could have matched the way Stanley Albert fought that night, his shirt off, and his black body shining with sweat, the muscles along his neck and shoulders twisting like grass snakes. There wasn't a finer-looking man and there wasn't a better: he proved that.

The first three fights were real orderly affairs. Everybody could see what was coming minutes ahead, and Willie got the two of them out in the yard before they got at each other. And everybody who was sober enough to walk went out on the porch and watched Stanley Albert pound first Ran Carey's and then Henry Johnson's head up and down in the dust. Alberta sat on the porch (Willie had brought her a chair from inside) and watched Stanley Albert roll around the dust of the yard and didn't even blink an eye, not even during the third fight when Tim Evans, who was Maggie Mary's brother, pull a razor. The razor got Stanley Albert all down one cheek, but Tim didn't have any teeth left and one side of his face got punched in so that it looked peculiar always afterward. Maggie Mary went running down into the yard, not bothering with her brother, to press her finger up against the little cut across Stanley Albert's cheek.

The fourth fight came up so suddenly nobody had time hardly to get out of the way: Joe Turner got one arm hooked around Stanley Albert's neck from behind. There wasn't any reason for it, except maybe that Joe was so drunk he didn't see who he had and that once there's been a couple of fights there's always more. Stanley Albert swung a bottle over his shoulder to break the hold and then nobody could see exactly what was happening: they were trying so hard to get clear. Willie pulled Alberta over the bar and pushed her down behind it and crouched alongside her, grinning. "That some fighter." And when it was all over they stood up again; first thing they saw was Joe Turner down on the floor and Stanley Albert leaning on a chair with Maggie dabbing at a cut on his hand with the edge of her petticoat.

He got a reputation from that Saturday night, and everybody was polite to him, and he could have had just about any of the girls he wanted. But he didn't seem to want them; at least he never took to coming to the houses to see them or to taking them home from Willie's. Maggie Mary Evans swore up and down that he had got her one day when she was fishing in Scanos River, but nobody paid her much attention. She liked to make up stories that way.

He had a little house in a valley to the east. Some boys who had gone out to shoot a cow for Christmas meat said they saw it. But they didn't go close even if there was three of them with a shotgun while Stanley Albert only carried a razor. Usually people only saw him on Saturday nights, and after a while they got used to him, though none of the men ever got to be friendly with him. There wasn't any mistaking the way the girls watched him. But after four or five Saturdays, by the time the summer was over, everybody expected him and waited for him, the way you'd wait for a storm to come or a freeze; not liking it, but not being able to do anything either. That's the way it went along: he'd buy his food for the coming week at Luther's Store, and then he'd come next door to Willie's.

He never stood up at the counter that was the bar. He'd take his glass and walk over to a table and sit down, and pull out a little bottle from his pocket, and add white lightning to the whisky. There wasn't anything could insult Willie more. He made the whisky and it was the best stuff in the county. He even had some customers drive clear out from Montgomery to buy some of his corn, and, being good stuff, there wasn't any call to add anything: it had enough kick of its own; raw and stinging to the throat. It was good stuff; nobody added anything to it—except Stanley Albert Thompson, while Willie looked at him and said things under his breath. But nothing ever came of it, because everybody remembered how good a job Stanley Albert had done the first night he came.

Stanley Albert always had money, enough of it to pay for the groceries and all the whisky he wanted. There was always the sound of silver jingling in his trouser pocket. Everybody could hear that. Once when Willie was standing behind the bar, shuffling a pack of cards with a wide fancy twirl—just for amusement—Stanley Albert, who had had a couple of drinks and was feeling especially good, got up and pulled a handful of coins out of his pocket. He began to shuffle them through the air, the way Willie had done

with the cards. Stanley Albert's black hands flipped the coins back and forth, faster and faster, until there was a solid silver ring hanging and shining in the air. Then Stanley Albert let one of his hands drop to his side and the silver ring poured back into the other hand and disappeared with a little clinking sound. And he dropped the money into his pocket with a short quick laugh.

That was the way Stanley Albert used his money: he had fun with it. Only thing, one night when Stanley Albert had had maybe a bit too much and sat dozing at his table, Morris Henry slipped a hand into the pocket. He wouldn't have ever dared to do that if Stanley Albert hadn't been dozing, leaning back in his chair, the bottle of white lightning empty in one hand. And Morris Henry slipped his little hand in the pocket and felt all around carefully. Then he turned his head slowly in a circle, looking at everybody in the room. He was a little black monkey Negro and his eyes were shiny and flat as mirrors. He slipped his hand back and scurried out into the yard and hid in the blackberry bushes. He wouldn't move until morning came; he just sat there, chewing on his little black fingers with his wide flaring yellow teeth. Anybody who wanted to know what was happening had to go out there and ask him. And ever afterwards Morris Henry swore that there hadn't been anything at all in Stanley Albert Thompson's pocket. But then everybody knew Morris Henry was crazy because just a few minutes later when Stanley Albert woke up and walked across to the bar, the change jingled in the pocket and he laid five quarters on the counter. And the money was good enough because Willie bounced it on the counter and it gave the clear ring of new silver.

Stanley Albert had money all right and he spent it; there wasn't anything short about him. He'd buy drinks for anybody who'd come over to his table; the only ones who came were the girls. And he didn't seem to care how much they drank. He'd just sit there, leaning way back in his chair, grinning, his teeth white and big behind his black lips, and matching them drink for drink, and every now and then running his eye up and down their length just to let them know he was appreciating their figures. Most often it was Maggie Mary who would be sitting there, warning all the other girls away with a little slanting of her eyes when they got near. And sometimes he'd sing a song: a song about whisky that would make everyone forget they didn't like him and laugh; or a song about poor boys who were going to be hanged in the morning. He had a good voice, strong and clear, and he pounded time with the flat of his hand on the table. And he'd always be looking at Alberta when he was singing until she'd get up, holding her head high and stiff, and march over to where Willie was and take hold of his arm real sweet and smile at him. And Willie would give Stanley Albert a quick mean look and then pour her a drink of his best whisky.

Stanley Albert had a watch, a big heavy gold one, round almost as a tomato, that would strike the hours. (That was how you could tell he was around sometimes—hearing his watch strike.) It was attached to a broad black ribbon and sometimes he held it up, let it swing before the eyes of whatever girl it happened to be at the time, let it swing slowly back and forth, up and down, so that her head moved with it. He had a ring too, on his right little finger: a white-colored band with a stone big as a chip of second coal and dark green. And when he fought, the first time he came into Willie's, the ring cut the same as a razor in his hand; it was maybe a little more messy, because its edges were jagged.

Those were two things—the watch and the ring—that must have cost more than all the money around here in a year. That was why all the women liked him so; they kept thinking of the nice things he could give them if he got interested. And that was why the men hated him. Things can go as smooth as glass if everybody's got about the same things and the same amount of money knocking around in a jean pocket on Saturday night. But when they don't, things begin happening. It would have been simpler maybe if they could have fought Stanley Albert Thompson, but there wasn't any man keen to fight him. That was how they started fighting each other. A feud that nobody'd paid any mind to for eight or ten years started up again.

It began one Sunday morning along toward dawn when everyone was feeling tired and leaving Willie's. Stanley Albert had gone out first and was sitting aside the porch railing. Jim Mastern was standing on the lowest step not moving, just staring across the fields, not being able to see anything in the dark, except may be the bright-colored patterns the whisky set shooting starwise before his eyes. And Randall Stevens was standing in the doorway, looking down at his own foot, which he kept moving in a little circle around and around on the floor boards. And Stanley Albert was looking hard at him. Randall Stevens didn't lift his head; he just had his razor out and was across the porch in one minute, bringing down his arm in a sweeping motion to get at Jim Mastern's neck. But he was too drunk to aim very straight and he missed; but he did cut the ear away so that it fell on the steps. Jim Mastern was off like a bat in the daylight, running fast, crashing into things, holding one hand to the side of his head. And Randall Stevens folded up the razor and slipped it back in his pocket and walked off slowly, his head bent over, as if he was sleepy. There wasn't any more sense to it than that; but it started the feud again.

Stanley Albert swung his legs over the railing and stretched himself and yawned. Nobody noticed except Alberta, they were so busy listening to the way Jim Mastern was screaming and running across the fields, and watching Randall Stevens march off, solemnly, like a priest.

And the next night Randall Stevens tumbled down the steps of his cabin with his head full of scatter shot. It was a Monday night in November. His mother came out to see and stepped square on him, and his blood spattered on the hoarfrost. Randall Stevens had six brothers, and the next night they rode their lanky burred horses five miles south and tried to set fire to the Mastern house. That was the beginning; the fighting kept up, off and on, all through the winter. The sheriff from Gloverston came down to investigate. He came driving down the road in the new shiny white state police patrol car— the only one in the county—stopped in Willie's Café for a drink and went back taking two gallons of home brew with him. That wasn't exactly right, maybe, seeing that he had taken an oath to uphold the law; but he couldn't have done much, except get killed. And that was certain.

The Stevenses and their friends took to coming to Willie's on Friday nights; the Masterns kept on coming on Saturday. That just made two nights Willie had to keep the place open and the lamps filled with kerosene; the crowd was smaller; shotguns were leaning against the wall.

That's the way it went all winter. Everybody got on one side or the other—everybody except Stanley Albert Thompson. They both wanted him: they had seen what he could do in a fight.

But Stanley Albert took to coming a night all by himself: Sunday night, and Willie had to light all the lamps for just him and stand behind the counter and watch him sit at the table adding lightning to the whisky.

Once along toward the end of February when Cy Mastern was killed and the roof of his house started burning with pine knots tossed from the ground, Stanley Albert was standing just on the rim of the light, watching. He helped the Masterns carry water, but Ed Stevens, who was hiding up in top of a pine to watch, swore that the water was like kerosene in his hands. Wherever he'd toss a bucketful, the fire would shoot up, brighter and hotter than before.

By March the frosts stopped, and there weren't any more cold winds. The farmers came out every noon, solemnly, and laid their hands on the bare ground to see if it was time to put in their earliest corn and potatoes. But the ground stayed cold a long time that year so that there wasn't any plowing until near May. All during that time from March till May there wasn't anything doing; that was the worst time for the fighting. In the winter your hand shakes so with the cold that you aren't much good with a gun or knife. But by March the air is warmer and you don't have any work to get you tired, so you spend all the time thinking.

That spring things got bad. There wasn't a crowd any more at Willie's though he kept the place open and the lights on for the three nights of the weekend. Neither the Stevenses nor the Masterns would come; they were too easy targets in a house with wall lamps burning. And on Sunday night the only person who ever came was Stanley Albert Thompson. He'd sit and drink his whisky and lightning and maybe sing a song or two for the girls who came over to see him. By the end of April that was changed too. He finally got himself the girl he wanted; the one he'd been waiting around nearly all winter for. And his courting was like this:

Thomas Henry Lacy and his sons, Luke and Tom, had gone for a walk, spoiling for a fight. They hadn't seen anything all evening, just some of the cows that had gone wild and went crashing away through the blueberry bushes. Alberta had taken herself along with them, since she was nearly as good as a man in a fight. They had been on the move all night but keeping in the range of a couple of miles and on the one side of the Scanos River. They were for Stevens and

there was no telling what sort of affair the Masterns had rigged up on their ground. They rested for a while on the bluff of the river. Tom had some bread in his pocket and they ate it there, wondering if there was anybody in the laurels across the river just waiting for them to show themselves. Then they walked on again, not saying very much, seeing nothing but the moon flat against the sky and its light shiny on the heavy dew.

Alberta didn't particularly care when they left her behind. She turned her head to listen to the plaintive gargling call of a night quail, and when she looked again her father and the boys were gone. She knew where she was: on the second ridge away from home. There was just the big high ridge there to the left. The house was maybe twenty minutes away, but a hard walk, and Alberta was tired. She'd been washing all day, trying to make the clear brook water carry off the dirt and grease from the clothes, her mother standing behind her, yelling at each spot that remained, her light face black almost as her husband's with temper, and her gray fuzzy hair tied into knots like a pickaninny's. The boys had spent the whole day dozing in the shed while they put a new shoe on the mule.

Alberta listened carefully; there was nothing but night noises; her father and the boys would be halfway home by now, scrambling down the rain-washed sides of the ridge. For a moment she considered following them. "Ain't no raving rush, girl," she told herself aloud. The night was cool, but there wasn't any wind. With her bare feet she felt the dry pine needles, then sat down on them, propping her back against a tree. She slipped the razor from the cord around her neck and held it open loosely in the palm of her hand; then she fell asleep.

She woke when the singing started, opening her eyes but not moving. The moon was right overhead, shining down so that the trunks of the pines stuck straight up out of the white shiny ground. There wasn't a man could hide behind a pine, yet she didn't see him. Only the singing going round and round her.

"*Alberta, what's on you mind,*
Alberta, why you treat me so unkind?
You keep me worried; you keep me blue
All the time,
Alberta, why you treat me so unkind?"

She pushed herself up to a sitting position, still looking straight ahead, not following the song around and around. She let the hand that held the razor fall in her lap, so that the moon struck on the blade.

"Alberta, why you treat me so unkind?"

Nothing grows under pines, not much grass even, not any bushes big enough to hide a man. Only pine trees, like black matches stuck in the moonlight. Black like matches, and thin like matches. There wasn't a man could hide behind a pine under a bright moon. There wasn't a man could pass a bright open space and not be seen.

"Alberta, let you hair hang low,
Alberta, let you hair hang low.
I'll give you more gold
Than you apron can hold."

"That ain't a very nice song," she said.

"I'll give you more gold
Than you apron can hold."

She lifted her right hand and turned the razor's edge slowly in the light. "I got silver of my own right here," she said. "That enough for me."
The song went round in a circle, round and round, weaving in and out of the pines, passing invisible across the open moon filled spaces.

"Alberta, let you hair hang low,
I'll give you more gold
Than you apron can hold
If you just let you hair hang low."

There wasn't a man alive could do that. Go round and round.

"Alberta, why you treat me so unkind?"

Round and round, in and out the thin black trees. Alberta stood up, following the sound, turning on her heel.

"You keep me worried, you keep me blue
All the time."

"I plain confused," she said. "I don't reckon I understand."

"I'll give you more gold
Than you apron can hold."

"I ain't got no apron," she said.

"Alberta, let you hair hang low,
Just let you hair hang low."

The song stopped and Stanley Albert Thompson came right out of a patch of bright moon ground, where there were only brown pine needles.
Alberta forgot she was tired; the moon-spotted ground rolled past her feet like the moon in the sky—effortless. She recognized the country they passed through: Blue Goose Lake, Scanos River, and the steeper rough ground of the north part of the country, toward the Tennessee border. It was a far piece to walk and she wondered at the lightness of her feet. By moonset they had got there—the cabin that the boys had seen one day while they were hunting cows. She hesitated a little then, not afraid, not reluctant, but just not sure how to go on. Stanley Albert Thompson had been holding her hand all evening; he still held it. Right at the beginning when he had first taken her along with him, she'd shook her head, no, she could walk; no man needed to lead her. But he'd grinned at her, and shook his head, imitating her gesture, so that the moon sparkled on his black curly hair, and his black broad forehead, and he took her hand and led her so that the miles seemed nothing and the hours like smooth water.
He showed her the cabin, from the outside first: mustard color, trimmed with white, like the cabins the railroad company builds. One room with high peaked roof.
"A real fine house," she said. "A real fine house. You work for the railroad?"
"No."
He took her inside. "You light with candles," she said.
"I ain't ever been able to stand the smell of lamps," he said.
"But it's a real nice house. I might could learn to like it."
"No might could about it." He smoothed the

cloth on the table with his fingers. "You going to like it."

She bent her head and looked at him through her eyelashes. "Now I don't rightly know. Seems as how I don't know you."

"Sure you do," he said. "I'm standing right here."

"Seems as how I don't know nothing. You might could have a dozen girls all over this here state."

"I reckon there's a dozen," he said.

She glared at him, hands on hips. "You old fool jackass," she said. "I reckon you can just keep everything."

He jammed his hands into the back pockets of his denim pants and bent backward staring at the ceiling.

"Ain't you gonna try to stop me?"

"Nuh-uh."

She leaned against the doorjamb and twisted her neck to look at him. "Ain't you sorry I going?"

"Sure." He was still staring upward at the ceiling with its four crossed beams. "Sure, I real sorry."

"I don't see as how I could stay though."

"Sure you could." He did not look at her.

"I don't see as how. You ain't give me none of the things you said."

"You a driving woman," he said, and grinned, his mouth wide and white in the dark of his face.

Then he sat down at the table. There were five candles there, stuck in bottles, but only one was lighted, the one in the center. Wax had run all down the side of the candle and down the bottle in little round blobs, nubby like gravel. He picked one off, dirty white between his black fingers. He rolled it slowly between his flat palms, back and forth. Then he flipped it toward Alberta. It flashed silvery through the circle of lamplight and thudded against her skirt. She bent forward to pick it up: a coin, new silver. As she bent there, another one struck her shoulder, and another. Stanley Albert Thompson sat at the table, grinning and tossing the coins to her, until she had filled both pockets of her dress.

He pushed the candle away from him. "You all right, I reckon, now."

She held one coin in her hands, turning it over and over.

"That ain't what you promised. I remember how you came and sang:

'I give you more gold
Than you apron can hold.' "

"Sure," he said and lifted a single eyebrow, very high. "I can do that all right, iffen you want it. I reckon I can do that."

She stood for a moment studying him. And Stanley Albert Thompson, from where he still sat at the table, curled up one corner of his mouth.

And very slowly Alberta began to smile. "I might could like it here," she said. "If you was real nice."

He got up then and rubbed her cheek very gently with his first finger. "I might could do that," he said. "I don't reckon it would be too heavy a thing to do."

The candle was on the table to one side. It caught the brightness of Alberta's eyes as she stood smiling at Stanley Albert Thompson. The steady yellow light threw her shadow over his body, a dark shadow that reached to his chin. His own shadow was on the wall behind. She glanced at it over his shoulder and giggled. "You better do something about your shadow there, Mr. Thompson. That there is a ugly shadow, sure."

He turned his head and glanced at it briefly. "Reckon so," he said.

It was an ugly shadow, sure. Alberta looked at Stanley Albert Thompson and shook her head. "I can't hardly believe it," she said. "You a right pretty man."

He grinned at her and shook himself so that the shadow on the wall spun around in a wild turn.

"I don't reckon you can do anything about it"

"No," he said briefly. "I can't go changing my shadow." He hunched his back so that the figure on the wall seemed to jump up and down in anger.

She stepped over to him, putting her hands behind her, leaning backward to see his face. "If he don't do any more than dance on a wall, I ain't complaining."

Stanley Albert stood looking down at her, looking down the length of his face at her, and rocking slowly back and forth on his heels. "No," he said. "He ain't gonna do more than wiggle around the wall sometimes. But you can bet I am."

The coins weighed down the pockets of her dress, and his hands were warm against her skin. "I reckon I'm satisfied," she said.

That was the way it began. That was the court-ing. The woman was young and attractive and strong. The man could give her whatever she wanted. There were other courtings like that in this country. Every season there were courtings like that.

People would see them around sometimes; or sometimes they'd only hear them when they were still far off. Sometimes it would be Stanley Albert Thompson singing:

> "*Alberta, let you hair hang low,*
> *Alberta, let you hair hang low.*
> *I'll give you more gold*
> *Than you apron can hold*
> *If you just let you hair hang low.*"

He had a strong voice. It could carry far in a quiet day or night. And if any of the people heard it, they'd turn and look at each other and nod their heads toward it, not saying anything, but just being sure that everyone was listening. And whenever Willie heard it, he'd close his eyes for a minute, seeing Alberta; and then he'd rub his hands all over his little black kinky head and whistle: "Euuuu," which meant that he was very, very sorry she had left him.

And sometimes all you could hear of them would be the chiming of Stanley Albert's watch every quarter-hour. One night that August, when the moon was heavy and hot and low, Maggie Mary was out walking with Jack Belden. She heard the clear high chime and remembered the nights at Willie's and the dangling gold watch. And she turned to Jack Belden, who had just got her comfortable in one arm, and jammed her fingers in his eyes and ran off after the sound. She didn't find them; and it wouldn't have much mattered if she had. Stanley Albert was much too gone on Alberta to notice any other woman in more than a passing appraising way.

And sometimes people would come on them walking alone, arms around each other's waist; or sitting in a shady spot during the day's heat, his head on her lap and both of them dozing and smiling a little. And everybody who saw them would turn around and get out of there fast; but neither of them turned a head or looked up: there might not have been anyone there.

And then every night they'd go down to Willie's. The first night they came—it was on a Thursday—the place was closed up tight. There wasn't ever anybody came on Thursday. Stanley Albert went around back to where Willie lived and pounded on the door, and when Willie didn't answer he went around to the front again where Alberta was waiting on the steps and kicked in the front panel of the wood door. Willie came scuttling out, his eyes round and bewildered like a suckling's and saw them sitting at one of the tables drinking his home brew, only first putting lightning into it. After that they came every night, just them. It was all most people could do to afford a drink on Saturday or the weekend, but some of them would walk over to Willie's just to look at Stanley Albert and Alberta sitting there. They'd stand at the windows and look in, sweating in the hot summer nights and looking. Maybe a few of them would still be there waiting when Stanley and Alberta got ready to go, along toward morning.

That's what they did every single night of the year or so they were together. If they fell asleep, Willie would just have to stand waiting. They'd go out with their arms around each other's waist, staggering some, but not falling. And an hour or so later, people who were going out before dawn to get a little work done in the cool would see them clear over on the other side of the county, at Goose Lake, maybe, a good three hours' walk for a man cold sober. Willie had his own version of how they got around. They just picked up their feet, he said, and went sliding off down the winds. Once, he said, when they were sitting over on the bench against the wall, Stanley Albert flat on it with his head on her lap, when the whisky made the man in him come up sud-den, so he couldn't wait, they went straight out the window, up the air, like a whistle sound. Willie had the broken glass to show the next morning, if you wanted to believe him.

Willie hated them, the two of them, maybe because they broke his glass, maybe because they made him stay up late every single night of the week, so that he had to hold his eyes open with his fingers, and watch them pour lightning into his very best whisky, maybe because he had wanted Alberta mighty bad himself. He'd been giving her presents—bottles of his best stuff—but he just couldn't match Stanley Albert. Those are three reasons; maybe he had others. And Maggie Mary hated them; and she had only one reason.

Once Pete Stokes shot at Stanley Albert Thompson. He hadn't wanted to: he was scared like everybody else. But Maggie Mary Evans talked him into it. She was a fine-looking girl: she could do things like that. He hid behind the privy and got a perfect bead on Stanley Albert as he came out the door. The bullet just knocked off a piece of Willie's doorframe. When Pete saw what happened he dropped the gun and began to run, jumping the rail fence and crashing face-first through the thick heavy berry bushes. Stanley Albert pursed his lips together and rubbed his hands on his chin, slow, like he was deciding what to do. Then he jumped down from the porch and went after Pete. He ran through the hackberries too; only with him it did not seem difficult: none of the crackling and crashing and waving arms. Stanley Albert just put his head down and moved his legs, and the sprays of the bushes, some of them thick as a rooster's spur, seemed to pull back and make way. Nobody saw the fight: the brave ones were too drunk to travel fast; and the sober ones didn't want to mix with a man like Stanley Albert, drunk and mad. Alberta, she just ran her hand across her mouth and then wiped it along the side of her green satin dress, yawning like she was tired. She stood listening for a while, her head cocked a little, though there wasn't anything to hear, then walked off, pulling down the dress across her hips. And the next night she and Stanley Albert were back at Wille's, and Pete never did turn up again. Willie used to swear that he ended up in the Scanos River and that if the water wasn't so yellow muddy, that if you could see to the bottom, you would see Pete lying there, along with all the others Stanley Albert had killed.

At the last it was Willie who got the idea. For a week, carefully, he put aside the coins Stanley Albert gave him. There were a lot of them, all new silver, because Stanley Albert always paid in silver. Then one morning very early, just after Stanley Albert and Alberta left, Willie melted the coins down, and using the molds he kept for his old outsized pistol, he cast four bullets.

He made a special little shelf for the pistol under the counter so that it would be near at hand. And he waited all evening, sometimes touching the heavy black handle with the tips of his fingers; and he waited, hoping that Stanley Albert would drink enough to pass out. But of course nothing like that happened. So Willie poured himself three or four fingers of his best stuff and swallowed it fast as his throat would

stand, then he blinked his little eyes fast for a second or so to clear his vision, and he reached for the gun. He got two shots over the bar, two good ones: the whole front of Stanley Albert's plaid shirt folded together and sank in, after the silver bullets went through. He got up, holding the table edge, unsteady, bending over, looking much smaller, his black skin gray-filmed and dull. His eyes were larger: they reached almost across his face—and they weren't dark any more; they were silver, two polished pieces of silver. Willie was afraid to fire again; the pistol shook where he held it in his two hands.

Then Stanley Albert walked out, not unsteady any more, but bent over the hole in his chest, walked out slowly with his eyes shining like flat metal, Alberta a few steps behind. They passed right in front of Willie, who still hadn't moved; his face was stiff with fear. Quietly, smoothly, in a single motion, almost without interrupting her step, Alberta picked up a bottle (the same one from which he had poured his drink moments before) and swung it against Willie's head. He slipped down in a quiet little heap, his legs folded under him, his black kinky head on top. But his idea had worked: over by Stanley Albert's chair there was a black pool of blood.

All that was maybe eight or ten years ago. People don't see them any more—Stanley and Alberta. They don't think much about them, except when something goes wrong—like weevils getting in the cotton, or Willie's burning down and Willie inside it—then they begin to think that those two had a hand in it. Brad Tedrow swore that he had seen Stanley Albert that night, just for a second, standing on the edge of the circle of light, with a burning faggot in his hand. And the next morning Brad went back to look, knowing that your eyes play tricks at night in firelight; he went back to look for footprints or some sign. All he found was a burnt-out stick of pine wood that anybody could have dropped.

And kids sometimes think they hear the jingle of silver in Stanley Albert's pocket, or the sound of his watch. And when women talk—when there's been a miscarriage or a stillbirth—they remember and whisper together.

And they all wonder if that's not the sort of work they do, the two of them. Maybe so; maybe not. The people themselves are not too sure. They don't see them around any more.

FOR ANALYSIS

1. This isn't a parable or an allegory or a ghost story, although it has elements of all of them. It does, however, have a theme. Try to abstract that theme by answering these questions:

   a. Who is the man with three names, Stanley Albert Thompson? His name is a kind of anagram. What are his three other names?

   b. Why does the author pick such a setting in which to introduce the Black Prince?

   c. Who narrates the story?

   d. What does the story say about the nature of evil?

POETRY

An Introduction

Poetry is the most highly organized and compressed form of expression. Because every word in a poem must contribute a greater weight of meaning than in prose, a poet must always assume that what does not positively add to his effect detracts from it. Therefore, every word in a poem must justify its existence or be eliminated.

Because a poem must be so compact, it is very dependent upon conventions. The following poem, a highly organized experience, illustrates how poetic conventions help to satisfy the reader's need for order.

JOHN KEATS

On First Looking into Chapman's Homer

Much have I travelled in the realms of gold,	*a*
And many goodly states and kingdoms seen;	*b*
Round many western islands have I been	*b*
Which bards in fealty to Apollo hold.	*a*
Oft of one wide expanse had I been told	*a*
That deep-browed Homer ruled as his demesne;	*b*
Yet did I never breathe its pure serene	*b*
Till I heard Chapman speak out loud and bold:	*a*
Then felt I like some watcher of the skies	*c*
When a new planet swims into his ken;	*d*
Or like stout Cortez when with eagle eyes	*c*
He stared at the Pacific—and all his men	*d*
Looked at each other with a wild surmise—	*c*
Silent, upon a peak in Darien.	*d*

This poem, written by John Keats when he was 21, expresses his surprise and delight at first reading George Chapman's translation of Homer's *Iliad*. Keats could not read Greek; other translations of Homer had not inspired him. Chapman's translation illuminated for him the greatness and the beauty of Homer. There is the

123

real experience, which sounds flat, badly stated, as do all summaries or paraphrases of works of art. It is Keats's problem to communicate that experience so that it seems urgent and important. He does this by organizing it. To organize, the writer must arrange the subject matter in a certain order, compare it with something else, or use both methods. (Notice how the methods of the scientist and the artist are identical in this respect.) Keats does both.

First, he employs several conventions. He chooses a highly organized and very familiar form for his poem—the Italian sonnet, a poem composed of fourteen lines which divide into two units of eight (the octave) and six (the sestet). The first eight rhyme always the same way, *abba*, *abba* (see marginal notes), whereas the sestet may rhyme any of several ways so long as it includes no more than three (*c, d, e*) new rhymes. Because of its two-part division, the Italian form, as opposed to the four-part English or Shakespearean form, is ideally adapted to dealing with an experience that involves describing an experience and commenting on it, asking a question and answering it, or posing a problem and solving it. Many readers will be familiar with this pattern. Thus, Keats establishes an expectation in the reader by deciding to use this form and then satisfies that expectation by using the form conventionally.

Next, he uses a metaphor, a figure of comparison, to describe his experience, since it is almost impossible to state emotion and emotional experience directly and flatly. He portrays himself as a traveler and explorer: the *Iliad* and the *Odyssey* deal often with the experience of Odysseus—one of the great travelers and explorers in literature. This figure of speech is maintained throughout the poem; all the references are to actions of some kind of traveler or explorer. Again Keats has satisfied the desire for order and symmetry.

Then Keats organizes the experience chronologically and spatially. Notice that the octave, while maintaining the explorer image, becomes increasingly specific with each line. The first two lines tell us that the poet has traveled much "in the realms of gold"—that is, he has read widely in literature—and has found many great books there—"goodly states and kingdoms." Then he narrows his compass. Apollo was the god of, among other things, poetry; therefore, in lines three and four Keats says that he has read a large amount of poetry. Becoming more specific, in lines five and six he says that he had been told of "one wide expanse" that Homer ruled. The reference here is to epic poetry. Finally, narrowing even farther, he tells us that he never really read Homer until he read Chapman's translation of Homer. This account has been expertly organized.

> lines 1 and 2 — literature as a whole
> lines 3 and 4 — poetry, one branch of literature
> line 5 — epic poetry, one branch of poetry
> line 6 — Homer, the greatest epic poet
> lines 7 and 8 — Chapman's translation of Homer

The octave is built like a pyramid standing on its apex. But the experience is incomplete. Thus far Keats has told us what he did but not how he felt about it. He does this in the sestet. Keeping the same figure, Keats says he felt like an astronomer who discovers a new planet (the only kind of space explorer possible in Keats's pre-astronaut days) or like Cortez when, first seeing the Pacific, he and his men were awed by the realization that here at last was the greatest body of water in the world. (Many readers will be bothered by the fact that Balboa, not Cortez, discovered the Pacific, but the lines, after all, do not say that Cortez discovered the Pacific, just as Keats was not the first discoverer of Chapman.) At that moment, Keats, like Cortez, stood alone on a peak of experience, seeing what few other men had seen.

Our account is still flat and stale because it is still paraphrase. No summary of a work of art ever approximates the experience of art. The paraphrase has not described the reader's pleasure of discovery as he recreates the experience line by line. Nor has it even mentioned the melody and the rhythm in the lines. It is not necessary to do those things here to illustrate how an experience is organized. A satisfactory account of the poem as a whole would certainly include these matters. Yet even such an account would not explain the experience fully because it would describe how all these elements appear separately when what is important—but impossible to communicate—is how all the elements work together simultaneously. This is one reason why poetry must be read, rather than discussed, to be appreciated. We will talk about it as briefly as possible.

We have remarked how Keats establishes an expectation in the reader and satisfies it. Any artist—painter, composer, sculptor, writer—establishes such a pattern. It works for him and the reader in two ways: by satisfying the expectation, he appeals to the sense of order, symmetry, unity in all of us; by breaking the pattern he stops the reader momentarily, that is, he emphasizes whatever happens at the break in the pattern. Let us illustrate how this works in poetry.

(1) A poet may break his rhythm and meter. When Shakespeare writes "To be or not to be, that is the question" he has taken a perfectly regular iambic line, that is, one in which each unaccented syllable is followed by an accented syllable ˣ/ˣ/ˣ/, and broken the pattern. The phrase "that is" is trochaic: It is made up of an accented syllable followed by an unaccented syllable, so that the meter goes this way ˣ/ˣ/ˣ//ˣˣ/ˣ. The word that stands out is the one that first breaks the meter. That is the one Shakespeare wants to emphasize.

(2) A poet may break his diction or vocabulary. Every poet in any specific poem writes on a certain level of usage in a fairly limited vocabulary. Emily Dickinson, for example, has a habit of breaking out of her vocabulary with the last word of the first line of a poem to arrest the reader and shock him into attention. She begins one poem (we omit the last word) "I heard a fly buzz when I _____." What word is expected? The rest of the words lead one to expect "opened the door" or "sat down." But her word is "died." The pattern is broken and the reader's attention has been focused. Another Dickinson poem begins "Because I could not stop for _____." The reader expects "coffee" or something innocuous. Dickinson's word is "death."

(3) A poet may break his image pattern. Keats maintained the image of the explorer all through his sonnet. However, Shakespeare wants to emphasize an idea when he has Macbeth say, "Tomorrow, and tomorrow, and tomorrow,/Creeps in this petty pace from day to day,/To the last syllable . . . ." The word "syllable" is attention-getting because "creeps" and "pace" have led the reader to expect

something physical, something snail-like. But "syllable" establishes a new line of thought: "to the last syllable of recorded time." It doesn't break the *sense* of the passage (it makes excellent sense) but it does command attention. Similarly, in the "Garden of Proserpine," after the poet Swinburne has almost soothed the reader to sleep with long, drowsy pictures of the underworld as a place of slow-growing, peaceful gardens, he suddenly interjects "Time stoops to no man's lure." This is an image from falconry, wherein the hawk is recalled by whirling a lure which the hawk "stoops" to, enabling the falconer to recapture him. This violent image, coming in the midst of the somnolent pattern, breaks that pattern and awakens the reader. Why? Because the idea in it—that no man controls time and therefore can never recapture the past—is central to the poem and the poet wants you to notice it.

(4) A poet may shift his tone. When a serious poem shifts to sarcasm or a satirical poem becomes solemn, the reader is immediately aware of the shift. This device is perhaps best illustrated in comic verse:

> There's the wonderful love of a beautiful maid,
>   And the love of a staunch true man,
> And the love of a baby that's unafraid—
>   All have existed since time began.
> But the most wonderful love, the Love of all loves,
>   Even greater than the love for Mother,
> Is the infinite, tenderest, passionate love
>   Of one dead drunk for another.

Any writer who does not pay attention to his patterns and to his departures from them is usually unsuccessful. Max Shulman parodies the bad modern poet when he writes:

> Tread quietly, Al,
> For the moon
> Is a half-slice of lemon
> On the teacup of the world.

The result here is that the reader is continually off balance—no pattern is ever established. The whole "poem" is a series of breaks. "Tread quietly" does not fit "Al," the "moon" doesn't fit "a half-slice of lemon/ On the teacup of the world." "Tread quietly" and "moon" go together. Nothing else does.

The point of this discussion is that the ability to distinguish pattern in a poem is the first step toward understanding the manipulated experience, the work itself.

Because poetry is compressed rather than diffuse, the poet must choose words that have the largest number of meanings. In practice, this means that he wants the word with the greatest number of relevant overtones to it. As a result, although a poet can achieve great precision of statement, he also often achieves ambiguity, that is, multiple meanings. A discussion of the causes of ambiguity follows.

Metaphor. Metaphor, in poetry, generally refers to any figure of comparison. It may be a metaphor proper ("There is a garden in her face"), a simile ("Her cheeks were like roses"), or even an analogy ("Her face was a storm cloud; and when the angry rain began to fall, lightning flashed from her eyes").

Metaphors are figurative, not literal, which means simply that their meaning consists largely of their overtones. Thomas Campion, for example, wrote:

> There is a garden in her face,
> Where roses and white lilies grow.

Obviously the reader is not meant to envision dirt and wheelbarrows. What the translated metaphor says is that the lady's cheeks are red and her skin is white. But the overtones suggest much more. "Garden," "roses," and "lilies" imply youth and health and natural, not artificial, loveliness. And they further suggest the temporary nature of that loveliness. Consider, for instance, the difference between the garden metaphor and:

> A face from alabaster carved
> That glowing rubies frame.

These two seventeenth-century poets have opposing ideas about how long beauty will endure. They may also be suggesting different degrees of accessibility in the lady, since the garden metaphor is in its overtones familiar and sweet, the statue metaphor, cold and rather distant.

Metaphoric ambiguity of this kind creates no special difficulties for the careful reader. And it enhances the pleasure of reading, since it provokes the reader's imagination, adds emotional coloring to intellectual perception, and makes sensuous what otherwise would be abstract.

But many ambiguities are more complex than these, and the reader grows uneasy because he feels he must make a choice between possible meanings. When Shakespeare, for example, in "Sonnet 75" writes that his love is to his thoughts as "sweet season'd showers are to the ground," "sweet season'd" can mean two things: "sweet scented" and "in the sweet season," that is, springtime. Both meanings are correct. They are complementary; the phrase has two parallel overtones instead of one.

Of course this is not to say that any random overtone sensed by any reader is legitimate. The overtone can usually be validated by the poem itself—the nature of the poem determines its relevance or irrelevance. For example, Shakespeare's "Sonnet 66" begins, "Tir'd with all these for restful death I cry." Now "Tir'd," that is, exhausted, gives the line a perfectly clear meaning. But Elizabethan English was a very flexible instrument, and "tir'd" is often a clipped form of a longer word, frequently of "attired" and "retired." Moreover, to twentieth-century ears, "with" seems at first an odd appendage to "tir'd"; one expects "of." Both "retired with" and "attired with" are linguistically proper, and used in the line, they make sensible metaphoric statements that in no way clash with the idea of exhaustion. But are they valid? Here is the total poem:

> Tir'd with all these for restful death I cry,
> As to behold desert a beggar borne,
> And needy Nothing trim'd in jollitie,
> And purest faith unhappily forsworn,
> And gilded honor shamefully misplaced,   5
> And maiden virtue rudely strumpeted,
> And right perfection wrongfully disgraced,
> And strength by limping sway disabled,
> And art made tongue-tied by authority,
> And Folly (Doctor-like) controlling skill,   10
> And simple Truth miscalled Simplicity,
> And captive good attending Captain ill.
>   Tir'd with all these, from these would I be gone,
> Save that to die, I leave my love alone.

Even a quick reading reveals that "retired" will not do. Of all possibilities, the speaker here definitely is not retired. His complaint is that he is too entangled in the hurly-burly of a dishonest and distasteful life. What about "attired"? There is validation for this metaphor in line 3: "needy Nothing trim'd in jollitie," that is, dressed in finery. The social evils he describes are then to be seen as a burdensome suit of clothes he would throw off in order to be again the natural man.

Thus overtones are accepted or rejected because they do or do not fit the facts of the poem.

Symbols. Symbols were explored briefly in the discussion of the short story (p. 15). A symbol is an emblem; it represents something else without ever announcing that an identification or a comparison is being made, as the metaphor does.

As in dealing with metaphor, the reader must exercise discretion in recognizing and accepting symbolic meaning. Again, the total poem must be the basis for accepting or rejecting symbolic meaning. One of the best known poetic symbols occurs in the concluding lines of Browning's "My Last Duchess" (p. 159). Because of what the reader knows of the Duke by the time he reaches these lines, he sees that, whatever the conscious reason for the Duke's mention of the statue of Neptune taming a sea horse, the statue symbolizes his cast of mind. The Duke is a man whose pride of ownership leads him to regard everything in his area of influence, including people, as property to be handled as he pleases. If these possessions do not conform to his desires, they must be "tamed."

Paradox.   A paradox is an apparent contradiction, a true statement that is made up of seemingly incompatible elements. Richard Lovelace's "I could not love thee dear so much/Loved I not honour more" is a paradox. Paradoxes are always emphatic because they demand inspection. Thus, John Donne concludes a sonnet with the striking paradox, "Death, thou shalt die," and Shakespeare with

> To give away your self, keeps your self still,
> And you must live drawn by your own sweet skill.

Many poetic paradoxes are far more complex than these. Probably the best known example in English literature is John Donne's "The Canonization," in which Donne proves the paradox that fleshly lovers are heavenly lovers, that is, saints. The same poet's "A Valediction Forbidding Mourning" (p. 199) argues that when lovers part, they do not part, another paradox.

Irony. Irony is the use of words that say one thing and mean another. It can occur variously in poetry. Occasionally, irony is a trick of phrasing, as when Byron in the *Don Juan* speaks of Coleridge

> Explaining metaphysics to the nation—
> I wish he would explain his Explanation.

Sometimes it is a result of a situation, as in Housman's "Is My Team Ploughing" (p. 205). In that poem, the questioner does not understand the significance of the answers he receives from his former friend, who is the one man who can, but who ought not, answer the questions truthfully. This is "dramatic irony," irony that evolves from a character's ignorance of the significance of what he is saying. "My Last Duchess" is a thoroughly ironic poem, in that the Duke never realizes the terrible portrait he draws of himself in his own words.

A more difficult kind of irony to explain is that appearing, for example, in John Crowe Ransom's "Bells for John Whiteside's Daughter" (p. 213). The speaker seems vexed at the little girl for not running and playing and refers to her present disposition as a "brown study," although both he and the reader know perfectly well that the little girl is dead. The mind of the speaker simply cannot assimilate this tragic fact, and he therefore uses logically inappropriate language in speaking of the child. He cannot say what he means.

Allusion. Like all writers, poets compress and add overtones by alluding, that is, referring, to facts outside the poem proper. Allusions are meant to deepen and illuminate a poem, but the careless reader may overlook them and therefore misread the poem. The impact of Yeats's "The Second Coming" (p. 206) depends partly on the reader's knowledge of the Nativity. No one is likely to misread this allusion. Part of the force and much of the logic of Milton's sonnet, "On His Blindness," (p. 172) depends on recognizing the allusion in the third line to the parable of the talents (*Matthew*, 25:26). Not many will miss this reference either. But many readers may pass over the significance of the allusions to Lazarus, Hamlet, and John the Baptist in Eliot's "The Love Song of J. Alfred Prufrock" (pp. 164). If so, the reader won't fully understand the character of Prufrock, since his comparisons of himself with these men illuminate his weaknesses.

Close-packed Imagery. An image in literature is a word or phrase that evokes a response in a reader by appealing to one or more of his five senses. It therefore arouses him physically and mentally. In the following example, which is the first thirteen lines of "Preludes" by T. S. Eliot, many senses are appealed to:

The winter evening settles down
With *smell of steaks* in passageways.   smell
Six o'clock.

The *burnt-out ends of smoky days*.	smell and sight (the image is of a cigarette or cigar)
And now a *gusty shower* wraps	sight and touch
The *grimy scraps*	touch
Of *withered leaves* about your feet	sight
And *newspapers from vacant lots;*	sight and touch
The *showers beat*	sight and sound
On *broken blinds and chimney-pots,*	sight
And at the corner of the street	
A *lonely cab-horse steams and stamps*.	sight, smell, and sound
And then the *lighting of the lamps*.	sight

Many of these are arguable—the newspapers blown about your feet could include sound imagery—but only the most obvious are mentioned. The reader's senses have a thorough exercise, which will probably create a reaction to the passage. But the passage hasn't said anything, that is, it contains no statement except the descriptive generalization in the first line. The images here create any feeling the reader may have, and they are able to do this because they are concrete. The more vague and abstract imagery becomes, the less effect it can produce. Compare, for example, the two following poems:

O wind, come soon	Western Wind, when wilt thou blow
Bringing rain from the sea;	So the small rain down can rain?
Then will the time arrive	Christ, that I were in my bed
When my love returns to me.	And my love in my arms again!

The poem on the left is a very poor twentieth-century imitation of the very good sixteenth-century poem on the right. The older poem is specific and concrete: the west wind (not just wind) brings the spring showers (not just rain); the love the speaker longs for is made real by a series of specific images: *Christ, bed, arms*—whereas the version on the left is vague and therefore unconvincing and lackluster. Literature, as defined before, is a manipulation of experience, and human beings experience things first through the five physical senses. Imagery, therefore, is an important device, so important that one school of poetry in America—the Imagist school—devoted itself to writing poems entirely in images, without any comment by the poet. The popularity of the Japanese *haiku* today (a three-line picture poem, the first line having five syllables, the second seven, and the third five, with the point of the poem growing out of the picture presented) is further evidence of the importance attached to imagery:

Blossoms on the pear—
a woman in the moonlight
reads a letter there.

CONVENTIONS OF DICTION

Since every poem in a sense establishes its own vocabulary and since fashions in poetic diction have changed so often in literary history, conventions of diction are fluid. The history of British poetry, for example, has been a series of reactions against the "poetic diction" of a preceding age, and each new school of poetry has claimed that it was restoring "natural" language to poetry. In fact, none of them did that; they simply replaced one set of conventions with another. The early nineteenth-century Romantics said they were returning to nature and natural language in opposition to the highly artificial diction of the eighteenth-century Neo-Classical school. The Neo-Classicists had argued that they were restoring natural language to poetry as a reaction against the rough, over-specialized language of the seventeenth-century Metaphysical school. In turn, the Metaphysicals were reacting against the artificial diction of the sixteenth-century sonneteers. This constant shift in diction makes a brief discussion of conventions of diction difficult. It is easier to give a couple of examples and generalize from them.

Older conventions sometimes trouble present-day readers. In much pretwentieth-century poetry, for example, the "neither . . . nor" construction familiar to us in prose was a "nor . . . nor" construction:

> Nor Mars his sword nor war's quick fire

The original reason for the use of this odd construction is lost; probably it was designed to produce metrical regularity, a balance, and a sonority that is lacking in the long *e* of *neither* but is supplied by the long *o* of *nor*. This minor example is representative of many conventional constructions that should cause no real difficulty once the convention is noted.

Other conventions are not so easily explained and accepted. Much eighteenth-century verse, for example, sounds to modern ears excessively wordy. Few nouns, so it seems, appear without adjectives, and often the same noun is linked to the same adjective. What the modern reader must realize is that the eighteenth-century poet was following a convention now discarded: The English construction was often a translation of a Latin construction. Its constant use was a kind of poetic shorthand peculiar to a society of writers and readers that set a high value on the classics. With second-rate poets the shorthand degenerated into an irritating mannerism, which even at its best displeases readers today. For example, a section of Gray's "Elegy Written in a Country Churchyard":

> Now fades the glimmering landscape on the sight,
> And all the air a solemn stillness holds,
> Save where the beetle wheels his droning flight,
> And drowsy tinklings lull the distant folds.

Today this might be called uneconomical diction because the four lines contain five nouns paired with adjectives for no apparent reason. An inventive reader can rewrite the lines for himself by leaving out an adjective in each line:

> Now fades the landscape on the sight,
> And all the air a stillness holds,
> Save where the beetle wheels his flight,
> And tinklings lull the distant folds.

Many readers will feel that the poem is not harmed by this editing. But they should also realize that it has now lost one of its conventions, one of the things that ties it to its period—that it is not the same poem reedited, but an entirely different poem.

The poetic diction of the eighteenth century looks peculiar today because we have virtually eliminated conventions of diction in our time by eliminating restrictions on subject matter. Present-day dogma could probably be stated thus: *Any word or phrase is poetic if it is appropriate to the subject matter; any subject matter is appropriate if it renders a significant experience vividly and concretely.* It is hard to imagine a twentieth-century reader objecting to a "low" subject in the manner of eighteenth- or nineteenth-century readers. It is equally hard to imagine another century writing about many of the subjects we deal with today. When the seventeenth-century poet John Donne, probably the most modern poet writing before our day, wrote poems which contained references to flies, he used the fly as a symbol of fleshly love (since the fly is short-lived and filthy); but several twentieth-century poets have written poems about flies simply as dirty little beasts.

If the present-day reader is irritated by the habits of diction of a previous century, he ought for a moment to reflect on how modern habits of diction would irritate readers of the past. In a very real sense, the absence of conventional diction is in itself a convention, probably no better and no worse than previous conventions. Taste does not improve; it only changes.

The responsibility of the reader, then, is to acclimate himself to the vocabulary the poet is using. *A good poem is one that is compatible with its own logic.* If the diction of the poem harmonizes with the subject matter and theme, it is probably appropriate. A very crude example of this could be a seventeenth-century poem which begins with an invocation to Apollo. Surely no reader will object to the passage simply because Apollo was a mythical figure and therefore could not possibly help the poet. The invocation was a convention and Apollo, as the god of poetry, was a conventional figure to be invoked; both were parts of the frame of reference of the past. Furthermore, if the passage begins, "O Apollo, on the wings of morning . . ." the reader has reason to dislike the phrase but not to condemn it entirely, since it is again part of an established convention and *it is compatible with the logic of invocation.* However, if the poet were to begin, "Hey, Apollo . . .," then the diction is obviously not compatible with the logic of the poem (unless it is a burlesque) and deserves condemnation.

CONVENTIONS OF RHYTHM AND METER

We are all rhythmical creatures: our pulse beats to a rhythm, we breathe in rhythm, we brush our teeth in rhythm. The poet takes natural rhythm and conventionalizes it; that is, he builds it into different artificial rhythms that we call *meter*. As we have said before, he establishes a pattern of regularity and then breaks that pattern for emphasis.

The study of meter is called prosody. Different kinds of poetry use different prosodic systems. Most systems rest on the counting of recurring sounds or stresses. A few do not: Syllabic verse, for example, is built on similar line length, as in the haiku. Marianne Moore, the American poet, writes syllabic verse; you cannot hear one sound recurring regularly in a line nor can you count a recurring number of stresses in a line, but you can count a recurring number of syllables in the line. This prosodic system, however, is unusual.

Most English verse is based on accentual-syllabic prosody, that is, on recurring stresses in combinations of two or three syllables. In English, it is difficult to pronounce three syllables successively without stressing ("accenting") one syllable more than the others. Thus stresses can be counted in units of two or three syllables. In English, four degrees of stress are possible, but in the interests of simplicity, let's limit our consideration to two possibilities—stress or no stress—and designate those two by ′ for stress and × for no stress. A word such as *undo* has two syllables, the first unstressed, the second stressed (ùndó). A word like *taken* reverses the pattern (tákèn). *Unaware* is a three-syllable word stressed in this fashion: ùnàwáre. *Sickening*, also three syllables, is stressed this way: síckènìng.

The patterns in *undo*, *taken*, *unaware*, and *sickening* are the most common in English verse; each of these words is a natural foot, that is, it contains in itself the smallest prosodic unit of measurement, the foot. A foot is a unit containing at least one stressed syllable and one or two unstressed syllables. The four feet illustrated above have these names:

× ′	(undo)	iambic foot
′ ×	(taken)	trochaic foot
× × ′	(unaware)	anapestic foot
′ × ×	(sickening)	dactylic foot

A good poet never composes a poem using only one kind of foot because it becomes monotonous and dead; the reader gets so hypnotized by the sing-song of the meter that he can pay no attention to anything else. However, in most poems one foot pattern predominates. The most common foot is the iambic; it occurs in natural speech more often than any other, and the poet who wants a conversational realism often adopts this one as the dominant foot. The trochaic foot sounds a little odd to English ears if it is repeated regularly, but it is a very emphatic foot because of the location of its stress ("Nó, Ì críed, ànd . . . ."). The anapest is a very rapid foot, useful in speeding up a line; when anapests are combined, they often result in a marching meter ("The Stars and Stripes Forever" begins with a strong trochaic foot and then shifts immediately into the marching anapest). The dactylic foot is the least common of the four; it is used chiefly for emphasis (it is simply a long trochaic foot) or for a galloping, lunging rhythm (in reading aloud Browning's "I galloped, Dirck galloped, we galloped all three" one can hear the horses' hooves).

There are also terms that describe the number of feet in a line.

one foot	monometer	"Ì dó"	(iambic monometer)
two feet	dimeter	"Tò thís wè cáme"	(iambic dimeter)
three feet	trimeter	"Ànd óne ùpón thè ráck"	(iambic trimeter)

four feet	tetrameter	"Síng nŏ grĕat sóngs ŏf thĕ bóld ănd thĕ bráve" (dactylic tetrameter [last foot shortened])
five feet	pentameter	"Wăs thís thĕ fáce thăt láunched ă thóusănd shíps?" (iambic pentameter)
six feet	hexameter	"Whére ăre Élmĕr, Hérmăn, Bért, Tóm, ănd Chárlĕy" (trochaic hexameter)
seven feet	heptameter	"Dýĭng, dýĭng, dýĭng, sínging dírgĕs fŏr ă sínkĭng sóul" (trochaic heptameter)

The commonest line in English verse is the iambic pentameter, probably because an adult male can pronounce that many syllables comfortably in one breath. Many women poets prefer tetrameter lines, a length better suited to their lung capacity, for one thing. Nursery rhymes are generally in dimeter or trimeter because a child can sustain that many syllables and no more comfortably in one breath. Hexameter and heptameter lines tend to be too long for one breath and too short for two and are therefore unpopular. But poets choose different line lengths for many other reasons. Short lines have a snap and sparkle that appeal to the poet who wants to write epigrams. Long iambic or trochaic lines, because they have a breath break in them, lend themselves to reflective utterances. Long anapestic lines have a dash and speed that work equally well for narrative or comic verse. The possible combinations of feet and line length for different effects are virtually inexhaustible.

After some practice in listening to verse, a reader begins to hear the music that an expert builds into his lines. For example, a poet sometimes syncopates a line: He plays off a natural rhythm against a metrical pattern. Take the following line:

A whirling, dipping, dancing, prancing girl.

In most aspects, that is probably an undistinguished line except for the fact that it moves and twists as you read it, not just because of the meaning of the words, but because of the syncopation. The four middle words are all natural trochaic feet: whírlĭng, díppĭng, dáncĭng, práncĭng. But the meter is not trochaic—it is iambic. The poet has placed one unaccented syllable at the beginning of the line and an accented monosyllable at the end so that in a line composed chiefly of natural trochees, there is an overriding iambic pattern; the ear hears the two rhythms going at the same time.

A poet can employ many rhythmic devices besides those already mentioned:

(1) Alliteration: the repetition of initial consonants to tie phrases and ideas together ("When to the sessions of sweet silent thought")

(2) Assonance: the repetition of vowel sounds ("Nŏr lĕt thĕ beetle nŏr thĕ death-moth be")

(3) Consonance: the repetition of consonant patterns ("Loving and living, I could not leave")

Rhyme is also a rhythmic device, basically the repetition of a similar vowel sound at the end of successive lines. A great deal of poetry does not rhyme. Many poets have felt that rhyme restricts them or destroys a natural sentence effect; they have therefore turned to unrhymed forms such as blank verse (unrhymed iambic pentameter) or free verse (unrhymed verse, usually without regular foot patterns). On the other hand, rhyme has great advantages to offer the poet: It appeals to the rhythmic demand in each of us; it organizes a poem in that rhyme is the basis of stanza forms; it offers a frame for a poem in much the same way that a picture frame enhances a portrait; and it is an effective mnemonic device.

Furthermore, the poet can use various kinds of rhyme.

(1) Slant rhyme: repetition of a similar but not identical vowel and an identical consonant: heel/ still

(2) Light rhyme: repetition of identical vowel sounds but with varying stress on the vowel: be/ silly

(3) Eye rhyme: repetition of different vowel sounds that appear identical to the eye: sentry/comply

(4) Full rhyme: repetition of an identical vowel sound and identical following consonants: hope/ scope

Rhyme and meter are the basis of stanza form. Like many formal conventions, stanza form can best be studied in the poems themselves.

The Modes of Poetry

Traditionally, poetry has been divided into three modes: (1) narrative; (2) dramatic; (3) lyric.

Narrative verse is used primarily to tell a story. It ranges in complexity from the simple folk ballad to the mock epic. Dramatic poetry may also tell a story, but it involves an identifiable speaker or speakers in a specific and identifiable situation that unfolds before the audience. Dramatic poetry, as generally defined today, includes plays in verse and the dramatic monologue, although one can argue that the dramatic monologue is as lyrical as it is dramatic. Lyric poetry, formally plotless, is the expression of feeling of a single speaker. It includes the sonnet, the ode, the elegy, and the song.

NARRATIVE POETRY

As we said, narrative poetry tells a story. Narratives can be extremely simple, as in some ballads, or they can be very complex. Lord Byron's *Don Juan*, for example, while it narrates the fictional adventures of a well-meaning but accident-prone young man, also comments, sometimes gently, sometimes savagely, on love, friendship, literature, politics, war, and morality. It is a kind of casebook of hypocrisy. Alexander Pope's *The Rape of the Lock*, a mock epic, tells the story of a flirtation but tells it ironically in the framework of the complicated conventions of heroic poetry. The *Iliad*, the *Odyssey, Paradise Lost*, all epics, are narrative poems.

Conventions of the ballad

The simplest narratives are the folk ballads. These ballads are the popular music of bygone days. How they came to be composed, who composed them, under what circumstances—these things are not known. Theoretically, they could have been composed by a group gathered around a campfire; practically, they were probably composed by individual authors and then passed through many hands and many voices until they were finally written down and solidified. The same ballad has usually many variant forms: "Lord Randal" in England may become "John Randal" in New England, "Johnnie Randolph" in the South, and "Jamie Rambo" in the Southwest. The basic story line is usually the same in all versions, but the special events are changed to fit the region.

From some of the more obvious conventions in the ballads, one can make additional inferences about their development. Many ballads, for example, have a refrain, sometimes a nonsense refrain: "with a hey and ho/ and a hey-nonny-no!" At other times, the refrain changes slightly each time to make use of *incremental repetition*, that is, each time the refrain repeats, it adds a little more to the narrative as a kind of progress report. Simply changing one word in a refrain can accomplish this. For example, in a ballad about a young man who goes to his wedding only to find his bride has died in the night (a common ballad theme), a refrain might in successive stanzas go like this:

(1) And onward he did go, oh!
(2) And quickly he did go, oh!
(3) And gladly he did go, oh!
(4) And sadly he did go, oh!
(5) And madly he did go, oh!

The change in the adverb reflects the change of mind in the main character.

This habitual use of a refrain implies two things: First, the ballad is basically an oral form; the refrain is used as a summary to pull together divisions of the story in a fashion that would not be necessary if the ballad were a printed form. Second, many ballads probably were dance forms: The nonsense refrain suggests that it allowed the dancers to regroup for the next "set" or pattern.

It is easy to see why the ballad is defined as the popular music of bygone days. Like most popular forms, its appeal rests largely on using material and techniques familiar to the audience: familiar themes, images, characters, phrases, actions—in other words, conventional material and methods. Following is a list of conventional folk ballad elements:

(1) Stanza form: usually iambic quatrains (four-line stanzas) with alternating lines of four feet and three feet—an abbreviated speech rhythm.
(2) Themes: the death of the young, the innocent, the beautiful, the good, often through no fault of their own.
(3) Images: stock figures, often connected by alliteration (hounds and hawks, dale and down, heath and hollow), sometimes alone (nut-brown maid, snow-white steed).

(4) Character: usually noble characters, either by birth or innate goodness. Kings, queens, princesses, lords, and ladies figure prominently in the ballads, as do folk heroes: Robin Hood, Jesse James, Allan-a-dale. Character itself is not developed; the hero or heroine is stereotyped.

(5) Phrasing: use of the refrain, stock comparisons (see also image); question and answer dialogue.

(6) Setting: very little attention to setting—the ballad is not nature poetry—because what matters is what happened, not where it happened.

(7) Point of view: the ballad is usually highly impersonal; the ballad sings itself. Usually there is no hint of the author's personality ("Jesse James" is a notable exception: the supposed originator, Billy Gashade, is clearly identified in the ballad itself). Part of the effect of the ballad comes from the starkly unemotional telling of an event that is fraught with strong emotion.

(8) Pace: ballads move very swiftly because of another very important convention. Although ballads deal more with action than with character, most of the action is not described but implied, that is, the real action occurs in the white spaces between the stanzas. Causes and effects get more attention than does the action itself.

Lord Randal

'O where hae ye been, Lord Randal, my son?
O where hae ye been, my handsome young man?'
'I hae been to the wild wood; mother, make my
    bed soon,
Fir I'm weary wi hunting, and fain wald lie down.'

'Where gat ye your dinner, Lord Randal, my
    son?   5
Where gat ye your dinner, my handsome young
    man?'
'I dined wi my true-love; mother, make my bed
    soon,
For I'm weary wi hunting, and fain wald lie down.'

'What gat ye to your dinner, Lord Randal, my son?
What gat ye to your dinner, my handsome young
    man?'   10
'I gat eels boiled in broo; mother, make my bed
    soon,
For I'm weary wi hunting, and fain wald lie down.'

'What became of your bloodhounds, Lord Randal,
    my son?

What became of your bloodhounds, my handsome
    young man?'
'O they swelled and they died; mother, make my
    bed soon,   15
For I'm weary wi hunting, and fain wald lie down.'

'O I fear ye are poisond, Lord Randal, my son!
O I fear ye are poisond, my handsome young man!'
'O yes! I am poisond; mother, make my bed soon,
For I'm sick at the heart and I fain wald lie
    down.'   20

FOR ANALYSIS

1. This typical ballad uses two kinds of repetition:
   (a) *simple*, as in the first two lines of each stanza;
   (b) *incremental*, as in the last two lines of each stanza.
   What "increment" do you find in each set of concluding lines? How does this make the ballad "sing itself"?
2. What double meaning do you find in the last increment, "For I'm sick at the heart"?
3. Why is Lord Randal unwilling to tell the story so that his mother must pry it out of him? What in the ballad tells you that he is unwilling?

Sir Patrick Spence

The king sits in Dumferling toune,
  Drinking the blude-reid wine:
'O whar will I get guid sailor,
  To sail this schip of mine?'

Up and spak an eldern knicht,   5
  Sat at the kings richt kne:
'Sir Patrick Spence is the best sailor,
  That sails upon the se.'

The king has written a braid letter,
  And signed it wi his hand,   10
And sent it to Sir Patrick Spence,
  Was walking on the sand.

The first line that Sir Patrick red,
  A loud lauch lauchèd he;
The next line that Sir Patrick red,   15
  The teir blinded his ee.

'O wha is this has don this deid,
  This ill deid don to me,
To send me out this time o' the yeir,
  To sail upon the se!   20

'Mak hast, mak haste, my mirry men all,
  Our guid schip sails the morne:'
'O say na sae, my master deir,
  For I feir a deadlie storme.

'Late, late yestreen I saw the new moone,   25
  Wi the auld moone in hir arme,
And I feir, I feir, my deir master,
  That we will cum to harme.'

O our Scots nobles wer richt laith
  To weet their cork-heild schoone;   30
Bot lang owre a' the play wer playd,
  Their hats they swam aboone.

O lang, lang may their ladies sit,
  Wi thair fans into their hand,
Or eir they se Sir Patrick Spence   35
  Cum sailing to the land.

O lang, lang may the ladies stand,

Wi thair gold kems in their hair,
Waiting for thar ain deir lords,
  For they 'll se thame na mair.   40

Haf owre, haf owre to Aberdour,
  It's fiftie fadom deip,
And thair lies guid Sir Patrick Spence,
  Wi the Scots lords at his feit.

FOR ANALYSIS

1. The abuse of power is a typical ballad theme.
   What about the circumstances of his mission
   makes the death of the hero more poignant than
   if he were, say, carrying troops to battle?
2. How is the passage of time handled in this ballad?
   How does this fit what you know of the conventions of the ballad?
3. Where and to what end is incremental repetition
   used in this ballad?

Jesse James

Jesse James was a lad that killed a-many a man;
He robbed the Danville train.
But that dirty little coward that shot Mr. Howard
Has laid poor Jesse in his grave.

Poor Jesse had a wife to mourn for his life,   5
Three children, they were brave.
But that dirty little coward that shot Mr. Howard
Has laid poor Jesse in his grave.

It was Robert Ford, that dirty little coward,
I wonder how he does feel,   10
For he ate of Jesse's bread and he slept in Jesse's bed,
Then laid poor Jesse in his grave.

Jesse was a man, a friend to the poor,
He never could see a man suffer pain:
And with his brother Frank he robbed the Chicago
  bank,   15
And stopped the Glendale train.

---

1 *toune:* town   9 *braid:* broad   29 *laith:* loath   30 *schoone:*
shoes   32 *aboone:* above

38 *kems:* combs

It was his brother Frank that robbed the Gallatin
    bank,
And carried the money from the town;
It was in this very place that they had a little race,
For they shot Captain Sheets to the ground.   20

They went to the crossing not very far from there,
And there they did the same;
With the agent on his knees, he delivered up the keys
To the outlaws, Frank and Jesse James.

It was on Wednesday night, the moon was shining
    bright,   25
They robbed the Glendale train;
The people they did say, for many miles away,
It was robbed by Frank and Jesse James.

It was on Saturday night, Jesse was at home
Talking with his family brave,   30
Robert Ford came along like a thief in the night
And laid poor Jesse in his grave.

The people held their breath when they heard of
    Jesse's death,
And wondered how he ever came to die.
It was one of the gang called little Robert Ford,   35
He shot poor Jesse on the sly.

Jesse went to his rest with his hand on his breast;
The devil will be upon his knee.
He was born one day in the county of Clay
And came from a solitary race.   40

This song was made by Billy Gashade,
As soon as the news did arrive;
He said there was no man with the law in his hand
Who could take Jesse James when alive.

FOR ANALYSIS

1. Ballads usually deal with the death of the young
   and innocent. Jesse James was not young when he
   was killed and by no stretch of the imagination
   could he be called "innocent" in the usual sense.
   How has the balladeer here preserved the convention without lying about Jesse James?
2. What in this relatively late ballad replaces the
   hawks and hounds of early ballads?
3. How has the figure of Jesse James been conventionalized into a ballad hero? Consider, for
   example, what elements in this ballad might fit
   Robin Hood or another folk hero.

JOHN KEATS

La Belle Dame Sans Merci

'O what can ail thee, knight-at-arms,
    Alone and palely loitering?
The sedge has wither'd from the lake,
    And no birds sing.

'O what can ail thee, knight-at-arms,   5
    So haggard and so woe-begone?
The squirrel's granary is full,
    And the harvest's done.

'I see a lily on thy brow
    With anguish moist and fever dew;   10
And on thy cheek a fading rose
    Fast withereth too.'

'I met a lady in the meads,
    Full beautiful—a faery's child,
Her hair was long, her foot was light,   15
    And her eyes were wild.

'I made a garland for her head,
    And bracelets too, and fragrant zone;
She look'd at me as she did love,
    And made sweet moan.   20

'I set her on my pacing steed
    And nothing else saw all day long,
For sidelong would she bend, and sing
    A faery's song.

'She found me roots of relish sweet,   25
    And honey wild, and manna dew,
And sure in language strange she said—
    "I love thee true."

'She took me to her elfin grot,
    And there she wept, and sigh'd full sore;   30
And there I shut her wild wild eyes
    With kisses four.

'And there she lullèd me asleep,
    And there I dream'd—Ah! woe betide!
The latest dream I ever dream'd   35
    On the cold hill's side.

'I saw pale kings and princes too,
  Pale warriors, death-pale were they all;
They cried—"La Belle Dame Sans Merci
  Hath thee in thrall!"   40

'I saw their starv'd lips in the gloom,
  With horrid warning gapèd wide,
And I awoke and found me here,
  On the cold hill's side.

'And this is why I sojourn here,   45
  Alone and palely loitering,
Though the sedge is wither'd from the lake,
  And no birds sing.'

FOR ANALYSIS

This is an *art ballad*, a form which uses some of the conventions of the *folk ballad* and some of its own. An art ballad is usually more tightly organized, more carefully constructed than a folk ballad. By answering the following questions, can you discover how this ballad differs from the folk tradition?

1. How is the supernatural treated in this poem? Matter-of-factly, as in the folk ballad?
2. Does the focus of the poem slowly shift from one actor to another or is it consistent as in the folk ballad? (All folk ballads are not consistent in focus, but when they shift, they shift abruptly.)
3. Does the content and form of the introductory and concluding stanzas show an attempt to unify this poem? How?

Other narratives

Except for the highly stylized ballad form, the narrative poet is his own master. He can choose his own stanzaic pattern, his own degree of subjectivity. He can make narrative verge on drama and incorporate lyrical elements.

The three narratives that follow, all nineteenth-century poems, all by romantic poets, illustrate this freedom. *The Rime of the Ancient Mariner*, ballad-like in form, is a philosophical narrative. "The Eve of St. Agnes," written in the elaborate Spenserian stanza (a nine-line stanza, rhyming *ababbcbcc*, the first eight lines pentameter, the last hexameter), subordinates its narrative to sensuous descriptive detail. "The Defence of Guenevere," written in intricate, interlocking terza rima stanzas (a succession of three-line pentameter stanzas rhyming *aba*, *bcb*, *cdc*, and so forth), approaches the dramatic monologue.

SAMUEL TAYLOR COLERIDGE

The Rime of the Ancient Mariner

ARGUMENT

How a Ship having passed the Line was driven by storms to the cold Country towards the South Pole; and how from thence she made her course to the tropical Latitude of the Great Pacific Ocean; and of the strange things that befell; and in what manner the Ancient Mariner came back to his own Country.

PART I

An ancient Mariner meeteth three Gallants bidden to a wedding-feast, and detaineth one.

It is an ancient Mariner,
And he stoppeth one of three.
"By thy long gray beard and glittering
        eye,
Now wherefore stopp'st thou me?

The Bridegroom's doors are opened
        wide,
And I am next of kin;
The guests are met, the feast is set:
May'st hear the merry din."

He holds him with his skinny hand,
"There was a ship," quoth he.   10

"Hold off! unhand me, graybeard
loon!"
Eftsoons his hand dropt he.

He holds him with his glittering eye—
The Wedding Guest stood still,
And listens like a three years' child:
The Mariner hath his will.

The Wedding Guest sat on a stone:
He cannot choose but hear;
And thus spake on that ancient man,
The bright-eyed Mariner.   20

"The ship was cheered, the harbor
cleared,
Merrily did we drop
Below the kirk, below the hill,
Below the lighthouse top.

The Sun came up upon the left,
Out of the sea came he!
And he shone bright, and on the right
Went down into the sea.

Higher and higher every day,
Till over the mast at noon—"   30
The Wedding Guest here beat his
breast,
For he heard the loud bassoon.

The bride hath paced into the hall,
Red as a rose is she;
Nodding their heads before her goes
The merry minstrelsy.

The Wedding Guest he beat his breast,
Yet he cannot choose but hear;
And thus spake on that ancient man,
The bright-eyed Mariner.   40

"And now the STORM-BLAST came, and
he
Was tyrannous and strong:
He struck with his o'ertaking wings,
And chased us south along.

With sloping masts and dipping prow,
As who pursued with yell and blow
Still treads the shadow of his foe,
And forward bends his head,

The ship drove fast, loud roared the
blast,
And southward aye we fled.   50

And now there came both mist and
snow,
And it grew wondrous cold:
And ice, mast-high, came floating by,
As green as emerald.

And through the drifts the snowy clifts
Did send a dismal sheen:
Nor shapes of men nor beasts we ken—
The ice was all between.

The ice was here, the ice was there,
The ice was all around: 60
It cracked and growled, and roared and
howled,
Like noises in a swound!

At length did cross an Albatross,
Through the fog it came;
As if it had been a Christian soul,
We hailed it in God's name.

It ate the food it ne'er had eat,
And round and round it flew.
The ice did split with a thunder-fit;
The helmsman steered us through!   70

And a good south wind sprung up be-
hind;
The Albatross did follow,
And every day, for food or play,
Came to the mariners' hollo!

In mist or cloud, on mast or shroud,
It perched for vespers nine;
Whiles all the night, through fog-smoke
white,
Glimmered the white Moon shine."

"God save thee, ancient Mariner!
From the fiends, that plague thee
thus!—   80

Why look'st thou so?"—With my
crossbow
I shot the ALBATROSS.

PART II

The Sun now rose upon the right:
Out of the sea came he,

Still hid in mist, and on the left
Went down into the sea.

And the good south wind still blew
　　behind,
But no sweet bird did follow,
Nor any day for food or play
Came to the mariners' hollo!　　90

And I had done a hellish thing,
And it would work 'em woe:
For all averred, I had killed the bird
That made the breeze to blow.
Ah wretch! said they, the bird to slay,
That made the breeze to blow!

Nor dim nor red, like God's own head,
The glorious Sun uprist:
Then all averred, I had killed the bird
That brought the fog and mist.　　100
'Twas right, said they, such birds to
　　slay,
That bring the fog and mist.

The fair breeze blew, the white foam
　　flew,
The furrow followed free;
We were the first that ever burst
Into that silent sea.

Down dropt the breeze, the sails dropt
　　down,
'Twas sad as sad could be;
And we did speak only to break
The silence of the sea!　　110

All in a hot and copper sky,
The bloody Sun, at noon,
Right up above the mast did stand,
No bigger than the Moon.

Day after day, day after day,
We stuck, nor breath nor motion;
As idle as a painted ship
Upon a painted ocean.

Water, water, everywhere,
And all the boards did shrink;　　120
Water, water, everywhere,
Nor any drop to drink.

The very deep did rot: O Christ!
That ever this should be!

Yea, slimy things did crawl with legs
Upon the slimy sea.

About, about, in reel and rout
The death-fires danced at night;
The water, like a witch's oils,
Burnt green, and blue and white.　　130

And some in dreams assurèd were
Of the Spirit that plagued us so;
Nine fathom deep he had followed us
From the land of mist and snow.

And every tongue, through utter
　　drought,
Was withered at the root;
We could not speak, no more than if
We had been choked with soot.

Ah! wel-a-day! what evil looks
Had I from old and young!　　140
Instead of the cross, the Albatross
About my neck was hung.

PART III

There passed a weary time. Each throat
Was parched, and glazed each eye.
A weary time! a weary time!
How glazed each weary eye,
When looking westward, I beheld
A something in the sky.

At first it seemed a little speck,
And then it seemed a mist;　　150
It moved and moved, and took at last
A certain shape, I wist.

A speck, a mist, a shape, I wist!
And still it neared and neared:
As if it dodged a water sprite,
It plunged and tacked and veered.

With throats unslaked, with black lips
　　baked,
We could nor laugh nor wail;
Through utter drought all dumb we
　　stood!
I bit my arm, I sucked the blood,　　160
And cried, A sail! a sail!

With throats unslaked, with black lips
　　baked,
Agape they heard me call:

A flash of joy;

Gramercy! they for joy did grin,
And all at once their breath drew in,
As they were drinking all.

And horror
follows. For
can it be a
ship that
comes onward
without wind
or tide?

See! see! (I cried) she tacks no more!
Hither to work us weal;
Without a breeze, without a tide,
She steadies with upright keel!   170

The western wave was all aflame.
The day was well nigh done!
Almost upon the western wave
Rested the broad bright Sun;
When that strange shape drove sud-
    denly
Betwixt us and the Sun.

It seemeth
him but the
skeleton of
a ship.
And its ribs
are seen as
bars on the
face of the
setting Sun.

And straight the Sun was flecked with
    bars,
(Heaven's Mother send us grace!)
As if through a dungeon grate he
    peered
With broad and burning face.   180

Alas! (thought I, and my heart beat
    loud)
How fast she nears and nears!
Are those *her* sails that glance in the
    Sun,
Like restless gossameres?

Are those *her* ribs through which the
    Sun

The Specter-
Woman and
her Death-
mate, and no
other on board
the skeleton
ship.

Did peer, as through a grate?
And is that Woman all her crew?
Is that a DEATH? and are there two?
Is DEATH that woman's mate?

Like vessel,
like crew!

Her lips were red, *her* looks were
    free,   190
Her locks were yellow as gold:
Her skin was as white as leprosy,
The Nightmare LIFE-IN-DEATH was she,
Who thicks man's blood with cold.

Death and
Life-in-Death
have diced for
the ship's
crew, and she
(the latter)
winneth the
ancient
Mariner.

The naked hulk alongside came,
And the twain were casting dice;
"The game is done! I've won! I've
    won!"
Quoth she, and whistles thrice.

No twilight
within the
courts of the
Sun.

The Sun's rim dips; the stars rush out:
At one stride comes the dark;   200
With far-heard whisper, o'er the sea,
Off shot the specter bark.

At the rising
of the Moon,

We listened and looked sideways up!
Fear at my heart, as at a cup,
My lifeblood seemed to sip!
The stars were dim, and thick the
    night,
The steersman's face by his lamp
    gleamed white;

From the sails the dew did drip—
Till clomb above the eastern bar
The hornèd Moon, with one bright
    star   210
Within the nether tip.

One after
another,

One after one, by the star-dogged
    Moon,
Too quick for groan or sigh,
Each turned his face with a ghastly
    pang,
And cursed me with his eye.

His shipmates
drop down
dead.

Four times fifty living men,
(And I heard nor sigh nor groan)
With heavy thump, a lifeless lump,
They dropped down one by one.

But Life-in-
Death begins
her work on
the ancient
Mariner.

The souls did from their bodies
    fly—   220
They fled to bliss or woe!
And every soul, it passed me by,
Like the whizz of my crossbow!

PART IV

The Wedding
Guest feareth
that a Spirit
is talking to
him;

"I fear thee, ancient Mariner!
I fear thy skinny hand!
And thou art long, and lank, and
    brown,
As is the ribbed sea-sand.

I fear thee and thy glittering eye,
And thy skinny hand, so brown."—

But the an-
cient Mariner
assureth him
of his bodily
life, and pro-
ceedeth to re-
late his hor-
rible penance.

Fear not, fear not, thou Wedding
    Guest!   230
This body dropt not down.

Alone, alone, all, all alone,
Alone on a wide wide sea!
And never a saint took pity on
My soul in agony.

He despiseth
the creatures
of the calm.

The many men, so beautiful!
And they all dead did lie:
And a thousand thousand slimy things
Lived on; and so did I.

And envieth
that *they*
should live,
and so many
lie dead.

I looked upon the rotting sea,   240
And drew my eyes away;
I looked upon the rotting deck,
And there the dead men lay.

I looked to heaven, and tried to pray;
But or ever a prayer had gusht,
A wicked whisper came, and made
My heart as dry as dust.

I closed my lids, and kept them close,
And the balls like pulses beat;
For the sky and the sea, and the sea
    and the sky   250
Lay like a load on my weary eye,
And the dead were at my feet.

But the curse
liveth for him
in the eye of
the dead men.

The cold sweat melted from their limbs,
Nor rot nor reek did they:
The look with which they looked on me
Had never passed away.

An orphan's curse would drag to hell
A spirit from on high;
But oh! more horrible than that
Is the curse in a dead man's eye!   260

In his lone-
liness and fix-
edness he
yearneth to-
wards the
journeying
Moon, and the
stars that still
sojourn, yet
still move on-
ward; and ev-
erywhere the
blue sky be-
longs to
them, and is
their ap-
pointed rest,
and their na-
tive country
and their
own natural
homes,
which they
enter unan-
nounced, as
lords that are
certainly ex-
pected and
yet there is a
silent joy at
their arrival.
By the light
of the Moon
he beholdeth
God's crea-
tures of the
great calm.

Seven days, seven nights, I saw that
    curse,
And yet I could not die.

The moving Moon went up the sky,
And nowhere did abide:
Softly she was going up,
And a star or two beside—

Her beams bemocked the sultry main,
Like April hoarfrost spread;
But where the ship's huge shadow
    lay,
The charmèd water burnt alway   270
A still and awful red.

Beyond the shadow of the ship,
I watched the water snakes:
They moved in tracks of shining white,
And when they reared, the elfish light
Fell off in hoary flakes.

Within the shadow of the ship
I watched their rich attire:
Blue, glossy green, and velvet black,
They coiled and swam; and every
    track   280
Was a flash of golden fire.

Their beauty
and their
happiness.

He blesseth
them in his
heart.

O happy living things! no tongue
Their beauty might declare:
A spring of love gushed from my heart,
And I blessed them unaware:
Sure my kind saint took pity on me,
And I blessed them unaware.

The spell
begins to
break.

The selfsame moment I could pray;
And from my neck so free
The Albatross fell off, and sank   290
Like lead into the sea.

PART V

Oh sleep! it is a gentle thing,
Beloved from pole to pole!
To Mary Queen the praise be given!
She sent the gentle sleep from Heaven,
That slid into my soul.

By grace of
the holy
Mother, the
ancient Mar-
iner is re-
freshed with
rain.

The silly buckets on the deck,
That had so long remained,
I dreamt that they were filled with dew;
And when I awoke, it rained.   300

My lips were wet, my throat was cold,
My garments all were dank;
Sure I had drunken in my dreams,
And still my body drank.

I moved, and could not feel my limbs:
I was so light—almost
I thought that I had died in sleep,
And was a blessèd ghost.

He heareth
sounds and
seeth strange
sights and
commotions
in the sky
and the ele-
ments.

And soon I heard a roaring wind:
It did not come anear;   310
But with its sound it shook the sails,
That were so thin and sere.

The upper air burst into life!
And a hundred fireflags sheen,
To and fro they were hurried about!
And to and fro, and in and out,
The wan stars danced between.

And the coming wind did roar more
    loud,
And the sails did sigh like sedge;
And the rain poured down from one
    black cloud;   320
The Moon was at its edge.

The thick black cloud was cleft, and still
The Moon was at its side:

Like waters shot from some high crag,
The lightning fell with never a jag,
A river steep and wide.

The bodies of
the ship's
crew are in-
spired and the
ship moves
on;
The loud wind never reached the ship,
Yet now the ship moved on!
Beneath the lightning and the Moon
The dead men gave a groan.   330

They groaned, they stirred, they all up-
rose,
Nor spake, nor moved their eyes;
It had been strange, even in a dream,
To have seen those dead men rise.

The helmsman steered, the ship moved
on;
Yet never a breeze upblew;
The mariners all 'gan work the ropes,
Where they were wont to do;
They raised their limbs like lifeless
tools—
We were a ghastly crew.   340

The body of my brother's son
Stood by me, knee to knee:
The body and I pulled at one rope,
But he said nought to me.

But not by
the souls of
the men, nor
by demons of
earth or mid-
dle air, but
by a blessed
troop of an-
gelic spirits,
sent down by
the invocation
of the guard-
ian saint.
"I fear thee, ancient Mariner!"
Be calm, thou Wedding Guest!
'Twas not those souls that fled in pain,
Which to their corses came again,
But a troop of spirits blest:

For when it dawned—they dropped
their arms,   350
And clustered round the mast;
Sweet sounds rose slowly through their
mouths,
And from their bodies passed.

Around, around, flew each sweet sound,
Then darted to the Sun;
Slowly the sounds came back again,
Now mixed, now one by one.

Sometimes a-dropping from the sky
I heard the skylark sing;
Sometimes all little birds that are,   360
How they seemed to fill the sea and air
With their sweet jargoning!

And now 'twas like all instruments,
Now like a lonely flute;

And now it is an angel's song,
That makes the heavens be mute.

It ceased; yet still the sails made on
A pleasant noise till noon,
A noise like of a hidden brook
In the leafy month of June,   370
That to the sleeping woods all night
Singeth a quiet tune.

Till noon we quietly sailed on,
Yet never a breeze did breathe:
Slowly and smoothly went the ship,
Moved onward from beneath.

The lonesome
Spirit from
the South
Pole carries
on the ship
as far as the
Line, in obedi-
ence to the
angelic troop,
but still re-
quireth venge-
ance.
Under the keel nine fathom deep,
From the land of mist and snow,
The spirit slid; and it was he
That made the ship to go.   380
The sails at noon left off their tune,
And the ship stood still also.

The Sun, right up above the mast,
Had fixed her to the ocean:
But in a minute she 'gan stir,
With a short uneasy motion—
Backwards and forwards half her length
With a short uneasy motion.

Then like a pawing horse let go,
She made a sudden bound: 390
It flung the blood into my head,
And I fell down in a swound.

How long in that same fit I lay,
I have not to declare;
But ere my living life returned,
I heard and in my soul discerned
Two voices in the air.

The Polar
Spirit's fel-
low-demons,
the invisible
inhabitants of
the element,
take part in
his wrong;
and two of
them relate,
one to the
other, that
penance long
and heavy
for the an-
cient Mariner
hath been ac-
corded to the
Polar Spirit,
who returneth
southward.
"Is it he?" quoth one, "Is this the man?
By him who died on cross,
With his cruel bow he laid full low   400
The harmless Albatross.

The spirit who bideth by himself
In the land of mist and snow,
He loved the bird that loved the man
Who shot him with his bow."

The other was a softer voice,
As soft as honeydew:
Quoth he, "The man hath penance
done,
And penance more will do."

PART VI

FIRST VOICE

"But tell me, tell me! speak again,   410
Thy soft response renewing—
What makes that ship drive on so fast?
What is the ocean doing?"

SECOND VOICE

"Still as a slave before his lord,
The ocean hath no blast;
His great bright eye most silently
Up to the Moon is cast—

If he may know which way to go;
For she guides him smooth or grim.
See, brother, see! how graciously   420
She looketh down on him."

FIRST VOICE

The Mariner hath been cast into a trance; for the angelic power causeth the vessel to drive northward faster than human life could endure.

"But why drives on that ship so fast,
Without or wave or wind?"

SECOND VOICE

"The air is cut away before,
And closes from behind.

Fly, brother, fly! more high, more high!
Or we shall be belated:
For slow and slow that ship will go,
When the Mariner's trance is abated."

The supernatural motion is retarded; the Mariner awakes, and his penance begins anew.

I woke, and we were sailing on   430
As in a gentle weather:
'Twas night, calm night, the moon was high;
The dead men stood together.

All stood together on the deck,
For a charnel-dungeon fitter:
All fixed on me their stony eyes,
That in the Moon did glitter.

The pang, the curse, with which they died,
Had never passed away:
I could not draw my eyes from theirs,   440
Nor turn them up to pray.

The curse is finally expiated.

And now this spell was snapt: once more
I viewed the ocean green,

And looked far forth, yet little saw
Of what had else been seen—

Like one, that on a lonesome road
Doth walk in fear and dread,
And having once turned round walks on,
And turns no more his head;
Because he knows, a frightful fiend   450
Doth close behind him tread.

But soon there breathed a wind on me,
Nor sound nor motion made:
Its path was not upon the sea,
In ripple or in shade.

It raised my hair, it fanned my cheek
Like a meadow-gale of spring—
It mingled strangely with my fears,
Yet it felt like a welcoming.

Swiftly, swiftly flew the ship,   460
Yet she sailed softly too:
Sweetly, sweetly blew the breeze—
On me alone it blew.

And the ancient Mariner beholdeth his native country.

Oh! dream of joy! is this indeed
The lighthouse top I see?
Is this the hill? is this the kirk?
Is this mine own countree?

We drifted o'er the harbor-bar,
And I with sobs did pray—
O let me be awake, my God!   470
Or let me sleep alway.

The harbor-bay was clear as glass,
So smoothly it was strewn!
And on the bay the moonlight lay,
And the shadow of the Moon.

The rock shone bright, the kirk no less,
That stands above the rock:
The moonlight steeped in silentness
The steady weathercock.

And the bay was white with silent light,   480
Till rising from the same,
Full many shapes, that shadows were,
In crimson colors came.

The angelic spirits leave the dead bodies,

And appear in their own forms of light.

A little distance from the prow
Those crimson shadows were:

I turned my eyes upon the deck—
Oh, Christ! what saw I there!

Each corse lay flat, lifeless and flat,
And, by the holy rood!
A man all light, a seraph man,   490
On every corse there stood.

This seraph band, each waved his hand:
It was a heavenly sight!
They stood as signals to the land,
Each one a lovely light;

This seraph band, each waved his hand,
No voice did they impart—
No voice; but oh! the silence sank
Like music on my heart.

But soon I heard the dash of oars,   500
I heard the Pilot's cheer;
My head was turned perforce away
And I saw a boat appear.

The Pilot and the Pilot's boy,
I heard them coming fast:
Dear Lord in Heaven! it was a joy
The dead men could not blast.

I saw a third—I heard his voice:
It is the Hermit good!
He singeth loud his godly hymns   510
That he makes in the wood.
He'll shrieve my soul, he'll wash away
The Albatross's blood.

PART VII

The Hermit of the Wood,

This Hermit good lives in that wood
Which slopes down to the sea.
How loudly his sweet voice he rears!
He loves to talk with mariners
That come from a far countree.

He kneels at morn, and noon, and eve—
He hath a cushion plump: 520
It is the moss that wholly hides
The rotted old oak stump.

The skiff boat neared: I heard them talk,
"Why, this is strange, I trow!
Where are those lights so many and fair,
That signal made but now?"

Approacheth the ship with wonder.

"Strange, by my faith!" the Hermit said—
"And they answered not our cheer!
The planks looked warped! and see those sails,
How thin they are and sere!   530
I never saw aught like to them,
Unless perchance it were

Brown skeletons of leaves that lag
My forest-brook along;
When the ivy tod is heavy with snow,
And the owlet whoops to the wolf below,
That eats the she-wolf's young."

"Dear Lord! it hath a fiendish look—
(The Pilot made reply)
I am afeared"—"Push on, push on!"   540
Said the Hermit cheerily.

The boat came closer to the ship,
But I nor spake nor stirred;
The boat came close beneath the ship,
And straight a sound was heard.

The ship suddenly sinketh.

Under the water it rumbled on,
Still louder and more dread:
It reached the ship, it split the bay;
The ship went down like lead.

The ancient Mariner is saved in the Pilot's boat.

Stunned by that loud and dreadful sound,   550
Which sky and ocean smote,
Like one that hath been seven days drowned
My body lay afloat;
But swift as dreams, myself I found
Within the Pilot's boat.

Upon the whirl, where sank the ship,
The boat spun round and round;
And all was still, save that the hill
Was telling of the sound.

I moved my lips—the Pilot shrieked   560
And fell down in a fit;
The holy Hermit raised his eyes,
And prayed where he did sit.

I took the oars: the Pilot's boy,
Who now doth crazy go,

Laughed loud and long, and all the
   while
His eyes went to and fro.
"Ha! ha!" quoth he, "full plain I see,
The Devil knows how to row."

And now, all in my own countree,   570
I stood on the firm land!
The Hermit stepped forth from the
   boat,
And scarcely he could stand.

The ancient Mariner earnestly entreateth the Hermit to shrieve him; and the penance of life falls on him.

"O shrieve me, shrieve me, holy man!"
The Hermit crossed his brow.
"Say quick," quoth he, "I bid thee say—
What manner of man art thou?"

Forthwith this frame of mine was
   wrenched
With a woful agony,
Which forced me to begin my tale;   580
And then it left me free.

And ever and anon throughout his future life an agony constraineth him to travel from land to land;

Since then, at an uncertain hour,
That agony returns:
And till my ghastly tale is told,
This heart within me burns.

I pass, like night, from land to land;
I have strange power of speech;
That moment that his face I see,
I know the man that must hear me:
To him my tale I teach.   590

What loud uproar bursts from that
   door!
The wedding guests are there:
But in the garden-bower the bride
And bridemaids singing are:
And hark the little vesper bell,
Which biddeth me to prayer!

O Wedding Guest! this soul hath been
Alone on a wide, wide sea:
So lonely 'twas, that God himself
Scarce seemèd there to be.   600

O sweeter than the marriage feast,
'Tis sweeter far to me,
To walk together to the kirk
With a goodly company!—

To walk together to the kirk,
And all together pray,

While each to his great Father bends,
Old men, and babes, and loving friends
And youths and maidens gay!

And to teach, by his own example, love and reverence to all things that God made and loveth.

Farewell, farewell! but this I tell   610
To thee, thou Wedding Guest!
He prayeth well, who loveth well
Both man and bird and beast.

He prayeth best, who loveth best
All things both great and small;
For the dear God who loveth us,
He made and loveth all."

The Mariner, whose eye is bright,
Whose beard with age is hoar,
Is gone: and now the Wedding
   Guest   620
Turned from the bridegroom's door.

He went like one that hath been
   stunned,
And is of sense forlorn:
A sadder and a wiser man,
He rose the morrow morn.

FOR ANALYSIS

1. What conventions of the folk ballad has Coleridge preserved in this poem?

2. As Coleridge himself argued, the moral dealing with loving all things is the Mariner's moral and not necessarily the theme of the poem. And even that moral is no solution to the Mariner's problem. What is his perpetual penance?

3. Why does the Mariner kill the albatross? Many readers have felt that the punishment for that deed is not proportionate to the crime. But the bird has been associated with Christ and humanity at large in the poem, which may help to explain the severity of the punishment. Moreover, if the Mariner's killing of the bird was an impulsive, irrational act, how does the punishment fit the crime?

4. As even Coleridge's friend Wordsworth noted, the Mariner is a curiously passive creature; most of the time he is acted upon rather than acting. At what crucial spots does he act?

5. What is it that the Mariner must learn to do before the worst of his punishment is over? Must he learn to do it rationally or instinctively? How does this match the crime?

6. In what way is the Wedding Guest a sadder and wiser man after listening to the Mariner? Is it important that he is a Wedding Guest? What

difference would it make if he were going to a funeral or were simply a man on the street?

JOHN KEATS

The Eve of St. Agnes

1

St. Agnes' Eve—Ah, bitter chill it was!
The owl, for all his feathers, was a-cold;
The hare limped trembling through the frozen grass,
And silent was the flock in woolly fold:
Numb were the Beadsman's fingers, while he told
His rosary, and while his frosted breath,
Like pious incense from a censer old,
Seemed taking flight for heaven, without a death,
Past the sweet Virgin's picture, while his prayer he saith.

2

His prayer he saith, this patient, holy man;   10
Then takes his lamp, and riseth from his knees,
And back returneth, meager, barefoot, wan,
Along the chapel aisle by slow degrees:
The sculptured dead, on each side, seem to freeze,
Emprisoned in black, purgatorial rails:
Knights, ladies, praying in dumb orat'ries,
He passeth by; and his weak spirit fails
To think how they may ache in icy hoods and mails.

3

Northward he turneth through a little door,
And scarce three steps, ere Music's golden tongue   20
Flattered to tears this aged man and poor;
But no—already had his deathbell rung:
The joys of all his life were said and sung:
His was harsh penance on St. Agnes' Eve:
Another way he went, and soon among
Rough ashes sat he for his soul's reprieve,
And all night kept awake, for sinner's sake to grieve.

4

That ancient Beadsman heard the prelude soft;
And so it chanced, for many a door was wide,
From hurry to and fro. Soon, up aloft,   30
The silver, snarling trumpets 'gan to chide:
The level chambers, ready with their pride,
Were glowing to receive a thousand guests:
The carvèd angels, ever eager-eyed,
Stared, where upon their heads the cornice rests,
With hair blown back, and wings put cross-wise on their breasts.

5

At length burst in the argent revelry,
With plume, tiara, and all rich array,
Numerous as shadows haunting fairily
The brain, new stuffed, in youth, with triumphs gay   40
Of old romance. These let us wish away,
And turn, sole-thoughted, to one Lady there,
Whose heart had brooded, all that wintry day,
On love, and winged St. Agnes' saintly care,
As she had heard old dames full many times declare.

6

They told her how, upon St. Agnes' Eve,
Young virgins might have visions of delight,
And soft adorings from their loves receive
Upon the honeyed middle of the night,
If ceremonies due they did aright;   50
As, supperless to bed they must retire,
And couch supine their beauties, lily white;
Nor look behind, nor sideways, but require
Of Heaven with upward eyes for all that they desire.

7

Full of this whim was thoughtful Madeline:
The music, yearning like a god in pain,
She scarcely heard: her maiden eyes divine,
Fixed on the floor, saw many a sweeping train
Pass by—she heeded not at all: in vain
Came many a tiptoe, amorous cavalier,   60
And back retired; not cooled by high disdain,
But she saw not: her heart was otherwhere:
She sighed for Agnes' dreams, the sweetest of the year.

8

She danced along with vague, regardless eyes,
Anxious her lips, her breathing quick and short:
The hallowed hour was near at hand: she sighs
Amid the timbrels, and the thronged resort
Of whispers in anger, or in sport;
'Mid looks of love, defiance, hate, and scorn,
Hoodwinked with faery fancy; all amort,   70
Save to St. Agnes and her lambs unshorn,
And all the bliss to be before to-morrow morn.

9

So, purposing each moment to retire,
She lingered still. Meantime, across the moors,
Had come young Porphyro, with heart on fire
For Madeline. Beside the portal doors,
Buttressed from moonlight, stands he, and
    implores
All saints to give him sight of Madeline,
But for one moment in the tedious hours,
That he might gaze and worship all unseen;   80
Perchance speak, kneel, touch, kiss—in sooth such
    things have been.

10

He ventures in: let no buzzed whisper tell:
All eyes be muffled, or a hundred swords
Will storm his heart, Love's fev'rous citadel:
For him, those chambers held barbarian hordes,
Hyena foemen, and hot-blooded lords,
Whose very dogs would execrations howl
Against his lineage; not one breast affords
Him any mercy, in that mansion foul,
Save one old beldame, weak in body and in soul.   90

11

Ah, happy chance! the aged creature came,
Shuffling along with ivory-headed wand,
To where he stood, hid from the torch's flame,
Behind a broad hall-pillar, far beyond
The sound of merriment and chorus bland:
He startled her: but soon she knew his face,
And grasped his fingers in her palsied hand,
Saying, "Mercy, Porphyro! hie thee from this
    place;
They are all here to-night, the whole blood-thirsty
    race!

12

"Get hence! get hence! there's dwarfish Hilde-
    brand;   100
He had a fever late, and in the fit
He cursèd thee and thine, both house and land:
Then there's that old Lord Maurice, not a whit
More tame for his gray hairs—Alas me! flit!
Flit like a ghost away."—"Ah, Gossip dear,
We're safe enough; here in this arm-chair sit,
And tell me how"—"Good Saints; not here, not
    here;
Follow me, child, or else these stones will be thy
    bier."

13

He followed through a lowly arched way,
Brushing the cobwebs with his lofty plume,   110
And as she muttered "Well-a—well-a-day!"
He found him in a little moonlight room,
Pale, latticed, chill, and silent as a tomb.
"Now tell me where is Madeline," said he,
"O tell me, Angela, by the holy loom
Which none but secret sisterhood may see,
When they St. Agnes' wool are weaving piously."

14

"St. Agnes! Ah! it is St. Agnes' Eve—
Yet men will murder upon holy days:
Thou must hold water in a witch's sieve,   120
And be liege-lord of all the Elves and Fays,
To venture so: it fills me with amaze
To see thee, Porphyro!—St. Agnes' Eve!
God's help! my lady fair the conjuror plays
This very night: good angels her deceive!
But let me laugh awhile, I've mickle time to grieve."

15

Feebly she laugheth in the languid moon,
While Porphyro upon her face doth look,
Like puzzled urchin on an aged crone
Who keepeth closed a wondrous riddle-
    book,   130
As spectacled she sits in chimney nook.
But soon his eyes grew brilliant, when she told
His lady's purpose; and he scarce could brook
Tears, at the thought of those enchantments cold,
And Madeline asleep in lap of legends old.

16

Sudden a thought came like a full-blown rose,
Flushing his brow, and in his painèd heart
Made purple riot: then doth he propose
A stratagem, that makes the beldame start:
"A cruel man and impious thou art: 140
Sweet lady, let her pray, and sleep, and dream
Alone with her good angels, far apart
From wicked men like thee. Go, go!—I deem
Thou canst not surely be the same that thou didst
    seem."

17

"I will not harm her, by all saints I swear,"
Quoth Porphyro: "O may I ne'er find grace
When my weak voice shall whisper its last prayer,

If one of her soft ringlets I displace,
Or look with ruffian passion in her face:
Good Angela, believe me by these tears;   150
Or I will, even in a moment's space,
Awake, with horrid shout, my foemen's ears,
And beard them, though they be more fanged than
    wolves and bears."

18

"Ah! why wilt thou affright a feeble soul?
A poor, weak, palsy-stricken, churchyard thing,
Whose passing-bell may ere the midnight toll;
Whose prayers for thee, each morn and evening,
Were never missed."—Thus plaining, doth she
    bring
A gentler speech from burning Porphyro;
So woeful, and of such deep sorrowing,   160
That Angela gives promise she will do
Whatever he shall wish, betide her weal or woe.

19

Which was, to lead him, in close secrecy,
Even to Madeline's chamber, and there hide
Him in a closet, of such privacy
That he might see her beauty unespied,
And win perhaps that night a peerless bride,
While legioned faeries paced the coverlet,
And pale enchantment held her sleepy-eyed.
Never on such a night have lovers met,   170
Since Merlin paid his Demon all the monstrous
    debt.

20

"It shall be as thou wishest," said the Dame:
"All cates and dainties shall be storèd there
Quickly on this feast-night: by the tambour frame
Her own lute thou wilt see: no time to spare,
For I am slow and feeble, and scarce dare
On such a catering trust my dizzy head.
Wait here, my child, with patience; kneel in prayer
The while: Ah! thou must needs the lady wed,
Or may I never leave my grave among the
    dead."   180

21

So saying, she hobbled off with busy fear.
The lover's endless minutes slowly passed:
The dame returned, and whispered in his ear
To follow her; with aged eyes aghast
From fright of dim espial. Safe at last,

Through many a dusky gallery, they gain
The maiden's chamber, silken, hushed, and
    chaste;
Where Porphyro took covert, pleased amain.
His poor guide hurried back with agues in her brain.

22

Her falt'ring hand upon the balustrade,   190
Old Angela was feeling for the stair,
When Madeline, St. Agnes' charmèd maid,
Rose, like a missioned spirit, unaware:
With silver taper's light, and pious care,
She turned, and down the aged gossip led
To a safe level matting. Now prepare,
Young Porphyro, for gazing on that bed;
She comes, she comes again, like ring-dove frayed
    and fled.

23

Out went the taper as she hurried in;
Its little smoke, in pallid moonshine, died: 200
She closed the door, she panted, all akin
To spirits of the air, and visions wide:
No uttered syllable, or, woe betide!
But to her heart, her heart was voluble,
Paining with eloquence her balmy side;
As though a tongueless nightingale should swell
Her throat in vain, and die, heart-stifled, in her dell.

24

A casement high and triple-arched there was,
All garlanded with carven imag'ries
Of fruits, and flowers, and bunches of knot-
    grass,   210
And diamonded with panes of quaint device,
Innumerable of stains and splendid dyes,
As are the tiger-moth's deep-damasked wings;
And in the midst, 'mong thousand heraldries,
And twilight saints, and dim emblazonings,
A shielded scutcheon blushed with blood of queens
    and kings.

25

Full on this casement shone the wintry moon,
And threw warm gules on Madeline's fair breast,
As down she knelt for heaven's grace and boon;
Rose-bloom fell on her hands, together
    pressed,   220
And on her silver cross soft amethyst,
And on her hair a glory, like a saint:

She seemed a splendid angel, newly dressed,
Save wings, for heaven:—Porphyro grew faint:
She knelt, so pure a thing, so free from mortal taint.

26

Anon his heart revives: her vespers done,
Of all its wreathèd pearls her hair she frees;
Unclasps her warmèd jewels one by one;
Loosens her fragrant bodice; by degrees
Her rich attire creeps rustling to her knees: 230
Half-hidden, like a mermaid in sea-weed,
Pensive awhile she dreams awake, and sees,
In fancy, fair St. Agnes in her bed,
But dares not look behind, or all the charm is fled.

27

Soon, trembling in her soft and chilly nest,
In sort of wakeful swoon, perplexed she lay,
Until the poppied warmth of sleep oppressed
Her soothèd limbs, and soul fatigued away;
Flown, like a thought, until the morrow-day;
Blissfully havened both from joy and pain;   240
Clasped like a missal where swart Paynims pray;
Blinded alike from sunshine and from rain,
As though a rose should shut, and be a bud again.

28

Stol'n to this paradise, and so entranced,
Porphyro gazed upon her empty dress,
And listened to her breathing, if it chanced
To wake into a slumberous tenderness;
Which when he heard, that minute did he bless,
And breathed himself: then from the closet crept,
Noiseless as fear in a wide wilderness,   250
And over the hushed carpet, silent, stepped,
And 'tween the curtains peeped, where, lo!—how
     fast she slept.

29

Then by the bed-side, where the faded moon
Made a dim, silver twilight, soft he set
A table, and, half anguished, threw thereon
A cloth of woven crimson, gold, and jet:—
O for some drowsy Morphean amulet!
The boisterous, midnight, festive clarion,
The kettle-drum, and far-heard clarinet,
Affray his ears, though but in dying tone:—   260
The hall door shuts again, and all the noise is gone.

30

And still she slept an azure-lidded sleep,
In blanchèd linen, smooth, and lavendered,

While he from forth the closet brought a heap
Of candied apple, quince, and plum, and gourd;
With jellies soother than the creamy curd,
And lucent syrops, tinct with cinnamon;
Manna and dates, in argosy transferred
From Fez; and spicèd dainties, every one,
From silken Samarkand to cedared Lebanon.   270

31

These delicates he heaped with glowing hand
On golden dishes and in baskets bright
Of wreathèd silver: sumptuous they stand
In the retired quiet of the night,
Filling the chilly room with perfume light.—
"And now, my love, my seraph fair, awake!
Thou art my heaven, and I thine eremite:
Open thine eyes, for meek St. Agnes' sake,
Or I shall drowse beside thee, so my soul doth
     ache."

32

Thus whispering, his warm, unnerved arm   280
Sank in her pillow. Shaded was her dream
By the dusk curtains:—'twas a midnight charm
Impossible to melt as icèd stream:
The lustrous salvers in the moonlight gleam;
Broad golden fringe upon the carpet lies:
It seemed he never, never could redeem
From such a stedfast spell his lady's eyes;
So mused awhile, entoiled in woofèd phantasies.

33

Awakening up, he took her hollow lute—
Tumultuous—and, in chords that tenderest
     be,   290
He played an ancient ditty, long since mute,
In Provence called, "La belle dame sans mercy":
Close to her ear touching the melody;—
Wherewith disturbed, she uttered a soft moan:
He ceased—she panted quick—and suddenly
Her blue affrayèd eyes wide open shone:
Upon his knees he sank, pale as smooth-sculptured
     stone.

34

Her eyes were open, but she still beheld,
Now wide awake, the vision of her sleep:
There was a painful change, that nigh
     expelled   300
The blisses of her dream so pure and deep
At which fair Madeline began to weep,
And moan forth witless words with many a sigh;

While still her gaze on Porphyro would keep;
Who knelt, with joinèd hands and piteous eye,
Fearing to move or speak, she looked so dreamingly.

35

"Ah, Porphyro!" said she, "but even now
Thy voice was at sweet tremble in mine ear,
Made tuneable with every sweetest vow;
And those sad eyes were spiritual and clear: 310
How changed thou art! how pallid, chill, and
    drear!
Give me that voice again, my Porphyro,
Those looks immortal, those complainings dear!
Oh leave me not in this eternal woe,
For if thou diest, my Love, I know not where to go."

36

Beyond a mortal man impassioned far
At these voluptuous accents, he arose,
Ethereal, flushed, and like a throbbing star
Seen mid the sapphire heaven's deep repose;
Into her dream he melted, as the rose   320
Blended its odor with the violet—
Solution sweet: meantime the frost-wind blows
Like Love's alarum pattering the sharp sleet
Against the window-panes; St. Agnes' moon hath
    set.

37

'Tis dark: quick pattereth the flaw-blown sleet:
"This is no dream, my bride, my Madeline!"
'Tis dark: the icèd gusts still rave and beat:
"No dream, alas! alas! and woe is mine!
Porphyro will leave me here to fade and pine.—
Cruel! what traitor could thee hither bring?   330
I curse not, for my heart is lost in thine,
Though thou forsakest a deceivèd thing;—
A dove forlorn and lost with sick unprunèd wing."

38

"My Madeline! sweet dreamer! lovely bride!
Say, may I be for aye thy vassal blest?
Thy beauty's shield, heart-shaped and vermeil
    dyed?
Ah, silver shrine, here will I take my rest
After so many hours of toil and quest,
A famished pilgrim—saved by miracle.
Though I have found, I will not rob thy nest   340
Saving of thy sweet self; if thou think'st well
To trust, fair Madeline, to no rude infidel.

39

"Hark! 'tis an elfin-storm from faery land,
Of haggard seeming, but a boon indeed:
Arise—arise! the morning is at hand;—
The bloated wassailers will never heed:—
Let us away, my love, with happy speed;
There are no ears to hear, or eyes to see—
Drowned all in Rhenish and the sleepy mead:
Awake! arise! my love, and fearless be,   350
For o'er the southern moors I have a home for thee."

40

She hurried at his words, beset with fears,
For there were sleeping dragons all around,
At glaring watch, perhaps, with ready spears—
Down the wide stairs a darkling way they
    found.—
In all the house was heard no human sound.
A chain-drooped lamp was flickering by each
    door;
The arras, rich with horseman, hawk, and hound,
Fluttered in the besieging wind's uproar;
And the long carpets rose along the gusty
    floor.   360

41

They glide, like phantoms, into the wide hall;
Like phantoms, to the iron porch, they glide;
Where lay the Porter, in uneasy sprawl,
With a huge empty flagon by his side:
The wakeful bloodhound rose, and shook his
    hide,
But his sagacious eye an inmate owns:
By one, and one, the bolts full easy slide:—
The chains lie silent on the footworn stones;—
The key turns, and the door upon its hinges groans.

42

And they are gone: aye, ages long ago   370
These lovers fled away into the storm.
That night the Baron dreamt of many a woe,
And all his warrior-guests, with shade and form
Of witch, and demon, and large coffin-worm,
Were long be-nightmared. Angela the old
Died palsy-twitched, with meager face deform;
The Beadsman, after thousands aves told,
For aye unsought-for slept among his ashes cold.

FOR ANALYSIS

1. The poem is based on the ancient legend that on
   St. Agnes' Eve, January 20, traditionally the

coldest night of the year, a virgin can see in a vision her future husband if she performs a stipulated ritual. How does this legend furnish a plot for the poem?

2. In an early version of the poem, Keats had Porphyro and Madeline actually consummate their visionary marriage in her room. His friends objected strenuously and he changed the poem. What would this episode do to the poem as it now stands?

3. What colors dominate the early part of the poem?

4. What colors are associated with Porphyro and Madeline? How do they contrast with the other colors?

5. Besides color imagery, what other sensuous appeal has Keats built into the poem? Take lines 262–271, for example. What sense impressions are heaped up there? Then consider just line 262. Notice the sound pattern of the vowels:

> And still she slept an azure-lidded sleep
>   *a*   *i* *e*   *a* *i*   *e*

Now take lines 98 and 99 and see how the vowels make a much more complicated pattern.

WILLIAM MORRIS

The Defence of Guenevere

But, knowing now that they would have her speak,
She threw her wet hair backward from her brow,
Her hand close to her mouth touching her cheek,

As though she had had there a shameful blow,
And feeling it shameful to feel aught but shame
All through her heart, yet felt her cheek burned so,

She must a little touch it; like one lame
She walked away from Gauwaine, with her head
Still lifted up; and on her cheek of flame

The tears dried quick; she stopped at last and said: 10
"O knights and lords, it seems but little skill
To talk of well-known things past now and dead.

"God wot I ought to say, I have done ill,
And pray you all forgiveness heartily!
Because you must be right, such great lords—still

"Listen, suppose your time were come to die,
And you were quite alone and very weak;
Yea, laid a dying while very mightily

"The wind was ruffling up the narrow streak
Of river through your broad lands running well: 20
Suppose a hush should come, then some one speak:

" 'One of these cloths is heaven, and one is hell,
Now choose one cloth for ever; which they be,
I will not tell you, you must somehow tell

" 'Of your own strength and mightiness; here, see!'
Yea, yea, my lord, and you to ope your eyes,
At foot of your familiar bed to see

"A great God's angel standing, with such dyes,
Not known on earth, on his great wings, and hands
Held out two ways, light from the inner skies   30

"Showing him well, and making his commands
Seem to be God's commands, moreover, too,
Holding within his hands the cloths on wands;

"And one of these strange choosing cloths was blue,
Wavy and long, and one cut short and red;
No man could tell the better of the two.

"After a shivering half-hour you said:
'God help! heaven's colour, the blue'; and he said: 'hell.'
Perhaps you then would roll upon your bed,

"And cry to all good men that loved you well,   40
'Ah Christ! if only I had known, known, known';
Launcelot went away, then I could tell,

"Like wisest man how all things would be, moan,
And roll and hurt myself, and long to die,
And yet fear much to die for what was sown.

"Nevertheless you, O Sir Gauwaine, lie,
Whatever may have happened through these years,
God knows I speak truth, saying that you lie."

Her voice was low at first, being full of tears,
But as it cleared, it grew full loud and shrill,   50
Growing a windy shriek in all men's ears,

A ringing in their startled brains, until
She said that Gauwaine lied, then her voice sunk,
And her great eyes began again to fill,

Though still she stood right up, and never shrunk,
But spoke on bravely, glorious lady fair!
Whatever tears her full lips may have drunk,

She stood, and seemed to think, and wrung her hair,
Spoke out at last with no more trace of shame,
With passionate twisting of her body there: 60

"It chanced upon a day that Launcelot came
To dwell at Arthur's court: at Christmas-time
This happened; when the heralds sung his name,

" 'Son of King Ban of Benwick,' seemed to chime
Along with all the bells that rang that day,
O'er the white roofs, with little change of rhyme.

"Christmas and whitened winter passed away,
And over me the April sunshine came,
Made very awful with black hail-clouds, yea

"And in the Summer I grew white with flame,   70
And bowed my head down—Autumn, and the sick
Sure knowledge things would never be the same,

"However often Spring might be most thick
Of blossoms and buds, smote on me, and I grew
Careless of most things, let the clock tick, tick,

"To my unhappy pulse, that beat right through
My eager body; while I laughed out loud,
And let my lips curl up at false or true,

"Seemed cold and shallow without any cloud.
Behold my judges, then the cloths were brought: 80
While I was dizzied thus, old thoughts would crowd,

"Belonging to the time ere I was bought
By Arthur's great name and his little love;
Must I give up for ever then, I thought,

"That which I deemed would ever round me move
Glorifying all things; for a little word,
Scarce ever meant at all, must I now prove

"Stone-cold for ever? Pray you, does the Lord
Will that all folks should be quite happy and good?
I love God now a little, if this cord   90

"Were broken, once for all what striving could
Make me love anything in earth or heaven?
So day by day it grew, as if one should

"Slip slowly down some path worn smooth and even,
Down to a cool sea on a summer day;
Yet still in slipping was there some small leaven

"Of stretched hands catching small stones by the
     way,
Until one surely reached the sea at last,
And felt strange new joy as the worn head lay

"Back, with the hair like sea-weed; yea all past   100
Sweat of the forehead, dryness of the lips,
Washed utterly out by the dear waves o'ercast,

"In the lone sea, far off from any ships!
Do I not know now of a day in Spring?
No minute of that wild day ever slips

"From out my memory; I hear thrushes sing,
And wheresoever I may be, straightway
Thoughts of it all come up with most fresh sting:

"I was half mad with beauty on that day,
And went without my ladies all alone,   110
In a quiet garden walled round every way;

"I was right joyful of that wall of stone,
That shut the flowers and trees up with the sky,
And trebled all the beauty: to the bone,

"Yea right through to my heart, grown very shy
With weary thoughts, it pierced, and made me glad;
Exceedingly glad, and I knew verily,

"A little thing just then had made me mad;
I dared not think, as I was wont to do,
Sometimes, upon my beauty; if I had   120

"Held out my long hand up against the blue,
And, looking on the tenderly darken'd fingers,
Thought that by rights one ought to see quite
     through,

"There, see you, where the soft still light yet lingers,
Round by the edges; what should I have done,
If this had joined with yellow spotted singers,

"And startling green drawn upward by the sun?
But shouting, loosed out, see now! all my hair,
And trancedly stood watching the west wind run

"With faintest half-heard breathing sound—why
     there   130
I lose my head e'en now in doing this;
But shortly listen—In that garden fair

"Came Launcelot walking; this is true, the kiss
Wherewith we kissed in meeting that spring day,
I scarce dare talk of the remember'd bliss,

"When both our mouths went wandering in one way,
And aching sorely, met among the leaves;
Our hands being left behind strained far away.

"Never within a yard of my bright sleeves
Had Launcelot come before—and now, so
        nigh!   140
After that day why is it Guenevere grieves?

"Nevertheless you, O Sir Gauwaine, lie,
Whatever happened on through all those years,
God knows I speak truth, saying that you lie.

"Being such a lady could I weep these tears
If this were true? A great queen such as I
Having sinn'd this way, straight her conscience sears;

"And afterwards she liveth hatefully,
Slaying and poisoning, certes never weeps,—
Gauwaine, be friends now, speak me lovingly.   150

"Do I not see how God's dear pity creeps
All through your frame, and trembles in your mouth?
Remember in what grave your mother sleeps,

"Buried in some place far down in the south,
Men are forgetting as I speak to you;
By her head sever'd in that awful drouth

"Of pity that drew Agravaine's fell blow,
I pray your pity! let me not scream out
For ever after, when the shrill winds blow

"Through half your castle-locks! let me not
        shout   160
For ever after in the winter night
When you ride out alone! in battle-rout

"Let not my rusting tears make your sword light!
Ah! God of mercy, how he turns away!
So, ever must I dress me to the fight;

"So—let God's justice work! Gauwaine, I say,
See me hew down your proofs: yea, all men know
Even as you said how Mellyagraunce one day,

"One bitter day in *la Fausse Garde*, for so
All good knights held it after, saw—   170
Yea, sirs, by cursed unknightly outrage; though

"You, Gauwaine, held his word without a flaw,
This Mellyagraunce saw blood upon my bed—
Whose blood then pray you? is there any law

"To make a queen say why some spots of red
Lie on her coverlet? or will you say,
'Your hands are white, lady, as when you wed,

" 'Where did you bleed?' and must I stammer out,
        'Nay,
I blush indeed, fair lord, only to rend
My sleeve up to my shoulder, where there lay   180

" 'A knife-point last night': so must I defend
The honor of the lady Guenevere?
Not so, fair lords, even if the world should end

"This very day, and you were judges here
Instead of God. Did you see Mellyagraunce
When Launcelot stood by him? what white fear

"Curdled his blood, and how his teeth did dance,
His side sink in? as my knight cried and said:
'Slayer of unarm'd men, here is a chance!

" 'Setter of traps, I pray you guard your head,   190
By God I am so glad to fight with you,
Stripper of ladies, that my hand feels lead

" 'For driving weight; hurrah now! draw and do,
For all my wounds are moving in my breast,
And I am getting mad with waiting so.'

"He struck his hands together o'er the beast,
Who fell down flat and grovell'd at his feet,
And groan'd at being slain so young—'at least.'

"My knight said: 'Rise you, sir, who are so fleet
At catching ladies, half-arm'd will I fight,   200
My left side all uncovered!' then I weet,

"Up sprang Sir Mellyagraunce with great delight
Upon his knave's face; not until just then
Did I quite hate him, as I saw my knight

"Along the lists look to my stake and pen
With such a joyous smile, it made me sigh
From agony beneath my waist-chain, when

"The fight began, and to me they drew nigh;
Ever Sir Launcelot kept him on the right,
And traversed warily, and ever high   210

"And fast leapt caitiff's sword, until my knight
Sudden threw up his sword to his left hand,
Caught it, and swung it; that was all the fight,

"Except a spout of blood on the hot land;

For it was hottest summer; and I know
I wonder'd how the fire, while I should stand,

"And burn, against the heat, would quiver so,
Yards above my head; thus these matters went;
Which things were only warnings of the woe

"That fell on me. Yet Mellyagraunce was
    shent,   220
For Mellyagraunce had fought against the Lord;
Therefore, my lords, take heed lest you be blent

"With all this wickedness; say no rash word
Against me, being so beautiful; my eyes,
Wept all away to grey, may bring some sword

"To drown you in your blood; see my breast rise,
Like waves of purple sea, as here I stand;
And how my arms are moved in wonderful wise,

"Yea also at my full heart's strong command,
See through my long throat how the words
    go up   230
In ripples to my mouth; how in my hand

"The shadow lies like wine within a cup
Of marvellously colour'd gold; yea now
This little wind is rising, look you up,

"And wonder how the light is falling so
Within my moving tresses: will you dare,
When you have looked a little on my brow,

"To say this thing is vile? or will you care
For any plausible lies of cunning woof,
When you can see my face with no lie there   240

"For ever? am I not a gracious proof—
'But in your chamber Launcelot was found'—
Is there a good knight then would stand aloof,

"When a queen says with gentle queenly sound:
'O true as steel, come now and talk with me,
I love to see your step upon the ground

" 'Unwavering, also well I love to see
That gracious smile light up your face, and hear
Your wonderful words, that all mean verily

" 'The thing they seem to mean: good friend,
    so dear   250
To me in everything, come here to-night,
Or else the hours will pass most dull and drear;

" 'If you come not, I fear this time I might

Get thinking over much of times gone by,
When I was young, and green hope was in sight:

" 'For no man cares now to know why I sigh;
And no man comes to sing me pleasant songs,
Nor any brings me the sweet flowers that lie

" 'So thick in the gardens; therefore one so longs
To see you, Launcelot; that we may be   260
Like children once again, free from all wrongs

" 'Just for one night.' Did he not come to me?
What thing could keep true Launcelot away
If I said 'Come'? There was one less than three

"In my quiet room that night, and we were gay;
Till sudden I rose up, weak, pale, and sick,
Because a bawling broke our dream up, yea

"I looked at Launcelot's face and could not speak,
For he looked helpless too, for a little while;
Then I remembered how I tried to shriek,   270

"And could not, but fell down; from tile to tile
The stones they threw up rattled o'er my head
And made me dizzier; till within a while

"My maids were all about me, and my head
On Launcelot's breast was being soothed away
From its white chattering, until Launcelot said—

"By God! I will not tell you more to-day,
Judge any way you will—what matters it?
You know quite well the story of that fray,

"How Launcelot still'd their bawling,
    the mad fit   280
That caught up Gauwaine—all, all, verily,
But just that which would save me; these things flit.

"Nevertheless you, O Sir Gauwaine, lie,
Whatever may have happen'd these long years,
God knows I speak truth, saying that you lie!

"All I have said is truth, by Christ's dear tears."
She would not speak another word, but stood
Turn'd sideways; listening, like a man who hears

His brother's trumpet sounding through the wood
Of his foes' lances. She lean'd eagerly,   290
And gave a slight spring sometimes, as she could

At last hear something really; joyfully
Her cheek grew crimson, as the headlong speed

Of the roan charger drew all men to see,
The knight who came was Launcelot at good need.

FOR ANALYSIS

1. Tennyson's Guenevere in *The Idylls of the King* is a much more familiar rendering of this character. Tennyson's queen crawls to Arthur, begging his forgiveness, sobbing her guilt. How does Morris' Guenevere differ?

2. What arguments does Guenevere use to save herself? Does she contradict herself? Where do you become aware that she has begun stalling for time? Does she offer logical argument or a blend of explanation, emotional appeal, and threat?

3. Is what she is really saying "I didn't do it" or "I won't be ashamed that I've done it"? In what sense is her repeated charge that Sir Gauwaine lied (in accusing her of adultery) true, in what sense false?

DRAMATIC POETRY

Narrowly defined, a dramatic poem is a play in verse. But today the dramatic monologue is usually included in this category, because it is sometimes much like a condensed play. In the monologue, a single speaker, having reached a crucial point in his life, reveals his character by speaking to a listener or listeners whose presence and characteristics we know only through signs the speaker gives us. Every word in the poem belongs to the single speaker.

The monologue, then, is like a compressed play in that it requires a dramatic situation and an invented speaker who is not the poet. It differs from a play in that only one character speaks, and from a soliloquy in that the speaker in the monologue does address a specific audience.

The popularity of the dramatic monologue is attributed to its "reality," its concentration on a single, vivid, human character, and its complexity. The reader is able to see the character as he sees himself, as we see him, and by implication, as others, usually the listeners, see him.

ALFRED, LORD TENNYSON

Ulysses

It little profits that an idle king,
By this still hearth, among these barren crags,
Match'd with an aged wife, I mete and dole
Unequal laws unto a savage race,
That hoard, and sleep, and feed, and know not me.
I cannot rest from travel; I will drink
Life to the lees. All times I have enjoy'd
Greatly, have suffer'd greatly, both with those
That loved me, and alone; on shore, and when
Thro' scudding drifts the rainy Hyades   10
Vext the dim sea. I am become a name;
For always roaming with a hungry heart
Much have I seen and known,—cities of men
And manners, climates, councils, governments,
Myself not least, but honor'd of them all,—
And drunk delight of battle with my peers,
Far on the ringing plains of windy Troy.
I am a part of all that I have met;
Yet all experience is an arch wherethro'
Gleams that untravel'd world whose margin fades   20
For ever and for ever when I move.
How dull it is to pause, to make an end,
To rust unburnish'd, not to shine in use!
As tho' to breathe were life! Life piled on life
Were all too little, and of one to me
Little remains; but every hour is saved
From that eternal silence, something more,
A bringer of new things; and vile it were
For some three suns to store and hoard myself,
And this gray spirit yearning in desire   30
To follow knowledge like a sinking star,
Beyond the utmost bound of human thought.

This is my son, mine own Telemachus,
To whom I leave the scepter and the isle,—
Well-loved of me, discerning to fulfil
This labor, by slow prudence to make mild
A rugged people, and thro' soft degrees
Subdue them to the useful and the good.
Most blameless is he, centered in the sphere
Of common duties, decent not to fail 40
In offices of tenderness, and pay
Meet adoration to my household gods,
When I am gone. He works his work, I mine.
  There lies the port; the vessel puffs her sail;
There gloom the dark, broad seas. My mariners,
Souls that have toil'd, and wrought, and thought with
    me,—
That ever with a frolic welcome took
The thunder and the sunshine, and opposed
Free hearts, free foreheads,—you and I are old;
Old age hath yet his honor and his toil. 50
Death closes all; but something ere the end,
Some work of noble note, may yet be done,
Not unbecoming men that strove with Gods.
The lights begin to twinkle from the rocks;
The long day wanes; the slow moon climbs; the deep
Moans round with many voices. Come, my friends,
'Tis not too late to seek a newer world.
Push off, and sitting well in order smite
The sounding furrows; for my purpose holds
To sail beyond the sunset, and the baths 60
Of all the western stars, until I die.
It may be that the gulfs will wash us down;
It may be we shall touch the Happy Isles,
And see the great Achilles, whom we knew.
Tho' much is taken, much abides; and tho'
We are not now that strength which in old days
Moved earth and heaven, that which we are, we are,—
One equal temper of heroic hearts,
Made weak by time and fate, but strong in will
To strive, to seek, to find, and not to yield. 70

FOR ANALYSIS

1. What seems to be the attitude of Ulysses toward
   his son? Love? Pride? Disdain? Supercilious-
   ness?
2. People who do not read very carefully often think
   "Ulysses" is a strong statement of courage, deter-
   mination, and hope. Probably they are concen-
   trating on the last few lines, which contain a typical Tennyson conclusion: a crashing close. Does
   the rest of the poem support the ending? In what
   way? Does the fact that no matter how hard you
   try to do otherwise, you have to read the poem

in a slow, almost dragging rhythm suggest something about the character of Ulysses in this poem?
3. The Ulysses you see here is the Ulysses of Dante,
   not the Ulysses of Homer. Whereas the Greeks
   sympathized with Ulysses, the Middle Ages
   (Dante's time) sympathized with the Trojans.
   Does this help you to draw a consistent portrait
   of Ulysses from the poem?

ROBERT BROWNING

My Last Duchess

That's my last Duchess painted on the wall,
Looking as if she were alive. I call
That piece a wonder, now: Frà Pandolf's hands
Worked busily a day, and there she stands.
Will 't please you sit and look at her? I said
'Frà Pandolf' by design, for never read
Strangers like you that pictured countenance,
The depth and passion of its earnest glance,
But to myself they turned (since none puts by
The curtain I have drawn for you, but I) 10
And seemed as they would ask me, if they durst,
How such a glance came there; so, not the first
Are you to turn and ask thus. Sir, 't was not
Her husband's presence only, called that spot
Of joy into the Duchess' cheek; perhaps
Frà Pandolf chanced to say, 'Her mantle laps
Over my lady's wrist too much,' or 'Paint
Must never hope to reproduce the faint
Half-flush that dies along her throat:' such stuff
Was courtesy, she thought, and cause enough 20
For calling up that spot of joy. She had
A heart—how shall I say?—too soon made glad,
Too easily impressed; she liked whate'er
She looked on, and her looks went everywhere.
Sir, 't was all one! My favor at her breast,
The dropping of the daylight in the West,
The bough of cherries some officious fool
Broke in the orchard for her, the white mule
She rode with round the terrace—all and each
Would draw from her alike the approving
    speech, 30
Or blush, at least. She thanked men,—good! but
    thanked
Somehow—I know not how—as if she ranked
My gift of a nine-hundred-years-old name
With anybody's gift. Who 'd stoop to blame

This sort of trifling? Even had you skill
In speech—(which I have not)—to make your will
Quite clear to such an one, and say, 'Just this
Or that in you disgusts me; here you miss,
Or there exceed the mark'—and if she let
Herself be lessoned so, nor plainly set   40
Her wits to yours, forsooth, and made excuse,
—E'en then would be some stooping; and I choose
Never to stoop. Oh, sir, she smiled, no doubt,
Whene'er I passed her; but who passed without
Much the same smile? This grew; I gave commands;
Then all smiles stopped together. There she stands
As if alive. Will 't please you rise? We 'll meet
The company below then. I repeat,
The Count your master's known munificence
Is ample warrant that no just pretense   50
Of mine for dowry will be disallowed;
Though his fair daughter's self, as I avowed
At starting, is my object. Nay, we 'll go
Together down, sir. Notice Neptune, though,
Taming a sea-horse, thought a rarity,
Which Claus of Innsbruck cast in bronze for me!

FOR ANALYSIS

1. Notice that although this poem reads as if it were
   in blank verse, it's really in heroic couplets. How
   does Browning achieve this blend of conventions
   —maintaining a strict form while getting a conversational naturalness at the same time?
2. The *dramatic monologue* allows the reader to see
   a character from at least two points of view. How
   do the following views of character differ?
   (a) The Duke as he sees himself *and* the Duke as
       the reader sees him.
   (b) The Duchess as the Duke sees her *and* the
       Duchess as the reader sees her.
3. What is the significance of the title? Is that the
   way one normally speaks of his wife? What does
   this tell you about the Duke's attitude toward
   his wife—or wives?

ROBERT BROWNING

Fra Lippo Lippi

I am poor brother Lippo, by your leave!
You need not clap your torches to my face.
Zooks, what's to blame? you think you see a monk!

What, 'tis past midnight, and you go the rounds,
And here you catch me at an alley's end
Where sportive ladies leave their doors ajar?
The Carmine's my cloister; hunt it up,
Do—harry out, if you must show your zeal,
Whatever rat, there, haps on his wrong hole,
And nip each softling of a wee white mouse,   10
Weke, weke, that's crept to keep him company!
Aha, you know your betters! Then, you'll take
Your hand away that's fiddling on my throat,
And please to know me likewise. Who am I?
Why, one, sir, who is lodging with a friend
Three streets off—he's a certain . . . how d' ye call?
Master—a . . . Cosimo of the Medici,
I' the house that caps the corner. Boh! you were best!
Remember and tell me, the day you're hanged,
How you affected such a gullet's gripe!   20
But you, sir, it concerns you that your knaves
Pick up a manner nor discredit you;
Zooks, are we pilchards, that they sweep the streets
And count fair prize what comes into their net?
He's Judas to a tittle, that man is!
Just such a face! Why, sir, you make amends.
Lord, I'm not angry! Bid your hangdogs go
Drink out this quarter-florin to the health
Of the munificent House that harbors me
(And many more beside, lads! more beside!)   30
And all's come square again. I'd like his face—
His, elbowing on his comrade in the door
With the pike and lantern—for the slave that holds
John Baptist's head a-dangle by the hair
With one hand ("Look you, now," as who should say)
And his weapon in the other, yet unwiped!
It's not your chance to have a bit of chalk,
A wood coal or the like? or you should see!
Yes, I'm the painter, since you style me so.
What, brother Lippo's doings, up and down,   40
You know them and they take you? like enough!
I saw the proper twinkle in your eye—
'Tell you, I liked your looks at very first.
Let's sit and set things straight now, hip to haunch.
Here's spring come, and the nights one makes up
    bands
To roam the town and sing out carnival,
And I've been three weeks shut within my mew,
A-painting for the great man, saints and saints
And saints again. I could not paint all night—
Ouf! I leaned out of window for fresh air.   50
There came a hurry of feet and little feet,
A sweep of lute strings, laughs, and whifs of song—
Flower o' the broom,
Take away love, and our earth is a tomb!
Flower o' the quince,

I let Lisa go, and what good in life since?
Flower o' the thyme—and so on. Round they went.
Scarce had they turned the corner when a titter
Like the skipping of rabbits by moonlight—three
    slim shapes,
And a face that looked up . . . zooks, sir, flesh and
    blood,   60
That's all I'm made of! Into shreds it went,
Curtain and counterpane and coverlet,
All the bed furniture—a dozen knots,
There was a ladder! Down I let myself,
Hands and feet, scrambling somehow, and so
    dropped,
And after them. I came up with the fun
Hard by St. Laurence, hail fellow, well met—
Flower o' the rose,
If I've been merry, what matter who knows?
And so as I was stealing back again   70
To get to bed and have a bit of sleep
Ere I rise up tomorrow and go work
On Jerome knocking at his poor old breast
With his great round stone to subdue the flesh,
You snap me of the sudden. Ah, I see!
Though your eye twinkles still, you shake your
    head—
Mine's shaved—a monk, you say—the sting's in
    that!
If Master Cosimo announced himself,
Mum's the word naturally; but a monk!
Come, what am I a beast for? tell us, now!   80
I was a baby when my mother died
And father died and left me in the street.
I starved there, God knows how, a year or two
On fig skins, melon parings, rinds and shucks,
Refuse and rubbish. One fine frosty day,
My stomach being empty as your hat,
The wind doubled me up and down I went.
Old Aunt Lapaccia trussed me with one hand,
(Its fellow was a stinger as I knew)
And so along the wall, over the bridge,   90
By the straight cut to the convent. Six words there,
While I stood munching my first bread that month:
"So, boy, you're minded," quoth the good fat father,
Wiping his own mouth, 'twas refection time—
"To quit this very miserable world?
Will you renounce" . . . "the mouthful of bread?"
    thought I;
By no means! Brief, they made a monk of me;
I did renounce the world, its pride and greed,
Palace, farm, villa, shop, and banking house,
Trash, such as these poor devils of Medici   100
Have given their hearts to—all at eight years old.
Well, sir, I found in time, you may be sure,

'Twas not for nothing—the good bellyful,
The warm serge and the rope that goes all round,
And day-long blessèd idleness beside!
"Let's see what the urchin's fit for"—that came next.
Not overmuch their way, I must confess.
Such a to-do! They tried me with their books;
Lord, they'd have taught me Latin in pure waste!
Flower o' the clove,   110
All the Latin I construe is "amo," I love!
But, mind you, when a boy starves in the streets
Eight years together, as my fortune was,
Watching folk's faces to know who will fling
The bit of half-stripped grape bunch he desires,
And who will curse or kick him for his pains—
Which gentleman processional and fine,
Holding a candle to the Sacrament,
Will wink and let him lift a plate and catch
The droppings of the wax to sell again,   120
Or holla for the Eight and have him whipped—
How say I?—nay, which dog bites, which lets drop
His bone from the heap of offal in the street—
Why, soul and sense of him grow sharp alike,
He learns the look of things, and none the less
For admonition from the hunger pinch.
I had a store of such remarks, be sure,
Which, after I found leisure, turned to use.
I drew men's faces on my copy books,
Scrawled them within the antiphonary's marge,   130
Joined legs and arms to the long music notes,
Found eyes and nose and chin for A's and B's,
And made a string of pictures of the world
Betwixt the ins and outs of verb and noun,
On the wall, the bench, the door. The monks looked
    black.
"Nay," quoth the Prior, "turn him out, d' ye say?
In no wise. Lose a crow and catch a lark.
What if at last we get our man of parts,
We Carmelites, like those Camaldolese
And Preaching Friars, to do our church up fine   140
And put the front on it that ought to be!"
And hereupon he bade me daub away.
Thank you! my head being crammed, the walls a
    blank,
Never was such prompt disemburdening.
First, every sort of monk, the black and white,
I drew them, fat and lean; then, folk at church,
From good old gossips waiting to confess
Their cribs of barrel droppings, candle ends—
To the breathless fellow at the altar foot,
Fresh from his murder, safe and sitting there   150
With the little children round him in a row
Of admiration, half for his beard and half
For that white anger of his victim's son

Shaking a fist at him with one fierce arm,
Signing himself with the other because of Christ
(Whose sad face on the cross sees only this
After the passion of a thousand years)
Till some poor girl, her apron o'er her head,
(Which the intense eyes looked through) came at eve
On tiptoe, said a word, dropped in a loaf,   160
Her pair of earrings and a bunch of flowers
(The brute took growling), prayed, and so was gone.
I painted all, then cried, " 'Tis ask and have;
Choose, for more's ready!"—laid the ladder flat,
And showed my covered bit of cloister wall.
The monks closed in a circle and praised loud
Till checked, taught what to see and not to see,
Being simple bodies—"That's the very man!
Look at the boy who stoops to pat the dog!
That woman's like the Prior's niece who comes   170
To care about his asthma; it's the life!"
But there my triumph's straw fire flared and funked;
Their betters took their turn to see and say;
The Prior and the learned pulled a face
And stopped all that in no time. "How? what's here?
Quite from the mark of painting, bless us all!
Faces, arms, legs, and bodies like the true
As much as pea and pea! it's devil's game!
Your business is not to catch men with show,
With homage to the perishable clay,   180
But lift them over it, ignore it all,
Make them forget there's such a thing as flesh.
Your business is to paint the souls of men—
Man's soul, and it's a fire, smoke . . . no, it's not . . .
It's vapor done up like a newborn babe—
(In that shape when you die it leaves your mouth)
It's . . . well, what matters talking, it's the soul!
Gives us no more of body than shows soul!
Here's Giotto, with his Saint a-praising God,
That sets us praising—why not stop with him?   190
Why put all thoughts of praise out of our head
With wonder at lines, colors, and what not?
Paint the soul, never mind the legs and arms!
Rub all out, try at it a second time.
Oh, that white smallish female with the breasts,
She's just my niece . . . Herodias, I would say—
Who went and danced and got men's heads cut off!
Have it all out!" Now, is this sense, I ask?
A fine way to paint soul, by painting body
So ill, the eye can't stop there, must go further   200
And can't fare worse! Thus, yellow does for white
When what you put for yellow's simply black,
And any sort of meaning looks intense
When all beside itself means and looks naught.
Why can't a painter lift each foot in turn,
Left foot and right foot, go a double step,

Make his flesh liker and his soul more like,
Both in their order? Take the prettiest face,
The Prior's niece . . . patron saint—is it so pretty
You can't discover if it means hope, fear,   210
Sorrow or joy? won't beauty go with these?
Suppose I've made her eyes all right and blue,
Can't I take breath and try to add life's flash,
And then add soul and heighten them threefold?
Or say there's beauty with no soul at all—
(I never saw it—put the case the same—)
If you get simple beauty and naught else,
You get about the best thing God invents:
That's somewhat; and you'll find the soul you have
    missed,
Within yourself, when you return him thanks.   220
"Rub all out!" Well, well, there's my life, in short,
And so the thing has gone on ever since.
I'm grown a man no doubt, I've broken bounds;
You should not take a fellow eight years old
And make him swear to never kiss the girls.
I'm my own master, paint now as I please—
Having a friend, you see, in the Corner-house!
Lord, it's fast holding by the rings in front—
Those great rings serve more purposes than just
To plant a flag in, or tie up a horse!   230
And yet the old schooling sticks, the old grave eyes
Are peeping o'er my shoulder as I work,
The heads shake still—"It's art's decline, my son!
You're not of the true painters, great and old;
Brother Angelico's the man, you'll find;
Brother Lorenzo stands his single peer;
Fag on at flesh, you'll never make the third!"
Flower o' the pine,
You keep your mistr . . . manners, and I'll stick to
    mine!
I'm not the third, then; bless us, they must
    know!   240
Don't you think they're the likeliest to know,
They with their Latin? So, I swallow my rage,
Clench my teeth, suck my lips in tight, and paint
To please them—sometimes do and sometimes
    don't;
For, doing most, there's pretty sure to come
A turn, some warm eve finds me at my saints—
A laugh, a cry, the business of the world—
(*Flower o' the peach,*
Death for us all, and his own life for each!)
And my whole soul revolves, the cup runs over,   250
The world and life's too big to pass for a dream,
And I do these wild things in sheer despite,
And play the fooleries you catch me at,
In pure rage! The old mill horse, out at grass
After hard years, throws up his stiff heels so,

Although the miller does not preach to him
The only good of grass is to make chaff.
What would men have? Do they like grass or no—
May they or mayn't they? all I want's the thing
Settled forever one way. As it is,   260
You tell too many lies and hurt yourself;
You don't like what you only like too much,
You do like what, if given you at your word,
You find abundantly detestable.
For me, I think I speak as I was taught;
I always see the garden and God there
A-making man's wife; and, my lesson learned,
The value and significance of flesh,
I can't unlearn ten minutes afterwards.

      You understand me; I'm a beast, I know.   270
But see, now—why, I see as certainly
As that the morning star's about to shine,
What will hap some day. We've a youngster here
Comes to our convent, studies what I do,
Slouches and stares and lets no atom drop.
His name is Guidi—he'll not mind the monks—
They call him Hulking Tom, he lets them talk—
He picks my practice up—he'll paint apace,
I hope so—though I never live so long,
I know what's sure to follow. You be judge!   280
You speak no Latin more than I, belike;
However, you're my man, you've seen the world
—The beauty and the wonder and the power,
The shapes of things, their colors, lights and shades,
Changes, surprises—and God made it all!
—For what? Do you feel thankful, aye or no,
For this fair town's face, yonder river's line,
The mountain round it and the sky above,
Much more the figures of man, woman, child,
These are the frame to? What's it all about?   290
To be passed over, despised? or dwelt upon,
Wondered at? oh, this last of course!—you say.
But why not do as well as say—paint these
Just as they are, careless what comes of it?
God's works—paint any one, and count it crime
To let a truth slip. Don't object, "His works
Are here already; nature is complete:
Suppose you reproduce her—(which you can't)
There's no advantage! you must beat her, then."
For, don't you mark? we're made so that we
      love   300
First when we see them painted, things we have
      passed
Perhaps a hundred times nor cared to see;
And so they are better, painted—better to us,
Which is the same thing. Art was given for that;
God uses us to help each other so,

Lending our minds out. Have you noticed, now,
Your cullion's hanging face? A bit of chalk,
And trust me but you should, though! How much
      more,
If I drew higher things with the same truth!
That were to take the Prior's pulpit-place,   310
Interpret God to all of you! Oh, oh,
It makes me mad to see what men shall do
And we in our graves! This world's no blot for us,
Nor blank; it means intensely, and means good:
To find its meaning is my meat and drink.
"Aye, but you don't so instigate to prayer!"
Strikes in the Prior; "when you meaning's plain
It does not say to folk—remember matins,
Or, mind you fast next Friday!" Why, for this
What need of art at all? A skull and bones,   320
Two bits of stick nailed crosswise, or, what's best,
A bell to chime the hour with, does as well.
I painted a St. Laurence six months since
At Prato, splashed the fresco in fine style;
"How looks my painting, now the scaffold's down?"
I ask a brother. "Hugely," he returns—
"Already not one phiz of your three slaves
Who turn the Deacon off his toasted side,
But's scratched and prodded to our heart's content,
The pious people have so eased their own   330
With coming to say prayers there in a rage;
We get on fast to see the bricks beneath.
Expect another job this time next year,
For pity and religion grow i' the crowd—
Your painting serves its purpose!" Hang the fools!
      —That is—you'll not mistake an idle word
Spoke in a huff by a poor monk, God wot,
Tasting the air this spicy night which turns
The unaccustomed head like Chianti wine!
Oh, the Church knows! don't misreport me,
      now   340
It's natural a poor monk out of bounds
Should have his apt word to excuse himself;
And hearken how I plot to make amends.
I have bethought me: I shall paint a piece
. . . There's for you! Give me six months, then go, see
Something in Sant' Ambrogio's! Bless the nuns!
They want a cast o' my office. I shall paint
God in the midst, Madonna and her babe,
Ringed by a bowery, flowery angel brood,
Lilies and vestments and white faces, sweet   350
As puff on puff of grated orris root
When ladies crowd to church at midsummer.
And then i' the front, of course a saint or two—
St. John, because he saves the Florentines,
St. Ambrose, who puts down in black and white
The convent's friends and gives them a long day,

And Job, I must have him there past mistake,
The man of Uz (and Us without the z,
Painters who need his patience). Well, all these
Secured at their devotion, up shall come   360
Out of a corner when you least expect,
As one by a dark stair into a great light,
Music and talking, who but Lippo! I!—
Mazed, motionless, and moonstruck—I'm the man!
Back I shrink—what is this I see and hear?
I, caught up with my monk's things by mistake,
My old serge gown and rope that goes all round,
I, in this presence, this pure company!
Where's a hole, where's a corner for escape?
Then steps a sweet angelic slip of a thing   370
Forward, puts out a soft palm—"Not so fast!"
—Addresses the celestial presence, "nay—
He made you and devised you, after all,
Though he's none of you! Could St. John there
    draw—
His camel hair make up a painting brush?
We come to brother Lippo for all that,
Iste perfecit opus!" So, all smile—
I shuffle sideways with my blushing face
Under the cover of a hundred wings
Thrown like a spread of kirtles when you're
    gay   380
And play hot cockles, all the doors being shut,

Till, wholly unexpected, in there pops
The hothead husband! Thus I scuttle off
To some safe bench behind, not letting go
The palm of her, the little lily thing
That spoke the good word for me in the nick,
Like the Prior's niece . . . St. Lucy, I would say.
And so all's saved for me, and for the church
A pretty picture gained. Go, six months hence!
Your hand, sir, and good-by; no lights, no
    lights!   390
The street's hushed, and I know my own way back,
Don't fear me! There's the gray beginning. Zooks!

FOR ANALYSIS

1. At a quick glance, Lippo seems to be a madcap
   monk. But there is much more to him than that.
   Why does he do the unmonklike things he does?
   Consider, for example, lines 97–101, 213–225,
   251–254, and 313–335. What is it that frustrates
   him?
2. Try to summarize Lippo's theory of art. Does it
   apply only to painting? What other art does it
   fit as well or better?
3. What holds this long poem together? Do you see
   hints of borrowed conventions here that unify
   what seems at first to be a rambling monologue?

T. S. ELIOT

The Love Song of J. Alfred Prufrock

epigraph: ties in with body of Poem "Dante's Inferno"

> *S'io credesse che mia risposta fosse*
> *A persona che mai tornasse al mondo,*
> *Questa fiamma staria senza piu scosse.*
> *Ma perciocche giammai di questo fondo*
> *Non torno vivo alcun, s'i'odo il vero,*
> *Senza tema d'infamia ti rispondo.**

Let us go then, you and I,
When the evening is spread out against the sky

He is emotionally paralyzed & has lost life

Like a patient etherized upon a table;
Let us go, through certain half-deserted streets,
The muttering retreats
Of restless nights in one-night cheap hotels   5

lonely

*S'io . . . rispondo. If I could believe that my answer might be to a person who should ever return into the world, this flame would stand without more quiverings; but inasmuch as, if I hear the truth, never from this depth did any living man return, without fear of infamy I answer thee (from Dante's *Inferno*, Canto XXVII, ll. 61–66).

And sawdust restaurants with oyster-shells:
Streets that follow like a tedious argument   *sees street like a map*
Of insidious intent   *like his mind.*
To lead you to an overwhelming question . . .   10
Oh, do not ask, 'What is it?' *doesn't want* *Question: To marry*
Let us go and make our visit. *to make up his* *her & he wants to*
                               mind.   *ask the woman.*

In the room the women come and go   *Jos is going to a party*
Talking of Michelangelo.

The yellow fog that rubs its back upon the window-panes,   15
The yellow smoke that rubs its muzzle on the window-panes
Licked its tongue into the corners of the evening,
Lingered upon the pools that stand in drains,
Let fall upon its back the soot that falls from chimneys,
Slipped by the terrace, made a sudden leap,   20
And seeing that it was a soft October night,
Curled once about the house, and fell asleep.

And indeed there will be time
For the yellow smoke that slides along the street,   *fog he is in*
Rubbing its back upon the window-panes;   25
There will be time, there will be time
To prepare a face to meet the faces that you meet;
There will be time to murder and create,
And time for all the works and days of hands
That lift and drop a question on your plate;   30
Time for you and time for me,
And time yet for a hundred indecisions,
And for a hundred visions and revisions,
Before the taking of a toast and tea.
In the room the women come and go   35
Talking of Michelangelo.

And indeed there will be time
To wonder, 'Do I dare?' and, 'Do I dare?'
Time to turn back and descend the stair,
With a bald spot in the middle of my hair—   40
(They will say: 'How his hair is growing thin!')
My morning coat, my collar mounting firmly to the chin,
My necktie rich and modest, but asserted by a simple pin—
(They will say: 'But how his arms and legs are thin!')
Do I dare   45
Disturb the universe?
In a minute there is time
For decisions and revisions which a minute will reverse.

For I have known them all already, known them all:—
Have known the evenings, mornings, afternoons,   50
I have measured out my life with coffee spoons;   *small, shallow life*
I know the voices dying with a dying fall
Beneath the music from a farther room.
   So how should I presume?

feels inferior

And I have known the eyes already, known them all—   55
The eyes that fix you in a formulated phrase,
And when I am formulated, sprawling on a pin,
When I am pinned and wriggling on the wall,
Then how should I begin

{ seen tensely like a bug under inspection }

To spit out all the butt-ends of my days and ways? - *has to get rid of all ways.*   60
    And how should I presume?

And I have known the arms already, known them all—
Arms that are braceleted and white and bare
(But in the lamplight, downed with light brown hair!)
Is it perfume from a dress   65
That makes me so digress?
Arms that lie along a table, or wrap about a shawl.
    And should I then presume?
    And how should I begin?

    . . . . . .

Shall I say, I have gone at dusk through narrow streets *appeals to her*   70
And watched the smoke that rises from the pipes *} sympathy*
Of lonely men in shirt-sleeves, leaning out of windows? . .
I should have been a pair of ragged claws *} can't do it*
Scuttling across the floors of silent seas.

Crazy - awkward fearful movements, not a whole animal, it's in a shell isolated

Cat { And the afternoon, the evening, sleeps so peacefully!   75
Smoothed by long fingers,
Asleep . . . tired . . . or it malingers,
Stretched on the floor, here beside you and me.
Should I, after tea and cakes and ices,
Have the strength to force the moment to its crisis?   80
But though I have wept and fasted, wept and prayed, *sacrificed*

Though I have seen my head (grown slightly bald) *Can't stop thinking about his hair*
    brought in upon a platter. *John the Baptist*
I am no prophet—and here's no great matter;

can't imagine

I have seen the moment of my greatness flicker, *seems to laugh ~ fate + death*
And I have seen the eternal Footman hold my coat, and snicker.   85
And in short, I was afraid. *afraid of being laughed at*
Direct statement.

And would it have been worth it, after all,
After the cups, the marmalade, the tea,
Among the porcelain, among some talk of you and me,
Would it have been worth while,   90
To have bitten off the matter with a smile,
To have squeezed the universe into a ball *Marvel asks lady to live with him but Prufrock can't*
To roll it toward some overwhelming question,
To say: 'I am Lazarus, come from the dead, *this love is the one flicker of life he has ever had*
Come back to tell you all, I shall tell you all'—   95
If one, settling a pillow by her head,
    Should say: 'That is not what I meant at all,
    That is not it, at all.' *afraid to ask in case he misread the signs*

And would it have been worth it, after all,
Would it have been worth while,   100

After the sunsets and the dooryards and the sprinkled streets,
After the novels, after the teacups, after the skirts that trail along the floor—
And this, and so much more?—
It is impossible to say just what I mean!
But as if a magic lantern threw the nerves in patterns on a screen: 105
Would it have been worth while
If one, settling a pillow or throwing off a shawl,   *Lady of high Station*
And turning toward the window, should say: *& She might say no*
  'That is not it at all,
  That is not what I meant, at all.'   110

INDECISIVE & gallant
No! I am not Prince Hamlet, nor was meant to be;
Am an attendant lord, one that will do
To swell a progress, start a scene or two,
Advise the prince; no doubt, an easy tool,
Deferential, glad to be of use,   *Can't be*   115
Politic, cautious, and meticulous;   *important*
Full of high sentence, but a bit obtuse;
At times, indeed, almost ridiculous—
Almost, at times, the Fool.

I grow old . . . I grow old . . .   120
I shall wear the bottoms of my trousers rolled.   *trivial decision*

Shall I part my hair behind? Do I dare to eat a peach? *Can make trivial decision*
I shall wear white flannel trousers, and walk upon the beach. *no freedom*
I have heard the mermaids singing, each to each.
                                                   lose of senses
I do not think that they will sing to me.   125

I have seen them riding seaward on the waves
Combing the white hair of the waves blown back   *sea is subconscious*
When the wind blows the water white and black.
We have lingered in the chambers of the sea   *caught up by a mermaid*
By sea-girls wreathed with seaweed red and brown   130
Till human voices wake us, and we drown.   *drowns in reality*
when he wakes from his dream
                                                      FOR ANALYSIS

The "I" and "you" of the poem are simply two sides of the same man, Prufrock, a
prototype of frustrated twentieth-century man. If the poem seems difficult, it is partly
because Prufrock is afraid to admit even to himself the extent of his own frustration.
Thus, it is important for the reader to answer to his own satisfaction at least three
basic questions about Prufrock:
(a) What is Prufrock afraid of?
(b) What kind of frustration does Prufrock suffer from?
(c) The conclusion says that "human voices wake us, and we drown." In what way
     are the characters in the poem not human?
The questions that follow attempt to guide you to the answers to the three questions
above.
1. In the first ten lines we learn that Prufrock is going to a rendezvous where he intends
    to ask someone a question. In what way do the figures of speech that Prufrock uses
    to describe the evening and the streets tell us that he is burdened by the thought of
    asking the question and apprehensive of the answer he may receive?

2. Prufrock reviews at length, in indirect fashion, his own real or imagined short-comings. In what way does the chorus, "In the room the women come and go/ Talking of Michelangelo," describe the kind of life he leads? In what way does his remark, "I have measured out my life with coffee spoons," sum up both his past and present existence? How does his remark, "I should have been a pair of ragged claws/ Scuttling across the floors of silent seas," summarize Prufrock's reaction to his review of his past and present existence?

3. What does the repeated "And would it have been worth it, after all" tell us of his intention to ask the question?

4. By line 110, the reader should understand what question Prufrock intended to ask, of whom he intended to ask it, and why he did not do so. The remainder of the poem explores the consequences of his not asking the question. What will his future life be like?

5. In the first half of the poem, Prufrock thinks chiefly of what he is and has been. In the second half he suggests what he has not been, is not, and will not be. His method in the latter half is that of allusive comparison. In what way is Prufrock not like John the Baptist (lines 81–83), or the lover of Marvell's "To His Coy Mistress" (lines 91–92), or Lazarus (lines 94–95), or Hamlet (line 111)? What resemblances, then, does Prufrock see between himself and these characters that cause him to introduce them for contrast?

LYRIC POETRY

Lyric poetry is personal song. Many older lyrics were set to music; the convention has persisted to the extent that the lyric, although it now has no musical accompaniment, has become a highly personal expression of both thought and feeling, usually in musical meters.

That expression, however, can be in any tone, mood, metrical form, and level of formality, from the limerick to the ode. The most common of the *fixed* lyric forms is the sonnet.

Conventions of the sonnet

A conventional sonnet is a fourteen-line poem dealing with a single subject, usually weighty in nature.

The convention of length varies. Some of the earliest sonnets in English (for example, Thomas Watson's "Hecatompathia" or "The Passionate Century of Love" [1582]) had eighteen lines; some more recent sonnets (George Meredith's "Modern Love" sequence) have sixteen lines. These exceptions are really not departures—basically, sonnet form is more a method of development than a stipulated length. Critics sometimes apply the term "sonnet structure" or "sonnet development" to a poem shorter or much longer than fourteen lines. They are referring, first, to the convention of the single weighty subject, and, second, to the pattern of discussion in the poem. This pattern may take either of two forms:

(1) Italian (or Petrarchan) form: a two-part development, consisting of an octave (eight lines) and a sestet (six lines). The octave of the Italian sonnet rhymes *abba abba;* the sestet may rhyme in almost any way (*cde cde; cdc dcd*, and so forth.)

(2) English (or Shakespearean) form: a four-part development, consisting of three quatrains (rhyming *abab cdcd efef*) and a closing couplet (*gg*).

Spenserian form has the same development as the English form, except that the rhyme scheme is interlocked (for instance, *abab bcbc cdcd ee*). This form is sometimes regarded as having more continuity than the English form because of its interlocked rhymes, but it has never been used much by British and American poets. It can be considered simply a variant of the English form.

The conventions of each form offer special advantages to the poet and reader.

The Italian form has several advantages:

(1) The two-part form of the Italian form is ideal for a pattern which involves asking a question and answering it, posing a problem and solving it, or describing an experience and commenting on it. A vast number of sonnets are argumentative; two-part development is the basic structure of argument.

(2) Italian form enables the poet to change direction easily (at the end of the octave) without changing his subject matter.

(3) Although the poet may have difficulty in composing enough rhymes, it is sufficient in a sonnet based on metaphorical comparison for him to use one metaphor for both the octave and sestet or a different one for each. The English form, however, requires *three* cogent metaphors for the three quatrains. This difficulty often causes a weakness in an English sonnet which appears in the third quatrain—the point where the poet's inspiration has lapsed and he is merely completing the form.

The English form has these advantages:

(1) The concluding couplet offers an opportunity for a neat, concise conclusion or summary, sometimes in epigrammatic form, of the whole sonnet. In the couplet, the poet can emphasize his main point, thus aiding the reader's comprehension.

(2) English is a difficult language for rhyming compared to, for example, French, Italian, and Spanish. Because the English form uses more varied rhymes, the poet is less handicapped by the resources of the language.

(3) The English form is a more complete unit than the Italian form since the three quatrains develop parallel or succeeding aspects of a single subject; in a sense, the English form uses a pattern of reinforcement.

These are generalizations, of course, and individual poets change conventions to avail themselves of the advantages and avoid the disadvantages of each form. For example, to create a more unified poem, Milton and Wordsworth often separated the Italian sonnet in the middle of the eighth or ninth line, rather than at the end of the eighth line. The outstanding innovator was probably Keats, who was dissatisfied with both forms. After much experimenting, he invented a ten-line sonnet stanza to use in his Odes, which consisted of a quatrain and a sestet—an English beginning and an Italian conclusion.

The Spenserian sonnet

EDMUND SPENSER

Sonnet 75

One day I wrote her name upon the strand,
But came the waves and washèd it away:
Again I wrote it with a second hand,
But came the tide, and made my pains his prey.
Vain man, said she, that dost in vain essay   5
A mortal thing so to immortalize;
For I myself shall like to this decay,
And eke my name be wipèd out likewise.
Not so, (quod I) let baser things devise,
To die in dust, but you shall live by fame;   10
My verse your virtues rare shall eternize,
And in the heavens write your glorious name:
Where, whenas death shall all the world subdue,
Our love shall live, and later life renew.

The English sonnet

WILLIAM SHAKESPEARE

Sonnet 73

That time of year thou mayst in me behold
When yellow leaves, or none, or few, do hang
Upon those boughs which shake against the
    cold,
Bare ruined choirs, where late the sweet birds
    sang.
In me thou see'st the twilight of such day   5
As after sunset fadeth in the west,
Which by and by black night doth take away,
Death's second self, that seals up all in rest.
In me thou see'st the glowing of such fire
That on the ashes of his youth doth lie,   10
As the death-bed whereon it must expire,
Consumed with that which it was nourished by.
This thou perceiv'st, which makes thy love more
    strong,
To love that well which thou must leave ere long.

MICHAEL DRAYTON

Sonnet 61

Since there's no help, come, let us kiss and part!
Nay, I have done; you get no more of me!
And I am glad, yea, glad, with all my heart,
That thus so cleanly I myself can free.
Shake hands for ever! Cancel all our vows!   5
And when we meet at any time again,
Be it not seen in either of our brows,
That we one jot of former love retain!
Now at the last gasp of Love's latest breath,
When, his pulse failing, Passion speechless lies;   10
When Faith is kneeling by his bed of death,
And Innocence is closing up his eyes,—
Now, if thou wouldst, when all have given him over,
From death to life thou might'st him yet recover!

FOR ANALYSIS

Sonnet 73

1. This is an example of classic English sonnet development: three separate quatrains using three separate metaphors, yet each metaphor related to the others, and all embodying the same idea, commented on in the couplet. What are the three metaphors and their common idea?
2. What color image is shared by each of the three quatrains?
3. Is the concluding couplet ambiguous? Is *thou* a specific person being spoken to? Or is it a general pronoun? What difference would it make to the sense of the sonnet?

Sonnet 61

1. In its development (not its rhyme scheme) is this closer to Italian or English sonnet form?
2. Explain the difference in tone of the first eight lines and the last six. How does Drayton get that effect?
3. The last six lines here contain an extended image. What is the image?

WILLIAM SHAKESPEARE

Sonnet 18

Shall I compare thee to a summer's day?
Thou art more lovely and more temperate:
Rough winds do shake the darling buds of May,

And summer's lease hath all too short a date:
Sometime too hot the eye of heaven shines   5
And often is his gold complexion dimmed;
And every fair from fair sometime declines,
By chance or nature's changing course untrimmed;
But thy eternal summer shall not fade
Nor lose possession of that fair thou owest;   10
Nor shall Death brag thou wanderest in his shade,
When in eternal lines to time thou growest:
So long as men can breathe or eyes can see,
So long lives this and this gives life to thee.

WILLIAM SHAKESPEARE
Sonnet 130

My mistress' eyes are nothing like the sun;
Coral is far more red than her lips' red;
If snow be white, why then her breasts are dun;
If hairs be wires, black wires grow on her head.
I have seen roses damasked, red and white,   5
But no such roses see I in her cheeks;
And in some perfumes is there more delight
Than in the breath that from my mistress reeks.
I love to hear her speak, yet well I know
That music hath a far more pleasing sound;   10
I grant I never saw a goddess go;
My mistress, when she walks, treads on the ground:
And yet, by heaven, I think my love as rare
As any she belied with false compare.

WILLIAM SHAKESPEARE
Sonnet 29

When in disgrace with fortune and men's eyes,
I all alone beweep my outcast state
And trouble deaf heaven with my bootless cries
And look upon myself and curse my fate,
Wishing me like to one more rich in hope,   5
Featured like him, like him with friends possessed,
Desiring this man's art and that man's scope,
With what I most enjoy contented least;
Yet in these thoughts myself almost despising,
Haply I think on thee, and then my state,   10

Like to the lark at break of day arising
From sullen earth, sings hymns at heaven's gate;
For thy sweet love remembered such wealth brings
That then I scorn to change my state with kings.

FOR ANALYSIS

Sonnet 18

1. Does Shakespeare use three separate metaphors for the three quatrains in this sonnet or does he simply use variations of a central metaphor? What does he gain by doing this?
2. What device familiar in the ballad form does Shakespeare use to make his concluding couplet stronger here?

Sonnet 130

1. This sonnet is a satire on the usual sonnet compliments to a lady. How does Shakespeare manage to laugh at the conventions without laughing at the lady?
2. Could he have done this as easily in the Italian form?

Sonnet 29

1. An important metaphor is buried in lines 9–14 of this sonnet. What is it? How does it set up a contrast with lines 1–8?
2. This is by its rhyme scheme an English sonnet. Yet there is something very odd about its development. What is that oddity?

The Italian sonnet

SIR THOMAS WYATT
The Lover Compareth His State to a Ship in Perilous Storm Tossed on the Sea

My galley charged with forgetfulness
Thorough sharp seas, in winter nights doth pass,
'Tween rock and rock; and eke my foe, alas,
That is my lord, steereth with cruelness,
And every hour, a thought in readiness,   5
As though that death were light in such a case.

An endless wind doth tear the sail apace
Of forcèd sighs, and trusty fearfulness.
A rain of tears, a cloud of dark disdain

Hath done the wearied cords great hinderance,   10
Wreathèd with error, and with ignorance.
The stars be hid that led me to this pain;
Drowned is reason that should be my comfort,
And I remain, despairing of the port.

JOHN DONNE

Holy Sonnet 14

Batter my heart, three personed God; for you
As yet but knock, breathe, shine, and seek to mend;
That I may rise and stand, o'erthrow me and bend
Your force to break, blow, burn and make me new.
I, like an usurped town, to another due,   5
Labor to admit you, but Oh, to no end,
Reason, your viceroy in me, me should defend,
But is captived, and proves weak or untrue.
Yet dearly I love you, and would be loved fain,
But am betrothed unto your enemy: 10
Divorce me, untie or break that knot again,
Take me to you, imprison me, for I
Except you enthrall me, never shall be free,
Nor ever chaste, except you ravish me.

JOHN MILTON

On His Blindness

When I consider how my light is spent
Ere half my days in this dark world and wide,
And that one talent which is death to hide
Lodged with me useless, though my soul more bent
To serve therewith my Maker, and present   5
My true account, lest he returning chide,
'Doth God exact day-labor, light denied?'
I fondly ask. But Patience, to prevent
That murmur, soon replies, 'God doth not need
Either man's work or his own gifts. Who best   10
Bear his mild yoke, they serve him best. His state
Is kingly: thousands at his bidding speed,

And post o'er land and ocean without rest;
They also serve who only stand and wait.'

FOR ANALYSIS

The Lover

1. Like many Italian sonnets, this one is based on a single metaphor extended into an analogy. What in the narrator's lovesick condition do these things represent:
   (a) the galley?   (d) the cords?
   (b) the enemy (steersman)?   (e) the stars?
   (c) the oars?   (f) the port?
2. What does Wyatt achieve by using a couplet ending, unusual in the Italian sonnet form? (Wyatt, incidentally, introduced the Italian sonnet into English.)

Holy Sonnet 14

1. In what traditional sense is God "three personed"?
2. In the first quatrain of the sonnet, what is the conception of God? (What kind of artisan batters, knocks, bends, breaks, blows, burns, breathes on and shines his work?)
3. In what shape is God conceived of in the second quatrain? In the third?
4. What paradox, common in Christian doctrine, is expressed in sexual terms in the concluding couplet?
5. How, then, does the phrase "three personed God" forecast and order the development of the sonnet?

On His Blindness

1. How does Milton give unusual unity to the Italian sonnet form here?
2. What is the *talent* of line three? What other talent, besides his own, is Milton referring to? (See *Matthew*, 25:26.)

PERCY BYSSHE SHELLEY

Ozymandias

I met a traveler from an antique land
Who said: Two vast and trunkless legs of stone
Stand in the desert. Near them, on the sand,
Half sunk, a shattered visage lies, whose frown,
And wrinkled lip, and sneer of cold command,   5
Tell that its sculptor well those passions read

Which yet survive, (stamped on these lifeless
    things),
The hand that mocked them and the heart that fed;
And on the pedestal these words appear:
'My name is Ozymandias, king of kings;   10
Look on my works, ye Mighty, and despair!'
Nothing beside remains. Round the decay
Of that colossal wreck, boundless and bare,
The lone and level sands stretch far away.

JOHN KEATS

When I Have Fears that I May Cease to Be

When I have fears that I may cease to be
Before my pen has gleaned my teeming brain,
Before high pilèd books, in charact'ry,
Hold like rich garners the full-ripened grain;
When I behold, upon the night's starred face,   5
Huge cloudy symbols of a high romance,
And think that I may never live to trace
Their shadows, with the magic hand of chance;
And when I feel, fair creature of an hour!
That I shall never look upon thee more,   10
Never have relish in the faery power
Of unreflecting love!—then on the shore
Of the wide world I stand alone, and think
Till Love and Fame to nothingness do sink.

WILLIAM WORDSWORTH

Composed Upon Westminster Bridge September 3, 1802

Earth has not anything to show more fair:
Dull would he be of soul who could pass by
A sight so touching in its majesty:
This city now doth like a garment wear
The beauty of the morning; silent, bare,   5
Ships, towers, domes, theaters, and temples lie

Open unto the fields, and to the sky;
All bright and glittering in the smokeless air.
Never did sun more beautifully steep
In his first splendor valley, rock, or hill;   10
Ne'er saw I, never felt, a calm so deep!
The river glideth at his own sweet will:
Dear God! the very houses seem asleep;
And all that mighty heart is lying still!

WILLIAM WORDSWORTH

The World Is Too Much with Us

The world is too much with us: late and soon,
Getting and spending, we lay waste our powers:
Little we see in Nature that is ours;
We have given our hearts away, a sordid boon!
This sea that bares her bosom to the moon;   5
The winds that will be howling at all hours,
And are up-gathered now like sleeping flowers;
For this, for everything, we are out of tune;
It moves us not.—Great God! I'd rather be
A pagan suckled in a creed outworn.   10
So might I, standing on this pleasant lea,
Have glimpses that would make me less forlorn;
Have sight of Proteus rising from the sea;
Or hear old Triton blow his wreathèd horn.

FOR ANALYSIS

Ozymandias

1. In what ways does this poem conform to sonnet conventions and in what ways does it differ?
2. Whose *hand* and whose *heart* are referred to in line 8?
3. What does Shelley gain by putting the poem in the mouth of someone else? How would the poem differ if the poet himself were speaking?

When I Have Fears

Although this poem is generally clear and uncomplicated, there are two points of difficulty:
1. What does Keats mean by "the magic hand of chance"?
2. What is "unreflecting love"?

Westminster Bridge

1. Wordsworth habitually preferred the country to the city. What is it about the city in this poem

that so surprises and attracts him? Consider what the words "beauty," "silent," "bare," "open," "bright," "calm" would usually be applied to.

2. What is the central metaphor on which the poem is built? Consider that the city here wears garments and has a mighty heart that is lying still.

3. Does Wordsworth say that the city always has the attributes he sees here? What are the implications of the metaphors he uses—implications of permanence or transience?

The World Is Too Much with Us

1. How does Wordsworth change the convention of the Italian sonnet form? Why?

2. Why is the poet "forlorn" in this poem? What advantage did the "pagan" have that we have not? Does the poet actually mean that the pagan saw Proteus and Triton? Or did those two figures symbolize something far deeper?

GERARD MANLEY HOPKINS

The Windhover

TO CHRIST OUR LORD

I caught this morning morning's minion, king-
   dom of daylight's dauphin, dapple-dawn-drawn Falcon, in his riding
   Of the rolling level underneath him steady air, and striding
High there, how he rung upon the rein of a wimpling wing
In his ecstasy! then off, off forth on swing,   5
   As a skate's heel sweeps smooth on a bow-bend: the hurl and gliding
   Rebuffed the big wind. My heart in hiding
Stirred for a bird,—the achieve of, the mastery of the thing!

Brute beauty and valor and act, oh, air, pride, plume, here
   Buckle! AND the fire that breaks from thee then, a billion   10
Times told lovelier, more dangerous, O my chevalier!

   No wonder of it: shéer plód makes plough down sillion
Shine, and blue-bleak embers, ah my dear,
   Fall, gall themselves, and gash gold-vermilion.

FOR ANALYSIS

1. A windhover is a small hawk, seen flying in the turbulent early morning air currents. In what figurative sense did the narrator "catch" the windhover? In what two senses is the hawk "drawn" by the dappled dawn? What is the hawk doing that so stirs the narrator?

2. The narrator is at first surprised by the hawk's mastery of and delight in the turbulent currents and asks that this same courage and joy be given to him. But then he says that he should not have been surprised: Simply plodding down a field behind a plow reveals a similar beauty—the plow and the sillion (the turned-back soil of the furrow) shine as the plowing goes on. Finally, he says, even the dying embers of a fire reveal a similar beauty, as in their last moment they collapse and throw a gold-vermilion flash of final fire. What do all these things—the flying hawk, the plodding plowman and plow, the falling embers—have in common? Why, therefore, should he not have been surprised by the hawk's beauty?

GERARD MANLEY HOPKINS

As Kingfishers Catch Fire

As kingfishers catch fire, dragonflies draw flame;
As tumbled over rim in roundy wells
Stones ring; like each tucked string tells, each hung
    bell's
Bow swung finds tongue to fling out broad its
    name;
Each mortal thing does one thing and the same; 5
Deals out that being indoors each one dwells;
Selves—goes itself; *myself*, it speaks and spells,
Crying *What I do is me; for that I came.*

I say more: the just man justices;
Keeps grace: that keeps all his goings graces; 10
Acts in God's eye what in God's eye he is—
Christ—for Christ plays in ten thousand places,
Lovely in limbs, and lovely in eyes not his
To the father through the features of men's faces.

FOR ANALYSIS

Hopkins is a difficult poet to read at first because although he was a nineteenth-century poet, he wrote in the fashion of some of the most adventurous twentieth-century poets. He omits simple connectives and runs words together for economy, borrows words from vocabularies old and new, coins words when he feels the need.

1. What do kingfishers catching fire, dragonflies drawing flame, stones ringing as they fall down a well, bells tolling as they swing, strings on instruments sounding as they are plucked, all have in common? What are they doing in terms of what they are? What are they doing in terms of what created them? (A kingfisher does not literally catch fire and a dragonfly does not literally draw flame; when the kingfisher dives, light reflects from his feathers and flashes, and as the dragonfly darts about the rays of the sun reflect on his wings.)

2. How does man share in this process of doing something that is uniquely his and yet is the same as all the rest? How does what a man does show what he is?

JOHN CIARDI

A Sonnet for Robert Frost but Not About Him

He'd heard in school about the Constitution
and what he thought he'd heard, or what he got
of what was said, and claimed he had been taught,
was that free government's an institution
for making all men equal. So equated 5
he set up an opinion, good as any,
on anything that didn't have too many
bunglesome facts about it. So he waited
for what was his by law of equal state.
It came to very few cents on the dollar. 10
Somehow his equalness kept getting smaller.
He died firmly bewildered by his fate.
Confusion's bound to be the mortal sequel
to letting children think they'll grow up equal.

FOR ANALYSIS

1. What characteristics of Frost's style and themes is Ciardi imitating here? See pp. 210–11 for some of Frost's poems.

Irregular sonnets

KENNETH FEARING

Art Review

Recently displayed at the Times Square Station, a new Vandyke on
    the face-cream girl,
(Artist unknown. Has promise, but lacks the brilliance shown by
    the great masters of the Elevated age)
That latest wood carving in a Whelan telephone booth, titled
    "O Mortal Fools WA 9–5090," shows two winged hearts above
    an ace of spades.
(His meaning is not entirely clear, but this man will go far)
A charcoal nude in the rear of Flatbush Ahearn's Bar & Grill,   5
    "Forward to the Brotherhood of Man," has been boldly con-
    ceived in the great tradition.
(We need more, much more of this)
Then there is the chalk portrait, on the walls of a waterfront
    warehouse, of a gentleman wearing a derby hat: "Bleecker
    Street Mike is a double-crossing rat."
(Morbid, but powerful. Don't miss)

Know then by these presents, know all men by these signs
    and omens, by these simple thumbprints on the throat of time,
Know that Pete, the people's artist, is ever watchful,   10
That Tuxedo Jim has passed among us, and was much displeased,
    as always,
That George the Ghost (no man has ever seen him) and Billy the
    Bicep boy will neither bend nor break,
That Mr. Harkness of Sunnyside still hopes for the best, and
    has not lost his human touch,
That Phantom Phil, the master of them all, has come and gone,
    but will return, and all is well.

FOR ANALYSIS

1. What is Fearing satirizing here? Conventional art reviewing? Or is it more
   involved than that? Consider, for example, the change in tone at the beginning
   of the sestet.
2. Ambiguity is a chief ingredient in this sonnet. "Elevated age" is obviously a
   humorous reference to the days when the elevated railway was an important means
   of transportation in New York; but has it also a more serious reference? The
   phrase, "thumbprints on the throat of time," is a parody of Longfellow's sen-
   tentious "footprints on the sands of time," but it has another significance. What
   would one be doing, figuratively speaking, to "time" if he left thumbprints on
   time's throat?
3. In what sense is the conclusion, "and all is well," ironic, in what sense straight-
   forward?

GEORGE MEREDITH
Sonnet 1

By this he knew she wept with waking eyes:
That, at his hand's light quiver by her head,
The strange low sobs that shook their common bed,
Were called into her with a sharp surprise,
And strangled mute, like little gaping snakes, 5
Dreadfully venomous to him. She lay
Stone-still, and the long darkness flowed away
With muffled pulses. Then, as midnight makes
Her giant heart of Memory and Tears
Drink the pale drug of silence, and so beat 10
Sleep's heavy measure, they from head to feet
Were moveless, looking through their dead black
 years,
By vain regret scrawled over the blank wall.
Like sculptured effigies they might be seen
Upon their marriage-tomb, the sword between; 15
Each wishing for the sword that severs all.

FOR ANALYSIS

1. In this sixteen-line sonnet, with what has Meredith replaced the final couplet of the English form? Can you suggest why he might have done this, knowing that the sequence, *Modern Love*, from which this sonnet is taken, is a narrative sequence?
2. What in the early part of the sonnet justifies that odd but effective image at the end of the carved effigies on the marriage tomb?
3. What sword is referred to in the last line?

Conventions of the pastoral

A pastoral is a poem dealing with country life as the "good life"; pastorals celebrate the virtues of the simple, uncomplicated, close-to-nature existence of carefree shepherds, swains, milkmaids. In other words, pastorals present country life in a highly idealized fashion. Pastorals are *not* rural poetry; they develop from a highly sophisticated society and are often a form of social criticism. They express the wish that human beings could exist so simply. Since life in the country was never like that described in pastorals, the implication in most pastorals is that the narrator longs for rest from the burdens of a complex society.

CHRISTOPHER MARLOWE
The Passionate Shepherd to His Love

Come live with me and be my love,
And we will all the pleasures prove
That valleys, groves, hills, and fields,
Woods, or steepy mountain yields.

And we will sit upon the rocks, 5
Seeing the shepherds feed their flocks,
By shallow rivers to whose falls
Melodious birds sing madrigals.

And I will make thee beds of roses
And a thousand fragrant posies, 10
A cap of flowers, and a kirtle
Embroidered all with leaves of myrtle;

A gown made of the finest wool
Which from our pretty lambs we pull;
Fair linèd slippers for the cold, 15
With buckles of the purest gold;

A belt of straw and ivy buds,
With coral clasps and amber studs:
And if these pleasures may thee move,
Come live with me, and be my love. 20

The shepherds' swains shall dance and sing
For thy delight each May morning:
If these delights thy mind may move,
Then live with me and be my love.

SIR WALTER RALEIGH

The Nymph's Reply
to the Shepherd

If all the world and love were young,
And truth in every shepherd's tongue,
These pretty pleasures might me move
To live with thee and be thy love.

Time drives the flocks from field to fold
When rivers rage and rocks grow cold,
And Philomel becometh dumb;
The rest complains of cares to come.

The flowers do fade, and wanton fields
To wayward winter reckoning yields;   10
A honey tongue, a heart of gall,
Is fancy's spring, but sorrow's fall.

Thy gowns, thy shoes, thy beds of roses,
Thy cap, thy kirtle, and thy posies
Soon break, soon wither, soon forgotten,—
In folly ripe, in reason rotten.

Thy belt of straw and ivy buds,
Thy coral clasps and amber studs,
All these in me no means can move
To come to thee and be thy love.   20

But could youth last and love still breed,
Had joys no date nor age no need,
Then these delights my mind might move
To live with thee and be thy love.

JOHN DONNE

The Bait

Come live with me, and be my love,
And we will some new pleasures prove
Of golden sands, and crystal brooks,
With silken lines, and silver hooks.

There will the river whispering run   5
Warmed by thy eyes, more than the Sun.
And there the enamoured fish will stay,

Begging themselves they may betray.
When thou wilt swim in that live bath,
Each fish, which every channel hath,   10
Will amorously to thee swim,
Gladder to catch thee, than thou him.

If thou, to be so seen, beest loath,
By Sun, or Moon, thou darknest both,
And if myself have leave to see,   15
I need not their light, having thee.

Let others freeze with angling reeds,
And cut their legs, with shells and weeds,
Or treacherously poor fish beset,
With strangling snare, or windowy net: 20

Let coarse bold hands, from slimy nest
The bedded fish in banks out-wrest,
Or curious traitors, sleavesilk flies
Bewitch poor fishes' wandering eyes.

For thee, thou needst no such deceit,   25
For thou thyself art thine own bait;
That fish, that is not catched thereby,
Alas, is wiser far than I.

CECIL DAY LEWIS

from A Time to Dance

Come, live with me and be my love,
And we will all the pleasures prove
Of peace and plenty, bed and board,
That chance employment may afford.

I'll handle dainties on the docks   5
And thou shalt read of summer frocks:
At evening by the sour canals
We'll hope to hear some madrigals.

Care on thy maiden brow shall put
A wreath of wrinkles, and thy foot   10
Be shod with pain: not silken dress
But toil shall tire thy loveliness.

Hunger shall make thy modest zone
And cheat fond death of all but bone—
If these delights thy mind may move,   15
Then live with me and be my love.

FOR ANALYSIS

Only the first of the preceding four poems is a genuine pastoral; the rest are parodies. The last three poems illustrate what happens to a convention when it loses its vitality. It either disappears or is altered to new ends.

1. Is Raleigh's poem a criticism of Marlowe's poem or a criticism of the pastoral convention as a whole? What primary assumption about Marlowe's poem is Raleigh making, tongue-in-cheek?

2. In what way is Donne's poem less pastoral, more sophisticated, than Marlowe's? Consider the odd coupling of words in the images: crystal brooks, silver hooks, and so forth. Is this just another technique for achieving Marlowe's goal or do the two poems have different ends in view?

3. What facets of his own society is Day Lewis most critical of? How does his poem differ from the "pure" pastoral of Marlowe?

4. Most pastorals are ironic by definition: They are implied contrasts of what ought to be with what is. Which of these four poems is the most ironic?

Conventions of the ode

A conventional ode is an elaborate lyrical poem of praise, elevated in tone and intricate in form. Once popular, the form has been used very little during the past hundred years.

The Pindaric ode is characterized by sets of three stanzas (strophe, antistrophe, epode); the strophe and antistrophe are metrically identical and the epode different. It largely disappeared in the seventeenth century, perhaps partly because the original reason for the three-part division became meaningless: a Greek chorus moving to the left while chanting the strophe, to the right for the antistrophe, and then remaining still to recite the epode.

Since the seventeenth century, the most frequently used form has been the irregular ode, first written by Abraham Cowley. It retains the previous tone and form, but it abandons the three-part organization and metrical repetition. See, for an example of the irregular ode, Wordsworth's "Ode: Intimations of Immortality" (p. 183).

Finally, the Horatian ode, an irregular ode with a less elevated tone and less intricate form, has attracted the talents of many excellent English and American poets. For an example, see Keats's "Ode on a Grecian Urn" (p. 182).

JOHN DRYDEN

Alexander's Feast

OR, THE POWER OF MUSIC; AN ODE IN HONOR OF
ST. CECILIA'S DAY

I

'Twas at the royal feast, for Persia won
    By Philip's warlike son:

      Aloft in awful state
      The godlike hero sate
        On his imperial throne:
    His valiant peers were placed around;
Their brows with roses and with myrtles bound:
    (So should desert in arms be crowned.)
    The lovely Thais, by his side,
Sate like a blooming Eastern bride   10
In flower of youth and beauty's pride.
      Happy, happy, happy pair!
      None but the brave,
      None but the brave,
      None but the brave deserves the fair.

St. Cecilia's Day: November 22. Dryden's ode was written in 1697 to celebrate the annual Feast of St. Cecilia, patroness of church music and legendary inventor of the organ. The ode compliments St. Cecilia obliquely by comparing her advantageously with Timotheus, the Theban flutist whose music entranced Alexander the Great, by popular legend the son of Jove and Olympias, wife of Philip of Macedon.

9 Thais: Alexander's mistress

CHORUS

Happy, happy, happy pair!
None but the brave,
None but the brave,
None but the brave deserves the fair.

II

Timotheus, placed on high   20
  Amid the tuneful choir,
    With flying fingers touched the lyre:
The trembling notes ascend the sky,
                And heavenly joys inspire.
The song began from Jove,
Who left his blissful seats above,
(Such is the power of mighty love.)
A dragon's fiery form belied the god:
Sublime on radiant spires he rode,
    When he to fair Olympia pressed;   30
    And while he sought her snowy breast:
Then, round her slender waist he curled,
And stamped an image of himself, a sovereign of the
    world.
The listening crowd admire the lofty sound;
"A present deity," they shout around;
"A present deity," the vaulted roofs rebound:
      With ravished ears
      The monarch hears,
      Assumes the god,
      Affects to nod,   40
And seems to shake the spheres.

CHORUS

With ravished ears
The monarch hears,
Assumes the god,
Affects to nod,
And seems to shake the spheres.

III

The praise of Bacchus then the sweet musician sung,
  Of Bacchus ever fair and ever young:
    "The jolly god in triumph comes;
    Sound the trumpets; beat the drums;   50
      Flushed with a purple grace
      He shews his honest face:
Now give the hautboys breath; he comes, he comes.
    Bacchus, ever fair and young,
      Drinking joys did first ordain;
    Bacchus' blessings are a treasure,
    Drinking is the soldier's pleasure:

    Rich the treasure,
    Sweet the pleasure,
    Sweet is pleasure after pain."   60

CHORUS

Bacchus' blessings are a treasure,
Drinking is the soldier's pleasure:
  Rich the treasure,
  Sweet the pleasure,
  Sweet is pleasure after pain.

IV

  Soothed with the sound, the king grew vain;
    Fought all his battles o'er again;
And thrice he routed all his foes; and thrice he slew
    the slain.
The master saw the madness rise;
His glowing cheeks, his ardent eyes;   70
And, while he heaven and earth defied,
Changed his hand, and checked his pride.
      He chose a mournful Muse,
        Soft pity to infuse:
He sung Darius great and good,
        By too severe a fate,
Fallen, fallen, fallen, fallen,
        Fallen from his high estate,
          And weltering in his blood;
Deserted, at his utmost need,   80
By those his former bounty fed;
On the bare earth exposed he lies,
With not a friend to close his eyes.

With downcast looks the joyless victor sate,
  Revolving in his altered soul
    The various turns of chance below;
  And, now and then, a sigh he stole;
    And tears began to flow.

CHORUS

Revolving in his altered soul
  The various turns of chance below;   90
And, now and then, a sigh he stole;
  And tears began to flow.

V

The mighty master smiled, to see
That love was in the next degree:

_____

75 *Darius:* King of Persia conquered by Alexander

'Twas but a kindred sound to move,
For pity melts the mind to love.
　Softly sweet, in Lydian measures,
　Soon he soothed his soul to pleasures.
　"War," he sung, "is toil and trouble;
　Honor, but an empty bubble;   100
　　Never ending, still beginning,
　Fighting still, and still destroying:
　　If the world be worth thy winning,
　Think, O think it worth enjoying;
　　Lovely Thais sits beside thee,
　　Take the good the gods provide thee."
The many rend the skies with loud applause;
So Love was crowned, but Music won the cause.
　The prince, unable to conceal his pain,
　　Gazed on the fair   110
　　Who caused his care,
　And sighed and looked, sighed and looked,
Sighed and looked, and sighed again:
At length, with love and wine at once oppressed,
The vanquished victor sunk upon her breast.

CHORUS

The prince, unable to conceal his pain,
　Gazed on the fair
　Who caused his care,
And sighed and looked, sighed and looked,
Sighed and looked, and sighed again: 120
At length, with love and wine at once oppressed,
The vanquished victor sunk upon her breast.

VI

Now strike the golden lyre again:
A louder yet, and yet a louder strain.
Break his bands of sleep asunder,
And rouse him, like a rattling peal of thunder.
　　Hark, hark, the horrid sound
　　Has raised up his head:
　　As awaked from the dead,
　　And amazed, he stares around.   130
"Revenge, revenge!" Timotheus cries,
　"See the Furies arise!
　See the snakes that they rear,
　How they hiss in their hair,
　And the sparkles that flash from their eyes!
　Behold a ghastly band,
　Each a torch in his hand!
Those are Grecian ghosts, that in battle were slain,

　　And unburied remain
　　Inglorious on the plain: 140
　　Give the vengeance due
　　To the valiant crew.
Behold how they toss their torches on high,
　How they point to the Persian abodes,
And glittering temples of their hostile gods!"
The princes applaud, with a furious joy;
And the king seized a flambeau with zeal to destroy;
　　Thais led the way,
　　To light him to his prey,
And, like another Helen, fired another Troy.   150

CHORUS

And the king seized a flambeau with zeal to destroy;
　Thais led the way,
　To light him to his prey,
And, like another Helen, fired another Troy.

VII

　　Thus, long ago,
　Ere heaving bellows learned to blow,
　　While organs yet were mute;
　Timotheus, to his breathing flute,
　　And sounding lyre,
Could swell the soul to rage, or kindle soft
　　desire.   160
　At last, divine Cecilia came,
　Inventress of the vocal frame;
The sweet enthusiast, from her sacred store,
　Enlarged the former narrow bounds,
　And added length to solemn sounds,
With nature's mother wit, and arts unknown before.
　Let old Timotheus yield the prize,
　　Or both divide the crown;
　He raised a mortal to the skies;
　　She drew an angel down.   170

GRAND CHORUS

At last, divine Cecilia came,
Inventress of the vocal frame;
The sweet enthusiast, from her sacred store,
　Enlarged the former narrow bounds,
　And added length to solemn sounds,
With nature's mother wit, and arts unknown before.
　Let old Timotheus yield the prize,
　　Or both divide the crown;

---

97 *Lydian:* soft and voluptuous, like the music of ancient Lydia
132 *Furies:* goddesses of revenge

148–150 Thais encouraged Alexander to burn the palace at Persepolis, capital of Persia.

He raised a mortal to the skies;
She drew an angel down.   180

FOR ANALYSIS

1. Although "Alexander's Feast" is not a Pindaric ode, there are traces of Pindaric features in it. Reread the brief description of the Pindaric ode at the beginning of this section, and then indicate what carry-over you find from that form in "Alexander's Feast."
2. Poets of the seventeenth century—notably Milton—often mixed references to Christian and pagan deities. How does Dryden separate them and use one to the advantage of the other?

JOHN KEATS

Ode on a Grecian Urn

Thou still unravished bride of quietness,
    Thou foster-child of silence and slow time,
Sylvan historian, who canst thus express
    A flowery tale more sweetly than our rhyme:
What leaf-fringed legend haunts about thy shape   5
    Of deities or mortals, or of both,
        In Tempe or the dales of Arcady?
    What men or gods are these? What maidens loath?
What mad pursuit? What struggle to escape?
    What pipes and timbrels? What wild
        ecstasy?   10

Heard melodies are sweet, but those unheard
    Are sweeter; therefore, ye soft pipes, play on:
Not to the sensual ear, but, more endeared,
    Pipe to the spirit ditties of no tone:
Fair youth, beneath the trees, thou canst not
    leave   15
    Thy song, nor ever can those trees be bare;
        Bold Lover, never, never canst thou kiss
Though winning near the goal—yet, do not grieve;
    She cannot fade, though thou hast not thy
        bliss,
    For ever wilt thou love, and she be fair!   20

Ah, happy, happy boughs! that cannot shed
    Your leaves, nor ever bid the Spring adieu;

And, happy melodist, unwearièd,
    For ever piping songs for ever new;
More happy love! more happy, happy love!   25
    For ever warm and still to be enjoyed,
        For ever panting, and for ever young;
All breathing human passion far above,
    That leaves a heart high-sorrowful and cloyed,
        A burning forehead, and a parching
            tongue.   30

Who are these coming to the sacrifice?
    To what green altar, O mysterious priest,
Lead'st thou that heifer lowing at the skies,
    And all her silken flanks with garlands dressed?
What little town by river or sea shore,   35
    Or mountain-built with peaceful citadel,
        Is emptied of this folk, this pious morn?
And, little town, thy streets for evermore
    Will silent be; and not a soul to tell
        Why thou art desolate, can e'er return.   40

O Attic shape! Fair attitude! with brede
    Of marble men and maidens over wrought,
With forest branches and the trodden weed;
    Thou, silent form, dost tease us out of thought
As doth eternity: Cold Pastoral!   45
    When old age shall this generation waste,
        Thou shalt remain, in midst of other woe
Than ours, a friend to man, to whom thou say'st,
    'Beauty is truth, truth beauty,'—that is all
        Ye know on earth, and all ye need to know. 50

FOR ANALYSIS

1. This poem attempts to express a basic paradox of life, phrased here in several ways. In what sense are the first two lines of the second stanza true?
2. What dissatisfaction with his own thoughts about the urn is the poet expressing when he calls it a "Cold Pastoral"?
3. There has been endless debate about the meaning of the "Beauty is truth, truth beauty" epigram. Considered by itself, it is not, at a rational level, true. One key to the difficulty lies in the pronoun "that" following the epigram. To what does *that* refer? To the epigram? Or to the whole sentence preceding it, "When old age shall this generation . . ."? Another key is the pronoun ye. To whom does this refer? The figures on the urn? Or the reader generally? Does the second ye refer to the same person as the one signified by the first ye?

WILLIAM WORDSWORTH

Ode : Intimations of Immortality
from Recollections
of Early Childhood

I

There was a time when meadow, grove, and stream,
    The earth, and every common sight,
        To me did seem
        Appareled in celestial light,
The glory and the freshness of a dream.   5
It is not now as it hath been of yore;—
        Turn wheresoe'er I may,
        By night or day,
The things which I have seen I now can see no more.

II

    The Rainbow comes and goes,   10
    And lovely is the Rose;
    The Moon doth with delight
Look round her when the heavens are bare;
      Waters on a starry night
      Are beautiful and fair;   15
    The sunshine is a glorious birth;
    But yet I know, where'er I go,
That there hath passed away a glory from the earth.

III

Now, while the birds thus sing a joyous song,
    And while the young lambs bound   20
      As to the tabor's sound,
To me alone there came a thought of grief:
A timely utterance gave that thought relief,
      And I again am strong:
The cataracts blow their trumpets from the steep;   25
No more shall grief of mine the season wrong;
I hear the Echoes through the mountains throng,
The Winds come to me from the fields of sleep,
      And all the earth is gay;
        Land and sea   30
    Give themselves up to jollity,
      And with the heart of May
      Doth every Beast keep holiday;—
        Thou Child of Joy,
Shout round me, let me hear thy shouts, thou happy Shepherd-boy! 35

IV

Ye blessèd Creatures, I have heard the call
      Ye to each other make; I see
The heavens laugh with you in your jubilee;
      My heart is at your festival,
      My head hath its coronal,   40
The fulness of your bliss, I feel—I feel it all.
      Oh, evil day! if I were sullen
      While Earth herself is adorning,
        This sweet May-morning,
      And the Children are culling   45
        On every side,
      In a thousand valleys far and wide,
Fresh flowers; while the sun shines warm,
And the Babe leaps up on his Mother's arm—
      I hear, I hear, with joy I hear!   50
      —But there's a Tree, of many, one,
A single Field which I have looked upon,
Both of them speak of something that is gone:
      The Pansy at my feet
      Doth the same tale repeat: 55
Whither is fled the visionary gleam?
Where is it now, the glory and the dream?

V

Our birth is but a sleep and a forgetting:
The Soul that rises with us, our life's Star,
      Hath had elsewhere its setting,   60
        And cometh from afar:
      Not in entire forgetfulness,
      And not in utter nakedness,
But trailing clouds of glory do we come
      From God, who is our home: 65
Heaven lies about us in our infancy!
Shades of the prison-house begin to close
      Upon the growing Boy,
But he beholds the light, and whence it flows
      He sees it in his joy;   70
The Youth, who daily farther from the east
      Must travel, still is Nature's priest,
      And by the vision splendid
      Is on his way attended;
At length the Man perceives it die away,   75
And fade into the light of common day.

VI

Earth fills her lap with pleasures of her own;
Yearnings she hath in her own natural kind,
And even with something of a Mother's mind,
      And no unworthy aim,   80
      The homely Nurse doth all she can

To make her Foster-child, her Inmate Man,
    Forget the glories he hath known,
And that imperial palace whence he came.

VII

Behold the Child among his new-born blisses,   85
A six years' Darling of a pigmy size!
See, where 'mid work of his own hand he lies,
Fretted by sallies of his mother's kisses,
With light upon him from his father's eyes!
See, at his feet, some little plan or chart,   90
Some fragment from his dream of human life,
Shaped by himself with newly-learnéd art;
    A wedding or a festival,
    A mourning or a funeral,
      And this hath now his heart,   95
    And unto this he frames his song:
      Then will he fit his tongue
To dialogues of business, love, or strife;
    But it will not be long
    Ere this be thrown aside,   100
    And with new joy and pride
The little Actor cons another part;
Filling from time to time his "humorous stage"
With all the Persons, down to palsied Age,
That Life brings with her in her equipage;   105
    As if his whole vocation
    Were endless imitation.

VIII

Thou, whose exterior semblance doth belie
    Thy Soul's immensity;
Thou best Philosopher, who yet dost keep   110
Thy heritage, thou Eye among the blind,
That, deaf and silent, read'st the eternal deep,
Haunted forever by the eternal mind—
    Mighty Prophet! Seer blest!
    On whom those truths do rest,   115
Which we are toiling all our lives to find,
In darkness lost, the darkness of the grave;
Thou, over whom thy Immortality
Broods like the Day, a Master o'er a Slave,
A Presence which is not to be put by;   120
Thou little Child, yet glorious in the might
Of heaven-born freedom on thy being's height,
Why with such earnest pains dost thou provoke
The years to bring the inevitable yoke,
Thus blindly with thy blessedness at strife?   125
Full soon thy Soul shall have her earthly freight,
And custom lie upon thee with a weight,
Heavy as frost, and deep almost as life!

IX

Oh, joy! that in our embers
    Is something that doth live,   130
    That nature yet remembers
    What was so fugitive!
The thought of our past years in me doth breed
Perpetual benediction: not indeed
For that which is most worthy to be blest;   135
Delight and liberty, the simple creed
Of Childhood, whether busy or at rest,
With new-fledged hope still fluttering in his breast—
    Not for these I raise
    The song of thanks and praise;   140
    But for those obstinate questionings
    Of sense and outward things,
    Falling from us, vanishings;
    Blank misgivings of a Creature
Moving about in worlds not realized,   145
High instincts before which our mortal nature
Did tremble like a guilty thing surprised:
    But for those first affections,
    Those shadowy recollections,
    Which, be they what they may,   150
Are yet the fountain light of all our day,
Are yet a master light of all our seeing;
  Uphold us, cherish, and have power to make
Our noisy years seem moments in the being
Of the eternal Silence: truths that wake,   155
    To perish never;
Which neither listlessness, nor mad endeavor,
    Nor Man nor Boy,
Nor all that is at enmity with joy,
Can utterly abolish or destroy!   160
    Hence in a season of calm weather
    Though inland far we be,
Our Souls have sight of that immortal sea
    Which brought us hither,
    Can in a moment travel thither,   165
And see the Children sport upon the shore,
And hear the mighty waters rolling evermore.

X

Then sing, ye Birds, sing, sing a joyous song!
    And let the young Lambs bound
    As to the tabor's sound!   170
We in thought will join your throng,
    Ye that pipe and ye that play,
    Ye that through your hearts today
    Feel the gladness of the May!
What though the radiance which was once so bright   175
Be now forever taken from my sight,
  Though nothing can bring back the hour
Of splendor in the grass, of glory in the flower;
    We will grieve not, rather find

Strength in what remains behind;   180
In the primal sympathy
Which having been must ever be;
In the soothing thoughts that spring
Out of human suffering;
In the faith that looks through death,   185
In years that bring the philosophic mind.

XI

And O, ye Fountains, Meadows, Hills, and Groves,
Forebode not any severing of our loves!
Yet in my heart of hearts I feel your might;
I only have relinquished one delight   190
To live beneath your more habitual sway.
I love the Brooks which down their channels fret,
Even more than when I tripped lightly as they;
The innocent brightness of a new-born Day
Is lovely yet;   195
The Clouds that gather round the setting sun
Do take a sober coloring from an eye
That hath kept watch o'er man's mortality.
Another race hath been, and other palms are won.
Thanks to the human heart by which we live,   200
Thanks to its tenderness, its joys, and fears,
To me the meanest flower that blows can give
Thoughts that do often lie too deep for tears.

FOR ANALYSIS

Wordsworth apparently conceives of an ode as being much less stylized than John Dryden does. Both poets observe the same elevation of subject, tone, and language, but where Dryden's ode is public and oratorical, Wordsworth's is personal and reflective, making the "Ode: Intimations of Immortality" a more difficult poem for the reader to deal with. Any serious reader of the poem will eventually have to answer to his own satisfaction questions such as the following:

1. What are the "things" that the poet says "I now can see no more"?
2. What is the "glory" that has passed away?
3. What is the "visionary gleam"?
4. In what way does a child live in a "dream of human life"? How does the dream differ from the reality?
5. What does the adult gain that partially makes up for the loss of the dream?

PERCY BYSSHE SHELLEY

Ode to the West Wind

I

O wild west wind, thou breath of Autumn's being,
Thou, from whose unseen presence the leaves dead
Are driven, like ghosts from an enchanter fleeing,

Yellow, and black, and pale, and hectic red,
Pestilence-stricken multitudes: O thou,   5
Who chariotest to their dark wintry bed

The wingéd seeds, where they lie cold and low,
Each like a corpse within its grave, until
Thine azure sister of the Spring shall blow

Her clarion o'er the dreaming earth, and fill   10
(Driving sweet buds like flocks to feed in air)
With living hues and odors plain and hill:

Wild Spirit, which art moving everywhere;
Destroyer and preserver; hear, oh, hear!

II

Thou on whose stream, mid the steep sky's commotion,   15
Loose clouds like earth's decaying leaves are shed,
Shook from the tangled boughs of Heaven and Ocean,

Angels of rain and lightning: there are spread
On the blue surface of thine aëry surge,
Like the bright hair uplifted from the head   20

Of some fierce Maenad, even from the dim verge
Of the horizon to the zenith's height,
The locks of the approaching storm. Thou dirge

Of the dying year, to which this closing night
Will be the dome of a vast sepulcher,   25
Vaulted with all thy congregated might

Of vapors, from whose solid atmosphere
Black rain, and fire, and hail will burst: oh, hear!

III

Thou who didst waken from his summer dreams
The blue Mediterranean, where he lay,   30
Lulled by the coil of his crystalline streams,

Beside a pumice isle in Baiae's bay,
And saw in sleep old palaces and towers
Quivering within the wave's intenser day,

All overgrown with azure moss and flowers   35
So sweet, the sense faints picturing them! Thou
For whose path the Atlantic's level powers

Cleave themselves into chasms, while far below
The sea-blooms and the oozy woods which wear
The sapless foliage of the ocean, know   40

Thy voice, and suddenly grow gray with fear,
And tremble and despoil themselves: oh, hear!

IV

If I were a dead leaf thou mightest bear,
If I were a swift cloud to fly with thee;
A wave to pant beneath thy power, and share   45

The impulse of thy strength, only less free
Than thou, O uncontrollable! If even
I were as in my boyhood, and could be

The comrade of thy wanderings over Heaven,
As then, when to outstrip thy skyey speed   50
Scarce seemed a vision; I would ne'er have striven

As thus with thee in prayer in my sore need.
Oh, lift me as a wave, a leaf, a cloud!
I fall upon the thorns of life! I bleed!

A heavy weight of hours has chained and bowed   55
One too like thee: tameless, and swift, and proud.

V

Make me thy lyre, even as the forest is:
What if my leaves are falling like its own!
The tumult of thy mighty harmonies

Will take from both a deep, autumnal tone,   60
Sweet though in sadness. Be thou, Spirit fierce,
My spirit! Be thou me, impetuous one!

Drive my dead thoughts over the universe
Like withered leaves to quicken a new birth!
And, by the incantation of this verse,   65

Scatter, as from an unextinguished hearth
Ashes and sparks, my words among mankind!
Be through my lips to unawakened earth

The trumpet of a prophecy! O Wind,
If Winter comes, can Spring be far behind?   70

FOR ANALYSIS

1. This poem is written in *terza rima*, a form that achieves continuity by interlocking rimes—*aba, bcb, cdc.* But does Shelley seem to have some other form also in mind? Consider the way he blocks the lines into larger units.
2. This poem is both an invocation and an incantation. Why does Shelley pick the West Wind as his object of supplication? What particularly does that wind do that makes it suitable? What similarities does Shelley see in himself and the West Wind?
3. The "statement" that the poem makes is obviously metaphorical: The poet could not actually become the wind or even use the wind. What, then, is Shelley saying in the poem?

The elegy

The elegy is a lyrical, meditative poem lamenting the death of a loved or honored person. Most common in English is the "pastoral elegy," a highly conventionalized lament borrowed from the Greeks. The dead person and his associates are rendered as shepherds in the pastoral elegy. The poem generally begins with an invocation, moves to a description of how all nature mourns the dead one, describes a procession of mourners, philosophizes on the justice and injustice of death, and ends positively with despair changed to hope, grief to acceptance. Woven into the conventional fabric may be digressions of various kinds; indeed, the best known parts of our better known English elegies are often from digressive passages.

JOHN MILTON

Lycidas

[*In this Monody the author bewails a learned friend, unfortunately drowned in his passage from Chester on the Irish Seas, 1637. And by occasion, foretells the ruin of our corrupted Clergy, then in their height.*]

Yet once more, O ye laurels, and once more,
Ye myrtles brown, with ivy never sear,
I come to pluck your berries harsh and crude,
And with forced fingers rude
Shatter your leaves before the mellowing year.
Bitter constraint and sad occasion dear
Compels me to disturb your season due;
For Lycidas is dead, dead ere his prime,
Young Lycidas, and hath not left his peer.
Who would not sing for Lycidas? He knew   10
Himself to sing, and build the lofty rime.
He must not float upon his watery bier
Unwept, and welter to the parching wind,
Without the meed of some melodious tear.
    Begin, then, Sisters of the sacred well,
That from beneath the seat of Jove doth spring;
Begin, and somewhat loudly sweep the string.
Hence with denial vain and coy excuse;
So may some gentle muse
With lucky words favor my destined urn,   20
And as he passes turn
And bid fair peace be to my sable shroud!
    For we were nursed upon the selfsame hill,
Fed the same flock, by fountain, shade, and rill;

Together both, ere the high lawns appeared
Under the opening eyelids of the Morn,
We drove afield, and both together heard
What time the gray-fly winds her sultry horn,
Battening our flocks with the fresh dews of night,
Oft till the star that rose at evening, bright,   30
Toward heaven's descent had sloped his westering
    wheel.
Meanwhile the rural ditties were not mute,
Tempered to the oaten flute;
Rough Satyrs danced, and Fauns with cloven heel
From the glad sound would not be absent long;
And old Damoetas loved to hear our song.
    But, oh! the heavy change, now thou art gone,
Now thou art gone, and never must return!
Thee, Shepherd, thee the woods and desert caves,
With wild thyme and the gadding vine   40
    o'ergrown,
And all their echoes, mourn.
The willows, and the hazel copses green,
Shall now no more be seen
Fanning their joyous leaves to thy soft lays.
As killing as the canker to the rose,
Or taint-worm to the weanling herds that graze,
Or frost to flowers, that their gay wardrobe wear,
When first the white-thorn blows—
Such, Lycidas, thy loss to shepherd's ear.
    Where were ye, Nymphs, when the   50
    remorseless deep
Closed o'er the head of your loved Lycidas?
For neither were ye playing on the steep
Where your old bards, the famous Druids, lie,
Nor on the shaggy top of Mona high,
Nor yet where Deva spreads her wizard stream.

Lycidas: a common name in pastoral verse; here Lycidas is Edward King, a young poet and Cambridge acquaintance of Milton   15 *Sisters, well:* the nine muses sit by the Pierian spring, fount of poetry

36 *Damoetus:* probably a college tutor   54 *Mona:* Isle of Anglesey, off the coast of Wales   55 *Deva:* Dee, the river harboring the port from which King sailed to his death

Aye me! I fondly dream
"Had ye been there"—for what could that have
   done?
What could the Muse herself that Orpheus bore,
The Muse herself, for her enchanting son,
Whom universal nature did lament, 60
When, by the rout that made the hideous roar,
His gory visage down the stream was sent,
Down the swift Hebrus to the Lesbian shore?
   Alas! what boots it with uncessant care
To tend the homely, slighted shepherd's trade,
And strictly meditate the thankless Muse?
Were it not better done as others use,
To sport with Amaryllis in the shade,
Or with the tangles of Neaera's hair?
Fame is the spur that the clear spirit doth raise 70
(That last infirmity of noble mind)
To scorn delights, and live laborious days;
But the fair guerdon when we hope to find,
And think to burst out into sudden blaze,
Comes the blind Fury with th' abhorrèd shears,
And slits the thin-spun life. "But not the praise,"
Phoebus replied, and touched my trembling ears;
"Fame is no plant that grows on mortal soil,
Nor in the glistering foil
Set off to the world, nor in broad rumor lies, 80
But lives and spreads aloft by those pure eyes
And perfect witness of all-judging Jove;
As he pronounces lastly on each deed,
Of so much fame in heaven expect thy meed."
   O fountain Arethuse, and thou honored flood,
Smooth-sliding Mincius, crowned with vocal reeds,
That strain I heard was of a higher mood.
But now my oat proceeds,
And listens to the Herald of the Sea
That came in Neptune's plea. 90
He asked the waves, and asked the felon winds,
What hard mishaps hath doomed this gentle swain?
And questioned every gust of rugged wings
That blows from off each beakèd promontory.
They knew not of his story;
And sage Hippotades their answer brings,
That not a blast was from his dungeon strayed;

The air was calm, and on the level brine
Sleek Panope with all her sisters played.
It was that fatal and perfidious bark, 100
Built in the eclipse, and rigged with curses dark,
That sunk so low that sacred head of thine.
   Next, Camus, reverend sire, went footing slow,
His mantle hairy, and his bonnet sedge,
Inwrought with figures dim, and on the edge
Like to that sanguine flower inscribed with woe.
"Ah! who hath reft," quoth he, "my dearest pledge?"
Last came, and last did go,
The Pilot of the Galilean Lake;
Two massy keys he bore of metals twain 110
(The golden opes, the iron shuts amain).
He shook his mitered locks, and stern bespake:
"How well could I have spared for thee, young
   swain,
Enow of such as, for their bellies' sake,
Creep, and intrude, and climb into the fold!
Of other care they little reckoning make
Than how to scramble at the shearers' feast,
And shove away the worthy bidden guest.
Blind mouths! that scarce themselves know how to
   hold
A sheep-hook, or have learned aught else the
   least 120
That to the faithful herdman's art belongs!
What recks it them? What need they? They are
   sped;
And when they list, their lean and flashy songs
Grate on their scrannel pipes of wretched straw;
The hungry sheep look up, and are not fed,
But swoln with wind and the rank mist they draw,
Rot inwardly, and foul contagion spread;
Besides what the grim wolf with privy paw
Daily devours apace, and nothing said.
But that two-handed engine at the door 130
Stands ready to smite once, and smite no more."
   Return, Alpheus, the dread voice is past
That shrunk thy streams; return, Sicilian Muse,
And call the vales, and bid them hither cast
Their bells and flowerets of a thousand hues.
Ye valleys low, where the mild whispers use
Of shades, and wanton winds, and gushing brooks,
On whose fresh lap the swart star sparely looks,
Throw hither all your quaint enameled eyes,

---

58 *Muse:* Calliope, muse of epic poetry, tried in vain to save her son Orpheus from the bacchanals, who dismembered him and sent his head and lyre floating down the Hebrus River and out to the Isle of Lesbos   68, 69 *Amaryllis, Neaera:* common names for shepherdesses in pastoral verse   75 *blind Fury:* Atropos, whose duty it was to cut the thread of life   77 *Phoebus:* god of poetry   85 *Arethuse:* river and pool near the birthplace of the pastoral poet Theocritus   86 *Mincius:* river near the birthplace of Virgil   88 *oat:* oat straw pipe, symbolizing pastoral poetry   89 *Herald of the Sea:* Triton, who blew on a conch shell   90 *Neptune's plea:* Triton defended Neptune, who had drowned Lycidas   96 *Hippotades:* Aeolus, god of the winds

99 *Panope:* one of the sea-god Nereus' fifty daughters   103 *Camus:* god of the river Cam, bordering Cambridge   106 *sanguine flower:* the hyacinth, whose markings look to some like the Greek characters for "Alas"   109 *Pilot:* St. Peter, the fisherman   110 *keys:* see *Matthew,* 16 : 19   130 *engine:* perhaps the two houses of Parliament   132 *Alpheus:* the underground river that rises and flows into the Arethuse   133 *Sicilian Muse:* the pastoral muse   138 *swart star:* Sirius, destructive to vegetation

That on the green turf suck the honeyed
    showers,   140
And purple all the ground with vernal flowers.
Bring the rathe primrose that forsaken dies,
The tufted crow-toe, and pale jessamine,
The white pink, and the pansy freaked with jet,
The glowing violet,
The musk-rose, and the well-attired woodbine,
With cowslips wan that hang the pensive head,
And every flower that sad embroidery wears;
Bid amaranthus all his beauty shed,
And daffodillies fill their cups with tears,   150
To strew the laureate hearse where Lycid lies.
For so, to interpose a little ease,
Let our frail thoughts dally with false surmise.
Aye me! Whilst thee the shores and sounding seas
Wash far away, where'er thy bones are hurled,
Whether beyond the stormy Hebrides,
Where thou perhaps under the whelming tide
Visit'st the bottom of the monstrous world;
Or whether thou, to our moist vows denied,
Sleep'st by the fable of Bellerus old,   160
Where the great Vision of the guarded mount
Looks toward Namancos and Bayona's hold.
Look homeward, Angel, now, and melt with ruth;
And, O ye dolphins, waft the hapless youth.

    Weep no more, woeful shepherds, weep no more,
For Lycidas, your sorrow, is not dead,
Sunk though he be beneath the watery floor;
So sinks the day-star in the ocean bed,
And yet anon repairs his drooping head,
And tricks his beams, and with new-spangled
    ore   170
Flames in the forehead of the morning sky.
So Lycidas sunk low, but mounted high,
Through the dear might of Him that walked the
    waves,
Where, other groves and other streams along,
With nectar pure his oozy locks he laves,
And hears the unexpressive nuptial song,
In the blest kingdoms meek of joy and love.
There entertain him all the Saints above,
In solemn troops, and sweet societies,
That sing, and singing in their glory move,   180
And wipe the tears forever from his eyes.
Now, Lycidas, the shepherds weep no more;
Henceforth thou art the Genius of the shore,

In thy large recompense, and shalt be good
To all that wander in that perilous flood.

    Thus sang the uncouth swain to the oaks and rills,
While the still morn went out with sandals gray;
He touched the tender stops of various quills,
With eager thought warbling his Doric lay.
And now the sun had stretched out all the
    hills,   190
And now was dropped into the western bay.
At last he rose, and twitched his mantle blue;
Tomorrow to fresh woods and pastures new.

FOR ANALYSIS

1. Samuel Johnson disliked "Lycidas" because its
grief seemed unreal; perhaps that is more a comment on the pastoral conventions than on
"Lycidas" in particular. What, however, in
"Lycidas" suggests that other things than Edward
King were on Milton's mind in the writing of the
poem?

MATTHEW ARNOLD

Thyrsis

*A Monody, to Commemorate the Author's Friend,
Arthur Hugh Clough, who Died at Florence, 1861*

How changed is here each spot man makes or fills!
    In the two Hinkseys nothing keeps the same;
        The village street its haunted mansion lacks,
    And from the sign is gone Sibylla's name,
        And from the roofs the twisted chimney stacks—
        Are ye too changed, ye hills?
    See, 'tis no foot of unfamiliar men
        Tonight from Oxford up your pathway strays!
    Here came I often, often, in old days—
Thyrsis and I; we still had Thyrsis then.   10

Runs it not here, the track by Childsworth Farm,
    Past the high wood, to where the elm tree crowns

---

160 *Bellerus:* invented by Milton from the Roman place-name for
Land's End, Bellerium   161 *Vision of the guarded mount:* St.
Michael's Mount near Land's End, guarded, legend has it, by
Michael   162 *Namancos, Bayona:* Spanish fortresses toward which
Michael would gaze from St. Michael's Mount   163 *dolphins:* in
legend, the Greek poet Arion was rescued from drowning by dolphins

---

189   *Doric:* Sicilian pastorals were written in the Doric dialect
monody: a lament sung or spoken by one voice   2 *two Hinkseys:*
North and South Hinksey, two villages near Oxford   4 *Sibylla:*
Sybylla Curr, proprietress of an inn in South Hinksey   10 *Thyrsis:*
Clough

The hill behind whose ridge the sunset flames?
The signal elm, that looks on Ilsley Downs,
The Vale, the three lone weirs, the youthful
Thames?—
This winter eve is warm,
Humid the air! leafless, yet soft as spring,
The tender purple spray on copse and briers!
And that sweet city with her dreaming spires,
She needs not June for beauty's heightening,   20

Lovely all times she lies, lovely tonight!—
Only, methinks, some loss of habit's power
Befalls me wandering through this upland dim.
Once passed I blindfold here, at any hour;
Now seldom come I, since I came with him.
That single elm tree bright
Against the west—I miss it! is it gone?
We prized it dearly; while it stood, we said,
Our friend, the Gypsy Scholar, was not dead;
While the tree lived, he in these fields lived
on.   30

Too rare, too rare, grow now my visits here,
But once I knew each field, each flower, each stick;
And with the countryfolk acquaintance made
By barn in threshing time, by new-built rick.
Here, too, our shepherd pipes we first assayed.
Ah me! this many a year
My pipe is lost, my shepherd's holiday!
Needs must I lose them, needs with heavy heart
Into the world and wave of men depart;
But Thyrsis of his own will went away.   40

It irked him to be here, he could not rest.
He loved each simple joy the country yields,
He loved his mates; but yet he could not keep,
For that a shadow lowered on the fields,
Here with the shepherds and the silly sheep.
Some life of men unblessed
He knew, which made him droop, and filled his
head.
He went; his piping took a troubled sound
Of storms that rage outside our happy ground;
He could not wait their passing, he is dead.   50

So, some tempestuous morn in early June,
When the year's primal burst of bloom is o'er,
Before the roses and the longest day—
When garden walks and all the grassy floor
With blossoms red and white of fallen May

And chestnut flowers are strewn—
So have I heard the cuckoo's parting cry,
From the wet field, through the vexed garden
trees,
Come with the volleying rain and tossing breeze:
The bloom is gone, and with the bloom go I!   60

Too quick despairer, wherefore wilt thou go?
Soon will the high Midsummer pomps come on,
Soon will the musk carnations break and swell,
Soon shall we have gold-dusted snapdragon,
Sweet William with his homely cottage smell,
And stocks in fragrant blow;
Roses that down the alleys shine afar,
And open, jasmine-muffled lattices,
And groups under the dreaming garden trees,
And the full moon, and the white evening
star.   70

He harkens not! light comer, he is flown!
What matters it? next year he will return,
And we shall have him in the sweet spring days,
With whitening hedges, and uncrumpling fern,
And bluebells trembling by the forest ways,
And scent of hay new mown.
But Thyrsis never more we swains shall see;
See him come back, and cut a smoother reed,
And blow a strain the world at last shall heed—
For Time, not Corydon, hath conquered thee!   80

Alack, for Corydon no rival now!—
But when Sicilian shepherds lost a mate,
Some good survivor with his flute would go,
Piping a ditty sad for Bion's fate;
And cross the unpermitted ferry's flow,
And relax Pluto's brow,
And make leap up with joy the beauteous head
Of Proserpine, among whose crownèd hair
Are flowers first opened on Sicilian air,
And flute his friends, like Orpheus, from the
dead.   90

O easy access to the hearer's grace
When Dorian shepherds sang to Proserpine!
For she herself had trod Sicilian fields,
She knew the Dorian water's gush divine,
She knew each lily white which Enna yields,
Each rose with blushing face;
She loved the Dorian pipe, the Dorian strain.

14, 15 *Ilsley Downs*, the Vale: hills and a vale near Oxford
35 *shepherd pipes:* poetry   40 *of his own will:* Clough voluntarily
left Oxford because of religious doubts   43 *keep:* stay   45 *silly:*
simple

80 *Corydon:* Arnold   84 *Bion:* Greek poet of the second century,
B. C., subject of an elegy by Moschus   81–97 The passage refers
to a Sicilian legend that poets descend into Hades to charm Proserpine into allowing their dead friends to return. Proserpine, gathering flowers in Sicily's valley of Enna, had been carried off by
Pluto to be queen of Hades. Doric: Sicilian pastoral poets wrote
in the Doric dialect

But ah, of our poor Thames she never heard!
Her foot the Cumner cowslips never stirred;
And we should tease her with our plaint in
        vain!   100

Well! wind-dispersed and vain the words will be,
Yet, Thyrsis, let me give my grief its hour
    In the old haunt, and find our tree-topped hill!
Who, if not I, for questing here hath power?
    I know the wood which hides the daffodil,
        I know the Fyfield tree,
I know what white, what purple fritillaries
    The grassy harvest of the river fields,
    Above by Ensham, down by Sandford, yields,
And what sedged brooks are Thames's
        tributaries;   110

I know these slopes; who knows them if not I?—
But many a dingle on the loved hillside,
    With thorns once studded, old, white-blossomed
        trees,
    Where thick the cowslips grew, and far descried
        High towered the spikes of purple orchises,
        Hath since our day put by
The coronals of that forgotten time;
    Down each green bank hath gone the plowboy's
        team,
    And only in the hidden brookside gleam
Primroses, orphans of the flowery prime.   120

Where is the girl, who by the boatman's door,
Above the locks, above the boating throng,
    Unmoored our skiff when through the Wytham
        flats,
    Red loosestrife and blond meadowsweet among
    And darting swallows and light water gnats,
        We tracked the shy Thames shore?
Where are the mowers, who, as the tiny swell
    Of our boat passing heaved the river grass,
    Stood with suspended scythe to see us pass?—
They all are gone, and thou art gone as well!   130

Yes, thou art gone! and round me too the night
In ever-nearing circle weaves her shade.
    I see her veil draw soft across the day,
    I feel her slowly chilling breath invade
    The cheek grown thin, the brown hair sprent
        with gray;
        I feel her finger light
Laid pausefully upon life's headlong train;—

The foot less prompt to meet the morning dew,
The heart less bounding at emotion new,
And hope, once crushed, less quick to spring
        again.   140

And long the way appears, which seemed so short
To the less practiced eye of sanguine youth;
    And high the mountaintops, in cloudy air,
    The mountaintops where is the throne of Truth,
    Tops in life's morning sun so bright and bare!
        Unbreachable the fort
Of the long-battered world uplifts its wall;
    And strange and vain the earthly turmoil grows,
    And near and real the charm of thy repose,
And night as welcome as a friend would fall.   150

But hush! the upland hath a sudden loss
Of quiet!—Look, adown the dusk hillside,
    A troop of Oxford hunters going home,
    As in old days, jovial and talking, ride!
    From hunting with the Berkshire hounds they
        come.
        Quick! let me fly, and cross
Into yon farther field!—'Tis done; and see,
    Backed by the sunset, which doth glorify
    The orange and pale violet evening sky,
Bare on its lonely ridge, the Tree! the Tree!   160

I take the omen! Eve lets down her veil,
    The white fog creeps from bush to bush about,
    The west unflushes, the high stars grow bright,
    And in the scattered farms the lights come out.
        I cannot reach the signal tree tonight,
            Yet, happy omen, hail!
Hear it from thy broad lucent Arno vale
    (For there thine earth-forgetting eyelids keep
    The morningless and unawakening sleep
Under the flowery oleanders pale),   170

Hear it, O Thyrsis, still our tree is there!—
    Ah, vain! These English fields, this upland dim,
    These brambles pale with mist engarlanded,
    That lone sky-pointing tree are not for him;
        To a boon southern country he is fled,
            And now in happier air,
Wandering with the great Mother's train divine
    (And purer or more subtle soul than thee,
    I trow, the mighty Mother doth not see)
Within a folding of the Apennine,   180

Thou hearest the immortal chants of old!—

Putting his sickle to the perilous grain
  In the hot cornfield of the Phrygian king,
For thee the Lityerses song again
    Young Daphnis with his silver voice doth sing;
    Sings his Sicilian fold,
His sheep, his hapless love, his blinded eyes—
And how a call celestial round him rang,
And heavenward from the fountain brink he
    sprang,
And all the marvel of the golden skies.   190

There thou art gone, and me thou leavest here
  Sole in these fields! yet will I not despair.
    Despair I will not, while I yet descry
  'Neath the mild canopy of English air
    That lonely tree against the western sky.
    Still, still these slopes, 'tis clear,
Our Gypsy Scholar haunts, outliving thee!
  Fields where soft sheep from cages pull the hay,
  Woods with anemones in flower till May,
Know him a wanderer still; then why not   200
  me?

A fugitive and gracious light he seeks,
  Shy to illumine; and I seek it too.
    This does not come with houses or with gold,
  With place, with honor, and a flattering crew;
    'Tis not in the world's market bought and sold—
    But the smooth-slipping weeks
Drop by, and leave its seeker still untired;
  Out of the heed of mortals he is gone,
  He wends unfollowed, he must house alone;
Yet on he fares, by his own heart inspired.   210

Thou too, O Thyrsis, on like quest wast bound;
  Thou wanderedst with me for a little hour!
    Men gave thee nothing; but this happy quest,
  If men esteemed thee feeble, gave thee power,
  If men procured thee trouble, gave thee rest.
    And this rude Cumner ground,
Its fir-topped Hurst, its farms, its quiet fields,
  Here cam'st thou in thy jocund youthful time,
  Here was thine height of strength, thy golden
    prime!
And still the haunt beloved a virtue yields.   220

What though the music of thy rustic flute
  Kept not for long its happy, country tone;
    Lost it too soon, and learned a stormy note

---

183 *Phrygian king:* Lityerses, King of Phrygia, put to death all travelers who could not surpass him in a reaping contest. Daphnis, a shepherd, defeated him by enlisting the aid of Hercules, who eventually killed Lityerses 217 *Hurst:* one of the Cumner hills

Of men contention-tossed, of men who groan,
  Which tasked thy pipe too sore, and tired thy
    throat—
    It failed, and thou wast mute!
Yet hadst thou always visions of our light,
  And long with men of care thou couldst not
    stay,
  And soon thy foot resumed its wandering way,
Left human haunt, and on alone till night.   230

Too rare, too rare, grow now my visits here!
  'Mid city noise, not, as with thee of yore,
    Thyrsis! in reach of sheepbells is my home.
  —Then through the great town's harsh, heart-
    wearying roar,
    Let in thy voice a whisper often come,
    To chase fatigue and fear:
Why faintest thou? I wandered till I died.
  Roam on! The light we sought is shining still.
  Dost thou ask proof? Our tree yet crowns the
    hill,
Our Scholar travels yet the loved hillside.   240

FOR ANALYSIS

1. Arnold, writing in the tradition of the pastoral elegy, must come to a positive conclusion. Thus, Clough is shown at the end of "Thyrsis" as a messenger of hope. But in lines 51–71, Clough is shown as a "Too quick despairer," like the cuckoo who mistakes an early summer storm for the onset of winter and flies to warmer regions. How does Arnold avoid what seems at first a flat contradiction?
2. A critic once remarked that "Thyrsis" sounded less like a lament for a dead friend than like a lament for a dead friendship. Is there a distinction to be made? Is it upheld by the poem?

ROBERT SOUTHWELL

The Burning Babe

As I in hoary winter's night stood shivering in the
  snow,
Surprised I was with sudden heat which made my
  heart to glow;
And lifting up a fearful eye to view what fire was
  near,

A pretty babe, all burning bright, did in the air ap-
pear,
Who scorchèd with exceeding heat such floods of
tears did shed,   5
As though his floods should quench his flames with
what his tears were fed;
'Alas!' quoth he, 'but newly born in fiery heats I fry,
Yet none approach to warm their hearts or feel my
fire but I!
My faultless breast the furnace is, the fuel wounding
thorns;
Love is the fire and sighs the smoke, the ashes shame
and scorns;   10
The fuel Justice layeth on, and Mercy blows the
coals;
The metal in this furnace wrought are men's defilèd
souls;
For which, as now on fire I am, to work them to
their good,
So will I melt into a bath, to wash them in my blood:'
With this he vanished out of sight, and swiftly
shrunk away,   15
And straight I callèd unto mind that it was Christ-
mas-day.

FOR ANALYSIS

1. Like many religious lyrics, this one contains an
allegory, a consistent presentation of one meaning
in the guise of another. Here the allegorical figure
explains his own allegorical attributes. Who is the
babe and why is he burning?
2. Explain the paradoxes in lines 9–11. If the "fuel"
is "wounding thorns," how can "Justice" be said
to lay that fuel on the fire? How can "Mercy" be
said to blow the coals?

GEORGE HERBERT
The Collar

I struck the board, and cried, 'No more;
I will abroad!
What! shall I ever sigh and pine?
My lines and life are free; free as the road,
Loose as the wind, as large as store.   5
Shall I be still in suit?
Have I no harvest but a thorn
To let me blood, and not restore
What I have lost with cordial fruit?
Sure there was wine   10

Before my sighs did dry it; there was corn
Before my tears did drown it;
Is the year only lost to me?
Have I no bays to crown it,
No flowers, no garlands gay? all blasted,   15
All wasted?
Not so, my heart, but there is fruit,
And thou hast hands.
Recover all thy sigh-blown age
On double pleasures; leave thy cold dispute   20
Of what is fit and not; forsake thy cage,
Thy rope of sands
Which petty thoughts have made; and made to thee
Good cable, to enforce and draw,
And be thy law,   25
While thou didst wink and wouldst not see.
Away! take heed;
I will abroad.
Call in thy death's head there, tie up thy fears:
He that forbears   30
To suit and serve his need
Deserves his load.'
But as I raved, and grew more fierce and wild
At every word,
Methought I heard one calling, 'Child';   35
And I replied, 'My Lord.'

FOR ANALYSIS

1. What is the significance of the title?
2. Notice the metrical difference between lines 1–31
and lines 32–35. Line 1 has at least six feet, line 2
only four, line 3 five, etc., and each of them
breaks somewhere into at least two pieces. Now
scan the last two lines. What effect is the poet
aiming at with these different metrical arrangements?
3. Why are there so many questions in the early part
of the poem? Are they rhetorical questions?
What answer to all of them is given later in the
poem?

JOHN DONNE
A Hymn to
God the Father

Wilt thou forgive that sin where I begun,
Which was my sin, though it were done before?
Wilt thou forgive that sin through which I run,

And do run still, though still I do deplore?
When thou hast done, thou hast not done;   5
    For I have more.

Wilt thou forgive that sin which I have won
  Others to sin, and made my sins their door?
Wilt thou forgive that sin which I did shun
  A year or two, but wallowed in a score?   10
When thou hast done, thou hast not done;
    For I have more.

I have a sin of fear, that when I've spun
  My last thread, I shall perish on the shore;
But swear by thyself that at my death thy Son   15
  Shall shine as he shines now and heretofore;
And having done that, thou hast done;
    I fear no more.

FOR ANALYSIS

1. What pun is Donne repeating throughout this poem? Can you find other puns in the poem?
2. The seventeenth century would have found pleasure in these puns. Has our attitude toward the punning convention changed since Donne's day?

THOMAS CAMPION
Cherry Ripe

There is a garden in her face,
Where roses and white lilies grow;
  A heavenly paradise is that place,
Wherein all pleasant fruits do flow.
    There cherries grow which none may buy   5
    Till cherry-ripe themselves do cry.

Those cherries fairly do enclose
Of orient pearl a double row,
  Which when her lovely laughter shows,
They look like rosebuds filled with snow.   10
    Yet them nor peer nor prince can buy,
    Till cherry-ripe themselves do cry.

Her eyes like angels watch them still;
Her brows like bended bows do stand,
  Threatening with piercing frowns to kill   15
All that attempt with eye or hand
    Those sacred cherries to come nigh,
    Till cherry-ripe themselves do cry.

ROBERT HERRICK
To the Virgins to Make Much of Time

Gather ye rosebuds while ye may,
  Old Time is still aflying;
And this same flower that smiles to-day,
  To-morrow will be dying.

The glorious lamp of heaven, the sun,   5
  The higher he's a-getting,
The sooner will his race be run,
  And nearer he's to setting.

That age is best which is the first,
  When youth and blood are warmer;   10
But being spent, the worse and worst
  Times still succeed the former.

Then be not coy, but use your time,
  And while ye may, go marry;
For, having lost but once your prime   15
  You may forever tarry.

ROBERT HERRICK
Delight in Disorder

A sweet disorder in the dress
Kindles in clothes a wantonness;
A lawn about the shoulders thrown
Into a fine distraction,
An erring lace, which here and there   5
Enthralls the crimson stomacher,
A cuff neglectful, and thereby
Ribands to flow confusedly,
A winning wave, deserving note,
In the tempestuous petticoat,   10
A careless shoe-string, in whose tie
I see a wild civility,
Do more bewitch me than when art
Is too precise in every part.

FOR ANALYSIS

Cherry Ripe

1. "Cherry ripe" was the cry of fruit vendors in London. What are the cherries in this poem?
2. What device from the ballad convention is used in this lyric?
3. What is Campion saying about the lady here, other than that she is beautiful?

To the Virgins

1. Herrick here makes his point by using two images: a rose and the sun. On the surface, they seem to have nothing in common. Why does he need them both to validate the point he makes in the first and last stanzas?
2. What paradox of existence does he point out in the second stanza?
3. Why does Herrick choose the rose as his symbolic flower instead of, say, a tulip or a geranium?

Delight in Disorder

1. In this poem the words applied to the clothes are not words that can literally apply to clothes— "sweet," "wantonness," "distraction," "erring," "enthralls," "neglectful," "confusedly," "winning," "tempestuous," "mild civility," "bewitch." To what do they really apply in the poem?
2. Does Herrick say that this disorder in dress is natural? Look closely at the last two lines.

ANDREW MARVELL

To His Coy Mistress

    Had we but world enough, and time,
This coyness, Lady, were no crime,
We would sit down and think which way
To walk and pass our long love's day.
Thou by the Indian Ganges' side   5
Shouldst rubies find; I by the tide
Of Humber would complain. I would
Love you ten years before the Flood,
And you should, if you please, refuse

Till the conversion of the Jews.   10
My vegetable love should grow
Vaster than empires, and more slow;
An hundred years should go to praise
Thine eyes and on thy forehead gaze,
Two hundred to adore each breast,   15
But thirty-thousand to the rest;
An age at least to every part,
And the last age should show your heart.
For, Lady, you deserve this state,
Nor would I love at lower rate.   20

    But at my back I always hear
Time's wingèd chariot hurrying near
And yonder all before us lie
Deserts of vast eternity.
Thy beauty shall no more be found,   25
Nor, in thy marble vault, shall sound
My echoing song; then worms shall try
That long preserved virginity,
And your quaint honor turn to dust,
And into ashes all my lust: 30
The grave's a fine and private place,
But none, I think, do there embrace.

    Now therefore, while the youthful hue
Sits on thy skin like morning dew,
And while thy willing soul transpires   35
At every pore with instant fires,
Now let us sport us while we may,
And now, like amorous birds of prey,
Rather at once our time devour
Than languish in his slow-chapt power.   40
Let us roll all our strength and all
Our sweetness up into one ball,
And tear our pleasures with rough strife
Thorough the iron gates of life:
Thus, though we cannot make our sun   46
Stand still, yet we will make him run.

FOR ANALYSIS

1. This poem divides into three parts which, taken together, resemble a logical argument: (a) If we had time; (b) But we don't; (c) Therefore, we should. . . . Try to identify the different *tone* which each of these sections has.
2. The image in lines 37–44 is of caged birds. In what are the lovers caged?
3. What do lines 33–36 tell you about the woman that you did not know before?

JOHN DONNE

Song

Go and catch a falling star,
   Get with child a mandrake root,
Tell me where all past years are,
   Or who cleft the devil's foot;
Teach me to hear mermaids singing,   5
   To keep off envy's stinging,
      And find
      What wind
Serves to advance an honest mind.

If thou be'st born to strange sights,   10
   Things invisible go see,
Ride ten thousand days and nights
   Till Age snow white hairs on thee;
Thou, when thou return'st, wilt tell me
All strange wonders that befell thee,   15
      And swear
      No where
Lives a woman true and fair.

If thou find'st one, let me know;
   Such a pilgrimage were sweet.   20
Yet do not; I would not go,
   Though at next door we might meet.
Though she were true when you met her,
And last till you write your letter,
      Yet she   25
      Will be
False, ere I come, to two or three.

FOR ANALYSIS

1. This is a remarkably strong and emphatic poem to be entitled "Song." What in the verbs particularly gives the poem this strength?
2. What do catching a falling star, impregnating a mandrake root, finding all past years, and the other things have in common? What does this imply about the possibility of any task or the validity of any belief raised later in the poem?
3. This poem is heavily rhymed but it has the ring of the spoken word at the same time. How does the poet get that seemingly contradictory effect?

JOHN DONNE

A Valediction
Forbidding Mourning

As virtuous men pass mildly away,
   And whisper to their souls to go,
Whilst some of their sad friends do say,
   "The breath goes now," and some say, "No,"

So let us melt and make no noise,   5
   No tear-floods nor sigh-tempests move;
'Twere profanation of our joys
   To tell the laity our love.

Moving of th' earth brings harms and fears;
   Men reckon what it did and meant,   10
But trepidation of the spheres,
   Though greater far, is innocent.

Dull sublunary lovers' love,
   Whose soul is sense, cannot admit
Absence, because it doth remove   15
   Those things which elemented it.

But we by a love so much refin'd
   That ourselves know not what it is,
Interassurèd of the mind,
   Care less eyes, lips, and hands to miss.   20

Our two souls, therefore, which are one,
   Though I must go, endure not yet
A breach, but an expansion,
   Like gold to airy thinness beat.

If they be two, they are two so   25
   As stiff twin compasses are two;
Thy soul, the fix'd foot, makes no show
   To move, but doth if th' other do.

And though it in the center sit,
   Yet when the other far doth roam,   30
It leans and hearkens after it,
   And grows erect as that comes home.

Such wilt thou be to me, who must,
   Like th' other foot, obliquely run;
Thy firmness makes my circle just,   35
   And makes me end where I begun.

FOR ANALYSIS

1. Metaphysical poetry abounds in strange and unusual metaphors. In this poem, the narrator tells his loved one why she should not grieve when he must leave her. What things are the two lovers compared to in successive stanzas? You should find at least five different metaphorical comparisons.
2. Now that you have isolated the metaphors, consider how they are related. Do they all have something in common? Does one generate another?

To lean in joy upon our father's knee;
And then I 'll stand and stroke his silver hair,
And be like him, and he will then love me.

FOR ANALYSIS

1. What does the cloud symbolize?
2. What is the precise meaning here of the repeated word "joy"?
3. In what way does the black boy consider himself superior to the white boy? What does he imply about the white boy by saying that he will shade him from the heat? The implication of line 23, after all, is that they will be free of their "clouds" at the same time.

WILLIAM BLAKE

The Little Black Boy

My mother bore me in the southern wild,
  And I am black, but O my soul is white;
White as an angel is the English child,
  But I am black, as if bereaved of light.

My mother taught me underneath a tree,   5
  And, sitting down before the heat of day,
She took me on her lap and kissèd me,
  And, pointing to the east, began to say:

'Look on the rising sun—there God does live,
  And gives his light, and gives his heat away;   10
And flowers and trees and beasts and men receive
  Comfort in morning, joy in the noonday.

'And we are put on earth a little space,
  That we may learn to bear the beams of love;
And these black bodies and this sunburnt face   15
  Is but a cloud, and like a shady grove.

'For when our souls have learned the heat to bear,
  The cloud will vanish, we shall hear his voice,
Saying: "Come out from the grove, my love and care,
  And round my golden tent like lambs
        rejoice." '   20

Thus did my mother say, and kissèd me;
  And thus I say to little English boy.
When I from black, and he from white cloud free,
  And round the tent of God like lambs we joy,

I'll shade him from the heat, till he can bear   25

SAMUEL TAYLOR COLERIDGE

Kubla Khan

In Xanadu did Kubla Khan
A stately pleasure-dome decree;
Where Alph, the sacred river, ran
Through caverns measureless to man
Down to a sunless sea.   5

So twice five miles of fertile ground
With walls and towers were girdled round:
And here were gardens bright with sinuous rills,
Where blossomed many an incense-bearing tree;
And here were forests ancient as the hills   10
Enfolding sunny spots of greenery.

But oh! that deep romantic chasm which slanted
Down the green hill athwart a cedarn cover!
A savage place! as holy and enchanted
As e'er beneath a waning moon was haunted   15
By woman wailing for her demon-lover!
And from this chasm, with ceaseless turmoil
        seething,
As if this earth in fast thick pants were breathing
A mighty fountain momently was forced:
Amid whose swift half-intermitted burst   20
Huge fragments vaulted like rebounding hail,
Or chaffy grain beneath the thresher's flail:
And 'mid these dancing rocks at once and ever
It flung up momently the sacred river.
Five miles meandering with a mazy motion   25
Through wood and dale the sacred river ran,

Then reached the caverns measureless to man,
And sank in tumult to a lifeless ocean:
And 'mid this tumult Kubla heard from far
Ancestral voices prophesying war! 30

    The shadow of the dome of pleasure
    Floated midway on the waves;
    Where was heard the mingled measure
    From the fountain and the caves.
It was a miracle of rare device, 35
A sunny pleasure-dome with caves of ice!

    A damsel with a dulcimer
    In a vision once I saw:
    It was an Abyssinian maid,
    And on her dulcimer she played, 40
    Singing of Mount Abora.
    Could I revive with me
    Her symphony and song,
    To such a deep delight 'twould win me,
That with music loud and long, 45
I would build that dome in air,
That sunny dome! those caves of ice!
And all who heard should see them there,—
And all should cry, Beware! Beware!—
His flashing eyes, his floating hair! 50
Weave a circle round him thrice,
And close your eyes with holy dread,
For he on honey-dew hath fed,
And drunk the milk of Paradise.

FOR ANALYSIS

Coleridge said he awoke from sleep with this poem
fully formed in his mind, sat down to write it, and
was interrupted by a caller. When he returned to
the poem he could remember no more of it than
this fragment. What the poem "means" has long
been a source of argument. A careful reader, however, can at least abstract the pattern of the poem,
whether or not he can supply a coherent meaning
to each exotic element.

1. The poem contains a strong conflict. What elements of contrast are here, besides "caves of ice"
   contrasting with the "sunny pleasure-dome"?
2. What in the poem indicates that these contrasting
   elements are in active conflict?
3. Who in the poem is going to resolve this conflict? How is he going to do it?

LORD BYRON

She Walks in Beauty

She walks in beauty, like the night
    Of cloudless climes and starry skies;
And all that's best of dark and bright
    Meet in her aspect and her eyes:
Thus mellowed to that tender light 5
    Which heaven to gaudy day denies.

One shade the more, one ray the less,
    Had half impaired the nameless grace
Which waves in every raven tress
    Or softly lightens o'er her face; 10
Where thoughts serenely sweet express
    How pure, how dear their dwelling-place.

And on that cheek, and o'er that brow
    So soft, so calm, yet eloquent,
The smiles that win, the tints that glow, 15
    But tell of days in goodness spent,
A mind at peace with all below,
    A heart whose love is innocent!

ALFRED, LORD TENNYSON

from The Princess

Tears, idle tears, I know not what they mean,
Tears from the depth of some divine despair
Rise in the heart, and gather to the eyes,
In looking on the happy Autumn-fields,
And thinking of the days that are no more. 5

Fresh as the first beam glittering on a sail,
That brings our friends up from the underworld,
Sad as the last which reddens over one
That sinks with all we love below the verge;
So sad, so fresh, the days that are no more. 10

Ah, sad and strange as in dark summer dawns
The earliest pipe of half-awakened birds
To dying ears, when unto dying eyes
The casement slowly grows a glimmering square;
So sad, so strange, the days that are no more. 15

Dear as remembered kisses after death,
And sweet as those by hopeless fancy feigned

On lips that are for others; deep as love,
Deep as first love, and wild with all regret;
O Death in Life, the days that are no more!   20

FOR ANALYSIS

She Walks in Beauty

1. Does there seem to be any pattern to the details in this poem? Or is it a catalogue of rather random thoughts about the woman? Is, for example, the comparison of the woman with the night carried throughout the poem?
2. Is there anything in the poem to justify the conclusion in the last two lines?
3. What do lines 11–12 mean?

from The Princess

1. What device from ballad convention is Tennyson using in the last line of each stanza here? What does the last line do for each of the stanzas?
2. The form here is very unusual: This is a blank verse lyric. What does Tennyson do inside the lines to make up for the lack of lyrical musicality in blank verse?
3. Readers often assume that these lines are spoken by an old man. As a matter of fact, they are spoken by a young woman. "Tears, Idle Tears" is one of the songs from *The Princess*. The lines are a lament by a young woman who does not wish to live apart from men as the Princess has forced her female subjects to do. Does this change the poem for you?

MATTHEW ARNOLD

Dover Beach

The sea is calm to-night,
The tide is full, the moon lies fair
Upon the Straits;—on the French coast, the light
Gleams, and is gone; the cliffs of England stand,
Glimmering and vast, out in the tranquil bay.   5
Come to the window, sweet is the night air!
Only, from the long line of spray
Where the ebb meets the moon-blanched sand,
Listen! you hear the grating roar
Of pebbles which the waves suck back, and fling,   10
At their return, up the high strand,
Begin, and cease, and then again begin,
With tremulous cadence slow, and bring
The eternal note of sadness in.

Sophocles long ago   15
Heard it on the Ægean, and it brought
Into his mind the turbid ebb and flow
Of human misery; we
Find also in the sound a thought,
Hearing it by this distant northern sea.   20

The sea of faith
Was once, too, at the full, and round earth's shore
Lay like the folds of a bright girdle furled;
But now I only hear
Its melancholy, long, withdrawing roar,   25
Retreating, to the breath
Of the night-wind down the vast edges drear
And naked shingles of the world.

Ah, love, let us be true
To one another! for the world, which seems   30
To lie before us like a land of dreams,
So various, so beautiful, so new,
Hath really neither joy, nor love, nor light,
Nor certitude, nor peace, nor help for pain;
And we are here as on a darkling plain   35
Swept with confused alarms of struggle and flight,
Where ignorant armies clash by night.

ARTHUR HUGH CLOUGH

Say Not the Struggle Nought Availeth

Say not the struggle nought availeth,
    The labor and the wounds are vain,
The enemy faints not, nor faileth,
    And as things have been they remain.

If hopes were dupes, fears may be liars;   5
    It may be, in yon smoke concealed,
Your comrades chase e'en now the fliers,
    And, but for you, possess the field.

For while the tired waves, vainly breaking,
    Seem here no painful inch to gain,   10
Far back, through creeks and inlets making,
    Comes silent, flooding in, the main.

And not by eastern windows only,
    When daylight comes, comes in the light,

In front, the sun climbs slow, how slowly,   15
But westward, look, the land is bright.

ARCHIBALD MACLEISH

"Dover Beach"
—A Note to That Poem

The Wave Withdrawing
Withers with seaward rustle of flimsy water
Sucking the sand down: dragging at empty shells:
The roil after it settling: too smooth: smothered. . .

After forty a man's a fool to wait in the   5
Sea's face for the full force and the roaring of
Surf to come over him: droves of careening water.
After forty the tug's out and the salt and the
Sea follow it: less sound and violence:
Nevertheless the ebb has its own beauty   10
Shells sand and all the whispering rustle.
There's earth in it then and the bubbles of foam
     gone.

Moreover—and this too has its lovely uses—
It's the outward wave that spills the inward forward
Tripping the proud piled mute virginal   15
Mountain of water in wallowing welter of light and
Sound enough—thunder for miles back: it's a fine
     and a
Wild smother to vanish in: pulling down—
Tripping with outward ebb the urgent inward.

Speaking alone for myself it's the steep hill
     and the   20
Toppling lift of the young men I am toward now—
Waiting for that as the wave for the next wave.
Let them go over us all I say with the thunder of
What's to be next in the world. It's we will be under
     it!

FOR ANALYSIS

"Dover Beach" is a famous statement of a universal problem: That things in this world are not what they seem and solutions to that problem are hard to find. Consider these questions about the three poems:
1. What solution does "Dover Beach" propose to the problem of illusion (what we see) versus reality (what is)? How are the images of sight and sound arranged to show this conflict?
2. MacLeish disagrees with Arnold. Does he disagree with Arnold's solution or with Arnold's statement of the problem? Consider what single image from "Dover Beach" he has selected as the basis of his poem.
3. Clough and Arnold were close friends in their youth; Arnold's "Thyrsis" is an elegy on Clough. But they differed on many things. Construct a detailed comparison and contrast of Clough's poem and Arnold's. What do they share? How do they differ?

WILLIAM WORDSWORTH

A Slumber
Did My Spirit Seal

A slumber did my spirit seal;
     I had no human fears;
She seemed a thing that could not feel
     The touch of earthly years.

No motion has she now, no force;   5
     She neither hears nor sees;
Rolled round in earth's diurnal course,
     With rocks, and stones, and trees.

A. E. HOUSMAN

The Night Is
Freezing Fast

The night is freezing fast,
     To-morrow comes December;
     And winterfalls of old
Are with me from the past;
     And chiefly I remember   5
     How Dick would hate the cold.

Fall, winter, fall; for he,
     Prompt hand and headpiece clever,
     Has woven a winter robe,

And made of earth and sea   15
  His overcoat for ever,
    And wears the turning globe.

FOR ANALYSIS

Both of these poems deal with death of a loved one,
but they are not elegies, since they center not on
the qualities of the dead person but on the feelings
of the narrator.

1. After reading both stanzas of the Wordsworth
poem, what do you think is the "slumber" that
Wordsworth says sealed his spirit? What did it
seal it off from? What are the "human fears" of
line 2?

2. Notice that the first stanza of the Wordsworth
poem speaks of the woman in human terms, but
the second speaks of her as a thing. Is this last
a natural way to speak of a loved one, dead or
not? What, then, can you infer about the state
of mind of the narrator?

3. The state of mind of the narrator in the Housman
poem is more complex than in the Wordsworth
poem. You can infer this by considering exactly
what he says: that Dick was lucky to die because
now he'll never be cold again since in his grave
he has the whole world as his overcoat. Again, is
this a natural way to speak of a dead loved one?
Or is it grotesque? Could the narrator mean
literally what he says? Then what is he trying to
do? In a similar but longer poem, "To an Athlete
Dying Young," Housman says that the athlete
was "smart" to die young because now he will
never see his records broken, never grow old and
lose his fine physical condition. Clearly this is not
meant literally; rational creatures do not wish
early death to those they love. Housman is trying to do the same thing in both poems.

EDGAR ALLAN POE

To Helen

Helen, thy beauty is to me
  Like those Nicèan barks of yore,
That gently, o'er a perfumed sea,
  The weary, way-worn wanderer bore
    To his own native shore.   5

On desperate seas long wont to roam,
  Thy hyacinth hair, thy classic face,

Thy Naiad airs have brought me home
  To the glory that was Greece
  And the grandeur that was Rome.   10

Lo! in yon brilliant window-niche
  How statue-like I see thee stand,
  The agate lamp within thy hand!
Ah, Psyche, from the regions which
  Are Holy Land!   15

DANTE GABRIEL ROSSETTI

The Woodspurge

The wind flapped loose, the wind was still,
Shaken out dead from tree and hill:
I had walked on at the wind's will,—
I sat now, for the wind was still.

Between my knees my forehead was,—   5
My lips, drawn in, said not Alas!
My hair was over in the grass,
My naked ears heard the day pass.

My eyes, wide open, had the run
Of some ten weeds to fix upon;   10
Among those few, out of the sun,
The woodspurge flowered, three cups in one.

From perfect grief there need not be
Wisdom or even memory:
One thing then learnt remains to me,—   15
The woodspurge has a cup of three.

FOR ANALYSIS

To Helen

1. Does this poem have a consecutive development?
Would it matter, for example, in what order the
stanzas came?

2. Do the words "Nicèan," "perfumed," "desperate,"
"hyacinth," "classic," "glory," "grandeur," point
to anything specific or concrete?

3. What can you conclude about the poem from
your answers to the preceding questions?

The Woodspurge

1. What is the narrator's state of mind?

2. What in that state of mind explains why the only

thing he remembers from this experience is that "The woodspurge has a cup of three"?

3. These are short lines, frequent rhymes. How does Rossetti avoid a jingly rhythm and sound that would destroy the mood? Look, for example, at the kind of rhymes he uses.

A. E. HOUSMAN

Is My Team Ploughing

"Is my team ploughing,
   That I was used to drive
And hear the harness jingle
   When I was man alive?"

Ay, the horses trample,
   The harness jingles now;
No change though you lie under
   The land you used to plough.

"Is football playing
   Along the river shore,   10
With lads to chase the leather,
   Now I stand up no more?"

Ay, the ball is flying,
   The lads play heart and soul;
The goal stands up, the keeper
   Stands up to keep the goal.

"Is my girl happy,
   That I thought hard to leave,
And has she tired of weeping
   As she lies down at eve?"   20

Ay, she lies down lightly,
   She lies not down to weep:
Your girl is well contented.
   Be still, my lad, and sleep.

"Is my friend hearty,
   Now I am thin and pine,
And has he found to sleep in
   A better bed than mine?"

Yes, lad, I lie easy,
   I lie as lads would choose;   30
I cheer a dead man's sweetheart,
   Never ask me whose.

FOR ANALYSIS

1. How does Housman break the pattern of expectation (and therefore attract attention and get emphasis) in the first line of the last stanza?

2. How has Housman made the reader's suspicions grow as the poem progresses so that the outcome is no surprise? For example, how does the reply to the third question differ from that to the first and second?

A. E. HOUSMAN

Loveliest of Trees

Loveliest of trees, the cherry now
Is hung with bloom along the bough,
And stands about the woodland ride
Wearing white for Eastertide.

Now, of my threescore years and ten,   5
Twenty will not come again,
And take from seventy springs a score,
It only leaves me fifty more.

And since to look at things in bloom
Fifty springs are little room,   10
About the woodlands I will go
To see the cherry hung with snow.

ROBERT FROST

Stopping by Woods on a Snowy Evening

Whose woods these are I think I know.
His house is in the village though;
He will not see me stopping here
To watch his woods fill up with snow.

My little horse must think it queer   5
To stop without a farmhouse near
Between the woods and frozen lake
The darkest evening of the year.

He gives his harness bells a shake
To ask if there is some mistake.   10
The only other sound's the sweep
Of easy wind and downy flake.

The woods are lovely, dark and deep.
But I have promises to keep,
And miles to go before I sleep,   20
And miles to go before I sleep.

FOR ANALYSIS

1. Although one can explore similarities and differ-
ences in these two poems at great length, the
greatest difference probably stems from a very
simple divergence in association: when Housman
looks at a natural scene just coming to life, he
thinks of death; and when Frost looks at a dead
or dormant natural scene he thinks of life. Both
poets feel that demands are being made upon
them. What are these demands and which ones
do the two poets decide to honor?

GERARD MANLEY HOPKINS
Spring and Fall

TO A YOUNG CHILD

Márgarét, are you griéving
Over Goldengrove unleaving?
Leáves, líke the things of man, you
With your fresh thoughts care for can you?
Áh! ás the heart grows older   5
It will come to such sights colder
By and by, nor spare a sigh
Though worlds of wanwood leafmeal lie;
And yet you wíll weep and know why.
Now no matter, child, the name: 10
Sórrow's spríngs áre the same.
Nor mouth had, no nor mind, expressed
What heart heard of, ghost guessed:
It ís the blight man was born for,
It is Margaret you mourn for.   15

FOR ANALYSIS

1. What is the meaning of "Goldengrove unleaving"? of "worlds of wanwood leafmeal lie"?

2. Why is Margaret crying? What is the "blight man
was born for"? (Don't immediately conclude
that it's death. Do the trees die when the leaves
fall? What is it that Margaret will lose as she
grows older?)

WILLIAM BUTLER YEATS
The Second Coming

Turning and turning in the widening gyre
The falcon cannot hear the falconer;
Things fall apart; the center cannot hold;
Mere anarchy is loosed upon the world,
The blood-dimmed tide is loosed, and everywhere 5
The ceremony of innocence is drowned;
The best lack all conviction, while the worst
Are full of passionate intensity.

Surely some revelation is at hand;
Surely the Second Coming is at hand.   10
The Second Coming! Hardly are those words out
When a vast image out of *Spiritus Mundi**
Troubles my sight: somewhere in sands of the desert
A shape with lion body and the head of a man,
A gaze blank and pitiless as the sun,   15
Is moving its slow thighs, while all about it
Reel shadows of the indignant desert birds.
The darkness drops again; but now I know
That twenty centuries of stony sleep
Were vexed to nightmare by a rocking cradle,   20
And what rough beast, its hour come round at last,
Slouches towards Bethlehem to be born?

WILLIAM BUTLER YEATS
Sailing to Byzantium

That is no country for old men. The young
In one another's arms, birds in the trees,
—Those dying generations—at their song,
The salmon-falls, the mackerel-crowded seas,
Fish, flesh, or fowl, commend all summer
        long   5

---

*For Yeats, a kind of collective unconscious, a racial memory.

Whatever is begotten, born, and dies.
Caught in that sensual music all neglect
Monuments of unageing intellect.

An aged man is but a paltry thing,
A tattered coat upon a stick, unless   10
Soul clap its hands and sing, and louder sing
For every tatter in its mortal dress,
Nor is there singing school but studying
Monuments of its own magnificence;
And therefore I have sailed the seas and
      come   15
To the holy city of Byzantium.

O sages standing in God's holy fire
As in the gold mosaic of a wall,
Come from the holy fire, perne in a gyre,
And be the singing-masters of my soul.   20
Consume my heart away; sick with desire
And fastened to a dying animal
It knows not what it is; and gather me
Into the artifice of eternity.

Once out of nature I shall never take   25
My bodily form from any natural thing,
But such a form as Grecian goldsmiths make
Of hammered gold and gold enamelling
To keep a drowsy Emperor awake;
Or set upon a golden bough to sing   30
To lords and ladies of Byzantium
Of what is past, or passing, or to come.

WILLIAM BUTLER YEATS

The Leaders
of the Crowd

They must to keep their certainty accuse
All that are different of a base intent;
Pull down established honour; hawk for news
Whatever their loose phantasy invent
And murmur it with bated breath, as though   5
The abounding gutter had been Helicon
Or calumny a song. How can they know
Truth flourishes where the student's lamp has shone,
And there alone, that have no solitude?

---

19 *Byzantium: perne in a gyre:* descend in a spiraling motion.

So the crowd come they care not what may
      come.   10
They have loud music, hope every day renewed
And heartier loves; that lamp is from the tomb.

FOR ANALYSIS

The Second Coming

1. A cyclical but not necessarily repetitive theory of history is imbedded in the poem. Consider, for example, the commonly accepted meaning of the phrase, "Second Coming," and compare it with what Yeats suggests it may mean. How do the two concepts differ?
2. Why does Yeats choose to cast the "beast" in the form of a sphinx?
3. Justify the phrase, "Mere anarchy." Identify the "tide" and then explain in what sense it can be said to be "blood-dimmed."

Sailing To Byzantium

1. Why does an aged man not belong in the world of the young? With what does he compensate his loss of youth?
2. What is the "artifice of eternity"? What connection has it with "Monuments of unageing intellect"? With the mechanical birds that sing?
3. What is Yeats saying about the difference between the world of the flesh and that of the intellect?

The Leaders of the Crowd

1. What paradox in all demagogues does Yeats point out in lines 1 and 2?
2. Why is it impossible, according to Yeats, for a demagogue ever to utter the truth?

EMILY DICKINSON

My Life Closed Twice
Before Its Close

My life closed twice before its close;
It yet remains to see
If Immortality unveil
A third event to me,

So huge, so hopeless to conceive   5
As these that twice befel.

Parting is all we know of heaven,
And all we need of hell.

EMILY DICKINSON

Tell All the Truth but Tell It Slant

Tell all the truth but tell it slant,
Success in circuit lies,
Too bright for our infirm delight
The truth's superb surprise;

As lightning to the children eased   5
With explanation kind,
The truth must dazzle gradually
Or every man be blind.

EMILY DICKINSON

A Bird Came Down the Walk

A Bird came down the Walk—
He did not know I saw—
He bit an Angleworm in halves
And ate the fellow, raw,

And then he drank a Dew   5
From a convenient Grass—
And then hopped sidewise to the Wall
To let a Beetle pass—

He glanced with rapid eyes
That hurried all around—   10
They looked like frightened Beads, I thought—
He stirred his Velvet Head

Like one in danger, Cautious,
I offered him a Crumb
And he unrolled his feathers   15
And rowed him softer home—

Than Oars divide the Ocean,

Too silver for a seam—
Or Butterflies, off Banks of Noon
Leap, plashless as they swim.   20

FOR ANALYSIS

1. Experiment with these three poems: try to isolate the idiom of the poet. After reading them, how would you describe a typical Dickinson poem?

DYLAN THOMAS

Fern Hill

Now as I was young and easy under the apple boughs
About the lilting house and happy as the grass was
            green,
   The night above the dingle starry,
      Time let me hail and climb
   Golden in the heydays of his eyes,   5
And honoured among wagons I was prince of the
            apple towns
And once below a time I lordly had the trees and
            leaves
      Trail with daisies and barley
   Down the rivers of the windfall light.

And as I was green and carefree, famous among the
            barns   10
About the happy yard and singing as the farm was
            home,
   In the sun that is young once only,
      Time let me play and be
   Golden in the mercy of his means,
And green and golden I was huntsman and herds-
            man, the calves   15
Sang to my horn, the foxes on the hills barked clear
            and cold,
      And the sabbath rang slowly
   In the pebbles of the holy streams.

All the sun long it was running, it was lovely, the hay
Fields high as the house, the tunes from the chim-
            neys, it was air   20
   And playing, lovely and watery
      And fire green as grass.
   And nightly under the simple stars
As I rode to sleep the owls were bearing the farm
            away,

All the moon long I heard, blessed among stables,
    the nightjars   25
  Flying with the ricks, and the horses
    Flashing into the dark.

And then to awake, and the farm, like a wanderer
    white
With the dew, come back, the cock on his shoulder:
    it was all
  Shining, it was Adam and maiden,   30
    The sky gathered again
    And the sun grew round that very day.
So it must have been after the birth of the simple
    light
In the first, spinning place, the spellbound horses
    walking warm
  Out of the whinnying green stable   35
    On to the fields of praise.

And honoured among foxes and pheasants by the
    gay house
Under the new made clouds and happy as the heart
    was long,
  In the sun born over and over,
    I ran my heedless ways,   40
    My wishes raced through the house high hay
And nothing I cared, at my sky blue trades, that
    time allows
In all his tuneful turning so few and such morning
    songs
  Before the children green and golden
    Follow him out of grace,   45

Nothing I cared, in the lamb white days, that time
    would take me
Up to the swallow thronged loft by the shadow of
    my hand,
  In the moon that is always rising,
    Nor that riding to sleep
  I should hear him fly with the high fields   50
And wake to the farm forever fled from the childless
    land.
Oh as I was young and easy in the mercy of his means,
    Time held me green and dying
    Though I sang in my chains like the sea.

FOR ANALYSIS

Dylan Thomas is much like Gerard Manley Hopkins; he adopts many of the same habits of poetic economy, habits that have become contemporary conventions.

1. If you assume that the narrator here tries to re-capture his thinking as it was when he was quite young, how does this help to explain such expressions as: "honoured among wagons I was prince of the apple towns" (what game was the boy playing all alone?); "Fields high as the house" (from the boy's perspective, how would they seem so?); horses walking "on to the fields of praise" (where is he pretending the horses are going?); "In the moon that is always rising" (does a boy falling asleep ever see the complete rising of the moon?)

2. What paradox of growing up is the poet describing in the poem?

DYLAN THOMAS

Do Not Go Gentle

Do not go gentle into that good night,
Old age should burn and rave at close of day;
Rage, rage against the dying of the light.

Though wise men at their end know dark is right,
Because their words had forked no lightning they   5
Do not go gentle into that good night.

Good men, the last wave by, crying how bright
Their frail deeds might have danced in a green bay,
Rage, rage against the dying of the light.

Wild men who caught and sang the sun in
    flight,   10
And learn, too late, they grieved it on its way,
Do not go gentle into that good night.

Grave men, near death, who see with blinding sight
Blind eyes could blaze like meteors and be gay,
Rage, rage against the dying of the light.   15

And you, my father, there on the sad height,
Curse, bless, me now with your fierce tears, I pray.
Do not go gentle into that good night.
Rage, rage against the dying of the light.

FOR ANALYSIS

1. This is a *villanelle*, a highly complicated verse form. Can you abstract its formal requirements by studying the poem—for example, how many rhymes can it have? where do certain lines have to repeat?

2. What pun do you find in "good night"? in "grave men"? What paradox in "blind eyes" that see?
3. Does the light really die, as Thomas says? What does?

ROY FULLER

January 1940

Swift had pains in his head.
Johnson dying in bed
Tapped the dropsy himself.
Blake saw a flea and an elf.
Tennyson could hear the shriek   5
Of a bat. Pope was a freak.
Emily Dickinson stayed
Indoors for a decade.
Water inflated the belly
Of Hart Crane, and of Shelley.   10
Coleridge was a dope.
Southwell died on a rope.
Byron had a round white foot.
Smart and Cowper were put
Away. Lawrence was a fidget.   15
Keats was almost a midget.
Donne, alive in his shroud,
Shakespeare, in the coil of a cloud,
Saw death very well as he
Came crab-wise, dark and massy.   20
I envy not only their talents
And fertile lack of balance
But the appearance of choice
In their sad and fatal voice.

JOHN CROWE RANSOM

Survey of Literature

In all the good Greek of Plato
I lack my roast beef and potato.

A better man was Aristotle
Pulling steady on the bottle.

I dip my hat to Chaucer   5
Swilling soup from his saucer,

And to Master Shakespeare
Who wrote big on small beer.

The abstemious Wordsworth
Subsisted on a curd's-worth.   10

But a slick one was Tennyson,
Putting gravy on his venison.

What these men had to eat and drink
Is what we say and what we think.

The flatulence of Milton   15
Came out of wry Stilton.

Sing a song for Percy Shelley,
Drowned in pale lemon jelly,

And for precious John Keats,
Dripping blood of pickled beets.   20

Then there was poor Willie Blake,
He foundered on sweet cake.

God have mercy on the sinner
Who must write with no dinner,

No gravy and no grub,   25
No pewter and no pub,

No belly and no bowels,
Only consonants and vowels.

FOR ANALYSIS

Compare the tone and theme of these two poems.

ROBERT FROST

The Road Not Taken

Two roads diverged in a yellow wood,
And sorry I could not travel both
And be one traveler, long I stood
And looked down one as far as I could
To where it bent in the undergrowth;

Then took the other, as just as fair,
And having perhaps the better claim,
Because it was grassy and wanted wear;

Though as for that the passing there
Had worn them really about the same, 10

And both that morning equally lay
In leaves no step had trodden black.
Oh, I kept the first for another day!
Yet knowing how way leads on to way,
I doubted if I should ever come back.

I shall be telling this with a sigh
Somewhere ages and ages hence:
Two roads diverged in a wood, and I—
I took the one less traveled by,
And that has made all the difference. 20

ROBERT FROST

Dust of Snow

The way a crow
Shook down on me
The dust of snow
From a hemlock tree

Has given my heart 5
A change of mood
And saved some part
Of a day I had rued.

ROBERT FROST

Fire and Ice

Some say the world will end in fire,
Some say in ice.
From what I've tasted of desire
I hold with those who favor fire.
But if it had to perish twice, 5
I think I know enough of hate
To say that for destruction ice
Is also great
And would suffice.

ARCHIBALD MACLEISH

Ars Poetica

A poem should be palpable and mute
As a globed fruit

Dumb
As old medallions to the thumb

Silent as the sleeve-worn stone 5
Of casement ledges where the moss has grown—

A poem should be wordless
As the flight of birds

A poem should be motionless in time
As the moon climbs 10

Leaving, as the moon releases
Twig by twig the night-entangled trees,

Leaving, as the moon behind the winter leaves,
Memory by memory the mind—

A poem should be motionless in time 15
As the moon climbs

A poem should be equal to:
Not true

For all the history of grief
An empty doorway and a maple leaf 20

For love
The leaning grasses and two lights above the sea—

A poem should not mean
But be.

MARIANNE MOORE

Poetry

I, too, dislike it: there are things that are important beyond all this fiddle.
    Reading it, however, with a perfect contempt for it, one discovers in
    it after all, a place for the genuine.
        Hands that can grasp, eyes
          that can dilate, hair that can rise   5
            if it must, these things are important not because a

high-sounding interpretation can be put upon them but because they are
    useful. When they become so derivative as to become unintelligible,
    the same thing may be said for all of us, that we
        do not admire what   10
        we cannot understand: the bat
            holding on upside down or in quest of something to

eat, elephants pushing, a wild horse taking a roll, a tireless wolf under
    a tree, the immovable critic twitching his skin like a horse that feels
        a flea, the base-   15
    ball fan, the statistician—
        nor is it valid
            to discriminate against "business documents and

school-books"; all these phenomena are important. One must make a distinction
    however: when dragged into prominence by half poets, the result is not   20
           poetry,
    nor till the poets among us can be
        "literalists of
        the imagination"—above
            insolence and triviality and can present   25

for inspection, imaginary gardens with real toads in them, shall we have
    it. In the meantime, if you demand on the one hand, the raw material of
           poetry in
        all its rawness and
        that which is on the other hand   30
            genuine, then you are interested in poetry.

FOR ANALYSIS

The two preceding poems have both described what a poem should be. After reading them separately, decide what Miss Moore thinks is the special function of poetry and what MacLeish thinks is the proper manner of writing a poem. Then compare them.

1. Do the poets have the same idea in mind when Miss Moore says poets should be "literalists of the imagination" and MacLeish says that "A poem should be palpable and mute"?

2. How does MacLeish's list of comparisons of poems with things harmonize with Miss Moore's definition of poetic content as "imaginary gardens with real toads in them"?

3. What would both poets say you must be interested in before you can be interested in poetry?

JOHN CROWE RANSOM

Janet Waking

Beautifully Janet slept
Till it was deeply morning. She woke then
And thought about her dainty-feathered hen,
To see how it had kept.

One kiss she gave her mother,   5
Only a small one gave she to her daddy
Who would have kissed each curl of his shining
    baby;
No kiss at all for her brother.

'Old Chucky, Old Chucky!' she cried,
Running on little pink feet upon the grass   10
To Chucky's house, and listening. But alas,
Her Chucky had died.

It was a transmogrifying bee
Came droning down on Chucky's old bald head
And sat and put the poison. It scarcely bled,   15

But how exceedingly

And purply did the knot
Swell with the venom and communicate
Its rigor! Now the poor comb stood up straight
But Chucky did not.   20

So there was Janet
Kneeling on the wet grass, crying her brown hen
(Translated far beyond the daughters of men)
To rise and walk upon it.

And weeping fast as she had breath   25
Janet implored us, 'Wake her from her sleep!'
And would not be instructed in how deep
Was the forgetful kingdom of death.

FOR ANALYSIS

1. In what two senses is Janet "waking" here?

2. If one assumes that the narrator of the poem is the father (only he could know the psychological fact of his own attitude mentioned early in the poem), how does this explain the odd, stilted words ("transmogrifying") and the bad jokes ("the comb stood up but Chucky did not") in the poem? What would be the state of mind of the narrator in the situation he outlines in the concluding lines?

3. What details early in the poem lead you to expect Janet's later reaction to the death of her hen?

JOHN CROWE RANSOM

Bells for John Whiteside's Daughter

There was such speed in her little body,
And such lightness in her footfall,
It is no wonder that her brown study
Astonishes us all.

Her wars were bruited in our high window.   5
We looked among orchard trees and beyond,
Where she took arms against her shadow,
Or harried unto the pond

The lazy geese, like a snow cloud
Dripping their snow on the green grass,   10
Tricking and stopping, sleepy and proud,
Who cried in goose, Alas,

For the tireless heart within the little
Lady with rod that made them rise
From their noon apple-dreams, and scuttle   15
Goose-fashion under the skies!

But now go the bells, and we are ready;
In one house we are sternly stopped
To say we are vexed at her brown study,
Lying so primly propped.   20

FOR ANALYSIS

These two poems deal with the same situation, the death of a young child. There all resemblances stop. Contrast the two poems by answering these questions:

1. What is the state of mind of the narrator in the Ransom poem? What can you infer about that state of mind from the use of the phrase "brown study" in this context? Can the narrator accept the fact of the child's death? What does he recall most about her—her sedateness or her constant vitality? How does this help to explain the odd ending? Is this a special kind of grief?

2. What is the narrator's state of mind in the Field poem? Is he sentimentalizing his recollections of the child? Is the focus of the poem on the child or on the narrator's grief? Is there fiction in this poem created by the narrator?

3. Which of the two poems implies the grief of the narrator more subtly and more exactly? Which of the poems seems sentimental? Which of the poems seems to you more successful?

EUGENE FIELD

Little Boy Blue

The little toy dog is covered with dust,
    But sturdy and staunch he stands;
And the little toy soldier is red with rust,
    And his musket moulds in his hands.
Time was when the little toy dog was new,   5
    And the soldier was passing fair;
And that was the time when our Little Boy Blue
    Kissed them and put them there.

"Now, don't you go till I come," he said,
    "And don't you make any noise!"   10
So, toddling off to his trundle-bed,
    He dreamt of the pretty toys;
And, as he was dreaming, an angel song
    Awakened our Little Boy Blue—
Oh! the years are many, the years are long,   15
    But the little toy friends are true!

Ay, faithful to Little Boy Blue they stand,
    Each in the same old place—
Awaiting the touch of a little hand,
    The smile of a little face;   20
And they wonder, as waiting the long years through
    In the dust of that little chair,
What has become of our Little Boy Blue,
    Since he kissed them and put them there.

W. H. AUDEN

The Unknown Citizen

TO JS/07/M/378
THIS MARBLE MONUMENT IS ERECTED BY THE STATE

He was found by the Bureau of Statistics to be
One against whom there was no official complaint,
And all the reports on his conduct agree
That, in the modern sense of an old-fashioned word,
    he was a saint,
For in everything he did he served the Greater Com-
    munity.   5
Except for the War till the day he retired
He worked in a factory and never got fired,
But satisfied his employers, Fudge Motors Inc.
Yet he wasn't a scab or odd in his views,
For his Union reports that he paid his dues,   10
(Our report on his Union shows it was sound)
And our Social Psychology workers found
That he was popular with his mates and liked a
    drink.
The Press are convinced that he bought a paper every
    day
And that his reactions to advertisements were normal
    in every way.   15

Policies taken out in his name prove that he was fully
    insured,
And his Health-card shows he was once in hospital
    but left it cured.
Both Producers Research and High-Grade Living
    declare
He was fully sensible to the advantages of the Install-
    ment Plan
And had everything necessary to the Modern
    Man,
A gramophone, a radio, a car and a frigidaire.   20
Our researchers into Public Opinion are content
That he held the proper opinions for the time of year;
When there was peace, he was for peace; when there
    was war, he went.
He was married and added five children to the popu-
    lation,
Which our Eugenist says was the right number for a
    parent of his generation,   25
And our teachers report that he never interfered with
    their education.
Was he free? Was he happy? The question is absurd:
Had anything been wrong, we should certainly have
    heard.

FOR ANALYSIS

1. What aspects of contemporary society is Auden
satirizing?
2. How does the form of the poem, especially the
rhymes, enhance the satire?

E. E. CUMMINGS

*if everything happens
that can't be done*

if everything happens that can't be done
(and anything's righter
than books
could plan)
the stupidest teacher will almost guess   5
(with a run
skip
around we go yes)
there's nothing as something as one

one hasn't a why or because or although   10
(and buds know better

than books
don't grow)
one's anything old being everything new
(with a what   15
which
around we come who)
one's everyanything so

so world is a leaf so tree is a bough
(and birds sing sweeter   20
than books
tell how)
so here is away and so your is a my
(with a down
up   25
around again fly)
forever was never till now

now i love you and you love me
(and books are shuter
than books   30
can be)
and deep in the high that does nothing but fall
(with a shout
each
around we go all)   35
there's somebody calling who's we

we're anything brighter than even the sun
(we're everything greater
than books
might mean)   40
we're everyanything more than believe
(with a spin
leap
alive we're alive)
we're wonderful one times one   45

FOR ANALYSIS

Cummings used capital letters, he said, only for
important things; he constructed, in other words,
his own conventions of typography.
1. Read this poem aloud for its rhythm. What is
this young girl, now in love for the first time,
doing as she sings this poem? The rhythm will
tell you.
2. What besides the recurring rhythm pattern holds
this poem together? Notice, for example, the last
word of each stanza and the first word of the
text.
3. After reading this poem, do you think that
disrupting natural syntax necessarily blocks
meaning?

E. E. CUMMINGS

if i

if i

or anybody don't
know where it her his

my next meal's coming from
i say to hell with that   5
that doesn't matter (and if

he she it or everybody gets a
bellyful without
lifting my finger i say to hell
with that i   10

say that doesn't matter)but
if somebody
or you are beautiful or

deep or generous what
i say is   15

whistle that
sing that yell that spell
that out big (bigger than cosmic
rays war earthquakes famine or the ex

prince of whoses diving into   20
a whatses to rescue miss nobody's
probably handbag) because i say that's not

swell (get me) babe not (understand me) lousy
kid that's something else my sweet (i feel that's
true)   25

FOR ANALYSIS

1. What are the important and valuable things that human beings ought to celebrate, according to this poem?
2. What is the narrator parodying when he talks of the rescue of the handbag?

KENNETH FEARING

Dirge

1-2-3 was the number he played but today the number
    came 3-2-1;
  bought his Carbide at 30 but it went to 29; had the
    favorite at Bowie but the track was slow—

O, executive type, would you like to drive a floating power,
    knee action, silk-upholstered six? Wed a Hollywood star?
  Shoot the course in 58? Draw to the ace, king, jack?
O, fellow with a will who won't take no, watch out for three
    cigarettes on the same, single match; O democratic voter
    born in August under Mars, beware of liquidated rails—

Dénouement to dénouement, he took a personal pride in the
    certain, certain way he lived his own, private life,
  but nevertheless, they shut off his gas; nevertheless,
    the bank foreclosed; nevertheless, the landlord called;
  nevertheless, the radio broke,

And twelve o'clock arrived just once too often,
    just the same he wore one gray tweed suit, bought one
      straw hat, drank one straight Scotch, walked one short
        step, took one long look, drew one deep breath,
    just one too many,

And wow he died as wow he lived,
   going whop to the office and blooie home to sleep and
      biff got married and bam had children and oof got fired,
  zowie did he live and zowie did he die,

With who the hell are you at the corner of his casket,
  . and where the hell we going on the right hand silver
  knob, and who the hell cares walking second from the
  end with an American Beauty wreath from why the hell
  not.

Very much missed by the circulation staff of the New York
  Evening Post; deeply, deeply mourned by the B.M.T.,

Wham, Mr. Roosevelt; pow, Sears Roebuck; awk, big dipper;
   bop, summer rain;
  bong, Mr., bong, Mr., bong, Mr., bong.

Pattern poems

The following poems show how some poets have gone far beyond the conventions of poetry as an oral form to approximate almost a sculptural form. We add no questions or comments, except to note that the Raleigh poem differs from the others in that it can be read horizontally or vertically without disturbing its form or content.

GEORGE HERBERT

Easter Wings

Lord, who createdst man in wealth and store,
  Though foolishly he lost the same,
    Decaying more and more
      Till he became
        Most poor;   5
        With Thee
       O let me rise
    As larks, harmoniously,
  And sing this day Thy victories;
Then shall the fall further the flight in me.   10

My tender age in sorrow did begin;
  And still with sickness and shame
    Thou didst so punish sin,
      That I became
        Most thin.   15
        With Thee
       Let me combine,
    And feel this day Thy victory;
  For if I imp my wing on Thine,
Affliction shall advance the flight in me.   20

ROBERT HERRICK

The Pillar of Fame

  Fame's pillar here at last we set,
  Out-during marble, brass, or jet;
    Charmed and enchanted so
    As to withstand the blow
      Of o v e r t h r o w;   5
      Nor shall the seas,
      Or o u t r a g e s
    Of storms, o'erbear
    What we uprear;
      Tho' kingdoms fall,   10
    This pillar never shall
    Decline or waste at all;
  But stand for ever by his own
  Firm and well-fixed foundatiòn.

To his book's end this last line he'd have placed:
Jocund his Muse was, but his life was chaste.

SIR WALTER RALEIGH

In the Grace of Wit,
of Tongue and Face

Your face	Your tongue	Your wit
So fair	So sweet	So sharp
First bent	Then drew	So hit
Mine eye	Mine ear	My heart
Mine eye	Mine ear	My heart
To like	To learn	To love
Your face	Your tongue	Your wit
Doth lead	Doth teach	Doth move
Your face	Your tongue	Your wit
With beams	With sound	With art
Doth blind	Doth charm	Doth rule
Mine eye	Mine ear	My heart
Mine eye	My ear	My heart
With life	With hope	With skill
Your face	Your tongue	Your wit
Doth feed	Doth feast	Doth fill
Oh face	O tongue	O wit
With frowns	With checks	With smart
Wrong not	Vex not	Wound not
Mine eye	My ear	My heart
This eye	This ear	This heart
Shall joy	Shall bend	Shall swear
Your face	Your tongue	Your wits
To serve	To trust	To fear

THE DRAMA

An Introduction

Drama employs more conventions than any other form of literature because of its two-part nature: It can be read as literature; however, its primary purpose is to portray people and events through action and dialogue which are performed. It adds to literary conventions a series of stage conventions. Staging devices—such as lighting, props, costumes—form an integral part of a play. Thus, the playwright includes stage directions not only for staging the play, but to help the reader visualize the scene and action.

Superficially, drama may seem less artificial, less conventional than other literary forms because it involves real people, words, and actions. But drama only seeks—it does not achieve—reality. The people are acting; the situations, conversations, and problems are simulated. Everything in drama is selected and manipulated to compress the experience just as in other literary forms. The physical characteristics of the theater itself create a situation which is vastly unreal—whether it is an open-air Greek stage, an Elizabethan platform stage projecting into the audience, a modern proscenium stage with a curtain, or a theater-in-the-round where the audience surrounds the stage.

The most familiar stage today is the proscenium stage. The audience sees a room with only three sides. People who have assumed personalities are talking to others about contrived problems and situations. Their dress is often affected, their words out of character, their actions unlikely.

The conventions of the theater, however, provide a context for the action of a play. The audience can overlook departures from actuality which are involved. If conventions were not accepted, the play would not seem plausible to the audience. The conventions of drama are numerous because the dramatist must concern himself with staging—music, costumes, lighting, movement, and so forth. He must be concerned with staging because drama involves a dimension which literature does not: Action has been added to words. One can read a play intelligently only if he considers the acting side along with the printed side; he must consider stage convention along with literary convention.

Conventions and their applications are more easily understood when their function is considered in a specific play. Tennessee Williams' *The Glass Menagerie* is a play about the problems of the Wingfield family and, by extension, of the society they represent. The family lives in a shabby apartment in St. Louis. The father long ago ran away from the family, unable to bear, among other things, his wife Amanda. Amanda, unable to cope with the present, lives in the past; her fondest recollection is of the night when seventeen gentlemen callers courted her. She lives by a code that died with the civilization she grew up in. Her daughter, Laura, is a shy, withdrawn cripple, who like her mother, cannot or will not cope with the outside world, and retires more and more into herself, spending hours with her collection of glass animals —the glass menagerie. Laura's brother, Tom, "a poet with a job in a warehouse" (says Williams in the stage directions) is torn between wanting to help Laura and needing to salvage his own identity.

The plot is simple: Amanda convinces Tom to invite an acquaintance, Jim O'Connor, to the Wingfield home for supper in hopes that he will be attracted to Laura. Jim, a normal but simple-minded young man, comes to supper; however, he is already engaged. Amanda's plan to help Laura only damages her; Laura retreats farther into unreality and Tom leaves.

Abstracted in this fashion, the play sounds weak. It is not. It had 563 performances on Broadway and won the New York Drama Critics' Circle Award as the best play of 1945. In creating this powerful comment on society and a tragic, touching portrayal of a family, Williams used almost every technique the drama offers.

CONVENTIONS OF SYMBOL

Williams used transparent walls on the set. As the curtain rises, the solid wall of the tenement becomes transparent and then rises slowly out of sight, not to be lowered again until Tom's final speech at the end of the play. This staging device is not a gimmick; Williams is illustrating symbolically the existence of a menagerie within a menagerie. Just as the beautiful glass animals stand imprisoned in their glass case, so these people live within their glass case. When the wall ascends, the menagerie is open for inspection. Here is a kind of symbol available only to the dramatist.

Another symbolic convention is the use of lighting in the play. As Williams says in the stage directions, "The lighting in the play is not realistic." Spotlights focus continually on Laura, even when she is not directly involved in the action. For example, when Tom and his mother argue about Tom's responsibility to Laura, the strong light is not on them but on Laura. Williams is again making a point symbolically: that although Tom has a problem, the central problem in the play is Laura—she is the center of everything.

Music also serves a symbolic purpose—by illustrating Laura's centrality. Williams demanded delicate, sad circus music, suggesting both nostalgia and the menagerie; he called it "Laura's music."

Williams had originally used an old vaudeville technique in the play. He wanted, at the beginning of each scene, a legend shown on a screen to suggest the mood and action of the scene to come. For example, the first scene when Amanda reminisces about her seventeen gentlemen callers, was to be preceded by the legend "*Où sont les neiges?*" part of the refrain ("Where are the snows of yesteryear?") of a poem by

François Villon, suggesting nostalgic and inevitably pointless recollections of a dead past. The screen device was never used, but it is included in the reading version of the play as another symbolic device.

Other symbolic devices are equally obvious. The animals in Laura's menagerie symbolize something to the audience—they also symbolize something to Laura. When her mother insists that she think of marriage, Laura reaches quickly for a glass animal. The gesture suggests that Laura realizes her retreat into unreality is being threatened. When Jim O'Connor comes to supper, Laura offers him her favorite glass animal to hold—an obvious gesture of love and trust. The animal is a unicorn, an animal traditionally connected with love and virgins. Jim clumsily breaks the horn from the unicorn as he and Laura dance, and Laura remarks that now the unicorn is just like all other horses, just as she is like other girls at the moment. Jim kisses her, then announces that he is engaged, and Laura insists that he take the broken unicorn as a souvenir.

The glass animal symbolism is strengthened by a recurring phrase that Jim uses to describe Laura: Blue Roses. Laura and her beauty have a highly unnatural quality: Roses, delicate and lovely, are not naturally blue.

Still another symbol is the use of candles. In the play Laura is associated with light, specifically with candles. At the end, long after he has fled from his family, Tom says that wherever he traveled, he always felt something pursuing him, especially when he heard music or saw a piece of transparent glass. As he speaks, Laura in the background (that is, in his memory) bends over candles and blows them out. Tom says he runs to movies or to a bar or to a stranger—"anything that can blow your candles out." As Laura blows out the candles, Tom says, "for nowadays the world is lit by lightning! Blow out your candles, Laura—and so, good-bye. . . ."

Tom, feeling guilt about leaving his sister, is here justifying his flight in the candles-lightning image. It's not a complicated image: Lightning is far more powerful and brilliant than candlelight, and Tom is saying that there are more important things for him than Laura's problems, that he must live in the present rather than die in the past. There is also an implication that Laura's problem is unsolvable—she herself blows out her candles, he does not. The basis for this explanation of his flight was developed early in the play when Tom says something that is repeated several times: that although in the U.S. there were labor squabbles and a slowly dissolving economy, "in Spain there was Guernica." The reference is to the Spanish city of Guernica, which was totally destroyed by the Fascists in the Spanish Civil War as a kind of threat to the enemy. However, to the Spanish Communists, Guernica became a battle-cry, a symbol of what they were fighting to overcome—it symbolized a cause to fight for. This is the lightning that lights the world: Tom feels he must face the lightning, not the candles in a St. Louis alley.

CONVENTIONS OF CHARACTER

Characters in plays can serve more functions than can characters in novels, poems, and short stories. Playwrights often use function characters, characters whose major importance is what they do, not what they are.

One of the oldest conventions and the earliest kind of function character is the chorus. A chorus is a group of actors (sometimes a single actor) speaking in unison and functioning as an expository device (for example, to give the audience necessary information which a character could not reveal because of limitations of time, place, or character consistency). Thus a chorus gives background information to the audience, comments on the action, or predicts what will happen. The convention requires that the audience believe what the chorus says—the chorus never lies.

When playwrights grew dissatisfied with the chorus device, they took three other character conventions and expanded them:

(1) The confidant: A character whose main function is to carry information to and from the main character and to provide an excuse for self-revelation by the main character. In the western movie, the hero talks to his horse or to a comical side-kick, both of them confidants. Hamlet talks to Horatio, a confidant. Antony talks to Enobarbus, a confidant. Juliet talks to the nurse, a confidant.

(2) The soliloquy: A character speaks his inmost thoughts directly to the audience. The chorus convention applies here with one difference: What the character says in soliloquy is what he sees as the truth. He may not, of course, know the truth or he may be deceiving himself.

(3) The aside: A character, in the midst of a group scene, suddenly turns to another character or to the audience and says something directed only to them. The convention requires that no one else hear the aside, even though the actor must shout to be heard in the back rows.

Some earlier plays have confidants, choruses, soliloquies, and asides. Modern playwrights have become more selective in using these devices. In *The Glass Menagerie* Williams has condensed all of them into the actions of one figure: Tom Wingfield. Consider what Tom does in this play:

(1) He is a character in the play.

(2) He is the narrator—the whole play is his memory of the action.

(3) He is a chorus. He goes to the front of the stage, speaks directly to the audience, and nobody else hears what he says; he speaks completely free of time and space.

(4) He is a confidant—an ironic one sometimes, but still a confidant. When he is with Amanda, he provokes her to reveal her paranoia, obviously not because he really did it in that situation, but because he wants the audience to see these qualities.

Another ancient convention of character, not limited to drama but especially noticeable there, is the use of a foil character. A foil is a function character whose personality contrasts with the main character to offset and clarify his qualities for the audience. In *Hamlet*, for example, Laertes, brother of Ophelia, son of Polonius, enemy of Hamlet, is a foil to Hamlet. Both men are in similar situations: each is a young student, each loves Ophelia in his own way, each has had a father murdered, each desires revenge. But where Hamlet must be sure that his revenge is just, Laertes resorts to trickery, poison, and possible damnation to achieve his. Thus, the relative nobility of Hamlet is emphasized.

In *The Glass Menagerie*, Jim O'Connor is a foil to Tom. Jim is a success in his own eyes and in Amanda's, a kind of all-American boy, but his own definition of success is stupid and depressing. Tom is a failure to everyone in the play, but unlike Jim, a success to the audience.

CONVENTIONS OF PLOT

Plays often employ a narrative structure similar in some respects to many novels and short stories. But because of its long history, drama is more conventionalized in the kind of plot is uses. Through the years, drama has built its own conventions—some of these have developed into so-called schools of playwriting: sentimental drama, expressionism, impressionism, theater of the absurd, and many others. But basically there are two kinds of plot structures and therefore two kinds of drama: comedy and tragedy.

Comedy is associated with happy endings and tragedy with sad endings—a vaguely correct, but nondefinitive description. Comedy is concerned less with individuals than with types, types involved in social situations. Comedy tends to be, then, a heavily plotted (although often episodic) form, since what happens rather than the persons involved is emphasized. A character in a comedy is usually trying desperately to adapt to a social situation; a tragic character is usually trying to establish his own identity or to live his life despite society's demands.

Comedy usually ends happily, with life triumphing over ruin and death—it ends with a beginning, that is, by suggesting a whole new story to come. "And they lived happily ever after" suggests a continuation, another story. Tragedy ends and ends finally, often with the death of the main character.

From these two forms have grown a series of subordinate forms. Each has its special conventions. Farce, for example, is highly exaggerated comedy wherein the playwright does not profess to maintain an illusion of reality. Melodrama is to tragedy what farce is to comedy: an exaggerated and therefore highly unreal rendering of a potentially tragic situation in which characters are so stereotyped and the plot so contrived that tragic characters seem almost funny. This is one of the paradoxes of the derivative forms: When the comic character becomes farcical, he loses much of the humor he would have had, and the audience almost despairs; comedy has taken on overtones of tragedy. When the tragic character becomes melodramatic, he loses much of the dignity he would have had; tragedy has taken on overtones of comedy.

To define tragedy and comedy in such limited fashion is sufficient for the purposes of this book. More specific explanation would involve numerous points that have been debated for two thousand years. For example, different ages have written different kinds of tragedy and have theorized differently about tragedy. The theory has usually been drawn from the practice. Aristotle defined tragedy as the imitation of a serious action of a man of noble but imperfect character, the action complete in itself, written poetically and dramatically, and aimed at arousing pity and fear in the audience so as to purge their emotions. His definition applies very well to the plays of Sophocles and Euripides, because those were the plays he was describing. But it cannot be applied to plays of all other ages. In the Middle Ages, tragedy was generally the case history of a man of high estate who fell from happiness to misery, usually to death. In the Renaissance, preeminently in Shakespeare, tragedy was sometimes Aristotelian (*King Lear*), sometimes not (*Macbeth*). During the late Renaissance, epic somehow became intertwined with tragedy—the characters of tragedy were often "Aristotelian," but the rest of the play's machinery was not. The eighteenth century eliminated even that resemblance by using middle-class heroes and heroines.

It cannot be said that writers since Aristotle have not been writing tragedy—it is just not tragedy as written in ancient Greece.

The same variety is observable in comedy. It is possible to distinguish two general types of comedy: high comedy (highly intellectualized, provoking laughter and scorn at the absurdity of men's conduct) and low comedy (slapstick). But this does not explain the variety of comic forms playwrights have developed through the centuries. Comedy during the Middle Ages mingled with romance and developed into romantic comedy, which involves uniting two (or four or six or eight) confused lovers despite outsiders' objections, tricks of fate, and their own indecisiveness. Whether this is high or low is debatable. Certainly high comedy is the "comedy of manners" developed in the seventeenth century, dealing with sophisticated characters and satirizing the absurdities of both fashionable conduct and deliberate violations of decorum. Sentimental comedy, which appeared in the eighteenth century, has elements of high and low comedy in its use of impossibly upright main characters who suffer indignity, embarrassment, and ill-fortune with surprising control that is even more surprising since these characters are not meant to be ridiculous but lovable.

At least two other derivative forms deserve mention. The history play or chronicle is based on an actual historical character or event, and on it is superimposed the form of tragedy or comedy. The problem play deals with a specific, usually contemporary social problem and explores solutions to the problem. By involving a major character in the problem, the playwright often superimposes the form of tragedy, less often comedy, as in the history play. The major difference is that the history play deals with the actual past, the problem play with the fictional present, and that the problem play is always argumentative.

The Glass Menagerie by this definition is a tragedy. With her brother's help, Laura tries to break out of her glass case into the real world and fails. Tom salvages what he can from the ruins of his family life—his own identity. If Tom were trying to adjust to a social situation (the mode of comedy) he would stay with the family through its progressive degeneration. But Tom must be true to his own nature (the mode of tragedy) no matter how callous that action may make him seem. In tragedy, ultimately we all stand alone, as Tom does. Like his father before him, who fled from Amanda and her refusal to face reality, Tom flees the now hopeless Laura. Tom is not happy in his choice; he has simply done what was necessary and has paid a heavy price for his freedom: a continual burden of guilt for what, against all reason, his conscience tells him is desertion. Laura is everyone's problem.

In the plays that follow, the playwrights use all the resources of stage and language. The plays differ greatly in type and therefore in technique. *Antigone* is tragedy in the Aristotelian sense. *Othello* is also a tragedy, but a special kind, usually called "domestic tragedy," since its central situation involves a man-and-wife conflict that determines all other action in the play. *The School for Scandal* is a comedy of manners, as is *The*

Importance of Being Earnest, but the two plays are very different. *The Glass Menagerie*, by our definition, is a twentieth-century tragedy in which the author has borrowed techniques from earlier forms in order to compress the action and the meaning of the action of years into minutes.

SOPHOCLES

*Antigone**

THE CHARACTERS

ANTIGONE, *daughter of Œdipus, former banished king.*

ISMENE, *her elder sister.*

CREON, *their maternal uncle, now King of Thebes.*

HAIMON, *Creon's son, beloved of Antigone.*

EURYDICE, *the Queen, his mother, whose other son has just been killed defending Thebes from attack.*

TEIRESIAS, *the old and blind seer or prophet.*

A SENTRY *and* A MESSENGER

THE CHORUS *of fifteen Thebans, elder citizens, among whom the* CHORAGOS *is the leader.*

TIME: *The legendary past of Ancient Greece.*

PLACE: *The walled city of Thebes with its seven gates.*

PROLOGUE

(SCENE: *Before the palace of* CREON, *King of Thebes. A central double door, and two lateral doors. A platform extends the length of the façade, and from this platform three steps lead down into the 'orchestra,' or chorus-ground. Time: Dawn of the day after the repulse of the Argive army from the assault on Thebes.*)

(ANTIGONE *and* ISMENE *enter from the central door of the Palace.*)

ANTIGONE.   Ismenê, dear sister,
You would think that we had already suffered enough
For the curse on Œdipus:
I cannot imagine any grief

---

*An English version by Dudley Fitts and Robert Fitzgerald.

That you and I have not gone through. And now—
Have they told you of the new decree of our King Creon?

ISMENE.   I have heard nothing: I know
That two sisters lost two brothers, a double death
In a single hour; and I know that the Argive army
Fled in the night; but beyond this, nothing.

ANTIGONE.   I thought so. And that is why I wanted you
To come out here with me. There is something we must do.

ISMENE.   Why do you speak so strangely?

ANTIGONE.   Listen, Ismenê:
Creon buried our brother Eteoclês
With military honours, gave him a soldier's funeral,
And it was right that he should; but Polyneicês,
Who fought as bravely and died as miserably,—
They say that Creon has sworn
No one shall bury him, no one mourn for him,
But his body must lie in the fields, a sweet treasure
For carrion birds to find as they search for food.
That is what they say, and our good Creon is coming here
To announce it publicly; and the penalty—
Stoning to death in the public square!
                                   There it is
And now you can prove what you are:
A true sister, or a traitor to your family.

ISMENE.   Antigonê, you are mad! What could I possibly do?

ANTIGONE.   You must decide whether you will help me or not.

ISMENE.   I do not understand you. Help you in what?

ANTIGONE.   Ismenê, I am going to bury him. Will you come?

ISMENE.   Bury him! You have just said the new law forbids it.

ANTIGONE.   He is my brother. And he is your brother, too.

SARCASt

ISMENE.   But think of the danger! Think what Creon will do!

ANTIGONE.   Creon is not strong enough to stand in my way.

ISMENE.   Ah sister!
Œdipus died. everyone hating him
For what his own search brought to light, his eyes
Ripped out by his own hand; and Iocastê died,
His mother and wife at once: she twisted the cords
That strangled her life; and our two brothers died,
Each killed by the other's sword. And we are left:
But oh, Antigonê,
Think how much more terrible than these
Our own death would be if we should go against Creon
And do what he has forbidden! We are only women,
We cannot fight with men, Antigonê!
The law is strong, we must give in to the law
In this thing, and in worse. I beg the Dead
To forgive me, but I am helpless: I must yield
To those in authority. And I think it is dangerous business
To be always meddling.

ANTIGONE.   If that is what you think,
I should not want you, even if you asked to come.
You have made your choice, you can be what you want to be.
But I will bury him; and if I must die,
I say that this crime is holy: I shall lie down
With him in death, and I shall be as dear
To him as he to me.
                    It is the dead,
Not the living, who make the longest demands:
We die for ever. . .
                    You may do as you like,
Since apparently the laws of the gods mean nothing to you.

ISMENE.   They mean a great deal to me; but I have no strength
To break laws that were made for the public good.

ANTIGONE.   That must be your excuse, I suppose. But as for me,
I will bury the brother I love.

ISMENE.   Antigonê,
I am so afraid for you!

ANTIGONE.   You need not be:
You have yourself to consider, after all.

ISMENE.   But no one must hear of this, you must tell no one!
I will keep it a secret, I promise!

ANTIGONE.   Oh, tell it! Tell everyone!
Think how they'll hate you when it all comes out
If they learn that you knew about it all the time!

ISMENE.   So fiery! You should be cold with fear.

ANTIGONE.   Perhaps. But I am doing only what I must.

ISMENE.   But can you do it? I say that you cannot.

ANTIGONE.   Very well: when my strength gives out, I shall do no more.

ISMENE.   Impossible things should not be tried at all.

ANTIGONE.   Go away, Ismenê:
I shall be hating you soon, and the dead will too,
For your words are hateful. Leave me my foolish plan:
I am not afraid of the danger; if it means death,
It will not be the worst of deaths—death without honour.

ISMENE.   Go then, if you feel that you must.
You are unwise,
But a loyal friend indeed to those who love you.

(*Exit into the Palace.* ANTIGONE *goes off,* L.)

(*Enter the* CHORUS.)

PÁRODOS *Entry of Chorus.*

CHORUS.   (*strophe* 1)
Now the long blade of the sun, lying
Level east to west, touches with glory
Thebes of the Seven Gates. Open, unlidded
Eye of golden day! O marching light
Across the eddy and rush of Dircê's stream,
Striking the white shields of the enemy
Thrown headlong backward from the blaze of morning!

CHORAGOS.   Polyneicês their commander
Roused them with windy phrases,
He the wild eagle screaming
Insults above our land,
His wings their shields of snow,
His crest their marshalled helms.

CHORUS.   (*antistrophe* 1)
Against our seven gates in a yawning ring
The famished spears came onward in the night;
But before his jaws were sated with our blood,
Or pinefire took the garland of our towers.

He was thrown back; and as he turned, great
    Thebes—
No tender victim for his noisy power—
Rose like a dragon behind him, shouting war.

    CHORAGOS. For God hates utterly *also*
The bray of bragging tongues; *aplicable*
And when he beheld their smiling, *to CREON*
Their swagger of golden helms,
The frown of his thunder blasted
Their first man from our walls.

    CHORUS.   (*strophe 2*) *fails in first test*
We heard his shout of triumph high in the air
Turn to a scream; far out in a flaming arc
He fell with his windy torch, and the earth
    struck him.
And others storming in fury no less than his
Found shock of death in the dusty joy of battle.

    CHORAGOS. Seven captains at seven gates
Yielded their clanging arms to the god
That bends the battle-line and breaks it.
These two only, brothers in blood,
Face to face in matchless rage,
Mirroring each the other's death,
Clashed in long combat.

    CHORUS.   (*antistrophe 2*)
But now in the beautiful morning of victory
Let Thebes of the many chariots sing for joy!
With hearts dancing we'll take leave of war:
Our temples shall be sweet with hymns of praise,
And the long night shall echo with our chorus.

SCENE 1

    CHORAGOS. But now at last our new King is
    coming:
Creon of Thebes, Menoiceus' son.
In this auspicious dawn of his reign
What are the new complexities *forecast of doom*
That shifting Fate has woven for him?
What is his counsel? Why has he summoned
The old men to hear him?
(*Enter* CREON *from the Palace, C. He addresses
the* CHORUS *from the top step.*)

    CREON. Gentlemen: I have the honour to
    inform you that our Ship of State, which
    recent storms have threatened to destroy,
    has come safely to harbour at last, guided
    by the merciful wisdom of Heaven. I have
    summoned you here this morning because
    I know that I can depend upon you: your
    devotion to King Laïos was absolute; you
    never hesitated in your duty to our late ruler

Œdipus; and when Œdipus died, your loy- *flatte people*
alty was transferred to his children. Unfortunately, as you know, his two sons, the
princes Eteoclês and Polyneicês, have killed
each other in battle; and I, as the next in
blood, have succeeded to the full power of
the throne.

    I am aware, of course, that no Ruler can
expect complete loyalty from his subjects
until he has been tested in office. Nevertheless, I say to you at the very outset that
I have nothing but contempt for the kind of
Governor who is afraid, for whatever reason, to follow the course that he knows is
best for the State; and as for the man who
sets private friendship above the public
welfare,—I have no use for him, either. I
call God to witness that if I saw my country
headed for ruin, I should not be afraid to
speak out plainly; and I need hardly remind
you that I would never have any dealings
with an enemy of the people. No one values
friendship more highly than I; but we must
remember that friends made at the risk of
wrecking our Ship are not real friends at all.

    These are my principles, at any rate, and
that is why I have made the following decision concerning the sons of Œdipus:
Eteoclês, who died as a man should die,
fighting for his country, is to be buried with
full military honours, with all the ceremony
that is usual when the greatest heroes die;
but his brother Polyneicês, who broke his
exile to come back with fire and sword
against his native city and the shrines of his
fathers' gods, whose one idea was to spill
the blood of his blood and sell his own
people into slavery—Polyneicês, I say, is *wants people to hate Polyneices & shows his*
to have no burial: no man is to touch him
or say the least prayer for him; he shall lie
on the plain, unburied; and the birds and
the scavenging dogs can do with him
whatever they like.

    This is my command, and you can see the
wisdom behind it. As long as I am King, *force by not bury. Polg.*
no traitor is going to be honoured with the
loyal man. But whoever shows by word
and deed that he is on the side of the State,
—he shall have my respect while he is living, and my reverence when he is dead.

    CHORAGOS. If that is your will, Creon son of
    Menoiceus,

speech justifies law he passed, sustaines position clearly. Reminder of loyalty.

You have the right to enforce it: we are yours.

CREON. That is my will. Take care that you do your part.

CHORAGOS. We are old men: let the younger ones carry it out.

CREON. I do not mean that: the sentries have been appointed.

CHORAGOS. Then what is it that you would have us do?

CREON. You will give no support to whoever breaks this law.

CHORAGOS. Only a crazy man is in love with death!

[handwritten margin: Suspicious of bribes]

CREON. And death it is; yet money talks, and the wisest

Have sometimes been known to count a few coins too many.

(*Enter* SENTRY *from L.*)

[handwritten margin: CREON accuses SENTRY + Prophet of taking BRIBES]

SENTRY. I'll not say that I'm out of breath from running, King, because every time I stopped to think about what I have to tell you, I felt like going back. And all the time a voice kept saying, 'You fool, don't you know you're walking straight into trouble?'; and then another voice: 'Yes, but if you let somebody else get the news to Creon first, it will be even worse than that for you!' But good sense won out, at least I hope it was good sense, and here I am with a story that makes no sense at all; but I'll tell it anyhow, because, as they say, what's going to happen's going to happen, and—

[handwritten margin: CREON's SENTRY waits to tell CREON because he knows CREON + for effect.]

CREON. Come to the point. What have you to say?

SENTRY. I did not do it. I did not see who did it. You must not punish me for what someone else has done.

CREON. A comprehensive defence! More effective, perhaps, If I knew its purpose. Come: what is it?

SENTRY. A dreadful thing . . . I don't know how to put it—

CREON. Out with it!

SENTRY.   Well, then;
The dead man—
               Polyneicês—

(*Pause. The* SENTRY *is overcome, fumbles for words.* CREON *waits impassively.*)

               out there—
               someone,—

New dust on the slimy flesh!

(*Pause. No sign from* CREON.)

Someone has given it burial that way, and Gone . . .

(*Long pause.* CREON *finally speaks with deadly control.*) *[handwritten: PAUSES to count to ten His first rule is BROKEN.]*

CREON. And the man who dared do this?

SENTRY.   I swear I
Do not know! You must believe me!
               Listen:
The ground was dry, not a sign of digging, no,
Not a wheeltrack in the dust, no trace of anyone.
It was when they relieved us this morning: and one of them,
The corporal, pointed to it.
               There it was,
The strangest—
       Look:
The body, just mounded over with light dust: you see?
Not buried really, but as if they'd covered it
Just enough for the ghost's peace. And no sign
Of dogs or any wild animal that had been there.

And then what a scene there was! Every man of us
Accusing the other: we all proved the other man did it,
We all had proof that we could not have done it.
We were ready to take hot iron in our hands,
Walk through fire, swear by all the gods,
It was not I!
I do not know who it was, but it was not I!

(CREON's *rage has been mounting steadily, but the* SENTRY *is too intent upon his story to notice it.*)

And then, when this came to nothing, someone said
A thing that silenced us and made us stare
Down at the ground: you had to be told the news,
And one of us had to do it! We threw the dice,
And the bad luck fell to me. So here I am,
No happier to be here than you are to have me:
Nobody likes the man who brings bad news.

CHORAGOS. I have been wondering, King: can it be that the gods have done this?

CREON (*furiously*). Stop.
Must you doddering wrecks
Go out of your heads entirely? 'The gods!'
Intolerable!

The gods favour this corpse? Why? How had
    he served them?
Tried to loot their temples, burn their images,
Yes, and the whole State, and its laws with it!
Is it your senile opinion that the gods love to
    honour bad men?
A pious thought!—
                No, from the very beginning
There have been those who have whispered
    together,
Stiff-necked anarchists, putting their heads to-
    gether,
Scheming against me in alleys. These are the
    men,
And they have bribed my own guard to do this
    thing. *falsely suspicious*
(*Sententiously*) Money!
There's nothing in the world so demoralising as
    money.
Down go your cities,
Homes gone, men gone, honest hearts corrupted,
Crookedness of all kinds, and all for money!
(*To* SENTRY)   But you—!
I swear by God and by the throne of God,
The man who has done this thing shall pay for
    it!
Find that man, bring him here to me, or your
    death
Will be the least of your problems: I'll string
    you up
Alive, and there will be certain ways to make you
Discover your employer before you die;
And the process may teach you a lesson you
    seem to have missed:
The dearest profit is sometimes all too dear:
That depends on the source. Do you understand
    me?
A fortune won is often misfortune.
SENTRY.   King, may I speak?
CREON.   Your very voice distresses me.
SENTRY.   Are you sure that it is my voice, and
    not your conscience?
CREON.   By God, he wants to analyse me
    now!
SENTRY.   It is not what I say, but what has
    been done, that hurts you.
CREON.   You talk too much.
SENTRY.   Maybe; but I've done nothing.
CREON.   Sold your soul for some silver:
    that's all you've done.
SENTRY.   "How dreadful it is when the right
    judge judges wrong!" *DRAMATIC IRONY*
CREON.   Your figures of speech

May entertain you now; but unless you bring me
    the man,
You will get little profit from them in the end.

(*Exit* CREON *into the Palace.*)

SENTRY.   'Bring me the man'—!
I'd like nothing better than bringing him the
    man!
But bring him or not, you have seen the last of
    me here.
At any rate, I am safe!

(*Exit* SENTRY.)

ODE I

related to play by exhaling

CHORUS. *man*   (*strophe 1*)
Numberless are the world's wonders, but none
More wonderful than man; the storm-gray sea
Yields to his prows, the huge crests bear him
    high;
Earth, holy and inexhaustible, is graven
With shining furrows where his plows have gone
Year after year, the timeless labour of stallions.

                      (*antistrophe 1*)
The lightboned birds and beasts that cling to
    cover,
The lithe fish lighting their reaches of dim water,
All are taken, tamed in the net of his mind;
The lion on the hill, the wild horse windy-maned,
Resign to him; and his blunt yoke has broken
The sultry shoulders of the mountain bull.

                      (*strophe 2*)
Words also, and thought as rapid as air,
He fashions to his good use; statecraft is his,
And his the skill that deflects the arrows of snow,
The spears of winter rain: from every wind
He has made himself secure—from all but one:
In the late wind of death he cannot stand.

                      (*antistrophe 2*)
O clear intelligence, force beyond all measure!
O fate of man, working both good and evil!
When the laws are kept, how proudly his city
    stands!
When the laws are broken, what of his city then?
Never may the anárchic man find rest at my
    hearth,
Never be it said that my thoughts are his
    thoughts.

SCENE 2

(*Re-enter* SENTRY *leading* ANTIGONE.)

[handwritten: REMINDS people who Antigone was]

CHORAGOS. What does this mean? Surely this captive woman
Is the Princess, Antigonê. Why should she be taken?
SENTRY. Here is the one who did it! We caught her
In the very act of burying him.—Where is Creon?
CHORAGOS. Just coming from the house.

(*Enter* CREON, C.)

CREON.   What has happened?
Why have you come back so soon?
SENTRY (*expansively*).   O King,
A man should never be too sure of anything:
I would have sworn
That you'd not see me here again: your anger
Frightened me so, and the things you threatened me with;
But how could I tell then
That I'd be able to solve the case so soon?

No dice-throwing this time: I was only too glad to come!

Here is this woman. She is the guilty one:
We found her trying to bury him.

Take her, then; question her; judge her as you will.
I am through with the whole thing now, and glád óf it.
CREON. But this is Antigonê! Why have you brought her here?
SENTRY. She was burying him, I tell you!
CREON. (*severely*). Is this the truth?
SENTRY. I saw her with my own eyes. Can I say more?
CREON. The details: come, tell me quickly!
SENTRY.   It was like this:
After those terrible threats of yours, King,
We went back and brushed the dust away from the body.
The flesh was soft by now, and stinking,
So we sat on a hill to windward and kept guard.
No napping this time! We kept each other awake.
But nothing happened until the white round sun
Whirled in the centre of the round sky over us:
Then, suddenly,

A storm of dust roared up from the earth, and the sky
Went out, the plain vanished with all its trees
In the stinging dark. We closed our eyes and endured it.
The whirlwind lasted a long time, but it passed;
And then we looked, and there was Antigonê!
I have seen
A mother bird come back to a stripped nest, heard
Her crying bitterly a broken note or two
For the young ones stolen. Just so, when this girl
Found the bare corpse, and all her love's work wasted,
She wept, and cried on heaven to damn the hands
That had done this thing.
                    And then she brought more dust
And sprinkled wine three times for her brother's ghost.
We ran and took her at once. She was not afraid,
Not even when we charged her with what she had done.
She denied nothing.
                    And this was a comfort to me,
And some uneasiness: for it is a good thing
To escape from death, but it is no great pleasure
To bring death to a friend.
                    Yet I always say
There is nothing so comfortable as your own safe skin!
CREON (*slowly*, *dangerously*). And you, Antigonê?
You with your head hanging,—do you confess this thing?
ANTIGONE. I do. I deny nothing.
CREON (*to* SENTRY). You may go.

(*Exit* SENTRY.)

(*To* ANTIGONE.) Tell me, tell me briefly:
Had you heard my proclamation touching this matter?
ANTIGONE. It was public. Could I help hearing it?
CREON. And yet you dared defy the law.
ANTIGONE.   I dared.
It was not God's proclamation. That final Justice
That rules the world below makes no such laws.
Your edict, King, was strong,
But all your strength is weakness itself against
The immortal unrecorded laws of God.

[handwritten: She defys King. First one who dares do it.]

They are not merely now: they were, and shall
   be,
Operative for ever, beyond man utterly.
I knew I must die, even without your decree:
I am only mortal. And if I must die
Now, before it is my time to die,
Surely this is no hardship: can anyone
Living, as I live, with evil all about me,
Think Death less than a friend? This death of
   mine
Is of no importance; but if I had left my brother
Lying in death unburied, I should have suffered.
Now I do not.
           You smile at me. Ah Creon,
Think me a fool, if you like; but it may well be
That a fool convicts me of folly.

   CHORAGOS.   Like father, like daughter: both
   headstrong, deaf to reason!
She has never learned to yield.

   CREON.   She has much to learn.
The inflexible heart breaks first, the toughest
   iron   *It also applies to Creon*
Cracks first, and the wildest horses bend their
   necks
At the pull of the smallest curb.
                   Pride? In a slave?
This girl is guilty of a double insolence,
Breaking the given laws and boasting of it.
Who is the man here,
She or I, if this crime goes unpunished?
Sister's child, or more than sister's child,
Or closer yet in blood—she and her sister
Win bitter death for this!
(*To* SERVANTS.)   Go, some of you,
Arrest Ismenê. I accuse her equally.
Bring her: you will find her sniffling in the house
   there.

Her mind's a traitor: crimes kept in the dark
Cry for light, and the guardian brain shudders;
But how much worse than this
Is brazen boasting of barefaced anarchy!

   ANTIGONE.   Creon, what more do you want
   than my death?

   CREON.   Nothing.
That gives me everything.

   ANTIGONE.   Then I beg you: kill me.
This talking is a great weariness: your words
Are distasteful to me, and I am sure that mine
Seem so to you. And yet they should not seem
   so:
I should have praise and honour for what I have
   done.

All these men here would praise me
Were their lips not frozen shut with fear of you.
   expresses hatred

(*Bitterly.*)   Ah the good fortune of kings,
Licensed to say and do whatever they please!

   CREON.   You are alone here in that opinion.

   ANTIGONE.   No they are with me. But they
   keep their tongues in leash.

   CREON.   Maybe. But you are guilty, and they
   are not.

   ANTIGONE.   There is no guilt in reverence for
   the dead.

   CREON.   But Eteoclês—was he not your
   brother too?

   ANTIGONE.   My brother too.

   CREON.   And you insult his memory?

   ANTIGONE (*softly*).   The dead man would not
   say that I insult it.

   CREON.   He would: for you honour a traitor
   as much as him.

   ANTIGONE.   His own brother, traitor or not,
   and equal in blood.

   CREON.   He made war on his country.
   Eteoclês defended it.

   ANTIGONE.   Nevertheless, there are honours
   due all the dead.

   CREON.   But not the same for the wicked as
   for the just.

   ANTIGONE.   Ah Creon, Creon.
Which of us can say what the gods hold wicked?

   CREON.   An enemy is an enemy, even dead.

   ANTIGONE.   It is my nature to join in love,
   not hate.   *Not true*

   CREON (*finally losing patience*).
Go join them, then; if you must have your love,
Find it in hell!

   CHORAGOS.   But see, Ismenê comes:

(*Enter* ISMENE, *guarded*.)

Those tears are sisterly, the cloud
That shadows her eyes rains down gentle sorrow.

   CREON.   You too, Ismenê,
Snake in my ordered house, sucking my blood
Stealthily—and all the time I never knew
That these two sisters were aiming at my throne!
                     Ismenê,
Do you confess your share in this crime, or
   deny it?
Answer me.

   ISMENE.   Yes, if she will let me say so. I am
   guilty.

   ANTIGONE (*coldly*).   No, Ismenê. You have
   no right to say so.

wants to sacrifice alone to get all the glory as a martyr

You would not help me, and I will not have you help me.

ISMENE. But now I know what you meant; and I am here
To join you, to take my share of punishment.

ANTIGONE. The dead man and the gods who rule the dead
Know whose act this was. Words are not friends.

ISMENE. Do you refuse me, Antigonê? I want to die with you:
I too have a duty that I must discharge to the dead.

ANTIGONE. You shall not lessen my death by sharing it.

ISMENE. What do I care for life when you are dead?

ANTIGONE. Ask Creon. You're always hanging on his opinions.

ISMENE. You are laughing at me. Why Antigonê?

ANTIGONE. It's a joyless laughter, Ismenê.

ISMENE.   But can I do nothing?

ANTIGONE. Yes. Save yourself. I shall not envy you.
There are those who will praise you; I shall have honour, too.

ISMENE. But we are equally guilty!

ANTIGONE.   No more, Ismenê.
You are alive, but I belong to Death.

CREON (*to the* CHORUS). Gentlemen, I beg you to observe these girls:
One has just now lost her mind; the other,
It seems, has never had a mind at all.

ISMENE. Grief teaches the steadiest minds to waver, King.

CREON. Yours certainly did, when you assumed guilt with the guilty!

ISMENE. But how could I go on living without her?

CREON.   You are.
She is already dead.

ISMENE. But, your own son's bride!

CREON. There are places enough for him to push his plow.
I want no wicked women for my sons!

ANTIGONE. O dearest Haimon, how your father wrongs you!

CREON. I've had enough of your childish talk of marriage!

CHORAGOS. Do you really intend to steal this girl from your son?

CREON. Nc; Death will do that for me.

CHORAGOS. Then she must die?

CREON (*ironically*).   You dazzle me.
             —But enough of this talk!
(*To* GUARDS.) You, there, take them away and guard them well:
For they are but women, and even brave men run
When they see Death coming.

(*Exeunt* ISMENE, ANTIGONE, *and* GUARDS.)

ODE II

CHORUS.   (*strophe 1*)
Fortunate is the man who has never tasted
  God's vengeance!
Where once the anger of heaven has struck, that
  house is shaken
For ever: damnation rises behind each child
Like a wave cresting out of the black northeast,
When the long darkness under sea roars up
And bursts drumming death upon the wind-
  whipped sand.

(*antistrophe 1*)
I have seen this gathering sorrow from time long
  past
Loom upon Œdipus' children: generation from
  generation
Takes the compulsive rage of the enemy god.
So lately this last flower of Œdipus' line
Drank the sunlight! but now a passionate word
And a handful of dust have closed up all its
  beauty.

(*strophe 2*)
    What mortal arrogance
    Transcends the wrath of Zeus?
Sleep cannot lull him, nor the effortless long
  months
Of the timeless gods: but he is young for ever,
And his house is the shining day of high
    Olympos.
    All that is and shall be,
    And all the past, is his.
No pride on earth is free of the curse of heaven.

(*antistrophe 2*)
    The straying dreams of men
    May bring them ghosts of joy:
But as they drowse, the waking embers burn
  them;
Or they walk with fixed eyes, as blind men walk.
But the ancient wisdom speaks for our own
  time:
Fate works most for woe
With Folly's fairest show.
Man's little pleasure is the spring of sorrow.

SCENE 3

CHORAGOS.   But here is Haimon, King, the last of all your sons.
Is it grief for Antigonê that brings him here,
And bitterness at being robbed of his bride?

(*Enter* HAIMON.)

CREON.   We shall soon see, and no need of diviners.
                        —Son,
You have heard my final judgment on that girl:
Have you come here hating me, or have you come
With deference and with love, whatever I do?
   HAIMON.   I am your son, father. You are my guide.
You make things clear for me, and I obey you.
No marriage means more to me than your continuing wisdom.
   CREON.   Good. That is the way to behave: subordinate
Everything else, my son, to your father's will.
This is what a man prays for, that he may get
Sons attentive and dutiful in his house,
Each one hating his father's enemies,
Honouring his father's friends. But if his sons
Fail him, if they turn out unprofitably,
What has he fathered but trouble for himself
And amusement for the malicious?
                        So you are right
Not to lose your head over this woman.
Your pleasure with her would soon grow cold, Haimon,
And then you'd have a hellcat in bed and elsewhere.
Let her find her husband in Hell!
Of all the people in this city, only she
Has had contempt for my law and broken it.

Do you want me to show myself weak before the people?
Or to break my sworn word? No, and I will not.
The woman dies.

I suppose she'll plead 'family ties.' Well, let her.
If I permit my own family to rebel,
How shall I earn the world's obedience?
Show me the man who keeps his house in hand,
He's fit for public authority.
                        I'll have no dealings
With law-breakers, critics of the government:
Whoever is chosen to govern should be obeyed—

Must be obeyed, in all things, great and small,
Just and unjust! O Haimon,
The man who knows how to obey, and that man only,
Knows how to give commands when the time comes.
You can depend on him, no matter how fast
The spears come: he's a good soldier, he'll stick it out.

Anarchy, anarchy! Show me a greater evil!
This is why cities tumble and the great houses rain down,
This is what scatters armies!
No, no: good lives are made so by discipline.
We keep the laws then, and the law-makers,
And no woman shall seduce us. If we must lose,
Let's lose to a man, at least! Is a woman stronger than we?
   CHORAGOS.   Unless time has rusted my wits,
What you say, King, is said with point and dignity.
   HAIMON (*boyishly earnest*).   Father.
Reason is God's crowning gift to man, and you are right
To warn me against losing mine. I cannot say—
I hope that I shall never want to say—that you
Have reasoned badly. Yet there are other men
Who can reason, too; and their opinions might be helpful.
You are not in a position to know everything
That people say or do, or what they feel:
Your temper terrifies them—everyone
Will tell you only what you like to hear.
But I, at any rate, can listen; and I have heard them
Muttering and whispering in the dark about this girl.
They say no woman has ever, so unreasonably,
Died so shameful a death for a generous act:
'She covered her brother's body. Is this indecent?
'She kept him from dogs and vultures. Is this a crime?
'Death?—She should have all the honour that we can give her!'

This is the way they talk out there in the city.

You must believe me:
Nothing is closer to me than your happiness.
What could be closer? Must not any son
Value his father's fortune as his father does his?
I beg you, do not be unchangeable:
Do not believe that you alone can be right.

The man who thinks that,
The man who maintains that only he has the
    power
To reason correctly, the gift to speak, the soul—
A man like that, when you know him, turns out
    empty.

It is not reason never to yield to reason!

In flood time you can see how some trees bend,
And because they bend, even their twigs are safe,
While stubborn trees are torn up, roots and all.
And the same thing happens in sailing:
Make your sheet fast, never slacken,—and over
    you go,
Head over heels and under: and there's your
    voyage.

Forget you are angry! Let yourself be moved!
I know I am young; but please let me say this:
The ideal condition
Would be, I admit, that men should be right by
    instinct;
But since we are all too likely to go astray,
The reasonable thing is to learn from those who
    can teach.
    CHORAGOS. You will do well to listen to
    him, King,
If what he says is sensible. And you, Haimon,
Must listen to your father.—Both speak well.
    CREON. You consider it right for a man of
    my years and experience
To go to school to a boy?
    HAIMON.   It is not right
If I am wrong. But if I am young, and right,
What does my age matter?
    CREON. You think it right to stand up for
    an anarchist?
    HAIMON. Not at all. I pay no respect to
    criminals.
    CREON. Then she is not a criminal?
    HAIMON. The City would deny it, to a man.
    CREON. And the City proposes to teach me
    how to rule?
    HAIMON. Ah. Who is it that's talking like
    a boy now?
    CREON. My voice is the one voice giving
    orders in this City!
    HAIMON. It is no City if it takes orders from
    one voice.
    CREON. The State is the King!
    HAIMON. Yes, if the State is a desert.

(*Pause.*)

    CREON. This boy, it seems, has sold out to
    a woman.
    HAIMON. If you are a woman: my concern
    is only for you.
    CREON. So? Your 'concern'! In a public
    brawl with your father!
    HAIMON. How about you, in a public brawl
    with justice?
    CREON. With justice, when all that I do is
    within my rights?
    HAIMON. You have no right to trample on
    God's right.
    CREON (*completely out of control*). Fool,
    adolescent fool! Taken in by a woman!
    HAIMON. You'll never see me taken in by
    anything vile.
    CREON. Every word you say is for her!
    HAIMON (*quietly, darkly*). And for you.
And for me. And for the gods under the earth.
    CREON. You'll never marry her while she
    lives.
    HAIMON. Then she must die.—But her death
    will cause another.
    CREON. Another?
Have you lost your senses? Is this an open
    threat?
    HAIMON. There is no threat in speaking to
    emptiness.
    CREON. I swear you'll regret this superior
    tone of yours!
You are the empty one!
    HAIMON. If you were not my father, I'd
I'd say you were perverse.
    CREON. You girlstruck fool, don't play at
    words with me!
    HAIMON. I am sorry. You prefer silence.
    CREON. Now, by God—!
I swear, by all the gods in heaven above us,
You'll watch it, I swear you shall!

(*To the* SERVANTS)   Bring her out!
Bring the woman out! Let her die before his
    eyes!
Here, this instant, with her bridegroom beside
    her!
    HAIMON. Not here, no; she will not die here,
    King.
And you will never see my face again.
Go on raving as long as you've a friend to endure
    you.

(*Exit* HAIMON.)

CHORAGOS.   Gone, gone.
Creon, a young man in a rage is dangerous!
  CREON.   Let him do, or dream to do, more
    than a man can.
He shall not save these girls from death.
  CHORAGOS.   These girls?
You have sentenced them both?
  CREON.   No, you are right.
I will not kill the one whose hands are clean.
  CHORAGOS.   But Antigonê?
  CREON (*somberly*).   I will carry her far away
Out there in the wilderness, and lock her
Living in a vault of stone. She shall have food,
As the custom is, to absolve the State of her
    death.
And there let her pray to the gods of hell:
They are her only gods:
Perhaps they will show her an escape from death,
Or she may learn,
                though late,
That pity shown the dead is pity in vain.

(*Exit* CREON.)

ODE III

CHORUS.   (*strophe*)
Love, unconquerable
Waster of rich men, keeper
Of warm lights and all-night vigil
In the soft face of a girl:
Sea-wanderer, forest-visitor!
Even the pure Immortals cannot escape you,
And mortal man, in his one day's dusk,
Trembles before your glory.
                          (*antistrophe*)
Surely you swerve upon ruin
The just man's consenting heart,
As here you have made bright anger
Strike between father and son—
And none has conquered but Love!
A girl's glánce wórking the will of heaven:
Pleasure to her alone who mocks us,
Merciless Aphroditê.

SCENE 4

CHORAGOS (*as* ANTIGONE *enters guarded*).
But I can no longer stand in awe of this,
Nor, seeing what I see, keep back my tears.
Here is Antigonê, passing to that chamber
Where all find sleep at last.
  ANTIGONE.   (*strophe 1*)
Look upon me, friends, and pity me
Turning back at the night's edge to say
Goodbye to the sun that shines for me no longer;
Now sleepy Death
Summons me down to Acheron, that cold shore:
There is no bridesong there, nor any music.

CHORUS.   Yet not unpraised, not without a
    kind of honour,
You walk at last into the underworld;
Untouched by sickness, broken by no sword.
What woman has ever found your way to death?

ANTIGONE.   (*antistrophe 1*)
How often I have heard the story of Niobê,
Tantalos' wretched daughter, how the stone
Clung fast about her, ivy-close: and they say
The rain falls endlessly
And sifting soft snow; her tears are never done.
I feel the loneliness of her death in mine.
  CHORUS.   But she was born of heaven, and
    you
Are woman, woman-born. If her death is yours,
A mortal woman's, is this not for you
Glory in our world and in the world beyond?

ANTIGONE.   (*strophe 2*)
You laugh at me. Ah, friends, friends,
Can you not wait until I am dead? O Thebes,
O men many-charioted, in love with Fortune,
Dear springs of Dircê, sacred Theban grove,
Be witness for me, denied all pity,
Unjustly judged! and think a word of love
For her whose path turns
Under dark earth, where there are no more tears.

CHORUS.   You have passed beyond human
    daring and come at last
Into a place of stone where Justice sits.
I cannot tell
What shape of your father's guilt appears in this.

ANTIGONE.   (*antistrophe 2*)
You have touched it at last: that bridal bed
Unspeakable, horror of son and mother min-
    gling:
Their crime, infection of all our family!
O Œdipus, father and brother!
Your marriage strikes from the grave to murder
    mine.

I have been a stranger here in my own land:
All my life
The blasphemy of my birth has followed me.

CHORUS.   Reverence is a virtue, but strength
Lives in established law: that must prevail.
You have made your choice,
Your death is the doing of your conscious hand.

ANTIGONE.   (epode)
Then let me go, since all your words are bitter,
And the very light of the sun is cold to me.
Lead me to my vigil, where I must have
Neither love nor lamentation; no song, but
   silence.

(CREON interrupts impatiently.)

CREON.   If dirges and planned lamentations
   could put off death,
Men would be singing for ever.
(To the SERVANTS)   Take her, go!
You know your orders: take her to the vault
And leave her alone there. And if she lives or
   dies,
That's her affair, not ours: our hands are clean.
   ANTIGONE.   O tomb, vaulted bridebed in
      eternal rock,
Soon I shall be with my own again
Where Persephonê welcomes the thin ghosts
   underground:
And I shall see my father again, and you, mother,
And dearest Polyneicês—
                         dearest indeed
To me, since it was my hand
That washed him clean and poured the ritual
   wine:
And my reward is death before my time!
And yet, as men's hearts know, I have done no
   wrong,
I have not sinned before God. Or if I have,
I shall know the truth in death. But if the guilt
Lies upon Creon who judged me, then, I pray,
May his punishment equal my own.
   CHORAGOS.   O passionate heart,
Unyielding, tormented still by the same winds!
   CREON.   Her guards shall have good cause to
      regret their delaying.
   ANTIGONE.   Ah! That voice is like the voice
      of death!
   CREON.   I can give you no reason to think
      you are mistaken.
   ANTIGONE.   Thebes, and you my fathers'
      gods,

And rulers of Thebes, you see me now, the last
Unhappy daughter of a line of kings,
Your kings, led away to death. You will re-
   member
What things I suffer, and at what men's hands,
Because I would not transgress the laws of
   heaven.
(To the GUARDS, simply) Come: let us wait no
   longer.

(Exit ANTIGONE, L., guarded.)

ODE IV

CHORUS.   (strophe 1)
All Danaê's beauty was locked away
In a brazen cell where the sunlight could not
   come:
A small room, still as any grave, enclosed her.
Yet she was a princess too,
And Zeus in a rain of gold poured love upon her.
O child, child,
No power in wealth or war
Or tough sea-blackened ships
Can prevail against untiring Destiny!

                              (antistrophe 1)
And Dryas' son also, that furious king,
Bore the god's prisoning anger for his bride:
Sealed up by Dionysos in deaf stone,
His madness died among echoes.
So at the last he learned what dreadful power
His tongue had mocked:
For he had profaned the revels,
And fired the wrath of the nine
Implacable Sisters that love the sound of the
   flute.

                              (strophe 2)
And old men tell a half-remembered tale
Of horror done where a dark ledge splits the sea
And a double surf beats on the gréy shóres:
How a king's new woman, sick
With hatred for the queen he had imprisoned,
Ripped out his two sons' eyes with her bloody
   hands
While grinning Arês watched the shuttle plunge
Four times: four blind wounds crying for
   revenge,

                              (antistrophe 2)
Crying, tears and blood mingled.—Piteously
   born,
Those sons whose mother was of heavenly birth!
Her father was the god of the North Wind

And she was cradled by gales,
She raced with young colts on the glittering
   hills
And walked untrammeled in the open light:
But in her marriage deathless Fate found means
To build a tomb like yours for all her joy.

SCENE 5

(*Enter blind* TEIRESIAS, *led by a boy. The opening
speeches of* TEIRESIAS *should be in singsong contrast to the realistic lines of* CREON.)

TEIRESIAS.   This is the way the blind man
   comes, Princess, Princess,
Lock-step, two heads lit by the eyes of one.
   CREON.   What new thing have you to tell us,
   old Teiresias?
TEIRESIAS.   I have much to tell you: listen to
   the prophet, Creon.
   CREON.   I am not aware that I have ever
   failed to listen.
TEIRESIAS.   Then you have done wisely, King,
   and ruled well.
   CREON.   I admit my debt to you. But what
   have you to say?
TEIRESIAS.   This, Creon: you stand once more
   on the edge of fate.
   CREON.   What do you mean? Your words
   are a kind of dread.
TEIRESIAS.   Listen, Creon:
I was sitting in my chair of augury, at the place
Where the birds gather about me. They were all
   a-chatter,
As is their habit, when suddenly I heard
A strange note in their jangling, a scream, a
Whirring fury; I knew that they were fighting,
Tearing each other, dying
In a whirlwind of wings clashing. And I was
   afraid.
I began the rites of burnt-offering at the altar,
But Hephaistos failed me: instead of bright
   flame,
There was only the sputtering slime of the fat
   thigh-flesh
Melting: the entrails dissolved in grey smoke,
The bare bone burst from the welter. And no
   blaze!

This was a sign from heaven. My boy described
   it,
Seeing for me as I see for others.

I tell you, Creon, you yourself have brought

This new calamity upon us. Our hearths and
   altars
Are stained with the corruption of dogs and
   carrion birds
That glut themselves on the corpse of Œdipus'
   son.
The gods are deaf when we pray to them, their
   fire
Recoils from our offering, their birds of omen
Have no cry of comfort, for they are gorged
With the thick blood of the dead.
                              O my son,
These are no trifles! Think: all men make
   mistakes,
But a good man yields when he knows his course
   is wrong,
And repairs the evil. The only crime is pride.
Give in to the dead man, then: do not fight with
   a corpse—
What glory is it to kill a man who is dead?
Think, I beg you:
It is for your own good that I speak as I do.
You should be able to yield for your own good.
   CREON.   It seems that prophets have made me
   their especial province.
All my life long
I have been a kind of butt for the dull arrows
Of doddering fortune-tellers!
                           No, Teiresias:
If your birds—if the great eagles of God him-
   self
Should carry him stinking bit by bit to heaven,
I would not yield. I am not afraid of pollution:
No man can defile the gods.
                        Do what you will,
Go into business, make money, speculate
In India gold or that synthetic gold from Sardis,
Get rich otherwise than by my consent to bury
   him.
Teiresias, it is a sorry thing when a wise man
Sells his wisdom, lets out his words for hire!
   TEIRESIAS.   Ah Creon! Is there no man left
   in the world—
   CREON.   To do what—Come, let's have the
   aphorism!
TEIRESIAS.   No man who knows that wisdom
   outweighs any wealth?
   CREON.   As surely as bribes are baser than
   any baseness.
TEIRESIAS.   You are sick, Creon! You are
   deathly sick!
   CREON.   As you say: it is not my place to
   challenge a prophet.

TEIRESIAS.   Yet you have said my prophecy is for sale.

CREON.   The generation of prophets has always loved gold.

TEIRESIAS.   The generation of kings has always loved brass.

CREON.   You forget yourself! You are speaking to your King.

TEIRESIAS.   I know it. You are a king because of me.

CREON.   You have a certain skill; but you have sold out.

TEIRESIAS.   King, you will drive me to words that—

CREON.   Say them, say them!
Only remember: I will not pay you for them.

TEIRESIAS.   No, you will find them too costly.

CREON.   No doubt. Speak:
Whatever you say, you will not change my will.

TEIRESIAS.   Then take this, and take it to heart!
The time is not far off when you shall pay back
Corpse for corpse, flesh of your own flesh.
You have thrust the child of this world into living night,
You have kept from the gods below the child that is theirs:
The one in a grave before her death, the other,
Dead, denied the grave. This is your crime:
And the Furies and the dark gods of Hell
Are swift with terrible punishment for you.

Do you want to buy me now, Creon?
                         Not many days,
And your house will be full of men and women weeping,
And curses will be hurled at you from far
Cities grieving for sons unburied, left to rot
Before the walls of Thebes.

These are my arrows, Creon: they are all for you.

(*To* BOY)   But come, child: lead me home
Let him waste his fine anger upon younger men.
Maybe he will learn at last
To control a wiser tongue in a better head.

(*Exit* TEIRESIAS.)

CHORAGOS.   The old man has gone, King, but his words
Remain to plague us. I am old, too,
But I cannot remember that he was ever false.

CREON.   That is true. . . . It troubles me.

Oh it is hard to give in! but it is worse
To risk everything for stubborn pride.

CHORAGOS.   Creon: take my advice.

CREON.   What shall I do?

CHORAGOS.   Go quickly: free Antigonê from her vault
And build a tomb for the body of Polyneicês.

CREON.   You would have me do this?

CHORAGOS.   Creon, yes!
And it must be done at once: God moves
Swiftly to cancel the folly of stubborn men.

CREON.   It is hard to deny the heart! But I
Will do it: I will not fight with destiny.

CHORAGOS.   You must go yourself, you cannot leave it to others.

CREON.   I will go.
                    —Bring axes, servants:
Come with me to the tomb. I buried her, I
Will set her free.
                    Oh, quickly!
My mind misgives—
The laws of the gods are mighty, and a man must serve them
To the last day of his life!

(*Exit* CREON.)

PÆAN

                                        (*strophe 1*)
CHORAGOS.   God of many names

CHORUS.   O Iacchos
                                        son
of Cadmeian Sémelê
                         O born of the Thunder!
Guardian of the West
                         Regent
of Eleusis' plain
                    O Prince of Mænad Thebes
and the Dragon Field by rippling Ismenos:

                                        (*antistrophe 1*)
CHORAGOS.   God of many names

CHORUS.   the flame of torches
flares on our hills
                         the nymphs of Iacchos
dance at the spring of Castalia:
from the vine-close mountain
                         come ah come in ivy:
Evohê evohê! sings through the streets of Thebes

                                        (*strophe 2*)
CHORAGOS.   God of many names

CHORUS.   Iacchos of Thebes
heavenly Child
            of Sémelê bride of the Thunderer!
The shadow of plague is upon us:
                                        come
with clement feet
            oh come from Parnasos
down the long slopes
            across the lamenting water

                        (*antistrophe 2*)
CHORAGOS.   Iô Fire! Chorister of the throb-
    bing stars!
O purest among the voices of the night!
Thou son of God, blaze for us!

CHORUS.   Come with choric rapture of circling
    Mænads
Who cry *Iô Iacche*!

                        God of many names!

        ÉXODUS

(*Enter* MESSENGER, *L.*)
    MESSENGER.   Men of the line of Cadmos,
        you who live
Near Amphion's citadel:
            I cannot say
Of any condition of human life 'This is fixed,
This is clearly good, or bad.' Fate raises up,
And Fate casts down the happy and unhappy
    alike:
No man can foretell his Fate.
            Take the case of Creon:
Creon was happy once, as I count happiness:
Victorious in battle, sole governor of the land,
Fortunate father of children nobly born.
And now it has all gone from him! Who can say
That a man is still alive when his life's joy fails?
He is a walking dead man. Grant him rich,
Let him live like a king in his great house:
If his pleasure is gone, I would not give
So much as the shadow of smoke for all he
    owns.
    CHORAGOS.   Your words hint at sorrow:
        what is your news for us?
    MESSENGER.   They are dead. The living are
        guilty of their death.
    CHORAGOS.   Who is guilty? Who is dead?
        Speak!
    MESSENGER.   Haimon.
Haimon is dead; and the hand that killed him
Is his own hand.
    CHORAGOS.   His father's? or his own?

    MESSENGER.   His own, driven mad by the
        murder his father had done.
    CHORAGOS.   Teiresias, how clearly you saw
        it all!
    MESSENGER.   This is my news: you must draw
        what conclusions you can from it.
    CHORAGOS.   But look: Eurydicê, our Queen:
Has she overheard us?

(*Enter* EURYDICE *from the Palace, C.*)

    EURYDICE.   I have heard something, friends:
As I was unlocking the gate of Pallas' shrine,
For I needed her help today, I heard a voice
Telling of some new sorrow. And I fainted
There at the temple with all my maidens about
    me.
But speak again: whatever it is, I can bear it:
Grief and I are no strangers.
    MESSENGER.   Dearest Lady,
I will tell you plainly all that I have seen.
I shall not try to comfort you: what is the use,
Since comfort could lie only in what is not true?
The truth is always best.
                        I went with Creon
To the outer plain where Polyneicês was lying,
No friend to pity him, his body shredded by dogs.
We made our prayers in that place to Hecatê
And Pluto, that they would be merciful. And we
    bathed
The corpse with holy water, and we brought
Fresh-broken branches to burn what was left
    of it,
And upon the urn we heaped up a towering
    barrow
Of the earth of his own land.
                        When we were done, we ran
To the vault where Antigonê lay on her couch
    of stone.
One of the servants had gone ahead,
And while he was yet far off he heard a voice
Grieving within the chamber, and he came back
And told Creon. And as the King went closer,
The air was full of wailing, the words lost,
And he begged us to make all haste. 'Am I a
    prophet?'
He said, weeping, 'And must I walk this road,
'The saddest of all that I have gone before?
'My son's voice calls me on. Oh quickly, quickly!
'Look through the crevice there, and tell me
'If it is Haimon, or some deception of the gods!'

We obeyed; and in the cavern's farthest corner
We saw her lying:

She had made a noose of her fine linen veil
And hanged herself. Haimon lay beside her,
His arms about her waist, lamenting her,
His love lost under ground, crying out
That his father had stolen her away from him.
When Creon saw him the tears rushed to his
     eyes
And he called to him: 'What have you done,
     child? Speak to me.
'What are you thinking that makes your eyes
     so strange?
'O my son, my son, I come to you on my knees!'
But Haimon spat in his face. He said not a word,
Staring—
                    And suddenly drew his sword
And lunged. Creon shrank back, the blade
     missed; and the boy,
Desperate against himself, drove it half its
     length
Into his own side, and fell. And as he died
He gathered Antigonê close in his arms again,
Choking, his blood bright red on her white
     cheek.
And now he lies dead with the dead, and she
     is his
At last, his bride in the houses of the dead.

(*Exit* EURYDICE *into the Palace.*)

CHORAGOS.   She has left us without a word.
     What can this mean?
MESSENGER.   It troubles me, too; yet she
     knows what is best,
Her grief is too great for public lamentation,
And doubtless she has gone to her chamber to
     weep
For her dead son, leading her maidens in dirge.
CHORAGOS.   It may be so: but I fear this deep
     silence.

(*Pause.*)

MESSENGER.   I will see what she is doing.
     I will go in.

(*Exit* MESSENGER *into the Palace.*)
(*Enter* CREON *with attendants, bearing* HAIMON'S
body.)

CHORAGOS.   But here is the King himself: oh
     look at him,
Bearing his own damnation in his arms.
CREON.   Nothing you say can touch me any
     more.

My own blind heart has brought me
From darkness to final darkness. Here you see
The father murdering, the murdered son—
And all my civic wisdom!

Haimon my son, so young, so young to die,
I was the fool, not you; and you died for me.
CHORAGOS.   That is the truth; but you were
     late in learning it.
CREON.   This truth is hard to bear. Surely
     a god
Has crushed me beneath the hugest weight of
     heaven,
And driven me headlong a barbaric way
To trample out the thing I held most dear.

The pains that men will take to come to pain!

(*Enter* MESSENGER *from the Palace.*)

MESSENGER.   The burden you carry in your
     hands is heavy,
But it is not all: you will find more in your
     house.
CREON.   What burden worse than this shall
     I find there?
MESSENGER.   The Queen is dead.
CREON.   O port of death, deaf world,
Is there no pity for me? And you, Angel of evil,
I was dead, and your words are death again.
Is it true, boy? Can it be true?
Is my life dead? Has death bred death?
MESSENGER.   You can see for yourself.

(*The doors are opened, and the body of* EURYDICE
is disclosed within.)
CREON.   Oh pity!
All true, all true, and more than I can bear!
O my wife, my son!
MESSENGER.   She stood before the altar, and
     her heart
Welcomed the knife her own hand guided,
And a great cry burst from her lips for Megareus
     dead,
And for Haimon dead, her sons; and her last
     breath
Was a curse for their father, the murderer of
     her sons.
And she fell, and the dark flowed in through her
     closing eyes.
CREON.   O God, I am sick with fear.
Are there no swords here? Has no one a blow
     for me?
MESSENGER.   Her curse is upon you for the
     deaths of both.

CREON. It is right that it should be. I alone
am guilty.
I know it, and I say it. Lead me in,
Quickly, friends.
I have neither life nor substance. Lead me in.
CHORAGOS. You are right, if there can be
right in so much wrong.
The briefest way is best in a world of sorrow.
CREON. Let it come,
Let death come quickly, and be kind to me.
I would not ever see the sun again.
CHORAGOS. All that will come when it will;
but we, meanwhile,
Have much to do. Leave the future to itself.
CREON. All my heart was in that prayer!
CHORAGOS. Then do not pray any more:
the sky is deaf.
CREON. Lead me away. I have been rash
and foolish.
I have killed my son and my wife.
I look for comfort; my comfort lies here dead.
Whatever my hands have touched has come to
nothing.
Fate has brought all my pride to a thought of
dust.

(As CREON is being led into the house, the
CHORAGOS advances and speaks directly to the
audience.)

CHORAGOS. There is no happiness where
there is no wisdom;
No wisdom but in submission to the gods.
Big words are always punished,
And proud men in old age learn to be wise.

FOR ANALYSIS

1. The conflicting forces are introduced immediately in this play. Antigone states her position
and the reasons for it, the Chorus provides a
brief exposition of how the situation developed,
and Creon states his position and the reasons for
it. At this point in the play, is it possible to say
that either Creon or Antigone is wrong?
2. Why is it necessary that Creon not change his
order? Why is it necessary that Antigone not
abandon her resolve?
3. What in the conversation of Creon with the
sentry indicates that the feelings of Polyneices's
family never entered Creon's thoughts when he
decided to forbid burial?
4. To what does the Chorus attribute the conflict
in this play? To two strong-minded people? Or

to something beyond that? Look carefully at
the second ode.
5. What secondary conflict of principle springs up
between Creon and Haimon?
6. What does Creon's releasing Ismene reveal of
the effect of Haimon's arguments? Does the way
Antigone is sentenced to die suggest more of
that effect?
7. In the third ode, love is described in terms usually reserved for another emotion. What is that
emotion? What does this foreshadow in the
play?
8. Why does the messenger report the death of
Haimon and Antigone? What convention of
the Greek stage would Sophocles apparently
violate if he were to show Creon's excavation
or the lovers' deaths dramatically?
9. At the end, Creon first assumes all the blame
himself and then blames Fate. Is this a reversal?
10. The play does not seem to be about Antigone
or Creon. What is the play about?
11. After having read the entire play, go back and
look at the choruses. What is their function? In
what way are they an economical device? What
would the twentieth-century playwright substitute for them?

WILLIAM SHAKESPEARE

Othello, the Moor of Venice*

CHARACTERS

DUKE OF VENICE
BRABANTIO, a senator, father to DESDEMONA
GRATIANO, brother to BRABANTIO
LUDOVICO, kinsman to BRABANTIO
OTHELLO, the Moor, General in the Venetian army
CASSIO, his honorable lieutenant
IAGO, OTHELLO'S ancient, a villain
RODERIGO, a gulled gentleman
MONTANO, governor of Cyprus
CLOWN, servant to OTHELLO
DESDEMONA, wife to OTHELLO
EMILIA, wife to IAGO

---

*Notes by Alan S. Downer, by permission of Alan S.
Downer and Holt, Rinehart & Winston, Inc.

BIANCA, *a courtesan, in love with* CASSIO.

SENATORS, GENTLEMEN OF CYPRUS, SAILORS, OFFICERS, MESSENGER, HERALD, MUSICIANS, *and* ATTENDANTS

SCENE: *Venice; Cyprus.*

ACT I.1 *Venice. A street.*

(*Enter* RODERIGO *and* IAGO.)

[handwritten margin notes: R gave Iago money to get Desdemona for him]

RODERIGO.   Tush, never tell me! I take
    it much unkindly
That thou, Iago, who hast had my purse
As if the strings were thine, shouldst
    know of this.
IAGO.   'Sblood, but you will not hear
    me.
If ever I did dream of such a matter,
Abhor me.
    RODERIGO.   Thou told'st me thou
    didst hold him in thy hate.
    IAGO.   Despise me, if I do not. Three
    great ones of the city,
In personal suit to make me his lieutenant,
Off-capp'd to him; and, by the faith of man, 10
I know my price; I am worth no worse
    a place.
But he, as loving his own pride and
    purposes,   *[margin: exposes his intention]*
Evades them with a bombast circumstance
Horribly stuff'd with epithets of war;
And, in conclusion,
Nonsuits my mediators; for, "Certes,"
    says he.
"I have already chose my officer."
And what was he?
Forsooth, a great arithmetician,
One Michael Cassio, a Florentine,   20
(A fellow almost damn'd in a fair wife)
That never set a squadron in the field,
Nor the division of a battle knows
More than a spinster; unless the bookish
    theoric,
Wherein the toged consuls can propose

As masterly as he. Mere prattle without
    practice
Is all his soldiership. But he, sir, had the
    election;
And I, of whom his eyes had seen the proof
At Rhodes, at Cyprus, and on other
    grounds,
Christian and heathen, must be be-lee'd
    and calm'd   30
By debitor and creditor; this counter-
    caster,
He, in good time, must his lieutenant be,
And I—God bless the mark!—his
    Moorship's ancient.
    RODERIGO.   By heaven, I rather would
    have been his hangman.
    IAGO.   Why, there's no remedy; 'tis the
    curse of service.
Preferment goes by letter and affection,
And not by old gradation, where each
    second
Stood heir to the first. Now, sir, be judge
    yourself
Whether I in any just term am affin'd
To love the Moor.
    RODERIGO.   I would not follow him
    then.   40
    IAGO.   O, sir, content you.
I follow him to serve my turn upon him.
We cannot all be masters, nor all masters
Cannot be truly follow'd. You shall mark
Many a duteous and knee-crooking knave,
That, doting on his own obsequious
    bondage,
Wears out his time, much like his master's
    ass,
For nought but provender, and when he's
    old, cashier'd.
Whip me such honest knaves. Others there
    are
Who, trimm'd in forms and visages of duty,   50
Keep yet their hearts attending on
    themselves,
And, throwing but shows of service
    on their lords,

ACT 1.1 2 *had:* used   4 *'Sblood:* by Christ's blood   11 *price:* value   13 *bombast circumstance:* circumlocutions padded out   16 *Nonsuits:* rejects the petitions of   16 *Certes:* certainly   19 *arithmetician:* i.e., student of books of military tactics (cf., Mercutio on Tybalt as a fencer, Romeo, II, 3)   21 *damn'd:* married to (?)   23 *division . . . battle:* organization of an army   24 *bookish theoric:* pedantic theory   25 *toged:* wearing a toga   25 *propose:* talk

27 *had the election:* was chosen   30 *be-lee'd:* "have the wind taken out of my sails"   31 *counter-caster:* arithmetician   33 *ancient:* ensign, third officer (after Othello and Cassio)   36 *Preferment:* promotion   36 *letter:* influence   36 *affection:* favoritism   37 *old gradation:* the old way of promoting from one rank to the next   39 *affin'd:* bound by affection   48 *cashier'd:* dismissed   50 *trimm'd:* costumed   52 *throwing but shows:* bestowing only the appearance

Do well thrive by 'em, and when they
   have lin'd their coats
Do themselves homage. These fellows
   have some soul; *VERBAL IRONY*
And such a one do I profess myself. For,
   sir,
It is as sure as you are Roderigo,
Were I the Moor, I would not be Iago.
In following him I follow but myself—
Heaven is my judge, not I for love and
   duty,
But seeming so, for my peculiar end.   60
For when my outward action does
   demonstrate
The native act and figure of my heart
In compliment extern, 'tis not long after
But I will wear my heart upon my sleeve
For daws to peck at: I am not what I am.
   RODERIGO.   What a full fortune does
    the thick-lips owe,
If he can carry't thus!
   IAGO.   Call up her father.
Rouse him, make after him, poison his
   delight,
Proclaim him in the streets. Incense her
   kinsmen,
And, though he in a fertile climate dwell,   70
Plague him with flies; though that his joy
   be joy,
Yet throw such changes of vexation on 't,
As it may lose some color.
   RODERIGO.   Here is her father's house.
    I'll call aloud.
   IAGO.   Do, with like timorous accent
    and dire yell
As when, by night and negligence, the fire
Is spied in populous cities.
   RODERIGO.   What, ho, Brabantio!
    Signior Brabantio, ho!
   IAGO.   Awake! what, ho, Brabantio!
    thieves! thieves!
Look to your house, your daughter, and
   your bags! (*MONEY*)   80
Thieves! thieves!

(*Enter* BRABANTIO *above, at a window.*)

   BRABANTIO.   What is the reason of this
    terrible summons?

What is the matter there?
   RODERIGO.   Signior, is all your family
    within?
   IAGO.   Are your doors lock'd?
   BRABANTIO.   Why,
    wherefore ask you this?
   IAGO.   'Zounds, sir, you're robb'd!
    For shame, put on your gown;
Your heart is burst, you have lost half
   your soul.
Even now, now, very now, an old black
   ram *DIRTY IMPLICATIONS OF SEX*
Is tupping your white ewe. Arise, arise!
Awake the snorting citizens with the bell,   90
Or else the devil will make a grandsire of
   you.
Arise, I say!
   BRABANTIO.   What, have you lost your wits?
   RODERIGO.   Most reverend signior, do you
    know my voice?
   BRABANTIO.   Not I. What are you?
   RODERIGO.   My name is Roderigo.   - *foolish*
   BRABANTIO.   The
    worser welcome.
I have charg'd thee not to haunt about
   my doors;
In honest plainness thou hast heard me say
My daughter is not for thee; and now, in
   madness,
Being full of supper and distempering
   draughts,
Upon malicious bravery dost thou come   100
To start my quiet.
   RODERIGO.   Sir, sir, sir,—
   BRABANTIO.   But thou must
    needs be sure
My spirits and my place have in them
   power
To make this bitter to thee.
   RODERIGO.   Patience, good sir.
   BRABANTIO.   What tell'st thou me of
    robbing? This is Venice;
My house is not a grange.
   RODERIGO.   Most grave
    Brabantio,
In simple and pure soul I come to you.
   IAGO.   'Zounds, sir, you are one of those
    that will not serve God, if the devil bid

---

54 *Do . . . homage:* serve themselves   60 *peculiar:* personal   62
native: secret   62 *figure:* purpose   63 *compliment extern:* outward appearance   65 *daws:* jackdaws, i.e., fools   72 *changes:* disturbances   75 *timorous accent:* voice of terror

86 *Zounds:* by Christ's wounds   86 *gown:* dressing gown   90 *snorting:* snoring   99 *distempering:* uninhibiting   100 *bravery:* defiance   101 *start:* disturb   103 *place:* position (as Senator)   106 *grange:* isolated farm

you. Because we come to do you service   110
and you think we are ruffians, you'll
have your daughter covered with a
Barbary horse; you'll have your nephews neigh to you; you'll have coursers
for cousins, and gennets for germans.

[handwritten margin note: ugly of Animal References]

BRABANTIO.   What profane wretch art
thou?

IAGO.   I am one, sir, that comes to tell
you your daughter and the Moor
are now making the beast with two
backs.

[handwritten margin note: changes subject so he won't have to tell who he is.]

BRABANTIO.   Thou art a villain.

IAGO.   You are
—a senator.

BRABANTIO.   This thou shalt answer.
I know thee, Roderigo.

RODERIGO.   Sir, I will answer anything.   120
But, I beseech you,
If 't be your pleasure and most wise
consent,
(As partly I find it is) that your fair
daughter,
At this odd-even and dull watch o' th' night,
Transported, with no worse nor better
guard
But with a knave of common hire, a
gondolier,
To the gross clasps of a lascivious Moor,—
If this be known to you and your allowance,
We then have done you bold and saucy
wrongs;
But if you know not this, my manners tell
me   130
We have your wrong rebuke. Do not
believe
That, from the sense of all civility,
I thus would play and trifle with your
reverence.
Your daughter, if you have not given
her leave,
I say again, hath made a gross revolt;
Tying her duty, beauty, wit, and fortunes
In an extravagant and wheeling stranger
Of here and everywhere. Straight satisfy
yourself.
If she be in her chamber or your house,
Let loose on me the justice of the state   140

For thus deluding you.

BRABANTIO.   Strike on the tinder,
ho!
Give me a taper! Call up all my people!
This accident is not unlike my dream.
Belief of it oppresses me already.
Light, I say! light!   (*Exit*)

IAGO.   Farewell; for I must
leave you.
It seems not meet, nor wholesome to my
place,
To be produc'd—as, if I stay, I shall—
Against the Moor; for, I do know, the
state,
However this may gall him with some
check,
Cannot with safety cast him, for he's
embark'd   150
With such loud reason to the Cyprus wars,
Which even now stands in act, that, for
their souls,
Another of his fathom they have none,
To lead their business; in which regard,
Though I do hate him as I do hell-pains,
Yet, for necessity of present life,
I must show out a flag and sign of love,
Which is indeed but sign. That you shall
surely find him,
Lead to the Sagittary the raised search;
And there will I be with him. So, farewell.   160
                              (*Exit.*)

(*Enter* BRABANTIO *in his night-gown, and
Servants with torches.*)

BRABANTIO.   It is too true an evil. Gone
she is;
And what's to come of my despised time
Is nought but bitterness. Now, Roderigo,
Where didst thou see her?—O unhappy
girl!—
With the Moor, say'st thou?—Who would
be a father!
How didst thou know 'twas she?—O, she
deceives me
Past thought! What said she to you?—
Get moe tapers;
Raise all my kindred—Are they married,
think you?

---

113 *gennets for germans:* ponies for relatives   118 *answer:* be
called to account for   124 *odd-even:* around midnight   128 *your
allowance:* a thing that you approve   132 *from:* contrary to   137
extravagant: vagabond

143 *taper:* candle   144 *meet:* fitting   148 *place:* i.e., as Othello's ensign   149 *check:* rebuke   150 *cast:* discharge   151 *loud:*
urgent   153 *fathom:* capacity   159 *Sagittary:* an inn (at the
sign of the Sagittarius, the Archer)   s.d. *night-gown:* dressing
gown   162 *despised time:* rest of my life   167 *moe:* more

RODERIGO.   Truly, I think they are.
BRABANTIO.   O heaven! How got she
out? O treason of the blood!   170
Fathers, from hence trust not your
daughters' minds
By what you see them act. Is there not
charms
By which the property of youth and
maidhood
May be abus'd? Have you not read,
Roderigo,
Of some such thing?
RODERIGO.   Yes, sir, I have indeed.
BRABANTIO.   Call up my brother.—O,
would you had had her!
Some one way, some another.—Do you
know
Where we may apprehend her and the
Moor?
RODERIGO.   I think I can discover him,
if you please
To get your guard and go along with me.   180
BRABANTIO.   Pray you, lead on. At every
house I'll call;
I may command at most.—Get weapons,
ho!
And raise some special officers of night.—
On, good Roderigo; I'll deserve your pains.
(*Exeunt.*)

ACT I.2   *Another street.*

(*Enter* OTHELLO, IAGO, *and* ATTENDANTS
with torches.)

tells people what they want to hear.

IAGO.   Though in the trade of war
I have slain men,
Yet do I hold it very stuff o' th' conscience
To do no contriv'd murder. I lack iniquity *says*
Sometimes to do me service. Nine or ten *he*
times *couldn't hurt anyone*
I had thought to have yerk'd him here
under the ribs.
OTHELLO.   'Tis better as it is.
IAGO.   Nay, but
he prated,
And spoke such scurvy and provoking
terms
Against your honor

That, with the little godliness I have,
I did full hard forbear him. But, I pray
you, sir,   10
Are you fast married? Be assur'd of this,
That the magnifico is much belov'd,
And hath in his effect a voice potential
As double as the Duke's. He will divorce *says Brabantio will end his marriage*
you;
Or put upon you what restraint or grievance
The law, with all his might to enforce it on,
Will give him cable.
OTHELLO.   Let him do his spite; *comes on as being nice compared to others on stage. + different from what people'll have said about them.*
My services which I have done the signiory
Shall out-tongue his complaints. 'Tis yet
to know,—
Which, when I know that boasting is an
honor,
I shall promulgate—I fetch my life and
being
From men of royal siege, and my demerits
May speak unbonneted to as proud a
fortune
As this that I have reach'd; for know,
Iago,
But that I love the gentle Desdemona,
I would not my unhoused free condition
Put into circumscription and confine
For the sea's worth. But, look! what lights
come yond?

(*Enter* CASSIO *and* OFFICERS, *with torches.*)

IAGO.   Those are the raised father and
his friends.
You were best go in.
OTHELLO.   Not I; I must be
found.   30
My parts, my title, and my perfect soul
Shall manifest me rightly. Is it they?
IAGO.   By Janus, I think no. *two faced (bottom)* ↓
OTHELLO.   The servants of the Duke,
and my lieutenant!
The goodness of the night upon you,
friends!
What is the news?
CASSIO.   The Duke does greet
you, general,

---

170 *of the blood:* against the family   173 *property:* nature   174
abus'd: deceived   182 *command:* find supporters
ACT 1.2   2 *very stuff'd:* strict scruple   5 *yerk'd:* thrust

---

10 *full hard forbear:* with difficulty spare   11 *fast:* securely   12
magnifico: i.e., senator   13 *effect:* ability to effect his wishes   13
voice potential: powerful voice   14 *As . . . Duke's:* like the Duke's
double vote   15 *grievance:* obstacles   18 *signiory:* the government   19 *yet to know:* not yet known   22 *royal siege:* throne   22
demerits: deserts   23 *unbonneted:* i.e., on equal terms   26
unhoused: free from domestic cares   29 *raised:* aroused   31
parts: abilities   33 *Janus:* Roman god with two faces

And he requires your haste-post-haste
    appearance,
Even on the instant.
    OTHELLO.   What is the matter,
    think you?
    CASSIO.   Something from Cyprus, as I
    may divine;
It is a business of some heat. The galleys   40
Have sent a dozen sequent messengers
This very night at one another's heels,
And many of the consuls, rais'd and met,
Are at the Duke's already. You have been
    hotly call'd for;
When, being not at your lodging to be
    found,
The Senate hath sent about three several
    quests
To search you out.
    OTHELLO.   'Tis well I am found by
    you.
I will but spend a word here in the house,
And go with you.   (*Exit*.)
    CASSIO.   Ancient, what makes he
    here?
    IAGO.   Faith, he to-night hath boarded
    a land carack: 50
If it proves lawful prize, he's made for ever.
    CASSIO.   I do not understand.
    IAGO.   He's married.
    CASSIO.   To who?

(*Re-enter* OTHELLO.)

    IAGO.   Marry, to—Come, captain, will
    you go?
    OTHELLO.   Have with you.
    CASSIO.   Here comes another troop to
    seek for you.

(*Enter* BRABANTIO, RODERIGO, *and* OFFICERS
with torches and weapons.)

    IAGO.   It is Brabantio. General, be
    advis'd;
He comes to bad intent.
    OTHELLO.   Holla! stand there!
    RODERIGO.   Signior, it is the Moor.
    BRABANTIO.   Down with him, thief!

(*They draw on both sides*.)
    IAGO.   You, Roderigo! come, sir, I am
    for you.
    OTHELLO.   Keep up your bright swords,
    for the dew will rust them.
Good signior, you shall more command
    with years   60
Than with your weapons.
    BRABANTIO.   O thou foul thief, where
    hast thou stow'd my daughter?
Damn'd as thou art, thou hast enchanted
    her;
For I'll refer me to all things of sense,
If she in chains of magic were not bound,
Whether a maid so tender, fair, and happy,
So opposite to marriage that she shunn'd
The wealthy curled darlings of our nation,
Would ever have, t' incur a general mock,
Run from her guardage to the sooty bosom 70
Of such a thing as thou—to fear, not to
    delight.
Judge me the world, if 'tis not gross in sense
That thou hast practis'd on her with foul
    charms,
Abus'd her delicate youth with drugs or
    minerals
That weaken motion. I'll have't disputed on;
'Tis probable, and palpable to thinking.
I therefore apprehend and do attach thee
For an abuser of the world, a practiser
Of arts inhibited and out of warrant.
Lay hold upon him; if he do resist,   80
Subdue him at his peril.
    OTHELLO.   Hold your hands,
Both you of my inclining, and the rest.
Were it my cue to fight, I should have
    known it
Without a prompter. Where will you that
    I go
To answer this your charge?
    BRABANTIO.   To prison, till fit time
Of law and course of direct session
Call thee to answer.
    OTHELLO.   What if I do obey?
How may the Duke be therewith satisfied,
Whose messengers are here about my side
Upon some present business of the state 90

---

37 *haste-post-haste*: speediest   40 *galleys*: warships   41 *sequent*:
one after another   46 *several*: separate   49 *makes he*: is he doing
50 *carack*: merchant ship   53 *Marry*: a mild oath   53 *captain*:
general   55 *advis'd*: cautious

---

59 *Keep up*: sheathe   64 *things of sense*: rational creatures   69
mock: ridicule   72 *gross in sense*: obvious to anyone's perception
74 *Abus'd*: deluded   75 *motion*: perception   75 *disputed on*:
argued at law   77 *attach*: arrest   79 *inhibited*: illegal   82 *of
my inclining*: my supporters   86 *direct*: regular   90 *present*:
immediate

To bring me to him?

OFFICER.   'Tis true, most worthy
signior.
The Duke's in council; and your noble self,
I am sure, is sent for.

BRABANTIO.   How? the Duke in
couneil?
In this time of the night? Bring him away;
Mine's not an idle cause. The Duke himself,
Or any of my brothers of the state,
Cannot but feel this wrong as 'twere their
own;
For if such actions may have passage free,
Bond-slaves and pagans shall our statesmen
be. *Rhymed couplet ends* *Act or scene.*   (*Exeunt.*)

ACT I.3   *A councilchamber.*

(*The* DUKE *and* SENATORS *sit at a table with
lights;* OFFICERS *and* ATTENDANTS.)

DUKE.   There is no composition in
these news
That gives them credit.

FIRST SENATOR.   Indeed, they are
disproportioned;
My letters say a hundred and seven galleys.

DUKE.   And mine, a hundred forty.

SECOND SENATOR.   And mine,
two hundred!
But though they jump not on a just
account,—
As in these cases, where the aim reports,
'Tis oft with difference—yet do they all
confirm
A Turkish fleet, and bearing up to Cyprus.

DUKE.   Nay, it is possible enough to
judgment.
I do not so secure me in the error   10
But the main article I do approve
In fearful sense.

SAILOR.   (*Within.*) What, ho! what, ho!
what, ho!

(*Enter a* SAILOR.)

OFFICER.   A messenger from the galleys.

DUKE.   Now, what's the bisiness?

SAILOR.   The Turkish preparation makes
for Rhodes;
So was I bid report here to the state
By Signior Angelo.

DUKE.   How say you by this change?

FIRST SENATOR.   This cannot be,
By no assay of reason. 'Tis a pageant,
To keep us in false gaze. When we consider
Th' importancy of Cyprus to the Turk,   20
And let ourselves again but understand
That, as it more concerns the Turk than
Rhodes,
So may he with more facile question bear it,
For that it stands not in such warlike brace,
But altogether lacks th' abilities
That Rhodes is dress'd in; if we make
thought of this,
We must not think the Turk is so unskilful
To leave that latest which concerns him first,
Neglecting an attempt of ease and gain
To wake and wage a danger profitless.   30

DUKE.   Nay, in all confidence, he's not
for Rhodes.

OFFICER.   Here is more news.

(*Enter a* MESSENGER.)

MESSENGER.   The Ottomites, reverend
and gracious,
Steering with due course toward the isle
of Rhodes,
Have there injointed them with an after
fleet.

FIRST SENATOR.   Ay, so I thought. How
many, as you guess?

MESSENGER.   Of thirty sail; and now
they do restem
Their backward course, bearing with
frank appearance
Their purposes toward Cyprus. Signior
Montano,
Your trusty and most valiant servitor,   40
With his free duty recommends you thus,
And prays you to believe him

DUKE.   'Tis certain, then, for Cyprus.
Marcus Lucchese, is not he in town?

FIRST SENATOR.   He's now in Florence.

DUKE.   Write from us to him; post-
post-haste dispatch.

---

95 *idle:* trivial   98 *passage free:* free allowance
ACT I.3   1 *composition:* consistency   5 *jump:* agree   6
aim: guesswork   10 *secure me in:* free me from anxiety because of
11 *main article:* general statement   11 *approve:* believe   12
fearful: to be feared

18 *no assay:* any test   18 *pageant:* a feint   19 *in false gaze:* looking in the wrong direction   23 *question:* contest   23 *bear:*
capture   24 *brace:* posture of defence   30 *wage:* risk   35
injointed: joined   35 *after:* second   37 *restem:* steer again
41 *free duty:* due respect

FIRST SENATOR.   Here comes Brabantio and the valiant Moor.

(*Enter* BRABANTIO, OTHELLO, CASSIO, IAGO, RODERIGO, *and* OFFICERS.)

DUKE.   Valiant Othello, we must straight employ you
Against the general enemy Ottoman.
(*To* BRABANTIO.)   I did not see you; welcome, gentle signior;   50
We lack'd your counsel and your help to-night.
BRABANTIO.   So did I yours. Good your Grace, pardon me;
Neither my place nor aught I heard of business
Hath rais'd me from my bed, nor doth the general care
Take hold on me; for my particular grief
Is of so flood-gate and o'erbearing nature
That it engluts and swallows other sorrows
And it is still itself.
DUKE.   Why, what's the matter?
BRABANTIO.   My daughter! O, my daughter!
SENATOR.   Dead?
BRABANTIO.   Ay, to me;
She is abus'd, stol'n from me, and corrupted   60
By spells and medicines bought of mountebanks;
For nature so preposterously to err,
Being not deficient, blind, or lame of sense,
Sans witchcraft could not.
DUKE.   Whoe'er he be that in this foul proceeding

SAYS BRAB. can do whAt he wants to who DiD it

Hath thus beguil'd your daughter of herself
And you of her, the bloody book of law
You shall yourself read in the bitter letter
After your own sense, yea, though our proper son
Stood in your action.
BRABANTIO.   Humbly I thank your Grace.   70
Here is the man,—this Moor, whom now, it seems,
Your special mandate for the state affairs
Hath hither brought.

ALL.   We are very sorry for 't.
DUKE.   (*To* OTHELLO.) What, in your own part, can you say to this?
BRABANTIO.   Nothing, but this is so.
OTHELLO.   Most potent, grave, and reverend signiors,
My very noble and approv'd good masters,
That I have ta'en away this old man's daughter,
It is most true; true, I have married her:
The very head and front of my offending   80
Hath this extent, no more. Rude am I in my speech,
And little bless'd with the soft phrase of peace;
For since these arms of mine had seven years' pith *taken from me at ag of 7*
Till now, some nine moons wasted, they have us'd *doesn't know much of women.*
Their dearest action in the tented field;
And little of this great world can I speak
More than pertains to feats of broils and battle;
And therefore little shall I grace my cause
In speaking for myself. Yet, by your gracious patience,
I will a round unvarnish'd tale deliver   90
Of my whole course of love—what drugs, what charms,
What conjuration, and what mighty magic,
(For such proceeding I am charg'd withal)
I won his daughter.
BRABANTIO.   A maiden never bold;
Of spirit so still and quiet, that her motion
Blush'd at herself; and she, in spite of nature,
Of years, of country, credit, everything,
To fall in love with what she fear'd to look on!
It is a judgment maim'd and most imperfect
That will confess perfection so could err   100
Against all rules of nature, and must be driven
To find out practices of cunning hell,
Why this should be. I therefore vouch again

---

55 *particular:* personal   57 *engluts:* swallows   61 *mountebanks:* quack docters   64 *Sans:* without   69 *proper:* own

77 *approv'd:* tested   80 *front:* forehead   81 *Rude:* unpolished   83 *pith:* marrow, i.e., strength   84 *moons wasted:* months gone by   85 *dearest:* most intense   88 *grace:* make attractive   90 *round:* direct   93 *withal:* with   95 *her motion ... herself:* the slightest cause made her blush   97 *credit:* reputation   102 *practices:* evil devices

That with some mixtures powerful o'er the
  blood,
Or with some dram conjur'd to this effect,
He wrought upon her.
   DUKE.   To vouch this is no proof,
Without more wider and more overt test
Than these thin habits and poor likelihoods
Of modern seeming do prefer against him.
   FIRST SENATOR.   But, Othello, speak.   110
Did you by indirect and forced courses
Subdue and poison this young maid's
  affections?
Or came it by request and such fair
  question
As soul to soul affordeth?
   OTHELLO.   I do beseech you,
Send for the lady to the Sagittary,
And let her speak of me before her father.
If you do find me foul in her report,
The trust, the office I do hold of you,
Not only take away, but let your sentence
Even fall upon my life.
   DUKE.   Fetch Desdemona hither.   120

   (*Exeunt two or three.*)

   OTHELLO.   Ancient, conduct them; you
     best know the place.   (*Exit* IAGO.)
And, till she come, as truly as to heaven
I do confess the vices of my blood,
So justly to your grave ears I'll present
How I did thrive in this fair lady's love,
And she in mine.
   DUKE.   Say it, Othello.
   OTHELLO.   Her father lov'd me, oft
     invited me;
Still question'd me the story of my life
From year to year, the battles, sieges,
  fortunes,   130
That I have pass'd.
I ran it through, even from my boyish days,
To th' very moment that he bade me tell it.
Wherein I spoke of most disastrous chances,
Of moving accidents by flood and field,
Of hair-breadth scapes i' th' imminent
  deadly breach,
Of being taken by the insolent foe
And sold to slavery, of my redemption
  thence,

And portance in my travel's history;
Wherein of antres vast and deserts idle,   140
Rough quarries, rocks, and hills whose
  heads touch heaven,
It was my hint to speak,—such was my
  process,—
And of the Cannibals that each other eat,
The Anthropophagi, and men whose heads
Do grow beneath their shoulders. This to
  hear
Would Desdemona seriously incline;
But still the house-affairs would draw her
  thence,
Which ever as she could with haste
  dispatch,
She'd come again, and with a greedy ear
Devour up my discourse. Which I
  observing,   150
Took once a pliant hour, and found good
  means
To draw from her a prayer of earnest heart
That I would all my pilgrimage dilate,
Whereof by parcels she had something
  heard,
But not intentively. I did consent,
And often did beguile her of her tears
When I did speak of some distressful
  stroke
That my youth suffer'd. My story being
  done,
She gave me for my pains a world of sighs.
She swore, in faith, 'twas strange, 'twas
  passing strange,   160
'Twas pitiful, 'twas wondrous pitiful.
She wish'd she had not heard it; yet she
  wish'd
That Heaven had made her such a man.
  She thank'd me,
And bade me, if I had a friend that lov'd
  her,
I should but teach him how to tell my
  story,
And that would woo her. Upon this hint
  I spake.
She lov'd me for the dangers I had pass'd,
And I lov'd her that she did pity them.
This only is the witchcraft I have us'd.

---

105 *conjur'd:* compounded with magic   108 *habits:* clothes, i.e.,
evidence   108 *poor:* unconvincing   109 *modern seeming:* slight
suspicion   111 *forced:* unnatural   113 *question:* speech   129
Still: continually   135 *accidents:* adventures   135 *flood:* sea

139 *portance:* my conduct   140 *antres:* caves   140 *idle:* uninhab-
ited   142 *hint:* occasion   142 *process:* narrative   144 *Anthropophagi:* man-eaters   151 *pliant:* suitable   153 *pilgrimage:*
wanderings (also, the Christian concept of man's life as a pilgrimage)
155 *intentively:* without distractions   160 *passing:* surpassingly
166 *hint:* opportunity (not, direct suggestion)

Poetry is used for elevated Characters & important speeches

Here comes the lady; let her witness it.   170

(*Enter* DESDEMONA, IAGO, *and* ATTENDANTS.)

DUKE.   I think this tale would win my
    daughter too.
Good Brabantio,
Take up this mangled matter at the best;
Men do their broken weapons rather use
Than their bare hands.
    BRABANTIO.   I pray you, hear
        her speak.
If she confess that she was half the wooer,
Destruction on my head, if my bad blame
Light on the man! Come hither, gentle
    mistress.
Do you perceive in all this noble company
Where most you owe obedience?
    DESDEMONA.   My noble father,   180
I do perceive here a divided duty.
To you I am bound for life and education;
My life and education both do learn me
How to respect you; you are lord of all my
    duty;
I am hitherto your daugher. But here's my
    husband;
And so much duty as my mother show'd
To you, preferring you before her father,
So much I challenge that I may profess
Due to the Moor, my lord.
    BRABANTIO.   God be with
        you! I have done.
Please it your Grace, on to the state-affairs.   190
I had rather to adopt a child than get it.
Come hither, Moor.
I here do give thee that with all my heart
Which, but thou hast already, with all my
    heart
I would keep from thee. For your sake,
    jewel,
I am glad at soul I have no other child;
For thy escape would teach me tyranny,
To hang clogs on them. I have done, my
    lord.
    DUKE.   Let me speak like yourself, and
        lay a sentence,
Which, as a grise or step, may help these
    lovers   200

Noble, strong willed self-possessed

Into your favour.
When remedies are past, the griefs are
    ended
By seeing the worst, which late on hopes
    depended.
To mourn a mischief that is past and gone
Is the next way to draw new mischief on.
What cannot be preserv'd when Fortune
    takes,
Patience her injury a mockery makes.
The robb'd that smiles steals something
    from the thief;
He robs himself that spends a bootless
    grief.
    BRABANTIO.   So let the Turk of Cyprus
        us beguile;   210
We lose it not, so long as we can smile.
He bears the sentence well that nothing
    bears
But the free comfort which from thence
    he hears,
But he bears both the sentence and the
    sorrow
That, to pay grief, must of poor patience
    borrow.
These sentences, to sugar, or to gall,
Being strong on both sides, are equivocal.
But words are words; I never yet did hear
That the bruis'd heart was pierced through
    the ear.
I humbly beseech you, proceed to th'
    affairs of state.   220
    DUKE.   The Turk with a most mighty
        preparation makes for Cyprus. Othello,
        the fortitude of the place is best known
        to you; and though we have there a
        substitute of most allowed sufficiency,
        yet opinion, a sovereign mistress of ef-
        fects, throws a more safer voice on you.
        You must therefore be content to slub-
        ber the gloss of your new fortunes with
        this more stubborn and boisterous ex-
        pedition.
    OTHELLO.   The tyrant custom, most
        grave senators,   230
Hath made the flinty and steel couch of war
My thrice-driven bed of down. I do agnize

---

173 *mangled:* confused   173 *at the best:* and make the best of it
183 *learn:* teach   187 *preferring . . . before:* placing you ahead of
188 *challenge:* claim the right   191 *get:* beget   198 *clogs:* weights
199 *like yourself:* as you ought   199 *sentence:* philosophical maxim
200 *grise:* step

203 *depended:* were supported   205 *next:* nearest   209 *bootless:*
unavailing   217 *equivocal:* ambiguous   219 *pierced:* reached
223 *substitute:* deputy commander (Montano)   224 *sufficiency:*
ability   224 *opinion:* public opinion   224 *effects:* results   225
more safer voice: vote of greater confidence   226 *slubber:* tarnish
232 *driven:* sifted   232 *agnize:* acknowledge

A natural and prompt alacrity
I find in hardness, and do undertake
These present wars against the Ottomites.
Most humbly therefore bending to your
    state,
I crave fit disposition for my wife,
Due reference of place and exhibition,
With such accommodation and besort
As levels with her breeding.
    DUKE.   If you please,   240
Be 't at her father's.
    BRABANTIO.   I'll not have it so.
    OTHELLO.   Nor I.
    DESDEMONA.   Nor I; I would not
    there reside,
To put my father in impatient thoughts
By being in his eye. Most gracious duke,
To my unfolding lend your prosperous ear;
And let me find a charter in your voice,
T' assist my simpleness.
    DUKE.   What would you, Desdemona?
    DESDEMONA.   That I did love the Moor
    to live with him,
My downright violence and storm of
    fortunes   250
May trumpet to the world. My heart's
    subdued
Even to the very quality of my lord:
I saw Othello's visage in his mind,
And to his honors and his valiant parts
Did I my soul and fortunes consecrate.
So that, dear lords, if I be left behind,
A moth of peace, and he go to the war,
The rites for why I love him are bereft me,
And I a heavy interim shall support
By his dear absence. Let me go with him.   260
    OTHELLO.   Let her have your voice.
Vouch for me, Heaven, I therefore beg it
    not
To please the palate of my appetite,
Nor to comply with heat the young
    affects—
In me defunct—and proper satisfaction;
But to be free and bounteous to her mind.
And Heaven defend your good souls, that
    you think

I will your serious and great business scant
When she is with me. No, when light-wing'd
    toys
Of feather'd Cupid seel with wanton   270
    dullness
My speculative and offic'd instruments
That my disports corrupt and taint my
    business,
Let housewives make a skillet of my helm,
And all indign and base adversities
Make head against my estimation!
    DUKE.   Be it as you shall privately
    determine,
Either for her stay or going. Th' affair
    cries haste,
And speed must answer it.
    FIRST SENATOR.   You must away
    to-night.
    DESDEMONA.   To-night, my lord!
    DUKE.   This night.
    OTHELLO.   With all my heart.
    DUKE.   At nine i' th' morning here   280
    we'll meet again.
Othello, leave some officer behind,
And he shall our commission bring to you,
And such things else of quality and respect
As doth import you.
    OTHELLO.   So please your Grace,
    my ancient;
A man he is of honesty and trust.
To his conveyance I assign my wife,
With what else needful your good Grace
    shall think
To be sent after me.
    DUKE.   Let it be so.
Good-night to every one. (*To* BRABANTIO.)
    And noble signior,   290
If virtue no delighted beauty lack,
Your son-in-law is far more fair than
    black.
    FIRST SENATOR.   Adieu, brave Moor;
    use Desdemona well.
    BRABANTIO.   Look to her, Moor, if
    thou hast eyes to see;
She has deceiv'd her father, and may thee.   *Iago's tool*

(*Exeunt* DUKE, BRABANTIO, SENATORS, OF-
FICERS, *etc.*)

---

233 *prompt alacrity:* spontaneous stimulus   234 *hardness:* hardship
238 *exhibition:* allowance (of money)   239 *besort:* attendants
239 *levels with:* suits   245 *unfolding:* plan   245 *prosperous:*
favorable   246 *charter:* permission   250 *storm of fortunes:*
taking my future in my own hands   252 *quality:* profession   257
moth: parasite   259 *heavy interim:* sad interval   264 *young
affects:* youthful passions   265 *defunct:* mortified   265 *proper:*
my own   267 *defend:* forbid

269 *toys:* trifles   270 *seel:* close up   271 *speculative . . . instruments:* power of sight and action   273 *indign:* unworthy   274
make head against: attack   286 *conveyance:* escort

OTHELLO. <u>My life upon her faith</u>! *Irony*
Honest Iago,
My Desdemona must I leave to thee.
I prithee, let thy wife attend on her;
And bring them after in the best advantage.
Come, Desdemona; I have but an hour
Of love, of worldly matters and direction,   300
To spend with thee. We must obey the
time.

(*Exeunt* OTHELLO *and* DESDEMONA.)

RODERIGO.   Iago,—
IAGO.   What say'st thou, noble heart?
RODERIGO.   What will I do, think'st
thou?
IAGO.   Why, go to bed, and sleep.
RODERIGO.   I will incontinently drown
myself.
IAGO.   If thou dost, I shall never love
thee after. Why, thou silly gentleman!
RODERIGO.   It is silliness to live when to
live is torment; and then have we a
prescription to die when Death is our   310
physician.
IAGO.   O villainous! I have looked upon
the world for four times seven years;
and since I could distinguish betwixt a
benefit and an injury, I never found man
that knew how to love himself. Ere I
would say I would drown myself for
the love of a guinea-hen, I would change
my humanity with a baboon.
RODERIGO.   What should I do? I confess
it is my shame to be so fond, but it is   320
not in my virtue to amend it.
IAGO.   Virtue! a fig! 'tis in ourselves that
we are thus or thus. Our bodies are our
gardens, to the which our wills are
gardeners; so that if we will plant net-
tles, or sow lettuce, set hyssop and weed
up thyme, supply it with one gender of
herbs, or distract it with many, either
to have it sterile with idleness, or ma-
nured with industry, why, the power
and corrigible authority of this lies in   330
our wills. If the balance of our lives had
not one scale of reason to poise another
of sensuality, the blood and baseness

of our natures would conduct us to
most preposterous conclusions. But we
have reason to cool our raging motions,
our carnal stings, our unbitted lusts,
whereof I take this that you call love to
be a sect or scion.
RODERIGO.   It cannot be.
IAGO.   It is merely a lust of the blood and
a permission of the will. Come, be a
man. Drown thyself? drown cats and   340
blind puppies. I have professed me thy
friend, and I confess me knit to thy
deserving with cables of perdurable
toughness; I could never better stead
thee than now. Put money in thy purse;
follow thou the wars; defeat thy favor
with an usurped beard. I say, put money
in thy purse. It cannot be long that
Desdemona should continue her love
to the Moor,—put money in thy purse,
—nor he his to her. It was a violent
commencement in her, and thou shalt   350
see an answerable sequestration: put
but money in thy purse. These Moors
are changeable in their wills;—fill thy
purse with money;—the food that to
him now is as luscious as locusts, shall
be to him shortly as bitter as colo-
quintida. She must change for youth;
when she is sated with his body, she
will find the error of her choice—she
must have change, she must—therefore
put money in thy purse. If thou wilt   360
needs damn thyself, do it a more delicate way than drowning. Make all the
money thou canst. If sanctimony and
a frail vow betwixt an erring barbarian
and a super-subtle Venetian be not too
hard for my wits and all the tribe of
hell, thou shalt enjoy her; therefore
make money. A pox of drowning thyself! it is clean out of the way. Seek
thou rather to be hanged in compassing
thy joy than to be drowned and go without her.
RODERIGO.   Wilt thou be fast to my

*Iago
projects
his own
qualities
on others*

---

hopes, if I depend on the issue?

IAGO.   Thou art sure of me—go, make money—I have told thee often, and I re-tell thee again and again, I hate the Moor. My cause is hearted; thine hath no less reason. Let us be conjunctive in our revenge against him. If thou canst cuckold him, thou dost thyself a pleasure, me a sport. There are many events in the womb of time which will be delivered. Traverse! go, provide thy money. We will have more of this tomorrow. Adieu.

RODERIGO.   Where shall we meet i' th' morning?

IAGO.   At my lodging.

RODERIGO.   I'll be with thee betimes.

IAGO.   Go to; farewell. Do you hear, Roderigo?

RODERIGO.   What say you?

IAGO.   No more of drowning, do you hear?

RODERIGO.   I am chang'd; I'll go sell all my land.

(*Exit.*)

IAGO.   Thus do I ever make my fool my purse;
For I mine own gain'd knowledge should profane
If I would time expend with such a snipe
But for my sport and profit. I hate the Moor;
And it is thought abroad that 'twixt my sheets
He has done my office. I know not if 't be true;
But I, for mere suspicion in that kind,
Will do as if for surety. He holds me well;
The better shall my purpose work on him.
Cassio's a proper man. Let me see now:
To get his place and to plume up my will
In double knavery—How, how?—Let's see:—
After some time, to abuse Othello's ear
That he is too familiar with his wife.
He hath a person and a smooth dispose
To be suspected, fram'd to make women false.

The Moor is of a free and open nature
That thinks men honest that but seem to be so,
And will as tenderly be led by th' nose
As asses are.
I have't. It is engender'd. Hell and night
Must bring this monstrous birth to the world's light.

(*Exit.*)

ACT II.1   *A sea-port in Cyprus. An open place.*

(*Enter* MONTANO *and two* GENTLEMEN.)

MONTANO.   What from the cape can you discern at sea?

FIRST GENTLEMAN.   Nothing at all; it is a high-wrought flood.
I cannot, 'twixt the heaven and the main,
Descry a sail.

MONTANO.   Methinks the wind hath spoke aloud at land;
A fuller blast ne'er shook our battlements,
If it hath ruffian'd so upon the sea,
What ribs of oak, when mountains melt on them,
Can hold the mortise? What shall we hear of this?

SECOND GENTLEMAN.   A segregation of the Turkish fleet.
For do but stand upon the foaming shore,
The chidden billow seems to pelt the clouds;
The wind-shak'd surge, with high and monstrous mane,
Seems to cast water on the burning Bear
And quench the Guards of th' ever-fixed pole.
I never did like molestation view
On the enchafed flood.

MONTANO.   If that the Turkish fleet
Be not enshelter'd and embay'd, they are drown'd;
It is impossible to bear it out.

(*Enter a third* GENTLEMAN.)

THIRD GENTLEMAN.   News, lads! our wars are done.

---

374 *hearted:* heartfelt   375 *conjunctive:* united   378 *Traverse:* forward march!   383 *betimes:* early   391 *snipe:* silly fellow   393 *thought abroad:* rumored   396 *for surety:* it were a proved fact   399 *plume up;* gratify   403 *smooth dispose:* easy way

407 *tenderly:* easily   409 *engender'd:* conceived
ACT II.1   9 *hold the mortise:* remain joined together   10 *segregation:* dispersal   14 *Bear:* Ursa Major, a constellation   15 *Guards:* stars in Ursa Major   17 *enchafed:* enraged   19 *bear it out:* weather the storm

The desperate tempest hath so bang'd the
    Turks,
That their designment halts. A noble ship
    of Venice
Hath seen a grievous wreck and sufferance
On most part of their fleet.
    MONTANO.   How? is this true?
    THIRD GENTLEMAN.   The ship
        is here put in,
A Veronesa. Michael Cassio,
Lieutenant to the warlike Moor Othello,
Is come on shore; the Moor himself at sea,
And is in full commission here for Cyprus.
    MONTANO.   I am glad on't; 'tis a worthy
        governor.   30
    THIRD GENTLEMAN.   But this same
        Cassio, though he speak of comfort
Touching the Turkish loss, yet he looks
    sadly,
And prays the Moor be safe; for they
    were parted
With foul and violent tempest.
    MONTANO.   Pray heavens he be;
For I have serv'd him, and the man com-
    mands
Like a full soldier. Let's to the seaside, ho!
As well to see the vessel that's come in
As to throw out our eyes for brave Othello,
Even till we make the main and th' aerial
    blue
An indistinct regard.
    THIRD GENTLEMAN.   Come, let's do so;   40
For every minute is expectancy
Of more arrivance.

(*Enter* CASSIO.)

    CASSIO.   Thanks, you the valiant of this
        warlike isle,
That so approve the Moor! O, let the
    heavens
Give him defense against the elements,
For I have lost him on a dangerous sea.
    MONTANO.   Is he well shipp'd?
    CASSIO.   His bark is stoutly timber'd,
        and his pilot
Of every expert and approv'd allowance;
Therefore my hopes, not surfeited to
    death,   50

Handwritten note at top: Can't have a war + a domestic tragedy at the same time.

Stand in bold cure.
                Within, "A sail, a sail, a sail!"

(*Enter a* MESSENGER.)

    CASSIO.   What noise?
    MESSENGER.   The town is empty; on
        the brow o' th' sea
Stand ranks of people, and they cry,
    "A sail!"
    CASSIO.   My hopes do shape him for
        the governor.

                                       (*A shot.*)

    SECOND GENTLEMAN.   They do dis-
        charge their shot of courtesy:
Our friends at least.
    CASSIO.   I pray you, sir, go forth,
And give us truth who 'tis that is arriv'd.
    SECOND GENTLEMAN.   I shall.   (*Exit.*)
    MONTANO.   But, good lieutenant, is
        your general wiv'd?   60
    CASSIO.   Most fortunately: he hath
        achiev'd a maid
That paragons description and wild fame;
One that excels the quirks of blazoning
    pens,
And in th' essential vesture of creation
Does tire the ingener.

(*Re-enter second* GENTLEMAN.)

                How now? who has put in?
    SECOND GENTLEMAN.   'Tis one Iago,
        ancient to the general.
    CASSIO.   Has had most favorable and
        happy speed.
Tempests themselves, high seas, and
    howling winds,
The gutter'd rocks and congregated sands,
Traitors ensteep'd to clog the guiltless keel,   70
As having sense of beauty do omit
Their mortal natures, letting go safely by
The divine Desdemona.
    MONTANO.   What is she?
    CASSIO.   She that I spake of, our great
        captain's captain,
Left in the conduct of the bold Iago,
Whose footing here anticipates our thoughts

---

22 *designment halts:* plan is checked   23 *sufferance:* disaster   29
in . . . commission: with full powers   36 *full:* perfect   38 *Even
till . . . regard:* until we can no longer distinguish between the blue of
the water and the blue of the sky   42 *arrivance:* arrivals   49
approv'd allowance: tested skill   50 *surfeited:* sickened

51 *bold:* confident expectation of   62 *paragons:* surpasses   63
quirks: elegant phrases   64 *essential . . . of creation:* her absolute
perfection   65 *ingener:* inventor, i.e., artist that could paint her as
she truly is   70 *ensteep'd:* submerged   71 *omit:* surrender tem-
porarily   72 *mortal:* deadly   76 *footing:* landing

A se'nnight's speed. Great Jove, Othello
    guard,
And swell his sail with thine own powerful
    breath,
That he may bless this bay with his tall
    ship,
Make love's quick pants in Desdemona's
    arms,   80
Give renew'd fire to our extincted spirits,
And bring all Cyprus comfort!

(*Enter* DESDEMONA, EMILIA, IAGO, RODERIGO,
and ATTENDANTS.)

                        O, behold,
The riches of the ship is come on shore!
You men of Cyprus, let her have your
    knees.
Hail to thee, lady! and the grace of heaven,
Before, behind thee, and on every hand,
Enwheel thee round!
    DESDEMONA.   I thank you, valiant
    Cassio.
What tidings can you tell me of my lord?
    CASSIO.   He is not yet arriv'd; nor know
    I aught
But that he's well and will be shortly here.   90
    DESDEMONA.   O, but I fear—How lost
    you company?
    CASSIO.   The great contention of the
    sea and skies
Parted our fellowship.—But, hark! a sail.
    (*Within*, "A sail, a sail!" *Guns heard.*)
    SECOND GENTLEMAN.   They give their
    greeting to the citadel:
This likewise is a friend.
    CASSIO.   See for the news.

                (*Exit* GENTLEMAN.)

Good ancient, you are welcome. (*To*
    EMILIA.) Welcome, mistress.
Let it not gall your patience, good Iago,
That I extend my manners; 'tis my breeding
That gives me this bold show of courtesy.   100
                        (*Kissing her.*)
    IAGO.   Sir, would she give you so much
    of her lips
As of her tongue she oft bestows on me,
You'd have enough.
    DESDEMONA.   Alas, she has no speech.

    IAGO.   In faith, too much;
I find it still, when I have list to sleep.
Marry, before your ladyship, I grant,
She puts her tongue a little in her heart,
And chides with thinking.
    EMILIA.   You have little cause to say so.
    IAGO.   Come on, come on; you are
    pictures out of doors,   110
Bells in your parlors, wild-cats in your
    kitchens,
Saints in your injuries, devils being
    offended,
Players in your housewifery, and
    housewives in your beds.
    DESDEMONA.   O, fie upon thee,
    slanderer!
    IAGO.   Nay, it is true, or else I am
    a Turk.
You rise to play and go to bed to work.
    EMILIA.   You shall not write my praise.
    IAGO.   No, let me not.
    DESDEMONA.   What wouldst thou write
    of me, if thou shouldst praise me?
    IAGO.   O gentle lady, do not put me
    to 't;
For I am nothing, if not critical.   120
    DESDEMONA.   Come on, assay.—There's
    one gone to the harbor?
    IAGO.   Ay, madam.
    DESDEMONA.   I am not merry; but I do
    beguile
The thing I am, by seeming otherwise.—
Come, how wouldst thou praise me?
    IAGO.   I am about it; but indeed my
    invention
Comes from my pate as birdlime does
    from frieze;
It plucks out brains and all. But my Muse
    labors,
And thus she is deliver'd:
        If she be fair and wise, fairness and   130
        wit,
        The one's for use, the other useth it.
    DESDEMONA.   Well prais'd! How if she
    be black and witty?
    IAGO.   If she be black, and thereto have a
    wit,
        She'll find a white that shall her
        blackness fit.

---

77 *se'nnight's:* week's   81 *extincted:* extinguished   87 *Enwheel:*
encompass   99 *extend:* show

106 *list:* desire   111 *Bells:* sweet-voiced   113 *housewives:* hussies
120 *critical:* censorious   126 *frieze:* cloth with a nap   135 *white:*
with a pun on wight, man

DESDEMONA.   Worse and worse.

EMILIA.   How if fair and foolish?

IAGO.   She never yet was foolish that was
    fair;
    For even her folly help'd her to an
    heir.

DESDEMONA.   These are old fond paradoxes to make fools laugh i' th' ale-   140
house. What miserable praise hast thou
for her that's foul and foolish?

IAGO.   There's none so foul and foolish
    thereunto,
    But does foul pranks which fair
    and wise ones do.

DESDEMONA.   O heavy ignorance! thou
praisest the worst best. But what praise
couldst thou bestow on a deserving
woman indeed, one that, in the authority of her merit, did justly put on the
vouch of very malice itself?

IAGO.   She that was ever fair and never
    proud,
    Had tongue at will and yet was
    never loud,   150
    Never lack'd gold and yet went
    never gay,
    Fled from her wish and yet said,
    "Now I may";
    She that being anger'd, her revenge
    being nigh,
    Bade her wrong stay and her dis-
    pleasure fly;
    She that in wisdom never was so
    frail
    To change the cod's head for the
    salmon's tail;
    She that could think and ne'er
    disclose her mind
    See suitors following and not look
    behind,
    She was a wight, if ever such
    wights were,—

DESDEMONA.   To do what?   160

IAGO.   To suckle fools and chronicle
small beer.

DESDEMONA.   O most lame and impotent
conclusion! Do not learn of him, Emilia,

though he be thy husband. How say you,
Cassio? Is he not a most profane and
liberal counsellor?

CASSIO.   He speaks home, madam. You
may relish him more in the soldier than
in the scholar.

IAGO.   (Aside.) He takes her by the palm;
ay, well said, whisper. With as little a
web as this will I ensnare as great a fly   170
as Cassio. Ay, smile upon her, do; I
will gyve thee in thine own courtship.—
You say true; 'tis so, indeed.—If such
tricks as these strip you out of your
lieutenantry, it had been better you had
not kissed your three fingers so oft,
which now again you are most apt to
play the sir in. Very good; well kissed!
an excellent curtsy! 'Tis so, indeed. Yet
again your fingers to your lips? Would
they were clyster-pipes for your sake!
(Trumpet within.)—The Moor! I know
his trumpet.   180

CASSIO.   'Tis truly so.

DESDEMONA.   Let's meet him and receive
him.

CASSIO.   Lo, where he comes!

(Enter OTHELLO and ATTENDANTS.)

OTHELLO.   O my fair warrior!

DESDEMONA.   My dear Othello!

OTHELLO.   It gives me wonder great as
    my content

To see you here before me. O my soul's
    joy!

If after every tempest come such calms,

May the winds blow till they have waken'd
    death!

And let the laboring bark climb hills of
    seas

Olympus-high, and duck again as low   190

As hell's from heaven! If it were now to
    die,

'Twere now to be most happy; for, I fear,

My soul hath her content so absolute

That not another comfort like to this

Succeeds in unknown fate.

DESDEMONA.   The heavens forbid

But that our loves and comforts should
    increase,

---

139 *folly:* foolishness and unchastity   140 *fond:* silly   141 *foul:*
ugly   149 *put on the vouch:* demand praise   153 *nigh:* readily
obtainable   156 *To change . . . tail:* to exchange the worthless part
of a cheap fish for the worthless part of an expensive one   161
chronicle small beer: keep household accounts

---

165 *liberal:* licentious   166 *home:* to the point   167 *relish:* like
172 *gyve:* handcuff   175 *kissed your three fingers:* a courtly gesture
178 *clyster:* enema   190 *Olympus:* mountain in Greece

Even as our days do grow!
  OTHELLO.   Amen to that, sweet
    powers!
I cannot speak enough of this content;
It stops me here; it is too much of joy.
And this, and this, the greatest discords be   200

                  (*They kiss.*)

That e'er our hearts shall make!
  IAGO.   (*Aside.*) O, you are well tun'd
    now!
But I'll set down the pegs that make this
    music,
As honest as I am.
  OTHELLO.   Come, let us to the castle.
News, friends; our wars are done, the
    Turks are drown'd.
How does my old acquaintance of this
    isle?
Honey, you shall be well desir'd in Cyprus;
I have found great love amongst them.
    O my sweet,
I prattle out of fashion, and I dote
In mine own comforts. I prithee, good Iago,
Go to the bay and disembark my coffers.   210
Bring thou the master to the citadel;
He is a good one, and his worthiness
Does challenge much respect. Come,
    Desdemona,
Once more, well met at Cyprus.

(*Exeunt* OTHELLO, DESDEMONA *and* ATTEN-
DANTS.)

  IAGO.   Do thou meet me presently at the
    harbor. Come hither. If thou be'st val-
    iant,—as, they say, base men being in
    love have then a nobility in their na-
    tures more than is native to them,—list
    me. The lieutenant tonight watches on
    the court of guard;—first, I must tell
    thee this: Desdemona is directly in love   220
    with him.
  RODERIGO.   With him? Why, 'tis not
    possible.
  IAGO.   Lay thy finger thus, and let thy
    soul be instructed. Mark me with what
    violence she first loved the Moor, but
    for bragging and telling her fantastical

lies. To love him still for prating,—let
not thy discreet heart think it. Her eye
must be fed; and what delight shall she
have to look on the devil? When the
blood is made dull with the act of sport,   230
there should be, again to inflame it, and
to give satiety a fresh appetite, loveliness in favor, sympathy in years, manners, and beauties; all which the Moor
is defective in. Now, for want of these
required conveniences, her delicate
tenderness will find itself abused, begin
to heave the gorge, disrelish and abhor
the Moor; very nature will instruct her
in it and compel her to some second
choice. Now, sir, this granted,—as it is
a most pregnant and unforced position
—who stands so eminent in the degree   240
of this fortune as Cassio does? a knave
very voluble; no further conscionable
than in putting on the mere form of
civil and humane seeming, for the better
compassing of his salt and most hidden
loose affection? Why, none; why, none;
a slipper and subtle knave, a finder of   *Projection*
occasion, that has an eye can stamp and
counterfeit advantages, though true
advantage never present itself; a devilish
knave. Besides, the knave is handsome,
young, and hath all those requisites in
him that folly and green minds look   250
after; a pestilent complete knave, and
the woman hath found him already.
  RODERIGO.   I cannot believe that in her;
    she's full of most blessed condition.
  IAGO.   Blessed fig's-end! The wine she
    drinks is made of grapes. If she had
    been blessed, she would never have
    loved the Moor. Blessed pudding!
    Didst thou not see her paddle with the
    palm of his hand? Didst not mark that?   260
  RODERIGO.   Yes, that I did; but that was
    but courtesy.
  IAGO.   Lechery, by this hand; an index
    and obscure prologue to the history of
    lust and foul thoughts. They met so near
    with their lips that their breaths em-

---

199 *here:* in the heart   203 *set down the pegs:* untune the strings of a musical instrument   209 *In:* on account of   211 *master:* ship's captain   215 *presently:* immediately   219 *court:* headquarters   222 *thus:* i.e. on the lips (be silent)

226 *still:* forever   229 *devil:* in popular art the devil was represented as black   232 *favor:* features   236 *heave the gorge:* retch   239 *pregnant:* obvious   242 *conscionable:* conscientious   244 *salt:* lustful   245 *slipper:* slippery   246 *stamp:* devise by craft   250 *green:* unsophisticated   254 *blessed condition:* heavenly qualities   262 *index:* forerunner

braced together. Villainous thoughts, Roderigo! When these mutualities so marshal the way, hard at hand comes the master and main exercise, th' incorporate conclusion. Pish! But, sir, be you ruled by me; I have brought you 270 from Venice. Watch you to-night; for the command, I'll lay 't upon you. Cassio knows you not. I'll not be far from you. Do you find some occasion to anger Cassio, either by speaking too loud, or tainting his discipline, or from what other course you please, which the time shall more favorably minister.

RODERIGO.   Well?

IAGO.   Sir, he's rash and very sudden in choler, and haply my strike at you. 280 Provoke him, that he may; for even out of that will I cause these of Cyprus to mutiny, whose qualification shall come into no true taste again but by the displanting of Cassio. So shall you have a shorter journey to your desires by the means I shall then have to prefer them; and the impediment most profitably removed, without the which there were no expectation of our prosperity.

RODERIGO.   I will do this, if you can bring it to any opportunity. 290

IAGO.   I warrant thee. Meet me by and by at the citadel; I must fetch his necessaries ashore. Farewell.

RODERIGO.   Adieu.   (*Exit.*)

IAGO.   That Cassio loves her, I do well believe 't;
That she loves him, 'tis apt and of great credit;
The Moor, howbeit that I endure him not,
Is of a constant, loving, noble nature,
And I dare think he'll prove to Desdemona
A most dear husband. Now, I do love her too; 300
Not out of absolute lust, though peradventure
I stand accountant for as great a sin,
But partly led to diet my revenge,
For that I do suspect the lusty Moor

Hath leap'd into my seat; the thought whereof
Doth, like a poisonous mineral, gnaw my inwards;
And nothing can or shall content my soul
Till I am even'd with him, wife for wife;
Or failing so, yet that I put the Moor
At least into a jealousy so strong 310
That judgment cannot cure. Which thing to do,
If this poor trash of Venice, whom I trash
For his quick hunting, stand the putting on,
I'll have our Michael Cassio on the hip,
Abuse him to the Moor in the rank garb—
For I fear Cassio with my night-cap too—
Make the Moor thank me, love me, and reward me,
For making him egregiously an ass
And practicing upon his peace and quiet
Even to madness. 'Tis here, but yet confus'd; 320
Knavery's plain face is never seen till us'd.
(*Exit.*)

ACT II.2 *A street.*

(*Enter* Othello's HERALD, *with a proclamation. People following.*)

HERALD.   It is Othello's pleasure, our noble and valiant general, that, upon certain tidings now arrived importing the mere perdition of the Turkish fleet, every man put himself into triumph; some to dance, some to make bonfires, each man to what sport and revels his addiction leads him; for, beside these beneficial news, it is the celebration of his nuptial. So much was his pleasure 10 should be proclaimed. All offices are open, and there is full liberty of feasting from this present hour of five till the bell have told eleven. Heaven bless the isle of Cyprus and our noble general Othello!   (*Exeunt.*)

ACT II.3 *A hall in the castle.*

(*Enter* OTHELLO, DESDEMONA, CASSIO, *and* ATTENDANTS.)

---

266 *mutualities:* reciprocal familiarities   269 *incorporate:* bodily   272 *the command:* your orders   278 *minister:* provide   280 *choler:* anger   280 *haply:* perhaps   283 *qualification:* appeasement   283 *come . . . taste:* not be attained   287 *prefer:* promote   296 *apt . . . credit:* probable and credible   303 *accountant:* accountable   304 *diet:* feed

311 *judgment:* reason   312 *trash For:* hold back from   315 *rank garb:* coarse fashion   318 *egregiously:* notably   319 *practising upon:* plotting against   320 *here:* i.e., in Iago's brain   ACT II. 2   4 *mere:* complete   11 *offices:* places to supply food and drink   14 *told:* counted

OTHELLO. Good Michael, look you to
  the guard to-night.
Let's teach ourselves that honorable stop,
Not to outsport discretion.
  CASSIO. Iago hath direction what to do;
But, notwithstanding, with my personal eye
Will I look to 't.
  OTHELLO. Iago is most honest.
Michael, good-night; to-morrow with your
  earliest
Let me have speech with you. (*To*
DESDEMONA.) Come, my dear love,
The purchase made, the fruits are to ensue;
That profit's yet to come 'tween me and
  you.   10
Good-night.

(*Exeunt* OTHELLO, DESDEMONA, *and* AT-
TENDANTS.)

(*Enter* IAGO.)

  CASSIO. Welcome, Iago; we must to the
  watch.
  IAGO. Not this hour, lieutenant; 'tis not
  yet ten o' th' clock. Our general cast us
  thus early for the love of his Desdemona; who let us not therefore
  blame: he hath not yet made wanton
  the night with her; and she is sport for
  Jove.
  CASSIO. She's a most exquisite lady.
  IAGO. And, I'll warrant her, full of game.
  CASSIO. Indeed, she's a most fresh and
  delicate creature.   20
  IAGO. What an eye she has! Methinks it
  sounds a parley to provocation.
  CASSIO. An inviting eye; and yet methinks right modest.
  IAGO. And when she speaks, is it not an
  alarum to love?
  CASSIO. She is indeed perfection.
  IAGO. Well, happiness to their sheets!
  Come, lieutenant, I have a stoup of
  wine; and here without are a brace of   30
  Cyprus gallants that would fain have a
  measure to the health of black Othello.
  CASSIO. Not to-night, good Iago. I have
  very poor and unhappy brains for

drinking; I could well wish courtesy
  would invent some other custom of
  entertainment.
  IAGO. O, they are our friends: but one
  cup; I'll drink for you.
  CASSIO. I have drunk but one cup to-
  night, and that was craftily qualified   40
  too, and, behold, what innovation it
  makes here. I am unfortunate in the infirmity, and dare not task my weakness
  with any more.
  IAGO. What, man! 'tis a night of revels.
  The gallants desire it.
  CASSIO. Where are they?
  IAGO. Here at the door; I pray you,
  call them in.
  CASSIO. I'll do 't; but it dislikes me.

(*Exit.*)

  IAGO. If I can fasten but one cup upon   50
  him,
With that which he hath drunk to-night
  already,
He'll be as full of quarrel and offense
As my young mistress' dog. Now, my sick
  fool Roderigo,
Whom love hath turn'd almost the wrong
  side out,
To Desdemona hath to-night carous'd
Potations pottle-deep; and he's to watch.
Three lads of Cyprus, noble swelling
  spirits
That hold their honors in a wary distance,
The very elements of this warlike isle,
Have I to-night fluster'd with flowing cups, 60
And they watch too. Now, 'mongst this
  flock of drunkards
Am I to put our Cassio in some action
That may offend the isle. But here they
  come.

(*Re-enter* CASSIO, *with him* MONTANO *and*
GENTLEMEN. *Servants follow with wine.*)

If consequence do but approve my dream,
My boat sails freely, both with wind and
  stream.

ACT II. 3   3 *outsport discretion:* overdo revelry   13 *cast:*
dismissed   26 *alarum:* call to arms, summons   29 *stoup:* large
goblet   31 *fain:* gladly

40 *craftily qualified:* diluted on the sly   42 *here:* i.e., in his face
55 *carous'd:* drunk off   56 *pottle-deep:* bottoms-up   58 *in a wary
distance:* i.e., are supersensitive (about their personal honor)   64
consequence: what follows

CASSIO. 'Fore God, they have given me a rouse already.

MONTANO. Good faith, a little one; not past a pint, as I am a soldier.

IAGO. Some wine, ho! 70

Sings. And let me the canakin clink, clink;
And let me the canakin clink.
A soldier's a man;
O, man's life's but a span;
Why, then, let a soldier drink.
Some wine, boys!

CASSIO. 'Fore God, an excellent song.

IAGO. I learned it in England, where, indeed, they are most potent in potting; your Dane, your German, and your swagbellied Hollander—Drink, ho!— 80 are nothing to your English.

CASSIO. Is your Englishman so exquisite in his drinking?

IAGO. Why, he drinks you, with facility, your Dane dead drunk; he sweats not to overthrow your Almain; he gives your Hollander a vomit ere the next pottle can be filled.

CASSIO. To the health of our general!

MONTANO. I am for it, lieutenant; and I'll do you justice. 90

IAGO. O sweet England!

King Stephen was and-a worthy peer,
His breeches cost him but a crown;
He held them sixpence all too dear,
With that he call'd the tailor lown.

He was a wight of high renown,
And thou art but of low degree.
'Tis pride that pulls the country down;
And take thy auld cloak about thee.

Some wine, ho! 100

CASSIO. Why, this is a more exquisite song than the other.

IAGO. Will you hear 't again?

CASSIO. No; for I hold him to be unworthy of his place that does those things. Well, God's above all; and there be souls must be saved, and there be souls must not be saved.

IAGO. It's true, good lieutenant.

CASSIO. For mine own part,—no offense to the general, nor any man of quality— 110 I hope to be saved.

IAGO. And so do I too, lieutenant.

CASSIO. Ay, but, by your leave, not before me; the lieutenant is to be saved before the ancient. Let's have no more of this; let's to our affairs.—God forgive us our sins!—Gentlemen, let's look to our business. Do not think, gentlemen, I am drunk. This is my ancient; this is my right hand, and this is my left. I am not drunk now; I can stand well enough, and I speak well enough. 120

GENTLEMEN. Excellent well.

CASSIO. Why, very well then; you must not think then that I am drunk.

(*Exit.*)

MONTANO. To th' platform, masters. Come, let's set the watch.

IAGO. You see this fellow that is gone before:
He is a soldier fit to stand by Caesar
And give direction; and do but see his vice.
'Tis to his virtue a just equinox,
The one as long as the other; 'tis pity of 130 him.
I fear the trust Othello puts him in,
On some odd time of his infirmity,
Will shake this island.

MONTANO. But is he often thus?

IAGO. 'Tis evermore his prologue to his sleep.
He'll watch the horologe a double set,
If drink rock not his cradle.

MONTANO. It were well
The general were put in mind of it.
Perhaps he sees it not; or his good nature
Prizes the virtue that appears in Cassio,
And looks not on his evils. Is not this true? 140

(*Enter* RODERIGO.)

IAGO. (*Aside to him.*) How now, Roderigo!
I pray you, after the lieutenant; go.

(*Exit* RODERIGO.)

MONTANO. And 'tis great pity that the noble Moor

---

67 *rouse:* drink   71 *canakin:* small drinking pot   80 *swagbellied:* "beer-bellied"   84 *sweats not:* does not have to exert himself   85 *Almain:* German   95 *lown:* lout   98 *pride:* extravagant dress   99 *auld:* old

124 *platform:* paved court where the guard is mustered   129 *just equinox:* exact equivalent   132 *odd time:* time or other   135 *watch . . . double set:* stay awake twenty-four hours

Should hazard such a place as his own
 second
With one of an ingraft infirmity:
It were an honest action to say
So to the Moor.
    IAGO.   Not I, for this fair island.
I do love Cassio well; and would do much
To cure him of this evil.—But, hark! what
 noise?
               Cry within: "Help! help!"

(*Re-enter* CASSIO, *pursuing* RODERIGO.)

    CASSIO. 'Zounds, you rogue! you rascal!
    MONTANO.   What's the matter,
     lieutenant?   150
    CASSIO. A knave teach me my duty! I'll
    beat the knave into a twiggen bottle.
    RODERIGO. Beat me?
    CASSIO. Dost thou prate, rogue?
                (*Striking* RODERIGO.)
    MONTANO. Nay, good lieutenant; (*Stay-
   ing him.*) I pray you, sir, hold your hand.
    CASSIO. Let me go, sir,
Or I'll knock you o'er the mazzard.
    MONTANO. Come, come, you're drunk.
    CASSIO. Drunk!   (*They fight.*)
    IAGO. (*Aside to* RODERIGO.) Away, I say;
   go out, and cry a mutiny.

                (*Exit* RODERIGO.)

Nay, good lieutenant,—God's will,
 gentlemen:—
Help, ho!—Lieutenant,—sir,—Montano,—
 sir;—
Help, masters!—Here's a goodly watch   160
 indeed!

                (*A bell rings.*)

Who's that which rings the bell?—Diablo,
 ho!
The town will rise. God's will, lieutenant,
 hold!
You will be sham'd for ever.

(*Re-enter* OTHELLO *and* ATTENDANTS.)

    OTHELLO.   What is the matter here?
    MONTANO. 'Zounds, I bleed still; I am
   hurt to th' death. He dies!
    OTHELLO. Hold, for your lives!
    IAGO. Hold, ho! Lieutenant,—sir,—

   Montano,—gentlemen,—
Have you forgot all sense of place and duty?
Hold! the general speaks to you; hold, for
 shame!
    OTHELLO. Why, how now, ho! from
   whence ariseth this?
Are we turn'd Turks, and to ourselves do   170
 that
Which Heaven hath forbid the Ottomites?
For Christian shame, put by this barbarous
 brawl.
He that stirs next to carve for his own rage
Holds his soul light; he dies upon his
 motion.
Silence that dreadful bell; it frights the isle
From her propriety. What is the matter,
 masters?
Honest Iago, that looks dead with grieving,
Speak, who began this? On thy love, I
 charge thee.
    IAGO. I do not know: friends all but
   now, even now,
In quarter, and in terms like bride and
 groom   180
Divesting them for bed; and then, but
 now—
As if some planet had unwitted men—
Swords out, and tilting one at other's
 breast,
In opposition bloody. I cannot speak
Any beginning to this peevish odds;
And would in action glorious I had lost
Those legs that brought me to a part of it!
    OTHELLO. How comes it, Michael, you
   are thus forgot?
    CASSIO. I pray you, pardon me; I can-
   not speak.
    OTHELLO. Worthy Montano, you were
   wont to be civil;   190
The gravity and stillness of your youth
The world hath noted, and your name is
 great
In mouths of wisest censure. What's the
 matter,
That you unlace your reputation thus,
And spend your rich opinion for the name
Of a night-brawler? Give me answer to it.
    MONTANO. Worthy Othello, I am hurt
   to danger.

---

145 *ingraft:* firmly fixed   151 *twiggen:* wicker-covered   155
mazzard: head   161 *bell:* alarm bell   161 *Diablo:* the devil

173 *carve for:* indulge   176 *propriety:* natural behavior   180
quarter: amity   183 *unwitted men:* struck men with madness
185 *peevish odds:* childish quarrel   188 *forgot:* forgetful of yourself
193 *censure:* judgment   195 *spend:* lose

Your officer, Iago, can inform you—
While I spare speech, which something now
    offends me—
Of all that I do know; nor know I aught   200
By me that's said or done amiss this night,
Unless self-charity be sometimes a vice,
And to defend ourselves it be a sin
When violence assails us.
    OTHELLO.   Now, by heaven,
My blood begins my safer guides to rule;
And passion, having my best judgment
    collied,
Assays to lead the way. If I once stir
Or do but lift this arm, the best of you
Shall sink in my rebuke. Give me to know
How this foul rout began, who set it on;   210
And he that is approv'd in this offense,
Though he had twinn'd with me, both at
    a birth,
Shall lose me. What! in a town of war,
Yet wild, the people's hearts brimful of
    fear,
To manage private and domestic quarrel,
In night, and on the court and guard of
    safety!
'Tis monstrous. Iago, who began 't?
    MONTANO.   If partially affin'd, or
    leagued in office,
Thou dost deliver more or less than truth,
Thou art no soldier.
    IAGO.   Touch me not so near.   220
I had rather have this tongue cut from my
    mouth
Than it should do offense to Michael
    Cassio;
Yet, I persuade myself, to speak the truth
Shall nothing wrong him. Thus it is,
    general:
Montano and myself being in speech,
There comes a fellow crying out for help;
And Cassio following him with determin'd
    sword
To execute upon him. Sir, this gentleman
Steps in to Cassio and entreats his pause;
Myself the crying fellow did pursue,   230
Lest by his clamor—as it so fell out—
The town might fall in fright. He, swift of
    foot,
Outran my purpose; and I return'd the
    rather
For that I heard the clink and fall of
    swords,
And Cassio high in oath; which till to-night
I ne'er might say before. When I came
    back—
For this was brief—I found them close
    together,
At blow and thrust; even as again they
    were
When you yourself did part them.
More of this matter cannot I report.   240
But men are men; the best sometimes
    forget.
Though Cassio did some little wrong to
    him,
As men in rage strike those that wish them
    best,
Yet surely Cassio, I believe, receiv'd
From him that fled some strange indignity
Which patience could not pass.
    OTHELLO.   I know, Iago,
Thy honesty and love doth mince this
    matter,
Making it light to Cassio. Cassio, I love
    thee;
But never more be officer of mine.

(*Re-enter* DESDEMONA, *attended.*)

Look, if my gentle love be not rais'd up!   250
I'll make thee an example.
    DESDEMONA.   What's the matter,
    dear?
    OTHELLO.   All's well now, sweeting;
    come away to bed.
Sir, [*To* MONTANO], for your hurts, myself
    will be your surgeon.—
Lead him off.   (MONTANO *is led off.*)
Iago, look with care about the town,
And silence those whom this vile brawl
    distracted.
Come, Desdemona; 'tis the soldiers' life
To have their balmy slumbers wak'd with
    strife.

(*Exeunt all but* IAGO *and* CASSIO.)

    IAGO.   What, are you hurt, lieutenant?
    CASSIO.   Ay, past all surgery.   260
    IAGO.   Marry, God forbid!

---

202 *self-charity:* care of one's self   207 *collied:* darkened   215 *manage:* engage in   218 *partially affin'd:* influenced by partiality   233 *rather:* sooner   246 *patience:* self-control   246 *pass:* endure   247 *mince:* extenuate

CASSIO.   Reputation, reputation, reputation! O, I have lost my reputation! I have lost the immortal part of myself, and what remains is bestial. My reputation, Iago, my reputation!

IAGO.   As I am an honest man, I thought you had received some bodily wound; there is more sense in that than in reputation. Reputation is an idle and most false imposition; oft got without merit, and lost without deserving. You have 270 lost no reputation at all, unless you repute yourself such a loser. What, man! there are more ways to recover the general again. You are but now cast in his mood, a punishment more in policy than in malice; even so as one would beat his offenseless dog to affright an imperious lion. Sue to him again, and he's yours.

CASSIO.   I will rather sue to be despised than to deceive so good a commander with so slight, so drunken, and so indis- 280 creet an officer. Drunk? and speak parrot? and squabble? swagger? swear? and discourse fustian with one's own shadow? O thou invisible spirit of wine, if thou hast no name to be known by, let us call thee devil!

IAGO.   What was he that you followed with your sword? What had he done to you?

CASSIO.   I know not.

IAGO.   Is't possible?

CASSIO.   I remember a mass of things, but 290 nothing distinctly; a quarrel, but nothing wherefore. O God, that men should put an enemy in their mouths to steal away their brains! That we should, with joy, pleasance, revel, and applause, transform ourselves into beasts!

IAGO.   Why, but you are now well enough. How came you thus recovered?

CASSIO.   It hath pleased the devil drunkenness to give place to the devil wrath. One unperfectness shows me another, to make me frankly despise myself. 300

IAGO.   Come, you are too severe a moraler. As the time, the place, and the condition of this country stands, I could heartily wish this had not befallen; but since it is as it is, mend if for your own good.

CASSIO.   I will ask him for my place again; he shall tell me I am a drunkard! Had I as many mouths as Hydra, such an answer would stop them all. To be now a sensible man, by and by a fool, and presently a beast! O strange! Every 310 inordinate cup is unblessed and the ingredient is a devil.

IAGO.   Come, come, good wine is a good familiar creature, if it be well used; exclaim no more against it. And, good lieutenant, I think you think I love you.

CASSIO.   I have well approved it, sir. I drunk!

IAGO.   You or any man living may be drunk at a time, man. I'll tell you what you shall do. Our general's wife is now the general;—I may say so in this re- 320 spect, for that he hath devoted and given up himself to the contemplation, mark, and denotement of her parts and graces;—confess yourself freely to her; importune her help to put you in your place again. She is of so free, so kind, so apt, so blessed a disposition, she holds it a vice in her goodness not to do more than she is requested. This broken joint between you and her husband entreat her to splinter; and, my fortunes against any lay worth naming, this 330 crack of your love shall grow stronger than it was before.

CASSIO.   You advise me well.

IAGO.   I protest, in the sincerity of love and honest kindness.

CASSIO.   I think it freely; and betimes in the morning I will beseech the virtuous Desdemona to undertake for me. I am desperate of my fortunes if they check me here.

IAGO.   You are in the right. Good-night, lieutenant; I must to the watch. 340

CASSIO.   Good-night, honest Iago.

---

268 *sense:* feeling   269 *imposition:* characteristic conferred by others   272 *recover:* win back   273 *cast in his mood:* dismissed because of his anger   282 *parrot:* without knowing what one says   283 *fustian:* nonsense   295 *pleasance:* merry-making

302 *moraler:* moralizer   307 *shall:* inevitably will   308 *Hydra:* a many-headed monster   311 *inordinate:* excessive   313 *familiar:* serviceable   323 *denotement:* observation   329 *splinter:* bind up with splints   330 *lay:* wager   339 *desperate:* hopeless   339 *check me:* hold me back

(Exit.)

IAGO.   And what's he then that says I
   play the villain?
When this advice is free I give and honest,
Probal to thinking and indeed the course
To win the Moor again? For 'tis most easy
The inclining Desdemona to subdue
In any honest suit; she's fram'd as fruitful
As the free elements. And then for her
To win the Moor, were't to renounce his
   baptism,
All seals and symbols of redeemed sin,   350
His soul is so enfetter'd to her love,
That she may make, unmake, do what she
   list,
Even as her appetite shall play the god
With his weak function. How am I then
   a villain
To counsel Cassio to this parallel course,
Directly to his good? Divinity of hell!
When devils will the blackest sins put on,
They do suggest at first with heavenly
   shows,
As I do now; for whiles this honest fool
Plies Desdemona to repair his fortunes   360
And she for him pleads strongly to the
   Moor,
I'll pour this pestilence into his ear,
That she repeals him for her body's lust;
And by how much she strives to do him
   good,
She shall undo her credit with the Moor.
So will I turn her virtue into pitch,
And out of her own goodness make the net
That shall enmesh them all.

(Re-enter RODERIGO.)

                          How now, Roderigo!
RODERIGO.   I do follow here in the chase,
   not like a hound that hunts, but one
   that fills up the cry. My money is al-   370
   most spent; I have been to-night exceedingly well cudgelled; and I think
   the issue will be, I shall have so much
   experience for my pains; and so, with
   no money at all and a little more wit,
   return again to Venice.
IAGO.   How poor are they that have not

patience!
What wound did ever heal but by degrees?
Thou know'st we work by wit, and not by
   witchcraft;
And wit depends on dilatory Time.
Does't not go well? Cassio hath beaten
   thee,   380
And thou, by that small hurt, hast cashier'd
   Cassio.
Though other things grow fair against the
   sun,
Yet fruits that blossom first will first be
   ripe.
Content thyself a while. By the mass, 'tis
   morning;
Pleasure and action make the hours seem
   short.
Retire thee; go where thou art billeted.
Away, I say; thou shalt know more
   hereafter.
Nay, get thee gone. *(Exit* RODERIGO.) Two
   things are to be done:
My wife must move for Cassio to her
   mistress;
I'll set her on;   390
Myself the while to draw the Moor apart,
And bring him jump when he may Cassio
   find
Soliciting his wife. Ay, that's the way;
Dull not device by coldness and delay.

                                          (Exit.)

ACT III.1   *Before the castle.*

(Enter CASSIO, *with* MUSICIANS.)

CASSIO.   Masters, play here; I will content
   your pains;
Something that's brief; and bid "Good
   morrow, General."

                                (They play.)

(Enter CLOWN.)

CLOWN.   Why, masters, have your instruments been in Naples, that they speak
   i' th' nose thus?
FIRST MUSICIAN.   How, sir, how?
CLOWN.   Are these, I pray you, wind-
   instruments?

---

344 *Probal to thinking:* approved by men of judgment   347 *fruitful:*
generous   354 *weak function:* feeble powers   359 *suggest:* tempt
363 *repeals:* would call back   370 *cry:* pack   375 *wit:* common
sense

378 *wit:* clever planning   379 *dilatory Time:* Time, who cannot be
hastened   381 *cashier'd:* brought about the dismissal of   389
move: petition   392 *jump:* just   394 *coldness:* lack of energy
ACT III. 1   4 *Naples:* i.e., have they acquired the Neapolitan
(venereal) disease

FIRST MUSICIAN. Ay, marry, are they, sir.

CLOWN. O, thereby hangs a tail.

FIRST MUSICIAN. Whereby hangs a tale, sir? 10

CLOWN. Marry, sir, by many a wind-instrument that I know. But, masters, here's money for you; and the General so likes your music, that he desires you, of all loves, to make no more noise with it.

FIRST MUSICIAN. Well, sir, we will not.

CLOWN. If you have any music that may not be heard, to 't again; but, as they say, to hear music the General does not greatly care.

FIRST MUSICIAN. We have none such, sir. 20

CLOWN. Then put up your pipes in your bag, for I'll away. Go, vanish into air, away! (Exeunt MUSICIANS.)

CASSIO. Dost thou hear, mine honest friend?

CLOWN. No, I hear not your honest friend; I hear you.

CASSIO. Prithee, keep up thy quillets. There's a poor piece of gold for thee. If the gentlewoman that attends the general's wife be stirring, tell her there's one Cassio entreats her a little favor of speech. Wilt thou do this?

CLOWN. She is stirring, sir: if she will 30 stir hither, I shall seem to notify unto her.

CASSIO. Do, good my friend.

(Exit CLOWN.)

(Enter IAGO.)

In happy time, Iago.

IAGO. You have not been a-bed, then?

CASSIO. Why, no; the day had broke Before we parted. I have made bold, Iago, To send in to your wife. My suit to her Is that she will to virtuous Desdemona Procure me some access.

IAGO. I'll send her to you presently; And I'll devise a mean to draw the Moor Out of the way, that your converse and business 40 May be more free.

CASSIO. I humbly thank you for 't. (Exit IAGO.) I never knew A Florentine more kind and honest.

(Enter EMILIA.)

EMILIA. Good morrow, good lieutenant: I am sorry For your displeasure; but all will sure be well. The General and his wife are talking of it, And she speaks for you stoutly. The Moor replies, That he you hurt is of great fame in Cyprus And great affinity, and that in wholesome wisdom He might not but refuse you; but he protests he loves you, 50 And needs no other suitor but his likings To take the safest occasion by the front To bring you in again.

CASSIO. Yet, I beseech you If you think fit, or that it may be done, Give me advantage of some brief discourse With Desdemona alone.

EMILIA. Pray you, come in; I will bestow you where you shall have time To speak your bosom freely.

CASSIO. I am much bound to you.

(Exeunt.)

ACT III.2 *A room in the castle.*

(*Enter* OTHELLO, IAGO, *and* GENTLEMEN.)

OTHELLO. These letters give, Iago, to the pilot; And by him do my duties to the Senate. That done, I will be walking on the works; Repair there to me.

IAGO. Well, my good lord, I'll do 't.

OTHELLO. This fortification, gentlemen, shall we see 't?

GENTLEMEN. We'll wait upon your lordship. 10

(Exeunt.)

ACT III.3 *The garden of the castle.*

(*Enter* DESDEMONA, CASSIO, *and* EMILIA.)

---

25 *keep up thy quillets:* keep your jokes to yourself   32 *in happy time:* well met

46 *displeasure:* disfavor   49 *affinity:* kindred   51 *likings:* affection   52 *take ... by the front:* "take Time by the forelock," seize the first good opportunity   58 *bosom:* inmost thoughts ACT III. 2   3 *works:* fortifications

DESDEMONA.   Be thou assur'd, good
Cassio, I will do
All my abilities in thy behalf.
  EMILIA.   Good madam, do. I warrant
it grieves my husband
As if the cause were his.
  DESDEMONA.   O, that's an honest fellow.
Do not doubt, Cassio,
But I will have my lord and you again
As friendly as you were.
  CASSIO.   Bounteous madam,
Whatever shall become of Michael Cassio,
He's never anything but your true servant.
  DESDEMONA.   I know 't; I thank you.
You do love my lord;   10
You have known him long; and be you
well assur'd
He shall in strangeness stand no farther off
Than in a politic distance.
  CASSIO.   Ay, but, lady,
That policy may either last so long,
Or feed upon such nice and waterish diet,
Or breed itself so out of circumstances,
That, I being absent and my place suppli'd,
My general will forget my love and service.
  DESDEMONA.   Do not doubt that; before
Emilia here
I give thee warrant of thy place. Assure
thee,   20
If I do vow a friendship, I'll perform it
To the last article. My lord shall never rest;
I'll watch him tame, and talk him out of
patience;
His bed shall seem a school, his board a
shrift;
I'll intermingle everything he does
With Cassio's suit. Therefore be merry,
Cassio;
For thy solicitor shall rather die
Than give thy cause away.

(*Enter* OTHELLO *and* IAGO.)

  EMILIA.   Madam, here comes my lord.
  CASSIO.   Madam, I'll take my leave.   30
  DESDEMONA.   Why, stay, and hear me
speak.
  CASSIO.   Madam, not now; I am very
ill at ease,

Unfit for mine own purposes.
  DESDEMONA.   Well, do your discretion.

(*Exit* CASSIO.)

first hint by Iago

  IAGO.   Ha! I like not that.
  OTHELLO.   What dost thou say?
  IAGO.   Nothing, my lord; or if—I know
not what.
  OTHELLO.   Was not that Cassio parted
from my wife?
  IAGO.   Cassio, my lord! No, sure, I can-
not think it,
That he would steal away so guilty-like,
Seeing your coming.
  OTHELLO.   I do believe 'twas he.   40
  DESDEMONA.   How now, my lord!
I have been talking with a suitor here,
A man that languishes in your displeasure.
  OTHELLO.   Who is 't you mean?
  DESDEMONA.   Why, your lieutenant,
Cassio. Good my lord,
If I have any grace or power to move you,
His present reconciliation take;
For if he be not one that truly loves you,
That errs in ignorance and not in cunning,
I have no judgment in an honest face.   50
I prithee, call him back.
  OTHELLO.   Went he hence now?
  DESDEMONA.   Yes, faith; so humbled
That he hath left part of his grief with me
To suffer with him. Good love, call him
back.
  OTHELLO.   Not now, sweet Desdemona;
some other time.
  DESDEMONA.   But shall 't be shortly?
  OTHELLO.   The sooner,
sweet, for you.
  DESDEMONA.   Shall 't be to-night at
supper?
  OTHELLO.   No, not to-night.
  DESDEMONA.   To-morrow dinner, then?
  OTHELLO.   I shall not dine at home;
I meet the captains at the citadel.
  DESDEMONA.   Why, then, to-morrow
night; on Tuesday morn;   60
On Tuesday morn, or night; on Wednesday
morn.
I prithee, name the time, but let it not
Exceed three days. In faith, he's penitent;
And yet his trespass, in our common

ACT III. 3   12 *strangeness:* estrangement   13 *than in . . . distance:* than policy requires   15 *nice and waterish:* trivial and insig-
nificant   16 *out of:* by (further)   19 *doubt:* fear   23 *watch
him:* keep awake until he is   24 *shrift:* place of admonition   28
away: up

33 *purposes:* best interests   47 *his present reconciliation take:*
accept his apology and become reconciled   51 *prithee:* pray you

reason—
Save that, they say, the wars must make
 example
Out of their best—is not almost a fault
T' incur a private check. When shall he
 come?
Tell me, Othello. I wonder in my soul,
What you would ask me, that I should
 deny,
Or stand so mamm'ring on. What!
 Michael Cassio,   70
That came a-wooing with you, and so
 many a time,
When I have spoke of you dispraisingly,
Hath ta'en your part,—to have so much
 to do
To bring him in! Trust me, I could do
 much,—
OTHELLO.   Prithee, no more; let him
 come when he will!
I will deny thee nothing.
DESDEMONA.   Why, this is not a boon.
'Tis as I should entreat you wear your
 gloves,
Or feed on nourishing dishes, or keep you
 warm,
Or sue to you to do a peculiar profit
To your own person. Nay, when I have
 a suit   80
Wherein I mean to touch your love indeed,
It shall be full of poise and difficult weight
And fearful to be granted.
OTHELLO.   I will deny thee nothing;
Whereon, I do beseech thee, grant me this,
To leave me but a little to myself.
DESDEMONA.   Shall I deny you? No.
 Farewell, my lord.
OTHELLO.   Farewell, my Desdemona;
 I'll come to thee straight.
DESDEMONA.   Emilia, come.—Be as your
 fancies teach you;
Whate'er you be, I am obedient.
            (Exeunt DESDEMONA and EMILIA.)
OTHELLO.   Excellent wretch! Perdition
 catch my soul,   90
But I do love thee! and when I love thee
 not,
Chaos is come again. *Irony*

IAGO.   My noble lord,—
OTHELLO.   What dost thou say, Iago?
IAGO.   Did Michael Cassio, when you
 woo'd my lady,
Know of your love?
OTHELLO.   He did, from first to last.
 Why dost thou ask?
IAGO.   But for a satisfaction of my
 thought;
No further harm.
OTHELLO.   Why of thy thought, Iago?
IAGO.   I did not think he had been
 acquainted with her.
OTHELLO.   O, yes; and went between us
 very oft.   100
IAGO.   Indeed!
OTHELLO.   Indeed! ay, indeed. Discern'st
 thou aught in that?
Is he not honest?
IAGO.   Honest, my lord?
OTHELLO.   Honest! ay, honest.
IAGO.   My lord, for aught I know.
OTHELLO.   What dost thou think?
IAGO.   Think, my lord?
OTHELLO.   Think, my lord!
By heaven, he echoes me,
As if there were some monster in his
 thought
Too hideous to be shown.—Thou dost
 mean something:
I heard thee say but now, thou lik'st not
 that,
When Cassio left my wife. What didst not
 like?   110
And when I told thee he was of my counsel
In my whole course of wooing, thou criedst,
 "Indeed!"
And didst contract and purse thy brow
 together,
As if thou then hadst shut up in thy brain
Some horrible conceit. If thou dost love me,
Show me thy thought.
IAGO.   My lord, you know I love you.
OTHELLO.   I think thou dost;
And, for I know thou'rt full of love and
 honesty,
And weigh'st thy words before thou giv'st
 them breath,
Therefore these stops of thine fright me
 the more;   120

---

64 *reason:* sense   65 *wars:* i.e., military discipline   66 *not almost:*
hardly   70 *mamm'ring on:* hesitating over   76 *boon:* great
favor to me   92 *Chaos:* the utter confusion that existed before the
order of the universe was established and that will accompany the end
of time

---

111 *of my counsel:* in my confidence   113 *purse:* draw   115 *conceit:* notion

For such things in a false disloyal knave
Are tricks of custom; but in a man that's
      just
They're close dilations, working from the
      heart
That passion cannot rule.
      IAGO.   For Michael Cassio,
I dare be sworn I think that he is honest.
      OTHELLO.   I think so too.
      IAGO.   Men should be what they seem;
Or those that be not, would they might
      seem none!
      OTHELLO.   Certain, men should be what
      they seem.
      IAGO.   Why, then, I think Cassio's an
      honest man.
      OTHELLO.   Nay, yet there's more in this.   130
I prithee, speak to me as to thy thinkings,
As thou dost ruminate, and give thy worst
      of thoughts
The worst of words.
      IAGO.   Good my lord, pardon me.
Though I am bound to every act of duty,
I am not bound to that all slaves are free
      to.
Utter my thoughts? Why, say they are vile
      and false;
As where's that palace whereinto foul things
Sometimes intrude not? Who has a breast
      so pure
But some uncleanly apprehensions
Keep leets and law-days and in sessions sit   140
With meditations lawful?
      OTHELLO.   Thou dost conspire against
      thy friend, Iago,
If thou but think'st him wrong'd and
      mak'st his ear
A stranger to thy thoughts.
      IAGO.   I do beseech you—
Though I perchance am vicious in my
      guess,
As, I confess, it is my nature's plague
To spy into abuses, and oft my jealousy
Shapes faults that are not—that your
      wisdom yet,
From one that so imperfectly conceits,
Would take no notice, nor build yourself

a trouble   150
Out of his scattering and unsure observance.
It were not for your quiet nor your good,
Nor for my manhood, honesty, and
      wisdom,
To let you know my thoughts.
      OTHELLO.   What dost thou mean?
      IAGO.   Good name in man and woman,
      dear my lord,
Is the immediate jewel of their souls.
Who steals my purse steals trash; 'tis
      Irony something, nothing;
'Twas mine, 'tis his, and has been slave to
      thousands;
But he that filches from me my good name
Robs me of that which not enriches him   160
And makes me poor indeed.
      OTHELLO.   By heaven, I'll know thy
      thoughts.
      IAGO.   You cannot, if my heart were in
      your hand;
Nor shall not, whilst 'tis in my custody.
      OTHELLO.   Ha!
      IAGO.   O, beware, my lord, of jealousy;
It is the green-ey'd monster which doth
      mock
The meat it feeds on. That cuckold lives in
      bliss
Who, certain of his fate, loves not his
      wronger;
But, O, what damned minutes tells he o'er
Who dotes, yet doubts, suspects, yet
      strongly loves!   170
      OTHELLO.   O misery!
      IAGO.   Poor and content is rich and rich
      enough,
But riches fineless is as poor as winter
To him that ever fears he shall be poor.
Good heaven, the souls of all my tribe
      defend
From jealousy!
      OTHELLO.   Why, why is this?
Think'st thou I'd make a life of jealousy,
To follow still the changes of the moon
With fresh suspicions? No! to be once in
      doubt
Is once to be resolv'd. Exchange me for
      a goat   180

---

122 *tricks of custom:* habitual tricks   123 *close dilations:* hidden
emotions that make the heart swell   127 *none:* i.e., not men, but
monsters   139 *apprehensions:* thoughts   140 *leets:* court sessions
140 *sit With:* sit on the bench beside   145 *vicious:* mistaken   147
jealousy: suspicious nature   149 *imperfectly conceits:* has such
vague ideas

---

151 *scattering:* casual   151 *observance:* observations   166 *mock:*
play cat and mouse with   168 *wronger:* faithless wife   169 *tells:*
counts   173 *fineless:* boundless   180 *to be resolv'd:* to discover
the truth

When I shall turn the business of my soul
To such exsufflicate and blown surmises,
Matching thy inference. 'Tis not to make
    me jealous
To say my wife is fair, feeds well, loves
    company,
Is free of speech, sings, plays, and dances
    well;
Where virtue is, these are more virtuous;
Nor from mine own weak merits will I
    draw
The smallest fear or doubt of her revolt;
For she had eyes, and chose me. No, Iago;
I'll see before I doubt; when I doubt, prove;   190
And on the proof, there is no more but
    this,—
Away at once with love or jealousy!
   IAGO.   I am glad of this, for now I shall
    have reason
To show the love and duty that I bear you
With franker spirit; therefore, as I am
    bound,
Receive it from me. I speak not yet of
    proof.
Look to your wife; observe her well with
    Cassio;
Wear your eyes thus, not jealous nor secure.
I would not have your free and noble
    nature,
Out of self-bounty, be abus'd; look to 't.   200
I know our country disposition well;
In Venice they do let God see the pranks
They dare not show their husbands. Their
    best conscience
Is not to leave 't undone, but keep 't
    unknown.
   OTHELLO.   Dost thou say so?
   IAGO.   She did deceive her father,
    marrying you;
And when she seem'd to shake and fear
    your looks,
She lov'd them most.
   OTHELLO.   And so she did.
   IAGO.   Why, go to then.
She that, so young, could give out such a
    seeming,
To seel her father's eyes up close as oak—   210
He thought 'twas witchcraft—but I am
    much to blame.
I humbly do beseech you of your pardon

For too much loving you.
   OTHELLO.   I am bound to thee for ever.
   IAGO.   I see this hath a little dash'd your
    spirits.
   OTHELLO.   Not a jot, not a jot.
   IAGO.   I' faith, I fear it has.
I hope you will consider what is spoke
Comes from my love. But I do see you're
    mov'd.
I am to pray you not to strain my speech
To grosser issues nor to larger reach
Than to suspicion.   220
   OTHELLO.   I will not.
   IAGO.   Should you do so, my lord,
My speech should fall into such vile success
Which my thoughts aim'd not at. Cassio's
    my worthy friend,—
My lord, I see you're mov'd.
   OTHELLO.   No, not much mov'd.
I do not think but Desdemona's honest.
   IAGO.   Long live she so; and long live
    you to think so!
   OTHELLO.   And yet, how nature erring
    from itself,—
   IAGO.   Ay, there's the point; as—to be
    bold with you—
Not to affect many proposed matches
Of her own clime, complexion, and degree,   230
Whereto we see in all things nature tends—
Foh! one may smell in such, a will most
    rank,
Foul disproportions, thoughts unnatural.
But pardon me; I do not in position
Distinctly speak of her; though I may fear
Her will, recoiling to her better judgment,
May fall to match you with her country
    forms,
And happily repent.
   OTHELLO.   Farewell, farewell!
If more thou dost perceive, let me know
    more;
Set on thy wife to observe. Leave me, Iago.   240
   IAGO.   (*Going.*) My lord, I take my leave.
   OTHELLO.   Why did I marry? This
    honest creature doubtless
Sees and knows more, much more, than
    he unfolds.
   IAGO.   (*Returning.*) My lord, I would

---

182 *exsufflicate:* odious   182 *blown:* flyspecked   200 *self-bounty:*
innate goodness   210 *as oak:* as the grain of oak

213 *bound:* indebted   219 *grosser issues:* worse conclusions   229
affect: care for, be inclined to   234 *position:* this principle   235
Distinctly: specifically   237 *match:* compare   237 *her country
forms:* men of her own country

*emotion dulls
Othello's mind.*

I might entreat your honor
To scan this thing no farther; leave it to
   time.
Although 'tis fit that Cassio have his place,
For, sure, he fills it up with great ability,
Yet, if you please to hold him off a while,
You shall by that perceive him and his
   means.
Note if your lady strain his entertainment   250
With any strong or vehement importunity;
Much will be seen in that. In the mean
   time,
Let me be thought too busy in my fears—
As worthy cause I have to fear I am—
And hold her free, I do beseech your honor.
   OTHELLO.   Fear not my government.
   IAGO.   I once more take my leave.
                                 (*Exit.*)
   OTHELLO.   This fellow's of exceeding
      honesty,
And knows all qualities, with a learned
   spirit,
Of human dealings. If I do prove her
   haggard,   260
Though that her jesses were my dear
   heartstrings,
I'd whistle her off and let her down the
   wind
To prey at fortune. Haply, for I am black
And have not those soft parts of conver-
   sation
That chamberers have, or for I am
   declin'd
Into the vale of years,—yet that's not
   much—
She's gone. I am abus'd; and my relief
Must be to loathe her. O curse of marriage,
That we can call these delicate creatures
   ours,
And not their appetites! I had rather be
   a toad   270
And live upon the vapor of a dungeon,
Than keep a corner in the thing I love
For others' uses. Yet, 'tis the plague of
   great ones;
Prerogativ'd are they less than the base:
'Tis destiny unshunnable, like death.
Even then this forked plague is fated to us

When we do quicken. Look where she
   comes.

(*Re-enter* DESDEMONA *and* EMILIA.)

If she be false, O, then heaven mocks
   itself!
I'll not believe 't.
   DESDEMONA.   How now, my dear
      Othello!
Your dinner, and the generous islanders   280
By you invited, do attend your presence.
   OTHELLO.   I am to blame.
   DESDEMONA.   Why do you
      speak so faintly?
Are you not well?
   OTHELLO.   I have a pain upon my
      forehead here.
   DESDEMONA.   Faith, that's with
      watching; 'twill away again.
Let me but bind it hard, within this hour
It will be well.
   OTHELLO.   Your napkin is too little;
      (*He puts the handkerchief from him;
      and it drops.*)
Let it alone. Come, I'll go in with you.
   DESDEMONA.   I am very sorry that you
      are not well.

(*Exeunt* OTHELLO *and* DESDEMONA.)

   EMILIA.   I am glad I have found this
      napkin;   290
This was her first remembrance from the
   Moor.
My wayward husband hath a hundred times
Woo'd me to steal it; but she so loves the
   token,
For he conjur'd her she should ever keep
   it,
That she reserves it evermore about her
To kiss and talk to. I'll have the work
   ta'en out,
And give 't Iago. What he will do with it
Heaven knows, not I;
I nothing but to please his fantasy.

(*Re-enter* IAGO.)

   IAGO.   How now! what do you here   300
      alone?
   EMILIA.   Do not you chide; I have a

---

250 *his entertainment:* that you reinstate him   256 *government:*
self-control   260 *haggard:* a wild hawk and an unchaste woman
261 *jesses:* straps on a falcon's legs   265 *chamberers:* gallants
274 *Prerogativ'd:* privileged

276 *forked:* horned   277 *do quicken:* are born   287 *napkin:*
handkerchief   292 *wayward:* capricious   296 *work:* embroidery
296 *ta'en out:* copied   299 *fantasy:* whim

thing for you.

IAGO. A thing for me? It is a common thing—

EMILIA. Ha!

IAGO. To have a foolish wife.

EMILIA. O, is that all? What will you give me now
For that same handkerchief?

IAGO. What handkerchief?

EMILIA. What handkerchief!
Why, that the Moor first gave to Desdemona;
That which so often you did bid me steal.

IAGO. Hast stol'n it from her? 310

EMILIA. No, faith; she let it drop by negligence,
And, to th' advantage, I, being here, took 't up.
Look, here it is.

IAGO. A good wench; give it me.

EMILIA. What will you do with 't, that you have been so earnest
To have me filch it?

IAGO. (Snatching it.) Why, what is that to you?

EMILIA. If it be not for some purpose of import,
Give 't me again. Poor lady, she'll run mad
When she shall lack it.

IAGO. Be not you acknown on 't; I have use for it.
Go, leave me. (Exit EMILIA.) 320
I will in Cassio's lodging lose this napkin
And let him find it. Trifles light as air
Are to the jealous confirmations strong
As proofs of holy writ; this may do something.
The Moor already changes with my poison.
Dangerous conceits are, in their nature, poisons,
Which at the first are scarce found to distaste,
But with a little act upon the blood,
Burn like the mines of sulphur. I did say so.

(Re-enter OTHELLO.)

Look, where he comes! Not poppy, nor 330
mandragora,
Nor all the drowsy syrups of the world
Shall ever medicine thee to that sweet sleep
Which thou ow'dst yesterday.

OTHELLO. Ha! ha! false to me?

IAGO. Why, how now, General! no more of that.

OTHELLO. Avaunt! be gone! thou hast set me on the rack.
I swear 'tis better to be much abus'd
Than but to know 't a little.

IAGO. How now, my lord!

OTHELLO. What sense had I of her stol'n hours of lust?
I saw 't not, thought it not, it harm'd not me.
I slept the next night well, fed well, was free and merry; 340
I found not Cassio's kisses on her lips.
He that is robb'd, not wanting what is stol'n,
Let him not know 't, and he's not robb'd at all.

IAGO. I am sorry to hear this.

OTHELLO. I had been happy, if the general camp,
Pioners and all, had tasted her sweet body,
So I had nothing known. O, now, for ever
Farewell the tranquil mind! farewell content!
Farewell the plumed troop, and the big wars,
That makes ambition virtue! O, farewell! 350
Farewell the neighing steed, and the shrill trump,
The spirit-stirring drum, th' ear-piercing fife,
The royal banner, and all quality,
Pride, pomp, and circumstance of glorious war!
And, O you mortal engines, whose rude throats
Th' immortal Jove's dread clamors counterfeit,
Farewell! Othello's occupation's gone!

IAGO. Is 't possible, my lord?

OTHELLO. Villain, be sure thou prove my love a whore,

---

312 *to th' advantage:* opportunity   313 *wench:* girl   317 *import:* importance   319 *lack:* miss   320 *Be not . . . on't:* don't admit any knowledge of it   328 *distaste:* taste bad   328 *with a little act:* having acted a little while   331 *drowsy syrups:* sleeping potions   333 *ow'dst:* possessed   335 *Avaunt:* Get out!   342 *wanting:* missing   346 *Pioners:* soldiers of the lowest rank   349 *big:* stately   353 *quality:* characteristics   354 *circumstance:* pageantry   355 *mortal engines:* deadly machines   356 *counterfeit:* imitate

Be sure of it; give me the ocular proof;   360
Or, by the worth of mine eternal soul,
Thou hadst been better have been born
     a dog
Than answer my wak'd wrath!
     IAGO.   Is't come to this?
     OTHELLO.   Make me to see 't; or, at the
     least, so prove it,
That the probation bear no hinge nor loop
To hang a doubt on; or woe upon thy life!
     IAGO.   My noble lord,—
     OTHELLO.   If thou dost slander her and
     torture me,
Never pray more; abandon all remorse;
On horror's head horrors accumulate;   370
Do deeds to make heaven weep, all earth
     amaz'd;
For nothing canst thou to damnation add
Greater than that.
     IAGO.   O grace! O Heaven forgive me!
Are you a man? Have you a soul or sense?
God buy you; take mine office. O wretched
     fool,
That lov'st to make thine honesty a vice!
O monstrous world! Take note, take note,
     O world,
To be direct and honest is not safe.
I thank you for this profit; and from hence
I'll love no friend, sith love breeds such
     offence.   380
     OTHELLO.   Nay, stay. Thou shouldst be
     honest.
     IAGO.   I should be wise, for honesty's
     a fool
And loses that it works for.
     OTHELLO.   By the world,
I think my wife be honest and think she is
     not;
I think that thou art just and think thou
     art not.
I'll have some proof. Her name, that was
     as fresh
As Dian's visage, is now begrim'd and
     black
As mine own face. If there be cords, or
     knives,
Poison, or fire, or suffocating streams,
I'll not endure it. Would I were satisfied!   390

     IAGO.   I see, sir, you are eaten up with
     passion;
I do repent me that I put it to you.
You would be satisfied?
     OTHELLO.   Would! nay, I will.
     IAGO.   And may; but, how? How
     satisfied, my lord?
Would you, the supervisor, grossly gape
     on—
Behold her tupp'd?
     OTHELLO.   Death and damnation! O!
     IAGO.   It were a tedious difficulty, I
     think,
To bring them to that prospect; damn them
     then,
If ever mortal eyes do see them bolster
More than their own! What then? How
     then?   400
What shall I say? Where's satisfaction?
It is impossible you should see this,
Were they as prime as goats, as hot as
     monkeys,
As salt as wolves in pride, and fools as
     gross
As ignorance made drunk. But yet, I say,
If imputation and strong circumstances,
Which lead directly to the door of truth,
Will give you satisfaction, you might
     have 't.
     OTHELLO.   Give me a living reason she's
     disloyal.   410
     IAGO.   I do not like the office;
But, sith I am enter'd in this cause so far,
Prick'd to 't by foolish honesty and love,
I will go on. I lay with Cassio lately;
And, being troubled with a raging tooth,
I could not sleep.
There are a kind of men so loose of soul
That in their sleeps will mutter their
     affairs;
One of this kind is Cassio.
In sleep I heard him say, "Sweet
     Desdemona,
Let us be wary, let us hide our loves";   420
And then, sir, would he gripe and wring
     my hand,
Cry, "O sweet creature!" and then kiss me
     hard,

---

363 *answer:* be exposed to   365 *probation:* proof   369 *remorse:* compassion   371 *amaz'd:* paralyzed with horror   375 *God buy you:* good-bye   379 *profit:* profitable lesson   384 *that:* i.e., trust   387 *Dian:* Diana, goddess of chastity

395 *supervisor:* as an eyewitness   399 *bolster:* lie together on a bolster (i.e., bed)   400 *More than:* other than   403 *prime:* lustful   404 *pride:* lust   406 *imputation . . . circumstances:* strong circumstantial evidence   411 *sith:* since

As if he pluck'd up kisses by the roots
That grew upon my lips; then laid his leg
Over my thigh, and sigh'd and kiss'd; and
then
Cried, "Cursed fate that gave thee to the
Moor!"
    OTHELLO. O monstrous! monstrous!
    IAGO.   Nay, this was but his dream.
    OTHELLO. But this denoted a foregone
conclusion.
'Tis a shrewd doubt, though it be but a
dream.
    IAGO. And this may help to thicken
other proofs   430
That do demonstrate thinly.
    OTHELLO.   I'll tear her all to pieces.
    IAGO. Nay, but be wise; yet we see
nothing done.
She may be honest yet. Tell me but this,
Have you not sometimes seen a
handkerchief
Spotted with strawberries in your wife's
hand?
    OTHELLO. I gave her such a one; 'twas
my first gift.
    IAGO. I know not that; but such a
handkerchief—
I am sure it was your wife's—did I to-day
See Cassio wipe his beard with.
    OTHELLO.   If it be that,—
    IAGO. If it be that, or any that was
hers,   440
It speaks against her with the other proofs.
    OTHELLO. O, that the slave had forty
thousand lives!
One is too poor, too weak for my revenge.
Now do I see 'tis true. Look here, Iago;
All my fond love thus do I blow to Heaven.
'Tis gone.
Arise, black Vengeance, from the hollow
hell!
Yield up, O love, thy crown and hearted
throne
To tyrannous hate! Swell, bosom, with thy
fraught,
For 'tis of aspics' tongues!
    IAGO.   Yet be content.   450
    OTHELLO. O, blood, blood, blood!

    IAGO. Patience, I say; your mind
perhaps may change.
    OTHELLO. Never, Iago. Like to the
Pontic Sea,
Whose icy current and compulsive course
Ne'er feels retiring ebb, but keeps due on
To the Propontic and the Hellespont,
Even so my bloody thoughts, with violent
pace,
Shall ne'er look back, ne'er ebb to humble
love,
Till that a capable and wide revenge
Swallow them up. Now, by yond marble
heaven,   460
In the due reverence of a sacred vow
I here engage my words.   (*Kneels.*)
    IAGO.   Do not rise yet.
Witness, you ever-burning lights above.
You elements that clip us round about,

                        (*Kneels.*)

Witness that here Iago doth give up
The execution of his wit, hands, heart,
To wrong'd Othello's service! Let him
command,
And to obey shall be in me remorse,
What bloody business ever.   (*They rise.*)
    OTHELLO.   I greet thy love,
Not with vain thanks, but with acceptance
bounteous,   470
And will upon the instant put thee to 't.
Within these three days let me hear thee say
That Cassio's not alive.
    IAGO. My friend is dead; 'tis done at
your request.
But let her live.
    OTHELLO.   Damn her, lewd minx! O,
damn her!
Come, go with me apart; I will withdraw
To furnish me with some swift means of
death
For the fair devil. Now art thou my
lieutenant.
    IAGO. I am your own for ever.   480

                      (*Exeunt.*)

ACT III.4 *Before the castle.*

(*Enter* DESDEMONA, EMILIA, *and* CLOWN.)

---

428 *foregone conclusion:* something already completed 429 *shrewd:*
cursed   435 *spotted with:* with a pattern of   442 *slave:* i.e.,
Cassio   448 *hearted throne:* throne in my heart   449 *fraught:*
burden   450 *aspic:* asp, poisonous snake

453 *Pontic:* Black   456 *Propontic:* Sea of Marmora   456 *Hellespont:* Bosporus   459 *capable:* all embracing   464 *clip:* embrace
466 *The execution:* all that can be done by   468 *remorse:* as if
only an act of pity

DESDEMONA.   Do you know, sirrah, where Lieutenant Cassio lies?

CLOWN.   I dare not say he lies anywhere.

DESDEMONA.   Why, man?

CLOWN.   He's a soldier, and for me to say a soldier lies, 'tis stabbing.

DESDEMONA.   Go to! Where lodges he?

CLOWN.   To tell you where he lodges, is to tell you where I lie.

DESDEMONA.   Can anything be made of this?   10

CLOWN.   I know not where he lodges, and for me to devise a lodging and say he lies here or he lies there, were to lie in mine own throat.

DESDEMONA.   Can you inquire him out, and be edified by report?

CLOWN.   I will catechize the world for him; that is, make questions, and by them answer.

DESDEMONA.   Seek him, bid him come hither. Tell him I have moved my lord on his behalf, and hope all will be well.   20

CLOWN.   To do this is within the compass of man's wit; and therefore I will attempt the doing it.   (*Exit.*)

DESDEMONA.   Where should I lose the handkerchief, Emilia?

EMILIA.   I know not, madam.

DESDEMONA.   Believe me, I had rather have lost my purse.
Full of crusadoes; and, but my noble Moor
Is true of mind and made of no such baseness
As jealous creatures are, it were enough
To put him to ill thinking.

EMILIA.   Is he not jealous?

DESDEMONA.   Who, he? I think the sun where he was born
Drew all such humors from him. *She idealizes of othello*

EMILIA.   Look, where he comes.

(*Enter* OTHELLO.)

DESDEMONA.   I will not leave him now till Cassio
Be call'd to him.—How is't with you, my lord?

OTHELLO.   Well, my good lady. (*Aside.*) O, hardness to dissemble!—

How do you, Desdemona?

DESDEMONA.   Well, my good lord.

OTHELLO.   Give me your hand. This hand is moist, my lady.

DESDEMONA.   It yet hath felt no age nor known no sorrow.

OTHELLO.   This argues fruitfulness and liberal heart;
Hot, hot, and moist. This hand of yours requires
A sequester from liberty, fasting and prayer,   40
Much castigation, exercise devout;
For here's a young and sweating devil here,
That commonly rebels. 'Tis a good hand,
A frank one.

DESDEMONA.   You may, indeed, say so;
For 'twas that hand that gave away my heart.

OTHELLO.   A liberal hand. The hearts of old gave hands;
But our new heraldry is hands, not hearts.

DESDEMONA.   I cannot speak of this. Come now, your promise.

OTHELLO.   What promise, chuck?

DESDEMONA.   I have sent to bid Cassio come speak with you.   50

OTHELLO.   I have a salt and sorry rheum offends me;
Lend me thy handkerchief.

DESDEMONA.   Here, my lord.

OTHELLO.   That which I gave you.

DESDEMONA.   I have it not about me.

OTHELLO.   Not?

DESDEMONA.   No, faith, my lord.

OTHELLO.   That's a fault. That handkerchief
Did an Egyptian to my mother give;
She was a charmer, and could almost read
The thoughts of people. She told her, while she kept it
'Twould make her amiable and subdue my father
Entirely to her love, but if she lost it,   60
Or made a gift of it, my father's eye
Should hold her loathed and his spirits should hunt
After new fancies. She, dying, gave it me;

ACT III. 4.   14 *edified:* instructed   26 *crusadoes:* gold coins
31 *humors:* whims

40 *sequester:* retirement   42 *devil:* i.e., sensual desire   47 *heraldry:* symbolism (hand joined to hand, rather than hand with a heart in it)   49 *chuck:* chick   51 *rheum:* head cold   56 *Egyptian:* gypsy

*humors { Phlegmatic - slow temperment
sanguine - optomistic - cheerful
choleric - hard to go along with*

And bid me, when my fate would have me
    wiv'd,
To give it her. I did so; and take heed on't;
Make it a darling like your precious eye.
To lose't or give't away were such
    perdition
As nothing else could match.
    DESDEMONA.   Is't possible?
    OTHELLO. 'Tis true; there's magic in
    the web of it.   70
A sibyl, that had number'd in the world
The sun to course two hundred compasses,
In her prophetic fury sew'd the work;
The worms were hallowed that did breed
    the silk;
And it was dy'd in mummy which the
    skilful
Conserv'd of maidens' hearts.
    DESDEMONA.   Indeed! is't true?
    OTHELLO. Most veritable; therefore
    look to't well.
    DESDEMONA. Then would to God that
    I had never seen 't.
    OTHELLO. Ha! wherefore?
    DESDEMONA. Why do you speak so
    startingly and rash?
    OTHELLO. Is't lost? Is't gone! Speak,
    is't out o' the way?   80
    DESDEMONA. Heaven bless us!
    OTHELLO.   Say you?
    DESDEMONA. It is not lost; but what an
    if it were?
    OTHELLO. How?
    DESDEMONA. I say, it is not lost.
    OTHELLO.   Fetch 't, let me see 't.
    DESDEMONA. Why, so I can, sir, but
    I will not now.
This is a trick to put me from my suit;
Pray you, let Cassio be receiv'd again.
    OTHELLO. Fetch me the handkerchief;
    my mind misgives.
    DESDEMONA. Come, come;   90
You'll never meet a more sufficient man.
    OTHELLO. The handkerchief!
    DESDEMONA. I pray, talk me of Cassio.
    OTHELLO. The handkerchief!
    DESDEMONA.   A man that all his time
Hath founded his good fortunes on your
    love,

Shar'd dangers with you,—
    OTHELLO. The handkerchief!
    DESDEMONA. I' faith, you are to blame.
    OTHELLO. 'Zounds!
                    (*Exit* OTHELLO.)
    EMILIA. Is not this man jealous?
    DESDEMONA. I ne'er saw this before.   100
Sure, there's some wonder in this
    handkerchief;
I am most unhappy in the loss of it.
    EMILIA. 'Tis not a year or two shows
    us a man:
They are all but stomachs, and we all but
    food;
They eat us hungerly, and when they are
    full
They belch us.

(*Enter* CASSIO *and* IAGO.)

        Look you, Cassio and my husband!
    IAGO. There is no other way, 'tis she
    must do 't;
And, lo, the happiness! Go, and importune
    her.
    DESDEMONA. How now, good Cassio!
    what's the news with you?

    CASSIO. Madam, my former suit. I do
    beseech you   110
That by your virtuous means I may again
Exist, and be a member of his love
Whom I with all the office of my heart
Entirely honor. I would not be delay'd.
If my offense be of such mortal kind
That nor my service past, nor present
    sorrows,
Nor purpos'd merit in futurity
Can ransom me into his love again,
But to know so must be my benefit;
So shall I clothe me in a forc'd content,   120
And shut myself up in some other course,
To Fortune's alms.
    DESDEMONA. Alas, thrice-gentle Cassio!
My advocation is not now in tune;
My lord is not my lord, nor should I know
    him
Were he in favor as in humor alter'd.
So help me every spirit sanctified
As I have spoken for you all my best

---

71 *sibyl:* prophetess   74 *mummy:* a concoction made of dried flesh
75 *Conserv'd:* prepared   79 *startingly:* by fits and starts   82 *an
if:* if

104 *all:* nothing   111 *virtuous means:* by means of virtue   113
office: devotion   119 *But:* only   119 *my benefit:* a favor to me
121 *To Fortune's alms:* to take what Fortune may give me

meloncholie — too thoughtful

And stood within the blank of his
    displeasure
For my free speech! You must a while be
    patient.
What I can do I will; and more I will   130
Than for myself I dare. Let that suffice
    you.
    IAGO.   Is my lord angry?
    EMILIA.   He went hence but now,
And certainly in strange unquietness.
    IAGO.   Can he be angry? I have seen the
    cannon
When it hath blown his ranks into the air,
And, like the devil, from his very arm
Puff'd his own brother—and can he be
    angry?
Something of moment then. I will go meet
    him.
There's matter in 't indeed, if he be angry.

                (*Exit* IAGO.)

    DESDEMONA.   I prithee, do so.
    Something, sure, of state,   140
Either from Venice, or some unhatch'd
    practice
Made demonstrable here in Cyprus to him,
Hath puddled his clear spirit; and in such
    cases
Men's natures wrangle with inferior things,
Though great ones are their object. 'Tis
    even so;
For let our finger ache, and it indues
Our other healthful members even to a
    sense
Of pain. Nay, we must think men are not
    gods,
Nor of them look for such observancy
As fits the bridal. Beshrew me much,   150
    Emilia,
I was, unhandsome warrior as I am,
Arraigning his unkindness with my soul;
But now I find I had suborn'd the witness,
And he's indicted falsely.
    EMILIA.   Pray Heaven it be state-matters,
    as you think,
And no conception nor no jealous toy
Concerning you.
    DESDEMONA.   Alas the day! I never gave

him cause.
    EMILIA.   But jealous souls will not be
    answer'd so;
They are not ever jealous for the cause,   160
But jealous for they're jealous. It is a
    monster
Begot upon itself, born on itself.
    DESDEMONA.   Heaven keep that monster
    from Othello's mind!
    EMILIA.   Lady, amen.
    DESDEMONA.   I will go seek him.
    Cassio, walk hereabout;
If I do find him fit, I'll move your suit
And seek to effect it to my uttermost.
    CASSIO.   I humbly thank your ladyship.

      (*Exeunt* DESDEMONA *and* EMILIA.)

(*Enter* BIANCA.)

    BIANCA.   Save you, friend Cassio!
    CASSIO.   What make you from home?
How is it with you, my most fair Bianca?   170
I' faith, sweet love, I was coming to your
    house.
    BIANCA.   And I was going to your lodg-
    ing, Cassio.
What, keep a week away? seven days and
    nights?
Eightscore eight hours? and lovers' absent
    hours,
More tedious than the dial eightscore times?
O weary reck'ning!
    Cassio.   Pardon me, Bianca.
I have this while with leaden thoughts been
    press'd;
But I shall, in a more continuate time,
Strike off this score of absence. Sweet
    Bianca,

(*Giving her* DESDEMONA'S *handkerchief.*)

Take me this work out.
    BIANCA.   O Cassio, whence came this?   180
This is some token from a newer friend;
To the felt absence now I feel a cause.
Is't come to this? Well, well.
    CASSIO.   Go to, woman!
Throw your vile guesses in the devil's teeth,
From whence you have them. You are
    jealous now

---

128 *blank:* direct aim   137 *Something:* some business   141 *un-hatch'd practice:* plot not yet matured   146 *indues:* brings into accord   149 *observancy:* attention   151 *unhandsome:* unfair 153 *suborn'd:* corrupted

175 *dial:* the whole round of the clock's hands   178 *more con-tinuate:* less interrupted   181 *friend:* mistress

That this is from some mistress, some
    remembrance.
No, by my faith, Bianca.
    BIANCA.   Why, whose is it?
    CASSIO. I know not, sweet; I found it
    in my chamber.
I like the work well; ere it be demanded—
As like enough it will—I'd have it copied.   190
Take it, and do't; and leave me for this
    time.
    BIANCA. Leave you! Wherefore?
    CASSIO. I do attend here on the
    General;
And think it no addition, nor my wish,
To have him see me woman'd.
    BIANCA.   Why, I pray you?
    CASSIO. Not that I love you not.
    BIANCA.   But that you do not love me.
I pray you, bring me on the way a little,
And say if I shall see you soon at night.
    CASSIO. 'Tis but a little way that I can
    bring you,
For I attend here; but I'll see you soon.   200
    BIANCA. 'Tis very good; I must be
    circumstanc'd.
                     (*Exeunt.*)

ACT IV.1 *Cyprus. Before the castle.*

(*Enter* OTHELLO *and* IAGO.)

    IAGO. Will you think so?
    OTHELLO.   Think so, Iago!
    IAGO.   What,
To kiss in private?
    OTHELLO.   An unauthoriz'd kiss.
    IAGO. Or to be naked with her friend in
    bed
An hour or more, not meaning any harm?
    OTHELLO. Naked in bed, Iago, and not
    mean harm!
It is hypocrisy against the devil:
They that mean virtuously, and yet do so,
The devil their virtue tempts, and they
    tempt heaven.
    IAGO. So they do nothing, 'tis a venial
    slip;
But if I give my wife a handkerchief,—   10

    OTHELLO. What then?
    IAGO. Why, then, 'tis hers, my lord;
    and, being hers,
She may, I think, bestow 't on any man.
    OTHELLO. She is protectress of her
    honor too;
May she give that?
    IAGO. Her honor is an essence that's
    not seen;
They have it very oft that have it not;
But, for the handkerchief,—
    OTHELLO. By heaven, I would most
    gladly have forgot it.
Thou said'st—O, it comes o'er my memory,   20
As doth the raven o'er the infected house,
Boding to all—he had my handkerchief.
    IAGO. Ay, what of that?
    OTHELLO.   That's not so good now.
    IAGO.   What
If I had said I had seen him do you wrong?
Or heard him say,—as knaves be such
    abroad,
Who having, by their own importunate
    suit,
Or voluntary dotage of some mistress,
Convinced or supplied them, cannot choose
But they must blab—
    OTHELLO.   Hath he said anything?
    IAGO. He hath, my lord; but be you
    well assur'd,   30
No more than he'll unswear.
    OTHELLO.   What hath he said?
    IAGO. Faith, that he did—I know not
    what he did.
    OTHELLO. What? what?
    IAGO. Lie—
    OTHELLO. With her?
    IAGO. With her, on her; what you will.
    OTHELLO. Lie with her! lie on her! We
    say lie on her, when they belie her. Lie
    with her! 'Zounds, that's fulsome!—
    Handkerchief—confessions—handker-
    chief!—To confess, and be hanged for
    his labor;—first, to be hanged, and then
    to confess.—I tremble at it. Nature
    would not invest herself in such shadow-   40
    ing passion without some destruction.
    It is not words that shake me thus.
    Pish! Noses, ears, and lips.—Is't possi-

---

186 *remembrance:* keepsake   193 *attend . . . on:* wait for   194
addition: credit   195 *woman'd:* with a woman   201 *be circum-*
stanc'd: submit to circumstances
ACT IV. 1   6 *hypocrisy against the devil:* appearing to do evil
without "meaning any harm"   8 *heaven:* i.e., heaven's power to
keep them from harm   9 *venial:* pardonable

---

17 *have it:* are reputed to have it   22 *Boding:* ominous   28
convinced or supplied: seduced or complied with   40 *invest herself:*
fill me with   41 *destruction:* actual cause

ble?—Confess—handkerchief!—O
devil!

(*Falls in a trance.*)

IAGO.   Work on,
My medicine, work! Thus credulous fools
are caught;
And many worthy and chaste dames even
thus,
All guiltless, meet reproach.—What, ho!
my lord!
My lord, I say! Othello!
(*Enter* CASSIO.)

How now, Cassio!

CASSIO.   What's the matter?   50
IAGO.   My lord is fall'n into an epilepsy.
This is his second fit; he had one yesterday.
CASSIO.   Rub him about the temples.
IAGO.   No, forbear;
The lethargy must have his quiet course;
If not, he foams at mouth and by and by
Breaks out to savage madness. Look, he
stirs.
Do you withdraw yourself a little while,
He will recover straight. When he is gone,
I would on great occasion speak with you.

(*Exit* CASSIO.)

How is it, general? Have you not hurt your   60
head?
OTHELLO.   Dost thou mock me?
IAGO.   I mock you not, by heaven.
Would you would bear your fortune like
a man!
OTHELLO.   A horned man's a monster
and a beast.
IAGO.   There's many a beast then in a
populous city,
And many a civil monster.
OTHELLO.   Did he confess it?
IAGO.   Good sir, be a man;
Think every bearded fellow that's but yok'd
May draw with you. There's millions now
alive
That nightly lie in those unproper beds
Which they dare swear peculiar; your case   70
is better.
O, 'tis the spite of hell, the fiend's arch-
mock,

To lip a wanton in a secure couch,
And to suppose her chaste! No, let me
know;
And knowing what I am, I know what she
shall be.
OTHELLO.   O, thou art wise; 'tis certain.
IAGO.   Stand you a while apart;
Confine yourself but in a patient list.
Whilst you were here o'erwhelmed with
your grief—
A passion most unsuiting such a man—
Cassio came hither. I shifted him away,
And laid good 'scuse upon your ecstasy;   80
Bade him anon return and here speak with
me,
The which he promis'd. Do but encave
yourself,
And mark the fleers, the gibes, and notable
scorns,
That dwell in every region of his face;
For I will make him tell the tale anew,
Where, how, how oft, how long ago, and
when
He hath, and is again to cope your wife.
I say, but mark his gesture. Marry,
patience;
Or I shall say you're all in all in spleen,
And nothing of a man.
OTHELLO.   Dost thou hear, Iago?   90
I will be found most cunning in my patience;
But—dost thou hear?—most bloody.
IAGO.   That's not amiss;
But yet keep time in all. Will you withdraw?

(OTHELLO *retires.*)

Now will I question Cassio of Bianca,
A housewife that by selling her desires
Buys herself bread and clothes. It is a
creature
That dotes on Cassio;—as 'tis the
strumpet's plague
To beguile many and be beguil'd by one;—
He, when he hears of her, cannot refrain
From the excess of laughter. Here he comes: 100

(*Re-enter* CASSIO.)

As he shall smile, Othello shall go mad;
And his unbookish jealously must construe

---

53 *forbear:* let him alone   54 *lethargy:* fit   61 *mock:* Othello
instantly thinks of the horns of a cuckold   66 *civil:* citizen   68
yok'd: married   68 *draw with:* share your fate   69 *unproper:*
not exclusively theirs   70 *peculiar:* theirs alone

72 *secure:* free from suspicion   76 *patient list:* in the bounds of
self-control   82 *encave:* conceal   87 *cope:* meet   89 *all in all
in spleen:* totally governed by impulses   93 *keep time:* act reason-
ably   95 *housewife:* hussy, harlot   102 *unbookish:* ignorant

Poor Cassio's smiles gestures, and light
  behaviors
Quite in the wrong. How do you,
  lieutenant?
CASSIO.   The worser that you give me
  the addition
Whose want even kills me.
IAGO.   Ply Desdemona well, and you are
  sure on't.
Now, if this suit lay in Bianca's power,
How quickly should you speed!
CASSIO.   Alas, poor caitiff!
OTHELLO.   Look, how he laughs already!   110
IAGO.   I never knew a woman love man
  so.
CASSIO.   Alas, poor rogue! I think, i'
  faith, she loves me.
OTHELLO.   Now he denies it faintly, and
  laughs it out.
IAGO.   Do you hear, Cassio?
OTHELLO.   Now he importunes him
To tell it o'er. Go to; well said, well said.
IAGO.   She gives it out that you shall
  marry her.
Do you intend it?
CASSIO.   Ha, ha, ha!   120
OTHELLO.   Do ye triumph, Roman? Do
  you triumph?
CASSIO.   I marry her! What? a customer!
  Prithee, bear some charity to my wit;
  do not think it so unwholesome. Ha,
  ha, ha!
OTHELLO.   So, so, so, so; Laugh that
  wins.
IAGO.   Faith, the cry goes that you shall
  marry her.
CASSIO.   Prithee, say true.
IAGO.   I am a very villain else.
OTHELLO.   Have you scor'd me? Well.   130
CASSIO.   This is the monkey's own giving
  out. She is persuaded I will marry her,
  out of her own love and flattery, not
  out of my promise.
OTHELLO.   Iago beckons me; now he
  begins the story.
CASSIO.   She was here even now; she
  haunts me in every place. I was the
  other day talking on the sea-bank with
  certain Venetians; and thither comes

the bauble, and, by this hand, she falls
  me thus about my neck—   140
OTHELLO.   Crying, "O dear Cassio!" as
  it were; his gesture imports it.
CASSIO.   So hangs, and lolls, and weeps
  upon me; so shakes and pulls me. Ha,
  ha, ha!
OTHELLO.   Now he tells how she plucked
  him to my chamber. O, I see that nose
  of yours, but not that dog I shall throw
  it to.
CASSIO.   Well, I must leave her company.
IAGO.   Before me! look, where she comes.

(*Enter* BIANCA.)

CASSIO.   'Tis such another fitchew!   150
  Marry, a perfumed one.—What do
  you mean by this haunting of me?
BIANCA.   Let the devil and his dam haunt
  you! What did you mean by that same
  handkerchief you gave me even now?
  I was a fine fool to take it. I must take
  out the work?—A likely piece of work,
  that you should find it in your chamber,
  and know not who left it there! This is
  some minx's token, and I must take out
  the work? There; give it your hobby-
  horse. Wheresoever you had it, I'll take   160
  out no work on't.
CASSIO.   How now, my sweet Bianca!
  how now! how now!
OTHELLO.   By heaven, that should be my
  handkerchief!
BIANCA.   If you'll come to supper to-
  night, you may; if you will not, come
  when you are next prepared for.

(*Exit.*)

IAGO.   After her, after her.   170
CASSIO.   Faith, I must; she'll rail in the
  streets else.
IAGO.   Will you sup there?
CASSIO.   Faith, I intend so.
IAGO.   Well, I may chance to see you; for
  I would very fain speak with you.
CASSIO.   Prithee, come; will you?
IAGO.   Go to; say no more.

(*Exit* CASSIO.)

---

105 *addition:* title   109 *caitiff:* wretch   121 *Roman:* i.e., proud
fellow   122 *customer:* harlot   130 *scor'd me:* summed me up

139 *bauble:* plaything   150 *fitchew:* polecat   152 *dam:* mother
159 *hobby-horse:* plaything

OTHELLO. (*Advancing.*) How shall I murder him, Iago? 180

IAGO. Did you perceive how he laughed at his vice?

OTHELLO. O Iago!

IAGO. And did you see the handkerchief?

OTHELLO. Was that mine?

IAGO. Yours, by this hand: and to see how he prizes the foolish woman your wife! She gave it him, and he hath given it his whore.

OTHELLO. I would have him nine years a-killing.
A fine woman! a fair woman! a sweet woman!

IAGO. Nay, you must forget that. 190

OTHELLO. Ay, let her rot, and perish, and be damned tonight; for she shall not live. No, my heart is turned to stone; I strike it, and it hurts my hand. O, the world hath not a sweeter creature! She might lie by an emperor's side and command him tasks.

IAGO. Nay, that's not your way.

OTHELLO. Hang her! I do but say what she is. So delicate with her needle! an admirable musician! O! she will sing the savageness out of a bear: of so high 200 and plenteous wit and invention!

IAGO. She's the worse for all this.

OTHELLO. O, a thousand thousand times! And then, of so gentle a condition!

IAGO. Ay, too gentle.

OTHELLO. Nay, that's certain. But yet the pity of it, Iago! O Iago, the pity of it, Iago!

IAGO. If you are so fond over her iniquity, give her patent to offend; for, if it touch not you, it comes near 210 nobody.

OTHELLO. I will chop her into messes. Cuckold me!

IAGO. O, 'tis foul in her.

OTHELLO. With mine officer!

IAGO. That's fouler.

OTHELLO. Get me some poison, Iago, this night. I'll not expostulate with her, lest her body and beauty unprovide my mind again. This night, Iago.

IAGO. Do it not with poison; strangle 220 her in her bed, even the bed she hath contaminated.

OTHELLO. Good, good; the justice of it pleases; very good.

IAGO. And for Cassio, let me be his undertaker: you shall hear more by midnight.

OTHELLO. Excellent good!

(*A trumpet.*)

What trumpet is that same?

IAGO. Something from Venice sure.

(*Enter* LODOVICO, DESDEMONA, *and* ATTENDANTS.)

'Tis Lodovico.
Come from the Duke; and, see, your wife is with him.

LODOVICO. God save you, worthy General!

OTHELLO. With all my heart, sir.

LODOVICO. The Duke and senators of Venice greet you. 230

(*Gives him a letter.*)

OTHELLO. I kiss the instrument of their pleasures.

(*Opens the letter and reads.*)

DESDEMONA. And what's the news, good cousin Lodovico?

IAGO. I am very glad to see you, signior; Welcome to Cyprus.

LODOVICO. I thank you. How does Lieutenant Cassio?

IAGO. Lives, sir.

DESDEMONA. Cousin, there's fall'n between him and my lord
An unkind breach; but you shall make all well.

OTHELLO. Are you sure of that?

DESDEMONA. My lord!

OTHELLO. (*Reads.*) "This fail you not to do, as you will"— 240

LODOVICO. He did not call; he's busy in the paper.

---

196 *Nay ... way:* you must not soften in your purpose   201 *invention:* originality   204 *condition:* disposition   209 *patent:* a charter

223 *be his undertaker:* manage his business   231 *kiss:* welcome

Is there division 'twixt my lord and Cassio?
DESDEMONA.   A most unhappy one.
  I would do much
T'atone them, for the love I bear to Cassio.
OTHELLO.   Fire and brimstone!
DESDEMONA.   My lord?
OTHELLO.   Are you wise?
DESDEMONA.   What, is he angry?
LODOVICO.   May be
  the letter mov'd him;
For, as I think, they do command him
  home,
Deputing Cassio in his government.
DESDEMONA.   Trust me, I am glad on 't.
OTHELLO.   Indeed!
DESDEMONA.   My lord?
OTHELLO.   I am glad to see you mad.
DESDEMONA.   Why, sweet Othello,— 250
OTHELLO.   (*Striking her.*) Devil!
DESDEMONA.   I have not deserv'd this.
LODOVICO.   My lord, this would not be
  believ'd in Venice
Though I should swear I saw't. 'Tis very
  much.
Make her amends: she weeps.
OTHELLO.   O devil, devil!
If that the earth could teem with a woman's
  tears,
Each drop she falls would prove a crocodile.
Out of my sight!
DESDEMONA.   I will not stay to offend
  you.

                  (*Going.*)

LODOVICO.   Truly, an obedient lady,
I do beseech your lordship, call her back. 260
OTHELLO.   Mistress!
DESDEMONA.   My lord?
OTHELLO.   What
  would you with her, sir?
LODOVICO.   Who, I, my lord?
OTHELLO.   Ay; you did wish that I would
  make her turn.
Sir, she can turn, and turn, and yet go on,
And turn again; and she can weep, sir, weep;
And she's obedient, as you say, obedient,
Very obedient. Proceed you in your tears.
Concerning this, sir,—O well-painted

passion!—
I am commanded home.—Get you away;
I'll send for you anon.—Sir, I obey the
  mandate,   270
And will return to Venice.—Hence,
  avaunt!—

              (*Exit* DESDEMONA.)

Cassio shall have my place. And, sir,
  to-night,
I do entreat that we may sup together.
You are welcome, sir, to Cyprus.—Goats
  and monkeys!
LODOVICO.   Is this the noble Moor whom
  our full Senate
Call all in all sufficient? Is this the nature
Whom passion could not shake? whose
  solid virtue
The shot of accident nor dart of chance
Could neither graze nor pierce?
IAGO.   He is much chang'd.
LODOVICO.   Are his wits safe? Is he not
  light of brain?   280
IAGO.   He's that he is; I may not breathe
  my censure
What he might be. If what he might he is
  not,
I would to heaven he were!
LODOVICO.   What, strike his wife!
IAGO.   Faith, that was not so well; yet
  would I knew
That stroke would prove the worst!
LODOVICO.   Is it his use?
Or did the letters work upon his blood,
And new-create this fault?
IAGO.   Alas, alas!
It is not honesty in me to speak
What I have seen and known. You shall
  observe him,
And his own courses will denote him so   290
That I may save my speech. Do but go
  after,
And mark how he continues.
LODOVICO.   I am sorry that I am deceiv'd
  in him.
                 (*Exeunt.*)

ACT IV.2 *A room in the castle.*

(*Enter* OTHELLO *and* EMILIA.)

---

244 *T'atone:* to reconcile   246 *wise:* i.e., sane   256 *teem:* bear offspring   257 *crocodile:* the crocodile was supposed to trap victims by weeping, and then devouring any who came to pity it   268 *well-painted:* cleverly imitated

277 *passion:* emotion   281 *censure:* opinion   285 *use:* habit
290 *courses:* behavior

OTHELLO.   You have seen nothing then?

EMILIA.   Nor ever heard, nor ever did suspect.

OTHELLO.   Yes, you have seen Cassio and she together.

EMILIA.   But then I saw no harm, and then I heard
Each syllable that breath made up between them.

OTHELLO.   What, did they never whisper?

EMILIA.   Never, my lord.

OTHELLO.   Nor send you out o' th' way?

EMILIA.   Never.

OTHELLO.   To fetch her fan, her gloves, her mask, nor nothing?

EMILIA.   Never, my lord.   10

OTHELLO.   That's strange.

EMILIA.   I durst, my lord, to wager she is honest,
Lay down my soul at stake. If you think other,
Remove your thought; it doth abuse your bosom.
If any wretch have put this in your head,
Let Heaven requite it with the serpent's curse!
For, if she be not honest, chaste, and true,
There's no man happy; the purest of their wives
Is foul as slander.

OTHELLO.   Bid her come hither; go.

(*Exit* EMILIA.)

She says enough yet she's a simple bawd   20
That cannot say as much. This is a subtle whore,
A closet lock and key of villanous secrets;
And yet she'll kneel and pray; I have seen her do 't.

(*Enter* DESDEMONA *with* EMILIA.)

DESDEMONA.   My lord, what is your will?

OTHELLO.   Pray, chuck, come hither.

DESDEMONA.   What is your pleasure?

OTHELLO.   Let me see your eyes;
Look in my face.

DESDEMONA.   What horrible fancy's this?

OTHELLO.   (*To* EMILIA.) Some of your function, mistress;
Leave procreants alone and shut the door;
Cough, or cry "hem," if anybody come.
Your mystery, your mystery; nay, dispatch.   30

(*Exit* EMILIA.)

DESDEMONA.   Upon my knees, what doth your speech import?
I understand a fury in your words,
But not the words.

OTHELLO.   Why, what art thou?

DESDEMONA.   Your wife, my lord; your true
And loyal wife.

OTHELLO.   Come, swear it, damn thyself.
Lest, being like one of heaven, the devils themselves
Should fear to seize thee; therefore be double damn'd,
Swear thou art honest.

DESDEMONA.   Heaven doth truly know it.

OTHELLO.   Heaven truly knows that thou art false as hell.

DESDEMONA.   To whom, my lord? With whom? How am I false?   40

OTHELLO.   Ah, Desdemona! Away! away! away!

DESDEMONA.   Alas the heavy day! Why do you weep?
Am I the motive of these tears, my lord?
If haply you my father do suspect
An instrument of this your calling back,
Lay not your blame on me. If you have lost him,
Why, I have lost him too.

OTHELLO.   Had it pleas'd Heaven
To try me with affliction; had they rain'd
All kinds of sores and shames on my bare head,
Steep'd me in poverty to the very lips,   50
Given to captivity me and my utmost hopes,
I should have found in some place of my soul
A drop of patience; but, alas, to make me

ACT IV. 2   9 *mask:* often worn by Elizabethan ladies in public places   13 *at stake:* as a wager   13 *other:* otherwise   16 *curse:* i.e., always to crawl on his belly; cf., the Snake in the Garden of Eden   20 *bawd:* proprietor of a brothel   22 *closet:* private room   22 *lock and key:* i.e., keeper

27 *Some:* perform some   27 *function:* office (of bawd)   30 *mystery:* trade   42 *heavy:* sorrowful

The fixed figure for the time of scorn
To point his slow unmoving finger at!
Yet could I bear that too, well, very well;
But there, where I have garner'd up my
      heart,
Where either I must live, or bear no life;
The fountain from the which my current
      runs,
Or else dries up to be discarded thence!   60
Or keep it as a cistern for foul toads
To knot and gender in! Turn thy complexion
      there,
Patience, thou young and rose-lipp'd
      cherubin,
Ay, there look grim as hell!
      DESDEMONA.   I hope my noble lord
      esteems me honest.
      OTHELLO.   O, ay; as summer flies are in
      the shambles,
That quicken even with blowing. O thou
      weed,
Who art so lovely fair and smell'st so sweet
That the sense aches at thee, would thou
      hadst ne'er been born!
      DESDEMONA.   Alas, what ignorant sin
      have I committed?   70
      OTHELLO.   Was this fair paper, this most
      goodly book,
Made to write "whore" upon? What
      committed?
Committed! O thou public commoner!
I should make very forges of my cheeks,
That would to cinders burn up modesty,
Did I but speak thy deeds. What
      committed?
Heaven stops the nose at it, and the moon
      winks,
The bawdy wind that kisses all it meets,
Is hush'd within the hollow mine of earth,
And will not hear it. What committed!   80
Impudent strumpet!
      DESDEMONA.   By heaven, you do me
      wrong.
      OTHELLO.   Are not you a strumpet?
      DESDEMONA.   No, as I am a Christian.
If to preserve this vessel for my lord

From any other foul unlawful touch
Be not to be a strumpet, I am none.
      OTHELLO.   What, not a whore?
      DESDEMONA.   No, as I shall be sav'd.
      OTHELLO.   Is 't possible?
      DESDEMONA.   O, Heaven forgive us!
      OTHELLO.   I cry you mercy, then.
I took you for that cunning whore of Venice
That married with Othello.—You, mistress,   90

(*Re-enter* EMILIA.)

That have the office opposite to Saint Peter,
And keeps the gate of hell! You, you, ay,
      you!
We have done our course; there's money for
      your pains.
I pray you, turn the key and keep our
      counsel.   (*Exit.*)
      EMILIA.   Alas, what does this gentleman
      conceive?
How do you, madam? How do you, my
      good lady?
      DESDEMONA.   Faith, half asleep.
      EMILIA.   Good madam, what's the
      matter with my lord?
      DESDEMONA.   With who?
      EMILIA.   Why, with my lord, madam.   100
      DESDEMONA.   Who is thy lord?
      EMILIA.   He that is yours, sweet lady.
      DESDEMONA.   I have none. Do not talk
      to me, Emilia;
I cannot weep, nor answers have I none
But what should go by water. Prithee,
      to-night
Lay on my bed my wedding sheets—
      remember;
And call thy husband hither.
      EMILIA.   Here's a change indeed!

                        (*Exit.*)

      DESDEMONA.   'Tis meet I should be us'd
      so, very meet.
How have I been behav'd, that he might
      stick
The small'st opinion on my least misuse?

(*Re-enter* EMILIA *with* IAGO.)

      IAGO.   What is your pleasure, madam?
      How is 't with you?   110

---

54 *time of scorn:* scornful world   55 *to point . . . finger at:* i.e., the finger is slow in "coming to point," but once fixed, is immoveable   57 *garnered up:* stored the harvest of   59 *fountain:* spring   60 *discarded thence:* rejected from it (i.e., her love)   61 *cistern:* cesspool   62 *gender:* mate   66 *shambles:* slaughterhouse   67 *quicken:* spring to life   67 *blowing:* laying of the eggs   73 *commoner:* prostitute   77 *winks:* shuts her eyes   79 *mine of earth:* cave whence the winds issued in classical legend

---

91 *Saint Peter:* gatekeeper of heaven   94 *counsel:* secret   104 *go by water:* be expressed by tears   107 *meet:* proper   109 *misuse:* slightest misconduct

DESDEMONA.   I cannot tell. Those that do
teach young babes
Do it with gentle means and easy tasks.
He might have chid me so; for, in good
faith,
I am a child to chiding.
    IAGO.   What's the matter, lady?
    EMILIA.   Alas, Iago, my lord hath so
bewhor'd her,
Thrown such despite and heavy terms upon
her,
That true hearts cannot bear.
    DESDEMONA.   Am I that name, Iago?
    IAGO.   What name, fair lady?
    DESDEMONA.   Such as she said my lord
did say I was.
    EMILIA.   He call'd her whore. A beggar
in his drink   120
Could not have laid such terms upon his
callet.
    IAGO.   Why did he so?
    DESDEMONA.   I do not know; I am sure
I am none such.
    IAGO.   Do not weep, do not weep. Alas
the day!
    EMILIA.   Hath she forsook so many noble
matches,
Her father and her country and her friends,
To be call'd whore? Would it not make one
weep?
    DESDEMONA.   It is my wretched fortune.
    IAGO.   Beshrew him for 't!
How comes this trick upon him?
    DESDEMONA.   Nay, Heaven doth know.
    EMILIA.   I will be hang'd, if some eternal
villain,   130
Some busy and insinuating rogue,
Some cogging, cozening slave, to get some
office,
Have not devis'd this slander; I'll be hang'd
else.
    IAGO.   Fie, there is no such man; it is
impossible.
    DESDEMONA.   If any such there be,
Heaven pardon him!
    EMILIA.   A halter pardon him and hell
gnaw his bones!
Why should he call her whore? Who keeps
her company?
What place? what time? what form? what

likelihood?
The Moor's abus'd by some most villainous
knave,
Some base notorious knave, some scurvy
fellow.   140
O heaven, that such companions thou 'dst
unfold,
And put in every honest hand a whip
To lash the rascals naked through the world
Even from the east to th' west!
    IAGO.   Speak within door.
    EMILIA.   O, fie upon them! Some such
squire he was
That turn'd your wit the seamy side without,
And made you to suspect me with the Moor.
    IAGO.   You are a fool; go to.
    DESDEMONA.   Alas, Iago,
What shall I do to win my lord again?
Good friend, go to him; for, by this light of
heaven,   150
I know not how I lost him. Here I kneel:
If e'er my will did trespass 'gainst his love,
Either in discourse of thought or actual
deed,
Or that mine eyes, mine ears, or any sense
Delighted them in any other form;
Or that I do not yet, and ever did,
And ever will—though he do shake me off
To beggarly divorcement—love him dearly,
Comfort forswear me! Unkindness may do
much;
And his unkindness may defeat my life,   160
But never taint my love. I cannot say
"whore."
It does abhor me now I speak the word;
To do the act that might the addition earn
Not the world's mass of vanity could make
me.
    IAGO.   I pray you, be content; 'tis but
his humor.
The business of the state does him offense,
And he does chide with you.
    DESDEMONA.   If 'twere no other,—
    IAGO.   It is but so, I warrant.

(*Trumpets within.*)

Hark, how these instruments summon to
supper!

---

121 *callet:* trull, "moll"   129 *trick:* freak   131 *busy:* med-
dlesome   132 *cogging:* cheating   136 *halter:* hangman's noose

140 *notorious:* notable   141 *companions:* knaves   141 *unfold:*
reveal   144 *within door:* more quietly   146 *seamy:* wrong
153 *discourse:* process   155 *them:* themselves   155 *form:* man
164 *vanity:* vain delights

The messengers of Venice stay the meat. 170
Go in, and weep not; all things shall be
  well.
    (*Exeunt* DESDEMONA *and* EMILIA.)

(*Enter* RODERIGO.)

How now, Roderigo!
  RODERIGO. I do not find that thou deal'st
    justly with me.
  IAGO. What in the contrary?
  RODERIGO. Every day thou daff'st me
    with some device, Iago; and rather, as
    it seems to me now, keep'st from me all
    conveniency than suppliest me with
    the least advantage of hope. I will indeed
    no longer endure it, nor am I yet per-
    suaded to put up in peace what already 180
    I have foolishly suffered.
  IAGO. Will you hear me, Roderigo?
  RODERIGO. Faith, I have heard too
    much, for your words and performances
    are no kin together.
  IAGO. You charge me most unjustly.
  RODERIGO. With nought but truth. I
    have wasted myself out of my means.
    The jewels you have had from me to
    deliver Desdemona would half have
    corrupted a votarist. You have told me 190
    she hath received them and returned me
    expectations and comforts of sudden
    respect and acquaintance, but I find
    none.
  IAGO. Well; go to; very well.
  RODERIGO. Very well! go to! I cannot go
    to, man; nor 'tis not very well. By this
    hand, I say 'tis scurvy, and begin to find
    myself fopped in it.
  IAGO. Very well.
  RODERIGO. I tell you 'tis not very well. I
    will make myself known to Desdemona: 200
    if she will return me my jewels, I will
    give over my suit and repent my un-
    lawful solicitation; if not, assure your-
    self I will seek satisfaction of you.
  IAGO. You have said now.
  RODERIGO. Ay, and said nothing but
    what I protest intendment of doing.
  IAGO. Why, now I see there's mettle in
    thee, and even from this instant do

build on thee a better opinion than ever
before. Give me thy hand, Roderigo. 210
Thou hast taken against me a most just
exception; but yet, I protest, I have dealt
most directly in thy affair.
  RODERIGO. It hath not appeared.
  IAGO. I grant indeed it hath not ap-
    peared, and your suspicion is not with-
    out wit and judgment. But, Roderigo,
    if thou hast that in thee indeed, which
    I have greater reason to believe now
    than ever—I mean purpose, courage,
    and valor—this night show it. If thou
    the next night following enjoy not 220
    Desdemona, take me from this world
    with treachery and devise engines for
    my life.
  RODERIGO. Well, what is it? Is it within
    reason and compass?
  IAGO. Sir, there is especial commission
    come from Venice to depute Cassio in
    Othello's place.
  RODERIGO. Is that true? Why, then
    Othello and Desdemona return again
    to Venice.
  IAGO. O, no; he goes into Mauretania
    and takes away with him the fair Desde- 230
    mona, unless his abode be lingered here
    by some accident; wherein none can be
    so determinate as the removing of
    Cassio.
  RODERIGO. How do you mean, remov-
    ing him?
  IAGO. Why, by making him uncapable
    of Othello's place; knocking out his
    brains.
  RODERIGO. And that you would have
    me to do? 240
  IAGO. Ay, if you dare do yourself a
    profit and a right. He sups to-night with
    a harlotry, and thither will I go to him:
    he knows not yet of his honorable for-
    tune. If you will watch his going thence,
    which I will fashion to fall out between
    twelve and one, you may take him at
    your pleasure. I will be near to second
    your attempt, and he shall fall between
    us. Come, stand not amazed at it, but
    go along with me; I will show you such

---

170 *meat:* supper   175 *daff'st me:* put me off   177 *conveniency:*
opportunity   190 *votarist:* nun   192 *sudden:* immediate   197
fopped: made a fool of   207 *mettle:* spirit

222 *engines for:* plots against   231 *abode be lingered:* stay be
lengthened   233 *determinate:* decisive   237 *uncapable of:* unable
to succeed to   243 *harlotry:* harlot

a necessity in his death that you shall
think yourself bound to put it on him.
It is now high suppertime, and the night
grows to waste. About it.   250
RODERIGO.   I will hear further reason for
this.
IAGO.   And you shall be satisfied.
                                        (*Exeunt.*)

ACT IV.3 *Another room in the castle.*

(*Enter* OTHELLO, LODOVICO, DESDEMONA,
EMILIA, *and* ATTENDANTS.)
LODOVICO.   I do beseech you, sir, trouble
yourself no further.
OTHELLO.   O, pardon me; 'twill do me
good to walk.
LODOVICO.   Madam, good-night; I
humbly thank your ladyship.
DESDEMONA.   Your honor is most
welcome.
OTHELLO.   Will you walk, sir?
O, Desdemona,—
DESDEMONA.   My lord?
OTHELLO.   Get you to bed on th' instant;
I will be returned forthwith. Dispatch
your attendant there. Look 't be done.
DESDEMONA.   I will, my lord.   10

                (*Exeunt* OTHELLO, LODOVICO, *and*
                                        ATTENDANTS.)

EMILIA.   How goes it now? He looks
gentler than he did.
DESDEMONA.   He says he will return
incontinent;
And hath commanded me to go to bed,
And bade me to dismiss you.
EMILIA.   Dismiss me?
DESDEMONA.   It was his bidding; there-
fore, good Emilia,
Give me my nightly wearing, and adieu.
We must not now displease him.
EMILIA.   I would you had never seen
him!
DESDEMONA.   So would not I. My love
doth so approve him,
That even his stubbornness, his checks, his
frowns,—   20
Prithee, unpin me,—have grace and favor

in them.
EMILIA.   I have laid those sheets you bade
me on the bed.
DESDEMONA.   All's one. Good faith, how
foolish are our minds!
If I do die before thee, prithee, shroud me
In one of those same sheets.
EMILIA.   Come, come, you talk.
DESDEMONA.   My mother had a maid
call'd Barbara;
She was in love, and he she lov'd prov'd mad
And did forsake her. She had a song of
"willow";
An old thing 'twas, but it express'd her
fortune,
And she died singing it. That song to-night   30
Will not go from my mind; I have much to
do
But to go hang my head all at one side
And sing it like poor Barbara. Prithee,
dispatch.
EMILIA.   Shall I go fetch your night-
gown?
DESDEMONA.   No, unpin me here.
This Lodovico is a proper man.
EMILIA.   A very handsome man.
DESDEMONA.   He speaks well.
EMILIA.   I know a lady in Venice would
have walked barefoot to Palestine for
a touch of his nether lip.   40
DESDEMONA.   (*Singing.*)

The poor soul sat sighing by a sycamore
tree,
    Sing all a green willow;
Her hand on her bosom, her head on
her knee,
    Sing willow, willow, willow.
The fresh streams ran by her, and murmur'd her moans;
    Sing willow, willow, willow;
Her salt tears fell from her, and soften'd
the stones;
    Sing willow, willow, willow;

Lay by these;—
(*Singing.*) "*Willow, willow;*"—
Prithee, hie thee; he'll come anon;—   50
(*Singing.*)

---

249 *high:* exactly
ACT IV. 3   8 *dispatch:* dismiss   12 *incontinent:* immediately
19 *approve:* commend

23 *All's one:* no matter   27 *mad:* wayward   28 "*willow*":
emblem of forlorn lovers   32 *But to go hang:* to keep from hanging
34 *night-gown:* dressing gown   41 *sycamore tree:* emblem of vain
hope

Sing all a green willow must be my
  garland.
Let nobody blame him, his scorn I approve,—

Nay, that's not next.—Hark! who is't that
  knocks?
EMILIA. It's the wind.
DESDEMONA. (*Singing*.)
  I call'd my love false love; but what
    said he then?
  Sing willow, willow, willow.

  If I court moe women, you'll couch with
    moe men.—
So, get thee gone; good-night. Mine eyes do
  itch;
Doth that bode weeping?
EMILIA.   'Tis neither here nor there.
DESDEMONA. I have heard it said so. O,
  these men, these men!   60
Dost thou in conscience think,—tell me,
  Emilia,—
That there be women do abuse their
  husbands
In such gross kind?
EMILIA.   There be some such, no
  question.
DESDEMONA. Wouldst thou do such a
  a deed for all the world?
EMILIA. Why, would not you?
DESDEMONA. No, by this heavenly light!
EMILIA. Nor I neither by this heavenly
  light; I might do 't as well i' th' dark.
DESDEMONA. Wouldst thou do such a
  deed for all the world?
EMILIA. The world's a huge thing; it is
  a great price for a small vice.
DESDEMONA. In troth, I think thou   70
  wouldst not.
EMILIA. In troth, I think I should; and
  undo 't when I had done. Marry, I would
  not do such a thing for a joint-ring, nor
  for measures of lawn, nor for gowns,
  petticoats, nor caps, nor any petty exhibition; but, for all the whole world,—
  'ud's pity, who would not make her
  husband a cuckold to make him a monarch? I should venture purgatory for 't.
DESDEMONA. Beshrew me, if I would do

such a wrong for the whole world.
EMILIA. Why, the wrong is but a wrong
  i' th' world; and having the world for   80
  your labor, 'tis a wrong in your own
  world, and you might quickly make it
  right.
DESDEMONA. I do not think there is any
  such woman.
EMILIA. Yes, a dozen; and as many to
  th' vantage as would store the world
  they play'd for.
But I do think it is their husbands' faults
If wives do fall. Say that they slack their
  duties
And pour our treasures into foreign laps,
Or else break out in peevish jealousies,   90
Throwing restraint upon us; or say they
  strike us,
Or scant our former having in despite;
Why, we have galls, and though we have
  some grace,
Yet have we some revenge. Let husbands
  know
Their wives have sense like them; they see
  and smell
And have their palates both for sweet and
  sour
As husbands have. What is it that they do
When they change us for others? Is it
  sport?
I think it is. And doth affection breed it?
I think it doth. Is't frailty that thus errs?   100
It is so too. And have not we affections,
Desires for sport, and frailty, as men have?
Then let them use us well; else let them
  know,
The ills we do, their ills instruct us so.
DESDEMONA. Good-night, good-night.
  Heaven me such uses send,
Not to pick bad from bad, but by bad mend.
                        (*Exeunt*.)

ACT V.1 *Cyprus. A street.*

(*Enter* IAGO *and* RODERIGO.)

IAGO. Here, stand behind this bulk;
  straight will he come.
Wear thy good rapier bare, and put it home.

---

57 *moe:* more   62 *abuse:* deceive   63 *kind:* way   72 *undo't:*
deny it   73 *joint-ring:* a love token   74 *lawn:* linen   76 *ud's
pity:* God's pity

85 *to th'vantage:* in addition   92 *having:* allowance   93 *galls:*
capacity for resentment   94 *revenge:* vindictiveness   98 *change:*
exchange   99 *affection:* desire for pleasure   106 *uses:* practices
107 *pick:* learn
ACT V. 1   1 *bulk:* projecting structure

Quick, quick; fear nothing; I'll be at thy elbow.
It makes us, or it mars us; think on that,
And fix most firm thy resolution.

RODERIGO.   Be near at hand; I may miscarry in 't.

IAGO.   Here, at thy hand; be bold, and take thy stand.

(*Retires.*)

RODERIGO.   I have no great devotion to the deed,
And yet he hath given me satisfying reasons—
'Tis but a man gone. Forth, my sword; he dies.   10

IAGO.   I have rubb'd this young quat almost to the sense,
And he grows angry. Now, whether he kill Cassio,
Or Cassio him, or each do kill the other,
Every way makes my gain. Live Roderigo,
He calls me to a restitution large
Of gold and jewels that I bobb'd from him,
As gifts to Desdemona;
It must not be. If Cassio do remain,
He hath a daily beauty in his life
That makes me ugly; and, besides, the Moor   20
May unfold me to him; there stand I in much peril.
No, he must die. Be't so. I hear him coming.

(*Enter* CASSIO.)

RODERIGO.   I know his gait, 'tis he.—
Villain, thou diest!

(*Makes a pass at* CASSIO.)

CASSIO.   That thrust had been mine enemy indeed,
But that my coat is better than thou know'st.
I will make proof of thine.
            (*Draws, and wounds* RODERIGO.)
RODERIGO.   O, I am slain.

(IAGO *from behind wounds* CASSIO *in the leg, and exit.*)

CASSIO.   I am maim'd for ever. Help, ho! murder! murder!

(*Falls.*)

(*Enter* OTHELLO.)

OTHELLO.   The voice of Cassio! Iago keeps his word.
RODERIGO.   O, villain that I am!
OTHELLO.   It is even so.
CASSIO.   O, help, ho! light! a surgeon!   30
OTHELLO.   'Tis he!—O brave Iago, honest and just,
That hast such noble sense of thy friends' wrong!
Thou teachest me. Minion, your dear lies dead,
And your unblest fate hies; strumpet, I come.
Forth of my heart those charms, thine eyes, are blotted;
Thy bed, lust-stain'd, shall with lust's blood be spotted.

(*Exit.*)

(*Enter* LODOVICO *and* GRATIANO.)

CASSIO.   What, ho! no watch? no passage? Murder! murder!
GRATIANO.   'Tis some mischance; the voice is direful.
CASSIO.   O, help!
LODOVICO.   Hark!   40
RODERIGO.   O wretched villain!
LODOVICO.   Two or three groan. It is a heavy night,
These may be counterfeits; let's think't unsafe
To come in to the cry without more help.
RODERIGO.   Nobody come? Then shall I bleed to death.

(*Re-enter* IAGO, *with a light.*)

LODOVICO.   Hark!
GRATIANO.   Here's one comes in his shirt, with light and weapons.
IAGO.   Who's there? Whose noise is this that cries on murder?
LODOVICO.   We do not know.
IAGO.   Do not you hear a cry?
CASSIO.   Here, here! for Heaven's sake, help me!
IAGO.   What's the matter?   50

---

6 *miscarry:* fail   11 *quat:* pimple   11 *sense:* quick   15 *large:* full   16 *bobb'd:* cheated   21 *unfold:* expose   25 *coat:* shirt of mail

33 *minion:* darling   34 *hies:* hastens   35 *of:* from   37 *passage:* passersby

GRATIANO.   This is Othello's ancient, as
I take it.

LODOVICO.   The same indeed; a very
valiant fellow.

IAGO.   What are you here that cry so
grievously?

CASSIO.   Iago? O, I am spoil'd, undone
by villains!
Give me some help.

IAGO.   O me, lieutenant! what villains
have done this?

CASSIO.   I think that one of them is
hereabout,
And cannot make away.

IAGO.   O treacherous villains!
What are you there?—Come in, and give
some help.

(*To* LODOVICO *and* GRATIANO.)

RODERIGO.   O, help me there!   60

CASSIO.   That's one of them.

IAGO.   O murderous slave! O villain!

(*Stabs* RODERIGO.)

RODERIGO.   O damn'd Iago! O inhuman
dog!

IAGO.   Kill men i' th' dark!—Where be
these bloody thieves?—
How silent is this town!—Ho! murder!
murder!—
What may you be? Are you of good or evil?

LODOVICO.   As you shall prove us, praise
us.

IAGO.   Signior Lodovico?

LODOVICO.   He, sir.

IAGO.   I cry you mercy. Here's Cassio
hurt by villains.

GRATIANO.   Cassio!   70

IAGO.   How is 't, brother!

CASSIO.   My leg is cut in two.

IAGO.   Marry, heaven forbid!
Light, gentlemen! I'll bind it with my shirt.

(*Enter* BIANCA.)

BIANCA.   What is the matter, ho? Who
is't that cried?

IAGO.   Who is't that cried!

BIANCA.   O my dear Cassio! my sweet
Cassio!
O Cassio, Cassio, Cassio!

IAGO.   O notable strumpet! Cassio, may
you suspect
Who they should be that have thus mangled
you?

CASSIO.   No.   80

GRATIANO.   I am sorry to find you thus;
I have been to seek you.

IAGO.   Lend me a garter. So. O, for a
chair,
To bear him easily hence!

BIANCA.   Alas, he faints! O Cassio,
Cassio, Cassio!

IAGO.   Gentlemen all, I do suspect this
trash
To be a party in this injury.
Patience a while, good Cassio. Come, come;
Lend me a light. Know we this face or no?
Alas, my friend and my dear countryman
Roderigo! No:—yes, sure:—O heaven!   90
Roderigo.

GRATIANO.   What, of Venice?

IAGO.   Even he, sir; did you know him?

GRATIANO.   Know him? ay.

IAGO.   Signior Gratiano? I cry you
gentle pardon;
These bloody accidents must excuse my
manners,
That so neglected you.

GRATIANO.   I am glad to see you.

IAGO.   How do you, Cassio? O, a chair,
a chair!

GRATIANO.   Roderigo!

IAGO.   He, he, 'tis he. (*A chair brought
in.*) O, that's well said; the chair.
Some good man bear him carefully from
hence;
I'll fetch the General's surgeon. (*To* BIANCA.)
For you mistress,   100
Save you your labor. He that lies slain here,
Cassio,
Was my dear friend. What malice was
between you?

CASSIO.   None in the world; nor do
I know the man.

IAGO.   (*To* BIANCA.) What, look you
pale? O, bear him out o' th' air.

(CASSIO *and* RODERIGO *are borne off.*)

Stay you, good gentlemen. Look you pale,
mistress?

---

54 *spoil'd:* crippled   59 *Come in:* approach   83 *chair:* litter

Do you perceive the gastness of her eye?
Nay, if you stare, we shall hear more anon.
Behold her well; I pray you, look upon her.
Do you see, gentlemen? Nay, guiltiness will speak,
Though tongues were out of use.   110

(*Enter* EMILIA.)

EMILIA.   Alas, what's the matter? What's the matter, husband?
IAGO.   Cassio hath here been set on in the dark
By Roderigo and fellows that are scap'd.
He's almost slain, and Roderigo dead.
EMILIA.   Alas, good gentlemen! alas, good Cassio!
IAGO.   This is the fruits of whoring. Prithee, Emilia,
Go know of Cassio where he supp'd to-night.
(*To* BIANCA.) What, do you shake at that?
BIANCA.   He supp'd at my house; but I therefore shake not.
IAGO.   O, did he so? I charge you, go with me.   120
EMILIA.   Oh, fie upon thee, strumpet!
BIANCA.   I am no strumpet, but of life as honest
As you that thus abuse me.
EMILIA.   As I? Fie upon thee!
IAGO.   Kind gentlemen, let's go see poor Cassio dress'd.
Come, mistress, you must tell's another tale.
Emilia, run you to the citadel,
And tell my lord and lady what hath happ'd.
Will you go on afore? (*Aside.*) This is the night

Rhyming couplet

That either makes me or fordoes me quite.
                                          (*Exeunt.*)

ACT V.2 *A bedchamber in the castle:*
         Desdemona in bed asleep.

(*Enter* OTHELLO *with a light.*)

OTHELLO.   It is the cause, it is the cause, my soul,—
Let me not name it to you, you chaste stars!—

It is the cause. Yet I'll not shed her blood,
Nor scar that whiter skin of hers than snow,
And smooth as monumental alabaster.
Yet she must die, else she'll betray more men.
Put out the light, and then put out the light.
If quench thee, thou flaming minister,
I can again thy former light restore,
Should I repent me; but once put out thy light,   10
Thou cunning'st pattern of excelling nature,
I know not where is that Promethean heat
That can thy light relume. When I have pluck'd the rose
I cannot give it vital growth again,
It needs must wither. I'll smell it on the tree.

(*Kisses her.*)

Oh, balmy breath, that dost almost persuade
Justice to break her sword! One more, one more.
Be thus when thou art dead, and I will kill thee
And love thee after. One more, and that's the last;
So sweet was ne'er so fatal. I must weep,   20
But they are cruel tears: this sorrow's heavenly;
It strikes where it doth love. She wakes.
DESDEMONA.   Who's there? Othello?
OTHELLO.   Ay, Desdemona.
DESDEMONA.   Will you come to bed, my lord?
OTHELLO.   Have you pray'd to-night, Desdemona?
DESDEMONA.   Ay, my lord.
OTHELLO.   If you bethink yourself of any crime
Unreconcil'd as yet to heaven and grace,
Solicit for it straight.
DESDEMONA.   Alack, my lord, what may you mean by that?
OTHELLO.   Well, do it, and be brief; I will walk by.   30
I would not kill thy unprepared spirit;
No; heaven forfend! I would not kill thy soul.

---

106 *gastness:* terrified look   107 *anon:* i.e., when she confesses
124 *dress'd:* i.e., his wounds treated   129 *foredoes:* ruins
ACT V. 2   1 *cause:* i.e., Desdemona's guilt

8 *minister:* servant   12 *Promethean heat:* heavenly fire (In classical legend, Prometheus stole fire from heaven to give life to a clay image)
13 *relume:* relight   21 *heavenly:* like God's, in both loving and chastening the sinner   30 *walk by:* step aside   32 *forfend:* forbid

DESDEMONA.   Talk you of killing?
OTHELLO.   Ay, I do.
DESDEMONA.   Then heaven
Have mercy on me!
OTHELLO.   Amen, with all my heart!
DESDEMONA.   If you say so, I hope you
    will not kill me.
OTHELLO.   Hum!
DESDEMONA.   And yet I fear you; for
    you're fatal then
When your eyes roll so. Why I should fear
    I know not,
Since guiltiness I know not; but yet I feel
    I fear.
OTHELLO.   Think on thy sins.
DESDEMONA.   They are
    loves I bear to you.   40
OTHELLO.   Ay, and for that thou diest.
DESDEMONA.   That death's unnatural
    that kills for loving.
Alas, why gnaw you so your nether lip?
Some bloody passion shakes your very
    frame.
These are portents; but yet I hope, I hope,
They do not point on me.
OTHELLO.   Peace, and be still!
DESDEMONA.   I will so. What's the
    matter?
OTHELLO.   That handkerchief which I so
    lov'd and gave thee
Thou gav'st to Cassio.
DESDEMONA.   No, by my life and soul!
Send for the man, and ask him.
OTHELLO.   Sweet soul, take heed,   50
Take heed of perjury; thou art on thy
    deathbed.
DESDEMONA.   Ay, but not yet to die.
OTHELLO.   Yes, presently,
Therefore confess thee freely of thy sin;
For to deny each article with oath
Cannot remove nor choke the strong
    conception
That I do groan withal. Thou art to die.
DESDEMONA.   Then Lord have mercy on
    me!
OTHELLO.   I say, amen.
DESDEMONA.   And have you mercy too!
    I never did
Offend you in my life; never lov'd Cassio
But with such general warranty of heaven   60

As I might love; I never gave him token.
    OTHELLO.   By heaven, I saw my
    handkerchief in's hand.
O perjur'd woman! thou dost stone my
    heart,
And mak'st me call what I intend to do
A murder, which I thought a sacrifice.
I saw the handkerchief.
    DESDEMONA.   He found it then;
I never gave it him. Send for him hither;
Let him confess a truth.
    OTHELLO.   He hath confess'd.
DESDEMONA.   What, my lord?
OTHELLO.   That he hath us'd thee.
DESDEMONA.   How? unlawfully?
OTHELLO.   Ay.   70
DESDEMONA.   He will not say so.
OTHELLO.   No, his mouth is stopp'd;
Honest Iago hath ta'en order for 't.
DESDEMONA.   O! my fear interprets.
    What, is he dead?
OTHELLO.   Had all his hairs been lives,
    my great revenge
Had stomach for them all.
DESDEMONA.   Alas! he is betray'd and
    I undone.
OTHELLO.   Out, strumpet? weep'st thou
    for him to my face?
DESDEMONA.   O, banish me, my lord, but
    kill me not!
OTHELLO.   Down, strumpet!
DESDEMONA.   Kill me to-morrow; let me
    live to-night!   80
OTHELLO.   Nay, if you strive,—
DESDEMONA.   But half an hour!
OTHELLO.   Being done, there is no
    pause.
DESDEMONA.   But while I say one prayer!
OTHELLO.   It is too late.

(*He smothers her.*)

EMILIA.   (*At the door.*) My lord, my lord!
    What, ho! my lord, my lord!
OTHELLO.   What noise is this? Not dead?
    not yet quite dead?
I that am cruel am yet merciful;
I would not have thee linger in thy pain.
So, so.

---

37 *fatal:* deadly   45 *portents:* ominous signs   52 *presently:* at
once   55 *conception:* belief   60 *warranty:* permission

63 *stone:* harden into stone   65 *sacrifice:* an act of justice   75
stomach: appetite   85 *What noise:* i.e., of a movement from Desdemona

EMILIA.   (*Within.*) What, ho! my lord,
my lord!

OTHELLO.   Who's there?

EMILIA.   (*Within.*) O, good my lord,
I would speak a word with you!   90

OTHELLO.   Yes:—'tis Emilia.—By and
by.—She's dead.

'Tis like she comes to speak of Cassio's
death.

The noise was high. Ha! no more moving?

Still as the grave. Shall she come in? Were
't good?—

I think she stirs again:—no. What's best
to do?

If she come in, she'll sure speak to my wife.

My wife! my wife! what wife? I have no
wife.

O, insupportable! O heavy hour!

Methinks it should be now a huge eclipse

Of sun and moon, and that th' affrighted
globe   100

Did yawn at alteration.

EMILIA.   (*Within.*) I do beseech you

That I may speak with you, O, good my
lord!

OTHELLO.   I had forgot thee. O, come
in, Emilia.

Soft; by and by.—Let me the curtains
draw.—

Where art thou?   (*Opens the door.*)

(*Enter* EMILIA.)

            What's the matter with thee now?

EMILIA.   O, my good lord, yonder's foul
murders done!   *Street brawl*

OTHELLO.   What, now?

EMILIA.   But now, my lord.

OTHELLO.   It is the very error of the
moon;

She comes more nearer earth than she was   110
wont,

And makes men mad.

EMILIA.   Cassio, my lord, hath kill'd
a young Venetian

Call'd Roderigo.

OTHELLO.   Roderigo kill'd!

And Cassio kill'd!

EMILIA.   No, Cassio is not kill'd.

OTHELLO.   Not Cassio kill'd! Then

murder's out of tune,

And sweet revenge grows harsh.

DESDEMONA.   O, falsely, falsely
murder'd!

EMILIA.   O Lord, what cry is that?

OTHELLO.   That! what?

EMILIA.   Out, and alas! that was my
lady's voice.

Help! help, ho! help! O lady, speak again!   120

Sweet Desdemona! O sweet mistress, speak!

DESDEMONA.   A guiltless death I die.

EMILIA.   O, who hath done this deed?

DESDEMONA.   Nobody; I myself.
Farewell!

Commend me to my kind lord. O, farewell!

                                            (*Dies.*)

OTHELLO.   Why, how should she be
murder'd?

EMILIA.   Alas, who knows?

OTHELLO.   You hear her say herself, it
was not I.

EMILIA.   She said so; I must needs report
the truth.

OTHELLO.   She's, like a liar, gone to
burning hell.

'Twas I that kill'd her.

EMILIA.   O, the more angel she,   130

And you the blacker devil!

OTHELLO.   She turn'd to folly, and she
was a whore.

EMILIA.   Thou dost belie her, and thou
art a devil.

OTHELLO.   She was false as water.

EMILIA.   Thou art rash as fire, to say

That she was false. O, she was heavenly
true!

OTHELLO.   Cassio did tup her; ask thy
husband else.

O, I were damn'd beneath all depth in hell

But that I did proceed upon just grounds

To this extremity. Thy husband knew it all.

EMILIA.   My husband?   140

OTHELLO.   Thy husband.

EMILIA.   That she was false to wedlock?

OTHELLO.   Ay, with Cassio. Nay, had she
been true,

If Heaven would make me such another
world

Of one entire and perfect chrysolite,

---

101 *alteration:* some change in nature   105 *curtains:* bed curtains
109 *error:* wandering from her course

132 *folly:* unchastity   145 *chrysolite:* a green stone

I'd not have sold her for it.

EMILIA.   My husband?

OTHELLO.   Ay, 'twas he that told me on
her first.

An honest man he is, and hates the slime
That sticks on filthy deeds.

EMILIA.   My husband?

OTHELLO.   What needs this iterance,
woman? I say thy husband.   150

EMILIA.   O mistress, villainy hath made
mocks with love!

My husband say that she was false?

OTHELLO.   He, woman;
I say thy husband; dost understand the
word?

My friend, thy husband, honest, honest
Iago.

EMILIA.   If he say so, may his pernicious
soul

Rot half a grain a day! He lies to th' heart:
She was too fond of her most filthy bargain.

OTHELLO.   Ha!

EMILIA.   Do thy worst!
This deed of thine is no more worthy heaven   160
Than thou wast worthy her.

OTHELLO.   Peace, you were best.

EMILIA.   Thou hast not half that power
to do me harm

As I have to be hurt. O gull! O dolt!
As ignorant as dirt! Thou hast done
a deed—

I care not for thy sword; I'll make thee
known,

Though I lost twenty lives.—Help! Help,
ho! help!

The Moor hath kill'd my mistress! Murder!
murder!

(*Enter* MONTANO, GRATIANO, IAGO, *and
others.*)

MONTANO.   What is the matter? How
now, General!

EMILIA.   O, are you come, Iago? You
have done well,

That men must lay their murders on your   170
neck.

GRATIANO.   What is the matter?

EMILIA.   Disprove this villain, if thou
be'st a man.

He says thou told'st him that his wife was

false;

I know thou didst not, thou'rt not such a
villain.

Speak, for my heart is full.

IAGO.   I told him what I thought, and
told no more

Than what he found himself was apt and
true.

EMILIA.   But did you ever tell him she
was false?

IAGO.   I did.

EMILIA.   You told a lie, an odious,
damned lie;   180

Upon my soul, a lie, a wicked lie.
She false with Cassio!—did you say with
Cassio?

IAGO.   With Cassio, mistress. Go to,
charm your tongue.

EMILIA.   I will not charm my tongue;
I am bound to speak.

My mistress here lies murdered in her bed,—

ALL.   O heavens forfend!

EMILIA.   And your reports have set the
murderer on.

OTHELLO.   Nay, stare not, masters; it is
true, indeed.

GRATIANO.   'Tis a strange truth.

MONTANO.   O monstrous act!

EMILIA.   Villainy, villainy, villainy!   190
I think upon 't, I think. I smell't,—O
villainy!

I thought so then,—I'll kill myself for
grief—

O villainy, villainy!

IAGO.   What, are you mad? I charge you
get you home.

EMILIA.   Good gentlemen, let me have
leave to speak;

'Tis proper I obey him, but not now.
Perchance, Iago, I will ne'er go home.

OTHELLO.   O! O! O!

(*He falls on the bed.*)

EMILIA.   Nay, lay thee down and roar;
For thou hast kill'd the sweetest innocent
That e'er did lift up eye.

OTHELLO.   (*Rising.*) O, she was foul!   200
I scarce did know you, uncle; there lies your
niece,

---

150 *iterance:* repetition   163 *gull:* dupe   183 *charm:* silence

Whose breath, indeed, these hands have
    newly stopp'd.
I know this act shows horrible and grim.
    GRATIANO.   Poor Desdemona! I am glad
    thy father's dead.
Thy match was mortal to him, and pure
    grief
Shore his old thread in twain. Did he live
    now,
This sight would make him do a desperate
    turn,
Yea, curse his better angel from his side,
And fall to reprobance.
    OTHELLO.   'Tis pitiful; but yet Iago
    knows   210
That she with Cassio hath the act of shame
A thousand times committed. Cassio
    confess'd it;
And she did gratify his amorous works
With that recognizance and pledge of love
Which I first gave her. I saw it in his hand;
It was a handkerchief, an antique token
My father gave my mother.
    EMILIA.   O God! O heavenly God!
    IAGO.   'Zounds, hold your peace.
    EMILIA.   'Twill out, 'twill out! I, peace!
No, I will speak as liberal as the north.   220
Let Heaven and men and devils, let them
    all,
All, all, cry shame against me, yet I'll speak.
    IAGO.   Be wise, and get you home.
    EMILIA.   I will not.

                (IAGO offers to stab EMILIA.)

    GRATIANO.   Fie!
Your sword upon a woman?
    EMILIA.   O thou dull Moor! that
    handkerchief thou speak'st of
I found by fortune and did give my
    husband;
For often, with a solemn earnestness,
More than indeed belong'd to such a trifle,
He begg'd of me to steal it.
    IAGO.   Villainous whore!
    EMILIA.   She give it Cassio! No, alas!
    I found it,   230
And I did give 't my husband.
    IAGO.   Filth, thou liest!
    EMILIA.   By heaven, I do not, I do not,

    gentlemen.
O murderous coxcomb! what should such
    a fool
Do with so good a wife?

(*The* MOOR *runs at* IAGO, *but is disarmed by*
MONTANO *and others.* IAGO *kills* EMILIA.)

    OTHELLO.   Are there no stones in
    heaven
But what serves for the thunder?—Precious
    villain!
    GRATIANO.   The woman falls; sure, he
    hath kill'd his wife.
    EMILIA.   Ay, ay! O, lay me by my
    mistress' side.

                              (*Exit* IAGO.)

    GRATIANO.   He's gone, but his wife's
    kill'd.
    MONTANO.   'Tis a notorious villain.
    Take you this weapon
Which I have here recover'd from the Moor.   240
Come, guard the door without; let him not
    pass,
But kill him rather. I'll after that same
    villain,
For 'tis a damned slave.
                (*Exeunt* MONTANO *and* GRATIANO.)
    OTHELLO.   I am not valiant neither,
But every puny whipster gets my sword.
But why should honor outlive honesty?
Let it go all.
    EMILIA.   What did thy song bode, lady?
Hark, canst thou hear me? I will play the
    swan
And die in music. (*Singing.*) "Willow,
    willow, willow!"—
Moor, she was chaste; she lov'd thee, cruel
    Moor;
So come my soul to bliss, as I speak true;   250
So speaking as I think, alas, I die.

                              (*Dies.*)

    OTHELLO.   I have another weapon in
    this chamber;
It was a sword of Spain, the ice-brook's
    temper,—

---

206 *Shore . . . twain:* cut his thread of life in two   209 *reprobance:*
utter damnation   213 *gratify:* reward   220 *liberal as the north:*
as freely as the harsh north winds

233 *coxcomb:* fool   234 *stones:* bolts   240 *recover'd:* secured
244 *whipster:* whippersnapper   245 *honor:* reputation   245
honesty: honorable character   247 *swan:* cf. "swan song" sung by
the dying bird   253 *ice-brook's temper:* tempered in ice-cold water,
as with some of the best Spanish swords

O, here it is. Uncle, I must come forth.
GRATIANO.   (*Within.*) If thou attempt
    it, it will cost thee dear.
Thou hast no weapon, and perforce must
    suffer.
OTHELLO.   Look in upon me then and
    speak with me,
Or, naked as I am, I will assault thee.

(*Re-enter* GRATIANO.)

GRATIANO.   What is the matter?
OTHELLO.   Behold, I have a weapon;
A better never did itself sustain   260
Upon a soldier's thigh. I have seen the day
That, with this little arm and this good
    sword,
I have made my way through more impedi-
    ments
Than twenty times your stop. But, O vain
    boast!   *Antigone*
Who can control his fate? 'tis not so now.
Be not afraid though you do see me
    weapon'd;
Here is my journey's end, here is my butt
And very sea-mark of my utmost sail.
Do you go back dismay'd? 'Tis a lost fear;
Man but a rush against Othello's breast   270
And he retires. Where should Othello go?
Now, how dost thou look now? O ill-starr'd
    wench!
Pale as thy smock! when we shall meet at
    compt,
This look of thine will hurl my soul from
    heaven,
And fiends will snatch at it. Cold, cold,
    my girl!
Even like thy chastity. O cursed, cursed
    slave!
Whip me, ye devils,
From the possession of this heavenly sight!
Blow me about in winds! roast me in
    sulphur!
Wash me in steep-down gulfs of liquid fire!   280
O Desdemona, Desdemona! dead!
Oh! Oh! Oh!

(*Enter* LODOVICO, MONTANO, CASSIO *carried
in a chair*, *and* OFFICERS, *with* IAGO *prisoner.*)

LODOVICO.   Where is this rash and most
    unfortunate man?
OTHELLO.   That's he that was Othello;
    here I am.
LODOVICO.   Where is that viper? Bring
    the villain forth.
OTHELLO.   I look down towards his feet;
    but that's a fable.
If that thou be'st a devil, I cannot kill thee.

(*Wounds* IAGO.)

LODOVICO.   Wrench his sword from him.
IAGO.   I bleed, sir; but not kill'd.
OTHELLO.   I am not sorry neither. I'd
    have thee live;
For, in my sense, 'tis happiness to die.   290
LODOVICO.   O thou Othello, that wert
    once so good,
Fallen in the practice of a cursed slave,
What shall be said to thee?
OTHELLO.   Why, anything.
An honorable murderer, if you will;
For nought did I in hate, but all in honor.
LODOVICO.   This wretch hath part
    confess'd his villainy.
Did you and he consent in Cassio's death?
OTHELLO.   Ay.
CASSIO.   Dear General, I never gave you
    cause.
OTHELLO.   I do believe it, and I ask your
    pardon.   300
Will you, I pray, demand that demi-devil
Why he hath thus ensnar'd my soul and
    body?
IAGO.   Demand me nothing; what you
    know, you know.
From this time forth I never will speak
    word.
LODOVICO.   What, not to pray?
GRATIANO.   Torments will ope your
    lips.
OTHELLO.   Well, thou dost best.
LODOVICO.   Sir, you shall understand
    what hath befall'n,
Which, as I think, you know not. Here is
    a letter
Found in the pocket of the slain Roderigo,
And here another. The one of them imports   310

---

258 *naked:* unarmed   267 *butt:* the end of my arrow's flight
268 *sea-mark:* landmark   268 *utmost sail:* end of my final voyage
270 *Man but a rush:* take up a reed as a spear   273 *compt:* judgment (day)   280 *steep-down gulfs:* whirlpools

286 *feet:* the devil has cloven hooves   290 *sense:* opinion   292
practice: stratagem   297 *consent in:* agree upon   310 *imports:*
concerns

The death of Cassio to be undertook
By Roderigo.
 OTHELLO. O villain!
 CASSIO.   Most heathenish
and most gross!
 LODOVICO. Now here's another dis-
contented paper,
Found in his pocket too; and this, it seems,
Roderigo meant t' have sent this damned
 villain;
But that belike Iago in the nick
Came in and satisfi'd him.
 OTHELLO. O thou pernicious caitiff!—
How came you, Cassio, by that handker-
chief
That was my wife's?
 CASSIO.   I found it in my chamber; 320
And he himself confess'd but even now
That there he dropp'd it for a special
 purpose
Which wrought to his desire.
 OTHELLO.   O fool! fool! fool!
 CASSIO. There is besides in Roderigo's
 letter
How he upbraids Iago, that he made him
Brave me upon the watch, whereon it came
That I was cast; and even but now he spake,
After long seeming dead, Iago hurt him,
Iago set him on.
 LODOVICO. You must forsake this room,
 and go with us. 330
Your power and your command is taken off,
And Cassio rules in Cyprus. For this slave,
If there be any cunning cruelty
That can torment him much and hold him
 long,
It shall be his. You shall close prisoner rest,
Till that the nature of your fault be known
To the Venetian state. Come, bring away.
 OTHELLO. Soft you; a word or two before
 you go.
I have done the state some service, and they
 know't—
No more of that. I pray you, in your letters, 340
When you shall these unlucky deeds relate,
Speak of me as I am; nothing extenuate,
Nor set down aught in malice. Then must
 you speak
Of one that lov'd not wisely but too well;
Of one not easily jealous, but being wrought

Perplex'd in the extreme; of one whose
 hand,
Like the base Indian, threw a pearl away
Richer than all his tribe; of one whose
 subdued eyes,
Albeit unused to the melting mood,
Drops tears as fast as the Arabian trees 350
Their med'cinable gum. Set you down
 this;
And say besides, that in Aleppo once,
Where a malignant and a turban'd Turk
Beat a Venetian and traduc'd the state,
I took by th' throat the circumcised dog,
And smote him, thus.

       (*Stabs himself.*)

 LODOVICO. O bloody period!
 GRATIANO. All that's spoke is marr'd.
 OTHELLO. I kiss'd thee ere I kill'd thee.
 No way but this,
Killing myself, to die upon a kiss.

    (*Falls on the bed, and dies.*)

 CASSIO. This did I fear, but thought 360
 he had no weapon;
For he was great of heart.
 LODOVICO. (*To* IAGO.) O Spartan dog,
More fell than anguish, hunger, or the sea!
Look on the tragic loading of this bed;
This is thy work. The object poisons sight;
Let it be hid. Gratiano, keep the house,
And seize upon the fortunes of the Moor,
For they succeed on you. To you, lord
 governor,
Remains the censure of this hellish villain;
The time, the place, the torture. O, enforce
 it!
Myself will straight aboard; and to the 370
 state
This heavy act with heavy heart relate.

        (*Exeunt.*)

Man of Station
Speaks last + States
a moral.

      FOR ANALYSIS

Act I

1. Othello is usually referred to as a *domestic
tragedy*, which means simply that the tragedy

---

317 *belike:* probably 318 *Came in:* interposed 323 *wrought
to:* worked out in accordance with 345 *easily:* naturally 345
wrought: worked upon

347 *Indian:* Indians proverbially had no knowledge of the value of
precious stones or gold 351 *med'cinable:* medicinal 357 *period:*
conclusion 362 *Spartan:* ferocious, but also, stony calm 363
fell: cruel

grows out of a family (domestic) situation and is acted out in that situation. What basic difficulties would the marriage of Desdemona and Othello have to overcome, even if Iago were not taken into consideration?

2. Shakespeare had a habit of taking a very strong main character and putting him into a situation where that strength was converted by the nature of the situation into a weakness. What obvious strength of Othello is turned against him here? Why, for example, does he so readily believe Iago?

3. A central problem in reading the play is Iago's motive. In the first scene, Iago speaks of his motives and several times during the play he repeats and adds to them. What do you regard as true in his statement of his motives?

4. What poetic device does Shakespeare use to make foreshadowings, warnings, important details stand out? See, for example, Brabantio's warning to Othello about his wife.

5. At the end of Act I, is Iago truthfully summarizing Othello's character?

Act II

1. So far as one can tell, is Othello's opinion of Iago shared by Desdemona and Cassio? What does this do to the audience's opinion of Othello?

2. What motives for villainy does Iago add in the first scene of this act? Are they credible?

Act III

1. What is the function of the short introductory scene with the clown and musicians?

2. Emilia is obviously a *function character* in the play. What functions does she perform?

3. To only one character in the play does Iago show flashes of his real, self-centered character. Who is that person?

4. How does Othello unknowingly force further villainy on Iago in this act?

5. Why does Desdemona not tell Othello the truth about the handkerchief?

Act IV

1. What has happened to Iago's original stated motive for revenge by this time? If he urges Othello to kill Desdemona, and Othello does it, then Othello will certainly suffer. Iago will never have Desdemona (assuming he was truthful in saying he wanted her) and he can never become Lieutenant to a man who no longer holds rank (assuming he was truthful in saying he wanted the post). What does this tell you of the nature of Iago and his motives?

Act V

1. Is Othello finally seeing the truth when he speaks of himself as "one who loved not wisely but too well"?

2. In what way is Roderigo not only Iago's dupe but also his foil?

3. Is it fitting in the play that Emilia should die? Notice that nobody in the play dies without clear cause. What is hers?

4. In what way is the marriage of Iago and Emilia used to show the attractiveness of the union of Desdemona and Othello?

5. Why, in terms of character development, should Shakespeare risk plausibility by having Desdemona speak after one assumes that she is dead (and surely stifling—whether it refers to strangling or smothering—would seem to hamper speech)?

6. One convention of Renaissance drama is that a play must end with a situation in balance—no loose ends must be left. How does this explain the anticlimax of Lodovico's last speech? (Cassio's last speech would be a better twentieth-century curtain line.)

7. One other convention of Renaissance drama is illustrated here: what is the rank, relatively, of the character who speaks last?

RICHARD BRINSLEY SHERIDAN

The School for Scandal

CHARACTERS

Sir Peter Teazle
Sir Oliver Surface
Joseph Surface
Charles Surface
Crabtree
Sir Benjamin Backbite
Rowley
Moses
Trip
Snake
Careless
Sir Harry Bumper
Lady Teazle
Maria
Lady Sneerwell
Mrs. Candour

Gentlemen, Maid, *and* Servants
SCENE: *London*
TIME: *Contemporary*

A PORTRAIT

Addressed to Mrs. Crewe, with the
Comedy of The School for Scandal

Tell me, ye prim adepts in Scandal's school,
Who rail by precept and detract by rule,
Lives there no character so tried, so known,
So decked with grace, and so unlike your own,
That even you assist her fame to raise,
Approve by envy, and by silence praise!
Attend!—a model shall attract your view—
Daughters of calumny, I summon you!
You shall decide if this a portrait prove,
Or fond creation of the Muse and Love.
Attend, ye virgin critics, shrewd and sage,
Ye matron censors of this childish age,
Whose peering eye and wrinkled front declare
A fixed antipathy to young and fair;
By cunning, cautious; or by nature, cold,
In maiden madness, virulently bold!—
Attend, ye skilled to coin the precious tale,
Creating proof, where innuendoes fail!
Whose practised memories, cruelly exact,
Omit no circumstance, except the fact!—
Attend, all ye who boast—or old or young—
The living libel of a slanderous tongue!
So shall my theme as far contrasted be
As saints by fiends, or hymns by calumny.
Come, gentle Amoret (for 'neath that name
In worthier verse is sung thy beauty's fame);
Come—for but thee who seeks the Muse?—and
    while
Celestial blushes check thy conscious smile,
With timid grace and hesitating eye,
The perfect model, which I boast, supply:
Vain Muse! couldst thou the humblest sketch
    create
Of her, or slightest charm couldst imitate—
Could thy blest strain in kindred colors trace
The faintest wonder of her form and face—
Poets would study the immortal line,
And Reynolds own *his* art subdued by thine;
That art, which well might added lustre give
To Nature's best, and Heaven's superlative:
On Granby's cheek might bid new glories rise,
Or point a purer beam from Devon's eyes!

Hard is the task to shape that beauty's praise,
Whose judgment scorns the homage flattery
    pays!
But praising Amoret we cannot err,
No tongue o'ervalues Heaven or flatters her!
Yet she by Fate's perverseness—she alone—
Would doubt our truth, nor deem such praise
    her own.
Adorning fashion, unadorned by dress,
Simple from taste, and not from carelessness;
Discreet in gesture, in deportment mild,
Not stiff with prudence, nor uncouthly wild:
No state has Amoret; no studied mien;
She frowns no *goddess*, and she moves no *queen*.
The softer charm that in her manner lies
Is framed to captivate, yet not surprise;
It justly suits the expression of her face;
'Tis less than dignity and more than grace!
On her pure cheek the native hue is such
That, formed by Heaven to be admired so much,
The hand divine, with a less partial care,
Might well have fixed a fainter crimson there
And bade the gentle inmate of her breast—
Inshrinèd Modesty—supply the rest.
But who the peril of her lips shall paint?
Strip them of smiles—still, still all words are
    faint,
But moving Love himself appears to teach
Their action, though denied to rule her speech;
And thou who seest her speak and dost not hear,
Mourn not her distant accents 'scape thine ear;
Viewing those lips, thou still may'st make
    pretence
To judge of what she says and swear 'tis sense:
Clothed with such grace, with such expression
    fraught,
They move in meaning and they pause in
    thought!
But dost thou farther watch, with charmed
    surprise,
The mild irresolution of her eyes,
Curious to mark how frequent they repose
In brief eclipse and momentary close—
Ah! seest thou not an ambushed Cupid there,
Too tim'rous of his charge, with jealous care
Veils and unveils those beams of heav'nly light,
Too full, too fatal else, for mortal sight?
Nor yet, such pleasing vengeance fond to meet,
In pard'ning dimples hope a safe retreat.
What though her peaceful breast should ne'er
    allow
Subduing frowns to arm her altered brow,

By Love, I swear, and by his gentle wiles,
More fatal still the mercy of her smiles!
Thus lovely, thus adorned, possessing all
Of bright or fair that can to woman fall,
The height of vanity might well be thought
Prerogative in her, and Nature's fault.
Yet gentle Amoret, in mind supreme
As well as charms, rejects the vainer theme;
And, half mistrustful of her beauty's store,
She barbs with wit those darts too keen before:—
Read in all knowledge that her sex should reach,
Though Greville, or the Muse, should deign to
    teach,
Fond to improve, nor timorous to discern
How far it is a woman's grace to learn;
In Millar's dialect she would not prove
Apollo's priestess, but Apollo's love;
Graced by those signs which truth delights to
    own—
The timid blush and mild submitted tone:
Whate'er she says, though sense appear through-
    out,
Displays the tender hue of female doubt;
Decked with that charm, how lovely wit ap-
    pears,
How graceful science when that robe she wears!
Such too her talents and her bent of mind,
As speak a sprightly heart by thought refined;
A taste for mirth, by contemplation schooled,
A turn for ridicule, by candor ruled,
A scorn of folly, which she tries to hide,
An awe of talent, which she owns with pride!
Peace, idle Muse! no more thy strain prolong,
But yield a theme thy warmest praises wrong;
Just to her merit, though thou canst not raise
Thy feeble verse, behold th'acknowledged praise
Has spread conviction through the envious
    train,
And cast a fatal gloom o'er Scandal's reign!
And lo! each pallid hag, with blistered tongue,
Mutters assent to all thy zeal has sung—
Owns all the colors just—the outline true,
Thee my inspirer and my model—CREWE!

PROLOGUE

WRITTEN BY MR. GARRICK

A School for Scandal! tell me, I beseech you,
Needs there a school this modish art to teach
    you?
No need of lessons now, the knowing think;
We might as well be taught to eat and drink.
Caused by a dearth of scandal, should the vapors
Distress our fair ones—let them read the
    papers;
Their powerful mixtures such disorders hit,
Crave what you will—there's *quantum sufficit*.
"Lord!" cries my Lady Wormwood (who loves
    tattle,
And puts much salt and pepper in her prattle),
Just ris'n at noon, all night at cards when
    threshing
Strong tea and scandal—"Bless me, how
    refreshing!
Give me the papers, Lisp—how bold and free!
(Sips.)
Last night Lord L. (sips) was caught with Lady D.
For aching heads what charming sal volatile!
    (Sips.)
If Mrs. B. will still continue flirting,
We hope she'll DRAW, *or we'll* UNDRAW *the*
    curtain.
Fine satire, poz—in public all abuse it,
But by ourselves *(sips)*, our praise we can't
    refuse it.
Now, Lisp, read you—there, at that dash and
    star."
"Yes, ma'am: *A certain lord had best beware,*
Who lives not twenty miles from Grosvenor
    Square;
For, should he Lady W. find willing,
Wormwood is bitter"—"Oh! that's me! the
    villain!
Throw it behind the fire, and never more
Let that vile paper come within my door."
Thus at our friends we laugh, who feel the dart;
To reach our feelings, we ourselves must smart.
Is our young bard so young, to think that he
Can stop the full spring-tide of calumny?
Knows he the world so little, and its trade?
Alas! the devil's sooner raised than laid.
So strong, so swift, the monster there's no
    gagging:
Cut Scandal's head off, still the tongue is
    wagging.
Proud of your smiles once lavishly bestowed,
Again our young Don Quixote takes the road;
To show his gratitude he draws his pen,
And seeks this hydra, Scandal, in his den.
For your applause all perils he would through—
He'll fight—that's write—a cavalliero true,
Till every drop of blood—that's ink—is spilt
    for you.

ACT I

SCENE 1

(LADY SNEERWELL'S *house.*)

(*Discovered,* LADY SNEERWELL *at her dressing-table;* SNAKE *drinking chocolate.*)

LADY S. The paragraphs, you say, Mr. Snake, were all inserted?

SNAKE. They were, madam; and, as I copied them myself in a feigned hand, there can be no suspicion whence they came.

LADY S. Did you circulate the report of Lady Brittle's intrigue with Captain Boastall?

SNAKE. That's in as fine a train as your ladyship could wish. In the common course of things, I think it must reach Mrs. Clackitt's ears within four-and-twenty hours; and then, you know, the business is as good as done.

LADY S. Why, truly, Mrs. Clackitt has a very pretty talent, and a great deal of industry.

SNAKE. True, madam, and has been tolerably successful in her day. To my knowledge, she has been the cause of six matches being broken off and three sons disinherited, of four forced elopements and as many close confinements, nine separate maintenances and two divorces. Nay, I have more than once traced her causing a tête-à-tête in the *Town and Country Magazine,* when the parties, perhaps, had never seen each other's face before in the course of their lives.

LADY S. She certainly has talents, but her manner is gross.

SNAKE. 'Tis very true. She generally designs well, has a free tongue and a bold invention; but her coloring is too dark and her outlines often extravagant. She wants that delicacy of tint and mellowness of sneer which distinguish your ladyship's scandal.

LADY S. You are partial, Snake.

SNAKE. Not in the least; everybody allows that Lady Sneerwell can do more with a word or look than many can with the most labored detail, even when they happen to have a little truth on their side to support it.

LADY S. Yes, my dear Snake; and I am no hypocrite to deny the satisfaction I reap from the success of my efforts. Wounded myself, in the early part of my life, by the envenomed tongue of slander, I confess I have since known no pleasure equal to the reducing others to the level of my own injured reputation.

SNAKE. Nothing can be more natural. But, Lady Sneerwell, there is one affair in which you have lately employed me, wherein, I confess, I am at a loss to guess your motives.

LADY S. I conceive you mean with respect to my neighbor, Sir Peter Teazle, and his family?

SNAKE. I do. Here are two young men to whom Sir Peter has acted as a kind of guardian since their father's death—the eldest possessing the most amiable character and universally well spoken of; the youngest, the most dissipated and extravagant young fellow in the kingdom, without friends or character: the former an avowed admirer of your ladyship, and apparently your favorite; the latter attached to Maria, Sir Peter's ward, and confessedly beloved by her. Now, on the face of these circumstances, it is utterly unaccountable to me why you, the widow of a city knight, with a good jointure, should not close with the passion of a man of such character and expectations as Mr. Surface; and more so, why you should be so uncommonly earnest to destroy the mutual attachment subsisting between his brother Charles and Maria.

LADY S. Then, at once to unravel this mystery, I must inform you that love has no share whatever in the intercourse between Mr. Surface and me.

SNAKE. No!

LADY S. His real attachment is to Maria, or her fortune; but, finding in his brother a favored rival, he has been obliged to mask his pretensions and profit by my assistance.

SNAKE. Yet still I am more puzzled why you should interest yourself in his success.

LADY S. How dull you are! Cannot you surmise the weakness which I hitherto, through shame, have concealed even from you? Must I confess that Charles—that libertine, that extravagant, that bankrupt in fortune and reputation—that he it is for whom I'm thus anxious and malicious, and to gain whom I would sacrifice everything?

SNAKE. Now, indeed, your conduct appears consistent; but how came you and Mr. Surface so confidential?

LADY S. For our mutual interest. I have found him out a long time since. I know him to be artful, selfish, and malicious—in short, a sentimental knave—while with Sir Peter, and indeed with all his acquaintance, he passes for a youthful miracle of prudence, good sense, and benevolence.

SNAKE. Yes; yet Sir Peter vows he has not his equal in England, and, above all, he praises him as a man of sentiment.

LADY S. True; and with the assistance of his sentiment and hypocrisy he has brought Sir Peter entirely into his interest with regard to Maria, while poor Charles has no friend in the house—though, I fear, he has a powerful one in Maria's heart, against whom we must direct our schemes.

(*Enter* SERVANT.)

SERV. Mr. Surface.

LADY S. Show him up.

(*Exit* SERVANT.)

(*Enter* JOSEPH SURFACE.)

JOSEPH. My dear Lady Sneerwell, how do you do to-day? Mr. Snake, your most obedient.

LADY S. Snake has just been rallying me on our mutual attachment, but I have informed him of our real views. You know how useful he has been to us, and, believe me, the confidence is not ill placed.

JOSEPH. Madam, it is impossible for me to suspect a man of Mr. Snake's sensibility and discernment.

LADY S. Well, well, no compliments now; but tell me when you saw your mistress, Maria—or, what is more material to me, your brother.

JOSEPH. I have not seen either since I left you, but I can inform you that they never meet. Some of your stories have taken a good effect on Maria.

LADY S. Ah, my dear Snake! the merit of this belongs to you. But do your brother's distresses increase?

JOSEPH. Every hour. I am told he has had another execution in the house yesterday. In short, his dissipation and extravagance exceed anything I have ever heard of.

LADY S. Poor Charles!

JOSEPH. True, madam; notwithstanding his vices, one can't help feeling for him. Poor Charles! I'm sure I wish it were in my power to be of any essential service to him; for the man who does not share in the distresses of a brother, even though merited by his own misconduct, deserves—

LADY S. O lud! you are going to be moral, and forget that you are among friends.

JOSEPH. Egad, that's true! I'll keep that sentiment till I see Sir Peter. However, it is certainly a charity to rescue Maria from such a libertine, who, if he is to be reclaimed, can be so only by a person of your ladyship's superior accomplishments and understanding.

SNAKE. I believe, Lady Sneerwell, here's company coming. I'll go and copy the letter I mentioned to you. Mr. Surface, your most obedient.

JOSEPH. Sir, your very devoted.

(*Exit* SNAKE.)

—Lady Sneerwell, I am very sorry you have put any farther confidence in that fellow.

LADY S. Why so?

JOSEPH. I have lately detected him in frequent conference with old Rowley, who was formerly my father's steward, and has never, you know, been a friend of mine.

LADY S. And do you think he would betray us?

JOSEPH. Nothing more likely. Take my word for't, Lady Sneerwell, that fellow hasn't virtue enough to be faithful even to his own villainy.—Ah, Maria!

(*Enter* MARIA.)

LADY S. Maria, my dear, how do you do? What's the matter?

MARIA. Oh! there's that disagreeable lover of mine, Sir Benjamin Backbite, has just called at my guardian's with his odious uncle, Crabtree; so I slipped out and ran hither to avoid them.

LADY S. Is that all?

JOSEPH. If my brother Charles had been of the party, madam, perhaps you would not have been so much alarmed.

LADY S. Nay, now you are severe, for I dare swear the truth of the matter is, Maria heard *you* were here.—But, my dear, what has Sir Benjamin done, that you would avoid him so?

MARIA. Oh, he has done nothing—but 'tis for what he has said; his conversation is a perpetual libel on all his acquaintance.

JOSEPH. Aye, and the worst of it is, there is no advantage in not knowing him; for he'll abuse a stranger just as soon as his best friend, and his uncle's as bad.

LADY S. Nay, but we should make allowance; Sir Benjamin is a wit and a poet.

MARIA. For my part, I confess, madam, wit loses its respect with me when I see it in company with malice. What do you think, Mr. Surface?

JOSEPH. Certainly, madam; to smile at the jest which plants a thorn in another's breast is to become a principal in the mischief.

LADY S. Pshaw! there's no possibility of being witty without a little ill nature. The malice of a good thing is the barb that makes it stick. What's your opinion, Mr. Surface?

JOSEPH. To be sure, madam; that conversation where the spirit of raillery is suppressed, will ever appear tedious and insipid.

MARIA. Well, I'll not debate how far scandal may be allowable, but in a man, I am sure, it is always contemptible. We have pride, envy, rivalship, and a thousand motives to depreciate each other, but the male slanderer must have the cowardice of a woman before he can traduce one.

(*Re-enter* SERVANT.)

SERV. Madam, Mrs. Candour is below, and if your ladyship's at leisure, will leave her carriage.

LADY S. Beg her to walk in.

(*Exit* SERVANT.)

—Now, Maria, here is a character to your taste, for though Mrs. Candour is a little talkative, everybody allows her to be the best-natured and best sort of woman.

MARIA. Yes, with a very gross affectation of good nature and benevolence, she does more mischief than the direct malice of old Crabtree.

JOSEPH. I'faith that's true, Lady Sneerwell; whenever I hear the current running against the characters of my friends, I never think them in such danger as when Candour undertakes their defence.

LADY S. Hush!—here she is!

(*Enter* MRS. CANDOUR.)

MRS. CAN. My dear Lady Sneerwell, how have you been this century?—Mr. Surface, what news do you hear?—though indeed it is no matter, for I think one hears nothing else but scandal.

JOSEPH. Just so, indeed, ma'am.

MRS. CAN. Oh, Maria! child—what, is the whole affair off between you and Charles? His extravagance, I presume—the town talks of nothing else.

MARIA. Indeed! I am very sorry, ma'am, the town is not better employed.

MRS. CAN. True, true, child, but there's no stopping people's tongues. I own I was hurt to hear it, as I indeed was to learn from the same quarter that your guardian, Sir Peter, and Lady Teazle have not agreed lately as well as could be wished.

MARIA. 'Tis strangely impertinent for people to busy themselves so.

MRS. CAN. Very true, child, but what's to be done? People will talk—there's no preventing it. Why, it was but yesterday I was told that Miss Gadabout had eloped with Sir Filigree Flirt. But, Lord! there's no minding what one hears—though, to be sure, I had this from very good authority.

MARIA. Such reports are highly scandalous.

MRS. CAN. So they are, child—shameful, shameful! But the world is so censorious, no character escapes. Lord, now who would have suspected your friend, Miss Prim, of an indiscretion? Yet such is the ill-nature of people, that they say her uncle stopped her last week, just as she was stepping into the York diligence with her dancing-master.

MARIA. I'll answer for't there are no grounds for that report.

MRS. CAN. Ah, no foundation in the world, I dare swear; no more, probably, than for the story circulated last month of Mrs. Festino's affair with Colonel Cassino—though, to be sure, that matter was never rightly cleared up.

JOSEPH. The licence of invention some people take is monstrous, indeed.

MARIA. 'Tis so; but in my opinion those who report such things are equally culpable.

MRS. CAN. To be sure they are; tale-bearers are as bad as the tale-makers—'tis an old observation, and a very true one: but what's to be done, as I said before? How will you prevent people from talking? To-day, Mrs. Clackitt assured me, Mr. and Mrs. Honeymoon were at last become mere man and wife, like the rest of their acquaintance. She likewise hinted that a certain widow, in the next street, had got rid of her dropsy and recovered her shape in a most surprising manner. And at the same time Miss Tattle, who was by, affirmed that Lord Buffalo had discovered his lady at a house of no extraordinary fame; and that Sir H. Bouquet and Tom Saunter were to measure swords on a similar provocation.—But Lord, do you think I would report these things! No, no! tale-bearers, as I said before, are just as bad as the tale-makers.

JOSEPH. Ah! Mrs. Candour, if everybody had your forbearance and good nature!

MRS. CAN. I confess, Mr. Surface, I cannot bear to hear people attacked behind their backs; and when ugly circumstances come out against our acquaintance, I own I always love to think the best. By-the-by, I hope 'tis not true that your brother is absolutely ruined?

JOSEPH. I am afraid his circumstances are very bad indeed, ma'am.

MRS. CAN. Ah! I heard so—but you must tell him to keep up his spirits: everybody almost is in the same way—Lord Spindle, Sir Thomas Splint, Captain Quinze, and Mr. Nickitt—all up, I hear, within this week; so, if Charles is undone, he'll find half his acquaintance ruined too, and that, you know, is a consolation.

JOSEPH. Doubtless, ma'am—a very great one.

(*Re-enter* SERVANT.)

SERV. Mr. Crabtree and Sir Benjamin Backbite. (*Exit* SERVANT.)

LADY S. So, Maria, you see your lover pursues you: positively, you sha'n't escape.

(*Enter* CRABTREE *and* SIR BENJAMIN BACKBITE.)

CRAB. Lady Sneerwell, I kiss your hand. Mrs. Candour, I don't believe you are acquainted with my nephew. Sir Benjamin Backbite? Egad, ma'am, he has a pretty wit, and is a pretty poet too; isn't he, Lady Sneerwell?

SIR BEN. Oh, fie, uncle!

CRAB. Nay, egad, it's true; I back him at a rebus or a charade against the best rhymer in the kingdom. Has your ladyship heard the epigram he wrote last week on Lady Frizzle's feather catching fire?—Do, Benjamin, repeat it, or the charade you made last night extempore at Mrs. Drowzie's conversazione. Come now; your first is the

name of a fish, your second a great naval commander, and—

SIR BEN. Uncle, now—prithee—

CRAB. I'faith, ma'am, 'twould surprise you to hear how ready he is at all these fine sort of things.

LADY S. I wonder, Sir Benjamin, you never publish anything.

SIR BEN. To say truth, ma'am, 'tis very vulgar to print; and as my little productions are mostly satires and lampoons on particular people, I find they circulate more by giving copies in confidence to the friends of the parties. However, I have some love elegies which, when favored with this lady's smiles, I mean to give the public. (*Turning to* MARIA.)

CRAB. (*to* MARIA). 'Fore Heaven, ma'am, they'll immortalise you!—you will be handed down to posterity, like Petrarch's Laura, or Waller's Sacharissa.

SIR BEN. Yes, madam, I think you will like them when you shall see them on a beautiful quarto page where a neat rivulet of text shall meander through a meadow of margin. 'Fore Gad, they will be the most elegant things of their kind!

CRAB. But, ladies, that's true—have you heard the news?

MRS. CAN. What, sir, do you mean the report of—

CRAB. No, ma'am, that's not it.— Miss Nicely is going to be married to her own footman.

MRS. CAN. Impossible!

CRAB. Ask Sir Benjamin.

SIR BEN. 'Tis very true, ma'am; everything is fixed and the wedding liveries bespoke.

CRAB. Yes—and they do say there were pressing reasons for it.

LADY S. Why, I have heard something of this before.

MRS. CAN. It can't be—and I wonder anyone should believe such a story of so prudent a lady as Miss Nicely.

SIR BEN. O lud! ma'am, that's the very reason 'twas believed at once. She has always been so cautious and so reserved that everybody was sure there was some reason for it at bottom.

MRS. CAN. Why, to be sure, a tale of scandal is as fatal to the credit of a prudent lady of her stamp as a fever is generally to those of the strongest constitutions. But there is a sort of puny, sickly reputation that is always ailing, yet will outlive the robuster characters of a hundred prudes.

SIR. BEN.   True, madam, there are valetudinarians in reputation as well as constitution, who, being conscious of their weak part, avoid the least breath of air and supply their want of stamina by care and circumspection.

MRS. CAN.   Well, but this may be all a mistake. You know, Sir Benjamin, very trifling circumstances often give rise to the most injurious tales.

CRAB.   That they do, I'll be sworn, ma'am. Did you ever hear how Miss Piper came to lose her lover and her character last summer at Tunbridge—Sir Benjamin, you remember it?

SIR BEN.   Oh, to be sure!—the most whimsical circumstance.

LADY S.   How was it, pray?

CRAB.   Why, one evening, at Mrs. Ponto's assembly, the conversation happened to turn on the breeding Nova Scotia sheep in this country. Says a young lady in company, "I have known instances of it; for, Miss Letitia Piper, a first cousin of mine, had a Nova Scotia sheep that produced her twins." "What!" cries the Lady Dowager Dundizzy (who you know is as deaf as a post), "has Miss Piper had twins?" This mistake, as you may imagine, threw the whole company into a fit of laughter. However, 'twas the next morning everywhere reported and in a few days believed by the whole town, that Miss Letitia Piper had actually been brought to bed of a fine boy and girl; and in less than a week there were some people who could name the father and the farm-house where the babies were put to nurse.

LADY S.   Strange, indeed!

CRAB.   Matter of fact, I assure you. O lud; Mr. Surface, pray, is it true that your uncle, Sir Oliver, is coming home?

JOSEPH.   Not that I know of, indeed, sir.

CRAB.   He has been in the East Indies a long time. You can scarcely remember him, I believe. Sad comfort, whenever he returns, to hear how your brother has gone on!

JOSEPH.   Charles has been imprudent, sir, to be sure, but I hope no busy people have already prejudiced Sir Oliver against him.

He may reform.

SIR BEN.   To be sure he may. For my part, I never believed him to be so utterly void of principle as people say, and, though he has lost all his friends, I am told nobody is better spoken of by the Jews.

CRAB.   That's true, egad, nephew. If the Old Jewry was a ward, I believe Charles would be an alderman; no man more popular there, 'fore Gad! I hear he pays as many annuities as the Irish tontine, and that, whenever he is sick, they have prayers for the recovery of his health in all the synagogues.

SIR BEN.   Yet no man lives in greater splendor. They tell me, when he entertains his friends he will sit down to dinner with a dozen of his own securities, have a score of tradesmen waiting in the ante-chamber, and an officer behind every guest's chair.

JOSEPH.   This may be entertainment to you, gentlemen, but you pay very little regard to the feelings of a brother.

MARIA (*aside*).   Their malice is intolerable!—(*Aloud.*) Lady Sneerwell, I must wish you a good morning; I'm not very well. (*Exit* MARIA.)

MRS. CAN.   Oh, dear! she changes color very much.

LADY S.   Do, Mrs. Candour, follow her; she may want your assistance.

MRS. CAN.   That I will, with all my soul, ma'am.—Poor dear girl, who knows what her situation may be! (*Exit* MRS. CANDOUR.)

LADY S.   'Twas nothing but that she could not bear to hear Charles reflected on, notwithstanding their difference.

SIR BEN.   The young lady's *penchant* is obvious.

CRAB.   But, Benjamin, you must not give up the pursuit for that; follow her and put her into good humor. Repeat her some of your own verses. Come, I'll assist you.

SIR BEN.   Mr. Surface, I did not mean to hurt you, but depend on't, your brother is utterly undone.

CRAB.   O lud, aye; undone as ever man was!—can't raise a guinea.

SIR BEN.   And everything sold, I'm told, that was movable.

CRAB.   I have seen one that was at his house.—Not a thing left but some empty bottles that were overlooked, and the family pictures, which I believe are framed in the wainscots.

SIR BEN (*going*). And I'm very sorry also to hear some bad stories against him.

CRAB. Oh, he has done many mean things, that's certain.

SIR BEN (*going*). But, however, as he's your brother—

CRAB. We'll tell you all another opportunity. (*Exeunt* CRABTREE *and* SIR BENJAMIN.)

LADY S. Ha! ha! 'tis very hard for them to leave a subject they have not quite run down.

JOSEPH. And I believe the abuse was no more acceptable to your ladyship than Maria.

LADY S. I doubt her affections are farther engaged than we imagine. But the family are to be here this evening, so you may as well dine where you are and we shall have an opportunity of observing farther; in the meantime, I'll go and plot mischief and you shall study sentiment. (*Exeunt.*)

SCENE 2

(*A room in* SIR PETER TEAZLE'S *House.*)
(*Enter* SIR PETER.)

SIR PET. When an old bachelor marries a young wife, what is he to expect? 'Tis now six months since Lady Teazle made me the happiest of men—and I have been the most miserable dog ever since. We tifted a little going to church, and fairly quarrelled before the bells had done ringing. I was more than once nearly choked with gall during the honeymoon, and had lost all comfort in life before my friends had done wishing me joy. Yet I chose with caution—a girl bred wholly in the country, who never knew luxury beyond one silk gown nor dissipation above the annual gala of a race ball. Yet she now plays her part in all the extravagant fopperies of the fashion and the town with as ready a grace as if she never had seen a bush or a grassplot out of Grosvenor Square! I am sneered at by all my acquaintance and paragraphed in the newspapers. She dissipates my fortune and contradicts all my humors; yet the worst of it is, I doubt I love her, or I should never bear all this. However, I'll never be weak enough to own it.

(*Enter* ROWLEY.)

ROW. Oh! Sir Peter, your servant; how is it with you, sir?

SIR PET. Very bad, Master Rowley, very bad. I meet with nothing but crosses and vexations.

ROW. What can have happened to trouble you since yesterday?

SIR PET. A good question to a married man!

ROW. Nay, I'm sure your lady, Sir Peter, can't be the cause of your uneasiness.

SIR PET. Why, has anybody told you she was dead?

ROW. Come, come, Sir Peter, you love her, notwithstanding your tempers don't exactly agree.

SIR PET. But the fault is entirely hers, Master Rowley. I am, myself, the sweetest-tempered man alive, and hate a teasing temper; and so I tell her a hundred times a day.

ROW. Indeed!

SIR PET. Aye; and what is very extraordinary, in all our disputes she is always in the wrong. But Lady Sneerwell and the set she meets at her house encourage the perverseness of her disposition. Then, to complete my vexation, Maria, my ward, whom I ought to have the power of a father over, is determined to turn rebel too, and absolutely refuses the man whom I have long resolved on for her husband—meaning, I suppose, to bestow herself on his profligate brother.

ROW. You know, Sir Peter, I have always taken the liberty to differ with you on the subject of these two young gentlemen. I only wish you may not be deceived in your opinion of the elder. For Charles, my life on't! he will retrieve his errors yet. Their worthy father, once my honored master, was, at his years, nearly as wild a spark; yet when he died, he did not leave a more benevolent heart to lament his loss.

SIR PET. You are wrong, Master Rowley. On their father's death, you know, I acted as a kind of guardian to them both till their uncle Sir Oliver's liberality gave them an early independence; of course, no person could have more opportunities of judging of their hearts, and I was never mistaken in my life. Joseph is indeed a model for the young men of the age. He is a man of sentiment and acts up to the *sentiments* he professes; but for the other, take my word for't, if he had any grain of virtue by descent, he has dissipated it with the rest of his inheritance. Ah! my old friend, Sir Oliver, will be deeply mortified when he finds how part of his bounty has been misapplied.

Row. I am sorry to find you so violent against the young man, because this may be the most critical period of his fortune. I came hither with news that will surprise you.

Sir Pet. What! let me hear.

Row. Sir Oliver is arrived and at this moment in town.

Sir Pet. How! you astonish me! I thought you did not expect him this month.

Row. I did not, but his passage has been remarkably quick.

Sir Pet. Egad, I shall rejoice to see my old friend. 'Tis fifteen years since we met. We have had many a day together. But does he still enjoin us not to inform his nephews of his arrival?

Row. Most strictly. He means before it is known to make some trial of their dispositions.

Sir Pet. Ah! there needs no art to discover their merits—he shall have his way; but pray, does he know I am married?

Row. Yes, and will soon wish you joy.

Sir Pet. What, as we drink health to a friend in a consumption! Ah! Oliver will laugh at me. We used to rail at matrimony together, but he has been steady to his text. Well, he must be soon at my house, though—I'll instantly give orders for his reception. But, Master Rowley, don't drop a word that Lady Teazle and I ever disagree.

Row. By no means.

Sir Pet. For I should never be able to stand Noll's jokes; so I'd have him think, Lord forgive me! that we are a very happy couple.

Row. I understand you; but then you must be very careful not to differ while he is in the house with you.

Sir Pet. Egad, and so we must—and that's impossible. Ah! Master Rowley, when an old bachelor marries a young wife, he deserves—no—the crime carries its punishment along with it. (*Exeunt.*)

ACT II

SCENE 1

(*A room in* Sir Peter Teazle's *house.*)
(*Enter* Sir Peter *and* Lady Teazle.)

Sir Pet. Lady Teazle, Lady Teazle, I'll not bear it!

Lady T. Sir Peter, Sir Peter, you may bear it or not, as you please; but I ought to have my own way in everything—and what's more I will, too. What! though I was educated in the country, I know very well that women of fashion in London are accountable to nobody after they are married.

Sir Pet. Very well, ma'am, very well; so a husband is to have no influence, no authority?

Lady T. Authority! No, to be sure. If you wanted authority over me, you should have adopted me, and not married me; I am sure you were old enough.

Sir Pet. Old enough!—aye, there it is. Well, well, Lady Teazle, though my life may be made unhappy by your temper; I'll not be ruined by your extravagance!

Lady T. My extravagance! I'm sure I'm not more extravagant than a woman of fashion ought to be.

Sir Pet. No, no, madam, you shall throw away no more sums on such unmeaning luxury. 'Slife! to spend as much to furnish your dressing-room with flowers in winter as would suffice to turn the Pantheon into a greenhouse, and give a *fête champêtre* at Christmas.

Lady T. And am I to blame, Sir Peter, because flowers are dear in cold weather? You should find fault with the climate, and not with me. For my part, I'm sure I wish it was spring all the year round and that roses grew under our feet.

Sir Pet. Oons! madam—if you had been born to this, I shouldn't wonder at your talking thus; but you forget what your situation was when I married you.

Lady T. No, no, I don't; 'twas a very disagreeable one, or I should never have married you.

Sir Pet. Yes, yes, madam, you were then in somewhat a humbler style—the daughter of a plain country squire. Recollect, Lady

Teazle, when I saw you first sitting at your tambour, in a pretty figured linen gown, with a bunch of keys at your side, your hair combed smooth over a roll, and your apartment hung round with fruits in worsted of your own working.

LADY T. Oh, yes! I remember it very well, and a curious life I led—my daily occupation to inspect the dairy, superintend the poultry, make extracts from the family receipt-book, and comb my aunt Deborah's lapdog.

SIR PET. Yes, yes, ma'am, 'twas so indeed.

LADY T. And then, you know, my evening amusements!—to draw patterns for ruffles, which I had not materials to make up; to play Pope Joan with the curate; to read a sermon to my aunt; or to be stuck down to an old spinet to strum my father to sleep after a fox-chase.

SIR PET. I am glad you have so good a memory. Yes, madam, these were the recreations I took you from; but now you must have your coach—vis-à-vis—and three powdered footmen before your chair; and, in the summer, a pair of white cats to draw you to Kensington Gardens. No recollection, I suppose, when you were content to ride double, behind the butler, on a docked coach-horse.

LADY T. No—I swear I never did that. I deny the butler and the coach-horse.

SIR PET. This, madam, was your situation; and what have I done for you? I have made you a woman of fashion, of fortune, of rank—in short, I have made you my wife.

LADY T. Well, then, and there is but one thing more you can make me to add to the obligation, and that is—

SIR PET. My widow, I suppose?

LADY T. Hem! hem!

SIR PET. I thank you, madam—but don't flatter yourself; for, though your ill conduct may disturb my peace, it shall never break my heart, I promise you: however, I am equally obliged to you for the hint.

LADY T. Then why will you endeavor to make yourself so disagreeable to me and thwart me in every little elegant expense?

SIR PET. 'Slife, madam, I say, had you any of these little elegant expenses when you married me?

LADY T. Lud, Sir Peter! would you have me be out of the fashion?

SIR PET. The fashion, indeed! what had you to do with the fashion before you married me?

LADY T. For my part, I should think you would like to have your wife thought a woman of taste.

SIR PET. Aye—there again—taste! Zounds! madam, you had no taste when you married me!

LADY T. That's very true, indeed, Sir Peter; and, after having married you, I should never pretend to taste again, I allow. But now, Sir Peter, if we have finished our daily jangle, I presume I may go to my engagement at Lady Sneerwell's.

SIR PET. Aye, there's another precious circumstance—a charming set of acquaintance you have made there!

LADY T. Nay, Sir Peter, they are all people of rank and fortune, and remarkably tenacious of reputation.

SIR PET. Yes, egad, they are tenacious of reputation with a vengeance, for they don't choose anybody should have a character but themselves! Such a crew! Ah! many a wretch has rid on a hurdle who has done less mischief than these utterers of forged tales, coiners of scandal, and clippers of reputation.

LADY T. What, would you restrain the freedom of speech?

SIR PET. Ah! they have made you just as bad as any one of the society.

LADY T. Why, I believe I do bear a part with a tolerable grace. But I vow, I bear no malice against the people I abuse; when I say an ill-natured thing, 'tis out of pure good humor, and I take it for granted they deal exactly in the same manner with me. But Sir Peter, you know you promised to come to Lady Sneerwell's too.

SIR PET. Well, well, I'll call in, just to look after my own character.

LADY T. Then, indeed, you must make haste after me, or you'll be too late. So good-bye to ye.

(*Exit* LADY TEAZLE.)

SIR PET. So—I have gained much by my intended expostulation! Yet with what a charming air she contradicts everything I say, and how pleasingly she shows her contempt for my authority! Well, though I can't make her love me, there is great satisfaction in quarrelling with her, and I think she never appears to such advantage as when she is doing everything in her power to plague me.

(*Exit.*)

SCENE 2

(*A room at* LADY SNEERWELL'S *house.*)

(*Enter* LADY SNEERWELL, MRS. CANDOUR, CRABTREE, SIR BENJAMIN BACKBITE, *and* JOSEPH SURFACE.)

LADY S.   Nay, positively, we will hear it.

JOSEPH.   Yes, yes, the epigram, by all means.

SIR BEN.   Oh, plague on't, uncle! 'tis mere nonsense.

CRAB.   No, no; 'fore Gad, very clever for an extempore!

SIR BEN.   But ladies, you should be acquainted with the circumstance. You must know that one day last week, as Lady Betty Curricle was taking the dust in Hyde Park, in a sort of duodecimo phaeton, she desired me to write some verses on her ponies; upon which, I took out my pocketbook, and in one moment produced the following:

Sure never were seen two such beautiful ponies;
Other horses are clowns, but these macaronies:
To give them this title I'm sure can't be wrong.
Their legs are so slim, and their tails are so long.

CRAB.   There, ladies, done in the smack of a whip, and on horseback too.

JOSEPH.   A very Phœbus, mounted—indeed, Sir Benjamin!

SIR BEN.   Oh! dear, sir! trifles—trifles.

(*Enter* LADY TEAZLE *and* MARIA.)

MRS. CAN.   I must have a copy.

LADY S.   Lady Teazle, I hope we shall see Sir Peter?

LADY T.   I believe he'll wait on your ladyship presently.

LADY S.   Maria, my love, you look grave. Come, you shall sit down to piquet with Mr. Surface.

MARIA.   I take very little pleasure in cards—however, I'll do as you please.

LADY T.   (*aside*). I am surprised Mr. Surface should sit down with her; I thought he would have embraced this opportunity of speaking to me before Sir Peter came.

MRS. CAN.   Now, I'll die, but you are so scandalous, I'll forswear your society.

LADY T.   What's the matter, Mrs. Candour?

MRS. CAN.   They'll not allow our friend Miss Vermilion to be handsome.

LADY S.   Oh, surely she is a pretty woman.

CRAB.   I am very glad you think so, ma'am.

MRS. CAN.   She has a charming fresh color.

LADY T.   Yes, when it is fresh put on.

MRS. CAN.   Oh, fie! I'll swear her color is natural; I have seen it come and go.

LADY T.   I dare swear you have, ma'am; it goes off at night and comes again in the morning.

SIR BEN.   True, ma'am; it not only comes and goes, but what's more, egad, her maid can fetch and carry it!

MRS. CAN.   Ha! ha! ha! how I hate to hear you talk so! But surely, now, her sister *is*, or *was*, very handsome.

CRAB.   Who? Mrs. Evergreen? O Lord! she's six-and-fifty if she's an hour!

MRS. CAN.   Now positively you wrong her; fifty-two or fifty-three is the utmost—and I don't think she looks more.

SIR BEN.   Ah! there's no judging by her looks unless one could see her face.

LADY S.   Well, well, if Mrs. Evergreen *does* take some pains to repair the ravages of time, you must allow she effects it with great ingenuity; and surely that's better than the careless manner in which the widow Ochre chalks her wrinkles.

SIR BEN.   Nay now, Lady Sneerwell, you are severe upon the widow. Come, come 'tis not that she paints so ill—but when she has finished her face, she joins it on so badly to her neck that she looks like a mended statue, in which the connoisseur may see at once that the head is modern, though the trunk's antique.

CRAB.   Ha! ha! ha! Well said, nephew!

MRS. CAN.   Ha! ha! ha! Well, you make me laugh; but I vow I hate you for it. What do you think of Miss Simper?

SIR BEN.   Why, she has very pretty teeth.

LADY T.   Yes, and on that account, when she is neither speaking nor laughing (which very seldom happens), she never absolutely shuts her mouth, but leaves it always on ajar, as it were—thus.

(*Shows her teeth.*)

MRS. CAN.   How can you be so ill-natured?

LADY T.   Nay, I allow even that's better

than the pains Mrs. Prim takes to conceal her losses in front. She draws her mouth till it positively resembles the aperture of a poor's-box, and all her words appear to slide out edgewise as it were—thus: "How do you do, madam? Yes, madam."

LADY S. Very well, Lady Teazle; I see you can be a little severe.

LADY T. In defence of a friend, it is but justice.—But here comes Sir Peter to spoil our pleasantry.

(*Enter* SIR PETER TEAZLE.)

SIR PET. Ladies, your most obedient.— (*Aside.*) Mercy on me, here is the whole set! a character dead at every word, I suppose.

MRS. CAN. I am rejoiced you are come, Sir Peter. They have been so censorious—and Lady Teazle as bad as anyone.

SIR PET. That must be very distressing to *you*, Mrs. Candour, I dare swear.

MRS. CAN. Oh, they will allow good qualities to nobody—not even good nature to our friend Mrs. Pursy.

LADY T. What, the fat dowager who was at Mrs. Quadrille's last night?

MRS. CAN. Nay, her bulk is her misfortune; and, when she takes so much pains to get rid of it, you ought not to reflect on her.

LADY S. That's very true, indeed.

LADY T. Yes, I know she almost lives on acids and small whey; laces herself by pulleys; and often, in the hottest noon in summer, you may see her on a little squat pony, with her hair plaited up behind like a drummer's and puffing round the Ring on a full trot.

MRS. CAN. I thank you, Lady Teazle, for defending her.

SIR PET. Yes, a good defence, truly.

MRS. CAN. Truly, Lady Teazle is as censorious as Miss Sallow.

CRAB. Yes, and she is a curious being to pretend to be censorious—an awkward gawky, without any one good point under heaven.

MRS. CAN. Positively you shall not be so very severe. Miss Sallow is a near relation of mine by marriage, and as for her person great allowance is to be made; for let me tell you, a woman labors under many disadvantages who tries to pass for a girl at six-and-thirty.

LADY S. Though surely, she is handsome still—and for the weakness in her eyes, considering how much she reads by candle-light, it is not to be wondered at.

MRS. CAN. True, and then as to her manner: upon my word, I think it is particularly graceful, considering she never had the least education; for you know her mother was a Welsh milliner, and her father a sugar-baker at Bristol.

SIR BEN. Ah! you are both of you too good-natured!

SIR PET. (*aside*). Yes, damned good-natured! This their own relation! mercy on me!

MRS. CAN. For my part, I own I cannot bear to hear a friend ill spoken of.

SIR PET. No, to be sure!

SIR BEN. Oh! you are of a moral turn. Mrs. Candour and I can sit for an hour and hear Lady Stucco talk sentiment.

LADY T. Nay, I vow Lady Stucco is very well with the dessert after dinner, for she's just like the French fruit one cracks for mottoes—made up of paint and proverb.

MRS. CAN. Well, I will never join in ridiculing a friend, and so I constantly tell my cousin Ogle—and you all know what pretensions she has to be critical on beauty.

CRAB. Oh, to be sure! she has herself the oddest countenance that ever was seen; 'tis a collection of features from all the different countries of the globe.

SIR BEN. So she has, indeed—an Irish front—

CRAB. Caledonian locks—

SIR BEN. Dutch nose—

CRAB. Austrian lips—

SIR BEN. Complexion of a Spaniard—

CRAB. And teeth *à la Chinoise*—

SIR BEN. In short, her face resembles a table d'hôte at Spa, where no two guests are of a nation—

CRAB. Or a congress at the close of a general war—wherein all the members, even to her eyes, appear to have a different interest, and her nose and chin are the only parties likely to join issue.

MRS. CAN. Ha! ha! ha!

SIR PET. (*aside*). Mercy on my life!—a person they dine with twice a week!

LADY S. Go, go; you are a couple of provoking toads.

MRS. CAN. Nay, but I vow you shall not

carry the laugh off so—for give me leave to say that Mrs. Ogle—

SIR PET. Madam, madam, I beg your pardon—there's no stopping these good gentlemen's tongues. But when I tell you, Mrs. Candour, that the lady they are abusing is a particular friend of mine, I hope you'll not take her part.

LADY S. Ha! ha! ha! well said, Sir Peter! but you are a cruel creature—too phlegmatic yourself for a jest and too peevish to allow wit in others.

SIR PET. Ah, madam, true wit is more nearly allied to good nature than your ladyship is aware of.

LADY T. True, Sir Peter; I believe they are so near akin that they can never be united.

SIR BEN. Or rather, madam, suppose them to be man and wife, because one seldom sees them together.

LADY T. But Sir Peter is such an enemy to scandal, I believe he would have it put down by Parliament.

SIR PET. 'Fore Heaven, madam, if they were to consider the sporting with reputation of as much importance as poaching on manors, and pass an act for the preservation of fame as well as game, I believe many would thank them for the bill.

LADY S. O lud! Sir Peter; would you deprive us of our privileges?

SIR PET. Aye, madam, and then no person should be permitted to kill characters and run down reputations but qualified old maids and disappointed widows.

LADY S. Go, you monster!

MRS. CAN. But surely you would not be quite so severe on those who only report what they hear?

SIR PET. Yes, madam, I would have law merchant for them too; and in all cases of slander currency, whenever the drawer of the lie was not to be found, the injured parties should have a right to come on any of the indorsers.

CRAB. Well, for my part, I believe there never was a scandalous tale without some foundation.

SIR PET. Oh, nine out of ten of the malicious inventions are founded on some ridiculous misrepresentation.

LADY S. Come, ladies, shall we sit down to cards in the next room?

(*Enter* SERVANT, *who whispers to* SIR PETER.)

SIR PET. I'll be with them directly.

(*Exit* SERVANT.)

(*Aside.*) I'll get away unperceived.

LADY S. Sir Peter, you are not going to leave us?

SIR PET. Your ladyship must excuse me; I'm called away by particular business. But I leave my character behind me.

(*Exit* SIR PETER.)

SIR BEN. Well—certainly, Lady Teazle, that lord of yours is a strange being. I could tell you some stories of him would make you laugh heartily if he were not your husband.

LADY T. Oh, pray don't mind that; come, do let's hear them. (*Joins the rest of the company going into the next room.*)

JOSEPH. Maria, I see you have no satisfaction in this society.

MARIA. How is it possible I should? If to raise malicious smiles at the infirmities or misfortunes of those who have never injured us be the province of wit or humor, Heaven grant me a double portion of dulness!

JOSEPH. Yet they appear more ill-natured than they are; they have no malice at heart.

MARIA. Then is their conduct still more contemptible, for in my opinion nothing could excuse the interference of their tongues but a natural and uncontrollable bitterness of mind.

JOSEPH. Undoubtedly, madam, and it has always been a sentiment of mine that to propagate a malicious truth wantonly is more despicable than to falsify from revenge. But can you, Maria, feel thus for others and be unkind to me alone? Is hope to be denied the tenderest passion?

MARIA. Why will you distress me by renewing this subject?

JOSEPH. Ah, Maria! you would not treat me thus and oppose your guardian Sir Peter's will but that I see that profligate Charles is still a favored rival.

MARIA. Ungenerously urged! But whatever my sentiments are for that unfortunate young man, be assured I shall not feel more bound to give him up because his distresses have lost him the regard even of a brother.

JOSEPH. Nay, but, Maria, do not leave me with a frown; by all that's honest, I swear—

(*Re-enter* LADY TEAZLE *behind.*)

—(*Aside.*) Gad's life, here's Lady Teazle.—(*Aloud to* MARIA.) You must not—no, you shall not—for though I have the greatest regard for Lady Teazle—

MARIA. Lady Teazle!

JOSEPH. Yet were Sir Peter to suspect—

(*Enter* LADY TEAZLE *and comes forward.*)

LADY T. What is this, pray? Do you take her for me?—Child, you are wanted in the next room.

(*Exit Maria.*)

—What is all this, pray?

JOSEPH. Oh, the most unlucky circumstance in nature! Maria has somehow suspected the tender concern I have for your happiness and threatened to acquaint Sir Peter with her suspicions, and I was just endeavoring to reason with her when you came in.

LADY T. Indeed! but you seemed to adopt a very tender mode of reasoning—do you usually argue on your knees?

JOSEPH. Oh, she's a child, and I thought a little bombast—but, Lady Teazle, when are you to give me your judgment on my library, as you promised?

LADY T. No, no! I begin to think it would be imprudent, and you know I admit you as a lover no farther than fashion requires.

JOSEPH. True—a mere Platonic cicisbeo—what every wife is entitled to.

LADY T. Certainly, one must not be out of the fashion. However, I have so much of my country prejudices left that though Sir Peter's ill humor may vex me ever so, it never shall provoke me to—

JOSEPH. The only revenge in your power. Well, I applaud your moderation.

LADY T. Go—you are an insinuating wretch! But we shall be missed—let us join the company.

JOSEPH. But we had best not return together.

LADY T. Well, don't stay; for Maria sha'n't come to hear any more of your reasoning, I promise you. (*Exit* LADY TEAZLE.)

JOSEPH. A curious dilemma my politics have run me into! I wanted, at first, only to ingratiate myself with Lady Teazle, that she might not be my enemy with Maria; and I have, I don't know how, become her serious lover. Sincerely I begin to wish I had never made such a point of gaining so very good a character, for it has led me into so many cursed rogueries that I doubt I

shall be exposed at last. (*Exit.*)

SCENE 3

(*A room in* SIR PETER TEAZLE'S *house.*)

(*Enter* ROWLEY *and* SIR OLIVER SURFACE.)

SIR O. Ha! ha! ha! so my old friend is married, hey?—a young wife out of the country. Ha! ha! ha! that he should have stood bluff to old bachelor so long and sink into a husband at last!

ROW. But you must not rally him on the subject, Sir Oliver; 'tis a tender point, I assure you, though he has been married only seven months.

SIR O. Then he has been just half a year on the stool of repentance!—Poor Peter! But you say he has entirely given up Charles—never sees him, hey?

ROW. His prejudice against him is astonishing, and I am sure greatly increased by a jealousy of him with Lady Teazle, which he has industriously been led into by a scandalous society in the neighborhood, who have contributed not a little to Charles's ill name. Whereas the truth is, I believe, if the lady is partial to either of them, his brother is the favorite.

SIR O. Aye, I know there are a set of malicious, prating, prudent gossips, both male and female, who murder characters to kill time and will rob a young fellow of his good name before he has years to know the value of it. But I am not to be prejudiced against my nephew by such, I promise you! No, no; if Charles has done nothing false or mean, I shall compound for his extravagance.

ROW. Then, my life on't, you will reclaim him. Ah, sir, it gives me new life to find that *your* heart is not turned against him, and that the son of my good old master has one friend, however, left.

SIR O. What! shall I forget, Master Rowley, when I was at his years myself? Egad, my brother and I were neither of us very prudent youths, and yet, I believe, you have not seen many better men than your old master was.

ROW. Sir, 'tis this reflection gives me assurance that Charles may yet be a credit to his family. But here comes Sir Peter.

SIR O. Egad, so he does! Mercy on me! he's

greatly altered, and seems to have a settled married look! One may read "husband" in his face at this distance.

(*Enter* SIR PETER TEAZLE).

SIR PET.   Ha! Sir Oliver—my old friend! Welcome to England a thousand times!

SIR O.   Thank you, thank you, Sir Peter! and i'faith, I am glad to find you well, believe me!

SIR PET.   Oh! 'tis a long time since we met—fifteen years, I doubt, Sir Oliver, and many a cross accident in the time.

SIR O.   Aye, I have had my share. But, what! I find you are married—hey? Well, well, it can't be helped, and so—I wish you joy with all my heart!

SIR PET.   Thank you, thank you, Sir Oliver.—Yes, I have entered into—the happy state; but we'll not talk of that now.

SIR O.   True, true, Sir Peter; old friends should not begin on grievances at first meeting—no, no, no.

ROW.   (*aside to* SIR OLIVER). Take care, pray, sir.

SIR. O.   Well, so one of my nephews is a wild fellow, hey?

SIR PET.   Wild! Ah! my old friend, I grieve for your disappointment there; he's a lost young man, indeed. However, his brother will make you amends; Joseph is, indeed, what a youth should be. Everybody in the world speaks well of him.

SIR O.   I am sorry to hear it; he has too good a character to be an honest fellow.—Everybody speaks well of him! Pshaw! then he has bowed as low to knaves and fools as to the honest dignity of genius and virtue.

SIR PET.   What, Sir Oliver! do you blame him for not making enemies?

SIR O.   Yes, if he has merit enough to deserve them.

SIR PET.   Well, well—you'll be convinced when you know him. 'Tis edification to hear him converse; he professes the noblest sentiments.

SIR O.   Oh, plague of his sentiments! If he salutes me with a scrap of morality in his mouth, I shall be sick directly. But, however, don't mistake me, Sir Peter; I don't mean to defend Charles's errors, but before I form my judgment of either of them, I intend to make a trial of their hearts, and my friend Rowley and I have planned something for the purpose.

ROW.   And Sir Peter shall own for once he has been mistaken.

SIR PET.   Oh, my life on Joseph's honor!

SIR O.   Well—come, give us a bottle of good wine, and we'll drink the lads' health and tell you our scheme.

SIR PET.   *Allons*, then!

SIR O.   And don't, Sir Peter, be so severe against your old friend's son. Odds my life! I am not sorry that he has run out of the course a little. For my part, I hate to see prudence clinging to the green suckers of youth; 'tis like ivy round a sapling, and spoils the growth of the tree. (*Exeunt.*)

ACT III

SCENE 1

(*A room in* SIR PETER TEAZLE'S *house.*)

(*Enter* SIR PETER TEAZLE, SIR OLIVER SURFACE, *and* ROWLEY.)

SIR PET.   Well then, we will see this fellow first and have our wine afterwards. But how is this, Master Rowley? I don't see the jet of your scheme.

ROW.   Why, sir, this Mr. Stanley, who I was speaking of, is nearly related to them by their mother. He was once a merchant in Dublin, but has been ruined by a series of undeserved misfortunes. He has applied, by letter, to Mr. Surface and Charles. From the former he has received nothing but evasive promises of future service, while Charles has done all that his extravagance has left him power to do; and he is, at this time, endeavoring to raise a sum of money, part of which, in the midst of his own distresses, I know he intends for the service of poor Stanley.

SIR O.   Ah! he is my brother's son.

SIR PET.   Well, but how is Sir Oliver personally to—

ROW.   Why, sir, I will inform Charles and his brother that Stanley has obtained permission to apply personally to his friends; and as they have neither of them ever seen him, let Sir Oliver assume his character and he will have a fair opportunity of judging, at least of the benevolence of their dispositions. And believe me, sir, you will find in the youngest brother one who, in the midst of folly and dissipation, has still, as our immortal bard expresses it,

> a heart to pity, and a hand
> Open as day for melting charity.

Sir Pet. Pshaw! What signifies his having an open hand or purse either when he has nothing left to give? Well, well—make the trial if you please. But where is the fellow whom you brought for Sir Oliver to examine relative to Charles's affairs?

Row. Below, waiting his commands, and no one can give him better intelligence.— This, Sir Oliver, is a friendly Jew, who, to do him justice, has done everything in his power to bring your nephew to a proper sense of his extravagance.

Sir Pet. Pray, let us have him in.

Row. (apart to Servant). Desire Mr. Moses to walk up stairs.

Sir Pet. But pray, why should you suppose he will speak the truth?

Row. Oh, I have convinced him that he has no chance of recovering certain sums advanced to Charles but through the bounty of Sir Oliver, who he knows is arrived; so that you may depend on his fidelity to his own interests. I have also another evidence in my power, one Snake, whom I have detected in a matter little short of forgery, and shall shortly produce him to remove some of your prejudices.

Sir Pet. I have heard too much on that subject.

Row. Here comes the honest Israelite.

(Enter Moses.)
—This is Sir Oliver.

Sir O. Sir, I understand you have lately had great dealings with my nephew Charles.

Moses. Yes, Sir Oliver, I have done all I could for him, but he was ruined before he came to me for assistance.

Sir O. That was unlucky, truly, for you have had no opportunity of showing your talents.

Moses. None at all; I hadn't the pleasure of knowing his distresses till he was some thousands worse than nothing.

Sir O. Unfortunate, indeed; But I suppose you have done all in your power for him, honest Moses?

Moses. Yes, he knows that. This very evening I was to have brought him a gentleman from the city, who does not know him and will, I believe, advance him some money.

Sir Pet. What, one Charles has never had money from before?

Moses. Yes—Mr. Premium of Crutched Friars, formerly a broker.

Sir Pet. Egad, Sir Oliver, a thought strikes me!—Charles, you say, does not know Mr. Premium?

Moses. Not at all.

Sir Pet. Now then, Sir Oliver, you may have a better opportunity of satisfying yourself than by an old romancing tale of a poor relation; go with my friend Moses and represent Premium, and then, I'll answer for it, you'll see your nephew in all his glory.

Sir O. Egad, I like this idea better than the other, and I may visit Joseph afterwards as old Stanley.

Sir Pet. True, so you may.

Row. Well, this is taking Charles rather at a disadvantage, to be sure. However, Moses, you understand Sir Peter and will be faithful?

Moses. You may depend upon me.—This is near the time I was to have gone.

Sir O. I'll accompany you as soon as you please, Moses—But hold! I have forgot one thing: how the plague shall I be able to pass for a Jew?

Moses. There's no need—the principal is Christian.

Sir O. Is he? I'm very sorry to hear it. But then again, an't I rather too smartly dressed to look like a moneylender?

Sir Pet. Not at all; 'twould not be out of character if you went in your own carriage— would it, Moses?

Moses. Not in the least.

Sir O. Well, but how must I talk? there's certainly some cant of usury and mode of treating that I ought to know.

Sir Pet. Oh, there's not much to learn. The great point, as I take it, is to be exorbitant enough in your demands. Hey, Moses?

Moses. Yes, that's a very great point.

Sir O. I'll answer for't I'll not be wanting in that. I'll ask him eight or ten per cent on the loan, at least.

Moses. If you ask him no more than that you'll be discovered immediately.

SIR O. Hey! what, the plague! how much then?

MOSES. That depends upon the circumstances. If he appears not very anxious for the supply, you should require only forty or fifty per cent; but if you find him in great distress and want the moneys very bad, you may ask double.

SIR PET. A good honest trade you're learning, Sir Oliver.

SIR O. Truly, I think so—and not unprofitable.

MOSES. Then, you know, you haven't the moneys yourself, but are forced to borrow them for him of a friend.

SIR O. Oh! I borrow it of a friend, do I?

MOSES. And your friend is an unconscionable dog, but you can't help that.

SIR O. My friend an unconscionable dog, is he?

MOSES. Yes, and he himself has not the moneys by him, but is forced to sell stock at a great loss.

SIR O. He is forced to sell stock at a great loss, is he? Well, that's very kind of him.

SIR PET. I'faith, Sir Oliver—Mr. Premium, I mean—you'll soon be master of the trade. But, Moses, would not you have him run out a little against the Annuity Bill? That would be in character, I should think.

MOSES. Very much.

ROW. And lament that a young man now must be at years of discretion before he is suffered to ruin himself?

MOSES. Aye, great pity!

SIR PET. And abuse the public for allowing merit to an act whose only object is to snatch misfortune and imprudence from the rapacious gripe of usury, and give the minor a chance of inheriting his estate without being undone by coming into possession.

SIR O. So, so—Moses shall give me farther instructions as we go together.

SIR PET. You will not have much time, for your nephew lives hard by.

SIR O. Oh, never fear! my tutor appears so able that though Charles lived in the next street, it must be my own fault if I am not a complete rogue before I turn the corner. (*Exit* SIR OLIVER SURFACE *and* MOSES.)

SIR PET. So, now, I think Sir Oliver will be convinced. You are partial, Rowley, and would have prepared Charles for the other plot.

ROW. No, upon my word, Sir Peter.

SIR PET. Well, go bring me this Snake, and I'll hear what he has to say presently. I see Maria, and want to speak with her. (*Exit* ROWLEY.) I should be glad to be convinced my suspicions of Lady Teazle and Charles were unjust. I have never yet opened my mind on this subject to my friend Joseph—I am determined I will do it; he will give me his opinion sincerely.

(*Enter* MARIA.)

—So, child, has Mr. Surface returned with you?

MARIA. No, sir; he was engaged.

SIR PET. Well, Maria, do you not reflect, the more you converse with that amiable young man, what return his partiality for you deserves?

MARIA. Indeed, Sir Peter, your frequent importunity on this subject distresses me extremely. You compel me to declare that I know no man who has ever paid me a particular attention whom I would not prefer to Mr. Surface.

SIR PET. So—here's perverseness!—No, no, Maria, 'tis Charles only whom you would prefer. 'Tis evident his vices and follies have won your heart.

MARIA. This is unkind, sir. You know I have obeyed you in neither seeing nor corresponding with him; I have heard enough to convince me that he is unworthy my regard. Yet I cannot think it culpable if, while my understanding severely condemns his vices, my heart suggests some pity for his distresses.

SIR PET. Well, well, pity him as much as you please, but give your heart and hand to a worthier object.

MARIA. Never to his brother!

SIR PET. Go, perverse and obstinate! But take care, madam: you have never yet known what the authority of a guardian is; don't compel me to inform you of it.

MARIA. I can only say, you shall not have just reason. 'Tis true, by my father's will I am for a short period bound to regard you as his substitute, but must cease to think you so when you would compel me to be miserable. (*Exit* MARIA.)

SIR PET. Was ever man so crossed as I am! everything conspiring to fret me! I had not been involved in matrimony a fortnight before her father, a hale and hearty man, died on purpose, I believe, for the pleasure of plaguing me with the care of his daughter. —But here comes my helpmate! She appears in great good humor. How happy I should be if I could tease her into loving me, though but a little!

(*Enter* LADY TEAZLE.)

LADY T. Lud! Sir Peter, I hope you haven't been quarrelling with Maria? It is not using me well to be ill-humored when I am not by.

SIR PET. Ah, Lady Teazle, you might have the power to make me good-humored at all times.

LADY T. I am sure I wish I had, for I want you to be in a charming sweet temper at this moment. Do be good-humored now and let me have two hundred pounds, will you?

SIR PET. Two hundred pounds! what, ain't I to be in a good humor without paying for it? But speak to me thus and, i'faith, there's nothing I could refuse you. You shall have it, but seal me a bond for the repayment.

LADY T. (*offering her hand*). Oh, no—there— my note of hand will do as well.

SIR PET. And you shall no longer reproach me with not giving you an independent settlement; I mean shortly to surprise you. But shall we always live thus, hey?

LADY T. If you please. I'm sure I don't care how soon we leave off quarrelling, provided you'll own you were tired first.

SIR PET. Well—then let our future contest be, who shall be most obliging.

LADY T. I assure you, Sir Peter, good nature becomes you. You look now as you did before we were married, when you used to walk with me under the elms and tell me stories of what a gallant you were in your youth; and chuck me under the chin, you would, and ask me if I thought I could love an old fellow who would deny me nothing— didn't you?

SIR PET. Yes, yes, and you were as kind and attentive—

LADY T. Aye, so I was, and would always take your part when my acquaintance used to abuse you and turn you into ridicule.

SIR PET. Indeed!

LADY T. Aye, and when my cousin Sophy has called you a stiff, peevish old bachelor, and laughed at me for thinking of marrying one who might be my father, I have always defended you and said I didn't think you so ugly by any means and I dared say you'd make a very good sort of a husband.

SIR PET. And you prophesied right; and we shall now be the happiest couple—

LADY T. And never differ again?

SIR PET. No, never!—though at the same time, indeed, my dear Lady Teazle, you must watch your temper very seriously; for in all our little quarrels, my dear, if you recollect, my love, you always began first.

LADY T. I beg your pardon, my dear Sir Peter; indeed, you always gave the provocation.

SIR PET. Now see, my angel! take care— contradicting isn't the way to keep friends.

LADY T. Then don't you begin it, my love!

SIR PET. There now! you—you are going on. You don't perceive, my life, that you are just doing the very thing which you know always makes me angry.

LADY T. Nay, you know if you will be angry without any reason, my dear—

SIR PET. There! now you want to quarrel again.

LADY T. No, I'm sure I don't, but if you will be so peevish—

SIR PET. There now! who begins first?

LADY T. Why, you, to be sure. I said nothing —but there's no bearing your temper.

SIR PET. No, no, madam, the fault's in your own temper.

LADY T. Aye, you are just what my cousin Sophy said you would be.

SIR PET. Your cousin Sophy is a forward, impertinent gipsy.

LADY T. You are a great bear, I'm sure, to abuse my relations.

SIR PET. Now may all the plagues of marriage be doubled on me if ever I try to be friends with you any more!

LADY T. So much the better.

SIR PET. No, no, madam: 'tis evident you never cared a pin for me, and I was a madman to marry you—a pert, rural coquette that had refused half the honest 'squires in the neighborhood.

LADY T. And I am sure I was a fool to marry you—an old dangling bachelor who was single at fifty only because he never could meet with anyone who would have him.

SIR PET. Aye, aye, madam, but you were pleased enough to listen to me; you never had such an offer before.

LADY T. No! didn't I refuse Sir Tivy Terrier, who everybody said would have been a better match? for his estate is just as good as yours, and he has broke his neck since we have been married.

SIR PET. I have done with you, madam! You are an unfeeling, ungrateful—but there's an end of everything. I believe you capable of everything that is bad. Yes, madam, I now believe the reports relative to you and Charles, madam. Yes, madam, *you* and Charles are, not without grounds—

LADY T. Take care, Sir Peter! you had better not insinuate any such thing! I'll not be suspected without cause, I promise you.

SIR PET. Very well, madam! very well! A separate maintenance as soon as you please. —Yes, madam, or a divorce! I'll make an example of myself for the benefit of all old bachelors. Let us separate, madam!

LADY T. Agreed! agreed! And now, my dear Sir Peter, we are of a mind once more, we may be the happiest couple and never differ again, you know—ha! ha! ha! Well, you are going to be in a passion, I see, and I shall only interrupt you—so, bye! bye! (*Exit.*)

SIR PET. Plagues and tortures! can't I make her angry either! Oh, I am the most miserable fellow! But I'll not bear her presuming to keep her temper—no! she may break my heart, but she shan't keep her temper. (*Exit.*)

SCENE 2

(*A room in* CHARLES SURFACE'S *house.*)

(*Enter* TRIP, MOSES, *and* SIR OLIVER SURFACE.)

TRIP. Here, Master Moses! if you'll stay a moment, I'll try whether—what's the gentleman's name?

SIR O. (*aside*). Mr. Moses, what is my name?

MOSES. Mr. Premium.

TRIP. Premium—very well. (*Exit* TRIP, *taking snuff.*)

SIR O. To judge by the servants, one wouldn't believe the master was ruined. But what!—sure, this was my brother's house?

MOSES. Yes, sir; Mr. Charles bought it of Mr. Joseph, with the furniture, pictures, etc., just as the old gentleman left it. Sir Peter thought it a piece of extravagance in him.

SIR O. In my mind, the other's economy in selling it to him was more reprehensible by half.

(*Re-enter* TRIP.)

TRIP. My master says you must wait, gentlemen; he has company and can't speak with you yet.

SIR O. If he knew who it was wanted to see him, perhaps he would not send such a message.

TRIP. Yes, yes, sir; he knows you are here—I did not forget little Premium. No, no, no!

SIR O. Very well; and I pray, sir, what may be your name?

TRIP. Trip, sir; my name is Trip, at your service.

SIR O. Well, then, Mr. Trip, you have a pleasant sort of place here, I guess?

TRIP. Why, yes—here are three or four of us pass our time agreeably enough; but then our wages are sometimes a little in arrear— and not very great either—but fifty pounds a year, and find our own bags and bouquets.

SIR O. (*aside*). Bags and bouquets? halters and bastinadoes!

TRIP. And à propos, Moses, have you been able to get me that little bill discounted?

SIR O. (*aside*). Wants to raise money too— mercy on me! Has his distresses too, I warrant, like a lord, and affects creditors and duns.

MOSES. 'Twas not to be done, indeed, Mr. Trip.

TRIP. Good lack, you surprise me! My friend Brush has indorsed it, and I thought when he put his name at the back of a bill 'twas the same as cash.

MOSES. No, 'twouldn't do.

TRIP. A small sum—but twenty pounds. Hark'ee, Moses, do you think you couldn't get it me by way of annuity?

SIR O. (*aside*). An annuity! ha! ha! a footman raise money by way of annuity! Well done, luxury, egad!

MOSES. Well, but you must insure your place.

TRIP. Oh, with all my heart! I'll insure my place, and my life too, if you please.

SIR O. (*aside*). It's more than I would your neck.

MOSES. But is there nothing you could deposit?

TRIP. Why, nothing capital of my master's wardrobe has dropped lately, but I could give you a mortgage on some of his winter clothes, with equity of redemption before November—or you shall have the reversion of the French velvet, or a post-obit on the blue and silver;—these, I should think, Moses, with a few pair of point ruffles as a collateral security—hey, my little fellow?

MOSES. Well, well. (*Bell rings.*)

TRIP. Egad, I heard the bell! I believe, gentlemen, I can now introduce you. Don't forget the annuity, little Moses!—This way, gentlemen.—I'll insure my place, you know.

SIR O. (*aside*). If the man be a shadow of the master, this is the temple of dissipation indeed! (*Exeunt.*)

SCENE 3

(*Another room in the same.*)

(CHARLES SURFACE *and his friends at a table with wine, etc.*)

CHARLES. 'Fore Heaven, 'tis true!—there's the great degeneracy of the age. Many of our acquaintance have taste, spirit, and politeness, but, plague on't, they won't drink.

CARE. It is so indeed, Charles! they give in to all the substantial luxuries of the table, and abstain from nothing but wine and wit. Oh, certainly society suffers by it intolerably! for now, instead of the social spirit of raillery that used to mantle over a glass of bright Burgundy, their conversation is become just like the Spa water they drink, which has all the pertness and flatulence of champagne without the spirit or flavor.

IST GENT. But what are they to do who love play better than wine?

CARE. True! there's Sir Harry diets himself for gaming, and is now under a hazard regimen.

CHARLES. Then he'll have the worst of it. What! you wouldn't train a horse for the course by keeping him from corn? For my part, egad, I am never so successful as when I am a little merry; let me throw on a bottle of champagne, and I never lose—at least I never feel my losses, which is exactly the same thing.

2D GENT. Aye, that I believe.

CHARLES. And then, what man can pretend to be a believer in love who is an abjurer of wine? 'Tis the test by which the lover knows his own heart. Fill a dozen bumpers to a dozen beauties, and she that floats a-top is the maid that has bewitched you.

CARE. New then, Charles, be honest and give us your real favorite.

CHARLES. Why, I have withheld her only in compassion to you. If I toast her, you must give a round of her peers, which is impossible—on earth.

CARE. Oh! then we'll find some canonised vestals or heathen goddesses that will do, I warrant!

CHARLES. Here then, bumpers, you rogues! bumpers! Maria! Maria!—

SIR H. Maria who?

CHARLES. Oh, damn the surname!—'tis too formal to be registered in Love's calendar.—But now, Sir Harry, beware, we must have beauty superlative.

CARE. Nay, never study, Sir Harry; we'll stand to the toast though your mistress should want an eye, and you know you have a song will excuse you.

SIR H. Egad, so I have! and I'll give him the song instead of the lady. (*Sings.*)

SONG

Here's to the maiden of bashful fifteen;
  Here's to the widow of fifty;
Here's to the flaunting extravagant quean
  And here's to the housewife that's thrifty

CHORUS.
    Let the toast pass,—
    Drink to the lass,
  I'll warrant she'll prove an excuse for the glass.

Here's to the charmer whose dimples we prize;
  Now to the maid who has none, sir;
Here's to the girl with a pair of blue eyes.
  And here's to the nymph with but one, sir.

CHORUS.
    Let the toast pass, etc.

Here's to the maid with a bosom of snow;
  Now to her that's as brown as a berry;
Here's to the wife with a face full of woe,
  And now to the damsel that's merry.

CHORUS.
    Let the toast pass, etc.

For let 'em be clumsy or let 'em be slim,
  Young or ancient, I care not a feather;
So fill a pint bumper quite up to the brim,
So fill up your glasses—nay, fill to the brim—.
  And let us e'en toast them together.
CHORUS.
    Let the toast pass, etc.

ALL.   Bravo! bravo!
(*Enter* TRIP *and whispers* CHARLES SURFACE.)
CHARLES.   Gentlemen, you must excuse me a little.—Careless, take the chair, will you?
CARE.   Nay, prithee, Charles, what now? This is one of your peerless beauties, I suppose, has dropped in by chance?
CHARLES.   No, faith! To tell you the truth, 'tis a Jew and a broker, who are come by appointment.
CARE.   Oh, damn it! let's have the Jew in.
1ST GENT.   Aye, and the broker too, by all means.
2D GENT.   Yes, yes, the Jew and the broker.
CHARLES.   Egad, with all my heart!—Trip, bid the gentlemen walk in.
(*Exit* TRIP.)
    —Though there's one of them a stranger, I can tell you.
CARE.   Charles, let us give them some generous Burgundy, and perhaps they'll grow conscientious.
CHARLES.   Oh, hang 'em, no! wine does but draw forth a man's natural qualities, and to make them drink would only be to whet their knavery.
(*Re-enter* TRIP, *with* SIR OLIVER SURFACE *and* MOSES.)
CHARLES.   So, honest Moses, walk in; walk in, pray, Mr. Premium—that's the gentleman's name, isn't it, Moses?
MOSES.   Yes, sir.
CHARLES.   Set chairs, Trip.—Sit down, Mr. Premium.—Glasses, Trip.
(TRIP *gives chairs and glasses, and exit.*)
    —Sit down, Moses.—Come, Mr. Premium, I'll give you a sentiment; here's *Success to usury!*—Moses, fill the gentlemen a bumper.
MOSES.   Success to usury! (*Drinks.*)
CARE.   Right, Moses—usury is prudence and industry, and deserves to succeed.
SIR O.   Then—here's all the success it deserves! (*Drinks.*)
CARE.   No, no, that won't do! Mr. Premium, you have demurred at the toast and must drink it in a pint bumper.
1ST GENT.   A pint bumper, at least.
MOSES.   Oh, pray, sir, consider—Mr. Premium's a gentleman.
CARE.   And therefore loves good wine.
2D GENT.   Give Moses a quart glass—this is mutiny, and a high contempt for the chair.
CARE.   Here, now for't! I'll see justice done, to the last drop of my bottle.
SIR O.   Nay, pray, gentlemen—I did not expect this usage.
CHARLES.   No, hang it, you shan't; Mr. Premium's a stranger.
SIR O. (*aside*).   Odd! I wish I was well out of their company.
CARE.   Plague on 'em then! if they won't drink, we'll not sit down with them. Come, Harry, the dice are in the next room.—Charles, you'll join us when you have finished your business with the gentlemen?
CHARLES.   I will! I will!
(*Exeunt* SIR HARRY BUMPER *and* GENTLEMEN, CARELESS *following.*)
    —Careless!
CARE. (*returning*).   Well!
CHARLES.   Perhaps I may want you.
CARE.   Oh, you know I am always ready; word, note, or bond, 'tis all the same to me. (*Exit.*)
MOSES.   Sir, this is Mr. Premium, a gentleman of the strictest honor and secrecy, and always performs what he undertakes. Mr. Premium, this is—
CHARLES.   Pshaw! have done. Sir, my friend Moses is a very honest fellow, but a little slow at expression; he'll be an hour giving us our titles. Mr. Premium, the plain state of the matter is this: I am an extravagant young fellow who wants to borrow money; you I take to be a prudent old fellow who have got money to lend. I am blockhead enough to give fifty per cent sooner than not have it; and you, I presume, are rogue enough to take a hundred if you can get it. Now, sir, you see we are acquainted at once, and may proceed to business without farther ceremony.
SIR O.   Exceeding frank, upon my word. I see, sir, you are not a man of many compliments.
CHARLES.   Oh, no, sir! plain dealing in business I always think best.
SIR O.   Sir, I like you the better for it.

However, you are mistaken in one thing; I have no money to lend, but I believe I could procure some of a friend—but then, he's an unconscionable dog. Isn't he, Moses?

MOSES.   But you can't help that.

SIR O.   And must sell stock to accommodate you—mustn't he, Moses?

MOSES.   Yes, indeed! You know I always speak the truth and scorn to tell a lie.

CHARLES.   Right. People that speak truth generally do. But these are trifles, Mr. Premium. What! I know money isn't to be bought without paying for't.

SIR O.   Well, but what security could you give? You have no land, I suppose?

CHARLES.   Not a mole-hill nor a twig but what's in the bough-pots out of the window.

SIR O.   Nor any stock, I presume?

CHARLES.   Nothing but live stock—and that only a few pointers and ponies. But pray, Mr. Premium, are you acquainted at all with any of my connections?

SIR O.   Why, to say truth, I am.

CHARLES.   Then you must know that I have a dev'lish rich uncle in the East Indies, Sir Oliver Surface, from whom I have the greatest expectations?

SIR O.   That you have a wealthy uncle, I have heard, but how your expectations will turn out is more, I believe, than you can tell.

CHARLES.   Oh, no!—there can be no doubt. They tell me I'm a prodigious favorite, and that he talks of leaving me everything.

SIR O.   Indeed! this is the first I've heard of it.

CHARLES.   Yes, yes, 'tis just so. Moses knows 'tis true; don't you, Moses?

MOSES.   Oh, yes! I'll swear to't.

SIR O.   (aside).   Egad, they'll persuade me presently I'm at Bengal.

CHARLES.   Now I propose, Mr. Premium, if it's agreeable to you, a post-obit on Sir Oliver's life—though at the same time the old fellow has been so liberal to me that I give you my word, I should be very sorry to hear that anything had happened to him.

SIR O.   Not more than I should, I assure you. But the bond you mention happens to be just the worst security you could offer me—for I might live to a hundred and never see the principal.

CHARLES.   Oh, yes, you would! the moment Sir Oliver dies, you know, you would come on me for the money.

SIR O.   Then I believe I should be the most unwelcome dun you ever had in your life.

CHARLES.   What! I suppose you're afraid that Sir Oliver is too good a life?

SIR O.   No, indeed I am not—though I have heard he is as hale and healthy as any man of his years in christendom.

CHARLES.   There again, now, you are misinformed. No, no, the climate has hurt him considerably, poor Uncle Oliver. Yes, yes, he breaks apace, I'm told—and is so much altered lately that his nearest relations don't know him.

SIR O.   No! Ha! ha! ha! so much altered lately that his nearest relations would not know him! Ha! ha! ha! egad—ha! ha! ha!

CHARLES.   Ha! ha!—you're glad to hear that, little Premium?

SIR O.   No, no, I'm not.

CHARLES.   Yes, yes, you are—ha! ha! ha!—you know that mends your chance.

SIR O.   But I'm told Sir Oliver is coming over; nay, some say he is actually arrived.

CHARLES.   Pshaw! sure I must know better than you whether he's come or not. No, no, rely on't he's at this moment at Calcutta. Isn't he, Moses?

MOSES.   Oh, yes, certainly.

SIR O.   Very true, as you say, you must know better than I, though I have it from pretty good authority—haven't I, Moses?

MOSES.   Yes, most undoubted!

SIR O.   But, sir, as I understand you want a few hundreds immediately, is there nothing you could dispose of?

CHARLES.   How do you mean?

SIR O.   For instance, now, I have heard that your father left behind him a great quantity of massy old plate.

CHARLES.   O lud! that's gone long ago. Moses can tell you how better than I can.

SIR O.   (aside).   Good lack! all the family race-cups and corporation-bowls!—(Aloud.) Then it was also supposed that his library was one of the most valuable and compact—

CHARLES.   Yes, yes, so it was—vastly too much so for a private gentleman. For my part, I was always of a communicative disposition; so I thought it a shame to keep so much knowledge to myself.

SIR. O.   (aside).   Mercy upon me! learning

that had run in the family like an heirloom! —(*Aloud.*) Pray, what are become of the books?

CHARLES. You must inquire of the auctioneer, Master Premium, for I don't believe even Moses can direct you.

MOSES. I know nothing of books.

SIR O. So, so, nothing of the family property left, I suppose?

CHARLES. Not much, indeed, unless you have a mind to the family pictures. I have got a room full of ancestors above, and if you have a taste for old paintings, egad, you shall have 'em a bargain.

SIR O. Hey! what the devil! sure, you wouldn't sell your forefathers, would you?

CHARLES. Every man of them, to the best bidder.

SIR O. What! your great-uncles and aunts?

CHARLES. Aye, and my great-grandfathers and grandmothers too.

SIR O. (*aside*). Now I give him up!—(*Aloud.*) What the plague, have you no bowels for your own kindred? Odds life! do you take me for Shylock in the play, that you would raise money of me on your own flesh and blood?

CHARLES. Nay, my little broker, don't be angry; what need you care, if you have your money's worth?

SIR O. Well, I'll be the purchaser; I think I can dispose of the family canvas.—(*Aside.*) Oh, I'll never forgive him this!—never!

(*Re-enter* CARELESS.)

CARE. Come, Charles, what keeps you?

CHARLES. I can't come yet. I'faith, we are going to have a sale above stairs; here's little Premium will buy all my ancestors!

CARE. Oh, burn your ancestors!

CHARLES. No, he may do that afterwards if he pleases. Stay, Careless, we want you: egad, you shall be auctioneer—so come along with us.

CARE. Oh, have with you, if that's the case.— [I can] handle a hammer as well as a dice-box!

SIR O. (*aside*). Oh, the profligates!

CHARLES. Come, Moses, you shall be appraiser if we want one. Gad's life, little Premium, you don't seem to like the business?

SIR O. Oh, yes, I do, vastly! Ha! ha! ha! yes, yes, I think it a rare joke to sell one's family by auction—ha! ha!—(*Aside.*) Oh, the prodigal!

CHARLES. To be sure! when a man wants money, where the plague should he get assistance if he can't make free with his own relations? (*Exeunt.*)

ACT IV

SCENE 1

(*Picture room at* CHARLES SURFACE'S *house.*)
(*Enter* CHARLES SURFACE, SIR OLIVER SURFACE, MOSES, *and* CARELESS.)

CHARLES. Walk in, gentlemen, pray walk in; here they are, the family of the Surfaces up to the Conquest.

SIR O. And in my opinion a goodly collection.

CHARLES. Aye, aye, these are done in the true spirit of portrait-painting; no *volontaire grâce* or expression. Not like the works of your modern Raphaels, who give you the strongest resemblance, yet contrive to make your portrait independent of you, so that you may sink the original and not hurt the picture. No, no; the merit of these is the inveterate likeness—all stiff and awkward as the originals, and like nothing in human nature besides.

SIR O. Ah! we shall never see such figures of men again.

CHARLES. I hope not. Well, you see, Master Premium, what a domestic character I am; here I sit of an evening surrounded by my family.—But come, get to your pulpit, Mr. Auctioneer; here's an old gouty chair of my grandfather's will answer the purpose.

CARE. Aye, aye, this will do. But, Charles, I haven't a hammer; and what's an auctioneer without his hammer?

CHARLES. Egad, that's true. What parchment have we here? Oh, our genealogy in full. Here, Careless, you shall have no common bit of mahogany; here's the family tree for you, you rogue! This shall be your hammer, and now you may knock down my ancestors with their own pedigree.

SIR O. (*aside*). What an unnatural rogue!— an *ex post facto* parricide!

CARE. Yes, yes, here's a list of your generation, indeed;—faith, Charles, this is the most convenient thing you could have found for the business, for 'twill not only serve as a hammer but a catalogue into the bargain. Come, begin—A-going, a-going, a-going!

CHARLES. Bravo! Careless! Well, here's my great-uncle, Sir Richard Raveline, a marvellous good general in his day, I assure you. He served in all the Duke of Marlborough's wars and got that cut over his eye at the battle of Malplaquet. What say you, Mr. Premium? look at him—there's a hero! not cut out of his feathers, as your modern clipped captains are, but enveloped in wig and regimentals, as a general should be. What do you bid?

MOSES. Mr. Premium would have *you* speak.

CHARLES. Why, then, he shall have him for ten pounds, and I'm sure that's not dear for a staff officer.

SIR O. (*aside*). Heaven deliver me! his famous uncle Richard for ten pounds!—Very well, sir, I take him at that.

CHARLES. Careless, knock down my uncle Richard.—Here, now, is a maiden sister of his, my great-aunt Deborah, done by Kneller, thought to be in his best manner and esteemed a very formidable likeness. There she is, you see, a shepherdess feeding her flock. You shall have her for five pounds ten—the sheep are worth the money.

SIR O. (*aside*). Ah! poor Deborah!—a woman who set such a value on herself!—Five pounds ten—she's mine.

CHARLES. Knock down my aunt Deborah! Here, now, are two that were a sort of cousins of theirs.—You see, Moses, these pictures were done some time ago, when beaux wore wigs and the ladies their own hair.

SIR O. Yes, truly, head-dresses appear to have been a little lower in those days.

CHARLES. Well, take that couple for the same.

MOSES. 'Tis [a] good bargain.

CHARLES. Careless!—This, now, is a grandfather of my mother's, a learned judge, well known on the western circuit.—What do you rate him at, Moses?

MOSES. Four guineas.

CHARLES. Four gineas! Gad's life, you don't bid me the price of his wig.—Mr. Premium, you have more respect for the woolsack; do let us knock his lordship down at fifteen.

SIR O. By all means.

CARE. Gone!

CHARLES. And there are two brothers of his, William and Walter Blunt, Esquires, both members of Parliament and noted speakers; and, what's very extraordinary, I believe, this is the first time they were ever bought or sold.

SIR O. That is very extraordinary, indeed! I'll take them at your own price, for the honor of Parliament.

CARE. Well said, little Premium! I'll knock them down at forty.

CHARLES. Here's a jolly fellow—I don't know what relation, but he was mayor of Manchester: take him at eight pounds.

SIR O. No, no; six will do for the mayor.

CHARLES. Come, make it guineas, and I'll throw you the two aldermen there into the bargain.

SIR O. They're mine.

CHARLES. Careless, knock down the mayor and aldermen. But, plague on't! we shall be all day retailing in this manner; do let us deal wholesale. What say you, little Premium? Give me three hundred pounds for the rest of the family in the lump.

CARE. Aye, aye, that will be the best way.

SIR O. Well, well, anything to accommodate you; they are mine. But there is one portrait which you have always passed over.

CARE. What, that ill-looking little fellow over the settee?

SIR O. Yes sir, I mean that—though I don't think him so ill-looking a little fellow, by any means.

CHARLES. What, that?—Oh, that's my uncle Oliver! 'twas done before he went to India.

CARE. Your uncle Oliver! Gad, then you'll never be friends, Charles. That, now, to me, is as stern a looking rogue as ever I saw—an unforgiving eye, and a damned disinheriting countenance!—an inveterate knave, depend on't. Don't you think so, little Premium?

SIR O. Upon my soul, sir, I do not; I think it is as honest a looking face as any in the room, dead or alive. But I suppose uncle Oliver goes with the rest of the lumber?

CHARLES. No, hang it; I'll not part with poor Noll. The old fellow has been very good to me and, egad, I'll keep his picture while I've a room to put it in.

SIR O. (*aside*). The rogue's my nephew after

all!—But, sir, I have somehow taken a fancy to that picture.

CHARLES. I'm sorry for't, for you certainly will not have it. Oons, haven't you got enough of them?

SIR O. (*aside*). I forgive him everything!—But, sir, when I take a whim in my head, I don't value money. I'll give you as much for that as for all the rest.

CHARLES. Don't tease me, master broker; I tell you I'll not part with it; and there's an end of it.

SIR O. (*aside*). How like his father the dog is!—Well, well, I have done.—(*Aside.*) I did not perceive it before, but I think I never saw such a striking resemblance.—Here is a draft for your sum.

CHARLES. Why, 'tis for eight hundred pounds!

SIR O. You will not let Sir Oliver go?

CHARLES. Zounds! no! I tell you once more.

SIR O. Then never mind the difference; we'll balance that another time. But give me your hand on the bargain. You are an honest fellow, Charles—I beg pardon, sir, for being so free.—Come, Moses.

CHARLES. Egad, this is a whimsical old fellow!—But hark'ee, Premium, you'll prepare lodgings for these gentlemen.

SIR O. Yes, yes, I'll send for them in a day or two.

CHARLES. But hold; do now send a genteel conveyance for them, for I assure you, they were most of them used to ride in their own carriages.

SIR O. I will, I will—for all but Oliver.

CHARLES. Aye, all but the little nabob.

SIR O. You're fixed on that?

CHARLES. Peremptorily.

SIR O. (*aside*). A dear extravagant rogue!—Good day!—Come, Moses.—(*Aside.*) Let me hear now who dares call him profligate! (*Exeunt* SIR OLIVER SURFACE *and* MOSES.)

CARE. Why, this is the oddest genius of the sort I ever saw!

CHARLES. Egad, he's the prince of brokers, I think. I wonder how Moses got acquainted with so honest a fellow.—Hah, here's Rowley.—Do, Careless, say I'll join the company in a few moments.

CARE. I will—but don't let that old blockhead persuade you to squander any of that money on old musty debts, or any such nonsense; for tradesmen, Charles, are the most exorbitant fellows.

CHARLES. Very true, and paying them is only encouraging them.

CARE. Nothing else.

CHARLES. Aye, aye, never fear. (*Exit* CARELESS.)

—So! this was an odd old fellow, indeed. Let me see, two-thirds of this is mine by right—five hundred and thirty odd pounds. 'Fore Heaven! I find one's ancestors are more valuable relations than I took them for!—Ladies and gentlemen, your most obedient and very grateful servant. (*Bows.*) (*Enter* ROWLEY.)

—Ha! old Rowley! egad, you are just come in time to take leave of your old acquaintance.

ROW. Yes, I heard they were a-going. But I wonder you can have such spirits under so many distresses.

CHARLES. Why, there's the point! my distresses are so many that I can't afford to part with my spirits; but I shall be rich and splenetic, all in good time. However, I suppose you are surprised that I am not more sorrowful at parting with so many near relations. To be sure, 'tis very affecting; but you see they never move a muscle; so why should I?

ROW. There's no making you serious a moment.

CHARLES. Yes, faith, I am so now. Here, my honest Rowley—here, get me this changed directly, and take a hundred pounds of it immediately to old Stanley.

ROW. A hundred pounds! Consider only—

CHARLES. Gad's life, don't talk about it! poor Stanley's wants are pressing, and if you don't make haste we shall have someone call that has a better right to the money.

ROW. Ah! there's the point! I never will cease dunning you with the old proverb—

CHARLES. "Be just before you're generous."—Why, so I would if I could, but Justice is an old, hobbling beldame, and I can't get her to keep pace with Generosity, for the soul of me.

ROW. Yet, Charles, believe me, one hour's reflection—

CHARLES. Aye, aye, it's all very true; but,

hark'ee, Rowley, while I have, by Heaven, I'll give; so, damn your economy—and now for hazard. (*Exeunt.*)

SCENE 2

(*The parlor.*)

(*Enter* SIR OLIVER SURFACE *and* MOSES.)

MOSES.   Well, sir, I think, as Sir Peter said, you have seen Mr. Charles in high glory; 'tis great pity he's so extravagant.

SIR O.   True, but he would not sell my picture.

MOSES.   And loves wine and women so much.

SIR O.   But he would not sell my picture.

MOSES.   And games so deep.

SIR O.   But he would not sell my picture!— Oh, here's Rowley.

(*Enter* ROWLEY.)

ROW.   So, Sir Oliver, I find you have made a purchase—

SIR O.   Yes, yes, our young rake has parted with his ancestors like old tapestry.

ROW.   And here has he commissioned me to re-deliver you part of the purchase money— I mean, though, in your necessitous character of old Stanley.

MOSES.   Ah! there is the pity of all; he is so damned charitable.

ROW.   And I left a hosier and two tailors in the hall, who, I'm sure, won't be paid, and this hundred would satisfy them.

SIR O.   Well, well, I'll pay his debts and his benevolence too. But now I am no more a broker, and you shall introduce me to the elder brother as old Stanley.

ROW.   Not yet awhile; Sir Peter, I know, means to call there about this time.

(*Enter* TRIP.)

TRIP.   Oh, gentlemen, I beg pardon for not showing you out; this way—Moses, a word. (*Exeunt* TRIP *and* MOSES.)

SIR O.   There's a fellow for you! Would you believe it, that puppy intercepted the Jew on our coming and wanted to raise money before he got to his master!

ROW.   Indeed!

SIR O.   Yes; they are now planning an annuity business. Ah, Master Rowley, in my days servants were content with the follies of their masters when they were worn a little threadbare; but now they have their

vices, like their birthday clothes, with the gloss on. (*Exeunt.*)

SCENE 3

(*A library in* JOSEPH SURFACE'S *house.*)

(*Enter* JOSEPH SURFACE *and* SERVANT.)

JOSEPH.   No letter from Lady Teazle?

SERV.   No, sir.

JOSEPH (*aside*).   I am surprised she has not sent if she is prevented from coming. Sir Peter certainly does not suspect me. Yet I wish I may not lose the heiress through the scrape I have drawn myself into with the wife; however, Charles's imprudence and bad character are great points in my favor.

(*Knocking without.*)

SERV.   Sir, I believe that must be Lady Teazle.

JOSEPH.   Hold! See whether it is or not before you go to the door. I have a particular message for you if it should be my brother.

SERV.   'Tis her ladyship, sir; she always leaves her chair at the milliner's in the next street.

JOSEPH.   Stay, stay; draw that screen before the window—that will do. My opposite neighbor is a maiden lady of so curious a temper.

(SERVANT *draws the screen, and exits.*) I have a difficult hand to play in this affair. Lady Teazle has lately suspected my views on Maria, but she must by no means be let into that secret—at least till I have her more in my power.

(*Enter* LADY TEAZLE.)

LADY T.   What, sentiment in soliloquy now? Have you been very impatient? O lud! don't pretend to look grave. I vow I couldn't come before.

JOSEPH.   O madam, punctuality is a species of constancy very unfashionable in a lady of quality.

LADY T.   Upon my word, you ought to pity me. Do you know Sir Peter is grown so ill-natured to me of late, and so jealous of Charles, too—that's the best of the story, isn't it?

JOSEPH (*aside*).   I am glad my scandalous friends keep that up.

LADY T.   I am sure I wish he would let Maria marry him, and then perhaps he would be convinced; don't you, Mr. Surface?

JOSEPH (*aside*). Indeed I do not.—Oh, certainly I do! for then my dear Lady Teazle would also be convinced how wrong her suspicions were of my having any design on the silly girl.

LADY T. Well, well, I'm inclined to believe you. But isn't it provoking to have the most ill-natured things said of one? And there's my friend Lady Sneerwell has circulated I don't know how many scandalous tales of me, and all without any foundation too; that's what vexes me.

JOSEPH. Aye, madam, to be sure, that is the provoking circumstance—without foundation; yes, yes, there's the mortification, indeed, for when a scandalous story is believed against one, there certainly is no comfort like the consciousness of having deserved it.

LADY T. No, to be sure; then I'd forgive their malice. But to attack me, who am really so innocent, and who never say an ill-natured thing of anybody—that is, of any friend; and then Sir Peter, too, to have him so peevish, and so suspicious, when I know the integrity of my own heart—indeed, 'tis monstrous!

JOSEPH. But, my dear Lady Teazle, 'tis your own fault if you suffer it. When a husband entertains a groundless suspicion of his wife and withdraws his confidence from her, the original compact is broken and she owes it to the honor of her sex to outwit him.

LADY T. Indeed! so that if he suspects me without cause, it follows that the best way of curing his jealousy is to give him reason for't?

JOSEPH. Undoubtedly—for your husband should never be deceived in you, and in that case it becomes you to be frail in compliment to his discernment.

LADY T. To be sure, what you say is very reasonable, and when the consciousness of my innocence—

JOSEPH. Ah, my dear madam, there is the great mistake! 'tis this very conscious innocence that is of the greatest prejudice to you. What is it makes you negligent of forms and careless of the world's opinion? why, the consciousness of your own in-

nocence. What makes you thoughtless in your conduct and apt to run into a thousand little imprudences? why, the consciousness of your own innocence. What makes you impatient of Sir Peter's temper and outrageous at his suspicions? why, the consciousness of your innocence.

LADY T. 'Tis very true!

JOSEPH. Now, my dear Lady Teazle, if you would but once make a trifling *faux pas*, you can't conceive how cautious you would grow, and how ready to humor and agree with your husband.

LADY T. Do you think so?

JOSEPH. Oh, I am sure on't; and then you would find all scandal would cease at once, for—in short, your character at present is like a person in a plethora, absolutely dying from too much health.

LADY T. So, so; then I perceive your prescription is that I must sin in my own defence and part with my virtue to preserve my reputation?

JOSEPH. Exactly so, upon my credit, ma'am.

LADY T. Well, certainly this is the oddest doctrine and the newest receipt for avoiding calumny!

JOSEPH. An infallible one, believe me. Prudence, like experience, must be paid for.

LADY T. Why, if my understanding were once convinced—

JOSEPH. Oh, certainly, madam, your understanding should be convinced. Yes, yes—Heaven forbid I should persuade you to do anything you thought wrong. No, no, I have too much honor to desire it.

LADY T. Don't you think we may as well leave honor out of the argument?

JOSEPH. Ah, the ill effects of your country education, I see, still remain with you.

LADY T. I doubt they do, indeed; and I will fairly own to you that if I could be persuaded to do wrong, it would be by Sir Peter's ill usage sooner than your *honorable logic*, after all.

JOSEPH (*taking her hand*). Then, by this hand, which he is unworthy of—

(*Re-enter* SERVANT.)

—'Sdeath, you blockhead—what do you want?

SERV. I beg your pardon, sir, but I thought you would not choose Sir Peter to come up without announcing him.

JOSEPH. Sir Peter!—Oons—the devil!

LADY T. Sir Peter! O lud!—I'm ruined! I'm ruined!

SERV. Sir, 'twasn't I let him in.

LADY T. Oh! I'm quite undone! What will become of me? Now, Mr. Logic—Oh! mercy, sir, he's on the stairs—I'll get behind here—and if ever I'm so imprudent again— (*Goes behind the screen.*)

JOSEPH. Give me that book. (*Sits down. Servant pretends to adjust his chair.*)

(*Enter Sir Peter.*)

SIR PET. Aye, ever improving himself—Mr. Surface, Mr. Surface—

JOSEPH. Oh, my dear Sir Peter, I beg your pardon—(*gaping, throws away the book*). I have been dozing over a stupid book. Well, I am much obliged to you for this call. You haven't been here, I believe, since I fitted up this room. Books, you know, are the only things in which I am a coxcomb.

SIR PET. 'Tis very neat, indeed. Well, well, that's proper; and you can make even your screen a source of knowledge—hung, I perceive, with maps.

JOSEPH. Oh, yes, I find great use in that screen.

SIR PET. I dare say you must, certainly, when you want to find anything in a hurry.

JOSEPH (*aside*). Aye, or to hide anything in a hurry either.

SIR PET. Well, I have a little private business—

JOSEPH (*to the* SERVANT). You need not stay.

SERV. No, sir.

JOSEPH. Here's a chair, Sir Peter—I beg—

SIR PET. Well, now we are alone, there is a subject, my dear friend, on which I wish to unburden my mind to you—a point of the greatest moment to my peace; in short, my good friend, Lady Teazle's conduct of late has made me very unhappy.

JOSEPH. Indeed! I am very sorry to hear it.

SIR PET. Yes, 'tis but too plain she has not the least regard for me; but what's worse I have pretty good authority to suppose she has formed an attachment to another.

JOSEPH. Indeed! you astonish me!

SIR PET. Yes! and, between ourselves, I think I've discovered the person.

JOSEPH. How! you alarm me exceedingly.

SIR PET. Aye, my dear friend, I knew you would sympathise with me!

JOSEPH. Yes—believe me, Sir Peter, such a discovery would hurt me just as much as it would you.

SIR PET. I am convinced of it. Ah! it is a happiness to have a friend whom we can trust even with one's family secrets. But have you no guess who I mean?

JOSEPH. I haven't the most distant idea. It can't be Sir Benjamin Backbite!

SIR PET. Oh, no! What say you to Charles?

JOSEPH. My brother!—impossible!

SIR PET. Oh, my dear friend, the goodness of your own heart misleads you. You judge of others by yourself.

JOSEPH. Certainly, Sir Peter, the heart that is conscious of its own integrity is ever slow to credit another's treachery.

SIR PET. True, but your brother has no sentiment—you never hear him talk so.

JOSEPH. Yet I can't but think Lady Teazle herself has too much principle.

SIR PET. Aye, but what is principle against the flattery of a handsome, lively young fellow?

JOSEPH. That's very true.

SIR PET. And there's, you know, the difference of our ages makes it very improbable that she should have any great affection for me; and if she were to be frail and I were to make it public, why, the town would only laugh at me—the foolish old bachelor who had married a girl.

JOSEPH. That's true, to be sure—they would laugh.

SIR PET. Laugh! aye, and make ballads, and paragraphs, and the devil knows what of me.

JOSEPH. No, you must never make it public.

SIR PET. But then again—that the nephew of my old friend, Sir Oliver, should be the person to attempt such a wrong, hurts me more nearly.

JOSEPH. Aye, there's the point. When ingratitude barbs the dart of injury, the wound has double danger in it.

SIR PET. Aye—I, that was, in a manner, left his guardian; in whose house he had been so often entertained; who never in my life denied him—my advice.

JOSEPH. Oh, 'tis not to be credited! There may be a man capable of such baseness, to be sure; but for my part till you can give me positive proofs, I cannot but doubt it.

However, if it should be proved on him, he is no longer a brother of mine—I disclaim kindred with him; for the man who can break the laws of hospitality and tempt the wife of his friend, deserves to be branded as the pest of society.

SIR PET.   What a difference there is between you! What noble sentiments!

JOSEPH.   Yet I cannot suspect Lady Teazle's honor.

SIR PET.   I am sure I wish to think well of her and to remove all ground of quarrel between us. She has lately reproached me more than once with having made no settlement on her, and in our last quarrel she almost hinted that she should not break her heart if I was dead. Now, as we seem to differ in our ideas of expense, I have resolved she shall have her own way and be her own mistress in that respect for the future; and if I were to die, she will find I have not been inattentive to her interest while living. Here, my friend, are the drafts of two deeds, which I wish to have your opinion on. By one she will enjoy eight hundred a year independent while I live, and by the other the bulk of my fortune at my death.

JOSEPH.   This conduct, Sir Peter, is indeed truly generous.—(*Aside*.) I wish it may not corrupt my pupil.

SIR PET.   Yes, I am determined she shall have no cause to complain, though I would not have her acquainted with the latter instance of my affection yet awhile.

JOSEPH (*aside*).   Nor I, if I could help it.

SIR PET.   And now, my dear friend, if you please, we will talk over the situation of your hopes with Maria.

JOSEPH (*softly*).   Oh, no, Sir Peter; another time, if you please.

SIR PET.   I am sensibly chagrined at the little progress you seem to make in her affections.

JOSEPH (*softly*).   I beg you will not mention it. What are my disappointments when your happiness is in debate!—(*Aside*). 'Sdeath, I shall be ruined every way!

SIR PET.   And though you are so averse to my acquainting Lady Teazle with your passion for Maria, I'm sure she's not your enemy in the affair.

JOSEPH.   Pray, Sir Peter, now oblige me. I am really too much affected by the subject we have been speaking of, to bestow a thought on my own concerns. The man who is entrusted with his friends' distresses can never—

(*Re-enter* SERVANT.)

—Well, sir?

SERV.   Your brother, sir, is speaking to a gentleman in the street, and says he knows you are within.

JOSEPH.   'Sdeath, blockhead, I'm not within. —I'm out for the day.

SIR PET.   Stay—hold—a thought has struck me;—you shall be at home.

JOSEPH.   Well, well, let him up.—

(*Exit* SERVANT.)

(*Aside*.) He'll interrupt Sir Peter, however.

SIR PET.   Now, my good friend, oblige me, I entreat you. Before Charles comes, let me conceal myself somewhere; then do you tax him on the point we have been talking, and his answer may satisfy me at once.

JOSEPH.   Oh, fie, Sir Peter! would you have me join in so mean a trick—to trepan my brother too?

SIR PET.   Nay, you tell me you are sure he is innocent; if so, you do him the greatest service by giving him an opportunity to clear himself, and you will set my heart at rest. Come, you shall not refuse me; here, behind the screen will be—Hey! what the devil! There seems to be one listener here already.—I'll swear, I saw a petticoat!

JOSEPH.   Ha! ha! ha! Well, this is ridiculous enough. I'll tell you, Sir Peter, though I hold a man of intrigue to be a most despicable character, yet, you know, it does not follow that one is to be an absolute Joseph either! Hark'ee, 'tis a little French milliner, a silly rogue that plagues me; and having some character to lose, on your coming, sir, she ran behind the screen.

SIR PET.   Ah, you rogue!—But, egad, she has overheard all I have been saying of my wife.

JOSEPH.   Oh, 'twill never go any farther, you may depend upon it!

SIR PET.   No? then, faith, let her hear it out.—Here's a closet will do as well.

JOSEPH.   Well, go in there.

SIR PET. (*going into the closet*).   Sly rogue! sly rogue!

JOSEPH.   A narrow escape, indeed! and a

curious situation I'm in, to part man and wife in this manner.

LADY T. (*peeping*).   Couldn't I steal off?

JOSEPH.   Keep close, my angel!

SIR PET. (*peeping*).   Joseph, tax him home.

JOSEPH.   Back, my dear friend!

LADY T. (*peeping*).   Couldn't you lock Sir Peter in?

JOSEPH.   Be still, my life!

SIR PET. (*peeping*).   You're sure the little milliner won't blab?

JOSEPH.   In, in, my dear Sir Peter!—'Fore Gad, I wish I had a key to the door.

(*Enter* CHARLES SURFACE.)

CHARLES.   Holla! brother, what has been the matter? Your fellow would not let me up at first. What! have you had a Jew or a wench with you?

JOSEPH.   Neither, brother, I assure you.

CHARLES.   But what has made Sir Peter steal off? I thought he had been with you.

JOSEPH.   He *was*, brother; but hearing you were coming, he did not choose to stay.

CHARLES.   What! was the old gentleman afraid I wanted to borrow money of him?

JOSEPH.   No, sir; but I am sorry to find, Charles, you have lately given that worthy man grounds for great uneasiness.

CHARLES.   Yes, they tell me I do that to a great many worthy men.—But how so, pray?

JOSEPH.   To be plain with you, brother, he thinks you are endeavoring to gain Lday Teazle's affection from him.

CHARLES.   Who, I? O lud! not I, upon my word.—Ha! ha! ha! ha! So the old fellow has found out that he has got a young wife, has he?—or, what is worse, Lady Teazle has found out she has an old husband?

JOSEPH.   This is no subject to jest on, brother. He who can laugh—

CHARLES.   True, true, as you were going to say—then, seriously, I never had the least idea of what you charge me with, upon my honor.

JOSEPH (*loudly*).   Well, it will give Sir Peter great satisfaction to hear this.

CHARLES.   To be sure, I once thought the lady seemed to have taken a fancy to me, but upon my soul I never gave her the least encouragement. Besides, you know my attachment to Maria.

JOSEPH.   But sure, brother, even if Lady Teazle had betrayed the fondest partiality for you—

CHARLES.   Why, look'ee, Joseph I hope I shall never deliberately do a dishonorable action, but if a pretty woman was purposely to throw herself in my way—and that pretty woman married to a man old enough to be her father—

JOSEPH.   Well—

CHARLES.   Why I believe I should be obliged to borrow a little of your morality that's all. But brother, do you know now that you surprise me exceedingly, by naming *me* with Lady Teazle; for, i'faith, I always understood you were her favorite.

JOSEPH.   Oh, for shame, Charles! This retort is foolish.

CHARLES.   Nay, I swear I have seen you exchange such significant glances—

JOSEPH.   Nay, nay, sir, this is no jest.

CHARLES.   Egad, I'm serious! Don't you remember one day when I called here—

JOSEPH.   Nay, prithee, Charles—

CHARLES.   And found you together—

JOSEPH.   Zounds, sir, I insist—

CHARLES.   And another time when your servant—

JOSEPH.   Brother, brother, a word with you! —(*Aside.*) Gad, I must stop him.

CHARLES.   Informed, I say that—

JOSEPH.   Hush! I beg your pardon, but Sir Peter has overheard all we have been saying. I knew you would clear yourself, or I should not have consented.

CHARLES.   How, Sir Peter! Where is he?

JOSEPH (*points to the closet*).   Softly!—there!

CHARLES.   Oh, 'fore Heaven, I'll have him out—Sir Peter, come forth!

JOSEPH.   No, no—

CHARLES.   I say, Sir Peter, come into court.— (*Pulls in* SIR PETER.) What! my old guardian! —What! turn inquisitor and take evidence incog?

SIR PET.   Give me your hand, Charles—I believe I have suspected you wrongfully; but you mustn't be angry with Joseph— 'twas my plan!

CHARLES.   Indeed!

SIR PET.   But I acquit you. I promise you I don't think near so ill of you as I did; what I have heard has given me great satisfaction.

CHARLES. Egad, then, 'twas lucky you didn't hear any more, (*apart to* JOSEPH) wasn't it, Joseph?

SIR PET. Ah! you would have retorted on him.

CHARLES. Ah, aye, that was a joke.

SIR PET. Yes, yes, I know his honor too well.

CHARLES. But you might as well have suspected *him* as *me* in this matter, for all that, (*apart to* JOSEPH) mightn't he, Joseph?

SIR PET. Well, well, I believe you.

JOSEPH (*aside*). Would they were both out of the room!

SIR PET. And in future, perhaps, we may not be such strangers.

(*Re-enter* SERVANT, *and whispers to* JOSEPH SURFACE.)

SERV. Lady Sneerwell is below, and says she will come up. (*Exit* SERVANT.)

JOSEPH. Gentlemen, I beg pardon—I must wait on you downstairs; here is a person come on particular business.

CHARLES. Well, you can see him in another room. Sir Peter and I have not met a long time, and I have something to say to him.

JOSEPH (*aside*). They must not be left together.—I'll send this man away, and return directly—(*Apart to* SIR PETER.) Sir Peter, not a word of the French milliner.

SIR PET. (*apart to* JOSEPH). I! not for the world! (*Exit* JOSEPH SURFACE.)—Ah, Charles, if you associated more with your brother one might indeed hope for your reformation. He is a man of sentiment.— Well, there is nothing in the world so noble as a man of sentiment.

CHARLES. Pshaw! he is too moral by half; and so apprehensive of his "good name," as he calls it, that I suppose he would as soon let a priest into his house as a girl.

SIR PET. No, no—come, come—you wrong him. No, no! Joseph is no rake, but he is no such saint either, in that respect.— (*Aside.*) I have a great mind to tell him—we should have a laugh at Joseph.

CHARLES. Oh, hang him! he's a very anchorite—a young hermit!

SIR PET. Hark'ee—you must not abuse him; he may chance to hear of it again, I promise you.

CHARLES. Why, you won't tell him?

SIR PET. No—but—this way.—(*Aside.*) Egad I'll tell him.—Hark'ee—have you a mind to have a good laugh at Joseph?

CHARLES. I should like it of all things.

SIR PET. Then, i'faith, we will! I'll be quit with him for discovering me. He had a girl with him when I called.

CHARLES. What! Joseph? you jest.

SIR PET. Hush!—a little French milliner; and the best of the jest is—she's in the room now.

CHARLES. The devil she is!

SIR PET. Hush! I tell you. (*Points.*)

CHARLES. Behind the screen! 'Slife, let's unveil her!

SIR PET. No, no, he's coming—you sha'n't, indeed!

CHARLES. Oh, egad, we'll have a peep at the little milliner!

SIR PET. Not for the world!—Joseph will never forgive me.

CHARLES. I'll stand by you—

SIR PET. Odds, here he is!

(JOSEPH SURFACE *enters just as* CHARLES SURFACE *throws down the screen.*)

CHARLES. Lady Teazle, by all that's wonderful!

SIR PET. Lady Teazle, by all that's damnable!

CHARLES. Sir Peter, this is one of the smartest French milliners I ever saw. Egad, you seem all to have been diverting yourselves here at hide and seek, and I don't see who is out of the secret. Shall I beg your ladyship to inform me? Not a word!— Brother, will you be pleased to explain this matter? What! is Morality dumb too? —Sir Peter, though I found you in the dark, perhaps you are not so now! All mute!— Well—though I can make nothing of the affair, I suppose you perfectly understand one another; so I'll leave you to yourselves. —(*Going.*) Brother, I'm sorry to find you have given that worthy man grounds for so much uneasiness.—Sir Peter! "there's nothing in the world so noble as a man of sentiment!" (*Exit* CHARLES.)

(*They stand for some time looking at each other.*)

JOSEPH. Sir Peter—notwithstanding—I confess—that appearances are against me—if you will afford me your patience—I make no doubt—but I shall explain everything to your satisfaction.

SIR PET. If you please, sir.

JOSEPH. The fact is, sir, that Lady Teazle,

knowing my pretensions to your ward Maria—I say, sir, Lady Teazle, being apprehensive of the jealousy of your temper—and knowing my friendship to the family—she, sir, I say—called here—in order that—I might explain these pretensions—but on your coming—being apprehensive—as I said —of your jealousy—she withdrew—and this, you may depend on it, is the whole truth of the matter.

SIR PET. A very clear account, upon my word, and I dare swear the lady will vouch for every article of it.

LADY T. For not one word of it, Sir Peter.

SIR PET. How! don't you think it worth while to agree in the lie?

LADY T. There is not one syllable of truth in what that gentleman has told you.

SIR PET. I believe you, upon my soul, ma'am!

JOSEPH (aside). 'Sdeath, madam, will you betray me?

LADY T. Good Mr. Hypocrite, by your leave, I'll speak for myself.

SIR PET. Aye, let her alone, sir; you'll find she'll make out a better story than you, without prompting.

LADY T. Hear me, Sir Peter!—I came here on no matter relating to your ward, and even ignorant of this gentleman's pretensions to her. But I came, seduced by his insidious arguments, at least to listen to his pretended passion, if not to sacrifice your honor to his baseness.

SIR PET. Now, I believe, the truth is coming, indeed!

JOSEPH. The woman's mad!

LADY T. No, sir; she has recovered her senses, and your own arts have furnished her with the means—Sir Peter, I do not expect you to credit me—but the tenderness you expressed for me when I am sure you could not think I was a witness to it, has so penetrated to my heart that had I left the place without the shame of this discovery, my future life should have spoken the sincerity of my gratitude. As for that smooth-tongued hypocrite, who would have seduced the wife of his too credulous friend while he affected honorable addresses to his ward—I behold him now in a light so truly despicable that I shall never again respect myself for having listened to him.

(*Exit* LADY TEAZLE.)

JOSEPH. Notwithstanding all this, Sir Peter, Heaven knows—

SIR PET. That you are a villain! and so I leave you to your conscience.

JOSEPH. You are too rash, Sir Peter; you shall hear me. The man who shuts out conviction by refusing to—(*Exeunt* SIR PETER *and* JOSEPH SURFACE *talking*.)

ACT V

SCENE 1

(*The library in* JOSEPH SURFACE'S *house*.)

(*Enter* JOSEPH SURFACE *and* SERVANT.)

JOSEPH. Mr. Stanley! and why should you think I would see him? You must know he comes to ask something.

SERV. Sir, I should not have let him in, but that Mr. Rowley came to the door with him.

JOSEPH. Pshaw! blockhead! to suppose that I should now be in a temper to receive visits from poor relations!—Well, why don't you show the fellow up?

SERV. I will, sir—Why, sir, it was not my fault that Sir Peter discovered my lady—

JOSEPH. Go, fool! (*Exit* SERVANT.)—Sure, Fortune never played a man of my policy such a trick before!—my character with Sir Peter, my hopes with Maria, destroyed in a moment! I'm in a rare humor to listen to other people's distresses! I sha'n't be able to bestow even a benevolent sentiment on Stanley.—So! here he comes, and Rowley with him. I must try to recover myself and put a little charity into my face, however. (*Exit*.)

(*Enter* SIR OLIVER SURFACE *and* ROWLEY.)

SIR O. What! does he avoid us? That was he, was it not?

ROW. It was, sir. But I doubt you are come a little too abruptly. His nerves are so weak that the sight of a poor relation may be too much for him. I should have gone first to break it to him.

SIR O. Oh, plague of his nerves! Yet this is he whom Sir Peter extols as a man of the most benevolent way of thinking!

ROW. As to his way of thinking, I cannot pretend to decide; for to do him justice he appears to have as much speculative benevolence as any private gentleman in the kingdom, though he is seldom so sensual as to indulge himself in the exercise of it.

SIR O.   Yet he has a string of charitable sentiments at his fingers' ends.

ROW.   Or rather, at his tongue's end, Sir Oliver; for I believe there is no sentiment he has such faith in as that "charity begins at home."

SIR O.   And his, I presume, is of that domestic sort which never stirs abroad at all.

ROW.   I doubt you'll find it so;—but he's coming. I mustn't seem to interrupt you; and you know, immediately as you leave him, I come in to announce your arrival in your real character.

SIR O.   True; and afterwards you'll meet me at Sir Peter's.

ROW.   Without losing a moment. (*Exit.*)

SIR O.   I don't like the complaisance of his features.

(*Re-enter* JOSEPH SURFACE.)

JOSEPH.   Sir I beg you ten thousand pardons for keeping you a moment waiting.—Mr. Stanley, I presume.

SIR O.   At your service.

JOSEPH.   Sir, I beg you will do me the honor to sit down—I entreat you, sir.

SIR O.   Dear sir—there's no occasion.— (*Aside.*) Too civil by half!

JOSEPH.   I have not the pleasure of knowing you, Mr. Stanley, but I am extremely happy to see you look so well. You were nearly related to my mother, I think, Mr. Stanley?

SIR O.   I was sir—so nearly that my present poverty, I fear, may do discredit to her wealthy children, else I should not have presumed to trouble you.

JOSEPH.   Dear sir, there needs no apology; he that is in distress, though a stranger, has a right to claim kindred with the wealthy. I am sure I wish I was one of that class, and had it in my power to offer you even a small relief.

SIR O.   If your uncle, Sir Oliver, were here, I should have a friend.

JOSEPH.   I wish he was, sir, with all my heart; you should not want an advocate with him, believe me, sir.

SIR O.   I should not need one—my distresses would recommend me. But I imagined his bounty would enable you to become the agent of his charity.

JOSEPH.   My dear sir, you were strangely misinformed. Sir Oliver is a worthy man— a very worthy man; but avarice, Mr. Stanley, is the vice of age. I will tell you, my good sir, in confidence, what he has done for me has been a mere nothing— though people, I know, have thought otherwise, and for my part I never chose to contradict the report.

SIR O.   What! has he never transmitted you bullion—repees—pagodas?

JOSEPH.   Oh, dear sir, nothing of the kind! No, no; a few presents now and then— china, shawls, congou tea, avadavats, and Indian crackers—little more, believe me.

SIR O.   (*aside*).   Here's gratitude for twelve thousand pounds!—avadavats and Indian crackers!

JOSEPH.   Then, my dear sir, you have heard, I doubt not, of the extravagance of my brother. There are very few would credit what I have done for that unfortunate young man.

SIR O.   (*aside*).   Not I, for one!

JOSEPH.   The sums I have lent him! Indeed I have been exceedingly to blame—it was an amiable weakness; however, I don't pretend to defend it—and now I feel it doubly culpable since it has deprived me of the pleasure of serving you, Mr. Stanley, as my heart dictates.

SIR O.   (*aside*).   Dissembler!—Then, sir, you can't assist me?

JOSEPH.   At present, it grieves me to say, I cannot; but whenever I have the ability, you may depend upon hearing from me.

SIR O.   I am extremely sorry—

JOSEPH.   Not more than I, believe me; to pity, without the power to relieve, is still more painful than to ask and be denied.

SIR O.   Kind sir, your modest obedient humble servant.

JOSEPH.   You leave me deeply affected, Mr. Stanley.—(*Calls to* SERVANT.) William, be ready to open the door.

SIR O.   Oh, dear sir, no ceremony.

JOSEPH.   Your very obedient.

SIR O.   Your most obsequious.

JOSEPH.   You may depend upon hearing from me whenever I can be of service.

SIR O.   Sweet sir, you are too good!

JOSEPH.   In the meantime I wish you health and spirits.

SIR O.   Your ever grateful and perpetual humble servant.

JOSEPH.   Sir, yours as sincerely.

SIR O.   (*aside*).   Charles, you are my heir! (*Exit.*)

JOSEPH.   This is one bad effect of a good character; it invites application from the unfortunate, and there needs no small degree of address to gain the reputation of benevolence without incurring the expense. The silver ore of pure charity is an expensive article in the catalogue of a man's good qualities; whereas the sentimental French plate I use instead of it makes just as good a show and pays no tax.

(*Re-enter* ROWLEY.)

Row.   Mr. Surface, your servant. I was apprehensive of interrupting you, though my business demands immediate attention, as this note will inform you.

JOSEPH.   Always happy to see Mr. Rowley. (*Reads the letter.*) Sir Oliver Surface—My uncle arrived!

Row.   He is, indeed; we have just parted—quite well, after a speedy voyage, and impatient to embrace his worthy nephew.

JOSEPH.   I am astonished!—William! stop Mr. Stanley if he's not gone.

Row.   Oh! he's out of reach, I believe.

JOSEPH.   Why did you not let me know this when you came in together?

Row.   I thought you had particular business. But I must be gone to inform your brother and appoint him here to meet your uncle. He will be with you in a quarter of an hour.

JOSEPH.   So he says. Well, I am strangely overjoyed at his coming.—(*Aside.*) Never, to be sure, was anything so damned unlucky!

Row.   You will be delighted to see how well he looks.

JOSEPH.   Oh! I'm overjoyed to hear it.—(*Aside.*) Just at this time!

Row.   I'll tell him how impatiently you expect him.

JOSEPH.   Do, do; pray, give my best duty and affection. Indeed, I cannot express the sensations I feel at the thought of seeing him.

(*Exit* ROWLEY.)

—Certainly his coming just at this time is the cruellest piece of ill-fortune. (*Exit.*)

SCENE 2

(*A room in* SIR PETER TEAZLE'S *house*.)

(*Enter* MRS. CANDOUR *and* MAID.)

MAID.   Indeed, ma'am, my lady will see nobody at present.

MRS. CAN.   Did you tell her it was her friend Mrs. Candour?

MAID.   Yes, ma'am, but she begs you will excuse her.

MRS. CAN.   Do go again; I shall be glad to see her, if it be only for a moment, for I am sure she must be in great distress.

(*Exit* MAID.)

—Dear heart, how provoking! I'm not mistress of half the circumstances! We shall have the whole affair in the newspapers, with the names of the parties at length, before I have dropped the story at a dozen houses.

(*Enter* SIR BENJAMIN BACKBITE.)

—Oh, dear Sir Benjamin! you have heard, I suppose—

SIR BEN.   Of Lady Teazle and Mr. Surface—

MRS. CAN.   And Sir Peter's discovery—

SIR BEN.   Oh, the strangest piece of business, to be sure!

MRS. CAN.   Well, I never was so surprised in my life. I am so sorry for all parties, indeed.

SIR BEN.   Now, I don't pity Sir Peter at all; he was so extravagantly partial to Mr. Surface.

MRS. CAN.   Mr. Surface! Why, 'twas with Charles Lady Teazle was detected.

SIR BEN.   No, no, I tell you—Mr. Surface is the gallant.

MRS. CAN.   No such thing! Charles is the man. 'Twas Mr. Surface brought Sir Peter on purpose to discover them.

SIR BEN.   I tell you I had it from one—

MRS. CAN.   And I have it from one—

SIR BEN.   Who had it from one who had it—

MRS. CAN.   From one immediately—But here comes Lady Sneerwell; perhaps she knows the whole affair.

(*Enter* LADY SNEERWELL.)

LADY S.   So, my dear Mrs. Candour, here's a sad affair of our friend Lady Teazle!

MRS. CAN.   Aye, my dear friend, who would have thought—

LADY S.   Well, there is no trusting appearances—though, indeed, she was always too lively for me.

MRS. CAN.   To be sure her manners were a little too free; but then, she was so young!

LADY S.   And had, indeed, some good qualities.

MRS. CAN.   So she had, indeed. But have you heard the particulars?

LADY S.   No, but everybody says that Mr. Surface—

SIR BEN.   Aye, there! I told you Mr. Surface was the man.

MRS. CAN.   No, no! indeed, the assignation was with Charles.

LADY S.   With Charles! You alarm me, Mrs. Candour!

MRS. CAN.   Yes, yes; he was the lover. Mr. Surface, to do him justice, was only the informer.

SIR BEN.   Well, I'll not dispute with you, Mrs. Candour, but be it which it may, I hope that Sir Peter's wound will not—

MRS. CAN.   Sir Peter's wound! Oh, mercy! I didn't hear a word of their fighting.

LADY S.   Nor I, a syllable.

SIR BEN.   No! what, no mention of the duel?

MRS. CAN.   Not a word.

SIR BEN.   Oh, yes! they fought before they left the room.

LADY S.   Pray, let us hear!

MRS. CAN.   Aye, do oblige us with the duel!

SIR BEN.   "Sir," says Sir Peter, immediately after the discovery, "you are a most ungrateful fellow."

MRS. CAN.   Aye to Charles—

SIR BEN.   No, no—to Mr. Surface—"a most ungrateful fellow; and old as I am, sir," says he, "I insist on immediate satisfaction."

MRS. CAN.   Aye, that must have been to Charles, for 'tis very unlikely Mr. Surface should fight in his own house.

SIR BEN.   Gad's life, ma'am, not at all— "giving me immediate satisfaction."—On this, ma'am, Lady Teazle, seeing Sir Peter in such danger, ran out of the room in strong hysterics, and Charles after her, calling out for hartshorn and water; then, madam, they began to fight with swords—

(*Enter* CRABTREE.)

CRAB.   With pistols, nephew—pistols! I have it from undoubted authority.

MRS. CAN.   Oh, Mr. Crabtree, then it is all true!

CRAB.   Too true, indeed, madam and Sir Peter is dangerously wounded—

SIR BEN.   By a thrust in second quite through his left side—

CRAB.   By a bullet lodged in the thorax.

MRS. CAN.   Mercy on me! Poor Sir Peter!

CRAB.   Yes, madam—though Charles would have avoided the matter if he could.

MRS. CAN.   I knew Charles was the person.

SIR BEN.   My uncle, I see, knows nothing of the matter.

CRAB.   But Sir Peter taxed him with the basest ingratitude—

SIR BEN.   That I told you, you know—

CRAB.   Do, nephew, let me speak!—and insisted on immediate—

SIR BEN.   Just as I said—

CRAB.   Odds life, nephew, allow others to know something too! A pair of pistols lay on the bureau (for Mr. Surface, it seems, had come home the night before late from Salthill, where he had been to see the Montem with a friend who has a son at Eton), so, unluckily, the pistols were left charged.

SIR BEN.   I heard nothing of this.

CRAB.   Sir Peter forced Charles to take one, and they fired, it seems, pretty nearly together. Charles's shot took effect, as I tell you, and Sir Peter's missed; but what is very extraordinary, the ball struck against a little bronze Shakespeare that stood over the fireplace, grazed out of the window at a right angle, and wounded the postman, who was just coming to the door with a double letter from Northamptonshire.

SIR BEN.   My uncle's account is more circumstantial, I confess; but I believe mine is the true one, for all that.

LADY S.   (*aside*).   I am more interested in this affair than they imagine, and must have better information.

(*Exit* LADY SNEERWELL.)

SIR BEN.   Ah! Lady Sneerwell's alarm is very easily accounted for.

CRAB.   Yes, yes, they certainly do say—but that's neither here nor there.

MRS. CAN.   But pray, where is Sir Peter at present?

CRAB. Oh! they brought him home, and he is now in the house, though the servants are ordered to deny him.

MRS. CAN. I believe so; and Lady Teazle, I suppose, attending him.

CRAB. Yes, yes; and I saw one of the faculty enter just before me.

SIR BEN. Hey! who comes here?

CRAB. Oh, this is he—the physician, depend on't.

MRS. CAN. Oh, certainly! it must be the physician; and now we shall know.

(*Enter* SIR OLIVER SURFACE.)

CRAB. Well, doctor, what hopes?

MRS. CAN. Aye, doctor, how's your patient?

SIR BEN. Now, doctor, isn't it a wound with a small-sword?

CRAB. A bullet lodged in the thorax, for a hundred!

SIR O. Doctor!—a wound with a small-sword! and a bullet in the thorax!—Oons! are you mad, good people?

SIR BEN. Perhaps, sir, you are not a doctor?

SIR O. Truly, I am to thank you for my degree if I am.

CRAB. Only a friend of Sir Peter's then, I presume. But sir, you must have heard of his accident?

SIR O. Not a word!

CRAB. Not of his being dangerously wounded?

SIR O. The devil he is!

SIR BEN. Run through the body—

CRAB. Shot in the breast—

SIR BEN. By one Mr. Surface—

CRAB. Aye, the younger.

SIR O. Hey! what the plague! you seem to differ strangely in your accounts; however, you agree that Sir Peter is dangerously wounded.

SIR BEN. Oh, yes, we agree in that.

CRAB. Yes, yes, I believe there can be no doubt of that.

SIR O. Then, upon my word, for a person in that situation, he is the most imprudent man alive; for here he comes, walking as if nothing at all was the matter.

(*Enter* SIR PETER TEAZLE.)

—Odds heart, Sir Peter, you are come in good time, I promise you, for we had just given you over!

SIR BEN. (*aside to* CRABTREE). Egad, uncle, this is the most sudden recovery!

SIR O. Why, man! what do you out of bed with a small-sword through your body and a bullet lodged in your thorax?

SIR PET. A small-sword and a bullet!

SIR O. Aye; these gentlemen would have killed you without law or physic, and wanted to dub me a doctor to make me an accomplice.

SIR PET. Why, what is all this?

SIR BEN. We rejoice, Sir Peter, that the story of the duel is not true, and are sincerely sorry for your other misfortune.

SIR PET. (*aside*). So, so—all over the town already!

CRAB. Though, Sir Peter, you were certainly vastly to blame to marry at your years.

SIR PET. Sir, what business is that of yours?

MRS. CAN.—Though, indeed, as Sir Peter made so good a husband, he's very much to be pitied.

SIR PET. Plague on your pity, ma'am! I desire none of it.

SIR BEN. However, Sir Peter, you must not mind the laughing and jests you will meet with on the occasion.

SIR PET. Sir, sir! I desire to be master in my own house.

CRAB. 'Tis no uncommon case, that's one comfort.

SIR PET. I insist on being left to myself—without ceremony, I insist on your leaving my house directly!

MRS. CAN. Well, well, we are going; and depend on't, we'll make the best report of it we can. (*Exit.*)

SIR PET. Leave my house!

CRAB.—And tell how hardly you've been treated. (*Exit.*)

SIR PET. Leave my house!

SIR BEN.—And how patiently you bear it. (*Exit.*)

SIR PET. Fiends! vipers! furies! Oh! that their own venom would choke them!

SIR O. They are very provoking indeed, Sir Peter.

(*Enter* ROWLEY.)

ROW. I heard high words; what has ruffled you, sir?

SIR PET. Pshaw! what signifies asking? Do I ever pass a day without my vexations?

ROW. Well, I'm not inquisitive.

SIR O. Well, Sir Peter, I have seen both my nephews in the manner we proposed.

SIR PET.   A precious couple they are!

ROW.   Yes, and Sir Oliver is convinced that your judgment was right, Sir Peter.

SIR O.   Yes, I find Joseph is indeed the man, after all.

ROW.   Aye, as Sir Peter says, he is a man of sentiment.

SIR O.   And acts up to the sentiments he professes.

ROW.   It certainly is edification to hear him talk.

SIR O.   Oh, he's a model for the young men of the age!—But how's this, Sir Peter? you don't join us in your friend Joseph's praise as I expected.

SIR PET.   Sir Oliver, we live in a damned wicked world, and the fewer we praise the better.

ROW.   What! do you say so, Sir Peter, who were never mistaken in your life?

SIR PET.   Pshaw! plague on you both! I see by your sneering you have heard the whole affair. I shall go mad among you!

ROW.   Then, to fret you no longer, Sir Peter, we are indeed acquainted with it all. I met Lady Teazle coming from Mr. Surface's so humbled that she deigned to request me to be her advocate with you.

SIR PET.   And does Sir Oliver know all this?

SIR O.   Every circumstance.

SIR PET.   What—of the closet and the screen, hey?

SIR O.   Yes, yes, and the little French milliner. Oh, I have been vastly diverted with the story! ha! ha! ha!

SIR PET.   'Twas very pleasant.

SIR O.   I never laughed more in my life, I assure you—ha! ha! ha!

SIR PET.   Oh, vastly diverting!—ha! ha! ha!

ROW.   To be sure, Joseph with his sentiments! ha! ha! ha!

SIR PET.   Yes, yes, his sentiments! ha! ha! ha!—Hypocritical villain!

SIR O.   Aye, and that rogue Charles to pull Sir Peter out of the closet: ha! ha! ha!

SIR PET.   Ha! ha! 'twas devilish entertaining, to be sure!

SIR O.   Ha! ha! ha! Egad, Sir Peter, I should like to have seen your face when the screen was thrown down—ha! ha!

SIR PET.   Yes, yes, my face when the screen was thrown down—ha! ha! ha! Oh, I must never show my head again!

SIR O.   But come, come, it isn't fair to laugh at you neither, my old friend—though, upon my soul, I can't help it.

SIR PET.   Oh, pray, don't restrain your mirth on my account; it does not hurt me at all. I laugh at the whole affair myself. Yes, yes, I think being a standing jest for all one's acquaintance a very happy situation. Oh, yes, and then of a morning to read the paragraphs about Mr. S——, Lady T——, and Sir P——, will be so entertaining!

ROW.   Without affectation, Sir Peter, you may despise the ridicule of fools. But I see Lady Teazle going towards the next room; I am sure you must desire a reconciliation as earnestly as she does.

SIR O.   Perhaps my being here prevents her coming to you. Well, I'll leave honest Rowley to mediate between you; but he must bring you all presently to Mr. Surface's, where I am now returning, if not to reclaim a libertine at least to expose hypocrisy.

SIR PET.   Ah, I'll be present at your discovering yourself there with all my heart, though 'tis a vile unlucky place for discoveries.

ROW.   We'll follow.

(*Exit* SIR OLIVER SURFACE.)

SIR PET.   She is not coming here, you see, Rowley.

ROW.   No, but she has left the door of that room open, you perceive. See, she is in tears.

SIR PET.   Certainly a little mortification appears very becoming in a wife. Don't you think it will do her good to let her pine a little?

ROW.   Oh, this is ungenerous in you!

SIR PET.   Well, I know not what to think. You remember the letter I found of hers evidently intended for Charles?

ROW.   A mere forgery, Sir Peter!—laid in your way on purpose. This is one of the points which I intend Snake shall give you conviction of.

SIR PET.   I wish I were once satisfied of that. She looks this way. What a remarkably elegant turn of the head she has! Rowley, I'll go to her.

ROW.   Certainly.

SIR PET.   Though when it is known that we are reconciled, people will laugh at me ten times more.

Row. Let them laugh, and retort their malice only by showing them you are happy in spite of it.

Sir Pet. I'faith, so I will; and, if I'm not mistaken, we may yet be the happiest couple in the country.

Row. Nay, Sir Peter, he who once lays aside suspicion—

Sir Pet. Hold, Master Rowley! if you have any regard for me, never let me hear you utter anything like a sentiment; I have had enough of them to serve me the rest of my life. (*Exeunt.*)

SCENE 3

(*The library in* Joseph Surface's *house.*)

(*Enter* Joseph Surface *and* Lady Sneerwell.)

Lady S. Impossible! Will not Sir Peter immediately be reconciled to Charles, and of course no longer oppose his union with Maria? The thought is distraction to me.

Joseph. Can passion furnish a remedy?

Lady S. No, nor cunning neither. Oh, I was a fool, an idiot, to league with such a blunderer!

Joseph. Sure, Lady Sneerwell, I am the greatest sufferer; yet you see. I bear the accident with calmness.

Lady S. Because the disappointment doesn't reach your heart; your interest only attached you to Maria. Had you felt for her what I have for that ungrateful libertine, neither your temper nor hypocrisy could prevent your showing the sharpness of your vexation.

Joseph. But why should your reproaches fall on me for this disappointment?

Lady S. Are you not the cause of it? Had you not a sufficient field for your roguery in imposing upon Sir Peter and supplanting your brother, but you must endeavor to seduce his wife? I hate such an avarice of crimes; 'tis an unfair monopoly, and never prospers.

Joseph. Well, I admit I have been to blame. I confess I deviated from the direct road of wrong, but I don't think we're so totally defeated neither.

Lady S. No!

Joseph. You tell me you have made a trial of Snake since we met, and that you still believe him faithful to us?

Lady S. I do believe so.

Joseph. And that he has undertaken, should it be necessary, to swear and prove that Charles is at this time contracted by vows and honor to your ladyship, which some of his former letters to you will serve to support.

Lady S. This, indeed, might have assisted.

Joseph. Come, come; it is not too late yet. —(*Knocking at the door.*) But hark! this is probably my uncle, Sir Oliver. Retire to that room; we'll consult farther when he is gone.

Lady S. Well, but if *he* should find you out too?

Joseph. Oh, I have no fear of that. Sir Peter will hold his tongue for his own credit's sake—and you may depend on it, I shall soon discover Sir Oliver's weak side!

Lady S. I have no diffidence of your abilities, only be constant to one roguery at a time.

Joseph. I will, I will!

(*Exit* Lady Sneerwell.)

—So! 'tis confounded hard, after such bad fortune, to be baited by one's confederate in evil. Well, at all events my character is so much better than Charles's that I certainly —hey!—what—this is not Sir Oliver, but old Stanley again. Plague on't that he should return to tease me just now! I shall have Sir Oliver come and find him here— and—

(*Enter* Sir Oliver Surface.)

—Gad's life, Mr. Stanley, why have you come back to plague me at this time? You must not stay now, upon my word.

Sir O. Sir, I hear your uncle Oliver is expected here, and though he has been so penurious to you, I'll try what he'll do for me.

Joseph. Sir, 'tis impossible for you to stay now; so I must beg—Come any other time, and I promise you, you shall be assisted.

Sir O. No; Sir Oliver and I must be acquainted.

Joseph. Zounds, sir! then I insist on your quitting the room directly.

Sir O. Nay, sir—

Joseph. Sir, I insist on't!—Here, William! show this gentleman out. Since you compel me, sir, not one moment—this is such insolence. (*Going to push him out.*)

(*Enter* CHARLES SURFACE.)

CHARLES. Heyday! what's the matter now? What the devil, have you got hold of my little broker here? Zounds, brother, don't hurt little Premium. What's the matter, my little fellow?

JOSEPH. So! he has been with you, too, has he?

CHARLES. To be sure, he has. Why, he's as honest a little—But sure, Joseph, you have not been borrowing money too, have you?

JOSEPH. Borrowing! no! But brother, you know we expect Sir Oliver here every—

CHARLES. O Gad, that's true! Noll mustn't find the little broker here, to be sure.

JOSEPH. Yet, Mr. Stanley insists—

CHARLES. Stanley! why, his name's Premium.

JOSEPH. No, sir, Stanley.

CHARLES. No, no, Premium.

JOSEPH. Well, no matter which—but—

CHARLES. Aye, aye, Stanley or Premium, 'tis the same thing, as you say; for I suppose he goes by half a hundred names, besides "A. B." at the coffee-house.

(*Knocking.*)

JOSEPH. 'Sdeath! here's Sir Oliver at the door. Now, I beg, Mr. Stanley—

CHARLES. Aye, aye, and I beg, Mr. Premium—

SIR O. Gentlemen—

JOSEPH. Sir, by Heaven, you shall go!

CHARLES. Aye, out with him, certainly!

SIR O. This violence—

JOSEPH. Sir, 'tis your own fault.

CHARLES. Out with him, to be sure! (*Both forcing* SIR OLIVER *out.*)

(*Enter* SIR PETER *and* LADY TEAZLE, MARIA, *and* ROWLEY.)

SIR PET. My old friend, Sir Oliver—Hey! what in the name of wonder—here are dutiful nephews—assault their uncle at a first visit!

LADY T. Indeed, Sir Oliver, 'twas well we came to rescue you.

ROW. Truly it was; for I perceive, Sir Oliver, the character of old Stanley was no protection to you.

SIR O. Nor of Premium either; the necessities of the former could not extort a shilling from that benevolent gentleman, and now, egad, with the other I stood a chance of faring worse than my ancestors,

and being knocked down without being bid for.

JOSEPH. Charles!

CHARLES. Joseph!

JOSEPH. 'Tis now complete!

CHARLES. Very!

SIR O. Sir Peter, my friend, and Rowley too—look on that elder nephew of mine. You know what he has already received from my bounty, and you also know how gladly I would have regarded half my fortune as held in trust for him; judge, then, my disappointment in discovering him to be destitute of faith, charity, and gratitude!

SIR PET. Sir Oliver, I should be more surprised at this declaration if I had not myself found him to be mean, treacherous, and hypocritical.

LADY T. And if the gentleman pleads not guilty to these, pray let him call *me* to his character.

SIR PET. Then I believe we need add no more. If he knows himself, he will consider it as the most perfect punishment, that he is known to the world.

CHARLES (*aside*). If they talk this way to Honesty, what will they say to me by and by?

SIR O. As for that prodigal, his brother, there—

CHARLES (*aside*). Aye, now comes my turn; the damned family pictures will ruin me!

JOSEPH. Sir Oliver—uncle, will you honor me with a hearing?

CHARLES (*aside*). Now, if Joseph would make one of his long speeches, I might recollect myself a little.

SIR O. (*to* JOSEPH). I suppose you would undertake to justify yourself entirely?

JOSEPH. I trust I could.

SIR O. (*to* CHARLES). Well, sir!—and you could justify yourself too, I suppose?

CHARLES. Not that I know of, Sir Oliver.

SIR O. What!—Little Premium has been let too much into the secret, I suppose?

CHARLES. True, sir; but they were *family* secrets, and should not be mentioned again, you know.

ROW. Come, Sir Oliver, I know you cannot speak of Charles's follies with anger.

SIR O. Odds heart, no more I can, nor with gravity either. Sir Peter, do you know the rogue bargained with me for all his ancestors—sold me judges and generals by the foot, and maiden aunts as cheap as broken china.

CHARLES. To be sure, Sir Oliver, I did make a little free with the family canvas, that's the truth on't. My ancestors may rise in judgment against me, there's no denying it; but believe me sincere when I tell you—and upon my soul I would not say so if I was not—that if I do not appear mortified at the exposure of my follies, it is because I feel at this moment the warmest satisfaction in seeing you, my liberal benefactor.

SIR O. Charles, I believe you. Give me your hand again. The ill-looking little fellow over the settee has made your peace.

CHARLES. Then, sir, my gratitude to the original is still increased.

LADY T. Yet, I believe, Sir Oliver, here is one whom Charles is still more anxious to be reconciled to.

SIR O. Oh, I have heard of his attachment there; and, with the young lady's pardon, if I construe right—that blush—

SIR PET. Well, child, speak your sentiments!

MARIA. Sir, I have little to say, but that I shall rejoice to hear that he is happy; for me, whatever claim I had to his attention, I willingly resign to one who has a better title.

CHARLES. How, Maria!

SIR PET. Heyday! what's the mystery now? While he appeared an incorrigible rake, you would give your hand to no one else; and now that he is likely to reform, I'll warrant you won't have him!

MARIA. His own heart and Lady Sneerwell know the cause.

CHARLES. Lady Sneerwell!

JOSEPH. Brother, it is with great concern I am obliged to speak on this point, but my regard to justice compels me and Lady Sneerwell's injuries can no longer be concealed. (*Opens the door.*)

(*Enter* LADY SNEERWELL.)

SIR PET. So! another French milliner! Egad, he has one in every room in the house, I suppose!

LADY S. Ungrateful Charles! Well may you be surprised, and feel for the indelicate situation your perfidy has forced me into.

CHARLES. Pray, uncle, is this another plot of yours? For, as I have life, I don't under-

stand it.

JOSEPH. I believe, sir, there is but the evidence of one person more necessary to make it extremely clear.

SIR PET. And that person, I imagine, is Mr. Snake.—Rowley, you were perfectly right to bring him with us, and pray let him appear.

ROW. Walk in, Mr. Snake.

(*Enter* SNAKE.)

I thought his testimony might be wanted; however, it happens unluckily that he comes to confront Lady Sneerwell, not to support her.

LADY S. A villain! Treacherous to me at last! Speak, fellow; have you too conspired against me?

SNAKE. I beg your ladyship ten thousand pardons; you paid me extremely liberally for the lie in question, but I unfortunately have been offered double to speak the truth.

SIR PET. Plot and counter-plot, egad!

LADY S. (*going*). The torments of shame and disappointment on you all!

LADY T. Hold, Lady Sneerwell—before you go, let me thank you for the trouble you and that gentleman have taken, in writing letters from me to Charles and answering them yourself; and let me also request you to make my respects to the scandalous college of which you are president, and inform term that Lady Teazle, licentiate, begs leave to return the diploma they granted her, as she leaves off practice and kills characters no longer.

LADY S. You, too, madam!—provoking—insolent! May your husband live these fifty years! (*Exit.*)

SIR PET. Oons! what a fury!

LADY T. A malicious creature, indeed!

SIR PET. What!—not for her last wish!

LADY T. Oh, no!

SIR O. Well, sir, and what have you to say now?

JOSEPH. Sir, I am so confounded to find that Lady Sneerwell could be guilty of suborning Mr. Snake in this manner to impose on us all, that I know not what to say; however, lest her revengeful spirit should prompt her to injure my brother, I had certainly better follow her directly. (*Exit.*)

SIR PET. Moral to the last drop!

SIR O. Aye, and marry her, Joseph, if you

can. Oil and vinegar, egad! you'll do very well together.

ROW. I believe we have no more occasion for Mr. Snake at present?

SNAKE. Before I go, I beg pardon once for all for whatever uneasiness I have been the humble instrument of causing to the parties present.

SIR PET. Well, well, you have made atonement by a good deed at last.

SNAKE. But I must request of the company that it shall never be known.

SIR PET. Hey! what the plague! are you ashamed of having done a right thing once in your life?

SNAKE. Ah, sir, consider—I live by the badness of my character; I have nothing but my infamy to depend on, and if it were once known that I had been betrayed into an honest action, I should lose every friend I have in the world.

SIR O. Well, well, we'll not traduce you by saying anything in your praise; never fear.

(*Exit* SNAKE.)

SIR PET. There's a precious rogue!

LADY T. See, Sir Oilver, there needs no persuasion now to reconcile your nephew and Maria.

SIR O. Aye, aye, that's as it should be, and, egad, we'll have the wedding to-morrow morning.

CHARLES. Thank you, dear uncle.

SIR PET. What, you rogue! don't you ask the girl's consent first?

CHARLES. Oh, I have done that a long time —a minute ago—and she has looked yes.

MARIA. For shame, Charles!—I protest, Sir Peter, there has not been a word.

SIR O. Well, then, the fewer the better; may your love for each other never know abatement!

SIR PET. And may you live as happily together as Lady Teazle and I intend to do!

CHARLES. Rowley, my old friend, I am sure you congratulate me; and I suspect that I owe you much.

SIR O. You do, indeed, Charles.

ROW. If my efforts to serve you had not succeeded, you would have been in my debt for the attempt; but deserve to be happy, and you overpay me.

SIR PET. Aye, honest Rowley always said you would reform.

CHARLES. Why, as to reforming, Sir Peter, I'll make no promises, and that I take to be a proof that I intend to set about it. But here shall be my monitor—my gentle guide.—Ah! can I leave the virtuous path those eyes illumine?

Though thou, dear maid, shouldst waive
    thy beauty's sway,
Thou still must rule, because I will obey:
An humble fugitive from Folly, view;
No sanctuary near but Love and you.

(*To the audience.*)

You can, indeed, each anxious fear remove,
For even Scandal dies if you approve.

(*Exeunt omnes.*)

EPILOGUE

BY MR. COLMAN
SPOKEN BY LADY TEAZLE

I, who was late so volatile and gay,
Like a trade-wind must now blow all one way,
Bend all my cares, my studies, and my vows,
To one dull rusty weathercock—my spouse!
So wills our virtuous bard—the motley Bayes
Of crying epilogues and laughing plays!
Old bachelors who marry smart young wives,
Learn from our play to regulate their lives;
Each brings his dear to town, all faults upon
    her—
London will prove the very source of honor.
Plunged fairly in, like a cold bath it serves,
When principles relax, to brace the nerves.
Such is my case; and yet I must deplore
That the gay dream of dissipation's o'er.
And say, ye fair! was ever lively wife,
Born with a genius for the highest life,
Like me, untimely blasted in her bloom,
Like me condemned to such a dismal doom?
Save money—when I just knew know to waste
    it!
Leave London—just as I began to taste it!
Must I then watch the early crowing cock,
The melancholy ticking of a clock,
In a lone rustic hall forever pounded,
With dogs, cats, rats, and squalling brats sur-
    rounded?
With humble curate can I now retire
(While good Sir Peter boozes with the squire),
And at backgammon mortify my soul
That pants for loo, or flutters at a vole?

"Seven's the main!" Dear sound that must
        expire,
Lost at hot cockles round a Christmas fire!
The transient hour of fashion too soon spent,
Farewell the tranquil mind, farewell content!
Farewell the plumèd head, the cushioned tête,
That takes the cushion from its proper seat!
That spirit-stirring drum!—card drums I mean,
Spadille—odd trick—pam—basto—king and
        queen!
And you, ye knockers, that, with brazen throat,
The welcome visitors' approach denote;
Farewell all quality of high renown,
Pride, pomp, and circumstance of glorious town!
Farewell! your revels I partake no more,
And Lady Teazle's occupation's o'er!
All this I told our bard; he smiled, and said
        'twas clear,
I ought to play deep tragedy next year.
Meanwhile he drew wise morals from his play,
And in these solemn periods stalked away:
"Bless'd were the fair like you; her faults who
        stopped
And closed her follies when the curtain dropped!
No more in vice or error to engage,
Or play the fool at large on life's great stage."

FOR ANALYSIS

Act I

1. What ancient convention of the drama is represented by the Prologue? What does the Prologue tell you about Sheridan's purpose in writing the play?
2. What common characteristic do the names of the characters have?
3. What is the purpose of the dialogue before the first entrance of the servant? What kind of *function* character is Snake?
4. Is there a difference between the methods of gossip introduced with each new character?
5. What older stage convention is embodied in Sir Peter's speech at the beginning of Scene 2?
6. What function does Rowley perform in Scene 2? Is this parallel to the early part of Scene 1?

Act II

1. By the end of Act II, what motives has the playwright suggested for the conduct of the scandalmongers?
2. How is the entrance of every major character prepared for by Sheridan? Why would a playwright prefer this method?

3. In what way is Lady Teazle's character more complicated than those of the others around her?

Act III

1. What targets of satire other than scandal begin to enter in Act III?
2. By the end of Act III does the scandal about Charles seem borne out? Who are the guides the audience uses at this point to distinguish admirable and despicable characters? Is there a conflict in opinion among these guides? Does this add to suspense in the play?
3. Besides having "guides," has the audience also been provided with a "measuring stick" character by which they can gauge good and bad men and women?
4. What seems to determine the point at which acts will end in this play? Length? Introduction of main characters? Divisions of plot structure? Change of scene?

Act IV

1. What quality in Charles appeals to his Uncle Oliver? Is there a difference between that and the quality that appeals to the audience?
2. Who by this time seem to be the *foil* characters in the play?
3. The device of having unsuspected listeners behind screens and in closets would seem farfetched in our day, but why is it necessary in this play?
4. At this point in the play, what does that muchadmired word "sentiment" mean to the audience?

Act V

1. What do all of the exposés of character have to do with Sheridan's purpose as announced in the Prologue?
2. What point about the motive behind scandal is made in Scene 2 when the gossips fabricate the wholly false account of the Teazle episode?
3. What quality of character triumphs in the play? Honesty? Charity? Goodness of heart? High principle?
4. What does the Epilogue do to the play? Is it there simply to balance the Prologue? Does it reinforce the ending of the play? Change the tone? Shift the moral emphasis?
5. Having read the play, consider the question of unity. What is the connection between the Sneerwell and Surface plots? Is the connection strong enough to justify the inclusion of both plots?

OSCAR WILDE

The Importance
of Being Earnest

THE PERSONS OF THE PLAY

JOHN WORTHING, J.P.
ALGERNON MONCRIEFF
REV. CANON CHASUBLE, D.D.
MERRIMAN, *Butler*
LANE, *Manservant*
LADY BRACKNELL
HON. GWENDOLEN FAIRFAX
CECILY CARDEW
MISS PRISM, *Governess*

THE SCENES OF THE PLAY

ACT ONE: *Algernon Moncrieff's Flat in Half-Moon Street, W.*

ACT TWO: *The Garden at the Manor House, Woolton*

ACT THREE: *Drawing-room at the Manor House, Woolton*

TIME: *The Present*

ACT I

SCENE: *Morning-room in Algernon's flat in Half-Moon Street. The room is luxuriously and artistically furnished. The sound of a piano is heard in the adjoining room.*

(LANE *is arranging afternoon tea on the table, and after the music has ceased,* ALGERNON *enters.*)

ALGERNON. Did you hear what I was playing, Lane?

LANE. I didn't think it polite to listen, sir.

ALGERNON. I'm sorry for that, for your sake. I don't play accurately—anyone can play accurately—but I play with wonderful expression. As far as the piano is concerned, sentiment is my forte. I keep science for Life.

LANE. Yes, sir.

ALGERNON. And, speaking of the science of Life, have you got the cucumber sandwiches cut for Lady Bracknell?

LANE. Yes, sir. (*Hands them on a salver.*)

ALGERNON. (*Inspects them, takes two, and sits down on the sofa.*) Oh! . . . by the way, Lane, I see from your book that on Thursday night, when Lord Shoreman and Mr. Worthing were dining with me, eight bottles of champagne are entered as having been consumed.

LANE. Yes, sir; eight bottles and a pint.

ALGERNON. Why is it that at a bachelor's establishment the servants invariably drink the champagne? I ask merely for information.

LANE. I attribute it to the superior quality of the wine, sir. I have often observed that in married households the champagne is rarely of a first-rate brand.

ALGERNON. Good heavens! Is marriage so demoralizing as that?

LANE. I believe it *is* a very pleasant state, sir. I have had very little experience of it myself up to the present. I have only been married once. That was in consequence of a misunderstanding between myself and a young person.

ALGERNON. (*Languidly.*) I don't know that I am much interested in your family life, Lane.

LANE. No, sir; it is not a very interesting subject. I never think of it myself.

ALGERNON. Very natural, I am sure. That will do, Lane, thank you.

LANE. Thank you, sir.

(LANE *goes out.*)

ALGERNON. Lane's views on marriage seem somewhat lax. Really, if the lower orders don't set us a good example, what on earth is the use of them? They seem, as a class, to have absolutely no sense of moral responsibility.

(*Enter* LANE.)

LANE. Mr. Ernest Worthing.

(*Enter* JACK. LANE *goes out.*)

ALGERNON. How are you, my dear Ernest? What brings you up to town?

JACK. Oh, pleasure, pleasure! What else should bring one anywhere? Eating as usual, I see, Algy!

ALGERNON. (*Stiffly.*) I believe it is customary in good society to take some slight refreshment at five o'clock. Where have you been since last Thursday?

JACK. (*Sitting down on the sofa.*) In the country.

ALGERNON.   What on earth do you do there?

JACK. (*Pulling off his gloves.*)   When one is in town one amuses oneself. When one is in the country one amuses other people. It is excessively boring.

ALGERNON.   And who are the people you amuse?

JACK. (*Airily.*)   Oh, neighbours, neighbours.

ALGERNON.   Got nice neighbours in your part of Shropshire?

JACK.   Perfectly horrid! Never speak to one of them.

ALGERNON.   How immensely you must amuse them! (*Goes over and takes sandwich.*) By the way, Shropshire is your county, is it not?

JACK.   Eh? Shropshire? Yes, of course. Hallo! Why all these cups? Why cucumber sandwiches? Why such reckless extravagance in one so young? Who is coming to tea?

ALGERNON.   Oh! merely Aunt Augusta and Gwendolen.

JACK.   How perfectly delightful!

ALGERNON.   Yes, that is all very well; but I am afraid Aunt Augusta won't quite approve of your being here.

JACK.   May I ask why?

ALGERNON.   My dear fellow, the way you flirt with Gwendolen is perfectly disgraceful. It is almost as bad as the way Gwendolen flirts with you.

JACK.   I am in love with Gwendolen. I have come up to town expressly to propose to her.

ALGERNON.   I thought you had come up for pleasure? . . . I call that business.

JACK.   How utterly unromantic you are!

ALGERNON.   I really don't see anything romantic in proposing. It is very romantic to be in love. But there is nothing romantic about a definite proposal. Why, one may be accepted. One usually is, I believe. Then the excitement is all over. The very essence of romance is uncertainty. If ever I get married, I'll certainly try to forget the fact.

JACK.   I have no doubt about that, dear Algy. The Divorce Court was specially invented for people whose memories are so curiously constituted.

ALGERNON.   Oh! there is no use speculating on that subject. Divorces are made in Heaven—(JACK *puts out his hand to take a sandwich.* ALGERNON *at once interferes.*) Please don't touch the cucumber sandwiches. They are ordered specially for Aunt Augusta. (*Takes one and eats it.*)

JACK.   Well, you have been eating them all the time.

ALGERNON.   That is quite a different matter. She is my aunt. (*Takes plate from below.*) Have some bread and butter. The bread and butter is for Gwendolen. Gwendolen is devoted to bread and butter.

JACK. (*Advancing to table and helping himself.*) And very good bread and butter it is too.

ALGERNON.   Well, my dear fellow, you need not eat as if you were going to eat it all. You behave as if you were married to her already. You are not married to her already, and I don't think you ever will be.

JACK.   Why on earth do you say that?

ALGERNON.   Well, in the first place, girls never marry the men they flirt with. Girls don't think it right.

JACK.   Oh, that is nonsense!

ALGERNON.   It isn't. It is a great truth. It accounts for the extraordinary number of bachelors that one sees all over the place. In the second place, I don't give my consent.

JACK.   Your consent!

ALGERNON.   My dear fellow, Gwendolen is my first cousin. And before I allow you to marry her, you will have to clear up the whole question of Cecily. (*Rings bell.*)

JACK.   Cecily! What on earth do you mean? What do you mean, Algy, by Cecily! I don't know anyone of the name of Cecily.

(*Enter* LANE.)

ALGERNON.   Bring me that cigarette case Mr. Worthing left in the smoking-room the last time he dined here.

LANE.   Yes, sir.

(LANE *goes out.*)

JACK.   Do you mean to say you have had my cigarette case all this time? I wish to goodness you had let me know. I have been writing frantic letters to Scotland Yard about it. I was very nearly offering a large reward.

ALGERNON.   Well, I wish you would offer one. I happen to be more than usually hard up.

JACK.   There is no good offering a large reward now that the thing is found.

(*Enter* LANE *with the cigarette case on a salver.* ALGERNON *takes it at once.* LANE *goes out.*)

ALGERNON. I think that is rather mean of you, Ernest, I must say. (*Opens case and examines it.*) However, it makes no matter, for, now that I look at the inscription inside, I find that the thing isn't yours after all.

JACK. Of course it's mine. (*Moving to him.*) You have seen me with it a hundred times, and you have no right whatsoever to read what is written inside. It is a very ungentlemanly thing to read a private cigarette case.

ALGERNON. Oh! it is absurd to have a hard and fast rule about what one should read and what one shouldn't. More than half of modern culture depends on what one shouldn't read.

JACK. I am quite aware of the fact, and I don't propose to discuss modern culture. It isn't the sort of thing one should talk of in private. I simply want my cigarette case back.

ALGERNON. Yes; but this isn't your cigarette case. This cigarette case is a present from someone of the name of Cecily, and you said you didn't know anyone of that name.

JACK. Well, if you want to know, Cecily happens to be my aunt.

ALGERNON. Your aunt!

JACK. Yes. Charming old lady she is, too. Lives at Tunbridge Wells. Just give it back to me, Algy.

ALGERNON. (*Retreating to back of sofa.*) But why does she call herself little Cecily if she is your aunt and lives at Tunbridge Wells? (*Reading.*) "From little Cecily with her fondest love."

JACK. (*Moving to sofa and kneeling upon it.*) My dear fellow, what on earth is there in that? Some aunts are tall, some aunts are not tall. That is a matter that surely an aunt may be allowed to decide for herself. You seem to think that every aunt should be exactly like your aunt! That is absurd. For Heaven's sake give me back my cigarette case. (*Follows* ALGERNON *round the room.*)

ALGERNON. Yes. But why does your aunt call you her uncle? "From little Cecily, with her fondest love to her dear Uncle Jack." There is no objection, I admit, to an aunt being a small aunt, but why an aunt, no matter what her size may be, should call her own nephew her uncle, I can't quite make out. Besides, your name isn't Jack at all; it is Ernest.

JACK. It isn't Ernest; it's Jack.

ALGERNON. You have always told me it was Ernest. I have introduced you to every one as Ernest. You answer to the name of Ernest. You look as if your name was Ernest. You are the most earnest-looking person I ever saw in my life. It is perfectly absurd your saying that your name isn't Ernest. It's on your cards. Here is one of them. (*Taking it from case.*) "Mr. Ernest Worthing, B.4, The Albany." I'll keep this as a proof that your name is Ernest if ever you attempt to deny it to me, or to Gwendolen, or to anyone else. (*Puts the card in his pocket.*)

JACK. Well, my name is Ernest in town and Jack in the country, and the cigarette case was given to me in the country.

ALGERNON. Yes, but that does not account for the fact that your small Aunt Cecily, who lives at Tunbridge Wells, calls you her dear uncle. Come, old boy, you had much better have the thing out at once.

JACK. My dear Algy, you talk exactly as if you were a dentist. It is very vulgar to talk like a dentist when one isn't a dentist. It produces a false impression.

ALGERNON. Well, that is exactly what dentists always do. Now, go on! Tell me the whole thing. I may mention that I have always suspected you of being a confirmed and secret Bunburyist; and I am quite sure of it now.

JACK. Bunburyist? What on earth do you mean by a Bunburyist?

ALGERNON. I'll reveal to you the meaning of that incomparable expression as soon as you are kind enough to inform me why you are Ernest in town and Jack in the country.

JACK. Well, produce my cigarette case first.

ALGERNON. Here it is. (*Hands cigarette case.*) Now produce your explanation, and pray make it improbable. (*Sits on sofa.*)

JACK. My dear fellow, there is nothing improbable about my explanation at all. In fact it's perfectly ordinary. Old Mr. Thomas Cardew, who adopted me when I was a little boy, made me in his will guardian to his granddaughter, Miss Cecily Cardew. Cecily, who addresses me as her uncle from motives of respect that you could not possibly appreciate, lives at my place in the country under the charge of her admirable governess, Miss Prism.

ALGERNON. Where is that place in the country, by the way?

JACK. That is nothing to you, dear boy. You are not going to be invited. . . . I may tell you candidly that the place is not in Shropshire.

ALGERNON. I suspected that, my dear fellow! I have Bunburyed all over Shropshire on two separate occasions. Now, go on. Why are you Ernest in town and Jack in the country?

JACK. My dear Algy, I don't know whether you will be able to understand my real motives. You are hardly serious enough. When one is placed in the position of guardian, one has to adopt a very high moral tone on all subjects. It's one's duty to do so. And as a high moral tone can hardly be said to conduce very much to either one's health or one's happiness, in order to get up to town I have always pretended to have a younger brother of the name of Ernest, who lives in The Albany, and gets into the most dreadful scrapes. That, my dear Algy, is the whole truth pure and simple.

ALGERNON. The truth is rarely pure and never simple. Modern life would be very tedious if it were either, and modern literature, a complete impossibility!

JACK. That wouldn't be at all a bad thing.

ALGERNON. Literary criticism is not your forte, my dear fellow. Don't try it. You should leave that to people who haven't been at a University. They do it so well in the daily papers. What you really are is a Bunburyist. I was quite right in saying you were a Bunburyist. You are one of the most advanced Bunburyists I know.

JACK. What on earth do you mean?

ALGERNON. You have invented a very useful younger brother called Ernest, in order that you may be able to come up to town as often as you like. I have invented an invaluable permanent invalid called Bunbury, in order that I may be able to go down into the country whenever I choose. Bunbury is perfectly invaluable. If it wasn't for Bunbury's extraordinary bad health, for in-

stance, I wouldn't be able to dine with you at Willis's to-night, for I have been really engaged to Aunt Augusta for more than a week.

JACK. I haven't asked you to dine with me anywhere to-night.

ALGERNON. I know. You are absurdly careless about sending out invitations. It is very foolish of you. Nothing annoys people so much as not receiving invitations.

JACK. You had much better dine with your Aunt Augusta.

ALGERNON. I haven't the smallest intention of doing anything of the kind. To begin with, I dined there on Monday, and once a week is quite enough to dine with one's own relations. In the second place, whenever I do dine there I am always treated as a member of the family, and sent down with either no woman at all, or two. In the third place, I know perfectly well whom she will place me next to, to-night. She will place me next Mary Farquhar, who always flirts with her own husband across the dinner-table. That is not very pleasant. Indeed, it is not even decent . . . and that sort of thing is enormously on the increase. The amount of women in London who flirt with their own husbands is perfectly scandalous. It looks so bad. It is simply washing one's clean linen in public. Besides, now that I know you to be a confirmed Bunburyist I naturally want to talk to you about Bunburying. I want to tell you the rules.

JACK. I'm not a Bunburyist at all. If Gwendolen accepts me, I am going to kill my brother, indeed I think I'll kill him in any case. Cecily is a little too much interested in him. It is rather a bore. So I am going to get rid of Ernest. And I strongly advise you to do the same with Mr. . . . with your invalid friend who has the absurd name.

ALGERNON. Nothing will induce me to part with Bunbury, and if you ever get married, which seems to me extremely problematic you will be very glad to know Bunbury. A man who marries without knowing Bunbury has a very tedious time of it.

JACK. That is nonsense. If I marry a charming girl like Gwendolen, and she is the only girl I ever saw in my life that I would marry, I certainly won't want to know Bunbury.

ALGERNON.   Then your wife will. You don't seem to realize, that in married life three is company and two is none.

JACK. (*Sententiously.*)   That, my dear young friend, is the theory that the corrupt French Drama has been propounding for the last fifty years.

ALGERNON.   Yes; and that the happy English home has proved in half the time.

JACK.   For heaven's sake, don't try to be cynical. It's perfectly easy to be cynical.

ALGERNON.   My dear fellow, it isn't easy to be anything nowadays. There's such a lot of beastly competition about. (*The sound of an electric bell is heard.*)   Ah! that must be Aunt Augusta. Only relatives, or creditors, ever ring in that Wagnerian manner. Now, if I get her out of the way for ten minutes, so that you can have an opportunity for proposing to Gwendolen, may I dine with you tonight at Willis's?

JACK.   I suppose so, if you want to.

ALGERNON.   Yes, but you must be serious about it. I hate people who are not serious about meals. It is so shallow of them.

(*Enter* LANE.)

LANE.   Lady Bracknell and Miss Fairfax.

(ALGERNON *goes forward to meet them. Enter* LADY BRACKNELL *and* GWENDOLEN.)

LADY BRACKNELL.   Good afternoon, dear Algernon, I hope you are behaving very well.

ALGERNON.   I'm feeling very well, Aunt Augusta.

LADY BRACKNELL.   That's not quite the same thing. In fact the two things rarely go together. (*Sees* JACK *and bows to him with icy coldness.*)

ALGERNON. (*To* GWENDOLEN.)   Dear me, you are smart!

GWENDOLEN.   I am always smart! Am I not, Mr. Worthing?

JACK.   You're quite perfect, Miss Fairfax.

GWENDOLEN.   Oh! I hope I am not that. It would leave no room for developments, and I intend to develop in many directions. (GWENDOLEN *and* JACK *sit down together in the corner.*)

LADY BRACKNELL.   I'm sorry if we are a little late, Algernon, but I was obliged to call on dear Lady Harbury. I hadn't been there since her poor husband's death. I never saw a woman so altered; she looks quite twenty years younger. And now I'll have a cup of tea, and one of those nice cucumber sandwiches you promised me.

ALGERNON.   Certainly, Aunt Augusta. (*Goes over to tea-table.*)

LADY BRACKNELL.   Won't you come and sit here, Gwendolen?

GWENDOLEN.   Thanks, mamma, I'm quite comfortable where I am.

ALGERNON. (*Picking up empty plate in horror.*) Good heavens! Lane! Why are there no cucumber sandwiches? I ordered them specially.

LANE. (*Gravely.*)   There were no cucumbers in the market this morning, sir. I went down twice.

ALGERNON.   No cucumbers!

LANE.   No, sir. Not even for ready money.

ALGERNON.   That will do, Lane, thank you.

LANE.   Thank you, sir. (*Goes out.*)

ALGERNON.   I am greatly distressed, Aunt Augusta, about there being no cucumbers, not even for ready money.

LADY BRACKNELL.   It really makes no matter, Algernon. I had some crumpets with Lady Harbury, who seems to me to be living entirely for pleasure now.

ALGERNON.   I hear her hair has turned quite gold from grief.

LADY BRACKNELL.   It certainly has changed its colour. From what cause I, of course, cannot say. (A"GérnÖn *crosses and hands tea.*) Thank you. I've quite a treat for you to-night, Algernon. I am going to send you down with Mary Farquhar. She is such a nice woman, and so attentive to her husband. It's delightful to watch them.

ALGERNON.   I am afraid, Aunt Augusta, I shall have to give up the pleasure of dining with you to-night after all.

LADY BRACKNELL. (*Frowning.*)   I hope not, Algernon. It would put my table completely out. Your uncle would have to dine upstairs. Fortunately he is accustomed to that.

ALGERNON.   It is a great bore, and, I need hardly say, a terrible disappointment to me, but the fact is I have just had a telegram to say that my poor friend Bunbury is very ill again. (*Exchanges glances with* JACK.) They seem to think I should be with him.

LADY BRACKNELL. It is very strange. This Mr. Bunbury seems to suffer from curiously bad health.

ALGERNON. Yes; poor Bunbury is a dreadful invalid.

LADY BRACKNELL. Well, I must say, Algernon, that I think it is high time that Mr. Bunbury made up his mind whether he was going to live or to die. This shilly-shallying with the question is absurd. Nor do I in any way approve of the modern sympathy with invalids. I consider it morbid. Illness of any kind is hardly a thing to be encouraged in others. Health is the primary duty of life. I am always telling that to your poor uncle, but he never seems to take much notice . . . as far as any improvement in his ailment goes. I should be much obliged if you would ask Mr. Bunbury, from me, to be kind enough not to have a relapse on Saturday, for I rely on you to arrange my music for me. It is my last reception, and one wants something that will encourage conversation, particularly at the end of the season when everyone has practically said whatever they had to say, which, in most cases, was probably not much.

ALGERNON. I'll speak to Bunbury, Aunt Augusta, if he is still conscious, and I think I can promise you be'll be all right by Saturday. Of course the music is a great difficulty. You see, if one plays good music, people don't listen, and if one plays bad music people don't talk. But I'll run over the programme I've drawn out, if you will kindly come into the next room for a moment.

LADY BRACKNELL. Thank you, Algernon. It is very thoughtful of you. (*Rising, and following* ALGERNON.) I'm sure the programme will be delightful, after a few expurgations. French songs I cannot possibly allow. People always seem to think that they are improper, and either look shocked, which is vulgar, or laugh, which is worse. But German sounds a thoroughly respectable language, and, indeed I believe is so. Gwendolen, you will accompany me.

GWENDOLEN. Certainly, mamma.

(LADY BRACKNELL *and* ALGERNON *go into the music-room*, GWENDOLEN *remains behind*.)

JACK. Charming day it has been, Miss Fairfax.

GWENDOLEN. Pray don't talk to me about the weather, Mr. Worthing. Whenever people talk to me about the weather, I always feel quite certain that they mean something else. And that makes me so nervous.

JACK. I do mean something else.

GWENDOLEN. I thought so. In fact, I am never wrong.

JACK. And I would like to be allowed to take advantage of Lady Bracknell's temporary absence. . . .

GWENDOLEN. I would certainly advise you to do so. Mamma has a way of coming back suddenly into a room that I have often had to speak to her about.

JACK. (*Nervously*.) Miss Fairfax, ever since I met you I have admired you more than any girl . . . I have ever met since . . . I met you.

GWENDOLEN. Yes, I am quite well aware of the fact. And I often wish that in public, at any rate, you had been more demonstrative. For me you have always had an irresistible fascination. Even before I met you I was far from indifferent to you. (JACK *looks at her in amazement*.) We live, as I hope you know, Mr. Worthing, in an age of ideals. The fact is constantly mentioned in the more expensive monthly magazines, and has reached the provincial pulpits, I am told; and my ideal has always been to love someone of the name of Ernest. There is something in that name that inspires absolute confidence. The moment Algernon first mentioned to me that he had a friend called Ernest, I knew I was destined to love you.

JACK. You really love me, Gwendolen?

GWENDOLEN. Passionately!

JACK. Darling! You don't know how happy you've made me.

GWENDOLEN. My own Ernest!

JACK. But you don't really mean to say that you couldn't love me if my name wasn't Ernest?

GWENDOLEN. But your name is Ernest.

JACK. Yes, I know it is. But supposing it was something else? Do you mean to say you couldn't love me then?

GWENDOLEN. (*Glibly*.) Ah! that is clearly a metaphysical speculation, and like most metaphysical speculations has very little reference at all to the actual facts of real life, as we know them.

JACK. Personally, darling, to speak quite candidly, I don't much care about the name of Ernest. . . . I don't think the name suits me at all.

GWENDOLEN. It suits you perfectly. It is a divine name. It has music of its own. It produces vibrations.

JACK. Well, really, Gwendolen, I must say that I think there are lots of other much nicer names. I think Jack, for instance, a charming name.

GWENDOLEN. Jack? . . . No, there is very little music in the name Jack, if any at all, indeed. It does not thrill. It produces absolutely no vibrations. . . . I have known several Jacks, and they all, without exception, were more than usually plain. Besides, Jack is a notorious domesticity for John! And I pity any woman who is married to a man called John. She would probably never be allowed to know the entrancing pleasure of a single moment's solitude. The only really safe name is Ernest.

JACK. Gwendolen, I must get christened at once—I mean we must get married at once. There is no time to be lost.

GWENDOLEN. Married, Mr. Worthing?

JACK. (*Astounded.*) Well . . . surely. You know that I love you, and you led me to believe, Miss Fairfax, that you were not absolutely indifferent to me.

GWENDOLEN. I adore you. But you haven't proposed to me yet. Nothing has been said at all about marriage. The subject has not even been touched on.

JACK. Well . . . may I propose to you now?

GWENDOLEN. I think it would be an admirable opportunity. And to spare you any possible disappointment, Mr. Worthing, I think it only fair to tell you quite frankly beforehand that I am fully determined to accept you.

JACK. Gwendolen!

GWENDOLEN. Yes, Mr. Worthing, what have you got to say to me?

JACK. You know what I have got to say to you.

GWENDOLEN. Yes, but you don't say it.

JACK. Gwendolen, will you marry me? (*Goes on his knees.*)

GWENDOLEN. Of course I will, darling. How long you have been about it! I am afraid you have had very little experience in how to propose.

JACK. My own one, I have never loved anyone in the world but you.

GWENDOLEN. Yes, but men often propose for practice. I know my brother Gerald does. All my girl-friends tell me so. What wonderfully blue eyes you have, Ernest! They are quite, quite blue. I hope you will always look at me just like that, especially when there are other people present.

(*Enter* LADY BRACKNELL.)

LADY BRACKNELL. Mr. Worthing! Rise, sir, from this semi-recumbent posture. It is most indecorous.

GWENDOLEN. Mamma! (*He tries to rise; she restrains him.*) I must beg you to retire. This is no place for you. Besides, Mr. Worthing has not quite finished yet.

LADY BRACKNELL. Finished what, may I ask?

GWENDOLEN. I am engaged to Mr. Worthing, mamma. (*They rise together.*)

LADY BRACKNELL. Pardon me, you are not engaged to anyone. When you do become engaged to someone, I, or your father, should his health permit him, will inform you of the fact. An engagement should come on a young girl as a surprise, pleasant or unpleasant, as the case may be. It is hardly a matter that she could be allowed to arrange for herself. . . . And now I have a few questions to put to you, Mr. Worthing. While I am making these inquiries, you, Gwendolen, will wait for me below in the carriage.

GWENDOLEN. (*Reproachfully.*) Mamma!

LADY BRACKNELL. In the carriage, Gwendolen! (GWENDOLEN *goes to the door. She and* JACK *blow kisses to each other behind* LADY BRACKNELL's *back.* LADY BRACKNELL *looks vaguely about as if she could not understand what the noise was. Finally turns round.*) Gwendolen, the carriage!

GWENDOLEN. Yes, mamma. (*Goes out, looking back at* JACK.)

LADY BRACKNELL. (*Sitting down.*) You can take a seat, Mr. Worthing.

(*Looks in her pocket for notebook and pencil.*)

JACK. Thank you, Lady Bracknell, I prefer standing.

LADY BRACKNELL. (*Pencil and notebook in hand.*) I feel bound to tell you that you are not down on my list of eligible young men, although I have the same list as the dear Duchess of Bolton has. We work together, in fact. However, I am quite ready to enter your name, should your answers be what a really affectionate mother requires. Do you smoke?

JACK. Well, yes, I must admit I smoke.

LADY BRACKNELL. I am glad to hear it. A man should always have an occupation of some kind. There are far too many idle men in London as it is. How old are you?

JACK. Twenty-nine.

LADY BRACKNELL. A very good age to be married at. I have always been of opinion that a man who desires to get married should know either everything or nothing. Which do you know?

JACK. (*After some hesitation.*) I know nothing, Lady Bracknell.

LADY BRACKNELL. I am pleased to hear it. I do not approve of anything that tampers with natural ignorance. Ignorance is like a delicate exotic fruit; touch it and the bloom is gone. The whole theory of modern education is radically unsound. Fortunately in England, at any rare, education produces no effect whatsoever. If it did, it would prove a serious danger to the upper classes, and probably lead to acts of violence in Grosvenor Square. What is your income?

JACK. Between seven and eight thousand a year.

LADY BRACKNELL. (*Makes a note in her book.*) In land, or in investments?

JACK. In investments, chiefly.

LADY BRACKNELL. That is satisfactory. What between the duties expected of one during one's lifetime, and the duties exacted from one after one's death, land has ceased to be either a profit or a pleasure. It gives one position, and prevents one from keeping it up. That's all that can be said about land.

JACK. I have a country house with some land, of course, attached to it, about fifteen hundred acres, I believe; but I don't depend on that for my real income. In fact, as far as I can make out, the poachers are the only people who make anything out of it.

LADY BRACKNELL. A country house! How many bedrooms? Well, that point can be cleared up afterwards. You have a town house, I hope? A girl with a simple, un-spoiled nature, like Gwendolen, could hardly be expected to reside in the country.

JACK. Well, I own a house in Belgrave Square, but it is let by the year to Lady Bloxham. Of course, I can get it back whenever I like, at six months' notice.

LADY BRACKNELL. Lady Bloxham? I don't know her.

JACK. Oh, she goes about very little. She is a lady considerably advanced in years.

LADY BRACKNELL. Ah, nowadays that is no guarantee of respectability of character. What number in Belgrave Square?

JACK. 149.

LADY BRACKNELL. (*Shaking her head.*) The unfashionable side. I thought there was something. However, that could easily be altered.

JACK. Do you mean the fashion, or the side?

LADY BRACKNELL. (*Sternly.*) Both, if necessary, I presume. What are your politics?

JACK. Well, I am afraid I really have none. I am a Liberal Unionist.

LADY BRACKNELL. Oh, they count as Tories. They dine with us. Or come in the evening, at any rate. Now to minor matters. Are your parents living?

JACK. I have lost both my parents.

LADY BRACKNELL. To lose one parent, Mr. Worthing, may be regarded as a misfortune; to lose both looks like carelessness. Who was your father? He was evidently a man of some wealth. Was he born in what the Radical papers call the purple of commerce, or did he rise from the ranks of the aristocracy?

JACK. I am afraid I really don't know. The fact is, Lady Bracknell, I said I had lost my parents. It would be nearer the truth to say that my parents seem to have lost me. . . . I don't actually know who I am by birth. I was . . . well, I was found.

LADY BRACKNELL. Found!

JACK. The late Mr. Thomas Cardew, an old gentleman of a very charitable and kindly disposition, found me, and gave me the name of Worthing, because he happened to have a first-class ticket for Worthing in his pocket at the time. Worthing is a place in Sussex. It is a seaside resort.

LADY BRACKNELL. Where did the charitable gentleman who had a first-class ticket for this seaside resort find you?

JACK. (*Gravely.*)   In a handbag.

LADY BRACKNELL.   A handbag?

JACK. (*Very seriously.*)   Yes, Lady Bracknell. I was in a handbag—a somewhat large, black leather handbag, with handles to it —an ordinary handbag in fact.

LADY BRACKNELL.   In what locality did this Mr. James, or Thomas, Cardew come across this ordinary handbag?

JACK.   In the cloakroom at Victoria Station. It was given to him in mistake for his own.

LADY BRACKNELL.   The cloakroom at Victoria Station?

JACK.   Yes. The Brighton line.

LADY BRACKNELL.   The line is immaterial. Mr. Worthing, I confess I feel somewhat bewildered by what you have just told me. To be born, or at any rate bred, in a handbag, whether it had handles or not, seems to me to display a contempt for the ordinary decencies of family life that reminds one of the worst excesses of the French Revolution. And I presume you know what that unfortunate movement led to? As for the particular locality in which the handbag was found, a cloakroom at a railway station might serve to conceal a social indiscretion —has probably, indeed, been used for that purpose before now—but it could hardly be regarded as an assured basis for a recognized position in good society.

JACK.   May I ask you then what you would advise me to do? I need hardly say I would do anything in the world to ensure Gwendolen's happiness.

LADY BRACKNELL.   I would strongly advise you, Mr. Worthing, to try and acquire some relations as soon as possible, and to make a definite effort to produce at any rate one parent, of either sex, before the season is quite over.

JACK.   Well, I don't see how I could possibly manage to do that. I can produce the handbag at any moment. It is in my dressing-room at home. I really think that should satisfy you, Lady Bracknell.

LADY BRACKNELL.   Me, sir! What has it to do with me? You can hardly imagine that I and Lord Bracknell would dream of allowing our only daughter—a girl brought up with the utmost care—to marry into a cloakroom, and form an alliance with a parcel. Good morning, Mr. Worthing!

(LADY BRACKNELL *sweeps out in majestic indignation.*)

JACK.   Good morning! (ALGERNON, *from the other room, strikes up the Wedding March.* JACK *looks perfectly furious, and goes to the door.*)   For goodness' sake don't play that ghastly tune, Algy! How idiotic you are!

(*The music stops and* ALGERNON *enters cheerily.*)

ALGERNON.   Didn't it go off all right, old boy? You don't mean to say Gwendolen refused you? I know it is a way she has. She is always refusing people. I think it is most ill-natured of her.

JACK.   Oh, Gwendolen is as right as a trivet. As far as she is concerned, we are engaged. Her mother is perfectly unbearable. Never met such a Gorgon. . . . I don't really know what a Gorgon is like, but I am quite sure that Lady Bracknell is one. In any case, she is a monster, without being a myth, which is rather unfair. . . . I beg your pardon, Algy, I suppose I shouldn't talk about your own aunt in that way before you.

ALGERNON.   My dear boy, I love hearing my relations abused. It is the only thing that makes me put up with them at all. Relations are simply a tedious pack of people, who haven't got the remotest knowledge of how to live, nor the smallest instinct about when to die.

JACK.   Oh, that is nonsense!

ALGERNON.   It isn't!

JACK.   Well, I won't argue about the matter. You always want to argue about things.

ALGERNON.   That is exactly what things were originally made for.

JACK.   Upon my word, if I thought that, I'd shoot myself. . . . (*A pause.*)   You don't think there is any chance of Gwendolen becoming like her mother in about a hundred and fifty years, do you, Algy?

ALGERNON.   All women become like their mothers. That is their tragedy. No man does. That's his.

JACK.   Is that clever?

ALGERNON.   It is perfectly phrased! and quite as true as any observation in civilized life should be.

JACK.   I am sick to death of cleverness. Everybody is clever nowadays. You can't go anywhere without meeting clever people.

The thing has become an absolute public nuisance. I wish to goodness we had a few fools left.

ALGERNON.   We have.

JACK.   I should extremely like to meet them. What do they talk about?

ALGERNON.   The fools? Oh! about the clever people, of course.

JACK.   What fools.

ALGERNON.   By the way, did you tell Gwendolen the truth about your being Ernest in town, and Jack in the country?

JACK.   (*In a very patronizing manner*.) My dear fellow, the truth isn't quite the sort of thing one tells to a nice, sweet, refined girl. What extraordinary ideas you have about the way to behave to a woman!

ALGERNON.   The only way to behave to a woman is to make love to her, if she is pretty, and to someone else, if she is plain.

JACK.   Oh, that is nonsense.

ALGERNON.   What about your brother? What about the profligate Ernest?

JACK.   Oh, before the end of the week I shall have got rid of him. I'll say he died in Paris of apoplexy. Lots of people die of apoplexy, quite suddenly, don't they?

ALGERNON.   Yes, but it's hereditary, my dear fellow. It's a sort of thing that runs in families. You had much better say a severe chill.

JACK.   You are sure a severe chill isn't hereditary, or anything of that kind?

ALGERNON.   Of course it isn't!

JACK.   Very well, then. My poor brother Ernest is carried off suddenly, in Paris, by a severe chill. That gets rid of him.

ALGERNON.   But I thought you said that . . . Miss Cardew was a little too much interested in your poor brother Ernest? Won't she feel his loss a good deal?

JACK.   Oh, that is all right. Cecily is not a silly romantic girl, I am glad to say. She has got a capital appetite, goes long walks, and pays no attention at all to her lessons.

ALGERNON.   I would rather like to see Cecily.

JACK.   I will take very good care you never do. She is excessively pretty, and she is only just eighteen.

ALGERNON.   Have you told Gwendolen yet that you have an excessively pretty ward who is only just eighteen?

JACK.   Oh! one doesn't blurt these things out to people. Cecily and Gwendolen are perfectly certain to be extremely great friends. I'll bet you anything you like that half an hour after they have met, they will be calling each other sister.

ALGERNON.   Women only do that when they have called each other a lot of other things first. Now, my dear boy, if we want to get a good table at Willis's, we really must go and dress. Do you know it is nearly seven?

JACK.   (*Irritably*.)   Oh! it always is nearly seven.

ALGERNON.   I'm hungry.

JACK.   I never knew you when you weren't. . . .

ALGERNON.   What shall we do after dinner? Go to a theatre?

JACK.   Oh no! I loathe listening.

ALGERNON.   Well, let us go to the Club?

JACK.   Oh, no! I hate talking.

ALGERNON.   Well, we might trot round to the Empire at ten?

JACK.   Oh, no! I can't bear looking at things. It is so silly.

ALGERNON.   Well, what shall we do?

JACK.   Nothing!

ALGERNON.   It is awfully hard work doing nothing. However, I don't mind hard work where there is no definite object of any kind.

(*Enter* LANE.)

LANE.   Miss Fairfax.

(*Enter* GWENDOLEN. LANE *goes out*.)

ALGERNON.   Gwendolen, upon my word!

GWENDOLEN.   Algy, kindly turn your back. I have something very particular to say to Mr. Worthing.

ALGERNON.   Really, Gwendolen, I don't think I can allow this at all.

GWENDOLEN.   Algy, you always adopt a strictly immoral attitude towards life. You are not quite old enough to do that. (ALGERNON *retires to the fireplace*.)

JACK.   My own darling!

GWENDOLEN.   Ernest, we may never be married. From the expression on mamma's face I fear we never shall. Few parents nowadays pay any regard to what their children say to them. The old-fashioned respect for the young is fast dying out. Whatever influence I ever had over mamma, I lost at the age of three. But although she may prevent us from becoming man and wife, and I may marry someone else, and marry often, nothing that she can possibly do can alter my eternal devotion to you.

JACK. Dear Gwendolen!

GWENDOLEN. The story of your romantic origin, as related to me by mamma, with unpleasing comments, has naturally stirred the deeper fibres of my nature. Your Christian name has an irresistible fascination. The simplicity of your character makes you exquisitely incomprehensible to me. Your town address at the Albany I have. What is your address in the country?

JACK. The Manor House, Woolton, Hertfordshire.

(ALGERNON, *who has been carefully listening, smiles to himself, and writes the address on his shirt-cuff. Then picks up the Railway Guide.*)

GWENDOLEN. There is a good postal service, I suppose? It may be necessary to do something desperate. That of course will require serious consideration. I will communicate with you daily.

JACK. My own one!

GWENDOLEN. How long do you remain in town?

JACK. Till Monday.

GWENDOLEN. Good! Algy, you may turn round now.

ALGERNON. Thanks, I've turned round already.

GWENDOLEN. You may also ring the bell.

JACK. You will let me see you to your carriage, my own darling?

GWENDOLEN. Certainly.

JACK. (*To* LANE, *who now enters.*) I will see Miss Fairfax out.

LANE. Yes, sir. (JACK *and* GWENDOLEN *go off.*)

(LANE *presents several letters on a salver to* ALGERNON. *It is to be surmised that they are bills, as* ALGERNON, *after looking at the envelopes, tears them up.*)

ALGERNON. A glass of sherry, Lane.

LANE. Yes, sir.

ALGERNON. To-morrow, Lane, I'm going Bunburying.

LANE. Yes, sir.

ALGERNON. I shall probably not be back till Monday. You can put up my dress clothes, my smoking jacket, and all the Bunbury suits . . . .

LANE. Yes, sir. (*Handing sherry.*)

ALGERNON. I hope to-morrow will be a fine day, Lane.

LANE. It never is, sir.

ALGERNON. Lane, you're a perfect pessimist.

LANE. I do my best to give satisfaction, sir.

(*Enter* JACK. LANE *goes off.*)

JACK. There's a sensible, intellectual girl! the only girl I ever cared for in my life. (ALGERNON *is laughing immoderately.*) What on earth are you so amused at?

ALGERNON. Oh, I'm a little anxious about poor Bunbury, that is all.

JACK. If you don't take care, your friend Bunbury will get you into a serious scrape some day.

ALGERNON. I love scrapes. They are the only things that are never serious.

JACK. Oh, that's nonsense, Algy. You never talk anything but nonsense.

ALGERNON. Nobody ever does.

(JACK *looks indignantly at him, and leaves the room.* ALGERNON *lights a cigarette, reads his shirt-cuff, and smiles.*)

ACT II

SCENE: *Garden at the Manor House. A flight of gray stone steps leads up to the house. The garden, an old-fashioned one, full of roses. Time of year, July. Basket chairs, and a table covered with books, are set under a large yew-tree.*

(MISS PRISM *discovered seated at the table.* CECILY *is at the back, watering flowers.*)

MISS PRISM. (*Calling.*) Cecily, Cecily! Surely such a utilitarian occupation as the watering of flowers is rather Moulton's duty than yours? Especially at a moment when intellectual pleasures await you. Your German grammar is on the table. Pray open it at page fifteen. We will repeat yesterday's lesson.

CECILY. (*Coming over very slowly.*) But I don't like German. It isn't at all a becoming language. I know perfectly well that I look quite plain after my German lesson.

MISS PRISM. Child, you know how anxious your guardian is that you should improve yourself in every way. He laid particular stress on your German, as he was leaving for town yesterday. Indeed, he always lays stress on your German when he is leaving for town.

CECILY. Dear Uncle Jack is so very serious! Sometimes he is so serious that I think he cannot be quite well.

MISS PRISM. (*Drawing herself up.*) Your guardian enjoys the best of health, and his gravity of demeanour is especially to be commended in one so comparatively young as he is. I know no one who has a higher sense of duty and responsibility.

CECILY. I suppose that is why he often looks a little bored when we three are together.

MISS PRISM. Cecily! I am surprised at you. Mr. Worthing has many troubles in his life. Idle merriment and triviality would be out of place in his conversation. You must remember his constant anxiety about that unfortunate young man his brother.

CECILY. I wish Uncle Jack would allow that unfortunate young man, his brother, to come down here sometimes. We might have a good influence over him, Miss Prism. I am sure you certainly would. You know German, and geology, and things of that kind influence a man very much. (CECILY *begins to write in her diary.*)

MISS PRISM. (*Shaking her head.*) I do not think that even I could produce any effect on a character that according to his own brother's admission is irretrievably weak and vacillating. Indeed I am not sure that I would desire to reclaim him. I am not in favour of this modern mania for turning bad people into good people at a moment's notice. As a man sows so let him reap. You must put away your diary, Cecily. I really don't see why you should keep a diary at all.

CECILY. I keep a diary in order to enter the wonderful secrets of my life. If I didn't write them down, I should probably forget all about them.

MISS PRISM. Memory, my dear Cecily, is the diary that we all carry about with us.

CECILY. Yes, but it usually chronicles the things that have never happened, and couldn't possibly have happened. I believe that Memory is responsible for nearly all the three-volume novels that Mudie sends us.

MISS PRISM. Do not speak slightingly of the three-volume novel, Cecily. I wrote one myself in earlier days.

CECILY. Did you really, Miss Prism? How wonderfully clever you are! I hope it did not end happily? I don't like novels that end happily. They depress me so much.

MISS PRISM. The good ended happily, and the bad unhappily. That is what Fiction means.

CECILY. I suppose so. But it seems very unfair. And was your novel ever published?

MISS PRISM. Alas! no. The manuscript unfortunately was abandoned. (CECILY *starts.*) I used the word in the sense of lost or mislaid. To your work, child, these speculations are profitless.

CECILY. (*Smiling.*) But I see dear Dr. Chasuble coming up through the garden.

MISS PRISM. (*Rising and advancing.*) Dr. Chasuble! This is indeed a pleasure.

(*Enter* CANON CHASUBLE.)

CHASUBLE. And how are we this morning? Miss Prism, you are, I trust, well?

CECILY. Miss Prism has just been complaining of a slight headache. I think it would do her so much good to have a short stroll with you in the Park, Dr. Chasuble.

MISS PRISM. Cecily, I have not mentioned anything about a headache.

CECILY. No, dear Miss Prism, I know that, but I felt instinctively that you had a headache. Indeed I was thinking about that, and not about my German lesson, when the Rector came in.

CHASUBLE. I hope, Cecily, you are not inattentive.

CECILY. Oh, I am afraid I am.

CHASUBLE. That is strange. Were I fortunate enough to be Miss Prism's pupil, I would hang upon her lips. (MISS PRISM *glares.*) I spoke metaphorically.—My metaphor was drawn from bees. Ahem! Mr. Worthing, I suppose, has not returned from town yet?

MISS PRISM. We do not expect him till Monday afternoon.

CHASUBLE. Ah yes, he usually likes to spend his Sunday in London. He is not one of those whose sole aim is enjoyment, as, by all accounts, that unfortunate young man his brother seems to be. But I must not disturb Egeria and her pupil any longer.

MISS PRISM. Egeria? My name is Laetitia, Doctor.

CHASUBLE. (*Bowing.*) A classical allusion merely, drawn from the Pagan authors. I shall see you both no doubt at Evensong?

MISS PRISM. I think, dear Doctor, I will have

a stroll with you. I find I have a headache after all, and a walk might do it good.

CHASUBLE.   With pleasure, Miss Prism, with pleasure. We might go as far as the schools and back.

MISS PRISM.   That would be delightful. Cecily, you will read your Political Economy in my absence. The chapter on the Fall of the Rupee you may omit. It is somewhat too sensational. Even these metallic problems have their melodramatic side.

(*Goes down the garden with* DR. CHASUBLE.)

CECILY. (*Picks up books and throws them back on table.*) Horrid Political Economy! Horrid Geography! Horrid, horrid German!

(*Enter* MERRIMAN *with a card on a salver.*)

MERRIMAN.   Mr. Ernest Worthing has just driven over from the station. He has brought his luggage with him.

CECILY. (*Takes the card and reads it.*)   "Mr. Ernest Worthing, B.4, The Albany, W." Uncle Jack's brother! Did you tell him Mr. Worthing was in town?

MERRIMAN.   Yes, Miss. He seemed very much disappointed. I mentioned that you and Miss Prism were in the garden. He said he was anxious to speak to you privately for a moment.

CECILY.   Ask Mr. Ernest Worthing to come here. I suppose you had better talk to the housekeeper about a room for him.

MERRIMAN.   Yes, Miss. (MERRIMAN *goes off.*)

CECILY.   I have never met any really wicked person before. I feel rather frightened. I am so afraid he will look just like everyone else.

(*Enter* ALGERNON, *very gay and debonair.*)

He does!

ALGERNON. (*Raising his hat.*)   You are my little cousin Cecily, I'm sure.

CECILY.   You are under some strange mistake. I am not little. In fact, I believe I am more than usually tall for my age. (ALGERNON *is rather taken aback.*) But I am your cousin Cecily. You, I see from your card, are Uncle Jack's brother, my cousin Ernest, my wicked cousin Ernest.

ALGERNON.   Oh! I am not really wicked at all, cousin Cecily. You mustn't think that I am wicked.

CECILY.   If you are not, then you have certainly been deceiving us all in a very in-excusable manner. I hope you have not been leading a double life, pretending to be wicked and being really good all the time. That would be hypocrisy.

ALGERNON. (*Looks at her in amazement.*)   Oh! Of course I have been rather reckless.

CECILY.   I am glad to hear it.

ALGERNON.   In fact, now you mention the subject, I have been very bad in my own small way.

CECILY.   I don't think you should be so proud of that, though I am sure it must have been very pleasant.

ALGERNON.   It is much pleasanter being here with you.

CECILY.   I can't understand how you are here at all. Uncle Jack won't be back till Monday afternoon.

ALGERNON.   That is a great disappointment. I am obliged to go up by the first train on Monday morning. I have a business appointment that I am anxious . . . to miss!

CECILY.   Couldn't you miss it anywhere but in London?

ALGERNON.   No: the appointment is in London.

CECILY.   Well, I know, of course, how important it is not to keep a business engagement, if one wants to retain any sense of the beauty of life, but still I think you had better wait till Uncle Jack arrives. I know he wants to speak to you about your emigrating.

ALGERNON.   About my what?

CECILY.   Your emigrating. He has gone up to buy your outfit.

ALGERNON.   I certainly wouldn't let Jack buy my outfit. He has no taste in neckties at all.

CECILY.   I don't think you will require neckties. Uncle Jack is sending you to Australia.

ALGERNON.   Australia! I'd sooner die.

CECILY.   Well, he said at dinner on Wednesday night, that you would have to choose between this world, the next world, and Australia.

ALGERNON.   Oh, well! The accounts I have received of Australia and the next world are not particularly encouraging. This world is good enough for me, cousin Cecily.

CECILY.   Yes, but are you good enough for it?

ALGERNON.   I'm afraid I'm not that. That is

why I want you to reform me. You might make that your mission, if you don't mind, cousin Cecily.

CECILY. I'm afraid I've not time, this afternoon.

ALGERNON. Well, would you mind my reforming myself this afternoon?

CECILY. It is rather Quixotic of you. But I think you should try.

ALGERNON. I will. I feel better already.

CECILY. You are looking a little worse.

ALGERNON. That is because I am hungry.

CECILY. How thoughtless of me. I should have remembered that when one is going to lead an entirely new life, one requires regular and wholesome meals. Won't you come in?

ALGERNON. Thank you. Might I have a buttonhole first? I have never any appetite unless I have a buttonhole first.

CECILY. A Maréchal Niel? (*Picks up scissors.*)

ALGERNON. No, I'd sooner have a pink rose.

CECILY. Why? (*Cuts a flower.*)

ALGERNON. Because you are like a pink rose, cousin Cecily.

CECILY. I don't think it can be right for you to talk to me like that. Miss Prism never says such things to me.

ALGERNON. Then Miss Prism is a shortsighted old lady. (CECILY *puts the rose in his buttonhole.*) You are the prettiest girl I ever saw.

CECILY. Miss Prism says that all good looks are a snare.

ALGERNON. They are a snare that every sensible man would like to be caught in.

CECILY. Oh, I don't think I would care to catch a sensible man. I shouldn't know what to talk to him about.

(*They pass into the house.* MISS PRISM *and* DR. CHASUBLE *return.*)

MISS PRISM. You are too much alone, dear Dr. Chasuble. You should get married. A misanthrope I can understand—a womanthrope, never!

CHASUBLE. (*With a scholar's shudder.*) Believe me, I do not deserve so neologistic a phrase. The precept as well as the practice of the Primitive Church was distinctly against matrimony.

MISS PRISM. (*Sententiously.*) That is ob-viously the reason why the Primitive Church has not lasted up to the present day. And you do not seem to realize, dear Doctor, that by persistently remaining single, a man converts himself into a permanent public temptation. Men should be more careful; this very celibacy leads weaker vessels astray.

CHASUBLE. But is a man not equally attractive when married?

MISS PRISM. No married man is ever attractive except to his wife.

CHASUBLE. And often, I've been told, not even to her.

MISS PRISM. That depends on the intellectual sympathies of the woman. Maturity can always be depended on. Ripeness can be trusted. Young women are green. (DR. CHASUBLE *starts.*) I spoke horticulturally. My metaphor was drawn from fruits. But where is Cecily?

CHASUBLE. Perhaps she followed us to the schools.

(*Enter* JACK *slowly from the back of the garden. He is dressed in the deepest mourning, with crepe hatband and black gloves.*)

MISS PRISM. Mr. Worthing!

CHASUBLE. Mr. Worthing?

MISS PRISM. This is indeed a surprise. We did not look for you till Monday afternoon.

JACK. (*Shakes* MISS PRISM'S *hands in a tragic manner.*) I have returned sooner than I expected. Dr. Chasuble, I hope you are well?

CHASUBLE. Dear Mr. Worthing, I trust this garb of woe does not betoken some terrible calamity?

JACK. My brother.

MISS PRISM. More shameful debts and extravagance?

CHASUBLE. Still leading his life of pleasure?

JACK. (*Shaking his head.*) Dead!

CHASUBLE. Your brother Ernest dead?

JACK. Quite dead.

MISS PRISM. What a lesson for him! I trust he will profit by it.

CHASUBLE. Mr. Worthing, I offer you my sincere condolence. You have at least the consolation of knowing that you were always the most generous and forgiving of brothers.

JACK. Poor Ernest! He had many faults, but it is a sad, sad blow.

CHASUBLE.   Very sad indeed. Were you with him at the end?

JACK.   No. He died abroad; in Paris, in fact. I had a telegram last night from the manager of the Grand Hotel.

CHASUBLE.   Was the cause of death mentioned?

JACK.   A severe chill, it seems.

MISS PRISM.   As a man sows, so shall he reap.

CHASUBLE.   (*Raising his hand.*)   Charity, dear Miss Prism, charity! None of us are perfect. I myself am peculiarly susceptible to draughts. Will the interment take place here?

JACK.   No. He seems to have expressed a desire to be buried in Paris.

CHASUBLE.   In Paris! (*Shakes his head.*)   I fear that hardly points to any very serious state of mind at the last. You would no doubt wish me to make some slight allusion to this tragic domestic affliction next Sunday. (JACK *presses his hand convulsively.*) My sermon on the meaning of the manna in the wilderness can be adapted to almost any occasion, joyful, or, as in the present case, distressing. (*All sigh.*) I have preached it at harvest celebrations, christenings, confirmations, on days of humiliation and festal days. The last time I delivered it was in the Cathedral, as a charity sermon on behalf of the Society for the Prevention of Discontent among the Upper Orders. The Bishop, who was present, was much struck by some of the analogies I drew.

JACK.   Ah! that reminds me, you mentioned christenings I think, Dr. Chasuble? I suppose you know how to christen all right? (DR. CHASUBLE *looks astounded.*) I mean, of course, you are continually christening, aren't you?

MISS PRISM.   It is, I regret to say, one of the Rector's most constant duties in this parish. I have often spoken to the poorer classes on the subject. But they don't seem to know what thrift is.

CHASUBLE.   But is there any particular infant in whom you are interested, Mr. Worthing? Your brother was, I believe, unmarried, was he not?

JACK.   Oh yes.

MISS PRISM.   (*Bitterly.*)   People who live entirely for pleasure usually are.

JACK.   But it is not for any child, dear Doctor. I am very fond of children. No! the fact is, I would like to be christened myself, this afternoon, if you have nothing better to do.

CHASUBLE.   But surely, Mr. Worthing, you have been christened already?

JACK.   I don't remember anything about it.

CHASUBLE.   But have you any grave doubts on the subject?

JACK.   I certainly intend to have. Of course I don't know if the thing would bother you in any way, or if you think I am a little too old now.

CHASUBLE.   Not at all. The sprinkling, and, indeed, the immersion of adults is a perfectly canonical practice.

JACK.   Immersion!

CHASUBLE.   You need have no apprehensions. Sprinkling is all that is necessary, or indeed I think advisable. Our weather is so changeable. At what hour would you wish the ceremony performed?

JACK.   Oh, I might trot round about five if that would suit you.

CHASUBLE.   Perfectly, perfectly! In fact I have two similar ceremonies to perform at that time. A case of twins that occurred recently in one of the outlying cottages on your own estate. Poor Jenkins the carter, a most hardworking man.

JACK.   Oh! I don't see much fun in being christened along with other babies. It would be childish. Would half-past five do?

CHASUBLE.   Admirably! Admirably! (*Takes out watch.*)   And now, dear Mr. Worthing, I will not intrude any longer into a house of sorrow. I would merely beg you not to be too much bowed down by grief. What seem to us bitter trials are often blessings in disguise.

MISS PRISM.   This seems to me a blessing of an extremely obvious kind.

(*Enter* CECILY *from the house.*)

CECILY.   Uncle Jack! Oh, I am pleased to see you back. But what horrid clothes you have got on. Do go and change them.

MISS PRISM.   Cecily!

CHASUBLE.   My child! my child. (CECILY *goes towards* JACK; *he kisses her brow in a melancholy manner.*)

CECILY.   What is the matter, Uncle Jack? Do look happy! You look as if you had toothache, and I have got such a surprise for you. Who do you think is in the dining-room? Your brother!

JACK. Who?

CECILY. Your brother Ernest. He arrived about half an hour ago.

JACK. What nonsense! I haven't got a brother.

CECILY. Oh, don't say that. However badly he may have behaved to you in the past he is still your brother. You couldn't be so heartless as to disown him. I'll tell him to come out. And you will shake hands with him, won't you, Uncle Jack? (*Runs back into the house.*)

CHASUBLE. These are very joyful tidings.

MISS PRISM. After we had all been resigned to his loss, his sudden return seems to me peculiarly distressing.

JACK. My brother is in the dining-room? I don't know what it all means. I think it is perfectly absurd.

(*Enter* ALGERNON *and* CECILY *hand in hand. They come slowly up to* JACK.)

JACK. Good heavens! (*Motions* ALGERNON *away*.)

ALGERNON. Brother John, I have come down from town to tell you that I am very sorry for all the trouble I have given you, and that I intend to lead a better life in the future. (JACK *glares at him and does not take his hand.*)

CECILY. Uncle Jack, you are not going to refuse your own brother's hand?

JACK. Nothing will induce me to take his hand. I think his coming down here disgraceful. He knows perfectly well why.

CECILY. Uncle Jack, do be nice. There is some good in everyone. Ernest has just been telling me about his poor invalid friend Mr. Bunbury whom he goes to visit so often. And surely there must be much good in one who is kind to an invalid, and leaves the pleasures of London to sit by a bed of pain.

JACK. Oh! he has been talking about Bunbury, has he?

CECILY. Yes, he has told me all about Mr. Bunbury and his terrible state of health.

JACK. Bunbury! Well, I won't have him talk to you about Bunbury or about anything else. It is enough to drive one perfectly frantic.

ALGERNON. Of course I admit that the faults were all on my side. But I must say that I think that Brother John's coldness to me is peculiarly painful. I expected a more enthusiastic welcome, especially considering it is the first time I have come here.

CECILY. Uncle Jack, if you don't shake hands with Ernest I will never forgive you.

JACK. Never forgive me?

CECILY. Never, never, never!

JACK. Well, this is the last time I shall ever do it. (*Shakes hands with* ALGERNON *and glares.*)

CHASUBLE. It's pleasant, is it not, to see so perfect a reconciliation? I think we might leave the two brothers together.

MISS PRISM. Cecily, you will come with us.

CECILY. Certainly, Miss Prism. My little task of reconciliation is over.

CHASUBLE. You have done a beautiful action today, dear child.

MISS PRISM. We must not be premature in our judgments.

CECILY. I feel very happy. (*They all go off except* JACK *and* ALGERNON.)

JACK. You young scoundrel, Algy, you must get out of this place as soon as possible. I don't allow any Bunburying here.

(*Enter* MERRIMAN.)

MERRIMAN. I have put Mr. Ernest's things in the room next to yours, sir. I suppose that is all right?

JACK. What?

MERRIMAN. Mr. Ernest's luggage, sir. I have unpacked it and put it in the room next to your own.

JACK. His luggage?

MERRIMAN. Yes, sir. Three portmanteaus, a dressing-case, two hat-boxes, and a large luncheon-basket.

ALGERNON. I am afraid I can't stay more than a week this time.

JACK. Merriman, order the dog-cart at once. Mr. Ernest has been suddenly called back to town.

MERRIMAN. Yes, sir. (*Goes back into the house.*)

ALGERNON. What a fearful liar you are, Jack. I have not been called back to town at all.

JACK. Yes, you have.

ALGERNON. I haven't heard anyone call me.

JACK. Your duty as a gentleman calls you back.

ALGERNON. My duty as a gentleman has never interfered with my pleasures in the smallest degree.

JACK. I can quite understand that.

ALGERNON. Well, Cecily is a darling.

JACK. You are not to talk of Miss Cardew like that. I don't like it.

ALGERNON. Well, I don't like your clothes. You look perfectly ridiculous in them. Why on earth don't you go up and change? It is perfectly childish to be in deep mourning for a man who is actually staying for a whole week with you in your house as a guest. I call it grotesque.

JACK. You are certainly not staying with me for a whole week as a guest or anything else. You have got to leave . . . by the four-five train.

ALGERNON. I certainly won't leave you so long as you are in mourning. It would be most unfriendly. If I were in mourning you would stay with me, I suppose. I should think it very unkind if you didn't.

JACK. Well, will you go if I change my clothes?

ALGERNON. Yes, if you are not too long. I never saw anybody take so long to dress, and with such little result.

JACK. Well, at any rate, that is better than being always over-dressed as you are.

ALGERNON. If I am occasionally a little over-dressed, I make up for it by being always immensely over-educated.

JACK. Your vanity is ridiculous, your conduct an outrage, and your presence in my garden utterly absurd. However, you have got to catch the four-five, and I hope you will have a pleasant journey back to town. This Bunburying, as you call it, has not been a great success for you.

(*Goes into the house.*)

ALGERNON. I think it has been a great success. I'm in love with Cecily, and that is everything.

(*Enter* CECILY *at the back of the garden. She picks up the can and begins to water the flowers.*) But I must see her before I go, and make arrangements for another Bunbury. Ah, there she is.

CECILY. Oh, I merely came back to water the roses. I thought you were with Uncle Jack.

ALGERNON. He's gone to order the dog-cart for me.

CECILY. Oh, is he going to take you for a nice drive?

ALGERNON. He's going to send me away.

CECILY. Then have we got to part?

ALGERNON. I am afraid so. It's a very painful parting.

CECILY. It is always painful to part from people whom one has known for a very brief space of time. The absence of old friends one can endure with equanimity. But even a momentary separation from anyone to whom one has just been introduced is almost unbearable.

ALGERNON. Thank you.

(*Enter* MERRIMAN.)

MERRIMAN. The dog-cart is at the door, sir.

(ALGERNON *looks appealingly at* CECILY.)

CECILY. It can wait, Merriman . . . for . . . five minutes.

MERRIMAN. Yes, miss.

(*Exit* MERRIMAN.)

ALGERNON. I hope, Cecily, I shall not offend you if I state quite frankly and openly that you seem to me to be in every way the visible personification of absolute perfection.

CECILY. I think your frankness does you great credit, Ernest. If you will allow me, I will copy your remarks into my diary. (*Goes over to table and begins writing in diary.*)

ALGERNON. Do you really keep a diary? I'd give anything to look at it. May I?

CECILY. Oh no. (*Puts her hand over it.*) You see, it is simply a very young girl's record of her own thoughts and impressions, and consequently meant for publication. When it appears in volume form I hope you will order a copy. But pray, Ernest, don't stop. I delight in taking down from dictation. I have reached "absolute perfection." You can go on. I am quite ready for more.

ALGERNON. (*Somewhat taken aback.*) Ahem! Ahem!

CECILY. Oh, don't cough, Ernest. When one is dictating one should speak fluently and not cough. Besides, I don't know how to spell a cough. (*Writes as* ALGERNON *speaks.*)

ALGERNON. (*Speaking very rapidly.*) Cecily, ever since I first looked upon your wonderful and incomparable beauty, I have dared to love you wildly, passionately, devotedly, hopelessly.

CECILY.   I don't think that you should tell me that you love me wildly, passionately, devotedly, hopelessly. Hopelessly doesn't seem to make much sense, does it?

ALGERNON.   Cecily.

(*Enter* MERRIMAN.)

MERRIMAN.   The dog-cart is waiting, sir.

ALGERNON.   Tell it to come round next week, at the same hour.

MERRIMAN.   (*Looks at* CECILY, *who makes no sign.*)   Yes, sir.

(MERRIMAN *retires.*)

CECILY.   Uncle Jack would be very much annoyed if he knew you were staying on till next week, at the same hour.

ALGERNON.   Oh, I don't care about Jack. I don't care for anybody in the whole world but you. I love you, Cecily. You will marry me, won't you?

CECILY.   You silly boy! Of course. Why, we have been engaged for the last three months.

ALGERNON.   For the last three months?

CECILY.   Yes, it will be exactly three months on Thursday.

ALGERNON.   But how did we become engaged?

CECILY.   Well, ever since dear Uncle Jack first confessed to us that he had a younger brother who was very wicked and bad, you of course have formed the chief topic of conversation between myself and Miss Prism. And of course a man who is much talked about is always very attractive. One feels there must be something in him, after all. I daresay it was foolish of me, but I fell in love with you, Ernest.

ALGERNON.   Darling. And when was the engagement actually settled?

CECILY.   On the 14th of February last. Worn out by your entire ignorance of my existence, I determined to end the matter one way or the other, and after a long struggle with myself I accepted you under this dear old tree here. The next day I bought this little ring in your name, and this is the little bangle with the true lover's knot I promised you always to wear.

ALGERNON.   Did I give you this? It's very pretty, isn't it?

CECILY.   Yes, you've wonderfully good taste, Ernest. It's the excuse I've always given for your leading such a bad life. And this is the box in which I keep all your dear letters. (*Kneels at table, opens box, and produces letters tied up with blue ribbon.*)

ALGERNON.   My letters! But, my own sweet Cecily, I have never written you any letters.

CECILY.   You need hardly remind me of that, Ernest. I remember only too well that I was forced to write your letters for you. I wrote always three times a week, and sometimes oftener.

ALGERNON.   Oh, do let me read them, Cecily?

CECILY.   Oh, I couldn't possibly. They would make you far too conceited. (*Replaces box.*) The three you wrote me after I had broken off the engagement are so beautiful, and so badly spelled, that even now I can hardly read them without crying a little.

ALGERNON   But was our engagement ever broken off?

CECILY   Of course it was. On the 22nd of last March. You can see the entry if you like. (*Shows diary.*) "To-day I broke off my engagement with Ernest. I feel it is better to do so. The weather still continues charming."

ALGERNON.   But why on earth did you break it off? What had I done? I had done nothing at all. Cecily, I am very much hurt indeed to hear you broke it off. Particularly when the weather was so charming.

CECILY.   It would hardly have been a really serious engagement if it hadn't been broken off at least once. But I forgave you before the week was out.

ALGERNON   (*Crossing to her, and kneeling.*) What a perfect angel you are, Cecily.

CECILY.   You dear romantic boy. (*He kisses her, she puts her fingers through his hair.*) I hope your hair curls naturally, does it?

ALGERNON.   Yes, darling, with a little help from others.

CECILY.   I am so glad.

ALGERNON.   You'll never break off our engagement again, Cecily?

CECILY.   I don't think I could break it off now that I have actually met you. Besides, of course, there is the question of your name.

ALGERNON.   Yes, of course. (*Nervously.*)

CECILY.   You must not laugh at me, darling, but it had always been a girlish dream of mine to love someone whose name was

Ernest. (ALGERNON *rises*, CECILY *also*.) There is something in that name that seems to inspire absolute confidence. I pity any poor married woman whose husband is not called Ernest.

ALGERNON   But, my dear child, do you mean to say you could not love me if I had some other name?

CECILY.   But what name?

ALGERNON.   Oh, any name you like—Algernon—for instance . . .

CECILY.   But I don't like the name of Algernon.

ALGERNON.   Well, my own dear, sweet, loving little darling, I really can't see why you should object to the name of Algernon. It is not at all a bad name. In fact, it is rather an aristocratic name. Half of the chaps who get into the Bankruptcy Court are called Algernon. But seriously, Cecily . . . (*Moving to her*.) if my name was Algy, couldn't you love me?

CECILY.   (*Rising*.) I might respect you, Ernest, I might admire your character, but I fear that I should not be able to give you my undivided attention.

ALGERNON.   Ahem! Cecily! (*Picking up hat*.) Your Rector here is, I suppose, thoroughly experienced in the practice of all the rites and ceremonials of the Church?

CECILY.   Oh, yes. Dr. Chasuble is a most learned man. He has never written a single book, so you can imagine how much he knows.

ALGERNON.   I must see him at once on a most important christening—I mean on most important business.

CECILY.   Oh!

ALGERNON.   I shan't be away more than half an hour.

CECILY.   Considering that we have been engaged since February the 14th, and that I only met you to-day for the first time, I think it is rather hard that you should leave me for so long a period as half an hour. Couldn't you make it twenty minutes?

ALGERNON.   I'll be back in no time. (*Kisses her and rushes down the garden*.)

CECILY.   What an impetuous boy he is! I like his hair so much. I must enter his proposal in my diary.

(*Enter* MERRIMAN.)

MERRIMAN.   A Miss Fairfax has just called to see Mr. Worthing. On very important business, Miss Fairfax states.

CECILY.   Isn't Mr. Worthing in his library?

MERRIMAN.   Mr. Worthing went over in the Rectory some time ago.

CECILY.   Pray ask the lady to come out here; Mr. Worthing is sure to be back soon. And you can bring tea.

MERRIMAN.   Yes, Miss.

(*Goes out*.)

CECILY.   Miss Fairfax! I suppose one of the many good elderly women who are associated with Uncle Jack in some of his philanthropic work in London. I don't quite like women who are interested in philanthropic work. I think it is so forward of them.

(*Enter* MERRIMAN.)

MERRIMAN.   Miss Fairfax.

(*Enter* GWENDOLEN. *Exit* MERRIMAN.)

CECILY.   (*Advancing to meet her*.) Pray let me introduce myself to you. My name is Cecily Cardew.

GWENDOLEN.   Cecily Cardew? (*Moving to her and shaking hands*.) What a very sweet name! Something tells me that we are going to be great friends. I like you already more than I can say. My first impressions of people are never wrong.

CECILY.   How nice of you to like me so much after we have known each other such a comparatively short time. Pray sit down.

GWENDOLEN.   (*Still standing up*.) I may call you Cecily, may I not?

CECILY.   With pleasure!

GWENDOLEN.   And you will always call me Gwendolen, won't you?

CECILY.   If you wish.

GWENDOLEN.   Then that is all quite settled, is it not?

CECILY.   I hope so. (*A pause. They both sit down together*.)

GWENDOLEN.   Perhaps this might be a favourable opportunity for my mentioning who I am. My father is Lord Bracknell. You have never heard of papa, I suppose?

CECILY.   I don't think so.

GWENDOLEN.   Outside the family circle, papa, I am glad to say, is entirely unknown. I think that is quite as it should be. The home seems to me to be the proper sphere for the man. And certainly once a man begins to neglect his domestic duties he becomes

painfully effeminate, does he not? And I
don't like that. It makes men so very attractive. Cecily, mamma, whose views on
education are remarkably strict, has brought
me up to be extremely short-sighted; it is
part of her system; so do you mind my
looking at you through my glasses?

CECILY. Oh! not at all, Gwendolen. I am
very fond of being looked at.

GWENDOLEN. (*After examining* CECILY *carefully through a lorgnette.*) You are here on
a short visit, I suppose.

CECILY. Oh, no! I live here.

GWENDOLEN. (*Severely.*) Really? Your
mother, no doubt, or some female relative
of advanced years, resides here also?

CECILY. Oh no! I have no mother, nor, in
fact, any relations.

GWENDOLEN. Indeed?

CECILY. My dear guardian, with the assistance of Miss Prism, has the arduous
task of looking after me.

GWENDOLEN. Your guardian?

CECILY. Yes, I am Mr. Worthing's ward.

GWENDOLEN. Oh! It is strange he never
mentioned to me that he had a ward. How
secretive of him! He grows more interesting
hourly. I am not sure, however, that the
news inspires me with feelings of unmixed
delight. (*Rising and going to her.*) I am very
fond of you, Cecily; I have liked you ever
since I met you! But I am bound to state
that now that I know that you are Mr.
Worthing's ward, I cannot help expressing
a wish you were—well, just a little older
than you seem to be—and not quite so very
alluring in appearance. In fact, if I may
speak candidly—

CECILY. Pray do! I think that whenever one
has anything unpleasant to say, one should
always be quite candid.

GWENDOLEN. Well, to speak with perfect
candour, Cecily, I wish that you were fully
forty-two, and more than usually plain for
your age. Ernest has a strong upright
nature. He is the very soul of truth and
honour. Disloyalty would be as impossible
to him as deception. But even men of the
noblest possible moral character are extremely susceptible to the influence of the
physical charms of others. Modern, no less
than Ancient History, supplies us with
many most painful examples of what I refer

to. If it were not so, indeed, History would
be quite unreadable.

CECILY. I beg your pardon, Gwendolen, did
you say Ernest?

GWENDOLEN. Yes.

CECILY. Oh, but it is not Mr. Ernest Worthing who is my guardian. It is his brother—
his elder brother.

GWENDOLEN. (*Sitting down again.*) Ernest
never mentioned to me that he had a
brother.

CECILY. I am sorry to say they have not
been on good terms for a long time.

GWENDOLEN. Ah! that accounts for it. And
now that I think of it I have never heard
any man mention his brother. The subject
seems distasteful to most men. Cecily, you
have lifted a load from my mind. I was
growing almost anxious. It would have
been terrible if any cloud had come across
a friendship like ours, would it not? Of
course you are quite, quite sure that it is
not Mr. Ernest Worthing who is your
guardian?

CECILY. Quite sure. (*A pause.*) In fact, I am
going to be his.

GWENDOLEN. (*Inquiringly.*) I beg your pardon?

CECILY. (*Rather shy and confidingly.*) Dearest
Gwendolen, there is no reason why I should
make a secret of it to you. Our little county
newspaper is sure to chronicle the fact next
week. Mr. Ernest Worthing and I are engaged to be married.

GWENDOLEN. (*Quite politely, rising.*) My
darling Cecily, I think there must be some
slight error. Mr. Ernest Worthing is engaged
to me. The announcement will appear in
the *Morning Post* on Saturday at the latest.

CECILY. (*Very politely, rising.*) I am afraid
you must be under some misconception.
Ernest proposed to me exactly ten minutes
ago. (*Shows diary.*)

GWENDOLEN. (*Examines diary through her
lorgnette carefully.*) It is very curious, for
he asked me to be his wife yesterday afternoon at 5.30. If you would care to verify
the incident, pray do so. (*Produces diary of
her own.*) I never travel without my diary.
One should always have something sensational to read in the train. I am so sorry,
dear Cecily, if it is any disappointment to
you, but I am afraid I have the prior claim.

CECILY. It would distress me more than I can tell you, dear Gwendolen, if it caused you any mental or physical anguish, but I feel bound to point out that since Ernest proposed to you he clearly has changed his mind.

GWENDOLEN. (*Meditatively.*) If the poor fellow has been entrapped into any foolish promise I shall consider it my duty to rescue him at once, and with a firm hand.

CECILY. (*Thoughtfully and sadly.*) Whatever unfortunate entanglement my dear boy may have got into, I will never reproach him with it after we are married.

GWENDOLEN. Do you allude to me, Miss Cardew, as an entanglement? You are presumptuous. On an occasion of this kind it becomes more than a moral duty to speak one's mind. It becomes a pleasure.

CECILY. Do you suggest Miss Fairfax, that I entrapped Ernest into an engagement? How dare you? This is no time for wearing the shallow mask of manners. When I see a spade I call it a spade.

GWENDOLEN. (*Satirically.*) I am glad to say that I have never seen a spade. It is obvious that our social spheres have been widely different.

(*Enter* MERRIMAN, *followed by the footman. He carries a salver, table cloth, and plate stand.* CECILY *is about to retort. The presence of the servants exercises a restraining influence, under which both girls chafe.*)

MERRIMAN. Shall I lay tea here as usual, Miss?

CECILY. (*Sternly, in a calm voice.*) Yes, as usual. (MERRIMAN *begins to clear table and lay cloth. A long pause.* CECILY *and* GWENDOLEN *glare at each other.*)

GWENDOLEN. Are there many interesting walks in the vicinity, Miss Cardew?

CECILY. Oh! yes! a great many. From the top of one of the hills quite close one can see five counties.

GWENDOLEN. Five counties! I don't think I should like that; I hate crowds.

CECILY. (*Sweetly.*) I suppose that is why you live in town?

(GWENDOLEN *bites her lip, and beats her foot nervously with her parasol.*)

GWENDOLEN. (*Looking round.*) Quite a well-kept garden this is, Miss Cardew.

CECILY. So glad you like it, Miss Fairfax.

GWENDOLEN. I had no idea there were any flowers in the country.

CECILY. Oh, flowers are as common here, Miss Fairfax, as people are in London.

GWENDOLEN. Personally I cannot understand how anybody manages to exist in the country, if anybody who is anybody does. The country always bores me to death.

CECILY. Ah! This is what the newspapers call agricultural depression, is it not? I believe the aristocracy are suffering very much from it just at present. It is almost an epidemic amongst them, I have been told. May I offer you some tea, Miss Fairfax?

GWENDOLEN. (*With elaborate politeness.*) Thank you. (*Aside.*) Detestable girl! But I require tea!

CECILY. (*Sweetly.*) Sugar?

GWENDOLEN. (*Superciliously.*) No, thank you. Sugar is not fashionable any more. (CECILY *looks angrily at her, takes up the tongs and puts four lumps of sugar into the cup.*)

CECILY. (*Severely.*) Cake or bread and butter?

GWENDOLEN. (*In a bored manner.*) Bread and butter, please. Cake is rarely seen at the best houses nowadays.

CECILY. (*Cuts a very large slice of cake and puts it on the tray.*) Hand that to Miss Fairfax.

(MERRIMAN *does so, and goes out with footman.* GWENDOLEN *drinks the tea and makes a grimace. Puts down cup at once, reaches out her hand to the bread and butter, looks at it, and finds it is cake. Rises in indignation.*)

GWENDOLEN. You have filled my tea with lumps of sugar, and though I asked most distinctly for bread and butter, you have given me cake. I am known for the gentleness of my disposition, and the extraordinary sweetness of my nature, but I warn you, Miss Cardew, you may go too far.

CECILY. (*Rising.*) To save my poor, innocent, trusting boy from the machinations of any other girl there are no lengths to which I would not go.

GWENDOLEN. From the moment I saw you I distrusted you. I felt that you were false and deceitful. I am never deceived in such matters. My first impressions of people are invariably right.

CECILY. It seems to me, Miss Fairfax, that I am trespassing on your valuable time.

No doubt you have many other calls of a similar character to make in the neighborhood.

(*Enter* JACK.)

GWENDOLEN. (*Catching sight of him.*) Ernest! My own Ernest!

JACK.   Gwendolen! Darling! (*Offers to kiss her.*)

GWENDOLEN. (*Drawing back.*) A moment! May I ask if you are engaged to be married to this young lady? (*Points to* CECILY.)

JACK. (*Laughing.*) To dear little Cecily! Of course not! What could have put such an idea into your pretty little head?

GWENDOLEN.   Thank you. You may! (*Offers her cheek.*)

CECILY. (*Very sweetly.*) I knew there must be some misunderstanding, Miss Fairfax. The gentleman whose arm is at present round your waist is my guardian, Mr. John Worthing.

GWENDOLEN.   I beg your pardon?

CECILY.   This is Uncle Jack.

GWENDOLEN. (*Receding.*) Jack! Oh!

(*Enter* ALGERNON.)

CECILY.   Here is Ernest.

ALGERNON. (*Goes straight over to* CECILY *without noticing anyone else.*) My own love! (*Offers to kiss her.*)

CECILY. (*Drawing back.*) A moment, Ernest! May I ask you—are you engaged to be married to this young lady?

ALGERNON. (*Looking round.*) To what young lady? Good heavens! Gwendolen!

CECILY.   Yes: to good heavens, Gwendolen, I mean to Gwendolen.

ALGERNON. (*Laughing.*) Of course not! What could have put such an idea into your pretty little head?

CECILY.   Thank you. (*Presenting her cheek to be kissed.*) You may. (ALGERNON *kisses her.*)

GWENDOLEN.   I felt there was some slight error, Miss Cardew. The gentleman who is now embracing you is my cousin, Mr. Algernon Moncrieff.

CECILY. (*Breaking away from* ALGERNON.) Algernon Moncrieff! Oh! (*The two girls move towards each other and put their arms round each other's waists as if for protection.*)

CECILY.   Are you called Algernon?

ALGERNON.   I cannot deny it.

CECILY.   Oh!

GWENDOLEN.   Is your name really John?

JACK. (*Standing rather proudly.*) I could deny it if I liked. I could deny anything if I liked. But my name certainly is John. It has been John for years.

CECILY. (*To* GWENDOLEN.) A gross deception has been practised on both of us.

GWENDOLEN.   My poor wounded Cecily!

CECILY.   My sweet wronged Gwendolen!

GWENDOLEN. (*Slowly and seriously.*) You will call me sister, will you not? (*They embrace.* JACK *and* ALGERNON *groan and walk up and down.*)

CECILY. (*Rather brightly.*) There is just one question I would like to be allowed to ask my guardian.

GWENDOLEN.   An admirable idea! Mr. Worthing, there is just one question I would like to be permitted to put to you. Where is your brother Ernest? We are both engaged to be married to your brother Ernest, so it is a matter of some importance to us to know where your brother Ernest is at present.

JACK. (*Slowly and hesitatingly.*) Gwendolen —Cecily—it is very painful for me to be forced to speak the truth. It is the first time in my life that I have ever been reduced to such a painful position, and I am really quite inexperienced in doing anything of the kind. However, I will tell you quite frankly that I have no brother Ernest. I have no brother at all. I never had a brother in my life, and I certainly have not the smallest intention of ever having one in the future.

CECILY. (*Surprised.*) No brother at all?

JACK. (*Cheerily.*) None!

GWENDOLEN. (*Severely.*) Had you never a brother of any kind?

JACK. (*Pleasantly.*) Never. Not even of any kind.

GWENDOLEN.   I am afraid it is quite clear, Cecily, that neither of us is engaged to be married to anyone.

CECILY.   It is not a very pleasant position for a young girl suddenly to find herself in. Is it?

GWENDOLEN.   Let us go into the house. They will hardly venture to come after us there.

CECILY.   No, men are so cowardly, aren't they?

(*They retire into the house with scornful looks.*)

JACK. This ghastly state of things is what you call Bunburying, I suppose?

ALGERNON. Yes, and a perfectly wonderful Bunbury it is. The most wonderful Bunbury I have ever had in my life.

JACK. Well, you've no right whatsoever to Bunbury here.

ALGERNON. That is absurd. One has a right to Bunbury anywhere one chooses. Every serious Bunburyist knows that.

JACK. Serious Bunburyist? Good heavens!

ALGERNON. Well, one must be serious about something, if one wants to have any amusement in life. I happen to be serious about Bunburying. What on earth you are serious about I haven't got the remotest idea. About everything, I should fancy. You have such an absolutely trivial nature.

JACK. Well, the only small satisfaction I have in the whole of this wretched business is that your friend Bunbury is quite exploded. You won't be able to run down to the country quite so often as you used to do, dear Algy. And a very good thing too.

ALGERNON. Your brother is a little off colour, isn't he, dear Jack? You won't be able to disappear to London quite so frequently as your wicked custom was. And not a bad thing either.

JACK. As for your conduct towards Miss Cardew, I must say that your taking in a sweet, simple, innocent girl like that is quite inexcusable. To say nothing of the fact that she is my ward.

ALGERNON. I can see no possible defence at all for your deceiving a brilliant, clever, thoroughly experienced young lady like Miss Fairfax. To say nothing of the fact that she is my cousin.

JACK. I wanted to be engaged to Gwendolen, that is all. I love her.

ALGERNON. Well, I simply wanted to be engaged to Cecily. I adore her.

JACK. There is certainly no chance of your marrying Miss Cardew.

ALGERNON. I don't think there is much likelihood, Jack, of you and Miss Fairfax being united.

JACK. Well, that is no business of yours.

ALGERNON. If it was my business, I wouldn't talk about it. (*Begins to eat muffins.*) It is very vulgar to talk about one's business.

Only people like stockbrokers do that, and then merely at dinner parties.

JACK. How you can sit there, calmly eating muffins when we are in this horrible trouble, I can't make out. You seem to me to be perfectly heartless.

ALGERNON. Well, I can't eat muffins in an agitated manner. The butter would probably get on my cuffs. One should always eat muffins quite calmly. It is the only way to eat them.

JACK. I say it's perfectly heartless your eating muffins at all, under the circumstances.

ALGERNON. When I am in trouble, eating is the only thing that consoles me. Indeed, when I am in really great trouble, as anyone who knows me intimately will tell you, I refuse everything except food and drink. At the present moment I am eating muffins because I am unhappy. Besides, I am particularly fond of muffins. (*Rising.*)

JACK. (*Rising.*) Well, there is no reason why you should eat them all in that greedy way. (*Takes muffins from* ALGERNON.)

ALGERNON. (*Offering tea-cake.*) I wish you would have tea-cake instead. I don't like tea-cake.

JACK. Good heavens! I suppose a man may eat his own muffins in his own garden.

ALGERNON. But you have just said it was perfectly heartless to eat muffins.

JACK. I said it was perfectly heartless of you, under the circumstances. That is a very different thing.

ALGERNON. That may be. But the muffins are the same. (*He seizes the muffin-dish from* JACK.)

JACK. Algy, I wish to goodness you would go.

ALGERNON. You can't possibly ask me to go without having some dinner. It's absurd. I never go without my dinner. No one ever does, except vegetarians and people like that. Besides I have just made arrangements with Dr. Chasuble to be christened at a quarter to six under the name of Ernest.

JACK. My dear fellow, the sooner you give up that nonsense the better. I made arrangements this morning with Dr. Chasuble to be christened myself at 5:30, and I naturally will take the name of Ernest. Gwendolen would wish it. We can't both be christened Ernest. It's absurd. Besides, I have a perfect right to be christened if I like. There is no evidence at all that I have ever been christened by anybody. I should think it extremely probable I never was, and so does Dr. Chasuble. It is entirely different in your case. You have been christened already.

ALGERNON. Yes, but I have not been christened for years.

JACK. Yes, but you have been christened. That is the important thing.

ALGERNON. Quite so. So I know my constitution can stand it. If you are not quite sure about your ever having been christened, I must say I think it rather dangerous your venturing on it now. It might make you very unwell. You can hardly have forgotten that someone very closely connected with you was very nearly carried off this week in Paris by a severe chill.

JACK. Yes, but you said yourself that a severe chill was not hereditary.

ALGERNON. It usen't to be, I know—but I daresay it is now. Science is always making wonderful improvements in things.

JACK. (*Picking up the muffin-dish.*) Oh, that is nonsense; you are always talking nonsense.

ALGERNON. Jack, you are at the muffins again! I wish you wouldn't. There are only two left. (*Takes them.*) I told you I was particularly fond of muffins.

JACK. But I hate tea-cake.

ALGERNON. Why on earth then do you allow tea-cake to be served up for your guests? What ideas you have of hospitality!

JACK. Algernon! I have already told you to go. I don't want you here. Why don't you go!

ALGERNON. I haven't quite finished my tea yet! and there is still one muffin left. (JACK *groans, and sinks into a chair.* ALGERNON *continues eating.*)

ACT III

SCENE: *Drawing-room at the Manor House.*

(GWENDOLEN *and* CECILY *are at the window, looking out into the garden.*)

GWENDOLEN. The fact that they did not follow us at once into the house, as anyone else would have done, seems to me to show that they have some sense of shame left.

CECILY. They have been eating muffins. That looks like repentance.

GWENDOLEN. (*After a pause.*) They don't seem to notice us at all. Couldn't you cough?

CECILY. But I haven't got a cough.

GWENDOLEN. They're looking at us. What effrontery!

CECILY. They're approaching. That's very forward of them.

GWENDOLEN. Let us preserve a dignified silence.

CECILY. Certainly. It's the only thing to do now.

(*Enter* JACK *followed by* ALGERNON. *They whistle some dreadful popular air from a British Opera.*)

GWENDOLEN. This dignified silence seems to produce an unpleasant effect.

CECILY. A most distasteful one.

GWENDOLEN. But we will not be the first to speak.

CECILY. Certainly not.

GWENDOLEN. Mr. Worthing, I have something very particular to ask you. Much depends on your reply.

CECILY. Gwendolen, your common sense is invaluable. Mr. Moncrieff, kindly answer me the following question. Why did you pretend to be my guardian's brother?

ALGERNON. In order that I might have an opportunity of meeting you.

CECILY. (*To* GWENDOLEN.) That certainly seems a satisfactory explanation, does it not?

GWENDOLEN. Yes, dear, if you can believe him.

CECILY. I don't. But that does not affect the wonderful beauty of his answer.

GWENDOLEN. True. In matters of grave importance, style, not sincerity, is the vital thing. Mr. Worthing, what explanation can you offer to me for pretending to have a brother? Was it in order that you might have an opportunity of coming up to town to see me as often as possible?

JACK. Can you doubt it, Miss Fairfax?

GWENDOLEN. I have the gravest doubts upon the subject. But I intend to crush them. This is not the moment for German scepticism. (*Moving to* CECILY.) Their explanations appear to be quite satisfactory, especially Mr. Worthing's. That seems to me to have the stamp of truth upon it.

CECILY.   I am more than content with what Mr. Moncrieff said. His voice alone inspires one with absolute credulity.

GWENDOLEN.   Then you think we should forgive them?

CECILY.   Yes. I mean no.

GWENDOLEN.   True! I had forgotten. There are principles at stake that one cannot surrender. Which of us should tell them? The task is not a pleasant one.

CECILY.   Could we not both speak at the same time?

GWENDOLEN.   An excellent idea! I nearly always speak at the same time as other people. Will you take the time from me?

CECILY.   Certainly. (GWENDOLEN *beats time with uplifted finger.*)

GWENDOLEN and CECILY. (*Speaking together.*) Your Christian names are still an insuperable barrier. That is all!

JACK and ALGERNON. (*Speaking together.*) Our Christian names! Is that all? But we are going to be christened this afternoon.

GWENDOLEN. (*To* JACK.) For my sake you are prepared to do this terrible thing?

JACK.   I am.

CECILY. (*To* ALGERNON.)   To please me you are ready to face this fearful ordeal?

ALGERNON.   I am!

GWENDOLEN.   How absurd to talk of the equality of the sexes! Where questions of self-sacrifice are concerned, men are infinitely beyond us.

JACK.   We are. (*Clasps hands with* ALGERNON.)

CECILY.   They have moments of physical courage of which we women know absolutely nothing.

GWENDOLEN. (*To* JACK.)   Darling!

ALGERNON. (*To* CECILY.)   Darling! (*They fall into each other's arms.*)

(*Enter* MERRIMAN. *When he enters he coughs loudly, seeing the situation.*)

MERRIMAN.   Ahem! Ahem! Lady Bracknell.

JACK.   Good heavens!

(*Enter* LADY BRACKNELL. *The couples separate in alarm. Exit* MERRIMAN.)

LADY BRACKNELL.   Gwendolen! What does this mean?

GWENDOLEN.   Merely that I am engaged to be married to Mr. Worthing, mamma.

LADY BRACKNELL.   Come here. Sit down. Sit down immediately. Hesitation of any kind is a sign of mental decay in the young, of physical weakness in the old. (*Turns to* JACK.) Apprised, sir, of my daughter's sudden flight by her trusty maid, whose confidence I purchased by means of a small coin, I followed her at once by a luggage train. Her unhappy father is, I am glad to say, under the impression that she is attending a more than usually lengthy lecture by the University Extension Scheme on the Influence of a Permanent Income on Thought. I do not propose to undeceive him. Indeed I have never undeceived him on any question. I would consider it wrong. But of course, you will clearly understand that all communication between yourself and my daughter must cease immediately from this moment. On this point, as indeed on all points, I am firm.

JACK.   I am engaged to be married to Gwendolen, Lady Bracknell!

LADY BRACKNELL.   You are nothing of the kind, sir. And now as regards Algernon! . . . Algernon!

ALGERNON.   Yes, Aunt Augusta.

LADY BRACKNELL.   May I ask if it is in this house that your invalid friend Mr. Bunbury resides?

ALGERNON. (*Stammering.*)   Oh! No! Bunbury doesn't live here. Bunbury is somewhere else at present. In fact, Bunbury is dead.

LADY BRACKNELL.   Dead! When did Mr. Bunbury die? His death must have been extremely sudden.

ALGERNON. (*Airily.*)   Oh! I killed Bunbury this afternoon. I mean poor Bunbury died this afternoon.

LADY BRACKNELL.   What did he die of?

ALGERNON.   Bunbury? Oh, he was quite exploded.

LADY BRACKNELL.   Exploded! Was he the victim of a revolutionary outrage? I was not aware that Mr. Bunbury was interested in social legislation. If so, he is well punished for his morbidity.

ALGERNON.   My dear Aunt Augusta, I mean he was found out! The doctors found out that Bunbury could not live, that is what I mean—so Bunbury died.

LADY BRACKNELL.   He seems to have had great confidence in the opinion of his physicians. I am glad, however, that he made up his mind at the last to some definite course of action, and acted under proper medical advice. And now that we have finally got rid of this Mr. Bunbury, may I ask, Mr. Worthing, who is that young person whose hand my nephew Algernon is now holding in what seems to me a peculiarly unnecessary manner?

JACK.   That lady is Miss Cecily Cardew, my ward. (LADY BRACKNELL *bows coldly to* CECILY.)

ALGERNON.   I am engaged to be married to Cecily, Aunt Augusta.

LADY BRACKNELL.   I beg your pardon?

CECILY.   Mr. Moncrieff and I are engaged to be married, Lady Bracknell.

LADY BRACKNELL. (*With a shiver, crossing to the sofa and sitting down.*) I do not know whether there is anything peculiarly exciting in the air of this particular part of Hertfordshire, but the number of engagements that go on seems to me considerably above the proper average that statistics have laid down for our guidance. I think some preliminary inquiry on my part would not be out of place. Mr. Worthing, is Miss Cardew at all connected with any of the larger railway stations in London? I merely desire information. Until yesterday I had no idea that there were any families or persons whose origin was a Terminus. (JACK *looks perfectly furious, but restrains himself.*)

JACK. (*In a cold, clear voice.*) Miss Cardew is the granddaughter of the late Mr. Thomas Cardew of 149 Belgrave Square, S.W.; Gervase Park, Dorking, Surrey; and the Sporran, Fifeshire, N.B.

LADY BRACKNELL.   That sounds not unsatisfactory. Three addresses always inspire confidence, even in tradesmen. But what proof have I of their authenticity?

JACK.   I have carefully preserved the Court Guides of the period. They are open to your inspection, Lady Bracknell.

LADY BRACKNELL. (*Grimly.*) I have known strange errors in that publication.

JACK.   Miss Cardew's family solicitors are Messrs. Markby, Markby, and Markby.

LADY BRACKNELL.   Markby, Markby, and Markby? A firm of the very highest position in their profession. Indeed I am told that one of the Mr. Markby's is occasionally to be seen at dinner parties. So far I am satisfied.

JACK. (*Very irritably.*) How extremely kind of you, Lady Bracknell! I have also in my possession, you will be pleased to hear, certificates of Miss Cardew's birth, baptism whooping cough, registration, vaccination, confirmation, and the measles; both the German and the English variety.

LADY BRACKNELL.   Ah! A life crowded with incident, I see; though perhaps somewhat too exciting for a young girl. I am not myself in favour of premature experiences. (*Rises, looks at her watch.*) Gwendolen! the time approaches for our departure. We have not a moment to lose. As a matter of form, Mr. Worthing, I had better ask you if Miss Cardew has any little fortune?

JACK.   Oh! about a hundred and thirty thousand pounds in the Funds. That is all. Good-bye, Lady Bracknell. So pleased to have seen you.

LADY BRACKNELL. (*Sitting down again.*) A moment, Mr. Worthing. A hundred and thirty thousand pounds! And in the Funds! Miss Cardew seems to me a most attractive young lady, now that I look at her. Few girls of the present day have any really solid qualities, any of the qualities that last, and improve with time. We live, I regret to say, in an age of surfaces. (*To* CECILY.) Come over here, dear. (CECILY *goes across.*) Pretty child! your dress is sadly simple, and your hair seems almost as Nature might have left it. But we can soon alter all that. A thoroughly experienced French maid produces a really marvellous result in a very brief space of time. I remember recommending one to young Lady Lancing, and after three months her own husband did not know her.

JACK.   And after six months nobody knew her.

LADY BRACKNELL. (*Glares at* JACK *for a few moments. Then bends, with a practised smile, to* CECILY.) Kindly turn round, sweet child. (CECILY *turns completely round.*) No, the side view is what I want. (CECILY *presents her profile.*) Yes, quite as I expected. There are distinct social possibilities in your profile. The two weak points in our age are its want of principle and its want of profile. The chin a little higher, dear. Style largely depends on the way the chin is worn. They are worn very high, just at present. Algernon!

ALGERNON. Yes, Aunt Augusta!

LADY BRACKNELL. There are distinct social possibilities in Miss Cardew's profile.

ALGERNON. Cecily is the sweetest, dearest, prettiest girl in the whole world. And I don't care twopence about social possibilities.

LADY BRACKNELL. Never speak disrespectfully of Society, Algernon. Only people who can't get into it do that. (*To* CECILY.) Dear child, of course you know that Algernon has nothing but his debts to depend upon. But I do not approve of mercenary marriages. When I married Lord Bracknell I had no fortune of any kind. But I never dreamed for a moment of allowing that to stand in my way. Well, I suppose I must give my consent.

ALGERNON. Thank you, Aunt Augusta.

LADY BRACKNELL. Cecily, you may kiss me!

CECILY. (*Kisses her.*) Thank you, Lady Bracknell.

LADY BRACKNELL. You may also address me as Aunt Augusta for the future.

CECILY. Thank you, Aunt Augusta.

LADY BRACKNELL. The marriage, I think, had better take place quite soon.

ALGERNON. Thank you, Aunt Augusta.

CECILY. Thank you, Aunt Augusta.

LADY BRACKNELL. To speak frankly, I am not in favour of long engagements. They give people the opportunity of finding out each other's character before marriage, which I think is never advisable.

JACK. I beg your pardon for interrupting you, Lady Bracknell, but this engagement is quite out of the question. I am Miss Cardew's guardian, and she cannot marry without my consent until she comes of age. That consent I absolutely decline to give.

LADY BRACKNELL. Upon what grounds, may I ask? Algernon is an extremely, I may almost say an ostentatiously, eligible young man. He has nothing, but he looks everything. What more can one desire?

JACK. It pains my very much to have to speak frankly to you, Lady Bracknell, about your nephew, but the fact is that I do not approve at all of his moral character. I suspect him of being untruthful. (ALGERNON and CECILY *look at him in indignant amazement.*)

LADY BRACKNELL. Untruthful! My nephew Algernon? Impossible! He is an Oxonian.

JACK. I fear there can be no possible doubt about the matter. This afternoon during my temporary absence in London on an important question of romance, he obtained admission to my house by means of the false pretence of being my brother. Under an assumed name he drank, I've just been informed by my butler, an entire pint bottle of my Perrier-Jouet, Brut, '89; wine I was specially reserving for myself. Continuing his disgraceful deception, he succeeded in the course of the afternoon in alienating the affections of my only ward. He subsequently stayed to tea, and devoured every single muffin. And what makes his conduct all the more heartless is, that he was perfectly well aware from the first that I have no brother, that I never had a brother, and that I don't intend to have a brother, not even of any kind. I distinctly told him so myself yesterday afternoon.

LADY BRACKNELL. Ahem! Mr. Worthing, after careful consideration I have decided entirely to overlook my nephew's conduct to you.

JACK. That is very generous of you, Lady Bracknell. My own decision, however, is unalterable. I decline to give my consent.

LADY BRACKNELL. (*To* CECILY.) Come here, sweet child. (CECILY *goes over.*) How old are you, dear?

CECILY. Well, I am really only eighteen, but I always admit to twenty when I go to evening parties.

LADY BRACKNELL. You are perfectly right in making some slight alteration. Indeed, no woman should ever be quite accurate about her age. It looks so calculating. . . . (*In a meditative manner.*) Eighteen, but admitting to twenty at evening parties. Well, it will not be very long before you are of age and free from the restraints of tutelage. So I don't think your guardian's consent is, after all, a matter of any importance.

JACK. Pray excuse me, Lady Bracknell, for interrupting you again, but it is only fair to tell you that according to the terms of her grandfather's will Miss Cardew does not come legally of age till she is thirty-five.

LADY BRACKNELL. That does not seem to me to be a grave objection. Thirty-five is a very attractive age. London society is full of women of the very highest birth who have, of their own free choice, remained thirty-five for years. Lady Dumbleton is an instance in point. To my own knowledge she has been thirty-five ever since she arrived at the age of forty, which was many years ago now. I see no reason why our dear Cecily should not be even still more attractive at the age you mention than she is at present. There will be a large accumulation of property.

CECILY. Algy, could you wait for me till I was thirty-five?

ALGERNON. Of course I could, Cecily. You know I could.

CECILY. Yes, I felt it instinctively, but I couldn't wait all that time. I hate waiting even five minutes for anybody. It always makes me rather cross. I am not punctual myself, I know, but I do like punctuality in others, and waiting, even to be married, is quite out of the question.

ALGERNON. Then what is to be done, Cecily?

CECILY. I don't know, Mr. Moncrieff.

LADY BRACKNELL. My dear Mr. Worthing, as Miss Cardew states positively that she cannot wait till she is thirty-five—a remark which I am bound to say seems to me to show a somewhat impatient nature—I would beg of you to reconsider your decision.

JACK. But my dear Lady Bracknell, the matter is entirely in your own hands. The moment you consent to my marriage with Gwendolen, I will most gladly allow your nephew to form an alliance with my ward.

LADY BRACKNELL. (*Rising and drawing herself up.*) You must be quite aware that what you propose is out of the question.

JACK. Then a passionate celibacy is all that any of us can look forward to.

LADY BRACKNELL. That is not the destiny I propose for Gwendolen. Algernon, of course, can choose for himself. (*Pulls out her watch.*) Come, dear (GWENDOLEN rises), we have already missed five, if not six, trains. To miss any more might expose us to comment on the platform.

(*Enter DR. CHASUBLE.*)

CHASUBLE. Everything is quite ready for the christenings.

LADY BRACKNELL. The christenings, sir! Is not that somewhat premature?

CHASUBLE. (*Looking rather puzzled, and pointing to* JACK *and* ALGERNON.) Both these gentlemen have expressed a desire for immediate baptism.

LADY BRACKNELL. At their age? The idea is grotesque and irreligious! Algernon, I forbid you to be baptized. I will not hear of such excesses. Lord Bracknell would be highly displeased if he learned that that was the way in which you wasted your time and money.

CHASUBLE. Am I to understand then that there are to be no christenings at all this afternoon?

JACK. I don't think that, as things are now, it would be of much practical value to either of us, Dr. Chasuble.

CHASUBLE. I am grieved to hear such sentiments from you, Mr. Worthing. They savour of the heretical views of the Anabaptists, views that I have completely refuted in four of my unpublished sermons. However, as your present mood seems to be one peculiarly secular, I will return to the church at once. Indeed, I have just been informed by the pew-opener that for the last hour and a half Miss Prism has been waiting for me in the vestry.

LADY BRACKNELL. (*Starting.*) Miss Prism! Did I hear you mention a Miss Prism?

CHASUBLE. Yes, Lady Bracknell. I am on my way to join her.

LADY BRACKNELL. Pray allow me to detain you for a moment. This matter may prove to be one of vital importance to Lord Bracknell and myself. Is this Miss Prism a female of repellent aspect, remotely connected with education?

CHASUBLE. (*Somewhat indignantly.*) She is the most cultivated of ladies, and the very picture of respectability.

LADY BRACKNELL. It is obviously the same person. May I ask what position she holds in your household?

CHASUBLE. (*Severely.*) I am a celibate, madam.

JACK. (*Interposing.*) Miss Prism, Lady Bracknell, has been for the last three years Miss Cardew's esteemed governess and valued companion.

LADY BRACKNELL.   In spite of what I hear of her, I must see her at once. Let her be sent for.

CHASUBLE. (*Looking off.*)   She approaches; she is nigh.

(*Enter* MISS PRISM *hurriedly.*)

MISS PRISM.   I was told you expected me in the vestry, dear Canon. I have been waiting for you there for an hour and three-quarters. (*Catches sight of* LADY BRACKNELL, *who has fixed her with a stony glare.* MISS PRISM *grows pale and quails. She looks anxiously round as if desirous to escape.*)

LADY BRACKNELL. (*In a severe, judicial voice.*) Prism! (MISS PRISM *bows her head in shame.*) Come here, Prism! (MISS PRISM *approaches in a humble manner.*) Prism! Where is that baby? (*General consternation. The* CANON *starts back in horror.* ALGERNON *and* JACK *pretend to be anxious to shield* CECILY *and* GWENDOLEN *from hearing the details of a terrible public scandal.*) Twenty-eight years ago, Prism, you left Lord Bracknell's house, Number 104, Upper Grosvenor Square, in charge of a perambulator that contained a baby of the male sex. You never returned. A few weeks later, through the elaborate investigations of the Metropolitan police, the perambulator was discovered at midnight standing by itself in a remote corner of Bayswater. It contained the manuscript of a three-volume novel of more than usually revolting sentimentality. (MISS PRISM *starts in involuntary indignation.*) But the baby was not there. (*Everyone looks at* MISS PRISM.) Prism! Where is that baby? (*A pause.*)

MISS PRISM.   Lady Bracknell, I admit with shame that I do not know. I only wish I did. The plain facts of the case are these. On the morning of the day you mention, a day that is forever branded on my memory, I prepared as usual to take the baby out in its perambulator. I had also with me a somewhat old, but capacious handbag in which I had intended to place the manuscript of a work of fiction that I had written during my few unoccupied hours. In a moment of mental abstraction, for which I can never forgive myself, I deposited the manuscript in the bassinette and placed the baby in the handbag.

JACK. (*Who has been listening attentively.*)   But where did you deposit the handbag?

MISS PRISM.   Do not ask me, Mr. Worthing.

JACK.   Miss Prism, this is a matter of no small importance to me. I insist on knowing where you deposited the handbag that contained that infant.

MISS PRISM.   I felt it in the cloakroom of one of the larger railway stations in London.

JACK.   What railway station?

MISS PRISM. (*Quite crushed.*)   Victoria. The Brighton line. (*Sinks into a chair.*)

JACK.   I must retire to my room for a moment. Gwendolen, wait here for me.

GWENDOLEN.   If you are not too long, I will wait here for you all my life. (*Exit* JACK *in great excitement.*)

CHASUBLE.   What do you think this means, LADY Bracknell?

LADY BRACKNELL.   I dare not even suspect, Dr. Chasuble. I need hardly tell you that in families of high position strange coincidences are not supposed to occur. They are hardly considered the thing.

(*Noises heard overhead as if someone was throwing trunks about. Everyone looks up.*)

CECILY.   Uncle Jack seems strangely agitated.

CHASUBLE.   Your guardian has a very emotional nature.

LADY BRACKNELL.   This noise is extremely unpleasant. It sounds as if he was having an argument. I dislike arguments of any kind. They are always vulgar, and often convincing.

CHASUBLE. (*Looking up.*)   It has stopped now. (*The noise is redoubled.*)

LADY BRACKNELL.   I wish he would arrive at some conclusion.

GWENDOLEN.   This suspense is terrible. I hope it will last.

(*Enter* JACK *with a handbag of black leather in his hand.*)

JACK. (*Rushing over to* MISS PRISM.)   Is this the handbag, Miss Prism? Examine it carefully before you speak. The happiness of more than one life depends on your answer.

MISS PRISM. (*Calmly.*)   It seems to be mine. Yes, here is the injury it received through the upsetting of a Gower Street omnibus in younger and happier days. Here is the stain on the lining caused by the explosion of a temperance beverage, an incident that occurred at Leamington. And here, on the lock, are my initials. I had forgotten that in an extravagant mood I had had them placed there. The bag is undoubtedly mine. I am delighted to have it so unexpectedly restored to me. It has been a great inconvenience being without it all these years.

JACK. (*In a pathetic voice.*) Miss Prism, more is restored to you than this handbag. I was the baby you placed in it.

MISS PRISM. (*Amazed.*) You?

JACK. (*Embracing her.*) Yes . . . mother!

MISS PRISM. (*Recoiling in indignant astonishment.*) Mr. Worthing. I am unmarried!

JACK. Unmarried! I do not deny that is a serious blow. But after all, who has the right to cast a stone against one who has suffered? Cannot repentance wipe out an act of folly? Why should there be one law for men, and another for women? Mother, I forgive you. (*Tries to embrace her again.*)

MISS PRISM. (*Still more indignant.*) Mr. Worthing, there is some error. (*Pointing to* LADY BRACKNELL.) There is the lady who can tell you who you really are.

JACK. (*After a pause.*) LADY Bracknell, I hate to seem inquisitive, but would you kindly inform me who I am?

LADY BRACKNELL. I am afraid that the news I have to give you will not altogether please you. You are the son of my poor sister, Mrs. Moncrieff, and consequently Algernon's elder brother.

JACK. Algy's elder brother! Then I have a brother after all. I knew I had a brother! I always said I had a brother! Cecily—how could you have ever doubted that I had a brother? (*Seizes hold of* ALGERNON.) Dr. Chasuble, my unfortunate brother. Miss Prism, my unfortunate brother. Gwendolen, my unfortunate brother. Algy, you young scoundrel, you will have to treat me with more respect in the future. You have never behaved to me like a brother in all your life.

ALGERNON. Well, not till to-day, old boy, I admit. I did my best, however, though I was out of practice.

(*Shakes hands.*)

GWENDOLEN. (*To* JACK.) My own! But what own are you? What is your Christian name, now that you have become someone else?

JACK. Good heavens! . . . I had quite forgotten that point. Your decision on the subject of my name is irrevocable, I suppose?

GWENDOLEN. I never change, except in my affections.

CECILY. What a noble nature you have, Gwendolen!

JACK. Then the question had better be cleared up at once. Aunt Augusta, a moment. At the time when Miss Prism left me in the handbag, had I been christened already?

LADY BRACKNELL. Every luxury that money could buy, including christening, had been lavished on you by your fond and doting parents.

JACK. Then I was christened! That is settled. Now, what name was I given? Let me know the worst.

LADY. BRACKNELL. Being the eldest son you were naturally christened after your father.

JACK. (*Irritably.*) Yes, but what was my father's Christian name?

LADY BRACKNELL. (*Meditatively.*) I cannot at the present moment recall what the General's Christian name was. But I have no doubt he had one. He was eccentric, I admit. But only in later years. And that was the result of the Indian climate, and marriage, and indigestion, and other things of that kind.

JACK. Algy! Can't you recollect what our father's Christian name was?

ALGERNON. My dear boy, we were never even on speaking terms. He died before I was a year old.

JACK. His name would appear in the Army Lists of the period, I suppose, Aunt Augusta?

LADY BRACKNELL. The General was essentially a man of peace, except in his domestic life. But I have no doubt his name would appear in any military directory.

JACK. The Army Lists of the last forty years are here. These delightful records should have been my constant study. (*Rushes to bookcase and tears the books out.*) M. Generals. . . Mallam, Maxbohm, Magley—what ghastly names they have—Markby, Migsby, Mobbs, Moncrieff! Lieutenant 1840, Captain, Lieutenant-Colonel, Colonel, General 1869, Christian names, Ernest John. (*Puts book very quietly down and speaks quite calmly.*) I always told you, Gwendolen, my name was Ernest, didn't I? Well, it is Ernest after all. I mean it naturally is Ernest.

LADY BRACKNELL.   Yes, I remember now that the General was called Ernest. I knew I had some particular reason for disliking the name.

GWENDOLEN.   Ernest! My own Ernest! I felt from the first that you could have no other name!

JACK.   Gwendolen, it is a terrible thing for a man to find out suddenly that all his life he has been speaking nothing but the truth. Can you forgive me?

GWENDOLEN.   I can. For I feel that you are sure to change.

JACK.   My own one!

CHASUBLE. (*To* MISS PRISM.) Laetitia! (*Embraces her.*)

MISS PRISM. (*Enthusiastically.*) Frederick! At last!

ALGERNON.   Cecily! (*Embraces her.*) At last!

JACK.   Gwendolen! (*Embraces her.*) At last!

LADY BRACKNELL.   My nephew, you seem to be displaying signs of triviality.

JACK.   On the contrary, Aunt Augusta, I've now realized for the first time in my life the vital Importance of Being Earnest.

FOR ANALYSIS

Act I

1. How does Wilde set the tone and mood of the whole play in the opening dialogue?
2. Where does Wilde use the *aside* early in the play?
3. Explain the pun in the title of the play, as much as you can after reading only the first act.
4. What conventions of polite society are being satirized in the conversations between Jack and Algernon and between Algernon and Lady Bracknell?
5. Do most of the characters speak in a distinctive manner or do they sound quite similar?

Act II

1. What is Wilde satirizing in the conversation of Miss Prism and Canon Chasuble?
2. Does Wilde take advantage of any stage conventions?
3. What is the chief advantage that an acted version of this play would have over a silent reading of

it?

4. One disadvantage of writing witty dialogue is that after every brilliant epigram or joke there comes a dead space, an anticlimax. How does Wilde try to avoid this dead space? How does the fact that this is a play help him avoid it?
5. Most of the sophisticated remarks in the play have two edges. For example, when Miss Prism says of her book, "The good ended happily, and the bad unhappily. That is what fiction means," there is an obvious criticism of fiction in the comment, but what is the major target of that remark?

Act III

1. The play is obviously a *farce*—no attempt is made to keep coincidence, contrivance, and caricature under control. Miss Prism's improbable revelation, for example, is introduced without any preparation, any attempt to make it logical and believable (although it was crudely foreshadowed in Act II). Why is it that this revelation, incredible as it is, does not really seem out of place in the play?
2. The play seems sometimes to exist merely for the sake of its epigrams. But does it not happen finally that the greatest lies are the honest truth in this situation—that Jack really was "earnest" about being "Ernest," even though he didn't know it? Is there another and greater paradox in this than one will find in the epigrams themselves?
3. Do you find the epigrams in the play simply a kind of surface smartness, or is there bitter truth in many of them? Take Jack's last epigram: "Gwendolen, it is a terrible thing for a man to find out suddenly that all his life he has been speaking nothing but the truth. Can you forgive me?" That is clever: is it also perceptive? In what way are these characters being "earnest" when they are being most contrary?

TENNESSEE WILLIAMS

The Glass Menagerie

CHARACTERS

AMANDA WINGFIELD, *the mother.* old aristocra life *A little woman of great but confused vitality clinging frantically to another time and place. Her characterization must be carefully created, not copied from type. She is not paranoiac, but her life is paranoia. There is much to admire in* AMANDA, *and as much to love and pity as there is to laugh at. Certainly she has endurance and a kind of heroism, and though her foolishness makes her unwittingly cruel at times, there is tenderness in her slight person.*

LAURA WINGFIELD, *her daughter.*

AMANDA, *having failed to establish contact with reality, continues to live vitally in her illusions, but* LAURA's *situation is even graver. A childhood illness has left her crippled, one leg slightly shorter than the other, and held in a brace. This defect need not be more than suggested on the stage. Stemming from this,* LAURA's *separation increases till she is like a piece of her own glass collection, too exquisitely fragile to move from the shelf.*

TOM WINGFIELD, *her son, and the narrator of the play. A poet with a job in a warehouse. His nature is not remorseless, but to escape from a trap he has to act without pity.*

JIM O'CONNOR, *the gentleman caller.*
A nice, ordinary, young man.

SCENE

An Alley in St. Louis
PART I.   Preparation for a Gentleman Caller.
PART II.   The Gentleman calls.
Time: Now and the Past.

PRODUCTION NOTES

Being a "memory play," *The Glass Menagerie* can be presented with unusual freedom of convention. Because of its considerably delicate or tenuous material, atmospheric touches and subtleties of direction play a particularly important part. Expressionism and all other unconventional techniques in drama have only one valid aim, and that is a closer approach to truth. When a play employs unconventional techniques, it is not, or certainly shouldn't be, trying to escape its responsibility of dealing with reality, or interpreting experience, but is actually or should be attempting to find a closer approach, a more penetrating and vivid expression of things as they are. The straight realistic play with its genuine frigidaire and authentic ice-cubes, its characters that speak exactly as its audience speaks, corresponds to the academic landscape and has the same virtue of a photographic likeness. Everyone should know nowadays the unimportance of the photographic in art: that truth, life, or reality is an organic thing which the poetic imagination can represent or suggest, in essence, only through transformation, through changing into other forms than those which were merely present in appearance.

These remarks are not meant as a preface only to this particular play. They have to do with a conception of a new, plastic theatre which must take the place of the exhausted theatre of realistic conventions if the theatre is to resume vitality as a part of our culture.

THE SCREEN DEVICE

There is *only one important difference between the original and acting versions of the play* and that is the *omission* in the latter of the device which I tentatively included in my *original* script. This device was the use of a screen on which were projected magic-lantern slides bearing images or titles. I do not regret the omission of this device from the Broadway production. The extraordinary power of Miss Taylor's performance made it suitable to have the utmost simplicity in the physical production. But I think it may be interesting to some readers to see how this device was conceived. So I am putting it into the published manuscript. These images and legends, projected from behind, were cast on a section of wall between the front-room and dining-room areas, which should be indistinguishable from the rest when not in use.

The purpose of this will probably be apparent. It is to give accent to certain values in each scene. Each scene contains a particular point (or several) which is structurally the most important. In an episodic play, such as this, the basic structure or narrative line may be obscured from the audience; the effect may seem fragmentary rather than architectural. This may not be the fault of the play so much as a lack of attention in the audience. The legend or image upon the screen will strengthen the effect of what is merely allusion in the writing and allow the primary point to be made more simply and lightly than if the entire responsibility were on the spoken lines. Aside from this structural value, I think the screen will have a definite emotional appeal, less definable but just as important. An imaginative producer or director may invent many other uses for this device than those indicated in the present script. In fact the possibilities of the device seem much larger to me than the instance of this play can possibly utilize.

THE MUSIC

Another extra-literary accent in this play is provided by the use of music. A single recurring tune, "The Glass Menagerie," is used to give emotional emphasis to suitable passages. This tune is like circus music, not when you are on the grounds or in the immediate vicinity of the parade, but when you are at some distance and very likely thinking of something else. It seems under those circumstances to continue almost interminably and it weaves in and out of your preoccupied consciousness; then it is the lightest, most delicate music in the world and perhaps the saddest. It expresses the surface vivacity of life with the underlying strain of immutable and inexpressible sorrow. When you look at a piece of delicately spun glass you think of two things: how beautiful it is and how easily it can be broken. Both of those ideas should be woven into the recurring tune, which dips in and out of the play as if it were carried on a wind that changes. It serves as a thread of connection and allusion between the narrator with his separate point in time and space and the subject of his story. Between each episode it returns as reference to the emotion, nostalgia, which is the first condition of the play. It is primarily Laura's music and therefore comes out most clearly when the play focuses upon her and the lovely fragility of glass which is her image.

THE LIGHTING

The lighting in the play is not realistic. In keeping with the atmosphere of memory, the stage is dim. Shafts of light are focused on selected areas or actors, sometimes in contradistinction to what is the apparent center. For instance, in the quarrel scene between Tom and Amanda, in which Laura has no active part, the clearest pool of light is on her figure. This is also true of the supper scene, when her silent figure on the sofa should remain the visual center. The light upon Laura should be distinct from the others, having a peculiar pristine clarity such as light used in early religious portraits of female saints or madonnas. A certain correspondence to light in religious paintings, such as El Greco's, where the figures are radiant in atmosphere that is relatively dusky, could be effectively used throughout the play. (It will also permit a more effective use of the screen.) A free, imaginative use of light can be of enormous value in giving a mobile, plastic quality to plays of a more or less static nature.

T.W.

SCENE I

The Wingfield apartment is in the rear of the building, one of those vast hive-like conglomerations of cellular living-units that flower as warty growths in overcrowded urban centers of lower middle-class population and are symptomatic of the impulse of this largest and fundamentally enslaved section of American society to avoid fluidity and differentiation and to exist and function as one interfused mass of automatism.

The apartment faces an alley and is entered by a fire-escape, a structure whose name is a touch of accidental poetic truth, for all of these huge buildings are always burning with the slow and implacable fires of human desperation. The fire-escape is included in the set—that is, the landing of it and steps descending from it.

The scene is memory and is therefore non-realistic. Memory takes a lot of poetic license. It omits some details; others are exaggerated, according to the emotional value of the articles it touches, for memory is seated predominantly in the heart. The interior is therefore rather dim and poetic.

At the rise of the curtain, the audience is faced with the dark, grim rear wall of the Wingfield tenement. This building, which runs parallel to the footlights, is flanked on both sides by dark, narrow alleys which run into murky canyons of tangled clotheslines, garbage cans, and the sinister lattice-work of neighboring fire-escapes. It is up and down these side alleys that exterior entrances and exits are made, during the play. At the end of TOM's *opening commentary, the dark tenement wall slowly reveals (by means of a transparency) the interior of the ground floor Wingfield apartment.*

Downstage is the living room, which also serves as a sleeping room for LAURA, *the sofa unfolding to make her bed. Upstage, center, and divided by a wide arch or second proscenium with transparent faded portieres (or second curtain), is the dining room. In an old-fashioned what-not in the living room are seen scores of transparent glass animals. A blown-up photograph of the father hangs on the wall of the living room, facing the audience, to the left of the archway. It is the face of a very handsome young man in a doughboy's First World War cap. He is gallantly smiling, ineluctably smiling, as if to say, "I will be smiling forever."*

The audience hears and sees the opening scene in the dining room through both the transparent fourth wall of the building and the transparent gauze portiers of the dining-room arch. It is during this revealing scene that the fourth wall slowly ascends, out of sight. This transparent exterior wall is not brought down again until the very end of the play, during TOM'S *final speech.*

The narrator is an undisguised convention of the play. He takes whatever license with dramatic convention is convenient to his purposes.

(TOM *enters dressed as a merchant sailor from alley, stage left, and strolls across the front of the stage to the fire-escape. There he stops and lights a cigarette. He addresses the audience.*)

TOM.   Yes, I have tricks in my pocket, I have things up my sleeve. But I am the opposite of a stage magician. He gives you illusion that has the appearance of truth. I give you truth in the pleasant disguise of illusion.

To begin with, I turn back time. I reverse it to that quaint period, the thirties, when the huge middle class of America was matriculating in a school for the blind. Their eyes had failed them, or they had failed their eyes, and so they were having their fingers pressed forcibly down on the fiery Braille alphabet of a dissolving economy.

In Spain there was revolution. Here there was only shouting and confusion.

In Spain there was Guernica. Here there

were disturbances of labor, sometimes pretty violent, in otherwise peaceful cities such as Chicago, Cleveland, Saint Louis . . .

This is the social background of the play.   (*Music.*)

The play is memory.

Being a memory play, it is dimly lighted, it is sentimental, it is not realistic.

In memory everything seems to happen to music. That explains the fiddle in the wings.

I am the narrator of the play, and also a character in it.

The other characters are my mother, Amanda, my sister, Laura, and a gentleman caller who appears in the final scenes.

He is the most realistic character in the play, being an emissary from a world of reality that we were somehow set apart from.

But since I have a poet's weakness for symbols, I am using this character also as a symbol; he is the long delayed but always expected something that we live for.

There is a fifth character in the play who doesn't appear except in this larger-than-life-size photograph over the mantel.

This is our father who left us a long time ago.

He was a telephone man who fell in love with long distances; he gave up his job with the telephone company and skipped the light fantastic out of town . . .

The last we heard of him was a picture post card from Mazatlan, on the Pacific coast of Mexico, containing a message of two words—

"Hello—— Good-bye!" and no address.

I think the rest of the play will explain itself . . .

(AMANDA'S *voice becomes audible through the portieres.* LEGEND ON SCREEN: "OÙ SONT LES NEIGES?" *He divides the portieres and enters the upstage area.* AMANDA *and* LAURA *are seated at a drop-leaf table. Eating is indicated by gestures without food or utensils.* AMANDA *faces the audience.* TOM *and* LAURA *are seated in profile. The interior has lit up softly and through the scrim we see* AMANDA *and* LAURA *seated at the table in the upstage area.*)

AMANDA.   (*Calling.*) Tom?

TOM.   Yes, Mother.

AMANDA. We can't say grace until you come to the table!

TOM. Coming, Mother.

(*He bows slightly and withdraws, reappearing a few moments later in his place at the table.*)

AMANDA. (*To her son.*) Honey, don't *push* with your *fingers*. If you have to push with something, the thing to push with is a crust of bread. And chew—chew! Animals have sections in their stomachs which enable them to digest food without mastication, but human beings are supposed to chew their food before they swallow it down. Eat food leisurely, son, and really enjoy it. A well-cooked meal has lots of delicate flavors that have to be held in the mouth for appreciation. So chew your food and give your salivary glands a chance to function! (TOM *deliberately lays his imaginary fork down and pushes his chair back from the table.*)

TOM. I haven't enjoyed one bite of this dinner because of your constant directions on how to eat it. It's you that make me rush through meals with your hawk-like attention to every bite I take. Sickening—spoils my appetite—all this discussion of—animals' secretion—salivary glands—mastication!

AMANDA. (*Lightly.*) Temperament like a Metropolitan star! (*He rises and crosses downstage.*) You're not excused from the table.

TOM. I'm getting a cigarette.

AMANDA. You smoke too much.

(LAURA *rises.*)

LAURA. I'll bring in the blanc mange.

(*He remains standing with his cigarette by the portieres during the following.*)

AMANDA. (*Rising.*) No, sister, no, sister—you be the lady this time and I'll be the darky.

LAURA. I'm already up.

AMANDA. Resume your seat, little sister—I want you to stay fresh and pretty—for gentlemen callers!

LAURA. I'm not expecting any gentlemen callers.

AMANDA. (*Crossing out to kitchenette. Airily.*) Sometimes they come when they are least expected! Why, I remember one Sunday afternoon in Blue Mountain—

(*Enters kitchenette.*)

TOM. I know what's coming!

LAURA. Yes. But let her tell it.

TOM. Again?

LAURA. She loves to tell it.

(AMANDA *returns with bowl of dessert.*)

AMANDA. One Sunday afternoon in Blue Mountain—your mother received—*seventeen!*—gentlemen callers! Why, sometimes there weren't chairs enough to accommodate them all. We had to send the nigger over to bring in folding chairs from the parish house.

TOM. (*Remaining at portieres.*) How did you entertain those gentlemen callers?

AMANDA. I understood the art of conversation!

TOM. I bet you could talk.

AMANDA. Girls in those days *knew* how to talk, I can tell you.

TOM. Yes?

(IMAGE: AMANDA AS A GIRL ON A PORCH, GREETING CALLERS.)

AMANDA. They knew how to entertain their gentlemen callers. It wasn't enough for a girl to be possessed of a pretty face and a graceful figure—although I wasn't slighted in either respect. She also needed to have a nimble wit and a tongue to meet all occasions.

TOM. What did you talk about?

AMANDA. Things of importance going on in the world! Never anything coarse or common or vulgar. (*She addresses* TOM *as though he were seated in the vacant chair at the table though he remains by portieres. He plays this scene as though he held the book.*) My callers were gentlemen—all! Among my callers were some of the most prominent young planters of the Mississippi Delta—planters and sons of planters! (TOM *motions for music and a spot of light on* AMANDA. *Her eyes lift, her face glows, her voice becomes rich and elegiac.* SCREEN LEGEND: "OÙ SONT LES NEIGES?")

There was young Champ Laughlin, who later became vice-president of the Delta Planters Bank.

Hadley Stevenson, who was drowned in Moon Lake and left his widow one hundred and fifty thousand in Government bonds.

There were the Cutrere brothers, Wesley

and Bates. Bates was one of my bright particular beaux! He got in a quarrel with that wild Wainwright boy. They shot it out on the floor of Moon Lake Casino. Bates was shot through the stomach. Died in the ambulance on his way to Memphis. His widow was also well-provided for, came into eight or ten thousand acres, that's all. She married him on the rebound—never loved her—carried my picture on him the night he died!

And there was that boy that every girl in the Delta had set her cap for! That beautiful, brilliant young Fitzhugh boy from Greene County!

TOM.   What did he leave his widow?

AMANDA.   He never married! Gracious, you talk as though all of my old admirers had turned up their toes to the daisies!

TOM.   Isn't this the first you've mentioned that still survives?

AMANDA.   That Fitzhugh boy went North and made a fortune—came to be known as the Wolf of Wall Street! He had the Midas touch, whatever he touched turned to gold! And I could have been Mrs. Duncan J. Fitzhugh, mind you! But—I picked your *father*!

LAURA.   (*Rising.*) Mother, let me clear the table.

AMANDA.   No, dear, you go in front and study your typewriter chart. Or practice your shorthand a little. Stay fresh and pretty!—It's almost time for our gentlemen callers · to start arriving. (*She flounces girlishly toward the kitchenette.*) How many do you suppose we're going to entertain this afternoon?

(TOM *throws down the paper and jumps up with a groan.*)

LAURA.   (*Alone in the dining room.*) I don't believe we 're going to receive any, Mother.

AMANDA.   (*Reappearing, airly.*) What? No one—not one? You must be joking! (LAURA *nervously echoes her laugh. She slips in a fugitive manner through the half-open portieres and draws them gently behind her. A shaft of very clear light is thrown on her face against the faded tapestry of the curtains.* MUSIC: "THE GLASS MENAGERIE" UNDER FAINTLY. *Lightly.*) Not one gentleman caller? It can't be true! There must be a flood, there must have been a tornado!

LAURA.   It isn't a flood, it's not a tornado, Mother. I'm just not popular like you were in Blue Mountain. . . . (TOM *utters another groan.* LAURA *glances at him with a faint, apologetic smile. Her voice catching a little.*) Mother's afraid I'm going to be an old maid.

THE SCENE DIMS OUT WITH "GLASS
MENAGERIE" MUSIC.

SCENE II

LEGEND: "LAURA, HAVEN'T YOU EVER LIKED SOME BOY?"

On the dark stage the screen is lighted with the image of blue roses.

Gradually LAURA'S *figure becomes apparent and the screen goes out. The music subsides.* LAURA *is seated in the delicate ivory chair at the small claw-foot table.*

She wears a dress of soft violet material for a kimono—her hair tied back from her forehead with a ribbon.

She is washing and polishing her collection of glass.

(AMANDA *appears on the fire-escape steps. At the sound of her ascent,* LAURA *catches her breath, thrusts the bowl of ornaments away and seats herself stiffly before the diagram of the typewriter keyboard as though it held her spell-bound.*

Something has happened to AMANDA. *It is written in her face as she climbs to the landing: a look that is grim and hopeless and a little absurd.*

She has on one of those cheap or imitation velvety-looking cloth coats with imitation fur collar. Her hat is five or six years old, one of those dreadful cloche hats that were worn in the late twenties, and she is clasping an enormous black patent-leather pocketbook with nickel clasps and initials. This is her full-dress outfit, the one she usually wears to the D.A.R.

Before entering she looks through the door. She purses her lips, opens her eyes very wide, rolls them upward and shakes her head.

Then she slowly lets herself in the door. Seeing her mother's expression LAURA *touches her lips with a nervous gesture.*)

LAURA.   Hello, Mother, I was—

(*She makes a nervous gesture toward the chart on the wall.* AMANDA *leans against the shut door and stares at* LAURA *with a martyred look.*)

AMANDA. Deception? Deception?

(*She slowly removes her hat and gloves, continuing the sweet suffering stare. She lets the hat and gloves fall on the floor—a bit of acting.*)

LAURA. (*Shakily.*) How was the D.A.R. meeting? (AMANDA *slowly opens her purse and removes a dainty white handkerchief which she shakes out delicately and delicately touches to her lips and nostrils.*) Didn't you go to the D.A.R. meeting, Mother?

AMANDA. (*Faintly, almost inaudibly.*)—No. —No. (*Then more forcibly.*) I did not have the strength—to go to the D.A.R. In fact, I did not have the courage! I wanted to find a hole in the ground and hide myself in it forever!

(*She crosses slowly to the wall and removes the diagram of the typewriter keyboard. She holds it in front of her for a second, staring at it sweetly and sorrowfully—then bites her lips and tears it in two pieces.*)

LAURA. (*Faintly.*) Why did you do that, Mother? (AMANDA *repeats the same procedure with the chart of the Gregg Alphabet.*) Why are you—

AMANDA. Why? Why? How old are you, Laura?

LAURA. Mother, you know my age.

AMANDA. I thought that you were an adult; it seems that I was mistaken.

(*She crosses slowly to the sofa and sinks down and stares at* LAURA.)

LAURA. Please don't stare at me, Mother. (AMANDA *closes her eyes and lowers her head. Count ten.*)

AMANDA. What are we going to do, what is going to become of us, what is the future?

(*Count ten.*)

LAURA. Has something happened, Mother? (AMANDA *draws a long breath and takes out the handkerchief again. Dabbing process.*) Mother, has—something happened?

AMANDA. I'll be all right in a minute, I'm just bewildered— (*Count five.*) —by life. . . .

LAURA. Mother, I wish that you would tell me what's happened!

AMANDA. As you know, I was supposed to be inducted into my office at the D.A.R. this afternoon. (IMAGE: A SWARM OF TYPEWRITERS.) But I stopped off at Rubi-

cam's Business College to speak to your teachers about your having a cold and ask them what progress they thought you were making down there.

LAURA. Oh. . . .

AMANDA. I went to the typing instructor and introduced myself as your mother. She didn't know who you were. Wingfield, she said. We don't have any such student enrolled at the school!

I assured her she did, that you had been going to classes since early in January.

"I wonder," she said, "if you could be talking about that terribly shy little girl who dropped out of school after only a few days' attendance?"

"No," I said, "Laura, my daughter, has been going to school every day for the past six weeks!"

"Excuse me," she said. She took the attendance book out and there was your name, unmistakably printed, and all the dates you were absent until they decided that you had dropped out of school.

I still said, "No, there must have been some mistake! There must have been some mix-up in the records!"

And she said, "No—I remember her perfectly now. Her hands shook so that she couldn't hit the right keys! The first time we gave a speed-test, she broke down completely—was sick at the stomach and almost had to be carried into the wash-room! After that morning she never showed up any more. We phoned the house but never got any answer"—while I was working at Famous and Barr, I suppose, demonstrating those——Oh!

I felt so weak I could barely keep on my feet!

I had to sit down while they got me a glass of water!

Fifty dollars' tuition, all of our plans— my hopes and ambitions for you—just gone up the spout, just gone up the spout like that.

(LAURA *draws a long breath and gets awkwardly to her feet. She crosses to the victrola and winds it up.*)

What are you doing?

LAURA. Oh!

(*She releases the handle and returns to her seat.*)

AMANDA. Laura, where have you been going when you've gone out pretending that you were going to business college?

LAURA. I've just been going out walking.

AMANDA. That's not true.

LAURA. It is. I just went walking.

AMANDA. Walking? Walking? In winter? Deliberately courting pneumonia in that light coat? Where did you walk to, Laura?

LAURA. All sorts of places—mostly in the park.

AMANDA. Even after you'd started catching that cold?

LAURA. It was the lesser of two evils, Mother. (IMAGE: WINTER SCENE IN PARK.) I couldn't go back up. I—threw up—on the floor!

AMANDA. From half past seven till after five every day you mean to tell me you walked around the park, because you wanted to make me think that you were still going to Rubicam's Business College?

LAURA. It wasn't as bad as it sounds. I went inside places to get warmed up.

AMANDA. Inside where?

LAURA. I went in the art museum and the bird-houses at the Zoo. I visited the penguins every day! Sometimes I did without lunch and went to the movies. Lately I've been spending most of my afternoons in the Jewel-box, that big glass house where they raise the tropical flowers.

AMANDA. You did all this to deceive me, just for deception? (LAURA looks down.) Why?

LAURA. Mother, when you're disappointed, you get that awful suffering look on your face, like the picture of Jesus' mother in the museum!

AMANDA. Hush!

LAURA. I couldn't face it.

(Pause. A whisper of strings. LEGEND: "THE CRUST OF HUMILITY.")

AMANDA. (Hopelessly fingering the huge pocketbook.) So what are we going to do the rest of our lives? Stay home and watch the parades go by? Amuse ourselves with the glass menagerie, darling? Eternally play those worn-out phonograph records your father left as a painful reminder of him?

We won't have a business career—we've given that up because it gave us nervous indigestion! (Laughs wearily.) What is there left but dependency all our lives? I know so well what becomes of unmarried women who aren't prepared to occupy a position. I've seen such pitiful cases in the South—barely tolerated spinsters living upon the grudging patronage of sister's husband or brother's wife!—stuck away in some little mouse-trap of a room—encouraged by one in-law to visit another— little birdlike women without any nest— eating the crust of humility all their life!

Is that the future that we've mapped out for ourselves?

I swear it's the only alternative I can think of!

It isn't a very pleasant alternative, is it?

Of course—some girls do marry. (LAURA twists her hands nervously.)

Haven't you ever liked some boy?

LAURA. Yes. I liked one once. (Rises.) I came across his picture a while ago.

AMANDA. (With some interest.) He gave you his picture?

LAURA. No, it's in the year-book.

AMANDA. (Disappointed.) Oh—a high-school boy.

(SCREEN IMAGE: JIM AS HIGH-SCHOOL HERO BEARING A SILVER CUP.)

LAURA. Yes. His name was Jim. (LAURA lifts the heavy annual from the claw-foot table.) Here he is in The Pirates of Penzance.

AMANDA. (Absently.) The what?

LAURA. The operetta the senior class put on. He had a wonderful voice and we sat across the aisle from each other Mondays, Wednesdays, and Fridays in the Aud. Here he is with the silver cup for debating! See his grin?

AMANDA. (Absently.) He must have had a jolly disposition.

LAURA. He used to call me—Blue Roses.

(IMAGE: BLUE ROSES.)

AMANDA. Why did he call you such a name as that?

LAURA. When I had that attack of pleurosis —he asked me what was the matter when I came back. I said pleurosis—he thought that I said Blue Roses! So that's what he always called me after that. Whenever he saw me, he'd holler, "Hello, Blue Roses!" I didn't care for the girl that he went out with. Emily Meisenbach. Emily was the best-dressed girl at Soldan. She never struck me, though, as being sincere . . . It says in the Personal Section—they're engaged. That's—six years ago! They must be married by now.

AMANDA.   Girls that aren't cut out for business careers usually wind up married to some nice man. (*Gets up with a spark of revival.*) Sister, that's what you'll do!
(LAURA *utters a startled, doubtful laugh. She reaches quickly for a piece of glass.*)

LAURA.   But, Mother——

AMANDA.   Yes? (*Crossing to photograph.*)

LAURA.   (*In a tone of frightened apology.*) I'm—crippled!   (IMAGE: SCREEN.)

AMANDA.   Nonsense! Laura, I've told you never, never to use that word. Why, you're not crippled, you just have a little defect— hardly noticeable, even! When people have some slight disadvantage like that, they cultivate other things to make up for it—develop charm—and vivacity—and—*charm!* That's all you have to do! (*She turns again to the photograph.*) One thing your father had *plenty of*—was *charm!*
(TOM *motions to the fiddle in the wings.*)

THE SCENE FADES OUT WITH MUSIC

SCENE III

(LEGEND ON SCREEN: "AFTER THE FIASCO——"
TOM *speaks from the fire-escape landing.*)

TOM.   After the fiasco at Rubicam's Business College, the idea of getting a gentleman caller for Laura began to play a more and more important part in Mother's calculations.

It became an obsession. Like some archetype of the universal unconscious, the image of the gentleman caller haunted our small apartment. . . .
(IMAGE: YOUNG MAN AT DOOR WITH FLOWERS.)

An evening at home rarely passed without some allusion to this image, this spectre, this hope. . . .

Even when he wasn't mentioned, his presence hung in Mother's preoccupied look and in my sister's frightened, apologetic manner—hung like a sentence passed upon the Wingfields!

Mother was a woman of action as well as words.

She began to take logical steps in the planned direction.

Late that winter and in the early spring— realizing that extra money would be needed to properly feather the nest and plume the bird—she conducted a vigorous campaign on the telephone, roping in subscribers to one of those magazines for matrons called *The Home-maker's Companion*, the type of journal that features the serialized sublimations of ladies of letters who think in terms of delicate cup-like breasts, slim, tapering waists, rich, creamy thighs, eyes like wood-smoke in autumn, fingers that soothe and caress like strains of music, bodies as powerful as Etruscan sculpture.
(SCREEN IMAGE: GLAMOR MAGAZINE COVER.
AMANDA *enters with phone on long extension cord. She is spotted in the dim stage.*)

AMANDA. Ida Scott? This is Amanda Wingfield!

We *missed* you at the D.A.R. last Monday!

I said to myself: She's probably suffering with that sinus condition! How is that sinus condition?

Horrors! Heaven have mercy!—You're a Christian martyr, yes, that's what you are, a Christian martyr!

Well, I just now happened to notice that your subscription to the *Companion's* about to expire! Yes, it expires with the next issue, honey!—just when that wonderful new serial by Bessie Mae Hopper is getting off to such an exciting start. Oh, honey, it's something that you can't miss! You remember how *Gone With the Wind* took everybody by storm? You simply couldn't go out if you hadn't read it. All everybody *talked* was Scarlett O'Hara. Well, this is a book that critics already compare to *Gone With the Wind*. It's the *Gone With the Wind* of the post-World War generation!— What?—Burning?—Oh, honey, don't let them burn, go take a look in the oven and I'll hold the wire! Heavens—I think she's hung up!

DIM OUT

(LEGEND ON SCREEN: "YOU THINK I'M IN LOVE WITH CONTINENTAL SHOEMAKERS?" *Before the stage is lighted the violent voices of* TOM *and* AMANDA *are heard. They are quarreling behind the portieres. In front of them stands* LAURA *with clenched hands and panicky expression. A clear pool of light on her figure throughout this scene.*)

TOM.   What in Christ's name am I——

AMANDA.   (*Shrilly.*) Don't you use that——

TOM.   Supposed to do!

AMANDA.   Expression! Not in my——

TOM.   Ohhh!

AMANDA.   Presence! Have you gone out of your senses?

TOM.   I have, that's true, *driven* out!

AMANDA.   What is the matter with you, you —big—big—IDIOT!

TOM.   Look!—I've got *no thing*, no single thing——

AMANDA.   Lower your voice!

TOM.   In my life here that I can call my OWN! Everything is——

AMANDA.   Stop that shouting!

TOM.   Yesterday you confiscated my books! You had the nerve to——

AMANDA.   I took that horrible novel back to the library—yes! That hideous book by that insane Mr. Lawrence. (TOM *laughs wildly.*) I cannot control the output of diseased minds or people who cater to them—(TOM *laughs still more wildly.*) BUT I WON'T ALLOW SUCH FILTH BROUGHT INTO MY HOUSE! No, no, no, no, no!

TOM.   House, house! Who pays rent on it, who makes a slave of himself to——

AMANDA.   (*Fairly screeching.*) Don't you DARE to——

TOM.   No, no, *I* mustn't say things! *I've* got to just——

AMANDA.   Let me tell you——

TOM.   I don't want to hear any more!

(*He tears the portieres open. The upstage area is lit with a turgid smoky red glow.* AMANDA's *hair is in metal curlers and she wears a very old bathrobe, much too large for her slight figure, a relic of the faithless Mr. Wingfield. An upright typewriter and a wild disarray of manuscripts is on the drop-leaf table. The quarrel was probably precipitated by* AMANDA's *interruption of his creative labor. A chair lying overthrown on the floor. Their gesticulating shadows are cast on the ceiling by the fiery glow.*)

AMANDA.   You *will* hear more, you——

TOM.   No, I won't hear more, I'm going out!

AMANDA.   You come right back in——

TOM.   Out, out, out! Because I'm——

AMANDA.   Come back here, Tom Wingfield! I'm not through talking to you!

TOM.   Oh go——

LAURA.   (*Desperately.*)—Tom!

AMANDA.   You're going to listen, and no more insolence from you! I'm at the end of my patience! (*He comes back toward her.*)

TOM.   What do you think I'm at? Aren't I supposed to have any patience to reach the end of, Mother? I know, I know. It seems unimportant to you, what I'm *doing*— what I *want* to do—having a little *difference* between them! You don't think that——

AMANDA.   I think you've been doing things that you're ashamed of. That's why you act like this. I don't believe that you go every night to the movies. Nobody goes to the movies night after night. Nobody in their right minds goes to the movies as often as you pretend to. People don't go to the movies at nearly midnight, and movies don't let out at two A.M. Come in stumbling. Muttering to yourself like a maniac! You get three hours' sleep and then go to work. Oh, I can picture the way you're doing down there. Moping, doping, because you're in no condition.

TOM.   (*Wildly.*) No, I'm in no condition!

AMANDA.   What right have you got to jeopardize your job? Jeopardize the security of us all? How do you think we'd manage if you were——

TOM.   Listen! You think I'm crazy *about* the *warehouse*? (*He bends fiercely toward her slight figure.*) You think I'm in love with the Continental Shoemakers? You think I want to spend fifty-five *years* down there in that—*celotex interior!* with—*fluorescent—tubes!* Look! I'd rather somebody picked up a crowbar and battered out my brains— than go back mornings! I *go!* Every time you come in yelling that God damn "*Rise and Shine!*" "*Rise and Shine!*" I say to myself, "How *lucky dead* people are!" But I get up. I *go!* For sixty-five dollars a month I give up all that I dream of doing and being *ever!* And you say self—*self's* all I ever think of. Why, listen, if self is what I thought of, Mother, I'd be where he is— GONE! (*Pointing to father's picture.*) As far as the system of transportation reaches! (*He starts past her. She grabs his arm.*) Don't grab at me, Mother!

AMANDA.   Where are you going?

TOM.   I'm going to the *movies!*

AMANDA.   I don't believe that lie!

TOM.   (*Crouching toward her, overtowering her tiny figure. She backs away, gasping.*) I'm going to opium dens! Yes, opium dens, dens of vice and criminals' hang-outs, Mother. I've joined the Hogan gang, I'm a hired assassin, I carry a tommy-gun in a violin case! I run a string of cat-houses in the Valley! They call me Killer, Killer Wingfield, I'm leading a double-life: a simple, honest warehouse worker by day, by night a dynamic *czar* of the *underworld, Mother.* I go to gambling casinos, I spin away fortunes on the roulette table! I wear a patch over one eye and a false mustache; sometimes I put on green whiskers. On those occasions they call me—*El Diablo!* Oh, I could tell you things to make you sleepless! My enemies plan to dynamite this place. They're going to blow us all sky-high some night! I'll be glad, very happy, and so will you! You'll go up, up on a broomstick, over Blue Mountain with seventeen gentlemen callers! You ugly—babbling old—*witch.* . . .

(*He goes through a series of violent, clumsy movements, seizing his overcoat, lunging to the door, pulling it fiercely open. The* WOMEN *watch him, aghast. His arm catches in the sleeve of the coat as he struggles to pull it on. For a moment he is pinioned by the bulky garment. With an outraged groan he tears the coat off again, splitting the shoulder of it, and hurls it across the room. It strikes against the shelf of* LAURA'S *glass collection, there is a tinkle of shattering glass.* LAURA *cries out as if wounded.* MUSIC. LEGEND: "THE GLASS MENAGERIE."*)

LAURA.   (*Shrilly.*) My glass!—menagerie. . . .
(*She covers her face and turns away. But* AMANDA *is still stunned and stupefied by the "ugly witch" so that she barely notices this occurrence. Now she recovers her speech.*)

AMANDA.   (*In an awful voice.*) I won't speak to you—until you apologize!
(*She crosses through portieres and draws them together behind her.* TOM *is left with* LAURA. LAURA *clings weakly to the mantel with her face averted.* TOM *stares at her stupidly for a moment. Then he crosses to shelf. Drops awkwardly on his knees to* collect the fallen glass, glancing at LAURA *as if he would speak but couldn't.*)
"THE GLASS MENAGERIE" *steals in as*

THE SCENE DIMS OUT

SCENE IV

The interior is dark. Faint light in the alley. A deep-voiced bell in a church is tolling the hour of five as the scene commences. (TOM *appears at the top of the alley. After each solemn boom of the bell in the tower, he shakes a little noise-maker or rattle as if to express the tiny spasm of man in contrast to the sustained power and dignity of the Almighty. This and the unsteadiness of his advance make it evident that he has been drinking.*
As he climbs the few steps to the fire-escape landing, light steals up inside. LAURA *appears in night-dress, observing* TOM'S *empty bed in the front room.*
TOM *fishes in his pockets for door-key, removing a motley assortment of articles in the search, including a perfect shower of movie-ticket stubs and an empty bottle. At last he finds the key, but just as he is about to insert it, it slips from his fingers. He strikes a match and crouches below the door.*)

TOM.   (*Bitterly.*) One crack—and it falls through!   (LAURA *opens the door.*)

LAURA.   Tom! Tom, what are you doing?

TOM.   Looking for a door-key.

LAURA.   Where have you been all this time?

TOM.   I have been to the movies.

LAURA.   All this time at the movies?

TOM.   There was a very long program. There was a Garbo picture and a Mickey Mouse and a travelogue and a newsreel and a preview of coming attractions. And there was an organ solo and a collection for the milk-fund—simultaneously—which ended up in a terrible fight between a fat lady and an usher!

LAURA.   (*Innocently.*) Did you have to stay through everything?

TOM.   Of course! And, oh, I forgot! There was a big stage show! The headliner on this stage show was Malvolio the Magician. He performed wonderful tricks, many of them, such as pouring water back and forth between pitchers. First it turned to wine and then it turned to beer and then it turned to whiskey. I know it was whiskey it finally turned into because he needed somebody to come up out of the audience to help him, and I came up—both shows! It was Kentucky Straight Bourbon. A very generous fellow, he gave souvenirs. (*He pulls from his back pocket a shimmering rainbow-colored scarf.*) He gave me this. This is his magic scarf. You can have it, Laura. You wave it over a canary cage and you get a bowl of gold-fish. You wave it over the gold-fish bowl and they fly away canaries. . . . But the wonderfullest trick of all was the coffin trick. We nailed him into a coffin and he got out of the coffin without removing one nail. (*He has come inside.*) There is a trick that would come in handy for me— get me out of this 2 by 4 situation!

(*Flops onto bed and starts removing shoes.*)

LAURA. Tom—Shhh!

TOM. What're you shushing me for?

LAURA. You'll wake up Mother.

TOM. Goody, goody! Pay 'er back for all those "Rise an' Shines." (*Lies down, groaning.*) You know it don't take much intelligence to get yourself into a nailed-up coffin, Laura. But who in hell ever got himself out of one without removing one nail?

(*As if in answer, the father's grinning photograph lights up.*)

SCENE DIMS OUT

(*Immediately following: The church bell is heard striking six. At the sixth stroke the alarm clock goes off in* AMANDA'S *room, and after a few moments we hear her calling: "Rise and Shine! Rise and Shine! Laura, go tell your brother to rise and shine!"*)

TOM. (*Sitting up slowly.*) I'll rise—but I won't shine.   (*The light increases.*)

AMANDA. Laura, tell your brother his coffee is ready.   (LAURA *slips into front room.*)

LAURA. Tom!—It's nearly seven. Don't make Mother nervous. (*He stares at her stupidly. Beseechingly.*) Tom, speak to Mother this morning. Make up with her, apologize, speak to her!

TOM. She won't to me. It's her that started not speaking.

LAURA. If you just say you're sorry she'll start speaking.

TOM. Her not speaking—is that such a tragedy?

LAURA. Please—please!

AMANDA. (*Calling from kitchenette.*) Laura, are you going to do what I asked you to do, or do I have to get dressed and go out myself?

LAURA. Going, going—soon as I get on my coat! (*She pulls on a shapeless felt hat with nervous, jerky movement, pleadingly glancing at* TOM. *Rushes awkwardly for coat. The coat is one of* AMANDA'S, *inaccurately made-over, the sleeves too short for* LAURA.) Butter and what else?

AMANDA. (*Entering upstage.*) Just butter. Tell them to charge it.

LAURA. Mother, they make such faces when I do that.

AMANDA. Sticks and stones can break our bones, but the expression on Mr. Garfinkel's face won't harm us! Tell your brother his coffee is getting cold.

LAURA. (*At door.*) Do what I asked you, will you, will you, Tom?

(*He looks sullenly away.*)

AMANDA. Laura, go now or just don't go at all!

LAURA. (*Rushing out.*) Going—going!

(*A second later she cries out.* TOM *springs up and crosses to door.* AMANDA *rushes anxiously in.* TOM *opens the door.*)

TOM Laura?

LAURA. I'm all right. I slipped, but I'm all right.

AMANDA. (*Peering anxiously after her.*) If anyone breaks a leg on those fire-escape steps, the landlord ought to be sued for every cent he possesses!

(*She shuts door. Remembers she isn't speaking and returns to other room. As* TOM *enters listlessly for his coffee, she turns her back to him and stands rigidly facing the window on the gloomy gray vault of the areaway. Its light on her face with its aged but childish features is cruelly sharp, satirical as a Daumier print.* MUSIC UNDER: "AVE MARIA." TOM *glances sheepishly but sullenly at her averted figure and slumps at the table. The coffee is scalding hot; he sips it and gasps and spits it back in the cup. At his gasp,* AMANDA *catches her breath and half turns. Then catches herself and turns back to window.* TOM *blows on his coffee, glancing sidewise at his mother. She clears her throat.* TOM *clears his. He starts to rise.*

Sinks back down again, scratches his head, clears his throat again. AMANDA *coughs.* TOM *raises his cup in both hands to blow on it, his eyes staring over the rim of it at his mother for several moments. Then he slowly sets the cup down and awkwardly and hesitantly rises from the chair.*)

TOM. (*Hoarsely.*) Mother. I—I apologize, Mother. (AMANDA *draws a quick shuddering breath. Her face works grotesquely. She breaks into childlike tears.*) I'm sorry for what I said, for everything that I said, I didn't mean it.

AMANDA. (*Sobbingly.*) My devotion has made me a witch and so I make myself hateful to my children!

TOM. *No*, you *don't*.

AMANDA. I worry so much, don't sleep, it makes me nervous!

TOM. (*Gently.*) I understand that.

AMANDA. I've had to put up a solitary battle all these years. But you're my right-hand bower! Don't fall down, don't fail!

TOM. (*Gently.*) I'll try, Mother.

AMANDA. (*With great enthusiasm.*) Try and you will SUCCEED! (*The notion makes her breathless.*) Why, you—you're just *full* of natural endowments! Both of my children —they're *unusual* children! Don't you think I know it? I'm so—*proud!* Happy and —feel I've—so much to be thankful for but——Promise me one thing, Son!

TOM. What, Mother?

AMANDA. Promise, son, you'll—never be a drunkard!

TOM. (*Turns to her, grinning.*) I will never be a drunkard, Mother.

AMANDA. That's what frightened me so, that you'd be drinking! Eat a bowl of Purina!

TOM. Just coffee, Mother.

AMANDA. Shredded wheat biscuit?

TOM. No. No, Mother, just coffee.

AMANDA. You can't put in a day's work on an empty stomach. You've got ten minutes —don't gulp! Drinking too-hot liquids makes cancer of the stomach. . . . Put cream in.

TOM. No, thank you.

AMANDA. To cool it.

TOM. No! No, thank you, I want it black.

AMANDA. I know, but it's not good for you. We have to do all that we can to build ourselves up. In these trying times we live in, all that we have to cling to is—each other. . . . That's why it's so important to— Tom, I——I sent out your sister so I could discuss something with you. If you hadn't spoken I would have spoken to you.

(*Sits down.*)

TOM. (*Gently.*) What is it, Mother, that you want to discuss?

AMANDA. *Laura!*

(TOM *puts his cup down slowly.* LEGEND ON SCREEN: "LAURA." MUSIC: "THE GLASS MENAGERIE.")

TOM. —Oh. —Laura. . .

AMANDA. (*Touching his sleeve.*) You know how Laura is. So quiet but—still water runs deep! She notices things and I think she—broods about them. (TOM *looks up.*) A few days ago I came in and she was crying.

TOM. What about?

AMANDA. You.

TOM. Me?

AMANDA. She has an idea that you're not happy here.

TOM. What gave her that idea?

AMANDA. What gives her any idea? However, you do act strangely. I—I'm not criticizing, understand *that!* I know your ambitions do not lie in the warehouse, that like everybody in the whole wide world—you've had to—make sacrifices, but—Tom—Tom—life's not easy, it calls for—Spartan endurance! There's so many things in my heart that I cannot describe to you! I've never told you but I—*loved* your father. . . .

TOM. (*Gently.*) I know that, Mother.

AMANDA. And you—when I see you taking after his ways! Staying out late—and—well, you *had* been drinking the night you were in that—terrifying condition! Laura says that you hate the apartment and that you go out nights to get away from it! Is that true, Tom?

TOM. No. You say there's so much in your heart that you can't describe to me. That's true of me, too. There's so much in my heart that I can't describe to *you!* So let's respect each other's——

AMANDA. But, why—*why*, Tom—are you always so *restless*? Where do you *go* to, nights?

TOM. I—go to the movies.

AMANDA. Why do you go to the movies so much, Tom?

TOM. I go to the movies because—I like adventure. Adventure is something I don't have much of at work, so I go to the movies.

AMANDA. But, Tom, you go to the movies *entirely* too *much!*

TOM. I like a lot of adventure.

(AMANDA *looks baffled, then hurt. As the familiar inquisition resumes he becomes hard and impatient again.* AMANDA *slips back into her querulous attitude toward him.* IMAGE ON SCREEN: SAILING VESSEL WITH JOLLY ROGER.)

AMANDA. Most young men find adventure in their careers.

TOM. Then most young men are not employed in a warehouse.

AMANDA. The world is full of young men employed in warehouses and offices and factories.

TOM. Do all of them find adventure in their careers?

AMANDA. They do or they do without it! Not everybody has a craze for adventure.

TOM. Man is by instinct a lover, a hunter, a fighter, and none of those instincts are given much play at the warehouse!

AMANDA. Man is by instinct! Don't quote instinct to me! Instinct is something that people have got away from! It belongs to animals! Christian adults don't want it!

TOM. What do Christian adults want, then, Mother?

AMANDA. Superior things! Things of the mind and the spirit! Only animals have to satisfy instincts! Surely your aims are somewhat higher than theirs! Than monkeys— pigs——

TOM. I reckon they're not.

AMANDA. You're joking. However, that isn't what I wanted to discuss.

TOM. (*Rising.*) I haven't much time.

AMANDA. (*Pushing his shoulders.*) Sit down.

TOM. You want me to punch in red at the warehouse, Mother?

AMANDA. You have five minutes. I want to talk about Laura.

(LEGEND: "PLANS AND PROVISIONS.")

TOM. All right! What about Laura?

AMANDA. We have to be making some plans and provisions for her. She's older than you, two years, and nothing has happened. She just drifts along doing nothing. It frightens me terribly how she just drifts along.

TOM. I guess she's the type that people call home girls.

AMANDA. There's no such type, and if there is, it's a pity! That is unless the home is hers, with a husband!

TOM. What?

AMANDA. Oh, I can see the handwriting on the wall as plain as I see the nose in front of my face! It's terrifying!

More and more you remind me of your father! He was out all hours without explanation!—Then *left! Good-bye!*

And me with the bag to hold. I saw that letter you got from the Merchant Marine. I know what you're dreaming of. I'm not standing here blindfolded.

Very well, then. Then *do* it!

But not till there's somebody to take your place.

TOM. What do you mean?

AMANDA. I mean that as soon as Laura has got somebody to take care of her, married, a home of her own, independent—why, then you'll be free to go wherever you please, on land, on sea, whichever way the wind blows you!

But until that time you've got to look out for your sister. I don't say me because I'm old and don't matter! I say for your sister because she's young and dependent.

I put her in business college—a dismal failure! Frightened her so it made her sick at the stomach.

I took her over to the Young People's League at the church. Another fiasco. She spoke to nobody, nobody spoke to her. Now all she does is fool with those pieces of glass and play those worn-out records. What kind of a life is that for a girl to lead?

TOM. What can I do about it?

AMANDA. Overcome selfishness!

Self, self, self is all that you ever think of! (TOM *springs up and crosses to get his coat. It is ugly and bulky. He pulls on a cap with earmuffs.*) Where is your muffler? Put your wool muffler on! (*He snatches it angrily from the closet and tosses it around his neck and pulls both ends tight.*) Tom! I haven't said what I had in mind to ask you.

TOM. I'm too late to——

AMANDA. (*Catching his arm—very importunately. Then shyly.*) Down at the warehouse, aren't there some—nice young men?

TOM. No!

AMANDA. There *must* be—*some* . . .

TOM. Mother—— (*Gesture.*)

AMANDA. Find out one that's clean-living—doesn't drink and—ask him out for sister!

TOM. What?

AMANDA. For *sister!* To *meet!* Get acquainted!

TOM. (*Stamping to door.*) Oh, my *go-osh!*

AMANDA. Will you? (*He opens door. Imploringly.*) Will you? (*He starts down.*) Will you? *Will* you, dear?

TOM. (*Calling back.*) YES!

(AMANDA *closes the door hesitantly and with a troubled but faintly hopeful expression.* SCREEN IMAGE: GLAMOR MAGAZINE COVER. *Spot* AMANDA *at phone.*)

AMANDA. Ella Cartwright? This is Amanda Wingfield!

How are you, honey?

How is that kidney condition?

(*Count five.*)

Horrors! (*Count five.*)

You're a Christian martyr, yes, honey, that's what you are, a Christian martyr!

Well, I just now happened to notice in my little red book that your subscription to the *Companion* has just run out! I knew that you wouldn't want to miss out on the wonderful serial starting in this new issue. It's by Bessie Mae Hopper, the first thing she's written since *Honeymoon for Three.*

Wasn't that a strange and interesting story? Well, this one is even lovelier, I believe. It has a sophisticated, society background. It's all about the horsey set on Long Island!

FADE OUT

SCENE V

LEGEND ON SCREEN: "ANNUNCIATION." *Fade with music.*

It is early dusk of a spring evening. Supper has just been finished in the Wingfield apartment. AMANDA *and* LAURA *in light-colored dresses are removing dishes from the table, in the upstage area, which is shadowy, their movements formalized almost as a*

dance or ritual, their moving forms as pale and silent as moths.

(TOM, *in white shirt and trousers, rises from the table and crosses toward the fire-escape.*)

AMANDA. (*As he passes her.*) Son, will you do me a favor?

TOM. What?

AMANDA. Comb your hair! You look so pretty when your hair is combed! (TOM *slouches on sofa with evening paper. Enormous caption "Franco Triumphs."*) There is only one respect in which I would like you to emulate your father.

TOM. What respect is that?

AMANDA. The care he always took of his appearance. He never allowed himself to look untidy. (*He throws down the paper and crosses to fire-escape.*) Where are you going?

TOM. I'm going out to smoke.

AMANDA. You smoke too much. A pack a day at fifteen cents a pack. How much would that amount to in a month? Thirty times fifteen is how much, Tom? Figure it out and you will be astounded at what you could save. Enough to give you a night-school course in accounting at Washington U! Just think what a wonderful thing that would be for you, Son!

(TOM *is unmoved by the thought.*)

TOM. I'd rather smoke.

(*He steps out on landing, letting the screen door slam.*)

AMANDA. (*Sharply.*) I know! That's the tragedy of it. . . .

(*Alone, she turns to look at her husband's picture.* DANCE MUSIC: "ALL THE WORLD IS WAITING FOR THE SUNRISE!") *a new chance*

TOM. (*To the audience.*) Across the alley from us was the Paradise Dance Hall. On evenings in spring the windows and doors were open and the music came outdoors. Sometimes the lights were turned out except for a large glass sphere that hung from the ceiling. It would turn slowly about and filter the dusk with delicate rainbow colors. Then the orchestra played a waltz or a tango, something that had a slow and sensuous rhythm. Couples would come outside, to the relative privacy of the alley. You could see them kissing behind ash-pits and telephone poles.

This was the compensation for lives that

passed like mine, without any change or adventure.

Adventure and change were imminent in this year. They were waiting around the corner for all these kids.

Suspended in the mist over Berchtesgaden, caught in the folds of Chamberlain's umbrella——

In Spain there was Guernica!

But here there was only hot swing music and liquor, dance halls, bars, and movies, and sex that hung in the gloom like a chandelier and flooded the world with brief, deceptive rainbows. . . .

All the world was waiting for bombardments!

(AMANDA *turns from the picture and comes outside.*)

AMANDA. (*Sighing.*) A fire-escape landing's a poor excuse for a porch. (*She spreads a newspaper on a step and sits down, gracefully and demurely as if she were settling into a swing on a Mississippi veranda.*) What are you looking at?

TOM. The moon.

AMANDA. Is there a moon this evening?

TOM. It's rising over Garfinkel's Delicatessen.

AMANDA. So it is! A little silver slipper of a moon. Have you made a wish on it yet?

TOM. Um-hum.

AMANDA. What did you wish for?

TOM. That's a secret.

AMANDA. A secret, huh? Well, I won't tell mine either. I will be just as mysterious as you.

TOM. I bet I can guess what yours is.

AMANDA. Is my head so transparent?

TOM. You're not a sphinx.

AMANDA. No, I don't have secrets. I'll tell you what I wished for on the moon. Success and happiness for my precious children! I wish for that whenever there's a moon, and when there isn't a moon, I wish for it, too.

TOM. I thought perhaps you wished for a gentleman caller.

AMANDA. Why do you say that?

TOM. Don't you remember asking me to fetch one?

AMANDA. I remember suggesting that it would be nice for your sister if you brought home some nice young man from the warehouse. I think that I've made that suggestion more than once.

TOM. Yes, you have made it repeatedly.

AMANDA. Well?

TOM. We are going to have one.

AMANDA. *What?*

TOM. A gentleman caller!

(*The annunciation is celebrated with music.* AMANDA *rises.* IMAGE ON SCREEN: CALLER WITH BOUQUET.)

AMANDA. You mean you have asked some nice young man to come over?

TOM. Yep. I've asked him to dinner.

AMANDA. You really did?

TOM. I did!

AMANDA. You did, and did he—*accept?*

TOM. He did!

AMANDA. Well, well—well, well! That's—lovely!

TOM. I thought that you would be pleased.

AMANDA. It's definite, then?

TOM. Very definite.

AMANDA. Soon?

TOM. Very soon.

AMANDA. For heaven's sake, stop putting on and tell me some things, will you?

TOM. What things do you want me to tell you?

AMANDA. *Naturally* I would like to know when he's *coming!*

TOM. He's coming tomorrow.

AMANDA. *Tomorrow?*

TOM. Yep. Tomorrow.

AMANDA. But, Tom!

TOM. Yes, Mother?

AMANDA. Tomorrow gives me no time!

TOM. Time for what?

AMANDA. Preparations! Why didn't you phone me at once, as soon as you asked him, the minute that he accepted? Then, don't you see, I could have been getting ready!

TOM. You don't have to make any fuss.

AMANDA. Oh, Tom, Tom, Tom, of course I have to make a fuss! I want things nice, not sloppy! Not thrown together. I'll certainly have to do some fast thinking, won't I?

TOM. I don't see why you have to think at all.

AMANDA. You just don't know. We can't have a gentleman caller in a pig-sty! All my wedding silver has to be polished, the monogrammed table linen ought to be laundered! The windows have to be washed and fresh curtains put up. And how about clothes? We have to *wear* something, don't we?

Tom.   Mother, this boy is no one to make a fuss over!

Amanda.   Do you realize he's the first young man we've introduced to your sister?

It's terrible, dreadful, disgraceful that poor little sister has never received a single gentleman caller! Tom, come inside!

(*She opens the screen door.*)

Tom.   What for?

Amanda.   I want to ask you some things.

Tom.   If you're going to make such a fuss, I'll call it off, tell him not to come!

Amanda.   You certainly won't do anything of the kind. Nothing offends people worse than broken engagements. It simply means I'll have to work like a Turk! We won't be brilliant, but we will pass inspection. Come on inside. (Tom *follows, groaning.*) Sit down.

Tom.   Any particular place you would like me to sit?

Amanda.   Thank heavens I've got that new sofa! I'm also making payments on a floor lamp I'll have sent out! And put the chintz covers on, they'll brighten things up! Of course I'd hoped to have these walls re-papered.... What is the young man's name?

Tom.   His name is O'Connor.

Amanda.   That, of course, means fish—tomorrow is Friday! I'll have that salmon loaf—with Durkee's dressing! What does he do? He works at the warehouse?

Tom.   Of course! How else would I——

Amanda.   Tom, he—doesn't drink?

Tom.   Why do you ask me that?

Amanda.   Your father *did!*

Tom.   Don't get started on that!

Amanda.   He *does* drink, then?

Tom.   Not that I know of!

Amanda.   Make sure, be certain! The last thing I want for my daughter's a boy who drinks!

Tom.   Aren't you being a little bit prema-ture? Mr. O'Connor has not yet appeared on the scene!

Amanda.   But will tomorrow. To meet your sister, and what do I know about his character? Nothing! Old maids are better off than wives of drunkards!

Tom.   Oh, my God!

Amanda.   Be still!

Tom.   (*Leaning forward to whisper.*) Lots of fellows meet girls whom they don't marry!

Amanda.   Oh, talk sensibly, Tom—and don't be sarcastic!

(*She has gotten a hairbrush.*)

Tom.   What are you doing?

Amanda.   I'm brushing that cow-lick down! What is this young man's position at the warehouse?

Tom.   (*Submitting grimly to the brush and the interrogation.*) This young man's position is that of a shipping clerk, Mother.

Amanda.   Sounds to me like a fairly re-sponsible job, the sort of a job *you* would be in if you just had more *get-up.*

What is his salary? Have you any idea?

Tom.   I would judge it to be approximately eighty-five dollars a month.

Amanda.   Well—not princely, but——

Tom.   Twenty more than I make.

Amanda.   Yes, how well I know! But for a family man, eighty-five dollars a month is not much more than you can just get by on. . . .

Tom.   Yes, but Mr. O'Connor is not a fam-ily man.

Amanda.   He might be, mightn't he? Some time in the future?

Tom.   I see. Plans and provisions.

Amanda.   You are the only young man that I know of who ignores the fact that the future becomes the present, the present the past, and the past turns into everlasting regret if you don't plan for it! REALISTIC AGAIN

Tom.   I will think that over and see what I can make of it.

Amanda.   Don't be supercilious with your mother! Tell me some more about this—what do you call him?

Tom.   James D. O'Connor. The D. is for Delaney.

Amanda.   Irish on *both* sides! *Gracious!* And doesn't drink?

Tom.   Shall I call him up and ask him right this minute?

Amanda.   The only way to find out about those things is to make discreet inquiries at the proper moment. When I was a girl in Blue Mountain and it was suspected that a young man drank, the girl whose atten-tions he had been receiving, if any girl *was,* would sometimes speak to the minister of his church, or rather her father would if her father was living, and sort of feel him out on the young man's character. That is the way such things are discreetly handled to keep a young woman from making a tragic mistake!

TOM.   Then how did you happen to make a tragic mistake?

AMANDA.   That innocent look of your father's had everyone fooled!

He *smiled*—the world was *enchanted!*

No girl can do worse than put herself at the mercy of a handsome appearance!

I hope that Mr. O'Connor is not too goodlooking.

TOM.   No, he's not too good-looking. He's covered with freckles and hasn't too much of a nose.

AMANDA.   He's not right-down homely, though?

TOM.   Not right-down homely. Just medium homely, I'd say.

AMANDA.   Character's what to look for in a man.

TOM.   That's what I've always said, Mother.

AMANDA.   You've never said anything of the kind and I suspect you would never give it a thought.

TOM.   Don't be so suspicious of me.

AMANDA.   At least I hope he's the type that's up and coming.

TOM.   I think he really goes in for self-improvement.

AMANDA.   What reason have you to think so?

TOM.   He goes to night school.

AMANDA.   (*Beaming.*) Splendid! What does he do, I mean study?

TOM.   Radio engineering and public speaking!

AMANDA.   Then he has visions of being advanced in the world!

Any young man who studies public speaking is aiming to have an executive job some day!

And radio engineering? A thing for the future!

Both of these facts are very illuminating. Those are the sort of things that a mother should know concerning any young man who comes to call on her daughter. Seriously or—not.

TOM.   One little warning. He doesn't know about Laura. I didn't let on that we had dark ulterior motives. I just said, why don't you come and have dinner with us? He said okay and that was the whole conversation.

AMANDA.   I bet it was! You're eloquent as an oyster.

However, he'll know about Laura when he gets here. When he sees how lovely and sweet and pretty she is, he'll thank his lucky stars he was asked to dinner.

TOM.   Mother, you mustn't expect too much of Laura.

AMANDA.   What do you mean?

TOM.   Laura seems all those things to you and me because she's ours and we love her. We don't even notice she's crippled any more.

AMANDA.   Don't say crippled! You know that I never allow that word to be used!

TOM.   But face facts, Mother. She is and—that's not all——

AMANDA.   What do you mean "not all"?

TOM.   Laura is very different from other girls.

AMANDA.   I think the difference is all to her advantage.

TOM.   Not quite all—in the eyes of others—strangers—she's terribly shy and lives in a world of her own and those things make her seem a little peculiar to people outside the house. *Tom here is realistic*

AMANDA.   Don't say peculiar.

TOM.   Face the facts. She is.

(THE DANCE-HALL MUSIC CHANGES TO A TANGO THAT HAS A MINOR AND SOMEWHAT OMINOUS TONE.)

AMANDA.   In what way is she peculiar—may I ask?

TOM.   (*Gently.*) She lives in a world of her own—a world of—little glass ornaments, Mother. . . . (*Gets up.* AMANDA *remains holding brush, looking at him, troubled.*) She plays old phonograph records and—that's about all——

(*He glances at himself in the mirror and crosses to door.*)

AMANDA.   (*Sharply.*) Where are you going?

TOM.   I'm going to the movies.

(*Out screen door.*)

AMANDA.   Not to the movies, every night to the movies! (*Follows quickly to screen door.*) I don't believe you always go to the movies!

(*He is gone.* AMANDA *looks worriedly after him for a moment. Then vitality and optimism return and she turns from the door. Crossing to portieres.*) Laura! Laura!
(LAURA *answers from kitchenette.*)

LAURA.   Yes, Mother.

AMANDA.   Let those dishes go and come in front! (LAURA *appears with dish towel. Gaily.*) Laura, come here and make a wish on the moon!   (SCREEN IMAGE: MOON.)

LAURA.   (*Entering.*) Moon—moon?

AMANDA.   A little silver slipper of a moon. Look over your left shoulder, Laura, and make a wish!
(LAURA *looks faintly puzzled as if called out of sleep.* AMANDA *seizes her shoulders and turns her at an angle by the door.*)
        Now!
        Now, darling, *wish!*

LAURA.   What shall I wish for, Mother?

AMANDA.   (*Her voice trembling and her eyes suddenly filling with tears.*) Happiness! Good fortune!
(*The violin rises and the stage dims out.*)

CURTAIN

SCENE VI

(IMAGE: HIGH-SCHOOL HERO.)

TOM.   And so the following evening I brought Jim home to dinner. I had known Jim slightly in high school. In high school Jim was a hero. He had tremendous Irish good nature and vitality with the scrubbed and polished look of white chinaware. He seemed to move in a continual spotlight. He was a star in basketball, captain of the debating club, president of the senior class and the glee club and he sang the male lead in the annual light operas. He was always running or bounding, never just walking. He seemed always at the point of defeating the law of gravity. He was shooting with such velocity through his adolescence that you would logically expect him to arrive at nothing short of the White House by the time he was thirty. But Jim apparently ran into more interference after his graduation from Soldan. His speed had definitely slowed. Six years after he left high school he was holding a job that wasn't much better than mine.

(IMAGE: CLERK.)

He was the only one at the warehouse with whom I was on friendly terms. I was valuable to him as someone who could remember his former glory, who had seen him win basketball games and the silver cup in debating. He knew of my secret practice of retiring to a cabinet of the wash-room to work on poems when business was slack in the warehouse. He called me Shakespeare. And while the other boys in the warehouse regarded me with suspicious hostility, Jim took a humorous attitude toward me. Gradually his attitude affected the others; their hostility wore off and they also began to smile at me as people smile at an oddly fashioned dog who trots across their path at some distance.

I knew that Jim and Laura had known each other at Soldan, and I had heard Laura speak admiringly of his voice. I didn't know if Jim remembered her or not. In high school Laura had been as unobtrusive as Jim had been astonishing. If he did remember Laura, it was not as my sister, for when I asked him to dinner, he grinned and said, "You know, Shakespeare, I never thought of you as having folks!"

He was about to discover that I did. . . .
(LIGHT UP STAGE. LEGEND ON SCREEN: "THE ACCENT OF A COMING FOOT." *Friday evening. It is about five o'clock of a late spring evening which comes "scattering poems in the sky." A delicate lemony light is in the Wingfield apartment.* AMANDA *has worked like a Turk in preparation for the gentleman caller. The results are astonishing. The new floor lamp with its rose-silk shade is in place, a colored paper lantern conceals the broken light fixture in the ceiling, new billowing white curtains are at the windows, chintz covers are on chairs and sofa, a pair of new sofa pillows make their initial appearance. Open boxes and tissue paper are scattered on the floor.* LAURA *stands in the middle with lifted arms while* AMANDA *crouches before her, adjusting the hem of the new dress, devout and ritualistic. The dress is colored and designed by memory. The arrangement of* LAURA'S *hair is changed; it is softer and more becoming. A fragile, unearthly prettiness has come out in* LAURA: *she is like a piece of translucent glass*

touched by light, given a momentary radiance, not actual, not lasting.)

AMANDA. (*Impatiently.*) Why are you trembling?

LAURA. Mother, you've made me so nervous!

AMANDA. How have I made you nervous?

LAURA. By all this fuss! You make it seem so important!

AMANDA. I don't understand you, Laura. You couldn't be satisfied with just sitting home, and yet whenever I try to arrange something for you, you seem to resist it.

(*She gets up.*)

Now take a look at yourself.

No, wait! Wait just a moment—I have an idea!

LAURA. What is it now?

(AMANDA *produces two powder puffs which she wraps in handkerchiefs and stuffs in* LAURA's *bosom.*)

LAURA. Mother, what are you doing?

AMANDA. They call them "Gay Deceivers"!

LAURA. I won't wear them!

AMANDA. You will!

LAURA. Why should I?

AMANDA. Because, to be painfully honest, your chest is flat.

LAURA. You make it seem like we were setting a trap.

AMANDA. All pretty girls are a trap, a pretty trap, and men expect them to be.

(LEGEND: "A PRETTY TRAP.")

Now look at yourself, young lady. This is the prettiest you will ever be!

I've got to fix myself now! You're going to be surprised by your mother's appearance!

(*She crosses through portieres, humming gaily.* LAURA *moves slowly to the long mirror and stares solemnly at herself. A wind blows the white curtains inward in a slow, graceful motion and with a faint, sorrowful sighing.*)

AMANDA. (*Off stage.*) It isn't dark enough yet.

(LAURA *turns slowly before the mirror with a troubled look.* LEGEND ON SCREEN: "THIS IS MY SISTER: CELEBRATE HER WITH STRINGS!" MUSIC.)

AMANDA. (*Laughing, off.*) I'm going to show you something. I'm going to make a spectacular appearance!

LAURA. What is it, Mother?

AMANDA. Possess your soul in patience— you will see!

Something I've resurrected from that old trunk! Styles haven't changed so terribly much after all. . . .

(*She parts the portieres.*)

Now just look at your mother!

(*She wears a girlish frock of yellowed voile with a blue silk sash. She carries a bunch of jonquils—the legend of her youth is nearly revived. Feverishly.*)

This is the dress in which I led the cotillion. Won the cakewalk twice at Sunset Hill, wore one spring to the Governor's ball in Jackson!

See how I sashayed around the ballroom, Laura?

(*She raises her skirt and does a mincing step around the room.*)

I wore it on Sundays for my gentlemen callers! I had it on the day I met your father——

I had malaria fever all that spring. The change of climate from East Tennessee to the Delta—weakened resistance—I had a little temperature all the time—not enough to be serious—just enough to make me restless and giddy!—Invitations poured in—parties all over the Delta!— "Stay in bed," said Mother, "you have fever!"—but I just wouldn't.—I took quinine but kept on going, going!—Evenings, dances!—Afternoons, long, long rides! Picnics—lovely!—So lovely, that country in May.—All lacy with dogwood, literally flooded with jonquils!—That was the spring I had the craze for jonquils. Jonquils became an absolute obsession. Mother said, "Honey, there's no more room for jonquils." And still I kept on bringing in more jonquils. Whenever, wherever I saw them, I'd say, "Stop! Stop! I see jonquils!" I made the young men help me gather the jonquils! It was a joke, Amanda and her jonquils! Finally there were no more vases to hold them; every available space was filled with jonquils. No vases to hold them? All right, I'll hold them myself! And then I——(*She stops in front of the picture.* MUSIC.) met your father!

Malaria fever and jonquils and then— this—boy. . . .

(*She switches on the rose-colored lamp.*)

I hope they get here before it starts to rain.

(*She crosses upstage and places the jonquils in bowl on table.*)

I gave your brother a little extra change so he and Mr. O'Connor could take the service car home.

LAURA. (*With altered look.*) What did you say his name was?

AMANDA. O'Connor.

LAURA. What is his first name?

AMANDA. I don't remember. Oh, yes, I do. It was—Jim.

(LAURA *sways slightly and catches hold of a chair.* LEGEND ON SCREEN: "NOT JIM!")

LAURA. (*Faintly.*) Not—Jim!

AMANDA. Yes, that was it, it was Jim! I've never known a Jim that wasn't nice!

(MUSIC: OMINOUS.)

LAURA. Are you sure his name is Jim O'Connor?

AMANDA. Yes. Why?

LAURA. Is he the one that Tom used to know in high school?

AMANDA. He didn't say so. I think he just got to know him at the warehouse.

LAURA. There was a Jim O'Connor we both knew in high school—— (*Then, with effort.*) If that is the one that Tom is bringing to dinner—you'll have to excuse me, I won't come to the table.

AMANDA. What sort of nonsense is this?

LAURA. You asked me once if I'd ever liked a boy. Don't you remember I showed you this boy's picture?

AMANDA. You mean the boy you showed me in the year book?

LAURA. Yes, that boy.

AMANDA. Laura, Laura, were you in love with that boy?

LAURA. I don't know, Mother. All I know is I couldn't sit at the table if it was him!

AMANDA. It won't be him! It isn't the least bit likely. But whether it is or not, you will come to the table. You will not be excused.

LAURA. I'll have to be, Mother.

AMANDA. I don't intend to humor your silliness, Laura. I've had too much from you and your brother, both!

So just sit down and compose yourself till they come. Tom has forgotten his key so you'll have to let them in, when they arrive.

LAURA. (*Panicky.*) Oh, Mother—*you* answer the door!

AMANDA. (*Lightly.*) I'll be in the kitchen—busy!

LAURA. Oh, Mother, please answer the door, don't make me do it!

AMANDA. (*Crossing into kitchenette.*) I've got to fix the dressing for the salmon. Fuss, fuss—silliness!—over a gentleman caller!

(*Door swings shut.* LAURA *is left alone.* LEGEND: "TERROR!" *She utters a low moan and turns off the lamp—sits stiffly on the edge of the sofa, knotting her fingers together.* LEGEND ON SCREEN: "THE OPENING OF A DOOR!" TOM *and* JIM *appear on the fire-escape steps and climb to landing. Hearing their approach,* LAURA *rises with a panicky gesture. She retreats to the portieres. The doorbell.* LAURA *catches her breath and touches her throat. Low drums.*)

AMANDA. (*Calling.*) Laura, sweetheart! The door!

(LAURA *stares at it without moving.*)

JIM. I think we just beat the rain.

TOM. Uh-huh.

(*He rings again, nervously.* JIM *whistles and fishes for a cigarette.*)

AMANDA. (*Very, very gaily.*) Laura, that is your brother and Mr. O'Connor! Will you let them in, darling?

(LAURA *crosses toward kitchenette door.*)

LAURA. (*Breathlessly.*) Mother—you go to the door!

(AMANDA *steps out of kitchenette and stares furiously at* LAURA. *She points imperiously at the door.*)

LAURA. Please, please!

AMANDA. (*In a fierce whisper.*) What is the matter with you, you silly thing?

LAURA. (*Desperately.*) Please, you answer it, *please!*

AMANDA. I told you I wasn't going to humor you, Laura. Why have you chosen this moment to lose your mind?

LAURA. Please, please, please, you go!

AMANDA. You'll have to go to the door because I can't!

LAURA. (*Despairingly.*) I can't either!

AMANDA. *Why?*

LAURA. I'm *sick!*

AMANDA. I'm sick, too—of your nonsense! Why can't you and your brother be normal people? Fantastic whims and behavior!

(TOM *gives a long ring*.)

Preposterous goings on! Can you give me one reason— (*Calls out lyrically*.) COMING! JUST ONE SECOND!—why you should be afraid to open a door? Now you answer it, Laura!

LAURA.   Oh, oh, oh . . .

(*She returns through the portieres. Darts to the victrola and winds it frantically and turns it on*.)

AMANDA.   Laura Wingfield, you march right to that door!

LAURA.   Yes—yes, Mother!

(*A faraway, scratchy rendition of "Dardanella" softens the air and gives her strength to move through it. She slips to the door and draws it cautiously open*. TOM *enters with the caller*, JIM O'CONNOR.)

TOM.   Laura, this is Jim. Jim, this is my sister, Laura.

JIM.   (*Stepping inside*.) I didn't know that Shakespeare had a sister!

LAURA.   (*Retreating stiff and trembling from the door*.) How—how do you do?

JIM.   (*Heartily extending his hand*.) Okay! (LAURA *touches it hesitantly with hers*.)

JIM.   Your hand's *cold*, Laura!

LAURA.   Yes, well—I've been playing the victrola. . . .

JIM.   Must have been playing classical music on it! You ought to play a little hot swing music to warm you up!

LAURA.   Excuse me—I haven't finished playing the victrola. . . .

(*She turns awkwardly and hurries into the front room. She pauses a second by the victrola. Then catches her breath and darts through the portieres like a frightened deer*.)

JIM.   (*Grinning*.) What was the matter?

TOM.   Oh—with Laura? Laura is—terribly shy.

JIM.   Shy, huh? It's unusual to meet a shy girl nowadays. I don't believe you ever mentioned you had a sister.

TOM.   Well, now you know. I have one. Here is the *Post Dispatch*. You want a piece of it?

JIM.   Uh-huh.

TOM.   What piece? The comics?

JIM.   Sports! (*Glances at it*.) Ole Dizzy Dean is on his bad behavior.

TOM.   (*Disinterest*.) Yeah?

(*Lights cigarette and crosses back to fire-escape door*.)

JIM.   Where are *you* going?

TOM.   I'm going out on the terrace.

JIM.   (*Goes after him*.) You know, Shakespeare—I'm going to sell you a bill of goods!

TOM.   What goods!

JIM.   A course I'm taking.

TOM.   Huh?

JIM.   In public speaking! You and me, we're not the warehouse type.

TOM.   Thanks—that's good news.

But what has public speaking got to do with it?

JIM.   It fits you for—executive positions!

TOM.   Awww.

JIM.   I tell you it's done a helluva lot for me.
(IMAGE: EXECUTIVE AT DESK.)

TOM.   In what respect?

JIM.   In every! Ask yourself what is the difference between you an' me and men in the office down front? Brains?—No!—Ability?—No! Then what? Just one little thing——

TOM.   What is that one little thing?

JIM.   Primarily it amounts to—social poise! Being able to square up to people and hold your own on any social level!

AMANDA.   (*Off stage*.) Tom?

TOM.   Yes, Mother?

AMANDA.   Is that you and Mr. O'Connor?

TOM.   Yes, Mother.

AMANDA.   Well, you just make yourselves comfortable in there.

TOM.   Yes, Mother.

AMANDA.   Ask Mr. O'Connor if he would like to wash his hands.

JIM.   Aw, no—no—thank you—I took care of that at the warehouse. Tom——

TOM.   Yes?

JIM.   Mr. Mendoza was speaking to me about you.

TOM.   Favorably?

JIM.   What do you think?

TOM.   Well——

JIM.   You're going to be out of a job if you don't wake up.

TOM.   I am waking up——

JIM.   You show no signs.

TOM.   The signs are interior.

(IMAGE ON SCREEN: THE SAILING VESSEL WITH JOLLY ROGER AGAIN.)

TOM.   I'm planning to change. (*He leans over the rail speaking with quiet exhilaration. The incandescent marquees and signs of the first-run movie houses light his face from across the alley. He looks like a voyager.*) I'm right at the point of committing myself to a future that doesn't include the warehouse and Mr. Mendoza or even a night-school course in public speaking.

JIM.   What are you gassing about?

TOM.   I'm tired of the movies.

JIM.   Movies!

TOM.   Yes, movies! Look at them—— (*A wave toward the marvels of Grand Avenue.*) All of those glamorous people— having adventures—hogging it all, gobbling the whole thing up! You know what happens? People go to the *movies* instead of *moving!* Hollywood characters are supposed to have all the adventures for everybody in America, while everybody in America sits in a dark room and watches them have them! Yes, until there's a war. That's when adventure becomes available to the masses! *Everyone's* dish, not only Gable's! Then the people in the dark room come out of the dark room to have some adventures them-selves—Goody, goody!—It's our turn now, to go to the South Sea Islands—to make a safari—to be exotic, far-off!—But I'm not patient. I don't want to wait till then. I'm tired of the *movies* and I am *about* to *move!*

JIM.   (*Incredulously.*) Move?

TOM.   Yes.

JIM.   When?

TOM.   Soon!

JIM.   Where? Where?

(THEME THREE MUSIC SEEMS TO ANSWER THE QUESTION, WHILE TOM THINKS IT OVER. HE SEARCHES AMONG HIS POCKETS.)

TOM.   I'm starting to boil inside. I know I seem dreamy, but inside—well, I'm boiling! —Whenever I pick up a shoe, I shudder a little thinking how short life is and what I am doing!—Whatever that means, I know it doesn't mean shoes—except as something to wear on a traveler's feet! (*Finds paper.*) Look——

JIM.   What?

TOM.   I'm a member.

JIM.   (*Reading.*) The Union of Merchant Seamen.

TOM.   I paid my dues this month, instead of the light bill.

JIM.   You will regret it when they turn the lights off.

TOM.   I won't be here.

JIM.   How about your mother?

TOM.   I'm like my father. The bastard son of a bastard! See how he grins? And he's been absent going on sixteen years!

JIM.   You're just talking, you drip. How does your mother feel about it?

TOM.   Shhh!—Here comes Mother! Mother is not acquainted with my plans!

AMANDA.   (*Enters portieres.*) Where are you all?

TOM.   On the terrace, Mother.

(*They start inside. She advances to them. TOM is distinctly shocked at her appearance. Even JIM blinks a little. He is making his first contact with girlish Southern vivacity and in spite of the night-school course in public speaking is somewhat thrown off the beam by the unexpected outlay of social charm. Certain responses are attempted by JIM but are swept aside by AMANDA's gay laughter and chatter. TOM is embarrassed but after the first shock JIM reacts very warmly. Grins and chuckles, is altogether won over.* IMAGE: AMANDA AS A GIRL.)

AMANDA.   (*Coyly smiling, shaking her girlish ringlets.*) Well, well, well, so this is Mr. O'Connor. Introductions entirely unneces-sary. I've heard so much about you from my boy. I finally said to him, Tom—good gracious!—why don't you bring this paragon to supper? I'd like to meet this nice young man at the warehouse!—In-stead of just hearing him sing your praises so much!

I don't know why my son is so stand-offish—that's not Southern behavior!

Let's sit down and—I think we could stand a little more air in here! Tom, leave the door open. I felt a nice fresh breeze a moment ago. Where has it gone to?

Mmm, so warm already! And not quite summer, even. We're going to burn up when summer really gets started.

However, we're having—we're having a very light supper. I think light things are better fo' this time of year. The same as light clothes are. Light clothes an' light food are what warm weather calls fo'. You know our blood gets so thick during th' winter—it takes a while fo' us to *adjust* ou'selves!—when the season changes . . .

It's come so quick this year. I wasn't prepared. All of a sudden—heavens! Already summer!—I ran to the trunk an' pulled out this light dress—Terribly old! Historical almost! But feels so good—so good an' co-ol, y'know. . . .

TOM. Mother——

AMANDA. Yes, honey?

TOM. How about—supper?

AMANDA. Honey, you go ask Sister if supper is ready! You know that Sister is in full charge of supper!

Tell her you hungry boys are waiting for it.   (*To* JIM.) Have you met Laura?

JIM. She——

AMANDA. Let you in? Oh, good, you've met already! It's rare for a girl as sweet an' pretty as Laura to be domestic! But Laura is, thank heavens, not only pretty but also very domestic. I'm not at all. I never was a bit. I never could make a thing but angel-food cake. Well, in the South we had so many servants. Gone, gone, gone. All vestige of gracious living! Gone completely! I wasn't prepared for what the future brought me. All of my gentlemen callers were sons of planters and so of course I assumed that I would be married to one and raise my family on a large piece of land with plenty of servants. But man proposes—and women accepts the proposal!—To vary that old, old saying a little bit—I married no planter! I married a man who worked for the telephone company!—That gallantly smiling gentleman over there! (*Points to the picture.*) A telephone man who—fell in love with long-distance!—Now he travels and I don't even know where!—But what am I going on for about my—tribulations? Tell me yours—I hope you don't have any!

Tom?

TOM. (*Returning.*) Yes, Mother?

AMANDA. Is supper nearly ready?

TOM. It looks to me like supper is on the table.

AMANDA. Let me look—— (*She rises prettily and looks through portieres.*) Oh, lovely! —But where is Sister?

TOM. Laura is not feeling well and she says that she thinks she'd better not come to the table.

AMANDA. What?—Nonsense!—Laura? Oh, Laura!

LAURA. (*Off stage, faintly.*) Yes, Mother.

AMANDA. You really must come to the table. We won't be seated until you come to the table!

Come in, Mr. O'Connor. You sit over there, and I'll——

Laura? Laura Wingfield!

You're keeping us waiting, honey! We can't say grace until you come to the table! (*The back door is pushed weakly open and* LAURA *comes in. She is obviously quite faint, her lips trembling, her eyes wide and staring. She moves unsteadily toward the table.* LEGEND: "TERROR!" *Outside a summer storm is coming abruptly. The white curtains billow inward at the windows and there is a sorrowful murmur and deep blue dusk.* LAURA *suddenly stumbles—she catches at a chair with a faint moan.*)

TOM. Laura!

AMANDA. Laura!

(*There is a clap of thunder.* LEGEND: "AH!" *Despairingly.*) Why, Laura, you *are* sick, darling! Tom, help your sister into the living room, dear! Sit in the living room, Laura—rest on the sofa.

Well!   (*To the gentleman caller.*) Standing over the hot stove made her ill!—I told her that it was just too warm this evening, but——

(*Tom comes back in.* LAURA *is on the sofa.*) Is Laura all right now?

TOM. Yes.

AMANDA. What *is* that? Rain? A nice cool rain has come up!

(*She gives the gentleman caller a frightened look.*)

I think we may—have grace—now . . .

                (*Tom looks at her stupidly.*) Tom, honey—you say grace!

TOM. Oh . . .

"For these and all thy mercies——

(*They bow their heads,* AMANDA *stealing a nervous glance at* JIM. *In the living room* LAURA, *stretched on the sofa, clenches her hand to her lips, to hold back a shuddering sob.*)
God's Holy Name be praised"——

THE SCENE DIMS OUT

SCENE VII

LEGEND: *A Souvenir.*
Half an hour later. Dinner is just being finished in the upstage area which is concealed by the drawn portieres.
As the curtain rises LAURA *is still huddled upon the sofa, her feet drawn under her, her head resting on a pale blue pillow, her eyes wide and mysteriously watchful. The new floor lamp with its shade of rose-colored silk gives a soft, becoming light to her face, bringing out the fragile, unearthly prettiness which usually escapes attention. There is a steady murmur of rain, but it is slackening and stops soon after the scene begins; the air outside becomes pale and luminous as the moon breaks out.*
A moment after the curtain rises, the lights in both rooms flicker and go out.

JIM. Hey, there, Mr. Light Bulb!
(AMANDA *laughs nervously.* LEGEND: "SUS-PENSION OF A PUBLIC SERVICE.")

AMANDA. Where was Moses when the lights went out? Ha-ha. Do you know the answer to that one, Mr. O'Conner?

JIM. No, Ma'am, what's the answer?

AMANDA. In the dark!
(JIM *laughs appreciatively.*)
Everybody sit still. I'll light the candles. Isn't it lucky we have them on the table? Where's a match? Which of you gentlemen can provide a match?

JIM. Here.

AMANDA. Thank you, sir.

JIM. Not at all, Ma'am!

AMANDA. I guess the fuse has burnt out. Mr. O'Connor, can you tell a burnt-out fuse? I know I can't and Tom is a total loss when it comes to mechanics.
(SOUND: GETTING UP: VOICES RECEDE A LITTLE TO KITCHENETTE.)
Oh, be careful you don't bump into something. We don't want our gentleman caller to break his neck. Now wouldn't

that be a fine howdy-do?

JIM. Ha-ha!
Where is the fuse-box?

AMANDA. Right here next to the stove. Can you see anything?

JIM. Just a minute.

AMANDA. Isn't electricity a mysterious thing?
Wasn't it Benjamin Franklin who tied a key to a kite?
We live in such a mysterious universe, don't we? Some people say that science clears up all the mysteries for us. In my opinion it only creates more!
Have you found it yet?

JIM. No, Ma'am. All these fuses look okay to me.

AMANDA. Tom!

TOM. Yes, Mother?

AMANDA. That light bill I gave you several days ago. The one I told you we got the notices about?
(LEGEND: "HA!")

TOM. Oh.—Yeah.

AMANDA. You didn't neglect to pay it by any chance?

TOM. Why, I——

AMANDA. Didn't! I might have known it!

JIM. Shakespeare probably wrote a poem on that light bill, Mrs. Wingfield.

AMANDA. I might have known better than to trust him with it! There's such a high price for negligence in this world!

JIM. Maybe the poem will win a ten-dollar prize.

AMANDA. We'll just have to spend the remainder of the evening in the nineteenth century, before Mr. Edison made the Mazda lamp!

JIM. Candlelight is my favorite kind of light.

AMANDA. That shows you're romantic! But that's no excuse for Tom.
Well, we got through dinner. Very considerate of them to let us get through dinner before they plunged us into everlasting darkness, wasn't it, Mr. O'Connor?

JIM. Ha-ha!

AMANDA. Tom, as a penalty for your carelessness you can help me with the dishes.

JIM. Let me give you a hand.

AMANDA. Indeed you will not!

JIM. I ought to be good for something.

AMANDA.   Good for something?

> (*Her tone is rhapsodic.*)

YOU? Why, Mr. O'Connor, nobody, *nobody's* given me this much entertainment in years—as you have!

JIM.   Aw, now, Mrs. Wingfield!

AMANDA.   I'm not exaggerating, not one bit! But Sister is all by her lonesome. You go keep her company in the parlor!

I'll give you this lovely old candelabrum that used to be on the altar at the Church of the Heavenly Rest. It was melted a little out of shape when the church burnt down. Lighting struck it one spring. Gypsy Jones was holding a revival at the time and he intimated that the church was destroyed because the Episcopalians gave card parties.

JIM.   Ha-ha.

AMANDA.   And how about you coaxing Sister to drink a little wine? I think it would be good for her! Can you carry both at once?

JIM.   Sure. I'm Superman!

AMANDA.   Now, Thomas, get into this apron!

[*The door of kitchenette swings closed on* AMANDA'S *gay laughter; the flickering light approaches the portieres.* LAURA *sits up nervously as he enters. Her speech at first is low and breathless from the almost intolerable strain of being alone with a stranger.* (THE LEGEND: "I DON'T SUPPOSE YOU REMEMBER ME AT ALL!") *In her first speeches in this scene, before* JIM'S *warmth overcomes her paralyzing shyness,* LAURA'S *voice is thin and breathless as though she has just run up a steep flight of stairs.* JIM'S *attitude is gently humorous. In playing this scene it should be stressed that while the incident is apparently unimportant, it is to* LAURA *the climax of her secret life.*]

JIM.   Hello, there, Laura.

LAURA.   (*Faintly.*) Hello.

> (*She clears her throat.*)

JIM.   How are you feeling now? Better?

LAURA.   Yes. Yes, thank you.

JIM.   This is for you. A little dandelion wine. (*He extends it toward her with extravagant gallantry.*)

LAURA.   Thank you.

JIM.   Drink it—but don't get drunk! (*He laughs heartily.* LAURA *takes the glass uncertainly, laughs shyly.*)

Where shall I set the candles?

LAURA.   Oh—oh, anywhere . . .

JIM.   How about here on the floor? Any objections?

LAURA.   No.

JIM.   I'll spread a newspaper under to catch the drippings. I like to sit on the floor, Mind if I do?

LAURA.   Oh, no.

JIM.   Give me a pillow?

LAURA.   What?

JIM.   A pillow!

LAURA.   Oh . . .   (*Hands him one quickly.*)

JIM.   How about you? Don't you like to sit on the floor?

LAURA.   Oh—yes.

JIM.   Why don't you, then?

LAURA.   I—will.

JIM.   Take a pillow! (LAURA *does. Sits on the other side of the candelabrum.* JIM *crosses his legs and smiles engagingly at her.*) I can't hardly see you sitting way over there.

LAURA.   I can—see you.

JIM.   I know, but that's not fair; I'm in the limelight. (LAURA *moves her pillow closer.*) Good! Now I can see you! Comfortable?

LAURA.   Yes.

JIM.   So am I. Comfortable as a cow! Will you have some gum?

LAURA.   No, thank you.

JIM.   I think that I will indulge, with your permission. (*Musingly unwraps it and holds it up.*) Think of the fortune made by the guy that invented the first piece of chewing gum. Amazing, huh? The Wrigley Building is one of the sights of Chicago.—I saw it summer before last when I went up to the Century of Progress. Did you take in the Century of Progress?

LAURA.   No, I didn't.

JIM.   Well, it was quite a wonderful exposition. What impressed me most was the Hall of Science. Gives you an idea of what the future will be in America, even more wonderful than the present time is! (*Pause. Smiling at her.*) Your brother tells me you're shy. Is that right, Laura?

LAURA.   I—don't know.

JIM.   I judge you to be an old-fashioned type of girl. Well, I think that's a pretty good type to be. Hope you don't think I'm being too personal—do you?

LAURA. (*Hastily, out of embarrassment.*) I believe I *will* take a piece of gum, if you—don't mind. (*Clearing her throat.*) Mr. O'Connor, have you—kept up with your singing?

JIM. Singing? Me?

LAURA. Yes. I remember what a beautiful voice you had.

JIM. When did you hear me sing?

(VOICE OFF STAGE IN THE PAUSE.)

VOICE. (*Off stage.*)

O blow, ye winds, heigh-ho,
A-roving I will go!
    I'm off to my love
    With a boxing glove—
Ten thousand miles away!

JIM. You say you've heard me sing?

LAURA. Oh, yes! Yes, very often . . . I—don't suppose—you remember me—at all?

JIM. (*Smiling doubtfully.*) You know I have an idea I've seen you before. I had that idea soon as you opened the door. It seemed almost like I was about to remember your name. But the name that I started to call you—wasn't a name! And so I stopped myself before I said it.

LAURA. Wasn't it—Blue Roses?

JIM. (*Springs up. Grinning.*) Blue Roses!—My gosh, yes—Blue Roses!
    That's what I had on my tongue when you opened the door!
    Isn't it funny what tricks your memory plays? I didn't connect you with high school somehow or other.
    But that's where it was; it was high school. I didn't even know you were Shakespeare's sister!
    Gosh, I'm sorry.

LAURA. I didn't expect you to. You—barely knew me!

JIM. But we did have a speaking acquaintance, huh?

LAURA. Yes, we—spoke to each other.

JIM. When did you recognize me?

LAURA. Oh, right away!

JIM. Soon as I came in the door?

LAURA. When I heard your name I thought it was probably you. I knew that Tom used to know you a little in high school. So when you came in the door—
    Well, then I was—sure.

JIM. Why didn't you *say* something, then?

LAURA. (*Breathlessly.*) I didn't know what to say, I was—too surprised!

JIM. For goodness' sake! You know, this sure is funny!

LAURA. Yes! Yes, isn't it, though . . .

JIM. Didn't we have a class in something together?

LAURA. Yes, we did.

JIM. What class was that?

LAURA. It was—singing—Chorus!

JIM. Aw!

LAURA. I sat across the aisle from you in the Aud.

JIM. Aw.

LAURA. Mondays, Wednesdays, and Fridays.

JIM. Now I remember—you always came in late.

LAURA. Yes, it was so hard for me, getting upstairs. I had that brace on my leg—it clumped so loud!

JIM. I never heard any clumping.

LAURA. (*Wincing at the recollection.*) To me it sounded like—thunder!

JIM. Well, well, well, I never even noticed.

LAURA. And everybody was seated before I came in. I had to walk in front of all those people. My seat was in the back row. I had to go clumping all the way up the aisle with everyone watching!

JIM. You shouldn't have been self-conscious.

LAURA. I know, but I was. It was always such a relief when the singing started.

JIM. Aw, yes, I've placed you now! I used to call you Blue Roses. How was it that I got started calling you that?

LAURA. I was out of school a little while with pleurosis. When I came back you asked me what was the matter. I said I had pleurosis—you thought I said Blue Roses. That's what you always called me after that!

JIM. I hope you didn't mind.

LAURA. Oh, no—I liked it. You see, I wasn't acquainted with many—people. . . .

JIM. As I remember you sort of stuck by yourself.

LAURA. I—I—never have had much luck at—making friends.

JIM. I don't see why you wouldn't.

LAURA. Well, I—started out badly.

JIM. You mean being——

LAURA. Yes, it sort of—stood between me——

JIM.   You shouldn't have let it!

LAURA.   I know, but it did, and——

JIM.   You were shy with people!

LAURA.   I tried not to be but never could——

JIM.   Overcome it?

LAURA.   No, I—I never could!

JIM.   I guess being shy is something you have to work out of kind of gradually.

LAURA.   (*Sorrowfully.*) Yes—I guess it——

JIM.   Takes time!

LAURA.   Yes——

JIM.   People are not so dreadful when you know them. That's what you have to remember! And everybody has problems, not just you, but practically everybody has got some problems.

   You think of yourself as having the only problems, as being the only one who is disappointed. But just look around you and you will see lots of people as disappointed as you are. For instance, I hoped when I was going to high school that I would be further along at this time, six years later, than I am now—— You remember that wonderful write-up I had in *The Torch*?

LAURA.   Yes!

   (*She rises and crosses to table.*)

JIM.   It said I was bound to succeed in anything I went into! (LAURA *returns with the annual.*) Holy Jeez! *The Torch!*

(*He accepts it reverently. They smile across it with mutual wonder.* LAURA *crouches beside him and they begin to turn through it.* LAURA's *shyness is dissolving in his warmth.*)

LAURA.   Here you are in *The Pirates of Penzance!*

JIM.   (*Wistfully.*) I sang the baritone lead in that operetta.

LAURA.   (*Raptly.*) So—*beautifully!*

JIM.   (*Protesting.*) Aw——

LAURA.   Yes, yes—beautifully—beautifully!

JIM.   You heard me?

LAURA.   All three times!

JIM.   No!

LAURA.   Yes!

JIM.   All three performances?

LAURA.   (*Looking down.*) Yes.

JIM.   Why?

LAURA.   I—wanted to ask you to—autograph my program.

JIM.   Why didn't you ask me to?

LAURA.   You were always surrounded by your own friends so much that I never had a chance to.

JIM.   You should have just——

LAURA.   Well, I—thought you might think I was——

JIM.   Thought I might think you was—what?

LAURA.   Oh——

JIM.   (*With reflective relish.*) I was beleaguered by females in those days.

LAURA.   You were terribly popular!

JIM.   Yeah——

LAURA.   You had such a—friendly way——

JIM.   I was spoiled in high school.

LAURA.   Everybody—liked you!

JIM.   Including you?

LAURA.   I—yes, I—I did, too——

   (*She gently closes the book in her lap.*)

JIM.   Well, well, well!—Give me that program, Laura. (*She hands it to him. He signs it with a flourish.*) There you are—better late than never!

LAURA.   Oh, I—what a—surprise!

JIM.   My signature isn't worth very much right now.

   But some day—maybe—it will increase in value!

   Being disappointed is one thing and being discouraged is something else. I am disappointed but I am not discouraged.

   I'm twenty-three years old.

   How old are you?

LAURA.   I'll be twenty-four in June.

JIM.   That's not old age!

LAURA.   No, but——

JIM.   You finished high school?

LAURA.   (*With difficulty.*) I didn't go back.

JIM.   You mean you dropped out?

LAURA.   I made bad grades in my final examinations. (*She rises and replaces the book and the program. Her voice strained.*) How is—Emily Meisenbach getting along?

JIM.   Oh, that kraut-head!

LAURA.   Why do you call her that?

JIM.   That's what she was.

LAURA.   You're not still—going with her?

JIM.   I never see her.

LAURA.   It said in the Personal Section that you were—engaged!

JIM.   I know, but I wasn't impressed by that—propaganda!

LAURA.   It wasn't—the truth?

JIM.   Only in Emily's optimistic opinion!

LAURA.   Oh——

(LEGEND: "WHAT HAVE YOU DONE SINCE

HIGH SCHOOL?" JIM *lights a cigarette and leans indolently back on his elbows smiling at* LAURA *with a warmth and charm which lights her inwardly with altar candles. She remains by the table and turns in her hands a piece of glass to cover her tumult.*)

JIM. (*After several reflective puffs on a cigarette.*) What have you done since high school? (*She seems not to hear him.*) Huh? (LAURA *looks up.*) I said what have you done since high school, Laura?

LAURA.   Nothing much.

JIM.   You must have been doing something these six long years.

LAURA.   Yes.

JIM.   Well, then, such as what?

LAURA.   I took a business course at business college——

JIM.   How did that work out?

LAURA.   Well, not very—well—I had to drop out, it gave me—indigestion——

(JIM *laughs gently.*)

JIM.   What are you doing now?

LAURA.   I don't do anything—much. Oh, please don't think I sit around doing nothing! My glass collection takes up a good deal of time. Glass is something you have to take good care of.

JIM.   What did you say—about glass?

LAURA.   Collection I said—I have one——

(*She clears her throat and turns away again, acutely shy.*)

JIM.   (*Abruptly.*) You know what I judge to be the trouble with you?

Inferiority complex! Know what that is? That's what they call it when someone low-rates himself!

I understand it because I had it, too. Although my case was not so aggravated as yours seems to be. I had it until I took up public speaking, developed my voice, and learned that I had an aptitude for science. Before that time I never thought of myself as being outstanding in any way whatsoever!

Now I've never made a regular study of it, but I have a friend who says I can analyze people better than doctors that make a profession of it. I don't claim that to be necessarily true, but I can sure guess a person's psychology, Laura! (*Takes out his gum.*) Excuse me, Laura. I always take

it out when the flavor is gone. I'll use this scrap of paper to wrap it in. I know how it is to get it stuck on a shoe.

Yep—that's what I judge to be your principal trouble. A lack of confidence in yourself as a person. You don't have the proper amount of faith in yourself. I'm basing that fact on a number of your remarks and also on certain observations I've made. For instance that clumping you thought was so awful in high school. You say that you even dreaded to walk into class. You see what you did? You dropped out of school, you gave up an education because of a clump, which as far as I know was practically non-existent! A little physical defect is what you have. Hardly noticeable even! Magnified thousands of times by imagination!

You know what my strong advice to you is? Think of yourself as *superior* in some way!

LAURA.   In what way would I think?

JIM.   Why, man alive, Laura! Just look about you a little. What do you see? A world full of common people! All of 'em born and all of 'em going to die!

Which of them has one-tenth of your good points? Or mine? Or anyone else's, as far as that goes——Gosh!

Everybody excels in some one thing. Some in many!

(*Unconsciously glances at himself in the mirror.*)

All you've got to do is discover in *what!*

Take me, for instance.

(*He adjusts his tie at the mirror.*)

My interest happens to lie in electrodynamics. I'm taking a course in radio engineering at night school, Laura, on top of a fairly responsible job at the warehouse. I'm taking that course and studying public speaking.

LAURA.   Ohhhh.

JIM.   Because I believe in the future of television!   (*Turning back to her.*)

I wish to be ready to go up right along with it. Therefore I'm planning to get in on the ground floor. In fact I've already made the right connections and all that remains is for the industry itself to get under way! Full steam——

(*His eyes are starry.*)

Knowledge—Zzzzzp! *Money*—Zzzzzzp!—*Power!*

That's the cycle democracy is built on! (*His attitude is convincingly dynamic.* LAURA *stares at him, even her shyness eclipsed in her absolute wonder. He suddenly grins.*)

I guess you think I think a lot of myself!

LAURA. No—o-o-o, I——

JIM. Now how about you? Isn't there something you take more interest in than anything else?

LAURA. Well, I do—as I said—have my—glass collection——

(*A peal of girlish laughter from the kitchen.*)

JIM. I'm not right sure I know what you're talking about.

What kind of glass is it?

LAURA. Little articles of it, they're ornaments mostly!

Most of them are little animals made out of glass, the tiniest little animals in the world. Mother calls them a glass menagerie!

Here's an example of one, if you'd like to see it!

This one is one of the oldest. It's nearly thirteen.

(MUSIC: "THE GLASS MENAGERIE." *He stretches out his hand.*)

Oh, be careful—if you breathe, it breaks!

JIM. I'd better not take it. I'm pretty clumsy with things.

LAURA. Go on, I trust you with him!

(*Places it in his palm.*)

There now—you're holding him gently!

Hold him over the light, he loves the light! You see how the light shines through him?

JIM. It sure does shine!

LAURA. I shouldn't be partial, but he is my favorite one.

JIM. What kind of a thing is this one supposed to be?

LAURA. Haven't you noticed the single horn on his forehead?

JIM. A unicorn, huh?

LAURA. Mmm-hmmm!

JIM. Unicorns, aren't they extinct in the modern world?

LAURA. I know!

JIM. Poor little fellow, he must feel sort of lonesome.

LAURA. (*Smiling.*) Well, if he does he doesn't complain about it. He stays on a shelf with some horses that don't have horns and all of them seem to get along nicely together.

JIM. How do you know?

LAURA. (*Lightly.*) I haven't heard any arguments among them!

JIM. (*Grinning.*) No arguments, huh? Well, that's a pretty good sign!

Where shall I set him?

LAURA. Put him on the table. They all like a change of scenery once in a while!

JIM. (*Stretching.*) Well well, well, well——

Look how big my shadow is when I stretch!

LAURA. Oh, oh, yes—it stretches across the ceiling!

JIM. (*Crossing to door.*) I think it's stopped raining. (*Opens fire-escape door.*) Where does the music come from?

LAURA. From the Paradise Dance Hall across the alley.

JIM. How about cutting the rug a little, Miss Wingfield?

LAURA. Oh, I——

JIM. Or is your program filled up? Let me have a look at it. (*Grasps imaginary card.*) Why, every dance is taken! I'll just have to scratch some out. (WALTZ MUSIC: "LA GOLONDRINA.") Ahh, a waltz!

(*He executes some sweeping turns by himself then holds his arms toward* LAURA.)

LAURA. (*Breathlessly.*) I—can't dance!

JIM. There you go, that inferiority stuff!

LAURA. I've never danced in my life!

JIM. Come on, try!

LAURA. Oh, but I'd step on you!

JIM. I'm not made out of glass.

LAURA. How—how—how do we start?

JIM. Just leave it to me. You hold your arms out a little.

LAURA. Like this?

JIM. A little bit higher. Right. Now don't tighten up, that's the main thing about it—relax.

LAURA. (*Laughing breathlessly.*) It's hard not to.

JIM. Okay.

LAURA. I'm afraid you can't budge me.

JIM. What do you bet I can't?

(*He swings her into motion.*)

LAURA.   Goodness, yes, you can!

JIM.   Let yourself go, now, Laura, just let yourself go.

LAURA.   I'm——

JIM.   Come on!

LAURA.   Trying!

JIM.   Not so stiff—— Easy does it!

LAURA.   I know but I'm——

JIM.   Loosen th' backbone! There now, that's a lot better.

LAURA.   Am I?

JIM.   Lots, lots better!

(*He moves her about the room in a clumsy waltz.*)

LAURA.   Oh, my!

JIM.   Ha-ha!

LAURA.   Oh, my goodness!

JIM.   Ha-ha-ha! (*They suddenly bump into the table.* JIM *stops.*) What did we hit on?

LAURA.   Table.

JIM.   Did something fall off it? I think——

LAURA.   Yes.

JIM.   I hope that it wasn't the little glass horse with the horn!

LAURA.   Yes.

JIM.   Aw, aw, aw. Is it broken?

LAURA.   Now it is just like all the other horses.

JIM.   It's lost its——

LAURA.   Horn!

It doesn't matter. Maybe it's a blessing in disguise.

JIM.   You'll never forgive me. I bet that that was your favorite piece of glass.

LAURA.   I don't have favorites much. It's no tragedy, Freckles. Glass breaks so easily. No matter how careful you are. The traffic jars the shelves and things fall off them.

JIM.   Still I'm awfully sorry that I was the cause.

LAURA.   (*Smiling.*) I'll just imagine he had an operation.

The horn was removed to make him feel less—freakish!   (*They both laugh.*)

Now he will feel more at home with the other horses, the ones that don't have horns . . .

JIM.   Ha-ha, that's very funny!

(*Suddenly serious.*)

I'm glad to see that you have a sense of humor.

You know—you're—well—very differ-ent!

Surprisingly different from anyone else I know!

(*His voice becomes soft and hesitant with a genuine feeling.*)

Do you mind me telling you that?

(LAURA *is abashed beyond speech.*)

I mean it in a nice way . . .

(LAURA *nods shyly, looking away.*)

You make me feel sort of—I don't know how to put it!

I'm usually pretty good at expressing things, but——

This is something that I don't know how to say!

(LAURA *touches her throat and clears it— turns the broken unicorn in her hands. Even softer.*)

Has anyone ever told you that you were pretty?

(PAUSE: MUSIC. LAURA *looks up slowly, with wonder, and shakes her head.*)

Well, you are! In a very different way from anyone else.

And all the nicer because of the differ-ence, too.

(*His voice becomes low and husky.* LAURA *turns away, nearly faint with the novelty of her emotions.*)

I wish that you were my sister. I'd teach you to have some confidence in yourself. The different people are not like other people, but being different is nothing to be ashamed of. Because other people are not such wonderful people. They're one hundred times one thousand. You're one times one! They walk all over the earth. You just stay here. They're common as—weeds, but—you—well, you're—*Blue Roses!*

(IMAGE ON SCREEN: BLUE ROSES. MUSIC CHANGES.)

LAURA.   But blue is wrong for—roses . . .

JIM.   It's right for you!—You're—pretty!

LAURA.   In what respect am I pretty?

JIM.   In all respects—believe me! Your eyes —your hair—are pretty! Your hands are pretty! (*He catches hold of her hand.*)

You think I'm making this up because I'm invited to dinner and have to be nice. Oh, I could do that! I could put on an act for you, Laura, and say lots of things without being very sincere. But this time I am. I'm talking to you sincerely. I happened to notice you had this inferiority complex that keeps you from feeling comfortable with people. Somebody needs to build your confidence up and make you proud instead of shy and turning away and—blushing——

Somebody—ought to——

Ought to—*kiss* you, Laura!

(*His hand slips slowly up her arm to her shoulder.* MUSIC SWELLS TUMULTUOUSLY. *He suddenly turns her about and kisses her on the lips. When he releases her,* LAURA *sinks on the sofa with a bright, dazed look.* JIM *backs away and fishes in his pocket for a cigarette.* LEGEND ON SCREEN: "SOUVENIR.")

Stumble-john!

(*He lights the cigarette, avoiding her look: There is a peal of girlish laughter from* AMANDA *in the kitchen.* LAURA *slowly raises and opens her hand. It still contains the little broken glass animal. She looks at it with a tender, bewildered expression.*)

Stumble-john!

I shouldn't have done that—— That was way off the beam.

You don't smoke, do you?

(*She looks up, smiling, not hearing the question. He sits beside her a little gingerly. She looks at him speechlessly—waiting. He coughs decorously and moves a little farther aside as he considers the situation and senses her feelings, dimly, with perturbation. Gently.*)

Would you—care for a—mint?

(*She doesn't seem to hear him but her look grows brighter even.*)

Peppermint—Life-Saver?

My pocket's a regular drug store— wherever I go . . .

(*He pops a mint in his mouth. Then gulps and decides to make a clean breast of it. He speaks slowly and gingerly.*)

Laura, you know, if I had a sister like you, I'd do the same thing as Tom. I'd bring out fellows and—introduce her to them. The right type of boys of a type to —appreciate her.

Only—well—he made a mistake about me.

Maybe I've got no call to be saying this. That may not have been the idea in having me over. But what if it was?

There's nothing wrong about that. The only trouble is that in my case—I'm not in a situation to—do the right thing.

I can't take down your number and say I'll phone.

I can't call up next week and—ask for a date.

I thought I had better explain the situation in case you—misunderstood it and —hurt your feelings. . . .

(*Pause. Slowly, very slowly,* LAURA'S *look changes, her eyes returning slowly from his to the ornament in her palm.* AMANDA *utters another gay laugh in the kitchen.*)

LAURA.   (*Faintly.*) You—won't—call again?

JIM.   No, Laura, I can't.

(*He rises from the sofa.*)

As I was just explaining, I've—got strings on me.

Laura, I've—been going steady!

I go out all of the time with a girl named Betty. She's a home-girl like you, and Catholic, and Irish, and in a great many ways we—get along fine.

I met her last summer on a moonlight boat trip up the river to Alton, on the *Majestic.*

Well—right away from the start it was —love!

(LEGEND: LOVE! LAURA *sways slightly forward and grips the arm of the sofa. He fails to notice, now enrapt in his own comfortable being.*)

Being in love has made a new man of me!

(*Leaning stiffly forward, clutching the arm of the sofa,* LAURA *struggles visibly with her storm. But* JIM *is oblivious; she is a long way off.*)

The power of love is really pretty tremendous!

Love is something that—changes the whole world, Laura!

(*The storm abates a little and* LAURA *leans back. He notices her again.*)

It happened that Betty's aunt took sick; she got a wire and had to go to Centralia. So Tom—when he asked me to dinner—I naturally just accepted the invitation, not knowing that you—that he —that I——

(*He stops awkwardly.*)

Huh—I'm a stumble-john!

(*He flops back on the sofa. The holy candles in the altar of* LAURA'S *face have been snuffed out. There is a look of almost infinite desolation.* JIM *glances at her uneasily.*)

I wish that you would—say something. (*She bites her lip which was trembling and then bravely smiles. She opens her hand again on the broken glass ornament. Then she gently takes his hand and raises it level with her own. She carefully places the unicorn in the palm of his hand, then pushes his fingers closed upon it.*) What are you—doing that for? You want me to have him?—Laura? (*She nods.*) What for?

LAURA.   A—souvenir . . .

(*She rises unsteadily and crouches beside the victrola to wind it up.* LEGEND ON SCREEN: "THINGS HAVE A WAY OF TURNING OUT SO BADLY!" OR IMAGE: "GENTLEMAN CALLER WAVING GOOD-BYE!—GAILY." *At this moment* AMANDA *rushes brightly back in the front room. She bears a pitcher of fruit punch in an old-fashioned cut-glass pitcher and a plate of macaroons. The plate has a gold border and poppies painted on it.*)

AMANDA.   Well, well, well! Isn't the air delightful after the shower?

I've made you children a little liquid refreshment.

(*Turns gaily to the gentleman caller.*)

Jim, do you know that song about lemonade? "Lemonade, lemonade
Made in the shade and stirred with a spade—Good enough for any old maid!"

JIM.   (*Uneasily.*) Ha-ha! No—I never heard it.

AMANDA.   Why, Laura! You look so serious!

JIM.   We were having a serious conversation.

AMANDA.   Good! Now you're better acquainted!

JIM.   (*Uncertainly.*) Ha-ha! Yes.

AMANDA.   You modern young people are much more serious-minded than my generation. I was so gay as a girl!

JIM.   You haven't changed, Mrs. Wingfield.

AMANDA.   Tonight I'm rejuvenated! The gaiety of the occasion, Mr. O'Connor!

(*She tosses her head with a peal of laughter. Spills lemonade.*)

Oooo! I'm baptizing myself!

JIM.   Here—let me——

AMANDA.   (*Setting the pitcher down.*) There now. I discovered we had some maraschino cherries. I dumped them in, juice and all!

JIM.   You shouldn't have gone to that trouble, Mrs. Wingfield.

AMANDA.   Trouble, trouble? Why, it was loads of fun!

Didn't you hear me cutting up in the kitchen? I bet your ears were burning! I told Tom how outdone with him I was for keeping you to himself so long a time! He should have brought you over much, much sooner! Well, now that you've found your way, I want you to be a very frequent caller! Not just occasional but all the time.

Oh, we're going to have a lot of gay times together! I see them coming!

Mmm, just breathe that air! So fresh, and the moon's so pretty!

I'll skip back out—I know where my place is when young folks are having a —serious conversation!

JIM.   Oh, don't go out, Mrs. Wingfield. The fact of the matter is I've got to be going.

AMANDA.   Going, now? You're joking! Why, it's only the shank of the evening, Mr. O'Connor!

JIM.   Well, you know how it is.

AMANDA.   You mean you're a young workingman and have to keep workingmen's hours. We'll let you off early tonight. But only on the condition that next time you stay later.

What's the best night for you? Isn't Saturday night the best night for you workingmen?

JIM.   I have a couple of time-clocks to punch, Mrs. Wingfield. One at morning, another one at night!

AMANDA.   My, but you *are* ambitious! You work at night, too?

JIM.   No, Ma'am, not work but—Betty!

(*He crosses deliberately to pick up his hat. The band at the Paradise Dance Hall goes into a tender waltz.*)

AMANDA.   Betty? Betty? Who's—Betty?

(*There is an ominous cracking sound in the sky.*)

JIM.   Oh, just a girl. The girl I go steady with!

(*He smiles charmingly. The sky falls.* LEGEND: "THE SKY FALLS.")

AMANDA.   (*A long-drawn exhalation.*) Ohhh . . . Is it a serious romance, Mr. O'Connor?

JIM.   We're going to be married the second Sunday in June.

AMANDA.   Ohhhh—how nice!

Tom didn't mention that you were engaged to be married.

JIM.   The cat's not out of the bag at the warehouse yet.

You know how they are. They call you Romeo and stuff like that.

(*He stops at the oval mirror to put on his hat. He carefully shapes the brim and the crown to give a discreetly dashing effect.*)

It's been a wonderful evening, Mrs. Wingfield. I guess this is what they mean by Southern hospitality.

AMANDA.   It really wasn't anything at all.

JIM.   I hope it don't seem like I'm rushing off. But I promised Betty I'd pick her up at the Wabash depot, an' by the time I get my jalopy down there her train'll be in. Some women are pretty upset if you keep 'em waiting.

AMANDA.   Yes, I know—— The tyranny of women!   (*Extends her hand.*)

Good-bye, Mr. O'Connor.

I wish you luck—and happiness—and success! All three of them, and so does Laura!—Don't you, Laura?

LAURA.   Yes!

JIM.   (*Taking her hand.*) Good-bye, Laura. I'm certainly going to treasure that souvenir. And don't you forget the good advice I gave you.

(*Raises his voice to a cheery shout.*)

So long, Shakespeare!

Thanks again, ladies—— Good night!

(*He grins and ducks jauntily out. Still bravely grimacing, AMANDA closes the door on the gentleman caller. Then she turns back to the room with a puzzled expression. She and LAURA don't dare to face each other. LAURA crouches beside the victrola to wind it.*)

AMANDA.   (*Faintly.*) Things have a way of turning out so badly.

I don't believe that I would play the victrola.

Well, well—well——

Our gentleman caller was engaged to be married!

Tom!

TOM.   (*From back.*) Yes, Mother?

AMANDA.   Come in here a minute. I want to tell you something awfully funny.

TOM.   (*Enters with macaroon and a glass of the lemonade.*) Has the gentleman caller gotten away already?

AMANDA.   The gentleman caller has made an early departure.

What a wonderful joke you played on us!

TOM.   How do you mean?

AMANDA.   You didn't mention that he was engaged to be married.

TOM.   Jim? Engaged?

AMANDA.   That's what he just informed us.

TOM.   I'll be jiggered! I didn't know about that.

AMANDA.   That seems very peculiar.

TOM.   What's peculiar about it?

AMANDA.   Didn't you call him your best friend down at the warehouse?

TOM.   He is, but how did I know?

AMANDA.   It seems extremely peculiar that you wouldn't know your best friend was going to be married!

TOM.   The warehouse is where I work, not where I know things about people!

AMANDA.   You don't know things anywhere! You live in a dream; you manufacture illusions!   (*He crosses to the door.*)

Where are you going?

TOM.   I'm going to the movies.

AMANDA.   That's right, now that you've had us make such fools of ourselves. The effort, the preparations, all the expense! The new floor lamp, the rug, the clothes for Laura! All for what? To entertain some other girl's fiancé!

Go to the movies, go! Don't think about us, a mother deserted, an unmarried sister who's crippled and has no job! Don't let anything interfere with your selfish pleasure!

Just go, go, go—to the movies!

TOM.   All right, I will! The more you shout about my selfishness to me the quicker I'll go, and I won't go to the movies!

AMANDA.   Go, then! Then go to the moon—you selfish dreamer!

(*TOM smashes his glass on the floor. He plunges out on the fire-escape, slamming the door. LAURA screams—cut off by door. Dance-hall music up. TOM goes to the rail and grips it desperately, lifting his face in the chill white moonlight penetrating the narrow abyss of the alley.* LEGEND ON SCREEN: "AND SO GOODBYE . . ." TOM'S *closing speech is timed with the interior pantomime. The interior scene is played as though viewed through soundproof glass.* AMANDA *appears to be making a comforting speech to* LAURA *who is huddled upon the sofa. Now that we cannot hear the mother's speech, her silliness is gone and she has dignity and tragic beauty.* LAURA'S *dark hair hides her face until at the end of the speech she lifts it to smile at her mother.* AMANDA'S *gestures are slow and graceful, almost dancelike, as she comforts the daughter. At the end of her speech she glances a moment at the father's picture—then withdraws through the portieres. At close of* TOM'S *speech,* LAURA *blows out the candles, ending the play.*)

TOM.   I didn't go to the moon, I went much further—for time is the longest distance between two places——

Not long after that I was fired for writing a poem on the lid of a shoe-box.

I left Saint Louis. I descended the steps of this fire-escape for the last time and followed, from then on, in my father's footsteps, attempting to find in motion what was lost in space——

I traveled around a great deal. The cities swept about me like dead leaves, leaves that were brightly colored but torn away from the branches.

I would have stopped, but I was pursued by something.

It always came upon me unawares, taking me altogether by surprise. Perhaps it was a familiar bit of music. Perhaps it was only a piece of transparent glass——

Perhaps I am walking along a street at night, in some strange city, before I have found companions. I pass the lighted window of a shop where perfume is sold. The window is filled with pieces of colored glass, tiny transparent bottles in delicate colors, like bits of a shattered rainbow.

Then all at once my sister touches my shoulder. I turn around and look into her eyes . . . .

Oh, Laura, Laura, I tried to leave you behind me, but I am more faithful than I intended to be!

I reach for a cigarette, I cross the street, I run into the movies or a bar, I buy a drink, I speak to the nearest stranger—anything that can blow your candles out!

(LAURA *bends over the candles.*)
—for nowadays the world is lit by lightning! Blow out your candles, Laura—and so goodbye . . . .

(*She blows the candles out.*)

Tom has to leave to survive

THE SCENE DISSOLVES

FOR ANALYSIS

For a discussion of this play, see the introduction to the drama section, pp. 219.

1. How is Tom's final escape foreshadowed and justified in the early scenes?
2. In what way is the father an actor in the play?
3. What developing figure characterizing first Amanda and then Laura begins in Scene II with Laura's remark about her mother's appearance? How is that figure continued in the scenes that follow by means of dialogue and the screen legends? How is it peculiarly fitting, if a little startling?
4. What do Jim and Amanda have in common?
5. How much truth is there in Jim's analysis of Laura's problem? of his own earlier problem?
6. Every character in this play has an escape hatch of some kind; for Laura it is the glass menagerie. What is it for Tom, before he leaves? for Amanda? for Jim?
7. The play is tied closely to the world situation of the 1930's. Is that setting necessary to the play? Or does the play have more universal validity than that?
8. What in Amanda's reaction to the dinner fiasco helps justify Tom's leaving?